On the Trail of Process

On the Trail of Process

A Historical Perspective on Cognitive Processes and Their Training

LESTER MANN, PH.D.

The Pennsylvania State University
Division of Special Education
Radnor, Pennsylvania

GRUNE & STRATTON
A Subsidiary of Harcourt Brace Jovanovich, Publishers
New York   San Francisco   London

Library of Congress Cataloging in Publication Data

Mann, Lester.
  On the trail of process.

  Bibliography: p. 553
  Includes index.
  1. Handicapped children—Education.
2. Remedial teaching. I. Title.
LC4015.M34   371.9   79–9936
ISBN 0–8089–1137–6

Grune & Stratton, Inc.
111 Fifth Avenue
New York, New York 10003

Distributed in the United Kingdom by
Academic Press, Inc. (London) Ltd.
24/28 Oval Road, London NW1

Library of Congress Catalog Number 79–9936
International Standard Book Number 0-8089-1137-6
Printed in the United States of America

We have become so involved with the psychological variables that we propose . . . , that we come to think as though those variables have a certain truth—a reality of the same order as that of physical variables. We fail to keep in mind that psychological variables are intellectual constructs, mere conventions. Generally, to be sure, they are useful conventions, for they provide meaningful descriptions of human behavior. Nevertheless, we must recognize the fact that psychological traits and properties that we formalize have a will-o'-the-wisp nature; perhaps they are there and perhaps they are not.

Edwin E. Ghiselli

CONTENTS

PART III: PROCESS TRAINING IN EDUCATION AND
          SPECIAL EDUCATION

PART IV: CONCLUSION

ACKNOWLEDGMENTS

Some personal acknowledgments: I have drawn upon the resources of The Pennsylvania State University library at Radnor and those of The University of Pennsylvania. Prise, King of Prussia, has also been most helpful. Much appreciation is herewith expressed to Jane G. Stevens and Constance Mann who assisted in the preparation of the manuscript; also to Deborah Garzone and Nancy States, who helped me in many crucial ways. Finally, I thank my editors at Grune & Stratton for managing the editing of a most difficult manuscript.

I would like to hereby express my appreciation to the following publishers and individuals for granting permission to reproduce specific passages:

From THE AGE OF ENLIGHTENMENT by I. Berlin. Copyright © 1956 by Houghton Mifflin Company. Reprinted by permission.

From APHASIA AND KINDRED DISORDERS OF SPEECH (VOL. I) by H. Head, by permission of Cambridge University Press, 1926a, Cambridge University Press.

From BRAIN MECHANISMS AND INTELLIGENCE by K. S. Lashley. The University of Chicago Press, Chicago, 1929. Used with permission.

From COMENIUS by M. W. Keatinge. Copyright © 1931 McGraw-Hill. Used with permission of McGraw-Hill Book Company.

From CONTEMPORARY SCHOOLS OF PSYCHOLOGY by R. S. Woodworth and M. R. Sheehan, 1964. Used with permission of John Wiley & Sons, Inc.

From "De Anima" trans. J. A. Smith from THE OXFORD TRANSLA- TION OF ARISTOTLE, ed. W. D. Ross, vol. 3 (1931). By permis- sion of Oxford University Press.

From DEMOCRACY AND EDUCATION by J. Dewey, 1916. Used with permission of MacMillan Publishing Co., Inc.

From DOCTRINES OF THE GREAT EDUCATORS by R. Rusk, 1969. Used with permission of St. Martin's Press, Incorporated.

From EDUCATIONAL PSYCHOLOGY (VOL. II), Teacher's College, Columbia University, 1913. Used with permission of R. L. Thorndike.

From EMILE by Jean-Jacques Rousseau, translated by B. Foxley, New York, 1911, Everyman's Library, E. P. Dutton as U.S. publisher. Used with permission.

From "The Evidence for the Concept of Intelligence" by C. Burt in the BRITISH JOURNAL OF EDUCATIONAL PSYCHOLOGY, 47, 1955a, published by Scottish Academic Press (Journals) Limited. Used with permission.

From FACTORS OF THE MIND by C. Burt, 1940. Used with permission of Hodder & Stoughton Educational.

From A HISTORY OF EDUCATIONAL THOUGHT by F. Mayer, 1960. Used with permission of Charles E. Merrill Publishing Co.

From HOW WE THINK by J. Dewey, Lexington, Mass.: D. C. Heath and Company, 1933. Reprinted by permission of D. C. Heath and Company.

From INTRODUCTION TO MODERN VIEWS OF EDUCATION by W. A. Saucier, Copyright © 1937 by W. A. Saucier. Used by permission of the publisher, Ginn and Company (Xerox Corporation).

From LIBERAL EDUCATION FOR FREE MEN by T. Woody, Philadelphia, 1951. Used with permission of publisher, University of Pennsylvania Press.

From THE LIVING THOUGHTS OF DESCARTES by P. Valery, Philadelphia, 1947. Used with permission of David McKay Co., Inc.

From "The Meaning and Assessment of Intelligence" in the EUGENICS REVIEW, 47, 1955b. Used with permission of the Eugenics Society.

From MENTAL TESTS by F. N. Freeman. © Copyright 1939 by Houghton Mifflin Co. Reprinted by permission.

From MIND, BRAIN AND ADAPTATION IN THE NINETEENTH CENTURY by R. M. Young. © Oxford University Press 1970. Reprinted by permission of Oxford University Press.

From "An Outline of a History of Ideas in Neurology" by W. Riese in BULLETIN OF THE HISTORY OF MEDICINE, XXIII (2), p. 118. The Johns Hopkins University Press. Reprinted by permission.

From PESTALOZZI AND EDUCATION by G. L. Gutek. New York: Random House, Inc., 1968. Reprinted by permission.

From THE PHILOSOPHY OF SPINOZA—SELECTED FROM HIS CHIEF WORKS by J. Ratner. New York: The Modern Library, 1927. Used with permission of J. Ratner.

From PHRENOLOGY FAD AND SCIENCE by J. Davies. New Haven: Yale University Press, 1955. Used with permission of J. Davies.

From THE PROCESS OF EDUCATION by J. S. Bruner. Cambridge, Mass.: Harvard University Press, 1961. Used with permission of publisher, Harvard University Press.

From PSYCHOLOGY OF SPECIAL ABILITIES AND DISABILITIES by A. Bronner, 1917, by permission of Little, Brown and Co.

From REMEDIAL TECHNIQUES IN BASIC SCHOOL SUBJECTS by G. Fernald. © Copyright 1943, McGraw-Hill. Used with permission of McGraw-Hill Book Company.

From THE REPUBLIC OF PLATO, trans. F. M. Cornford (1941). By permission of Oxford University Press.

From SELECTIONS FROM THE NOTEBOOKS OF LEONARDO DA VINCI, ed. Irma A. Richter (1952). By permission of Oxford University Press.

From A SHORT HISTORY OF EDUCATIONAL IDEAS by S. J. Curtis and M. E. Boultwood, London, 1953. By permission of University Tutorial Press, Ltd.

From A SOCIAL HISTORY OF HELPING SERVICES: Clinic, Court, School, and Community by M. Levine and A. Levine, New York, 1970. By permission of Prentice-Hall, Inc.

From SOME PAPERS ON THE CEREBRAL CORTEX, trans. G. von-Bonin, 1960. Courtesy of Charles C Thomas, Publisher, Springfield, Illinois.

From TEACHING, LEARNING, AND THE MIND by Young Pai. Copyright © 1973 by Houghton Mifflin Co. Reprinted by permission.

From THREE THOUSAND YEARS OF EDUCATIONAL WISDOM/ SELECTIONS FROM GREAT DOCUMENTS by R. Ulich. Cambridge, Mass.: Harvard University Press, 1947. Used with permission of publisher, Harvard University Press.

From THE WILD BOY OF AVEYRON by H. Lane. Cambridge, Mass.: Harvard University Press, 1976. Used with permission of publisher, Harvard University Press.

From THE WORKING BRAIN: An Introduction to Neuropsychology by A. R. Luria, trans. Basil Haigh. © Penquin Books Ltd. 1973, translation © Penquin Books Ltd. 1973, Basic Books, Inc., Publishers, New York. Used with permission.

PREFACE

This book is an outgrowth of the author's concerns about process training, which were first expressed in 1967. It was originally intended to be a part of a broader history of exceptionalities and special education, but conceptually became of sufficient proportions to warrant its publication as a separate treatise.

There is a need for special education to obtain a historical perspective as to the cognitive processes with which it is so often concerned. Levine and Levine, in their preface to *A Social History of Helping Services* (1970), expressed their concern about the social sciences:

> It is a regrettable tendency of our field to neglect the history of research problems. We adopt the physical science model with its assumption that earlier knowledge is fully incorporated into the most recent theory and technology. (p. 3)

A clear parallel may be made for special education. Its problems in the past continue to be approached through technologies that have repeatedly failed, yet have often gone unrecognized as failures. A little historical understanding may help prevent a great deal of future waste.

By specifically addressing cognitive processes and process training as they have been construed within special (and remedial) education, the problem is approached from several standpoints: the nature of processes, brain localization theory, and cognitive training.

The book begins with the Greeks and terminates approximately mid-twentieth century. The reasons for what may appear to be premature closure are several: The years since 1950 do, in fact, receive good coverage in a number of currently available psychological, remedial, and special education texts. Additionally, the current process scene is muddled. Somewhat worn and beaten down within special education, processes are alive and flourishing in cognitive psychology and split-brain halves. They now require political or philosophical commentary, rather than a historical review. Finally, the process/antiprocess battle within special education is currently one which has taken on a clearly *ad hominem* tone. Despite my own biases, which are clearly on view in the book, I do wish to avoid the general battle.

Much of this book is drawn from secondary sources, particularly in the first part. It is not quite the scholarly thing to do, but inevitable when one pursued his livelihood as I did when writing it, in other than academic settings. As an apology, I wish to note that I have, in fact, read many of the original sources. Even in such cases, however, I have often chosen to indicate the secondary sources that first drew my attention to their writings, or (in the case of translations from foreign languages) that capture an element or flavor I may have missed in my primary source readings. My borrowings and indebtedness are clearly indicated in the text of this book. I wish to call particular attention to five authors whose work has clearly guided my own conceptions: Charles Spearman, Cyril Burt, Robert M. Young, Thomas Woody, and S. S. Colvin.

The second part of the book, particularly the later stages, are distinguished from the first by the greater emphasis on and, indeed, the singular attention paid to singular authors. This is done for several reasons: First, their books captured the message for their times of what process training was about. Second, their often elaborate rationales and technologies of process training deserve special review for our age, when equally elaborate rationales and technologies, often of great similitude, are again offered.

I have exhaustively reviewed my topics, but I have not exhaustively written about them. There are many other topics and people important to conceptualizations of process, who did not appear to be immediately germane to the specific focus of this book. Their neglect does not intend disrespect.

My casting of this history is, in part, based upon personal interpretation of various developments within it, my interpretation of what happened and why. I hope I did not unduly distort the facts that I have also recorded. As to errors in scholarship, quotes, conceptualizations, and syntax, may my friends correct me quietly!

Lester Mann, Ph.D.

On the Trail of Process

Part I

The Concept of Processes

1

Introduction

Much of the endeavor of childhood exceptionality and special education for the past decade and a half has been devoted to the principles and practices of what has been, in recent parlance, described as *process training*.

Webster's Third New International Dictionary defines process as follows:

1a: the action of moving forward progressively from one point to another on the way to completion; the action of passing through continuing development from a beginning to a contemplated end; the action of continuously going along through each of a succession of acts, events, or developmental stages, etc.

Process has been defined in the simplified *Random House Dictionary of the English Language* as follows:

1. A systematic series of actions directed to some end.
2. A continuous action, operation, or series of changes taking place in a definite manner.

The term "process"—more specifically psychological process—within the context of special education is usually identified with, and frequently replaces, the term "ability."[1] Sometimes these two terms are used interchangeably. Thus a child may have a learning disability which is corrected through process training.

Semantically, ability has a more enduring structural quality than

---

[1] Both terms are also largely synonymous with what earlier educators called power, potential, factor, capacity, or faculty.

3

process; witness Guilford's morphological approach to intelligence in which he talks about abilities relative to the structure of intellect. Process usually implies motion and becoming, even in its early uses by Aristotle. It is frequently favored because it suggests

> . . . the transitional as opposed to the substantive nature of mental events . . . and serves to safeguard against the intrusion of the fallacy of reification incident to the hazards of regarding abstract words like . . . perception, attention . . . and other psychological terms as references to things or entities akin to objects like tables or shoes. (Klein, 1970, p. 88)

For all practical purposes, however, the two terms, ability and process have been treated as identical in special education, with process losing much of its transitional quality.[2]

There are ultimately as many abilities or processes as there are things that one does or acts that one engages in. There is the ability to walk—the process of walking; the ability to digest food—the process of digesting food; the ability to do crossword puzzles; the process of reading income tax forms. There is an endless list of processes, abilities, and their fellow travelers—powers, capacities, faculties, factors, dispositions, traits—of constructs used to explain the hows in reading, arithmetic, perception, hog calling, and psychological depression. All that is needed to stretch the list toward infinity is to catalog everything past, present, and potential that plant, animal, or man can do, or will do—or cause to happen.

But what are processes? The answer, historically, has been a disputed one. For some process theorists, they are merely hypothetical constructs—convenient fictions—useful in summarizing data and in drawing generalizations therefrom. To others, however, they suggest substantive realities—actual components or powers of the soul or mind. Processes and process constructs have always been central to man's attempt at self-understanding. Galton tried to sink measurement shafts to measure them. Freud discovered warring ones struggling for supremacy within the psyche. We in special education have developed test profiles to chart their vicissitudes.

The story of processes and process training is integral to an understanding of special education, since process doctrines have dominated education's agendas, manifest or hidden, over the centuries. However, it is a story that cannot be told in isolation, for its doctrines journey through history with a neurological traveling companion—the doctrine(s) of brain localization. The association of the two is a natural one. If we may be permitted to shift metaphors, let us rhetorically pose the question—a process has to live somewhere, doesn't it? Nowadays processes are content, most of the time, to hang about subtests of such instruments as their ITPA and DTVP. But they also claim residencies within the brain.

---

[2] The reader will have difficulty finding any definitions of processes or abilities in most special education textbooks. Perhaps it is a matter of leaving well enough alone.

We all know that visual perception resides in the occipital lobe, that sensory and motor processes confront each other over the central fissure, and that speech processes have Broca and Wernicke as their landlords. Higher cognitive processsses live high in the cortex. Lower cognitive processes—do they live lower down? Neurologists, physiologists, psychologists, and you and I have always been prone to place cognitive processes—perception and the like—within specific corners of the brain. To repeat our rhetorical question—a process has to live somewhere, doesn't it?

With this in mind, we will proceed to examine both the historical course of process concepts and that of brain localization; we shall, in due course, also historically review process training practices.

Before we begin our narrative proper, however, I would like to remind the reader that processes through the centuries have been called by many names. Plato and Aristotle favored powers, but also used forms and principles. The Romans created the terms "potentiae" and "faculties." The medievalists, especially the Arabians, were to write of the psyche's different *virtutes* or *vires,* or its *aptitudines.* After the Renaissance, capacities *(capacites, capacitates)* and abilities came into popular parlance. However, *facultas* and *facultes,* i.e., faculty and faculties (introduced by Cicero to translate the Greek word for power for Latin uses) were destined to become the most widely used process terms into the early decades of the current century (Spearman, 1937a). Faculty will become a most familiar term to our readers ere this book is over.[4]

I should also like to observe that processes do not have to be large. During the eighteenth century, for example, Bonnet claimed every individual idea or sensory event was assignable to a specific process residing within an individual nerve fiber. Usually, however, process terms imply broad scopes of action, e.g.,

. . . a single potentiality governing a multitude of manifestations representing: . . . countless transient mental experiences by a small number of relatively permanent—particularly innate—different principles. (Spearman, 1937a, p. 108)[3]

This is the way process is usually employed in special education. It is in this sense that process is also generally construed in this book.[5]

---

[3] When used with other process terms, faculty was usually supraordinate to them, e.g., it usually was regarded as a higher order term than ability or power. It, in turn, was subordinated to the broader, more encompassing processes of mind and soul.

[4] Such varying process terms usually carried particular shades of meaning and specific intents that distinguished them, one from the other. For example, power, on different occasions, has been distinguished from faculty. Distinctions like these, however, have typically been vague and shifting.

[5] Modern process theorists—perhaps to disavow any faculty connotations, perhaps to insist upon the pluralistic nature of their variables or their dynamic active qualities—talk of "processes" rather than "a process," but they still really intend to represent "countless transient mental experiences by a small number of . . . principles," as Spearman would have it. Thus memory processes imply memory, perceptual processes perception, and so on.

2
The Beginnings of Process Theory

THE SOUL AS PROCESS

The soul[1] is the ultimate process activating the body and causing behavior. All religions are preoccupied with it, the essence of life. Reduced to its simplest terms, the soul produces movement, and its presence is identified with activity (Murphy & Kovach, 1972).

Conceptions of a separate detachable soul seemed plausible to primitive man. The dramatic differences he perceived between a sleeping man and a waking one invited the idea that something had departed and later returned. Also in illness, particularly delirium or coma, something seemed to disappear from a man that reappeared upon his recovery. Hallucinations, apparitions, and delusions further provided witness to a separable soul substance.

The conception of a detachable soul implied a distinction between it and the body it inhabited. Soul and body could be conceived as being in continuous interaction, yet distinct as substances. Or the soul could be conceptualized as having both physical and immaterial, or ghost, aspects.

THE LOCATION OF THE SOUL

Where is the soul located? The Egyptians and the Jews favored the heart and the region thereabout.[2] There is but scant allusion to the head as

[1] Soul originally appears to have had the meaning of a vital principle or life force, with no necessary theological connotation. We shall discuss this point in some detail when we review Descartes's contributions to process theory.
[2] The liver was also assigned cognitive functions on occasion by the Egyptians.

6

a possible location in the Old Testament.[3] The early Greeks, who equated thoughts with words, words with breath, and breath with soul, usually preferred the *phrenum* (diaphragm).

It was also the Greeks who first localized "mind" in the brain. Pythagoras (ca. sixth century B.C.) is usually given credit for this theoretical innovation. He did so by dividing the soul into two parts—the rational and irrational. The first, localized in the brain, the second, in the heart.[4]

Alcameon (ca. sixth century B.C.), a follower of Pythagoras, identified soul as a unitary central psychological agency seated in the brain, with separate capacities—perception and intelligence. All sentient creatures have sense perception. It is man alone, however, who understands. Alcameon's distinction between higher and lower cognitive processes, and between sense perception and thought, would be repeated by later Greek theorists, Plato and Aristotle most prominently. The distinction has, of course, continued into our own age.

Democritus (ca. 420 B.C.), a Greek protobehaviorist, insisted that the soul, rather than being localized in any given organ or set of organs, is diffused throughout the body. It is not a separate, unique force, apart from the corporeal structure that houses it. Like the body, it is composed of atoms. But while the atoms of the body are large and slow moving, soul atoms are small and extremely movable. They are thus able to penetrate the interstices between the larger atoms of the body and, by doing so, they become very much one with the body they activate. Global thinker to this point, Democritus then went the route of localization. He relegated thought atoms to the brain, ego ones to the heart, and those of desire to the liver. His tripartite soul model was to be a favored one for later generations of Greek philosophers.

Hippocrates (460–357 B.C.) was suspicious and scornful of a psychology without anatomy or physiology to underpin and support it. The brain, he remarked, was a gland like any other gland, and it secreted thought. In *De Morbo Sacro* we read:

> The head has glands; the brain itself resembles a gland. It is white, it is separated in small masses, like other glands. It possesses the same advantages. . . . (Hunt, 1868, p. 334)

Hippocrates, in some of his statements, seemed to be attempting to establish the brain as the seat of a single unitary mind or soul process:

---

[3] According to Delitzch, the head of the seat of intellect is referred to but once in the Old Testament and then only in Daniel, "The dream and the visions of my head are these. . . Daniel had a dream and vision of his head," and "the visions of my head troubled me" (Hunt, 1868, p. 333). These references to the head in Daniel probably reflect Hellenic influences on the writers of this section of the Bible.

[4] His selection of the heart as a location for the "lower" soul may have been influenced by Egyptian psychology.

It is necessary to know that man has only pleasure, gaiety, laughter, by the brain. From the same part came also pain, trouble, and inflictions. By this part we are wise, intelligent, we see, and hear, and discern what is good and bad, what is agreeable or disagreeable. . . . It is by the brain that we fall into delirium and insanity, that we feel terror and fear by day or in the night, by dreams or errors of all kinds. (Hunt, 1868, p. 334)[5]

With Plato (427?–347 B.C.), physical soul processes were clearly distinguished from those of a spiritual and essentially nonmaterial nature, and the separation of higher from lower processes, earlier suggested by Alcameon, was definitively established as a premise of psychological functioning. At least this holds true on the basis of his most widely accepted—tripartite—conceptualization of the soul. In this theory, a higher soul (capable of transcending the concrete immediacy of physical objects and having the capacity to deal with abstract universal thoughts) is distinguished from two lower souls, more directly engaged with the body as a physical, sentient, moving organism. There are the rational soul[6] and the irrational souls of desire and appetite. The three are situated on and linked by the cerebro-spinal column. The immortal, immaterial, rational soul is in the brain, while the mortal, irrational souls are situated, respectively, in the thoracic and abdominal cavities. Blood vessels serve as avenues of communication between the three souls and convey sensations throughout the body.[7]

Plato assigned the rational soul (mind) to the brain, but for superficial

[5] Another Hippocratic passage (in his book on the heart) states:

The human mind is placed by nature in the left ventricle, whence it governs
the rest of the soul. (Hunt, 1868, p. 334)

This passage raises two issues: Does this statement mean that Hippocrates also flirted with the notion of localizing the soul in the heart, contrary to previous commitment to brain localization? Further, was he intending to subdivide the soul and localize the rational intellect in the left ventricle placing the lower parts of the soul elsewhere? Most scholars have it that this second statement is to be attributed either to Hippocrates's son or to his son-in-law rather than to Hippocrates himself. On the other hand, it is not certain Hippocrates wrote *De Morbo Sacro*.

[6] That is, mind, reason, and thought—all practically equivalent terms for Plato. The rational soul later came to be described as the intellect in Roman times.

[7] Plato was by no means consistent in his statements about the soul. Thus in *Phaedo* the soul is conceived of as being unitary and simple. In *Timaeus* a twofold division of the soul is discussed in one place, i.e., there is a rational soul concerned with the reasoning and an irrational soul consisting of desire and appetite. Elsewhere in *Timaeus*, however, and in *The Republic* and *The Phaedrus*, the soul is conceived of as being tripartite. It is possible to reconcile these contradictory concepts by interpeting Plato's first view as emphasizing the essential unity of the soul and the second and third views as describing the soul's varied aspects. From this standpoint, the Platonic soul may be conceived of as a unity, yet manifesting diversity in its functions (Watson, 1971).

reasons. It was put there by the gods because the head was the bodily part nearest heaven and possessed the most graceful form. Their decision appeared a propitious one:

> Now fearing, no doubt, to pollute the divine part on their account, save in so far as was altogether necessary, they housed the mortal apart from it in a different dwelling-place in the body, building between head and breast, as an isthmus and boundary, the neck, which they placed between to keep the two apart. In the breast, then, and the trunk (as it is called) they confined the mortal kind of soul. And since part of it has a nobler nature, part a baser, they built another partition across the hollow of the trunk, as if marking off the men's apartment from the women's and set the midriff as a fence between them. . . . (Cornford, 1948, p. 74)

THE POWERS OF THE SOUL

Plato's various souls had various powers.[8] It is with him that the history of processes as we understand them today may be said to have officially begun.[9] We read in *The Republic* of the different powers attributed to the rational soul:

> I will begin by placing faculties in a class by themselves: they are powers in us, and in all other things, by which we do as we do. . . . In speaking of a faculty I think only of its sphere and its result; and that which has the same sphere and the same result I call the same faculty, but that which has another sphere and another result I call different. . . . (Edman, 1928, p. 437)

Did Plato regard his faculties as separate and distinct processes? Remember that he could not even agree whether there were one, two, or three souls.

> This is truly hard [to decide] whether we perform our separate acts by one and the same power, or whether . . . we perform one by one, and another by another; that is, learn by one, get angry by another, and by a third covet the pleasures of nutrition and propagation, and others akin to these; or whether, when we devote ourselves to them, we act on each with the whole soul; these matters are difficult adequately to determine. (Spearman, 1937a, p. 107)[10]

---

[8] The term "power" was meant originally as a capacity or propensity for an act rather than a force, as it eventually came to signify. Most translators use the term "faculty," developed by Cicero, for the Greek word "power."

[9] It would be more appropriate, perhaps, to indicate that Plato was the first to clearly formalize this conception of separate powers, for even the pre-Homeric Greeks had talked of the soul as having separate functions (Brett, 1912) and earlier Greek philosophers, such as Pythagoras, spoke in a similar vein.

[10] One must always be aware, however, of artifacts and misrepresentations appearing in translations. The development of process conceptions has been strongly influenced by vagaries of translation—no less so the above passage in Plato. Spearman notes:

The same question was to also trouble Aristotle (384–322 B.C.), who stated the problem of psychology as being that of ascertaining ". . . the nature and essence of soul, and its attributes" (MacLeod, 1975, p. 68). After which he went on to ponder:

We must consider also whether the soul is divisible or is without parts, and whether it is everywhere homogeneous or not; and if not homogeneous, whether its various forms are different specifically or generically. . . . We must be careful not to ignore the question whether soul can be defined in a single unambiguous formula . . . or whether we must not give a separate formula for each sort of it. . . . Further, if what exists is not a plurality of soul, but a plurality of parts of one soul, which ought we to investigate first, the whole soul or its parts? (It is also a difficult problem to decide which of these parts are in nature distinct from one another.) Again, which ought we to investigate first, these parts or their functions, mind or thinking, the faculty or the act of sensation, and so on? . . . Is each of these a soul or a part of a soul? And if a part, a part in which sense? A part merely distinguishable by definition or a part distinct in local situation as well? In the case of certain of these powers, the answers to these questions are easy; in the case of others we are puzzled what to say. (Smith, 1931, p. 402)

The divisibility of the soul has always been, and continues to be a pressing concern for process theorists and their antagonists. It is one of several major unresolved issues that we shall consider in the following chapter.

About this remarkable passage, we may specially note that the word "power" is really the product of the translator's imagination. Another rendering (Lindsay) substituted "principle." Another (Jowett), "element." And yet another (Shorley) "thing." What Plato himself wrote was only "one and the same," warily leaving us to choose for ourselves. One and the same. What? (Spearman, 1937a, p. 107)

3
Some Basic Questions About Processes

THE DIVISIBILITY OF THE SOUL

Is the soul divisible? On the part of process advocates through the centuries, the answer usually has been a horrified no, just as it usually is with today's process theorists. After all, many process theorists were theologians, and to espouse other than a unified soul would have been heretical. Medieval Christians, such as Augustine and Thomas Aquinas, and medieval Moslems, too, such as Avicenna and Averroës, disclaimed any intent of other than total indivisibility for the immortal soul. Hear thus the argument proffered by Maimonides (1135–1204), Jewish–Arab physician–philosopher, insisting upon the oneness of the human soul:

> Know that the human soul is one, but that it has many diversified activities. Some of these activities have, indeed, been called souls, which has given rise to the opinion that man has many souls, as was the belief of the physicians, with the result that the most distinguished of them states in the introduction to his book that there are three souls, the physical, the vital, and the psychical. These activities are called *faculties* and *parts*, so that the phrase "parts of the soul," frequently employed by philosophers, is commonly used. By the word "parts," however, they do not intend to imply that the soul is divided into parts as are bodies, but they merely enumerate the different activities of the soul as being parts of a whole, the union of which makes up the soul (Gorfinkle, 1912, pp. 36–37).

Yet, after making all proper apologies to the contrary, almost all process theorists have proceeded to talk of cognitive, affective, and other psychological processes as if they are, in fact, separate and distinct—one from the other—and can be addressed or manipulated individually.

11

Similarly, the learning-disability specialists of today often break out profiles of various perceptual, visual, auditory-perceptual, and language skills upon which they presume to base training directed to the "whole" child; a whole child dealt with, in their schemes of things, in his parts.

THE REALITY OF PROCESSES

The broader and more basic question to which the divisibility of the soul (or mind) into distinct processes refers itself is, of course, the reality of its processes. In the writings of many of the major process theorists of the past, we find disclaimers against considering the processes with which they were concerned as "real," but at the same time we see them talking about them in substantive terms. See again the contradictions in the following writings of Maimonides. After insisting upon the non-substantive status of faculties, he discusses them in a fashion that would suggest they *are* substantive.

The *appetitive* is that faculty by which a man desires, or loathes a thing, and from which there arise the following activities: the pursuit of an object or flight from it, inclination and avoidance, anger and affection, fear and courage, cruelty and compassion, love and hate, and many other similar psychic qualities (Gorfinkle, 1912, pp. 42–43).

Reason, that faculty peculiar to man, enables him to understand, reflect, acquire knowledge of the sciences, and to discriminate between proper and improper actions. Its functions are partly *practical* and partly *speculative* (theoretical), the *practical* being, in turn, either *mechanical* or *intellectual. . . .* (Gorfinkle, 1912, pp. 42–43)

The situation has not changed much in our own day. In discussing factors—modern-day faculties—Guilford defines a factor first as "an intervening variable, conceived by the investigator, and . . . inferred from observed data" (Guilford, 1967, p. 37). He proceeds to say it "is also a psychological function," which casts it in terms of activity. But then he places his factors in a structure of intellect; and it hardly sounds as if he intends his model altogether metaphorically. So, too, in their discussion of "cognitive" processes, Kagan and Kogan first tell us that cognitive processes are hypothetical, but then discuss them as causative, hence substantive, agents. First:

. . . *cognition stands for those hypothetical psychological processes invoked to explain*[1] overt verbal and motor behavior as well as certain physiological reactions. Cognitive process is a superordinate term subsuming the more famil-

_____
[1] Italics have been added by the author.

iar titles of imagery, perception, free association, thought, mediation, prolifera-
tion of hypotheses, reasoning, reflection, and problem solving. (Kagan & Kogan,
1970, p. 1275)

Then, in the course of the same short paragraph:

> *All* verbal *behavior must be a product of cognitive processes, as are dreams
> and intelligence test performances.* (Kagan & Kogan, 1970, p. 1275)

Are processes real? We can be sure that no matter what answer to the
contrary process theorists offer, their processes, in due course, assume
the flesh of reality. Reification, in fact, is almost impossible to avoid when
talking about processes; one falls into its traps even when warring against
them. The workings of reification are clearly manifest in the evolution of
the word "faculty" itself—the most popular process term of all over the
centuries. This word, or rather its original Latin equivalent, *facultas,* was
intended originally as an abbreviation of *facilitas* (facility), which meant
the facility to do something or to express the possiblity of a particular
event occurring. While Cicero first introduced the term *"facultas,"* to
express the Greek word for power into psychology, he defined its meaning
in terms of the original *facilis*. Nevertheless, in due course, it came to
mean an active causative agent with substantive properties (Spearman,
1937a). The tautological deployment of faculties is explained by Woodworth and Sheehan:

> Aristotle employed verbal nouns equivalent to our *remembering, willing,*
> etc., as names for his classes. When his works were translated into Latin, a slight
> change of form was required to fit the Latin idiom. The translation became
> "faculty of remembering," "faculty of willing," etc. . . . the list of faculties was
> nothing more or less than a list of classes of "things done," an answer . . . to the
> question "What?" . . . the great thinkers who spoke of the faculties of the mind
> were perfectly clear on this matter, but many lesser men . . . were betrayed by
> the form of expression into supposing that the faculties were processes, an answer
> to the question "How?" (Woodworth & Sheehan, pp. 14–15)

THE EVOLUTION AND DEVOLUTION OF PROCESSES

Our concern with the specificities and reality of processes may be
more clearly understood if we attempt to understand the ways and means
by which, and through which, processes are identified.[2]

---

[2] We are, in our discourse, concerned with behavioral processes (more specifically we shall
usually limit that interest even further—to cognitive processes). We should, nevertheless,
not forget that there are other areas of inquiry wherein process terms are used and have been
most valuable: for example, electricity, energy, the atom, gravity—all are process terms. It
would take us too far afield to compare the use of process terms in man's various areas of

Behavioral or psychological processes are, whatever their validity, hypothetical "inner" events or entity constructs. They are usually used to explain behavior, i.e., presumed to cause behavior.[3] While there is nothing that precludes process theorists from identifying their processes with numerical codes, say 45 D,[4] they have usually chosen to name their constructs in a commonsense way—as would the man on the street; the name of a process is usually assigned to it on the basis of the behavior it is presumed to generate. "Intelligent behavior" is the result of intelligence. "Remembering" is brought about by memory; we "perceive" with our perceptual abilities. The famed Roman medical authority Galen (130–200) noted a given faculty "exists only in relation to its own effect" (Riese, 1959, p. 22). Earlier, Aristotle had attempted a similar operational definition: "Mind must be related to what is thinkable as sense is to what is sensible." Frostig similarly defined perceptual processes, centuries later.

During the decade leading up to America's bicentennial, there was a process explosion as new areas of psychological investigation proliferated. Witness Neisser's list of cognitive processes. In the visual area, we find transient iconic memory, verbal coding, perceptual set, span of apprehension, displacement and rotation in pattern recognition, backward masking, template matching, decision time, visual search, feature analysis, focal attention, preattentive control figural synthesis, figural synthesis, perceptual defense, etc. In the auditory area, Neisser lists segmentation, echoic memory, filtering, auditory synthesis, recoding, slotting, decay, linguistics, gestalts, and grammatical structure (Neisser, 1967).

Processes come and go; they are evoked or evolved to explain phenomena of interest and then discarded to die or disappear if no one any longer cares about the phenomena they "explain." They are often absorbed into other, newer processes or assume new names according to the changing times and fashions. Frequently they are reinterpreted and given new meanings. Many of the old processes are no longer with us. Where have they gone? Where were the newest of today's processes when we needed *them* years ago?

With this in mind, let us examine the vicissitudes of some popular process constructs.

The Rational Soul

Plato found it necessary to subdivide the rational soul into superior and lower parts in order to account for the diversity of its activities.

discourse, to muse upon their great value in physical science, their considerably lesser value in behavioral science.
[3] Though also used as intervening variables.
[4] We would undoubtedly be less prone to reify our processes if they were simply coded. . . . Numbers don't take on conceptual flesh as readily as words.

Aristotle made a somewhat different division into (1) an active intellect which can "become all things," never ceases to function, and is immortal; and (2) a passive intellect which perishes with the body. When such subprocesses of the reasonable faculty were later found still to be insufficient to account for all the phenomena of thought, a later theorist, Alexander of Aphrodiasis, created a third type of reason, "habit," which he hypothesized as developing out of the active and passive reasoning powers. Six hundred years later, Alkindin added a fourth. And on it went. During the Middle Ages, the scholastics, seeking to reenthrone Aristotelean theory, restored Aristotle's original two types of mind, with Thomas Aquinas (1225–1274) calling one the *intellectus* and the other the *ratio*.[5] But they found it necessary to bolster the two with a variety of "lower" cognitive processes operating under the title of inner senses. In later centuries, the addition of "super-rational thought" was proposed by Gioberti. Immanuel Kant (1724–1804) distinguished between *Verstand*, which was perceptually based and consisted of the power to conceive and judge, and *Vernunft*, not dependent on perceptual information and having the power to draw conclusions and establish principles. Herbert Spencer (1820–1903), working within the framework of evolutionary psychology, raised intelligence to a full faculty status, earlier defined by St. Thomas Aquinas as the "intellect's very act, which is to understand." Spencer gave an important role to intelligence's role in "Instinct, Reason, Perception, Conception, Memory, Will, etc." (Spearman, 1937a, p. 12)

Perception

Sensory information was clearly identified by the Greeks as a major source of knowledge. The doctrine of the five senses, which received its imprimatur from Aristotle, established five basic "external" senses, each with its particular type of physical organs and faculties, to convey information about the physical world to the psyche. These were: vision, hearing, smell, taste, and touch. However, these external senses were found to require assistance in managing information. Aristotle joined Plato in pointing out that different types of sensory input, while having unique characteristics, e.g., color, weight, taste, also possessed some characteristics in common, such as those of position and size. He argued that there then had to exist beyond the special senses a general or

---

[5] Process theories boil down to attempts to derive multitudinous behaviors from a few basic variables. Because of the vastness of sensory experience, the ancients were sometimes unsure whether sense perception should be ascribed faculty status. Debate over this continued into the Middle Ages, when separate faculties were clearly agreed upon for each of the senses. Aquinas insisted the respective senses belonged to different faculties because "by their very nature" they are directed to diverse qualities.

common sense[6] (sensus communis) to account for such communalities. The common sense, an internal sense, however, was not to be left off with the relatively simple duty of dealing with communalities and cross modality integration. Aristotle also assigned to it the responsibility of restoring sensory inputs, i.e., creating images (a sequel common to all senses), and authority for creating consciousness of sensory experiences.

Memory

Memory, in its various forms, is a process that has always engaged both theoretical and practical interest. Is memory a separate faculty? Plato considered it as such for a while, but then rejected the notion as superfluous. Since knowing and remembering meant much the same to him, he conceived of memory as being in one part joined up with sensory perception, the other part joined to reasoning. Aristotle paid small notice to memory in *De Anima*, wherein it was described as little more than the persistence of sense impressions. While in *De Memoria*, he elevated the process to a position of great importance, he was nevertheless reluctant to accord it full faculty status and so split it between sense (the common sense) and reasoning (Spearman, 1937a, p. 107).[7] Aristotle also distinguished between what he specifically called "memory" (shared by both animals and men), essentially the ability to remain aware of past perceptions (assigned to the common sense) and recollection or recall, an active search for past information (assigned to reason), which is only proper to man.

The first psychologist who clearly recognized memory as a full and separate faculty was Plotinus (204–270). Later, Augustine (354–436) and Avicenna (980–1037) also accepted it as a full-blown faculty, but in the face of other scholarly opinion. The majority of scholastics supported Aristotle in denying memory full faculty status. Renaissance psychologists debated its status at length. Huarte (1529–1588) and Bacon (1561–1626) thought it a full-fledged faculty; others did not. Today we talk of visual memory, auditory memory, short-term memory, distant memory, and rote memory. Are they all separate, distinct processes, or merely aspects of a broader monarchical one called memory? This, too, is debated.

[6] Diogenes of Appalonia, Greek philosopher of the fifth century B.C. who was concerned with the physiological bases of sensation and perception, has been accorded some precedence relative to this construct and notion of sensory integration.
[7] There is some uncertainty about this. Thus Watson believes that he did regard it as a separate faculty. The ambiguity of Aristotle's writings makes a sure interpretation impossible.

Imagination

A faculty with a particularly checkered history is imagination. It was originally identified as sensory memory by the Greeks, who considered images the sole means by which sensory information could be recalled. Imagination later came to mean two distinct sets of functions—one resulting in the passive recall of sensory information and the other organizing and developing this remembered information into visible forms for the intellect. On such grounds, Immanuel Kant declared it to be a transcendent power interposed between sense and intellect. Today we still distinguish between sensory image making—imagery—and imagination of a "productive" sort, though we are usually prone to associate the process of imagination with the latter usage.

Attention

Nowhere else are the vagaries of process creation better illustrated than with the faculty of attention. It all began rather innocently with an ancient Greek phrase, τὸν νοῦν προσέχειν, which is translated "to direct the intellect toward." Such a phrase appears 36 times in Plato's writings. In due course, however, it passed from the Greek language into the Latin as *animum adverte, animum adjicere,* and became *animum attendere* (at a period when the Latin term *"animus"* was the equivalent of *intellectus,* or intellect). But while *adverte* and *adivere* simply meant *to direct, attendere* introduced a new shade of meaning, implying that the directing of the intellect involved "tension." (Spearman, 1937a)

By the time the original Greek phrase "direct the intellect toward" reached the age of Cicero (106–43 B.C.), we find the substantive *attentio animi* and *intentis animi* being used to express it in Latin terms. The sad tale of familiarity breeding abbreviation eventuated in *attentio* (attention) being casually used without the accompanying term *animi*. After three or four centuries this omission became customary, and a new process, *attention,* was ensconced. There were protests. Philoponus exclaimed in the sixth century A.D.:

> But the more recent interpreters, standing not in awe of the frown of Alexander, not listening to Plutarch, even repelling Aristotle himself, have devised a new interpretation . . . According to them, the rational soul not only comprehends the faculties of the intellect . . ., thought . . . opinion . . . will . . . and election . . .; they also thrust into it another sixth faculty, which they call that of Attention. (Spearman, 1937a, p. 143)

Possibly because of criticisms like that above there was relatively little attention paid to the process of attention during the Middle Ages. St. Thomas Aquinas, for one, gave it no place in his list of faculties. But with the Renaissance, attention was to achieve full recognition as a faculty, and went on to great heights of popularity in subsequent centuries.

Thus with processes over the ages there have been chronic debates over their nature, indeed over their reality, their partitioning into ever more finite and precise forms, their elaboration into new variants, the discarding of the old, the creation of new ones. So has it been as man has sought to explain man.

4
Early Faculty Theories

CLASSICAL FACULTY DOCTRINE

Aristotle established the basic forms that process doctrines were to take over many subsequent centuries—the *five major faculties*[1] subsuming various potentials:[2] (1) the faculty of absorbing food and procreation—possessed by all living things, plant, animal, and man; (2) the faculty of locomotion—restricted to animal and man; (3) the faculty(ies) of sensory perception—subsuming the five internal senses and the common sense; (4) the faculty of reason (intellect)—divided into active and passive parts; and (5) the faculty of desire—consisting of appetite and will.

These conceptions served as the departure point for most later faculty theories. The first two of Aristotle's original five faculties were soon relegated to the realm of physiology by his followers, leaving the latter three (sensation, reason, and desire) to philosophy and its offspring, psychology. (Spearman, 1927)

During Rome's imperial ascendancy, the major schools of philosophy, e.g., Epicurean and Stoic, agreed that the psyche had broad specific powers, i.e., faculties, to which were endowed specific subcapacities or functions. Intellect, attention, and language were popular faculties during

[1] Aristotle usually fluctuated between two and five major faculties in his narratives, depending on his intentions. However, he is almost always identified with the five above.
[2] Potential, the possibility or capacity for an act, i.e., as precedent state necessary for achievement, is also an Aristotelean notion.

the time of the Roman Empire. We might pause to comment here upon the ancients' relative lack of interest in language as a faculty. It appears to have been introduced by the Stoics but, though quite popular for awhile, doesn't appear to have been of much theoretical interest as a faculty in its own right. Language's neglect was perhaps due to its cognitive aspects being assigned to the rational faculty; nineteenth century interest in it would, in due time, make up for its early ugly-duckling status.

During the Christian era, when Judeo-Christian doctrines temporarily dimmed the luminosities of Greek and Roman learning, classical faculty doctrine faltered awhile, but survived, nonetheless—thanks in large part to Neoplatonic influences upon early Christian doctrine.[3]

Later, St. Augustine, influenced by both Aristotle and Plato, clearly embraced faculty doctrines—though with variations of his own. The rational soul, he said, is a unity, but carries out diverse functions through its faculties of reason, memory, and will.[4] Imagination, which mediates between memory and reason, is a lesser faculty. Augustine's authority invested faculty doctrine with new stature and helped it to pass into the early Middle Ages as a regnant psychological theory.

During the later Middle Ages, Aristotle reigned as the supreme authority in matters of the psyche among both Muslim and Christian psychological theorists, who, despite their extreme divergences in religious belief, developed quite similar faculty models. Since scholastic conceptions were to prominently influence early brain localization theories, it behooves us to examine them more closely—specifically those proposed by St. Thomas Aquinas.

MEDIEVAL FACULTY CONCEPTIONS

St. Thomas clearly distinguished between the soul, a unitary affair, and its faculties, or powers. The soul is not its faculties, but exercises its functions through these agencies that are separate and distinct from its (the soul's) essence. There is order and priority among the soul's three major faculties—the rational, the sensitive, and the vegetative (Aristotle's

---

[3] By such as Plotinus, who, while not a Christian himself, strongly influenced the thinking of the early Christian fathers. Plotinus's conception of an incorporeal soul, free of the body and physical restraints, had many echoes within doctrines of the Catholic church.

[4] The concept of willpower is one that was certainly popularized by Augustine, if not necessarily original with him. In his writings he speaks of his struggle to control his willful will very much as if he experienced it as an independent force operating within him. However, Brett has called attention to Augustine's recognition of *will* as ". . . a function of the whole nature of man . . ." (Brett, 1912). Augustine's opposition to the free-will doctrine of Pelagius is supportive of this interpretation. Nevertheless, Augustine very frequently wrote about the will as if it were an independent faculty.

nutritive faculty). The rational faculty, the highest faculty, is found only in man and embraces and controls the sensitive faculty, which is present in both man and animal, but not in plants. The sensitive faculty is superior to and controls the vegetative faculty, which is present in all three. The vegetative faculty has the subpowers of nutrition, growth, and reproduction. The sensitive faculty includes the subfaculties that manage information from the five exterior senses, the four interior senses, appetite, and locomotion; it also subsumes the common sense, which exercises additional functions. The rational faculty, or intellect, the most spiritual of the major faculties, subsumes the higher cognitive powers (Watson, 1963).

Despite its fundamental reliance upon Aristotle's original faculty theories, St. Thomas Aquinas's process theory was anything but a slavish imitation of the ancient master's work.[5] The interior senses do not react to any bodily stimulations, whether from sources external or internal, but rather to the products of this stimulation. The first of the interior senses is Aristotle's common sense, which is responsible for sensory qualities not specific to any single sense, e.g., softness, length. The second is the *vis aestimativa*, or estimative power, an inner sense that informs animals of what is harmful or useful to them and does not depend upon any previous training or experience; in man, this process is affected by reason and so given a distinctive name, the *vis cogitativa*. There is also the imaginative sense through which both animals and humans conserve sensory data, i.e., produce imagery. Finally, St. Thomas postulated an inner sense of sensory memory which provides for recognition of images (reproduced sensations) as items of personal experience.

St Thomas Aquinas also modified Aristotelean concepts of appetite, or desire. According to the medieval scholar, the faculty of appetite is twofold, involving sensitive appetites at the sensory level and volitional ones, or will, at the rational level. Will, he said, is necessarily influenced by the rational faculty since it requires knowledge of purpose. "Nothing is willed," St. Thomas said, "unless known" (Watson, 1963, p. 125)—something with which Freud would have disagreed.

Aquinas purified the Aristotelean concept of the rational faculty which had become adulterated over the years. According to St. Thomas, this faculty involves two powers: the power of the active intellect, the *intellectus*, which carries out abstractions and that of the possible intellect, the *ratio*, which is directed toward understanding, judgment, and reasoning. The first power is active and creative; the second, passive and receptive. Sensory information, to become intelligible, must first be processed by

[5] The notions of Arab philosopher–physicians such as Avicenna and Averroës, however, find easy echoes in those of St. Thomas Aquinas and other scholastics who, indeed, often acknowledged Muslim precedence in such theory.

the active intellect, which through abstraction[6] develops concepts such as color and species. It would not take much to make the great scholastic's process theories fit into a modern textbook on cognitive functioning!

This sort of model was the starting point of faculty theory and brain localization efforts for the later Middle Ages, the Renaissance, and the sixteenth century.

RENAISSANCE FACULTY CONCEPTUALIZATIONS

During the Renaissance, there was a general conceptual loosening in faculty conceptualizations. Renaissance man, seeking to escape from theological constraints and scholastic nit-picking, was more willing to speculate and play with process concepts than were his predecessors, and he was less insistent upon excruciating precision and niceties in their development and exposition. If a class of activity sufficiently engaged the interest of a particular philosopher, it was likely to be a candidate for faculty status, a situation very much like today.

During the Renaissance, we find the first clear utilization of faculties to interpret individual differences (Spearman, 1927), as opposed to their use nomothetically. Earlier faculty theorists had employed faculties to explain how men were alike, rather than the ways in which they varied. For example, the rational faculty had been assigned to man and denied to lower animals in an all-or-none fashion. While early faculty theorists had certainly recognized variations in aptitudes, abilities, and penchants from one individual to another in their day-to-day practices and, in fact, in other aspects of their writings, these variations were not generally recognized from the standpoint of their formal theories.[7]

The Renaissance, which glorified individualism rectified this, for with Renaissance individualism came an interest in individual differences and a recognition of differences in the strength and qualities of the various faculties. The impetus toward the utilization of faculties to explain individual differences came, however, from the Renaissance man in the street, rather than from the halls of academia; it was he, not the scholar, who was

---

[6] The senses do some degree of work in this as well. The perception of a specific color, for example, involves perceptual abstraction.

[7] An exception was memory, which received early recognition as varying in degree, or quality. Plato wrote of a man having a "naturally good memory." Aristotle discussed differences in memory as related to his personal characteristics and differences—apparently physiological differences.

Neither very quick-witted nor very slow people seem to have good memories, in the one class there is too much fluidity, in the other too much density. . . . (Spearman, 1927)

inclined to concern himself with human intra-species variations—what made him stronger or better or more sagacious than his fellows, for instance. Coming from the streets, this new language of individual differences was expressed in the vernacular, alienating it from the faculty theories of the scholars, who expressed themselves only in Latin. As a result, the doctrine of individual (faculty) differences was to grow for a while without academic approval. In due time, of course, even academia would succumb to the obvious and recognize that people differed in their abilities (faculties).[8]

---

[8] However, as late as the nineteenth century, Gall was to complain that academic faculty psychologies still ignored individual differences.

5

Early Efforts at Brain Localization

The ventricles of the brain fascinated ancient physician and philosopher alike. They were containers, obviously, but of what and for what purpose—humors or something else? And if something else, what else? Cavities they might have been, but filled with speculations as well as fluids.

The idea of spirits carrying out life processes is implicit in many of the writings of the ancients and received clear expression in the writings of Erasistratus (ca. 310–250 B.C.), who postulated two kinds of *pneuma* (spirits) in the human body governing its functions. Herophilius (ca. 300 B.C.), who preferred four, may have been the first to specifically locate the spirits in the ventricles, wherefrom they regulated the body. It is on this basis that he is sometimes credited as also being the first to specifically locate cognitive faculties within the ventricles (though the spirits may be more appropriately conceived of as agents of the faculties, rather than as faculties themselves).

If Herophilius is frequently accorded priority in localizing the cognitive faculties within the ventricles, so Galen (130–200) is credited with their initial localization within the substance of the brain; though Erasistratus, who appears to have chosen the brain's membranes for this duty, may possibly be awarded priority here. Galen noted that the brain was soft, as a receiving organ should be, and that it pulsated as befitted its role in creating movement. To it Galen assigned various faculties of imagination (forebrain), cogitation (midbrain), sensation, memory, and voluntary motion (hindbrain).[1]

Like his predecessors, Galen attributed all motion to spirits. There are natural spirits, prepared in the lungs; animal spirits, which derive from the heart and arteries; and finer, psychic spirits causing bodily movement, which collect in the ventricles of the brain wherein they are acted upon by the "cognitive faculties" (Riese, 1959).[2]

MEDIEVAL AND RENAISSANCE CONCEPTS
OF BRAIN LOCALIZATION

Conflicting propositions concerning the localization of faculties were generally resolved in favor of the ventricles by the fourth century within Christendom, when the Christian father, Nemesius, clearly identified the ventricles as repositories of cognitive processes.

The "anterior ventricle" of the brain was established as the seat of perception and imagination (*cellula phantastica*), the middle ventricle as the seat of the intellect proper (*cellula logistica*), and the posterior ventricle as the seat of the memory (*cellula memoralis*). Later developments in medieval faculty theory saw a continued emphasis upon ventricular localization within both Christian and Arab camps, though it appears that some writers thereof intended to locate their processes within the walls of the ventricles rather than in its fluids, e.g., in the writings of Averroës (1126–1198) and Avicenna (980–1037) (Murphy & Murphy, 1969).

During the fourteenth century, Mundinus associated the anterior compartment of the lateral ventricle with fantasy or retention, the middle ventricle with special senses, and the posterior one with imagination and the ability to combine things perceived separately. The third ventricle was endowed with the powers of cognition and prognostication; the fourth ventricle was the receptacle of impressions and memory. The choroid plexus, known as the *vermis* because of its wormlike appearance, was

[1] As to the ventricles, Galen, like Herophilius, was impressed by the four interconnecting chambers containing a clear fluid and credited them as the reservoir in which the *pneuma psychicon* were created and stored and from which they caused the body's movements. It is on these grounds that Luria credits him as a ventricular localizationist (Luria, 1966). However, he has been generally accepted as a solidist (McHenry, 1969 and Riese, 1959).
[2] Though Galen assigned faculties to all anatomical organs and accounted for all bodily and mental effects by faculties, he clearly recognized their speculative status. He observed ". . . one would be mistaken in conceiving a faculty as something real, residing in a substance as we reside in our houses" (Riese 3, p. 22) and ". . . so long as we are ignorant of the true essence of the cause which is operating, we call it a faculty" (Riese, 1959, p. 24).

supposed to open and close the passage to these chambers and thus regulate mental powers (McHenry, 1969).[3]

The first European writer of the medieval period to illustrate the ventricular theory of process localization was Albertus Magnus, considered the Aristotle of his time (1193–1280). In Reisch's *Margarita Philosophica* (1513), there is a particularly famous engraving, generally faithful to that of Albertus. In the *Dialogues* (ca. 1562), Ludovici Dolci depicts an instructor discussing Reisch's Renaissance SOI model (and engraving) with a student, in ways anticipatory of our current scene. Hortensius queries:

> You see in this figure where is the common sense, where is the imagination, where the estimative power, where the power of memory and also where is smell and taste.

Fabricus, the student, replies:

> I see all this remarkably well, and everything is put into its proper place. (Hunt, 1869, p. 342)

Even Leonardo da Vinci (1452–1519), master anatomist, subscribed to ventricular conceptions. He located sensations, cognition, and memory in the lateral, third, and fourth ventricles, respectively, and speculated on mental functions:

> The common sense is set in movement by . . . the organ of perception . . . situated in the center between it and the senses. The organ of perception acts by means of the images of the things presented to it by the superficial instruments, that is, the senses, which are placed in the middle between the external things and the organ of perception. . . . (MacCurdy, 1941)

Andreas Vesalius (1514–1564), who made the first detailed study of the solid structures of the brain, viewed the prospects of brain localization differently. His anatomical investigations had led him to speculate on the dominance of a cerebral power (*virtus*), whose strength depended on the opportune balancing of the elements of brain structure. The animal spirits, which in Galenic tradition he assigned to the ventricles, were used for the operations of this *virtus* and for the divine operations of the Reigning Soul. Vesalius was unwilling, however, to commit himself to any specific doctrine of localization, saying:

> How the brain performs its functions, in imagination, in reasoning, in thinking

---

[3] Shakespeare was also taken with such ideas. In *Love's Labour's Lost* (Act IV, Sc. II), Holofernes describes his talent:

> This is a gift! have . . . a foolish extravagant spirit, full of forms, figures, shapes, objects, ideas, apprehension, motions, revolutions: these are begat in the ventricle of memory, nourished in the womb of the pia mater. . . .

and in memory (or in whatever way following the dogma of this or that man you prefer to classify or name the several actions of the chief soul) I can form no opinion whatsoever. Nor do I think that anything more will be found out by anatomy. . . . (Head, 1926, p. 2))

It would seem that he, like Galen, placed processes, in an ill-defined way, in the solid matter of the brain.

LATER VENTRICULAR AND SOLIDIST CONCEPTIONS OF BRAIN LOCALIZATION

Just when ventricular conceptions of brain localization were super-seded in popularity by solidist doctrines is not entirely clear. During the Middle Ages, Western European and Arab physicians and philosophers popularly espoused ventricular localization, though Greek Byzantine physicians' doctrines (still influential at the beginning of the seventeenth century) often argued that the processes were rather to be found within the brain's tissues. It is likely that the advancing science of medical anatomy was responsible for the eventual triumph of substance over cavity. Just as the ventricles had, earlier, logically suggested themselves as the recepta-cles for the processes, the later study of anatomy continued to reveal differentiated brain structures and tissues that manifestly had specific purposes, of which the containment of faculties seemed to be one. As we have seen, Vesalius resisted the temptation to confuse structure with function. Other anatomists, however, were not as sophisticated. Thus the process speculations of the new age of anatomical investigation (Renais-sance and beyond) increasingly turned to the solidities of the cerebrum for the answers as to where this and that faculty, or power, originated and abided.

Ventricular localization of processes diminished sharply by the mid-dle of the seventeenth century. Their last hurrah came with Soemmerring's treatise on the *Organ of the Soul* (1796). In this widely read and discussed treatise dedicated to Kant, Soemmerring postulated that the fluid within the cerebral ventricles is the "immediate organ of the soul (mind)"; the nerve endings he found in the ventricular walls evidenced the soul's direct contact with the sensory and motor activities of the body; the ventricular soul fluid united the nerves and associated them with con-scious experiences. What about the varying cerebral structures which Soemmerring, an eminent neuroanatomist, could certainly not ignore? How were they to be explained? He had an answer: the "power" acting through the fluid used the various cerebral structures as resistors to channel itself.

Immanuel Kant, to whom Soemmerring's work was dedicated, did not at all agree with his admirer's conclusions. He allowed that the ventricular fluid provided a reasonable medium for the collective unity of sensations, i.e., the *sensus communis*, now known as the *sensorium commune*. However, the soul, he said, did not have a specific seat. He rejected the possibility of the "thinking self" being in "a given region of my body." "My soul," Kant expounded: ". . . is everywhere in my body and in its entirety in each of its parts" (Riese, 1959, p. 88).[4] At this point, with Kant's general rejection of Soemmerring's thesis, ventricular localization passes out of history as a tenable concept.

However, while ventricular conceptions of processes were doomed to eventual extinction, their demise does not appear to have been an all-or-none process. Compromises were made here and there between ventricular and solidist positions. We find mixed positions expressed regularly through the centuries. During the thirteenth century, Bartolomaeus Anglicus, Minorite friar and professor of theology in Paris, spoke about derangement of the faculties because of infections and disturbances in "certain *skynnes* [membranes] and *selles* [ventricles] of the brayne" but worst of all when the ". . . problame be in the substaunce of the braine—then is the frenesie worst and most grevous, and therefore most peryllous" (Hunter & MacAlpine, 1963, pp. 2, 3).

A mixed position respecting the roles of ventricles and brain tissue vis-à-vis brain localization is also to be found in the work of Juan Huarte (1529–1588). Prolegomenous of conclusions to be later drawn by Flourens and Lashley, he decided that inasmuch as the understanding could not act without memory and imagination could not act without understanding, all powers resided in each of the ventricles. Attempting to explain nature's purpose in providing more than one ventricle if each held the same processes, he stated that it was for the same reason Nature made two eyes and two ears—so that when one fails there will be other backup structures to carry out necessary functions. So much for Huarte's ventricular concepts. Elsewhere, he wrote about the various sensations being impressed in the brain. Understanding required a dry brain; memory, a moist brain. As the brain substance became too hard in old age, it was unable to properly receive impressions. All this in a solidist Galenic tradition (Hunt, 1869).

Solidist and ventricular coexistence could still be found as late as 1649—in the *Traité de l'esprit de l'homme* of Le Sieur Chanet. In describing imagination, he commented, "The images being brought by the spirits [nerves] to the interior ventricle of the brain excite the faculty which here resides. It is called imagination . . ." (Hunt, 1868, p. 343). Ventricular

---

[4] He did admit to the possibility that the soul could exercise its activity more intensely at specific points of the anatomy.

localization. No? Yes! But then Chanet spoke of the sensory stimulation also leaving "traces and delineations in the brain" (Hunt, 1868, p. 344). Though too cautious to make any grand attempt at specifically localizing processes with the brain's solid parts, Chanet further noted, "Anatomy shows that the brain is composed of a number of small organs we see dispersed in different parts of the brain, though we may not know the use of these different parts . . ." (Hunt, 1868, p. 344). Then he grew bolder and tried to localize memory in cerebellum, exclaiming, "What a marvelous composition must have, then, that organ which is the direct instrument of our mental operations" (Hunt, 1868, p. 344)—solidist localization, to be sure!

So there is no clear demarcation point where ventricular and solidist advocations of process localization abruptly waxed or waned—at least as far as I can determine—rather, there was a fading out of the first as the second became more prominent. By the middle of the seventeenth century, however, solidist doctrines were clearly ascendant.

The outstanding neuroanatomist of the seventeenth century was Thomas Willis (1620–1675), whose *Cerebri Anatome* (1664) introduced a new precision to conceptualizations of brain functions (McHenry, 1969) and to brain localization doctrine. Willis reasoned that the cerebrum was the organ of thought and that the cerebellum was the center of vital functions and the controller of involuntary mechanisms, such as heartbeat, respiration, and digestion. He assigned perception to the corpus striatum, imagination to the corpus callosum, memory to the gyri, and instinct to the midbrain—all in a solidist tradition. Vieussens (1685) preferred the white matter of the cerebral hemispheres for his processes, Lancise (1739) the corpus callosum (Luria, 1966, McHenry, 1969, Riese, 1959).[5]

The great French philosopher, René Descartes (1596–1650), also contributed to solidist tradition. Descartes described the mind (soul) as purely spiritual in constitution and outside the physical order of matter.[6] The functions, or faculties of this soul, he said, are to be considered the ways this insubstantial entity employs itself through its own powers.

Descartes's list of processes was not anything dramatically new. He allowed for the usual faculties—i.e., the external five, the internal senses, the appetites, and the like.

What was new and compelling, however, was his search for a physical abode, or seat, for the soul. Insubstantial as the soul might be, it needed a specific physical point where it could particularly influence the

---

[5] Luria states that "a common feature of the work of all investigations at this early stage was the desire to localize mental phenomena in one particular point of the brain . . . to find a single 'cerebral organ' for all mental processes" (Luria, 1966, p. 1).

[6] The Cartesian theory of mind–body relationships will be discussed more fully in the following chapter.

total body, where its activity and influences could be most accentuated. Riese and Hoff pointed out:

> . . . the doctrine of . . . localization remains the legitimate child of the doctrine of the seat of the soul, a doctrine originated and developed by Descartes in a planned attempt to relate the soul to a distinct region of the brain. (Riese & Hoff, 1950, p. 51)[7]

The region of the brain upon which Descartes bestowed the honor of being the seat of the soul, from whence it regulated the connections between sensory and motor impulses and controlled the body was, of course, the pineal gland, or conarium . . . a rather inconsequential organ. Paul Valery traced the course of Descartes's thinking on the matter:

> . . . despite his separation of the psyche from the body and from the extension, he contrived . . . to find for the psyche a localized position in the brain and to prove that this location is indispensable for the admission of sensory perceptions. He remarks that there exists in the brain a small gland which would seem to him to be this seat of the soul, and the reason he gives for it is that the other parts of the brain are by pairs, just as the eyes and ears are by pairs. Surely there must be "some place where the two images which come to us through our eyes can be joined together before reaching the soul," and he finds no other place in the body where they might be joined except in this gland. . . . (Valéry, 1947, pp. 28–29)

This thesis that one part of the brain harbors the soul, besides contributing to the triumph of solodist conceptions of brain functioning, also held, as we have noted, the basic elements of the classic doctrine of localization—namely, allotment of limited divisions of physical space to specific psychic qualities (Riese & Hoff, 1950). But Descartes went beyond the seating of the soul in the pineal gland. He also took steps to distribute some of its discrete functions over distinct regions of the brain. While the pineal gland was assigned the duty of receiving new impressions into the *sensorium commune,* which Descartes located there, "corporeal" memory required a more extended abode, and the rest of the brain, even nerves and muscles, shared in the housing of this faculty. However, Descartes's forays into brain localization did not go beyond bodily memory. "Intellectual," or "spiritual," memory depended on the soul, as did all higher cognitive processes, and could not be specifically localized. We again see here a distinction being made between higher and lower processes. It was to be a particularly important point of contention for localizationist and anti-localizationist forces in later centuries.[8]

---

[7] A position somewhat toned down by Riese's reconceptualizations of brain localization efforts in later years (Riese, 1959).

[8] We have seen this distinction repeated throughout the earlier part of this history; by Plato, for example, who is perhaps most notably responsible for its wide adoption. Descartes modernized the distinction in a form that was to profoundly influence Western European civilization. We shall observe influences of the Cartesian distinction between lower and higher psychological processes throughout the rest of this historical narrative.

6

The Travails of Faculty Psychology

THE DESCARTIAN SOUL

The towering figure of Descartes casts its shadow on faculty psychology, as elsewhere in the world of ideas. The importance of his conception of mind for process theory extends far beyond the boundaries of brain localization doctrine. For it is to Descartes that we owe the version of *mind* that most of us in the Western world still accept as personally, if not scientifically, valid. Philosophy, psychology or medicine have not been able to fully rid themselves of that mind, the *res cogitans*—a thing that thinks! Nor of his solution of mind–body relationships, a solution culminating many centuries of inquiry and debate and inaugurating new centuries of inquiry and debate. Man's conception of soul was originally an explanatory rather than a theological principle. It was an attempt to explain the difference between living and nonliving things or between inanimate and animate things. The Greek conception of *pneuma* initially meant breath or air, as did *psyche*. *Pneuma* later came to be translated as spirit, *psyche* as soul. In Aristotle's writings *pneuma* came to be a partial manifestation of *psyche*, the fiery spirit that distinguishes living from nonliving things. *Pneuma* in its various forms was then postulated to activate living things, and, in the case of animate things like animals and humans, to move them and direct them in their movements. It was described as a nonmaterial force directing material objects. Later, *vital* and *animal spirits* were to be invoked for similar explanatory reasons. Like *pneuma*, spirits and the like emanate from the soul to control life processes, create animation, direct behavior, etc. The espousal of pneumatic principles by the famed Roman medical authority Galen and by the medieval Christian church—which found Galen's conceptions most compatible with its own—meant their wide acceptance in theological, learned, and lay societies; heresy being a chancy thing through most of history.

A major problem persisted for such explanatory schemes, however. It was much the same for a seventeenth century philosopher such as Descartes as it had been for the Greek philosophers of the fifth century B.C. Are these life forces spiritual in nature, i.e., spiritual in terms that we of today would use, or material, i.e., physical? Aristotle had offered a solution, in which the soul is a life principle identifiable with the structures and functions of living things: Aristotle's solution served to philosophically resolve the distinction between the physical and the spiritual. But it was not truly compatible with the developments of Christian theology which conceptualized a free immaterial soul, associated and identified with the body within which it resides, but immortal and striving toward union with God; with its ties to the physical body dissolved upon death. Nor was it entirely satisfactory to the New Science whose conceptions of Natural Law had been broadened to encompass the functioning of the human body, and which invited a materialistic interpretation of the functioning of that body. Somehow soul and body had to be separated and yet allowed to interact. If this could be done, both the imperatives of theology and the demands of science would be satisfied. Descartes formulated an answer, that of psycho–physical dualism, that seemed to do this.

Descartes developed his theories on mind–body relationships at a time when the frontiers of scientific and technological knowledge were rapidly expanding. Despite the wary eye of the Church, new medical discoveries were being made that made it increasingly possible to interpret physiology and behavior entirely in materialistic terms; Harvey's discovery of the circulation of blood dealt, for one, a mortal blow to Galen's pneumatic theories. In addition to increasing scientific—and materialistic—knowledge concerning the human body, there was the new wonder of Descartes's age—mechanical models. The more elaborate gardens of the day were adorned with statues that moved and instruments that played music by proper direction and redirection of the flow of water through them. If statues could move and instruments play in the absence of any voluntary action, could not the movements of the human body take place without any conscious intent on the part of an individual?

Descartes became convinced that bodies, animal and human, are machines, able to operate in a self-contained way without invoking the concept or principle of soul to account for their activation or behavior. Whatever spirits operate an animal or human body, they operate within the closed system of that body, and are not part of the soul system.

Animals do not possess souls at all; they are altogether automata and belong entirely to the realm of physical phenomena. Human bodies are also self-contained machines able to function automatically. They too do not require souls to function. Nor is the soul dependent upon the body. It, unlike the body, is free and unextended, immaterial and immortal. It resides in all parts of the body but reaches out to its creator. After death it departs its corruptible human container and goes to join the creator. Soul and body interact in the pineal gland. (In later centuries the cerebral cortex would replace the gland as the site of interaction.) The human soul, can direct the human body's movements by moving the pineal gland about. The human body, however, is capable of movement without the human soul being engaged; Descartes inaugurated the idea of reflex action with his thoughts on this latter point.

Descartes thus freed the human soul—from physical constraints. He clearly made it into a mind substance. It became after his ministrations very much a cognitive affair replete with innate ideas inviting empirical study and analysis; it is the Cartesian mind that we evaluate through intelligence tests (Chomsky, 1966). It was the Cartesian mind that led the way into modern conceptualizations of process; both from the standpoint of the ideas Descartes elaborated and the challenges that were mounted to them.

As we have reviewed in the previous chapter, Descartes's *res cogitans* was supplied with faculties by the Frenchman. His soul needed memory, reason and will, etc., to operate. However, Descartes was also insistent that this soul was unitary and indivisible. He called attention to its oneness.

> . . . I cannot discover in myself any parts, but I clearly know and conceive that I am a thing absolutely one and complete. (Young, 1970, p. 72)

What were, then, the Descartian soul's faculties? Were they simply generalizations—abstractions—categorizing various communalities in thought and behavior? Were they the soul's potentials for various types of action? Were they separate and special capacities? Were they independently definable psychic structures? Descartes was irritated at the latter notion, piquishly commenting:

> There are in us as many faculties as there are truths to be known. . . . But I do not think that any useful application can be made of this way of thinking; and it seems to me rather more likely to be mischievous, by giving to the ignorant occasion for imagining an equal number of little entities in the soul. (Flourens, 1846, p. xi)

But what always seems to happen with processes, inevitably happened with the faculties of post-Descartian years. The insidious process of reification soon turned them into psychic things, which, given the influence of Descartes, came to be regarded as innately determined. Carte-

sians were likely to hail, in the master's name, both the inviolability of the
soul and the faculties as discrete and causative agents within that soul.

ASSOCIATIONISM[1]

Such practices were to be challenged by psychologists who can be
loosely categorized as associationistic. The first in this new tradition was
the British empiricist, Thomas Hobbes (1588–1679), a contemporary and
acquaintance of Descartes and a steadfast foe of religion and super-
naturalism—who was influenced by Galileo's conceptions of motion.
Hobbes held that almost all mental activities result from the movement of atoms in the brain that are set off by sensory experiences. All of
the mind's activities and contents can be so explained. No soul is required, nor any innate controlling faculties; the mind is the result of

. . . the *motion,* agitation or alteration which the object worketh in the
brain or spirits, or some internal substance of the head. (Murphy & Kovach,
1972, p. 28)

How do the movements of atoms cause mental processes—which are,
after all, phenomenologically different? Hobbes did not concern himself
with the issue, but what he did say was enough to inspire a movement that
would rock the foundations of faculty psychology.

Hobbes's successor, in what came to be the British empiricist tradition,[2] was John Locke (1632–1704), who, despite having written "We
are born with faculties and powers capable of anything," nevertheless
attempted to reduce the mind to elementaristic sensations and their products. Locke was after big game in his "Essay on the Nature of Human
Conduct": the scholasticism that had burdened him when he was a
student some 30 years earlier and Descartes's doctrine of innate ideas. He
insisted, contrary to accepted Descartian rule, that we are not born with
any preconceived, i.e., innate, ideas, moral, theological, logical, or
mathematical principles or faculties. Instead, he pointed out, in the tradition of Hobbes, that the mind is derived from sense impressions:

How comes it (the mind) to be furnished? Whence has it all the materials of
reason and knowledge? To this I answer, in one word, from *experience.* In that all
our knowledge is founded, and from that it ultimately derives itself. (Boring, 1950,
p. 172)

---

[1] Locke first coined the term "association of ideas." Associationism is, variously, a theory,
a doctrine, an empirical phenomenon. I have chosen not to clearly distinguish such aspects,
one from the other, in this book.
[2] The term "empiricist" refers to the belief that knowledge is derived from experience.

But in what manner? In his explanations, Locke seemed to lose his nerve or some of his convictions, for he acknowledged that the mind actively combines and manages sensations and impressions they leave and that a process called reflection accounts for the complexities of thought. He also held, much in the tradition of faculty psychology, that the mind employs the powers of perception, reasoning, judgment, etc., How so, John Locke, arch antifacultist? Why, with proper explanations and apologies! Thus he told his readers, regarding such powers, that the ordinary way of speaking

. . . is that the understanding and the will are two faculties of the mind, a word proper enough if it be used . . . so as not to breed any confusion in man's thoughts by being supposed to stand for some real beings in the soul that performed those actions of understanding and volition. . . . For if it be reasonable to suppose and talk of faculties as distinct beings that can act as we do when we say "The will orders" and "The will is free" it is fit that we shall make a speaking faculty, and a walking faculty, and a dancing faculty, by which these actions are produced, which are but several modes of motion . . . the fault has been that faculties have been spoken of and represented as so many distinct agents. For it being asked, what it was that digested the meat in our stomachs, it was a ready and very satisfactory answer to say that it was the digestive faculty . . . and so on in the mind, the intellectual faculty, or the understanding, understood; and the elective faculty, or the will, willed or commanded; which is, in short, to say that the ability to digest, digested; and the ability to move, moved; and the ability to understand, understood. For "faculty, ability, and power," I think, "are but different names for the same thing." (Rusk, 1969, pp. 132, 133)

It would appear that Locke was trying to have his cake and eat it, too, with regard to his formulations and that he could not rid himself of faculty conceptions despite his earnest denial of them—a situation not uncommon to other critics of faculty psychology.[3]

David Hume (1715–1776), another of the early British empiricists, was to take a harder, more radical (and more consistent) approach to the problem of faculties than that of Locke's in his *Treatise of Human Nature* (1738). Locke had allowed for the "acts of the mind" exerting control over ideas that resulted from sensations. He had also talked about the mind's exercising control over sensory information, through its powers, etc. Hume denied the need for any mind agents at all, saying, ". . . there is not, in any particular instance of cause and effect, anything which can suggest the idea of power . . . or necessary connection" (Sahakian, 1975, p. 43). He reduced all mental contents to impressions left by the sensations caused by the kaleidoscope of events to which the organism was

---

[3] This use of alternate terms has always been common to those who rely on faculty constructs while being unwilling to be identified as faculty psychologists.

exposed. These impressions are controlled by an external force called association, which operates according to specific laws.[4] No other forces or processes, he said, are needed to explain cognition. The mind is just another name for "a heap or collection of different perceptions . . ." (Sahakian, 1975, p. 43). Memory, imagination, and the other so-called faculties are but different names for the ideas derived from sensory impressions. Unlike Locke, Hume had no afterthoughts, apologies, or regrets for his position.

The soul–mind and its faculties having been properly reduced to elementary sensations by Hume, a systematic formulation of the new principles of what was to be called associationism was required, and it came from the mind and hands of David Hartley (1705–1757).

Hartley transformed the "laws" of associationism into a psychology of association (Mandler & Mandler, 1964).

Boring speaks of Hartley's contributions:

> He is important because he was the founder of associationism. He was not the originator; that was Aristotle, or Hobbes, or Locke, as one pleases. The principle had been used effectively and greatly developed by Berkeley and Hume. Hartley merely established it as a doctrine. He took Locke's little-used title for a chapter, "The Association of Ideas," made it the name of a fundamental law, reiterated it, wrote a psychology around it, and thus created a formal doctrine with a definite name, so that a school could repeat the phrase after him for a century and thus implicitly constitute him its founder. (Boring, 1950, pp. 193, 194)

Associationism, in its various forms, has always sought to explain away faculty psychology.[5] So it is from this standpoint that Hartley is particularly important for a history of processes. He is additionally important because, being a physician interested in neurology, he extended the laws of association to include motor phenomena, i.e., muscular movements, and ideas derived therefrom, all of which could be "associated." The association of sensory and motor elements brings voluntary and semivoluntary actions, he said, under the control of sensations. S-R theory was aborning. In Corollary VII of Proposition XX of Hartley's *Observations on Man,* we read the theorem making it all possible.

> If any sensation A, idea B, or muscular motion C, be associated for a sufficient number of times with any other sensation D, idea E, or muscular motion F, it will, at last, excited, the simple idea belonging to the sensation D, the very idea E, or the very muscular motion F. (Mandler & Mandler, 1964, p. 87)

---

[4] The concept of *natural laws,* like Newton's laws of gravity, strongly influenced Hume. There was no need to posit inner organizing forces, e.g., faculties to account for cognitive events. They obeyed the same external laws as did the universe outside of man.

[5] Though as we shall see, in the long run, it provided faculty psychology with the means of metaphrasing its doctrines in ways which allowed them to survive into the age of "scientific psychology."

This theorem was to find its way, consciously and unconsciously, into the theories of a variety of Hartley's neurological and psychological successors. It was to eventually be of great import, though neglected for the while.[6]

Hartley was no more tolerant of cognitive faculties than was Hume. The only thing tantamount to a process, or faculty, that he would allow was the capacity of children to have sensations. That was all that was needed, because, as Murphy and Kovach remark:

> Sensory experience, in due time by making proper connections would build up to more complex objects of thought and finally arrive at systems of higher cognitive thinkings, morals, and whatever else was needed to explain man. . . . (Murphy & Kovach, 1972, p. 35)

With Hartley there was the arrival in psychology at almost complete physical atomism, a reduction of mental life to sensation-derived elements, which, in combinations, through association yield all observable events.

FRENCH SENSATIONALISM

The French sensationalists[7] followed the example of their British empiricist-associationistic colleagues by also attacking faculty psychology. However, while in their broad intents as radically reductionistic as Hume, they, like Locke, could not altogether do away with faculty concepts in their formulations. In a certain sense, they became facultists—despite themselves. Among other things, their insistence upon inner organizing structures being required to manage the flux and flow of experiential data sensations would lay the groundwork for one of the most prominent of all faculty theories—phrenology. Let us sketch several of their ambivalencies.

The importance of Etienne de Condillac (1750–1780) to a history of process training—or for that matter to the history of special education—should not be underestimated. We will consider his role in these respects in the second part of the book. What we are immediately concerned with at this particular stage are his conceptualizations as a process theorist, wherein associationism's struggles and the compromises with faculty psychology are both clearly manifest.

Condillac, an influential French philosopher, adapted Locke's ideas to Gallic ways, making Lockean concepts familiar ones to French thinkers. He was even more radical than Locke in his conception of the mind as a tabula rasa. Locke was willing to endow the newborn child with

---

[6] The motor side of the equation was relatively ignored by many important later associationists (the Mills, for example, giving it minor notice).

[7] Call them empiricists if you will, or associationists too!

capacities both for sensation and reflection (which could create ideas). Condillac thought sensation was enough—hence, his famous statue. It was a sentient one, with a soul capable of experiencing sensations of smell but with its other modalities inoperative.[8]

Condillac's statue began "life" with no knowledge of any kind, certainly not the innate ideas, which Descartes had attributed to the human mind and which Locke and Condillac were trying, above all else, to deny. The first impression on its tabula rasa would be the smell of a rose. Since the statue was sentient, it had to be conscious of the rose's smell. To be conscious of the smell meant to notice it, that is, pay attention to it. If a second kind of smell were introduced, the statue would compare it with the first. Thus judgment would be created. As the number of smells increased, the statue would encounter some that were pleasant, others unpleasant, arousing desire and aversion, out of which, preferences would be developed. With the emergence of preferences, there would be approach and avoidance, i.e., motivation. As particular smells recurred, the statue could come to recognize their earlier occurrences, with memory the consequence. In comparing past and present smells, the statue would be associating them. Once olfaction developed into a form of cognition in the statue, the provision of tactual sensations would allow the statue to greatly expand its knowledge about external objects by developing additional associations. Then, as further information from the other modalities was added, the statue could develop a human mind. And this mind would have faculties, though Condillac, unlike Locke would have them derive from sensations, rather than be construed as innate organizing principles (Bentley, 1916).

However by allowing a "negative" mind to this statue, i.e., one capable of reviewing and organizing experiences, Condillac admitted the existence of "inner" processes—despite his denial of innate faculties. Nor could Charles Bonnet (1720–1793), another major French sensationalist, do without such "organizing" principles, even though he, too, derived them from sensory information.

The need for "organizers" also appears, in somewhat compromised form in the work of Pierre Jean George Cabanis (1757–1808) (Bentley, 1916). Cabanis, like the other French sensationalists, emphasized that the sense organs on the outside of the body provide the data that ultimately make up the mind. Nevertheless, the organism's basic needs require that it have innate faculties. These faculties emerge from a mental constitution that is determined by physical anatomy, i.e., the brain, which carries out

---

[8] Condillac chose to begin with the sense of smell because he regarded it as the least valuable of three senses in contributing knowledge. He was handicapping his statue by making it begin at rock bottom in respect to obtaining information.

the diverse functions of combining and rearranging sensory impressions, attaching signs to them, and producing thought.

THE REAFFIRMATION OF FACULTY PSYCHOLOGY

Attack! Counter attack!—First by Gottfried Wilhelm Liebnitz (1646–1716), who responded to Locke's "An Essay Concerning the Human Understanding" with a reaffirmation of Descartes's doctrine of innate processes.

Observing, as did Aristotle, Descartes, and sundry others, that animals share sense experience with humans, yet are lacking in scientific knowledge, he challenged the empiricists that the human mind had to be more than a tabula rasa. "There is nothing in the intellect which was not previously in the senses," he observed, ". . . provided we make the reservation, except the intellect itself" (Sahakian, 1975, p. 28).

Leibnitz emphasized the unity of the mind, as did Descartes before him, a mind which, persistently active, is also continuous. The so-called faculties he observed are abstractions from this mind's complex unified whole, or *unitas multiplex,* so that perception, memory, attention, thought, and a multitude of other functions are expressed concurrently in any specific activity. Thus Leibnitz's importance for faculty psychology does not lie in his endorsement of reified faculties. It is, rather, due to his endorsement of the Descartian mind as an innately given, active, dynamic, organizing psychological entity.

It was in this respect that his formulations prepared the way for a new and aggressive restatement of faculty theory. This was provided by the German psychologist Christian Wolff (1679–1754), whose work earned him the title of "Father of Faculty Psychology" (the modern father, we should more appropriately say).[9]

Wolff's central doctrine was simple and clear-cut. The soul is unitary but it has distinct, more or less independent, faculties through which it acts, just as the whole body enters at different times into widely different acts. Faculties create possibilities for action (*Vermögen*). They are the soul's means of carrying out certain activities. An act of remembering, for example, is made possible by the faculty of remembering. Wolff's faculties are gentle creatures, *nudae agendi possibilitates,* very much in the manner that Plato had originally intended, not aggressive causative agents.

From these modest beginnings, however, Wolff proceeded on the

---

[9] Most familiar to most readers in the form of his caricature is Dr. Pangloss in Voltaire's *Candide.*

road to reification by comparing his faculties to bodily organs such as the heart, stomach, and lungs. Wolff's faculty "organs" are interdependent in their functions, as are the anatomical organs of the body. And while the soul's "unifying force" synthesizes their activities (Klein, 1970), they are separate and distinct.

Wolff postulated two major groups of faculties—the cognitive and appetitive—within which there are subfaculties. Following Platonic tradition, he distinguished between higher and lower processes. The cognitive faculty was higher than the appetitive; each of these faculties was itself divided into a number of higher and lower faculties. Thus the faculty of reason was given higher status within the cognitive faculty than that of memory.

Johann Nikolaus Tetens (1736–1807), one of Wolff's major followers, replaced his mentor's bipartite faculty model with a tripartite one. The affective and conative components of Wolff's appetitive faculty became the separate faculties of feeling and willing. Tetens' tripartite scheme, because of its espousal by Immanuel Kant, became the classic way of approaching the mind in modern times, i.e., in terms of knowing, feeling, and willing[10] (Watson, 1963).

It is difficult to overestimate the influence of Kant upon the thinking of his time. Accordingly, his endorsement of faculty psychology gave it high credibility. The faculty approach was congenial to the religious mind—Kant was religious—because it accepted certain fundamental functions of intellectual and moral importance as givens and rejected the anarchistic policies of the British associationists and French sensationalists, who sought to reduce psychic phenomena to sensory bits, thus ultimately denying the soul.

It was Hume's attack upon the innate givens of cognitive behavior that made Kant decide to discover what the mind is and what it does. He concluded from his speculations that knowledge and understanding are products created by the mind, rather than mere accretions and complications of sensory impressions. He determined that the mind (soul) works in certain inherent ways, utilizing three great faculties—knowing, feeling, and willing—each of which exercises specific subpowers. (The subpower of judgment was given particular love and care by Kant, which may have accounted for its prominence in later educational psychology texts.) In addition, Liebnitz's monadal concept of apperception became, in Kantian theory, an a priori synthesizing power of the mind that operates as a principle of "transcendental unity."

Thus the existence of innate processes governing man's behavior was reaffirmed by Kant. The later elaboration of his doctrines by Hegel

---

[10] These became the traditional organizing principles of subsequent psychology texts.

(1770–1831) and Friess[11] (1773–1843) spread the gospel of faculty psychology throughout Western Europe.

Elsewhere, there was also a rallying of support to faculties. Hume's radical empiricism had not only wakened Kant from his dogmatic slumbers on the European continent. It had also stirred up negative reactions in the British Isles, especially in the Scottish universities. There, the mechanistic writings of Hobbes, the sensationalistic doctrines of Locke, and—most of all—Hume's indifference to the soul and its higher powers created a strong protest movement. Hume's skepticism was anathema to those raised within the pale of Scottish Presbyterianism. They found a particularly cogent spokesman and leader in the person of philosopher–psychologist Thomas Reid (1710–1796).

Reid's opinions are important, not only because of their influence within Britain, but also because of their influence abroad. In addition to affecting British psychology, they stimulated a counterreaction against Condillac's sensationalism in France. Reid's influences are further to be found in cognitive and educational theories developed in the United States—even in the thinking of such American psychologists as William James, Mary Calkins, and Gordon Allport. It is on these grounds that our narrative considers his contributions in some detail.

Hume's skepticism led Reid to even question the existence of the external world. He argued, however, that a simple and undeniable perception tells us that this external world does, in fact, exist and that Hume's doubts flew in the face of all human experience. Having established the existence of the objective world on a commonsensical basis, Reid promulgated his doctrine of faculties, again on a commonsensical basis:

> The words *power* and *faculty*, which are often used in speaking of the mind, need little explication. Every operation supposes a power in the being that operates; for to suppose anything to operate, which has no power to operate, is manifestly absurd. (Young, 1970, p. 22)

There have been heated debates about the nature of Reid's faculties. Did he conceive them as actual structures, as Warren suggested in his *History of Association*? In Warren's book, Reid was criticized for having regarded ". . . mind as a collection of faculties, each fully capable of performing its functions from the beginning" (Warren, 1921, p. 19). Several of Reid's apologists have credited him with more defensible positions. Klein (1970) believed that Reid meant to define his faculties as psychological activities, rather than as "independent things or objects." And, indeed, Reid did describe his faculties and powers as "operations of

---

[11] Friess tried to refer these processes to physiological processes. On this basis, he can be considered a brain localizationist, though he is rarely acknowledged as such.

the mind." Albrecht (1970) maintained that Reid used the term "faculty" only in a classificatory sense and to establish topics for his mental (cognitive) analyses, rather than as ". . . an agent or substance . . . of . . . explanatory value" (Albrecht, 1970, p. 36). It is not quite clear, however, how such apologies void his statement above or others such as ". . . as I believe that every effect has a cause, I believe there is some power or faculty which enables me to remember" (Albrecht, 1970, p. 38).

Another of the problems that confronts Reid's apologists lies in his interpretation of process terms. Thus Reid, rather than using Wolff's notion of *nudae agendi possibilites* for his faculties or the Latin word *potentia* (which would have suggested capacity for certain types of action), chose to use the English word "power" in its modern sense—a word that implies an active agent. It is also difficult to claim that Reid used his faculties only for classificatory purposes, when he spoke about strong and weak faculties, e.g., of good or bad memory.

There are, in fact, many ways of viewing Reid's intentions concerning his faculty constructs, for he seems to have used them variously: as classificatory principles and as capacities and structures, or functions. Also, how his faculty conceptions come across depends upon where in Reid you wish to read and your own preconceptions on the subject. His writings on "process" were anything but simple.

Reid distinguished between the mind's operations (activities) and the powers that cause them. The mind's operations can be observed through introspection, but its underlying powers are not immediately observable. Every operation presupposes a power, but the existence of a power does not mean that an operation will necessarily be performed, since a power implies *potential* rather than *actual* activity.[12] He noted that we cannot observe the powers directly but only infer them from perceived operations; that the same operations may be the result of different powers, and that the powers often operate in conjunction with each other, so that it may be impossible to isolate one from the other.

Reid distinguished between *power* and *faculty*, though recognizing they were often used synonymously. Power, he said, is the more general term, relative to the ability to do many things, while faculties are those powers which are ". . . original and natural, and which make a part of the constitution of the mind" (Brooks, 1976, p. 69). Powers developed by use, exercise, or study, he called habits. While instinct is innately determined like a faculty, he made it a power rather than a faculty, though not distinguishing clearly one from the other. The behavior determined by a faculty is more complex than that determined by an instinct. Faculties

---

[12] Herein Reid falls in line with Wolff and classical faculty psychology, returning to the original ancient usage of *potentia*.

require experience before they are transformed into efficient behavior. No such practice is necessary with instincts. The characteristics of the mind that allow us to acquire new powers in the form of habits he termed *capacities*.

While powers differ in both kind and degree, Reid insisted that they are but different aspects of the same unifying principle[13] and function in conjunction with one another, so that their effects never appear in isolation. The exertion of a component of a specific class of powers influences the activities of the rest of the powers in that class. Was he intimating transfer of training?

Reid's broadest division of psychic processes was into intellectual and active powers, i.e., those involving sensory perception and information processing and those that prompt us to action. These two types of powers operate in conjunction with each other. Both types are employed "in most, perhaps in all of the operations of the mind." Moreover, the intellectual powers have active components, and the active powers have intellectual components. Respecting the latter, when there is activity, the intellectual powers help determine the appropriate action, and so are necessarily involved in volition.

Reid's active powers divide into the mechanical, animal, and rational. The mechanical powers further subdivide into instincts and habits; the animal powers into appetites, desires, and benevolent and malevolent affections. Desires are acquired appetites; affections are complex emotionally toned attitudes involving other people. Desires also subsume rational powers, which include the moral faculty (moral sense, or conscience) and resentment (rational anger). There are other unclassified powers that have intellectual components, such as attention, deliberation, imitation, and faculty of resolution (fixed purpose) (Brooks, 1976).

Reid did not proceed to any exhaustive listing of powers. He was more systematic with those of the intellectual class than with the members of the active class, since he wished to build a picture of the successive steps by which the mind proceeds in the acquisition of its knowledge and he thought the active powers were more individual, hence less easily cataloged.

The intellectual powers are fewer in number than the active, and they are not provided with subclassifications. Reid enumerated them, beginning with the simplest intellectual activities and moving gradually to the more complex processes. It is unclear which of these intellectual powers are to be considered faculties—perhaps all of them. However, Reid's writing is generally casual and unsystematic. Thus it is difficult to deter-

---

[13] He was certainly no more willing than Wolff, Tetens, Kant (or any of their predecessors) to violate the invisibility of the unitary human soul.

mine the exact number of his intellectual powers and faculties; the reader is further baffled in trying to do so by confusions in the use of terms. He used the term imagination, for example, as a synonym for two different powers: simple apprehension and invention. Reid also forgot to include in his catalog certain obvious faculties and powers, such as that of speech.

Reid was aware of his problems in identifying and specifying his powers.[14] His *writings* include remarks to the effect that since powers are, after all, not directly observable, they are impossible to accurately isolate. And, then, the same power had been labeled in many ways by different and even the same writers. Reid did not blame himself for such faulty conceptualizations, though he was as guilty as any.

Reid's process conceptions are considerably more complex than our sketch might indicate. A more extensive consultation of his doctrines or of Stewart's later elaborations would take us too far off the major track we seek to follow. The reader interested in learning more about it is referred elsewhere (Albrecht, 1970, Ross, 1976, Klein, 1970) and to Reid himself. It should be clear, even from our brief review, that Reid was an elaborate, if often disorganized, process theorist and that in him faculty theory once again had found a doughty champion.

---

[14] Remember that faculties were subclasses of powers.

7
Phrenology

THE BEGINNINGS OF PHRENOLOGY AND THE DESCARTIAN BRAIN

The doctrine of phrenology began the modern era of brain localization efforts. It is a "science" which is associated, usually infamously, with the name of Franz Joseph Gall (1758–1828), who attempted to correlate skull configurations (and through them, brain structures) with behavioral functions. Although Gall himself used the term "craniology," *phrenology* was preferred by his erstwhile associate, Spurzheim (1776–1832). The latter term came to be the preferred one.

As with almost all concepts of the past there are usually harbingers of that past, if not facsimiles, to be found in a still more distant past. So was it with Gall's ideas.

The idea that the functions of the brain could be inferred from its structure was perhaps never as enthusiastically espoused as by Le Sieur Chanet in his *Traité de l'esprit de l'homme* (1649).

An intelligence fully acquainted with the whole mechanism of the brain could read it like a book. The prodigious number of minute organs appropriated to sensations and thoughts would be, for such an intelligence, what, for us, are printed characters. We turn over the leaves of books; we study them. The aforesaid intelligence would merely contemplate the brain. (Hunt, 1868, p. 343)

The belief that the size and shape of the brain and its parts and the nature of its functions can be read from the size and shape of the skull can be traced back to the ancients. Among them, Galen claimed that the brain could be inferred from the shape of a head, which should be like a round ball compressed "a little on the sides," to suggest a proper intelligence (Hunt, 1869, p. 103).

It was also expressed during the Renaissance by Juan Huarte in *An Examination of Geniuses for the Sciences*, discussing the differences of aptitudes among men and what sort of learning would best suit different types.[1] Huarte suggested a man who has ". . . his forehead very plain, the back of his head very flat, has not his brain so figured as is requisite for wit and ability." For a man to be intelligent, his ". . . brain should be well formed, and of sufficient quantity. The four ventricles should be distinct and severed, each in its proper place, and of appropriate capacity" (Hunt, 1869, p. 103). Like Galen, Huarte agreed that smallness of head meant a deficiency in brains. Unlike Galen, Huarte was disinclined to think that big heads implied big brains, since size might be due to the thickness of bone and the quality of flesh, rather than a large brain; in the same way big oranges may have thick hard skin but little juice.

That the skull may give clues to more specific aspects of mental function can be found in a later book, *Examen de l'Examen des Esprits* (1631) by Jourdain Guibelet. In the last chapter, entitled "By What Signs the Character of Children May Be Known," Guibelet espoused the doctrine of physiognomy, that doctrine by which facts of personality, character, and intelligence are to be deduced from an individual's physical appearance, and specifically from his head (cephalonomy). The Frenchman noted that there is such an intimate connection between the soul and its organ, the body, that we are able to judge the mental capacity of a child by his face, "the mirror of the soul," when he is seven or eight years old; the chief marks, however, of a child's mind are to be found about the head. Since the brain is the seat of the faculties, it is reasonable to suppose that the external head should show what is going on within, just as a dial outwardly represents what is hidden. A large, square head proportioned to the size of the face was thought to demonstrate strong faculties, since a large brain was a sign of good sense and a sound mind (Hunt, 1869).[2]

Similar views were discussed elsewhere in the seventeenth century by Marion Cureau de la Chambre (1549–1669), physician to Louis XIV, and the Englishman Richard Saunders, who in 1653 in his book *Physiognomie, Chiromancie, Metoscopie, etc.* clearly adumbrated and anticipated Gall's researches:

> Now, in our science of Physiognomie, the form, the proportion, and dimensions of the head are to be considered; for by it, and its form, we judge of the mind contained therein.

---

[1] We have noted Huarte's brain localization efforts earlier.

[2] Guibelet believed in ventricular localization. Large heads being required, he perceived, to accommodate large ventricles.

A little head is never without vice, and most commonly, is guilty of little wisdom, but rather full of folly, which is naught and malicious.

The best form of a head is moderate, has greatness and thickness, and of a decent and convenient roundness, which, before and behind, is tempered with a little depression . . . .

The brain, one of the noblest parts of the body, is according to the form of the cranium; for if the cranium be corrupted, the brain is so too. The head of man has proportionately more brains than all other living creatures; and men have more brains than women; and the head of man has more joynts than any other creature. So the well-formed head is like a mallet, or sphear, there being some eminence before and behinde; the form of the middle ventricle should be a little compressed, so the cogitative faculty is the more notable. If the forepart be depressed, the man is of no judgment: if the hinder, he has no memory. . . . When the head is big, proportionately to the body, the sinews of the neck big, and the neck itself strong, it is a sign of strength, choler, magnanimity, and a martial humour. . . . A head having the middle ventricle somewhat compressed towards the side, denotes the cogitative faculty, natural diligently comprehensive, rationative, and eloquent, which proceeds from the union of the spirits that are in that place; those who have a head thus are learned and knowing. The head, very little, is necessarily an evil sign; and the less it is, the more folly there is. (Hunt, 1869, pp. 109, 110)

Assuredly, speculations regarding the relationship between skull size and contour and the brain (and through the brain, its functions) have a long history.

By the eighteenth century there was general consensus that the brain was the organ of the mind, the seat of its processes. However, interest in the nature of brain/process relationships was essentially speculative. Bichat, as late as 1799, was still able to exposit a Platonic distinction between cognitive and affective processes. He held that the brain was the center for intelligence, memory, perception, imagination, and judgment, but that the emotions had their seats in the internal organs (Boring, 1950).

One could choose to continue in the tradition of the faculty psychologists and elect the brain as the seat of a number of major faculties, or one could reduce the mind to minute elements, the impressions left by sensations, and assign these to small changes in the nervous system caused by vibrations of nervous fibers, as suggested by British and French associationists. Better still, one could play both elementarist and factulist. So Charles Bonnet, in the eighteenth century, assigned specific functions to each nerve fiber . . . every word recorded by one's ears had its own sensory fiber. Yet Bonnet also considered the mind to be an aggregation of larger faculties, each of which was assigned a specific bundle of nerve fibers.

But there was no intensive searching to validate these propositions. Instead, there prevailed a generally languid acceptance of rational arguments and possible explanations as to how the mind's functions and the brain were related, with little hope held out for better. So Czech physiologist, George Prochaskas wrote in his *Dissertation on the Functions of the Nervous System* (1784) of the "divisions of the intellect," each of which had "its allotted organ in the brain . . . understanding . . . the will, imagination and memory."

Prochaskas remarked that

. . . since the brain, as well as the cerebellum, is composed of many parts, variously figured, it is probable that nature, which never works in vain, has destined those parts to various uses, so that the various faculties of the mind seem to require different portions of the cerebrum and cerebellum for their production.

Nevertheless,

Hitherto it has not been possible to determine what portions of the cerebrum or cerebellum are specially subservient to this or that faculty of the mind. The conjectures by which eminent men have attempted to determine these are extremely improbable, and that department of physiology is as obscure now as ever it was. (Prochaskas, 1851, p. 446)

The German physiologist, Albrecht von Haller, in his epochal work *Elementa Physiologiae* (1757–1765), agreed. He had conducted experiments on the brain and concluded that the cortex must feel, though he elicited no movement from it upon excitation. He admitted that experiments, the phenomena of disease, and anatomical evidence supported the concept of brain localization. Nevertheless, he decided:

Our present knowledge does not permit us to speak with any show of truth about the more complicated functions of the mind or to assign in the brain to imagination its seat, to common sensation its seat, to memory its seat. Hypotheses of this kind have in great numbers reigned in the writings of physiologists from all time. But all of them alike have been feeble, fleeting, and of a short life. (Foster, 1924, p. 292)

Haller was writing along the lines of the generally accepted neurological tradition of his day. The cerebral hemispheres were considered insensitive and as having no motor functions; rather, they constituted the seat of the *sensorium commune;* Aristotle's *common sense* was still in business. The mind directed the body's movements by acting upon lower brain centers. There were no specific localizations of functions within the cortex itself, despite knowledge, extending back into antiquity, that injury to one side of the brain caused paralysis of the limbs on the opposite side. Opposition to the concept of localization continued in the face of evidence to the contrary, even current evidence.

François Pourfoir de Petit (1664–1771), a French surgeon, opened the skull of an officer who had died from a rapier thrust beneath his right orbit and before death had sustained a complete hemiplegia; de Petit found pus pouring from a right anterior abscess. Following similar postmortem observations, he began to operate on dogs, destroying various parts of their brains through trephine holes, observing their loss of powers, and then examining their brains. His observation that there was paralysis of the opposite side of the brain clearly supported "localization of motor functions" in the cerebrum (Tizard, 1959). His work was largely overlooked.

Nicolas Saucerotte (1741–1814), another French army surgeon, further confirmed the facts of contralateral innervation through some 28 experiments with dogs. His work also suggested somatotopic localization, since cerebral lesions made through anteriorly placed trephines caused paralysis of the opposite hindlimbs. Weakness of forelimbs was found to result from a posteriorly placed lesion (McHenry, 1969). Again, there was neglect of these findings that clearly supported the thesis of brain localization. So also with the experimental efforts of Zinn and Cabanis.

Neurologists were disinclined to accept such evidence for various reasons. It was, for one, based on research that was sporadic and lacked systematic replication. There was, however, a second, more persuasive, reason for their reluctance to accept the premise that processes could be precisely located within the brain. It was the theological-philosophical spirit of the age, a Descartian spirit, which insisted that the mind was a unitary, immaterial, organ, whose physical seat—the brain—was not to be precisely dissected as per so many cubic centimeters of tissue. Research such as Pourfoir de Petit's and Saucerotte's, or Willis's anatomical attempts to associate distinct functions with specific cerebral locales, was decried on grounds that it violated the principle of a unified soul.

Over the years, the accumulation of evidence finally mounted to the point where lower functions were allowed to be localized in the lower sections of the nervous system; after all, Descartes permitted this. But higher processes still could only be allowed to mysteriously interact within the unity of the mind, which expressed itself through a unitary physical organ, the cerebrum. It was a Descartian mind that dominated conventional neurological theory. And it operated within a Descartian cerebrum, which when conceived as a unity displaced the pineal gland from its exalted place as the seat of the soul.[3]

In its broadest terms, this antilocalizationist position, prominent even when Gall appeared on the scene, held that the mind was unitary and indivisible, even though it expressed itself through various faculties. It was also independent of the brain, but effected its union with the body

---

[3] The reader will remember that the pineal gland had been selected by Descartes to seat his *res cogitans* on the basis of its singularity. An indivisible soul required an indivisible organ. The elevation of the cerebrum to *its* role as throne for the Descartian mind required that it, too, (despite its bi-lobed structure) be considered a unitary organ.

amidst the undifferentiated mass of the cerebrum, within which it received sensory inputs arriving from lower sensory centers and through which it created motor effects by playing on the motor centers, located on the lower levels of the central nervous system.

The mind is an independent unity utilizing a unified cerebrum. This Descartian premise established the broad philosophical platform upon which the enemies of localization were to stand and fight for many years! So was the great German physiologist, Johannes Mueller (1838), to argue against localization:

> . . . the mind is a substance independent of the brain and hence . . . a change in the structure of the brain cannot produce a change in the mental principle itself, but can only modify its actions. . . . The loss of portions of the cerebral substance . . . cannot deprive the mind of certain masses of ideas, but diminishes the brightness and clearness of conceptions generally. (Tizard, 1959, p. 135)

So was the great French experimental neurologist, Flourens, (1824) to insist:

> . . . all sensation, all perception, and all volition occupy concurrently the same seat . . . (in the cerebrum . . .) The faculty of sensation, perception and volition is then essentially the same faculty. (Tizard, 1959, p. 133)

GALL AND HIS OPPONENTS

On this scene of doubts that psychological processes could or should be localized within the cerebrum, Franz Joseph Gall (1758–1828) appeared. Some of the major neurological controversies of the nineteenth and twentieth centuries emerged out of his work and the negative reactions to it.

About 1770, Gall made his legendary discovery that schoolmates of his who had good memories also had prominent protruding eyes. It prompted him to speculate why and to investigate. His lines of inquiry were initially physiognomical rather than anatomical. Physiognomical study had been earlier defined by Lavater as the study of "the exterior, or superficies of man, in motion or at rest." Such study also called attention to the configuration of the skull, though not in any explicit fashion. Physiognomical inquiry, however, simply sought to establish connections between man's superficies and his characterological qualities. Gall found such a simplistic enumeration of correspondences unsatisfactory for his purposes.

The defects of physiognomy led Gall to embrace a more ambitious course of investigation, which dates from approximately 1785. This time he wanted to investigate "the basis of the whole physiology of the brain," which provided the basis of all mental functions.

Gall recognized the importance of structure: "A doctrine of the functions of the brain which is incompatible with the structure of the brain must . . . of necessity be false," he stated, and since ". . . the structure of the parts of the brain has an essential and immediate bearing upon their functions . . . it is natural to consider these two together and to treat them as a single and identical body of doctrine" (Lesky, 1946, p. 279). All that was required now for Gall was a short step from this position in order to iterate that individual differences in animal and human dispositions are created by variations of specific brain structures and that these variations, in turn, are manifested in cranial differences. The play of Gall's speculations, however, caused him to eventually ignore the facts of brain anatomy and, finally, to decry them when they were used against him.

There were three basic tenets to Gall's theoretical position:

1. The mind is divided into specific, innately determined, though modifiable, faculties. The strength of these faculties varies from one individual to another, based upon inheritance, the effects of various life vicissitudes, and practice.
2. Each of these faculties is precisely and uniformly located in a specific area of the cerebral cortex. A faculty's state of development, its strength or weakness, is directly dependent on development and integrity of the cortical area that generates it.
3. The third of Gall's basic tenets—the one that has earned his efforts both their greatest fame and greatest derision—was that the outer cranial surface of the brain faithfully reflects the brain beneath and that by examining the external cranium, its protuberances and depressions, the state of the cerebrum and its faculties can be assessed.

Now Gall could easily explain the bulgy eyes of his friends who had good memories—the brain area behind their eyes, which mediated the faculty of verbal memory, was overdeveloped, causing their eyes to bulge.

More precisely, Gall's formulations were expressed in six principles that came to be known as "Gall's laws." Two of these are anatomical: (1) the size of a cerebral "organ" is a measure of its power and (2) the exterior of the skull conforms in general to the shape of the brain. The other four principles, which are psychophysiological, were stated by Gall in these words:

The moral and intellectual dispositions are innate; their manifestation depends on organization; the brain is exclusively the organ of the mind; the brain is composed of as many particular and independent organs, as there are fundamental powers of the mind—these four incontestable principles form the basis of the whole physiology of the brain. (Spoerl, 1935–36, pp. 217, 218)

Gall was, of course, contesting Descartian doctrine—that of the unity of the mind—but he did so without any immediate intention of confronting the French philosopher. His attack was rather against doctrines of British and French sensationalism and associationism, which had sought to reduce men's minds to a "heap" of impressions, as Hume would have had it.

Gall insisted that the mind is more than a compound of sensations. He insisted upon its innate organization and chided the associationists and sensationists for overconcentrating upon the senses to the neglect of the brain. He also observed quite accurately that though all of them rejected faculties, they still required organizing principles for their theories.

Bacon, Locke, Hume, Helvetius and Condillac found themselves obliged, in order to comprehend in some manner the possibility of the functions of the understanding, to have recourse not only to the senses which certain of these authors have so greatly exalted, but to a recognition of the association of sensations, or to attention, or to experience, or to reflection, or to induction. Although they have at times contradicted each other, they have nevertheless perceived that none of the faculties which we have just enumerated could appertain to any one of the senses. But if, in this life, no faculty at all could exercise itself without a material condition—as we shall later prove beyond a doubt—then there must of necessity be presupposed a material basis for the exercise of the intellectual faculties. The investigation of those organs through which animals and men receive their material impressions of the external world has always been regarded as very important. Will it be less interesting, less noble, to try to discover the organs of the superior faculties of the spirit? (Bentley, 1916, pp. 107, 108)[4]

How did Gall come to his pursuits? The atmosphere in which Gall matured, i.e., Strasbourg and Vienna, was one in which Wolff's faculty theories were highly influential, and it is likely he was influenced by them or by other current speculative faculty theories. His interest in the investigation of faculties may also have been stimulated by the scholar, Crusius, who died in 1775 just before Gall reached maturity. Crusius had rejected Wolff's faculties, which merely provided capacities and potentials for action—the *nudae agendi possibilitates*—as being too feeble to explain behavioral phenomena and substituted for them the forces (*Krafte*) of thought, judgment, imagination, and the like, i.e., faculties that were active-causative. It is likely that Gall was also responding to the theories of physiologist–psychologist Karl Franz von Irving (1728–1801), who had declared that the most abstract integration of ideas as well as

---

[4] Note that this argument did not reject the importance of sensory information. It was rather a reaffirmation of the central directing functions of the nervous system.

sensations had a basis in the brain and that over these, the mind presided with the faculties of analysis, synthesis, and comparison, etc. Irving had also promulgated feelings and impulses as providing the springs of mental activity, and this quite likely drew Gall's attention to the affective and conative qualities of cognitive experience and the latter's basis in instinct and impulse.

Gall appears also to have had his opinions shaped by concepts less close to home, those of French sensationalists, who espoused the existence of neurological centers to account for the complexities of behavior.

He was very critical of the efforts of previous faculty psychologists, both continental and British, on a variety of grounds. Their faculties, he protested, were mere generalities on one hand and yet at the same time too specific and finite to properly explain the true complexities of behavior:[5]

Whether we admit, one, two, three, four, five, six or seven faculties of the soul, we shall see, in the sequel, that the error is always essentially the same, since all these faculties are mere abstractions. None of the faculties mentioned, describes either an instinct, a propensity, a talent, nor any other determinate faculty, moral or intellectual. How are we to explain, by sensation in general, by attention, by comparison, by reasoning, by desire, by preference, and by freedom, the origin and exercise of the principle of propagation; that of the love of offspring, of the instinct of attachment? How explain, by all these generalities, the talents for music, for mechanics, for a sense of the relations of space, for painting, poetry, etc.? (Gall et al., 1835a, p. 84)

Previous faculty theories, furthermore, did not truly enable one to understand the differences that characterized either a species as a whole or individual differences therein: the faculties they proposed:

. . . are not applicable to the detailed study of a species, or an individual. Every man, except an idiot, enjoys all these faculties. Yet all men have not the same intellectual or moral character. *We need faculties, the different distribution of which shall determine the different species of animals, and their different proportions of which explain the difference in individuals* . . . the philosophers with their generalities. From most ancient to the most modern, they have not made a step further, one than another, in the exact knowledge of the true nature of man, of his inclinations and talents, of the source and motive of his determinations. (Gall et al., 1835a, pp. 88, 89)

The faculties of his predecessors were not up to the job of explaining what fascinated Gall, i.e., exaggerations in human behavior—positive and

[5] As Condillac explained the growth of knowledge as dependent upon the recruitment of stages of growth of sensory information, so did Gall declare that the faculties of the soul grew in correspondence with the development of its "organs" in the brain.

negative. They were too abstract, generalized, insufficiently distinctive, and not "determinate."

It is on the basis of the complexities of his own faculties that it has been stated that Gall was seeking to isolate and locate, cerebrally, traits rather than narrow functions (Spoerl, 1936, Lesky, 1946) and that his behavioral theories are far more sophisticated—and modern—than is usually recognized. His theories have been, unfortunately, confused (too often) with those of Spurzheim, with whom he at one time collaborated and whose excesses in espousing phrenology are, in considerable part, to blame for the postmortem discreditation of Gall.

From where did Gall obtain his faculties? This is a much disputed issue. It is sometimes suggested that he borrowed his lists from the Scottish facultists, either Reid or Stewart. However, it is not at all clear whether he was knowledgeable of their works. We do know that he was familiar with that of continental faculty psychologists. In their writings, Gall encountered such processes as

. . . understanding, will, sensibility, desire—voluntary motion, intelligence, reason, imagination, liberty, thought, sentiment, attention, comparison, memory, judgment, reflection, preference . . . among others. (Spoerl, 1936, p. 220)

However, as we have seen, he decried earlier facultists' work as being too abstract and indeterminate to explain behavior and individual differences. And so it is unlikely that he used more than their inspiration to create his list of the 27 determinate faculties or "radical powers" that he believed served as the fundamental processes of the mind. For the most part, these appear to be original with him. They are, in the order he named them:

1. Instance of generation
2. Love of offspring
3. Friendship, attachment
4. Courage, self-defense
5. Wish to destroy
6. Cunning
7. Sentiment of property
8. Pride, self-esteem
9. Vanity, ambition
10. Cautiousness
11. Educability
12. Local memory
13. Memory for persons
14. Verbal memory
15. Memory for languages

16. Sense of colors
17. Music
18. Mathematics
19. Mechanical aptitude
20. Comparative sagacity
21. Metaphysical depth
22. Wit
23. Poetry
24. Good nature
25. Mimicry
26. Theosophy, religion
27. Firmness of character[6]

Gall did not deny that the mind performed the functions denoted by the abstract faculties of his predecessors, e.g., perception, memory, attention, imagination, or the great suprafaculties made sacrosanct by Kant—cognition, affection, and conation. However, he did not identify these earlier faculties as faculties, but rather as general attributes whose qualities, strengths, and weaknesses modified the operations of the determinant faculties he proposed (Spoerl, 1936).

Gall's theories were really quite sophisticated and anything but "a caricature of" the Wolffian theories of faculties which Mueller, Wundt, and later James, accused them of being.[7] If his faculty theories were sophisticated, however, his methods of investigating them and verifying them, were anything but. While his craniology was absurd, there have been worse absurdities voiced before and after him. But what cannot be forgiven him is the fact that, though Gall was a fine neurologist and clinician, he did not utilize his considerable skills to seek empirical proof for his hypotheses. Instead, lamentably credulous or intellectually dishonest, he sought out the most superficial and shabbiest of proofs to support his theses and applied the scientific tenets of his day to his evidence in such a way as to caricature them.

There were nine specific ways by which Gall proceeded to verify the operations of his faculties or their localization (Young, 1970):

---

[6] Spurzheim modified Gall's faculties along more traditional lines. He cataloged them under the rubrics of affective faculties and intellectual faculties, further broken down into propensities and sentiments and then further broken down into perceptive and reflective faculties. Each of Spurzheim's 37 powers of the mind corresponded to an equal number of organs of the mind, the development of which might cause enlargements of the skull, which was therefore divided into 37 contiguous patches, some large and others small. The familiar phrenologists' busts, with which most readers are familiar, express Spurzheim's conceptions.
[7] At the time of their criticisms, these latter worthies were reprimanding Spurzheim's theories, which they mistook to be Gall's (Spoerl, 1936).

1. Whenever he met or heard of animals or men who had striking endowments, i.e., propensities, sentiments or talents, he first of all verified whether truly fundamental faculties were at work within them. He then examined their heads to determine which cranial prominences were associated with these faculties, prominent protuberances being interpreted as signifying strong or overdeveloped underlying cerebral areas (organs).
2. He examined individuals who either lacked or were weakly endowed in such faculties to assure that they lacked the cranial prominences found in the well endowed.
3. Seeing a person with a striking head prominence, he would try to determine his propensities and talents; he traveled to schools, hospitals, prisons, and lunatic asylums to study remarkable heads and the talents or tendencies (positive or negative) associated with them.[8]
4. He collected and measured head casts of hundreds of individuals remarkable either for their personal characteristics or their skull formations and compared the first with the second.
5. He tried to find common characteristics in groups of ten or 20 skulls or their casts and to associate specific faculties with these.
6. He studied comparative anatomy and physiology; thus he arrived at differences in species' behavior that were related to their cranial makeup.
7. He accepted accidental injury to parts of the brain as providing confirmation for localizations that had already been established, but not as independent proofs.
8. Experimental ablations, as well as clinical-pathological correlations, were to be used as evidence to support localizations that had already been established.
9. He studied the succession and arrangement of the cerebral organs in the brain, believing (based upon his contention that he had already discovered the faculties and their organs by other means) that the harmonious arrangement and grouping of these organs provided yet another proof of his theses.

The "anecdotal" method was an accepted scientific procedure of Gall's age. Gall also employed it dramatically to support his views. Stories about patients, famous people, criminals, quotations from the writings of others, incidents reported in the press, all were given credence if they appeared to support his views. Seeking confirmations of his observations, he found them everywhere.

The most important of Gall's criteria for the correlation of a faculty

---

[8] Thus, he found the bump on the head that represented the faculty of acquisitiveness particularly pronounced in pickpockets.

with a cerebral and skull localization was exaggeration of a given quality in geniuses and maniacs. Gall argued that there was a monomania for each of his faculties. And he drew heavily from the extremes of society to support his theories: prodigies, geniuses, criminals, and lunatics. He observed:

> In conformity to principles, I have more than once announced, we may infer, that when in disease, some particular quality is manifested in a much higher degree of activities than the others, it is fundamental.[9] (Gall et al., 1835d, p. 162)

In all fairness, Gall was attempting, in the first long-range, consistent research of its kind, to empirically study processes, and the methods he used were not outlandish for his day. But in his attempt to provide a ". . . complete list of human powers, faculties, tendencies, in terms of which the whole human mind could be fully and accurately described," he was willing to go to almost any extent of self-deceit. So the slightest of proofs, hearsay, casual evidence, or outlandish inference sufficed to verify his hypotheses. His discovery of the fundamental "carnivorous instinct" or "disposition to murder" was based on two findings: One was the comparison of carnivorous to frugivorous species. ". . . in the carnivora, there are cerebral parts about and behind the ear, not possessed by the frugivora. . . ." Then the skulls of a parricide and a murderer were made available to him and ". . . there was, in each, a prominence strongly swelling out immediately over the external opening of the ear" (Young, 1970, p. 39). On such "evidence," Gall concluded that specific regions in the brains of carnivores and murderers, because of their high development, were associated with the heightened inclination to kill. He then confirmed his conclusions by additional studies upon collections of cat and dog skulls and observed that man's frequent cruelties to other men clearly established ". . . in man an innate propensity, which leads him to the destruction of his own species" (Young, 1970, p. 40); subsequent examination of criminal skulls proved this latter point! Gall, however, unwilling to make more than a modest claim about this faculty of "wishing to destroy," which he had discovered, cautioned:

> All we can confidently maintain is, that, *caeteris paribus*, a person who has this organ large, will be more easily induced to commit homicide, than one not naturally disposed to it by his organization. (Gall et al., 1835d, p. 110)

When skulls were not available to prove a point, paintings and sculpted busts sufficed. He accused painters and sculptors of often underplaying physiognomical correlates of brain characteristics.

> . . . painters, draftsmen, engravers, and sculptors, sacrifice truth to errone-

---

[9] Gall seemed to favor pathological accentuations. Spurzheim preferred positive ones.

ous notions of beauty, and endeavor to render less striking those uncommon forms, which they sometimes meet with in their models. (Gall et al., 1835d, pp. 117, 118)

Nevertheless, even they could not always avoid the true portrayal of appropriate skull configurations, for

. . . there occur, from time to time, forms so striking, that the likeness absolutely depends on it, and then the artist is obliged, in spite of himself, to remain true to nature. In this way we obtain some faithful portraits of remarkable persons. The busts and portraits of Caligula, Nero . . . all bear the outward mark of a cruel and bloody character. (Gall et al., 1835e, p. 153)

If arguments were made to the effect that the busts of such great or hallowed figures as Homer, Socrates, and Christ—from which he sought support for the cranial correlates of the more positive faculties—were artists' conceptions rather than true images, Gall had a ready answer. He agreed that their busts were not taken from originals. However, since the sculptors of such busts undoubtedly used the greatest analogous men of their own times as models, the "facts" of craniology were still confirmed by their renditions.

Gall had few doubts about his contentions. Discussing the organ which represented the wish to destroy, he noted: "Since the discovery of this organ, hardly a day has passed that I have not discovered confirmation either positive or negative of this truth . . . I have made thousands of observations on this subject and have never found an exception" (Gall et al., 1835e, p. 183).

What about negative evidence, when, for example, a protuberance did not properly fit the characteristic that was supposed to accompany it? When, for example, a murderer did not have proper cranial enlargement over the external opening of the ear, it was readily explained away by circumstance (a father murdering a man who had raped his daughter), brain disease, the overriding activity of other organs, education, habit, example, and so forth. If poor memory were found with protruding eyes, rickets or hydrocephalus was to blame.

Other phrenologists similarly had facile explanations when their theories were contradicted. When in Paris a young boy was found with remarkable mathematical skills and a skull depression where a prominence associated with numbers was expected, phrenologists Broussais and Domoutier explained that other faculties made up for the deficit. When a cast of Napoleon's skull didn't measure up to predictions, the cast was criticized as being a poor rendition. When it was reported to Spurzheim that Descartes's skull was remarkably small in the anterior and superior regions of the forehead (where the rational faculties were localized) he retorted that Descartes was overrated as a great thinker.

And so it went . . . confirmatory evidence reconfirmed and negative evidence negated (Young, 1970).

Why didn't Gall, a neurologist, seek confirmatory experimental or clinical evidence? He did eventually, to confound his enemies, but he did so reluctantly. He found many reasons why direct examination of cerebral functions did not work. The blood, the shock of experimental ablations, and the imprecision of clinical study of head injuries made it difficult, Gall said, to arrive at sound conclusions. More than that, he viewed with extreme skepticism the attempt to derive functional relationships directly from structure.

Only very rarely can the anatomist determine function to some extent from the structure of the parts, in bone and ligaments for instance; even here the functional potentialities can only be conjectured. (Lesky, 1946, p. 299)

Gall pointed out that for centuries tendons and ligaments were confused with nerves and that, until Harvey's time, the arteries were believed to be only air vessels. What, then, could be expected from a purely anatomical consideration of the brain, where there were no nerves, no excretory ducts, no visible fluids to suggest functions, but rather, masses of seemingly directionless fibers varying from gray to white, from hard to soft, and going one way and the other? No wonder earlier anatomists who carved up this organ with their crude techniques saw only broken pieces without functional attributes. Gall claimed his intuitive inductive methods, based on the gathering of great masses of correlative data, were far better.

Gall further insisted that discovery of the brain's functions should be made independently of knowledge relative to the brain's anatomy, and that this would eventually result in increased understanding of the brain's structures that created them. The reason previous attempts at cerebral localization had failed was that no one had sought to discover what its ". . . radical, fundamental, primitive faculties were . . ." which could only be accomplished by observing the habits of animals and the moral and intellectual qualities of man, i.e., his ". . . diversity of mechanical aptitudes, instincts, propensities and faculties" (Gall et al., 1835f, p. 192). Gall's case for the study of function prior to structure had merit, though not enough to offset his malpractices in technique and inference.

Most surely, Gall's work set the stage for a first-class outbreak of charlatanism and quackery, but his positive accomplishments must also be acknowledged. First, he clearly established the brain as the seat of the mind. Even Flourens, his arch critic, conceded that:

The proposition that the brain is the exclusive seat of the soul is not a new proposition and hence does not originate with Gall. The merit of Gall, and it is by no means a slender merit, consists in having understood better than any of his predecessors the whole of its importance, and in having devoted himself to its demonstration. It existed in science before Gall appeared—it may be said to reign there ever since his appearance. (Flourens, 1846, pp. 27, 28)

Gall also focused scientific attention on the question of the specific brain localizations of behavioral functions. He further took the abstract faculties of his predecessors and made of them broad behavioral traits, which could be used to interpret both brain functions and individual differences. Chiefly, he removed the study of processes from the realm of speculation and placed it on an empirical basis. Whatever his faults and excesses, he made an enormous contribution to the study of man.

During his lifetime, Gall's excesses earned him a great deal of abuse and eventual discreditation (except in the eyes of a few). His work was attacked by the Church, which found his materialistic efforts to reduce faculties to brain functions untenable—so much so that he moved from a most Catholic Austria to a more tolerant France. More devastatingly, he was set upon by colleagues and successors—Rolando, Mueller, and Magendie—who manifoldly derided his work. But the brutal assaults upon him by Flourens made all other criticism pale into insignificance.

Pierre Flourens (1794–1867) was an experimental anatomist; Gall was a clinician. While Gall depended upon the most casual observations and hearsay for the support of his theory, Flourens was a precise and methodical investigator. While Gall spoke for specificity, Flourens spoke of the unity of the soul and dedicated his book to Descartes on the basis of that indivisible unity. Whereas Gall spoke of determinate processes, Flourens derided the concept of many precise faculties. He agreed that men and animals show very different propensities, talents, and so forth:

> No doubt of it. But what sort of philosophy is that, that thinks to explain a fact by a word? You observe such or such a penchant in an animal, such or such a taste or talent in a man; *presto*, a particular faculty is produced for each one of these peculiarities, and you suppose the whole matter to be settled. You deceive yourself; your *faculty* is only a word—it is the name of the fact—and all the difficulty remains just where it was before. (Flourens, 1846, p. 39)

Unlike Gall, Flourens always insisted upon experimental evidence; his observations were based on a number of subjects, and then were repeated. He was not an antilocalizationist. Far from decrying specificity of function in the central nervous system, he was the first to demonstrate experimentally, on the basis of extirpation and stimulation of his subjects' brains, that different parts of the nervous system have different functions. He concluded that the spinal cord's function is conduction, that movement is controlled by the cerebellum, the vital functions by the medulla, and that perception, memory, and will—higher functions—are all seated in the cerebral hemispheres. But in the spirit of Descartes, he insisted:

All sensations, all perceptions, and all volition occupy concurrently the same seat in these organs. The faculty of sensation, perception and volition is then essentially one faculty. (Tizard, 1959, p. 133)[10]

Flourens's observations were, of course, limited by the limited neurological knowledge base of his time and the crude technology then available to him. The only parts of the brain anatomically differentiated in any definitive fashion were the medulla, corpora quadrigemina, cerebellum, and hemispheres; it was not known how gray and white matter differed in function. Despite Flourens's elegant and precise (for the time) methods of excision and his careful observation, which led to many classical neurological discoveries, he still did violence to the nervous system of his subjects, e.g., his method of studying cortical functions by peeling away the cerebrum layer by layer, i.e., through successive slicing of its substance, could not have revealed Gall's organs, even if they were there. He appears, on occasion, to have cut away more than he intended. He rejected the use of electricity, which might have yielded more precise effects in stimulating the brain.[11] His subjects were lower species; birds were scarcely proper subjects for the study of higher faculties.

No matter, Flourens was decidedly on the side of classical neurological doctrine, which we have observed was commensurate with Descartian doctrine. Flourens's attack upon phrenology, the *Examen de la Phrenologie* was dedicated to Descartes in adulatory fashion:

I frequently quote Descartes: I even go further; for I dedicate my work to his memory. I am writing in opposition to a bad philosophy [Gall's] while I am endeavoring to recall a sound one. (Flourens, 1846, p. xiv)

Flourens's conclusions that the cortex acts as one organ and that all its faculties, the higher faculties, are indivisible, supported Descartes's conception of a unitary soul, which in Flourens's view, requires a unitary cortex as its basis of operation. His biases were so strong that this great observer overlooked what was his to readily see. He even insisted that the cortex is not the origin of any nerve, a claim that could not be reconciled with the state of contemporary knowledge at the time of his investigations. But he was determined to protect the cerebral cortices from indecent attacks upon their *unitas* by Gall, at all costs, even if it meant blunting his own intellectual activity.

Experimental neurologists, by and large, rallied to the cause of cerebral globalism espoused by Flourens. François Magendie (1783–1855), codiscoverer of the Bell-Magendie law, followed closely in Flourens's

---

[10] This was a statement of what later came to be known as equipotentiality of the cerebral hemispheres and the principle of mass action, though intended from different standpoints.
[11] He criticized Rolando, who did use it thus providing some evidence for cerebral localization of motor functions, for not having controlled "overflow" stimulation.

footsteps and proposed that the mind resides in unitary fashion within the cerebral cortices, from which it responds to and acts upon the sensory and motor centers that lie at "lower" levels of the nervous system.[12]

Johannes Mueller (1801–1858), the greatest German experimental physiologist of the age, also rejected cerebral localization and Gall's faculties. The mind, Mueller said, the highest expression of the soul, can not be localized anywhere specifically in the brain, though it acts through the brain to carry out its bodily missions. Most important, Mueller rejected the notion that the cerebral cortices, directly and within their own substance, mediate motor functions. He was somewhat unsure whether it was correct to deny the cortex as the seat of sensory functions. But motor functions? No, never. These were to remain evermore in the lower levels of the central nervous system.

> The fibres of all the motor, cerebral and spinal nerves may be imagined as spread out in the medulla oblongata, and exposed to the influence of the will like the keys of a piano-forte. (Mueller, 1842, p. 934)[13]

Descartes's view had generally prevailed. Carpenter's British text on physiology, the standard of its day, reiterated through all its editions (as late as 1874) the concept of the cortex as a unitary organ superimposed on lower sensory-motor centers.[14]

THE TIDE BEGINS TO TURN

Neurological science, however, kept advancing, and with its advance new physiological facts clamored for attention. It was becoming apparent that the nervous system functioned on a "chemicophysical basis" and had electrical qualities (Tizard, 1959). In 1848, de Bois Reymond demonstrated the electrical nature of the nervous impulse. In 1850, Helmholz measured its speed. The measurement of reaction time followed shortly.

New neuroanatomical evidence appeared that made it clear that the brain was anything but a set of simple unelaborated structures. The gray matter of the brain was discovered to be cellular; the white matter, fibrous—beginning and ending in the gray cells. It was becoming increasingly difficult to deny the possibility of differentiated brain "centers" and the possibility that such differentiated structures could serve differentiated functions.

---

[12] Bell, a clinician, was willing to allow for sensory representation but disallowed motor representation.

[13] He never quite developed his doctrine of the specific energies of the nerves into a sensory localization theory.

[14] We shall discuss the great reluctance of nineteenth century neurologists to localize motor functions within the brain in a later chapter.

Clinical evidence was also mounting to support localization of cerebral functions. Even in the days of darkest discreditation of Gall's theories, there had been clinical neurologists who were willing to support his contentions. As far back as 1825, Bouillaud, a great admirer of Gall, called attention to the apparent link between loss of speech and damage to the anterior lobes of the cerebrum. In the face of Flourens's assertions that the brain exerts no direct or specific motor control on speech, he produced evidence to show that verbal articulation may be paralyzed by selective brain surgery without loss of power in other regions of the body.

Bouillaud, on the basis of such observations, proposed a distinct and independent cerebral center for regulation of the organs of speech. He distinguished, further, between the faculty (and its localization) of creating words as signs of ideas and retaining them in memory and the faculty which articulated language. His work, he said, was a clear vindication of ". . . Gall's opinion on the seat of the organ of articulate language" (Walker, 1967, p. 103).[15] He was confident enough to offer a prize of 500 francs to anyone who could disprove his (Bouillaud's) thesis that speech disorders were associated with lesions of the frontal lobe. Eleven years later, Marc Dax was also to argue the case for a unilateral speech center.[16] Broca, in due course, would also make his appearance.

---

[15] He also pointed out that a number of highly coordinated acts ordinarily associated with the right hand implied special functions for the left hemisphere.

[16] This was contrary to Gall's thesis that the brain, like other paired organs of the body, had equivalent functions for each of its lobes.

8

Recasting Cerebral Localization in Sensory-Motor Terms

EARLY S-R ASSOCIATIONISM

Associationism was to recast both the doctrines of faculty psychology and brain localization into new forms that were credible by the tenets of the scientific age of psychology and the advancements in neurology that were hallmarks of the latter part of the nineteenth century. In order to accomplish this, it had to have a clear motor formulation of its doctrines.

Associationism, as we have seen, reduced all mental (behavioral) phenomena to elementary units that were aggregated or combined in various ways according to the "laws" of association. Despite Hartley's admission of "muscular motions" into association theory, most associationistic psychologists followed Locke's lead and emphasized the association of sensations and derivations therefrom. Hartley's interest in motor phenomena was to be virtually ignored by psychologists until the work of Bain, well into the middle of the nineteenth century.[1]

Nor did associationistic psychology show any great interest in the significance of nervous functioning for mental "associations"—at least

---

[1] True, a number of theorists, including the Frenchman Pierre J. G. Cabanis (1805), the Scotsman Thomas Brown (1820), wrote about a muscle sense. But they were concentrating on the sensations created by motor behavior rather than on the motor behavior itself. And when, finally, Englishman James Bain (1869) had his attention called to motor phenomena, it was because of the writings of physiologists, rather than psychologists; physiologists had minded Hartley's writings. We should note, however, that educational interest in motor behavior was originally strongly influenced by theoretical formulations that almost entirely ignored neurological fact and theory. This will become apparent in later chapters of this book.

from the standpoint of British associationists,[2] who approached their doctrines, more likely than not, from an epistemological rather than empirical standpoint. Again, Hartley stands out as an exception. His mental sensations and motions were paralled by "vibrations" or "elemental" particles in the nervous system. Locke didn't concern himself with the nervous system, remarking: "I shall not . . . meddle with the physical consideration of the mind, or trouble myself to examine wherein its essence consists . . ." (Young, 1970, p. 98). Thomas Brown's mental physiology was no physiology at all. Both James Mill and J. S. Mill essentially stood with Locke.

THE BELL-MAGENDIE PARADIGM AND ITS EXTENSIONS

The ascendance of motor phenomena into prominence within associationistic doctrines and the anchoring of sensory-motor associationism within the nervous system began with the monumental discoveries of Charles Bell (1774–1842) and Francois Magendie (1783–1855), which resulted in the Bell-Magendie law (1822), i.e., spinal nerve roots are divided into sensory and motor categories.[3] And out of this law emerged, in due time, a modern reformulation of phrenology, a rejustification of Gall's doctrines on the basis of associationistic doctrines.

The Bell-Magendie principle of differentiated sensory-motor neural function was applied by neurologists, after its discovery, to successively higher parts of the nervous system. Bell and Magendie focused upon the functions of the spinal cord itself, i.e., the spinal nerves. Then Flourens and Mueller applied the law to the medulla oblongata. Following them, Todd and Bowman (1845) extended the sensory-motor paradigm further up the neuraxis into the thalami (for sensation) and the corpora striata (for movement). Only the cerebral cortices—the home of the Descartian soul—finally remained to be invaded by the Bell-Magendie principle. But before this could be accomplished neurologically, that principle would have to be translated into psychological—specifically, associationistic—terms. The first attempts in this direction were surprisingly provided by a cerebral globalist, Mueller, who surely would have been surprised at the final outcome of his speculations. (Young, 1970)

[2] French associationists, as we have seen, took an early neurological interest in associationism.

[3] This functional division accomplished by the two men was not truly a novelty. It was known by Greek physicians in antiquity. Hippocrates, Herophilus, Erasistratus, and Galen, knew about it. So later on, did, Vesalius. Nevertheless, the first definitive clinical (Bell's) and experimental (Magendie's) evidence for it appeared in the early part of the nineteenth century.

Johannes Mueller, in his *Elements of Physiology* (1842), clearly proposed the psychological notion that behavior emerges from the association of sensory and motor activities. He did so in his discussion of the development of volition in a fetus or infant:

> Thus a connection is established in the yet void mind between certain sensations and certain motions. When subsequently a sensation is excited from without in any one part of the body, the mind will be already aware that the voluntary motion which is in consequence executed will manifest itself in the limb which was the seat of the sensation; the foetus in utero will move the limb that is pressed upon, and not all the limbs simultaneously. The voluntary movements of animals must be developed in the same manner. (Mueller, 1842, pp. 936, 937)

Mueller was saying, in effect, that movements gave rise to sensations and the association of the latter effects, with their motor causes, resulted in the organism's deliberate (voluntary) control of its movement; this is a basic concept of S-R psychology.[4] Turning to the association of ideas and movements, Mueller proposed:

> The connection between ideas and movements is sometimes as close as that between different ideas; thus, when an idea and a movement have frequently occurred in connection with each other, the idea often excites the involuntary production of the movement. . . . It is a general rule that the more frequently ideas and movements are voluntarily associated together, the more prone are the movements to be excited by those ideas rather than by the will, or to be withdrawn from the influence of the will. This kind of association plays as important a part as the association of movements with each other in the production of mechanical dexterity and perfection in the mechanical arts. (Mueller, 1842, p. 944)

LATER S-R ASSOCIATIONISM

Mueller was, of course, restating Hartley's "muscular motion" theorem. And, like Hartley, he was relating sensations and movements and the "ideas" derived therefrom, as well as the "associations" that

---

[4] Mueller acknowledged the precedence of Erasmus Darwin for this concept:

> The law laid down by Darwin is, that "all the fibrous motions, whether muscular or sensual, which are frequently brought into action together, either in combined tribes or in successive trains, become so connected by habit, that when one of them is reproduced the others have a tendency to succeed or accompany it. (Mueller, 1842, p. 243)

Mueller also was influenced by J. C. Reil in his S-R formulations. Both Darwin and Reil, in turn, had adapted theirs from Hartley's work. It was in this way that Hartley's S-R conceptions would come to influence both associationistic psychology and brain localization doctrine.

bound them all together, to the workings of the nervous system.[5] Mueller's motor and neurological association conceptions, however, unlike Hartley's, were to receive wide audience among neurologists everywhere. They were to influence, through English translation and expositions by English neurologists, a young psychologist who, in 1851, expressed the wish to place psychology on a physiological basis. In fact, to

. . . unite psychology and physiology that physiologists may be made to appreciate the true ends and drift of their researches into the nervous system. . . (Bain, 1855, p. v)

That young psychologist was Alexander Bain (1818–1903), the first to devote a specific chapter in a psychology text to the "Physiology of the Brain and Nerves," i.e., in his book *The Senses and the Intellect*. The impact of this then-daring wedding of physiology and psychology was such that by 1873, Ribot, an eminent French psychologist, would say:

Every study of experimental psychology, whose object is the exact description of facts, and research into their laws, must henceforth set out with a physiological exposition, that of the nervous system. Mr. Bain has done this. . . . (Young, 1970, p. 119)

Alexander Bain had come to associationistic psychology via an early flirtation with phrenology, whose influences never quite left him. While he vehemently insisted, in his first edition of *Senses and the Intellect* (which expressed his allegiance to associationistic doctrines), that "in treating of the intellect, the subdivision into faculties is abandoned" and by minutely applying the laws of association, one can explain all the phenomena implied by the so-called faculties of ". . . Memory, Reason, Imagination, etc." (Bain, 1855, p. v), he could not quite fully let go of phrenology. So in later editions of his book we find, despite his associationistic "yea saying," his discussion as well, in most supportive terms, of Gall's musical faculties:

Phrenology has very naturally laid hold of this faculty, and has, with confidence, assigned its local habitation. Musicians are found to agree in an enlargement of the lateral parts of the forehead. The analysis of the musical faculty has been made with great care, and we believe with success, by the leading phrenologists. . . . No objection can be taken to the tracing out of a cerebral conformation agreeing with this peculiar sensibility. (Bain, 1861, p. 162)

When Bain later developed his own threefold division of cognitive functioning under the rubrics of emotion, volition, and intellect, he re-

---

[5] Though Mueller was an antilocalizationist (as respects the cerebrum), he did not accept motor functions within the cerebrum. Nor did he, a psychophysical dualist, attempt to directly explain psychic functions on a physical basis.

sorted to faculty concepts. (True, he used names such as powers and attributes rather than faculties, but a change of name does not mean a change in ideas, and if that were all Bain had done, he still would have warranted notice for his wedding of neurology and psychology. Otherwise he might have been dismissed as a closet facultist, at least from the standpoint of this book.) However, Bain was also responsible for the later emphasis upon motor functions in associationistic psychology, a feat that was to have major ramifications (some well beyond the scope of this chapter). He provided the missing element to the associationist paradigm—the R(response) element, i.e., a motor element that would open up entirely new vistas of inquiry and thought in brain localization theory and investigation, as well as in psychology.[6]

The importance of the Bell-Magendie law for both Bain and associationistic tradition is revealed in J. S. Mill's review of Bain's work (in his book *Bain's Psychology,* 1867):

> What may be called the outward action of the nervous system is twofold— sensation and muscular motion; and one of the great physiological discoveries of the present age is that these two functions are performed by means of two distinct sets of nerves, in close juxtaposition; one of which, if separately severed or paralyzed, puts an end to sensation in the part of the body it supplies, but leaves the power of motion unimpaired; the other destroys the power of motion, but does not affect sensation. That the central organ of the nervous system, the brain, must in some way or other cooperate in all sensation, and in all muscular motion (except for reflex responses) is also certain (for if continuity with the brain is interrupted, sensation and motion in that part cease to exist). (Mill, 1867, p. 117)

The Bell-Magendie law had been applied to the mind, in a very real sense, by Alexander Bain. Thanks to Bain, the mind now clearly had motor as well as sensory components. And even higher cognitive activities could be construed in sensory-motor terms. A salient statement in all four editions of Bain's *The Senses and the Intellect* reads as follows:

> Actions, sensations or states of feeling, occurring together or in close succession tend to grow together or cohere in such a way that when any one of them is afterwards presented to the mind, the others are apt to be brought up. (Watson, 1963, p. 214)

Bain's sensory-motor association was a dynamic one. He compared the nervous system to the most advanced communication technology of the day, stating, "a system of telegraph wires might represent exactly what takes place in the brain" (Drever, 1968, p. 26). However, with shades of his old phrenological inclinations, Bain also suggested that various of

---

[6] Bain's work is being selectively used for the purposes of this particular history, attention being specifically directed to those writings that influenced the course of localization and associationistic writings relative to process conceptions.

the sensory-motor associationistic nexuses that constituted cognitive processes might have specific representations within the brain—a faculty-phrenological rather than a traditional associationistic construct.

> . . . it is most reasonable to suppose that, the brain being constituted on a uniform plan, the same parts serve the same functions in different individuals. (Bain, 1868, p. 46)

And he went on to speculate about the localization of centers for muscular movement, spontaneous energy, and sensory modalities.

Bain came close to a sensory-motor formulation of Gall's cerebral "organs." He had expressed the Bell-Magendie law in psychological terms, and then applied the resulting S-R associationistic theorem to explain the functioning of the nervous system. However, Descartes's ghost was still about: Bain was reluctant to extend his theorem to the cerebral cortices. The last sentence of Mill's quotation reflects the uncertainty that Bain and others of his generation felt concerning the localization of sensory and, particularly, motor functions in the cerebrum. By 1868 he was still saying that the thalamus was primarily a sensory ganglion and that the corpora striata were ". . . believed to contain principally the motor fibres" (Bain, 1868, p. 44).[7] As Young points out, the consequences of his position were that ". . . the intellect and its cerebral substrate were still set apart" (Young, 1970, p. 120). And so the cerebrum still remained the inviolate center of unified, indivisible, higher cognitive functioning—a global organ wherein was seated and mystically reigned Descartes's *res cogitans.*

To sum up and reflect: Bain clearly interpreted the Bell-Magendie law in psychological associationistic terms and elevated Hartley's "muscular motion" theorem to its rightful place in associationistic theory. He applied his S-R formulation to explain neurological functioning, but was reluctant to extend it to include cerebral functioning. This final, bold step was to be taken by an even more influential British psychologist, Herbert Spencer (1820–1903).

Like Bain, Spencer initially approached psychology via phrenology. And, again like Bain, his interest in phrenology continued to express itself throughout his career. In 1846 he tried to improve upon phrenological technology by developing ways of more exactly measuring head proportions. His subscription to the principles of faculty psychology is clearly evident in his first book, *Social Statistics,* published in 1851, wherein he argued that social bodies were analagous to the organic organization of men and other organisms:

---

[7] Bain was only to reluctantly admit to the possibilities of S-R Cerebral Localization at the end of his career.

Man . . . consists of congeries of faculties, qualifying him for surrounding conditions. Each of these faculties, if normally developed, yields to him, when exercised, a gratification constituting part of his happiness; whilst, in the act of exercising it, some deed is done subserving the wants of the man as a whole, and affording to the other faculties the opportunity of performing in turn their respective functions, and of producing every one its peculiar pleasure: so that, when healthily balanced, each subserves all, and all subserve each. (Spencer, 1851, p. 5)

His subscription to localizationist tenets emerged from that early belief in phrenology. It received bold statement:

A Function to each organ, and each organ to its own function, is the law of all organization. To do its work well, an apparatus must possess special fitness for that work; and this will amount to *un*fitness for any other work. (Spencer, 1851, p. 274)

Eventually, disillusioned with his early faculty-psychology-phrenologic allegiances, Spencer embraced the principles of sensory-motor associationism. His mature doctrine, that of *evolutionary associationism*, amounted to his making the associative law of frequency (a major law of associationism) operate phylogenetically with sensations and motions.

Whereas Bain moved associationism out of its position of passive sensationalism, Spencer removed from it the necessity to explain human behavior and all of its complexities on the basis of the human experiences of a single lifetime inscribed on a *tabula rasa* empty at birth. On the basis of Spencer's theories man could be conceived not only as learning from the numerous associations he forms in his own life, but also from associations formed through the aeon-long vicissitudes of his species and, within that species, from the associations peculiar to his race. When an association is repeated with sufficient frequency in organisms, Spencer theorized, it is fixed in their nervous systems and becomes cumulative over successive generations, i.e., a hereditary tendency. Acquired associations may thus become inheritable and passed on, generation to generation. Moving up into higher species of animals, and, later, into the higher races of man, such acquired hereditary associations become more and more complex. At the bottom of the ontogenetic-phylogenetic ladder, sensory-motor associations evolve, through heredity, into reflex actions, which are at the base of psychic life. At a higher stage, instincts are formed out of certain reflex actions, and voluntary actions are formed out of others. At still higher stages, cognition and memory evolve from instinct.

This evolutionary psychological hierarchy is facsimiled in the nervous system itself. In the nervous system, increasingly higher levels of sophistication are achieved out of the same basic sensory-motor associations that existed at lower levels—through the ever-increasing complexity of their interrelations.

Beyond constituting a comprehensive explanation of why man functions as he does, the principles of hierarchical, evolutionary development allowed Spencer to at last extend the Bell-Magendie sensory-motor paradigm into the cerebrum itself.

Using his rationale, all neurological phenomena, as well as all mental phenomena, could be explained by sensory-motor associations. The functional division of the spinal cord into sensory and motor components is the physical counterpart of the sensations and motions of which Bain spoke. The basic sensory-motor building blocks of both psyche and nervous system are organized continuously and hierarchically into units of ever-greater complexity and sophistication in the progression from lower to higher species within the animal world, from lower to higher races within mankind, and within individual man himself, caudocephalically, from lower to higher levels of neurological and behavioral functioning.

Spencer's original belief in Gall's "organ" psychology could now be expressed within the gospel of associationism, with neural ganglia substituting for Gall's cerebral organs in providing the neurological "centers" required to coordinate cognitive functioning. Spencer wrote:

> . . . an organized tendency towards certain complex aggregations of psychical states, supposes a structural modification of the nervous system—a special set of complex nervous connections whereby the numerous excitations . . . may be co-ordinated. . . . As every student of the nervous system knows, the combination of any set of impressions, or motions, or both, implies a ganglion in which the various nerve-fibres concerned are put in connection. (Spencer, 1855, pp. 606, 607)[8]

As to the possible accusation that phrenology was once again afoot, Spencer agreed that the unscientific reasoning of the phrenologists deserved rejection.

> But no physiologist who calmly considers the question in connection with the general truths of his science, can long resist the conviction that different parts of

---

[8] A similar point of view, it should be noted, had been expressed even earlier by the British neurophysiologist Thomas Laycock, who in 1840 proffered a hypothesis of reflex cerebral action. Laycock, in his formulation, stated:

> . . . that the *brain* . . . *is subject to the laws of reflex action, and* . . . *in this respect does not differ from the other ganglia in the nervous system* . . . being a continuation of the spinal cord . . . (and) . . . regulated . . . *by laws identical with those governing the spinal ganglia, and their analogies in lower animals.* (Young, 1970, p. 294)

It is not at all certain, however, that Spencer knew of his work.

the cerebrum subserve different kinds of mental action. Localization of function is the law of all organization whatever: separateness of duty is universally accompanied with separateness of structure: and it would be marvelous were an exception to exist in the cerebral hemispheres. Let it be granted that the cerebral hemispheres are the seat of the higher psychical activities; let it be granted that among these higher psychical activities there are distinctions of kind, which, though not definite, are yet practically recognizable; and it cannot be denied, without going in direct opposition to established physiological principles, that these more or less distinct kinds of psychical activity must be carried on in more or less distinct parts of the cerebral hemispheres. (Spencer, 1855, p. 607)

Everything known about the peripheral nervous system supported this view, he said:

It is proved experimentally, that every bundle of nerve fibres and every ganglion, has a special duty; and that each part of every such bundle and every such ganglion, has a duty still more special. Can it be, then, that in the great hemispherical ganglia alone, this specialization of duty does not hold? (Spencer, 1855, p. 608)

And so Spencer, even though an avowed associationist, accepted the "fundamental proposition" of cerebral localization.

Indeed, any other hypothesis seems to me, on the face of it, untenable. Either there is some arrangement, some organization in the cerebrum, or there is none. If there is no organization, the cerebrum is a chaotic mass of fibres, incapable of performing any orderly action. If there is some organization, it must consist in the same "physiological division of labour" in which all organization consists; and there is no division of labour, physiological or other, of which we have any example, or can form any conception, but what involves the concentration of special kinds of activity in special places. (Spencer, 1855, p. 608)

But faced with possible charges of heresy to associationistic principles, Spencer was quick to criticize the phrenologists' closemindedness. He decried their rigid faculties and their attempts to demarcate precise functional centers within the brain; his own undogmatic views on these points were to particularly appeal to Hughlings Jackson. He argued further against the fixedness of the facultists' beliefs, attacking the simple view that there was one cerebral organ to one faculty, and suggested instead that the so-called faculties were rather based on "centres of coordination" of numbers of complex aggregates of sensory and motor fibers distributed through the cerebrum.

Spencer comprehensively applied the S-R paradigm to neurological functioning and to the problems of cerebral localization. His themes, however, were too diffuse to permit precise application. It remained to Hughlings Jackson (1835–1911), an avant-garde clinical neurologist, to take Spencer's ambitious but vague notions of sensory-motor neuropsychology and translate them into terms that could explain both normal and pathological neurological phenomena.

Jackson was influenced by Bain, more so by Laycock, and most of all by Spencer. Of the latter, he remarked in his *Selected Writings,* "I need scarcely mention the name of Herbert Spencer except to express my vast indebtedness to him" (Young, 1970, p. 198). Throughout Jackson's writings there appear acknowledgments of Spencer as source, inspiration, and authority. This is as it should be, for Jackson's provocative innovations in neurology clearly relied upon the application of Spencer's evolutionary psychology to the structure, functions, and diseases of the nervous system. It is on the basis of Spencer's theories that Jackson rhetorized:

If the doctrine of evolution be true, all nervous centres must be of sensori-motor constitution. *A priori,* it seems reasonable to suppose that, if the highest centres have the same composition as the lower, being, like the lower, made up of cells and fibres, they have also the same constitution. It would be marvellous if, at a certain level, whether we call it one of evolution or not, there were a sudden change into centres of a different *kind* of constitution. Is it not enough difference that the highest centres of one nervous system are greatly more complicated than the lower. (Jackson, 1931b, p. 63)

Elsewhere he said,

I cannot conceive of what other materials the cerebral hemispheres can be composed than of nervous arrangements representing impressions and movements. (Jackson, 1931a, p. 42)

Jackson translated Spencer's rather vague notions into a comprehensive sensory-motor theory of all mental processes. Like Spencer, he committed himself to the notion of *hierarchical continuity*[9] expressed in ever-greater complexity of sensory-motor associations—from lowest to highest levels of the nervous system and behavior. There were three major levels: a spinal (low) level, a brainstem (middle) level, and a level in the frontal regions of the brain, the cerebrum (the highest).

Armed with this theory, Jackson assaulted the conception of the cerebrum as dwelling place for an unsubstantial mind, i.e., that Descartian entity so ably defended by Flourens, Mueller, and, the British physiologist Carpenter. He criticized those who

. . . speak as if at some place in the higher parts of the nervous system we abruptly cease to have to do with impressions and movements, and begin all at once to have to do with mental states. (Jackson, 1931a, p. 48)

[9] Cabanis should be accorded priority in the conception of the central nervous system as a hierarchical affair of ever greater complexity, though his actual influence upon later workers such as Jackson does not appear to have been a direct one.

Jackson insisted upon the motor constituencies of the cerebrum—and the mind—and appealed to the phenomena of normal psychology and neuropathology to support his position.

It is asserted by some that the cerebrum is the organ of mind, and that it is not a *motor* organ. Some think the cerebrum is to be likened to an instrumentalist, and the motor centres to the instrument; one part is for ideas, and the other for movements. . . . But of what "substance" can the convolutions differ from the inferior centres, except as parts representing *more* intricate coordinations of impressions and movements in time and space than they do? Are we to believe that the hemisphere is built on a plan *fundamentally* different from that of the motor tract? What can an "idea," say of a ball, be, except a process representing certain impressions of surface and particular muscular adjustments? What is recollection, but a revivification of such processes which, in the past, have become part of the organism itself? What is delirium, except the *disorderly* revival of sensori-motor processes received in the past: What is a mistake in a word, but a wrong movement, a chorea? Giddiness can be but the temporary loss or disorder of certain relations in space, chiefly made up of muscular feelings. Surely the conclusion is irresistible, that "mental" symptoms from disease of the hemisphere are fundamentally like hemiplegia, chorea and convulsions, however specially different. They must all be due to lack, or to disorderly development, of sensori-motor processes. (Jackson, 1931a, p. 26)

As to the so-called classical faculties and other processes, e.g., volition, ideation, reasoning, and emotion, these, Jackson observed, are artificially distinguished aspects of consciousness. Their "centres" in the cerebrum do not represent what Gall had called cerebral organs, but rather sensory-motor processes:

. . . "ideation," "consciousness," etc. Sensori-*motor* processes are the physical side of, or, as I prefer to say, form the anatomical substrata of, mental states. (Jackson, 1931a, p. 49)

The proper activity of the physiologist, was to explain the functions of the brain in terms of sensory-motor processes—mothing more;[10] the mind's "faculties" were to be discussed as simple associationistic phenomena. The localization of faculties in the cerebrum was a matter of identifying sensory-motor complexes whose functioning paralleled the behaviors identified as caused by faculties.

In summary, the accumulation of new physiological and anatomical

---

[10] Jackson held to the beliefs of psychophysical parallelism in which the phenomena of the body paralleled but did not explain the cause of psychical phenomena. Hence:

Neural physiology is concerned only with the varying conditions of the anatomical arrangements of nerve cells and fibres—with the physics of the nervous system. (Jackson, 1931a, p. 52)

evidence, the continuing accretion of clinical evidence—even experimental evidence demonstrating that specific lesions disrupted specific behaviors—and the advancement of the S-R paradigm all weakened the beliefs of the past, that the cerebrum was the unitary seat of a unitary soul. The cerebral cortices, like the lower levels of the central nervous system before them, were ready to succumb to scientific analysis. This is a topic for a later chapter.

9
Latter-Day Faculty Psychology

THE DISCREDITATION OF FACULTY PSYCHOLOGY

Following its espousement by Wolff, Kant, Reid, and other eminents, faculty psychology enjoyed vast popularity within philosophical, psychological, and educational, as well as medical, circles. Even Flourens had not denied the existence of faculties—rather, he objected to the absurdities perpetrated in their name and their being used to deny the unity of Descartes's *res cogitans*. Even the British and French associationist critics of the faculty doctrine often ended up explaining and reinterpreting faculties on the basis of their theories, rather than doing away with them altogether. Faculty psychology was popular among the masses. It was the man in the street's way of understanding himself and others. There was broad acceptance in popular texts of psychology, education, and psychiatry of faculty explanations. The mind was made up of faculties. One trained them in school and corrected them when they were deranged.

The situation was described by Stout, a British psychologist, writing at a later date.

The human mind has always been prone to mistake abstractions for realities, even when the corresponding concretes stand out in clear and definite detail. This propensity becomes almost irresistible in a case in which concrete details are shadowy and evasive. Hence we find that the faculty psychologists, unable to make legitimate use of their generalizations in the explanation of particular phenomena, treated them as if they were real forces producing these phenomena. Thus in their hands psychology became transformed into a kind of mythology which was none the less mischievous because scarcely anyone overtly and explicitly professed to believe in it. (Rusk, p. 232)

During the period when Gall was formulating his hypotheses but Flourens had not yet released his thunderbolts against them, George Frederick Herbart (1774–1841), who wore many hats, many mantles, including those of philosopher, psychologist, and educator, entered the scene. He was determined, once and for all, to destroy the concept of the mind as substance. He wanted to destroy Descartian innate ideas, and along with them psychic structures, and faculties.

A German associationist, Herbart, like his British and French brethren, was influenced by Newton's concepts of a lawful universe operating outside of, but affecting specific objects, which he intended to apply to the psyche. Like the physical world, the mind's operations were governed by laws. External forces ". . . were the true causes . . . in the mind . . . whose laws were to be external to itself" (Wolman, 1968, p. 31). Herbart's intention of applying Newtonian principles to the psyche was contrary to Kant's theory of a transcendent mind which viewed the world through inherent prisms and functioned through innately endowed faculties. The latter were consigned by Herbart, after due acknowledgment of his debts to Kant, to the dustbins of history. The soul, i.e., mind, Herbart wrote, is not

. . . a substance . . . for it has no original activity . . . it possesses no categories of thought and intention, nor faculties of will and action. The soul has originally no predispositions whatever. (Wolman, 1968, p. 35)

Its nature is ". . . wholly unknown and must remain unknown." Its contents derive from the association of elements (sensations), which, impinging upon its originally passive nature, force it to protect itself against disequilibrium by forming ideas. Ideas are units of energy that merge, combine, or inhibit one another. Ideas that lose are repressed, hence forgotten. Those that win achieve consciousness. Every new idea is assimilated by the previously established general body of ideas in a process called apperception. It could be, and was, exposited mathematically.[1]

Faculties had no place in Herbart's scheme of things. The entire doctrine of faculties, he said, was meretricious. a conceptual sleight-of-

---

[1] Herbart's ideas were, we know, extremely influential in education, particularly his doctrine of apperception which was to dominate many a later curriculum. It was not, however, interpreted by him as an original synthesizing natural power a la Kant but rather in terms of the way new ideas were interpreted in terms of ideas previously received by the mind; the faculty or power implications of the Kantian interpretation of apperception are diminished in Herbart's version. Herbart's apperception is more in the way of an activity or a frame of reference than a faculty (Hamlyn, 1961).

hand that transformed logical constructs and abstractions into active powers. The soul, he insisted ". . . has no innate tendencies nor faculties . . . it is an error . . . to look upon the human soul as an aggregate of all sorts of faculties." What we call "faculties," such as imagination, reasoning, and memory are formed within the individual mind (soul) by presentations from the social and physical world. Memory is the reproduction of percepts formed through sense activity.[2] The contacts of a child with external objects cause him to ask questions and create the ideas we associate with the power of reasoning. Imagination simply refers to the mental representations of remembered impressions from the external world. All are the result of dynamic laws governing the relationship of ideas to each other. The so-called faculty of will indicates a disposition of the mind for a certain action. As to the training of these "hypothetical faculties," stuff and nonsense, indeed!

Such attacks against faculties were not novel. Other associationists had struck hard against faculty constructs on similar grounds. The artificial nature of faculties had been warned against by Avicenna and Maimonides, even by Descartes and Aristotle.

Herbart's writings, in fact, in many ways paraphrased the earlier protests of the Jewish philosopher, Bernard Spinoza (1632–1677) who warned against the reification of faculties and said that:

> . . . faculties are . . . altogether fictitious, or else are nothing but metaphysical or universal entities, which we are in the habit of forming from individual cases. The intellect and will, therefore, are related to this or that idea or volition as rockiness is related to this or that rock, or as man is related to Peter or Paul. . . .
>
> In the mind there exists no absolute faculty of willing or not willing. Only individual volitions exist, that is to say, this and that affirmation and this and that negation. . . .
>
> The will and the intellect are nothing but the individual volitions and ideas themselves. (Ratner, 1927, pp. 191–193)

Why, then, were Herbart's antifaculty statements so influential? Partly because he developed such an elaborate and ingenious theory to support them and partly because he was such a dominant figure in psychology and education in his day, and had a vast horde of disciples.

> Practically all neurological and psychological research workers in the second part of the Nineteenth Century were influenced by Herbart. . . . (Wolman, 1968, p. 43)

Following his discreditation of faculty theories, a great number of

---

[2] He also decried the idea that there are subfaculties such as distinct memories of a verbal, numerical, visual, or personal nature. What would he have said if he had seen the variety of "memory" processes popular today?

eminent scholars all vied with one another in invective, both against the faculties in general and against Wolff and Fries in particular (Spearman, 1927, p. 185). Kant was treated more leniently by the new horde of antifacultists out of respect for his awesome self and was excused on grounds that he had been led astray by Wolff. St. Thomas Aquinas escaped criticism because he had been forgotten.

C. A. Hart observed ". . . few psychologists or educators . . . have not taken a fling at its (faculty psychology's) supposed absurdities" (Spearman, 1927, p. 185). Yet, despite discreditation, the fundamentals of faculty doctrine managed to persist and even to prosper. Spearman was to comment upon their survival into the twentieth century.

One curious feature about these formal faculties has yet to be mentioned. The doctrine loses every battle—so to speak—but always wins the war. It will bend to the slightest breath of criticism; but not the most violent storm can break it. The attacks made long ago by the Herbartians appeared to be irresistible; no serious defence was even attempted. Yet the sole permanent effect of these attacks was only to banish the word "faculty," leaving the doctrine represented by this word to escape scot free. (Spearman, 1927, pp. 38, 39)

Spearman's statement is clearly illustrated by the theory and research of Wilhelm Wundt (1832–1820), father of experimental psychology. Wundt insisted that cognitive functioning should be thought of in active, dynamic, nonstructural terms. He construed its elements in terms of processes rather than structures, which denied the attribution of objective "more or less permanent character to the contents of psychical experiences." Yet, as Boring remarked, Wundt's word ". . . has not always kept its meaning" (Boring, 1950, p. 334). Despite his antifaculty stance Wundt, lapsed into the use of faculty terminology and, inevitably, concepts—his own version of apperception being a particular favorite. His laboratory efforts, attempting to isolate different mental operations, had a phrenological quality in certain of their descriptions.

And so it was that in the years succeeding those of Herbart's attacks on them, faculty theory and practices, though wounded, survived, albeit often in disguised or larvated forms. Man persistently seeks agents to explain the phenomena he finds in his world and in himself. How, then, could he forego the use of process explanations? It was one thing to scorn faculties theoretically, following the hallowed Herbart's onslaughts upon them; it was quite another thing to kick the habit of using them or their bootlegged variants. In particular, education seemed unable to let them go, and from nursery school into university, one was to hear educators enthusiastically espousing faculty training as a major goal of education. We shall see this all too well in the later chapters of this book.

In the twentieth century, faculty doctrine received several additional blows that, at the time, seriously affected its applications in educational practice—this time from American quarters where William James, not altogether unsympathetic to faculty doctrine, and Edward Thorndike, its sworn foe, both carried out transfer of training experiments whose outcomes denied that broad processes such as memory could be trained. In his 1903 edition of *Educational Psychology*, a most influential work, Thorndike insisted:

> The science of education should at once rid itself of its conception of the mind as a sort of machine, different parts of which sense, perceive, discriminate, imagine, remember, conceive, associate, reason about, desire, choose, form habits, attend to. . . . There is no power of sense discrimination to be delicate or coarse. . . . There are only the connections between separate sense stimuli and our separate senses and human judgments thereof. . . . There is no memory to hold in a uniformly tight and loose grip the experiences of the past. There are only the particular connections between particular mental events and others. (Klein, 1970, p. 662)

It was Spinoza or Herbart all over again, but this time an attack backed by experimental evidence; hence scientific, hence oh so convincing!

The effect of Thorndike's attacks upon faculty training, the process training of its day, was devastating. Vast numbers of curricula, textbooks, philosophy of education, were all discredited. Thorndike was able to proclaim triumphantly the demise of faculty theory:

> This opinion . . . is vanishing from the world of expert thought and no more need be said about it than that it is false and would not be useful to human welfare if true. (Pratt, 1929, p. 143)[3]

If Thorndike, speaking from the vantage point of an educational psychologist were not enough to finally dispatch the faculty demon, there were others also proclaiming its departure, immediate or imminent, from the world of psychology. Following Wundt's attacks upon traditional faculty psychology demons American psychologists of note also moved to deny it any further reasons for existence. Thus Titchner (1867–1927) charged it "with impotence" and ". . . seeking by false pretences to conceal its impotence." The doctrine of mental faculties, he said, was one of "utter emptiness" (Pratt, 1929, p. 144). Then came the behaviorists. John Watson was out . . . for the last dramatic extirpation of Cartesian "unextended substance" (Boring, 1950).

Behaviorism, as espoused by Watson and his earlier followers, sim-

---

[3] Though an out-and-out antifacultist, Thorndike, interestingly enough, could not shake the ingrained habit of his times of speaking about "faculties." Thus he described his bonds as faculties in the 1903 edition of *Educational Psychology* (p. 39) ". . . the mind is a host of highly particularized and independent faculties" (Spearman, 1927, p. 36).

ply disallowed the mind, its processes, and contents. And what of the behavioral phenomena that were identified by "mentalistic" names? They sought to reduce these to behavioral terms. Everything was to be identified via responses, there was no need for mental bits a la Wundt or Titchner and most certainly no need for faculties either. B. F. Skinner was later to go even further, denying the need for any type of process constructs:

> I never attacked a problem by constructing a hypothesis. I never deduced theorems . . . I had no preconceived model of behavior—certainly not a physiological or mentalist one and, I believe, not a conceptual one. (Woodworth & Sheehan, 1964, p. 227)

There was little room for faculty constructs in Gestalt psychology either. Gestalt psychology tenets emphasized neurological-psychological isomorphism, field theory, and dynamic self-distribution of cognitive forces and "wholes." None of this was particularly conducive to any interest in or tolerance of traditional faculty doctrine. Gestalt psychology research into perception, however, eventually stimulated a particularly popular variant of faculty psychology during the 1960s. Several theories of perceptual training then reified Gestalt variables into very traditional types of faculties, though hardly anyone gave notice to the contradictions implicit in so doing.[4]

Faculty psychology did receive acceptance here and there during the early decades of the twentieth century, despite its rude rejection by most of the ruling class of psychology and education. What has been called functional psychology was concerned with an examination of the "adaptive functions of mind" and some of the tenets of facultism with its formulations continued within functionalism, albeit in considerably altered form (though many functionalists would have been undoubtedly horrified at the thought of being considered inheritors of faculty tradition). Faculty tradition also continued unabashedly among Catholic psychological circles, where it has never ceased to hold a place of importance. But Catholic psychology was basically out of the mainstream of traditional scientific psychology. Certain renowned educators of humanist persuasion, such as Adler and Hutchins, proclaimed its value well into the twentieth century. Moreover, its hold upon the popular mind and even the nonscientific thinking of scientific psychologists continued. The textbooks studied by generation after generation of psychologists, even those who were ardent behaviorists, until quite recently had their topics grouped in chapters whose titles and contents were inspired by faculty traditions.

---

[4] No matter that Gestalt psychologists such as Kohler insisted that perception was a "unitary process, a functional whole."

If our treatise at this point seems to be adumbrating a final decline in faculty psychology (with an occasional flash of success emerging), on the dunkling plains of its defeats, let our readers immediately dissuade themselves from such a belief. Faculty psychology was, in fact, even during its darkest years of discreditation at the hands of psychologists, educators, and physicians, moving into new realms of operation wherein it was to receive empirical and scientific credibility, e.g., correlational psychology.

FACULTY PSYCHOLOGY AND PSYCHOMETRICS

Psychometrics formally began with Sir Francis Galton (1822–1911), who was the first to apply scientific methods to the study of individual differences. Galton was interested in genetics and the transmission of "hereditary genius." Influenced by Spencer's evolutionary theories, which posited that the basic characteristics of the human mind are innate and transmitted as part of a common racial endowment, Galton went one step further and maintained that individual differences in such characteristics might also be inherited.

Galton established an anthropometric laboratory to assist in his inquiries "for the measurement of human form and faculty" about 1884. At first, his measurements were largely of the physical variety. Later, he added psychological assessments, using tests of discrimination, reaction time, and questionnaires.

When Galton first began his inquiries, the regnant theories of individual differences were still those of traditional faculty doctrines, which he found unsatisfactory. As an associationist, he believed that knowledge is derived from the senses—" good senses, good intellect."[5] As an associationist influenced by Alexander Bain, he also emphasized the importance of motor processes. So Galton devised both sensory and motor tests to assess the human faculty—tests of sensory threshold, both absolute and differential, and simple psycho-motor tests, such as strength of hand grip and reaction time. He hoped through the study of such elementary components of mental functioning to achieve an understanding of the broader and more complex aspects of the mind as well. He was doing what Bain, Spencer, and Jackson had all suggested. His testing approaches were consonant with the tenets of evolutionary association, which postulated that the same S-R psychological elements are to be found at every level of "cognitive" functioning. He described his techniques as measuring "mental faculties" (Burt, 1955).

On the basis of his inquiries, Galton described what, in essence, is a

[5] A notion that he confirmed by his observation that "idiots" have very poor sensory functioning.

superfaculty which he called "general ability," assigning to this faculty the name *intelligence* (a term popularized by Spencer). Galton distinguished this superfaculty from special aptitudes. He was more interested in the first, since he believed that general ability inevitably set a limit to accomplishment of any kind. He complained that most writers emphasized specific aptitudes or skills, that they

> . . . lay too much stress upon apparent specialties, thinking that because a man is devoted to some particular pursuit, he could not have succeeded in anything else; they might as well say that, because a youth has fallen in love with a brunette, he could not possibly have fallen in love with a blonde. He may or may not have had any more natural liking for the former type of beauty than for the latter; but it is as probable as not that the affair was mainly or wholly due to a *general* amorousness. It is just the same with intellectual pursuits. (Burt, 1955, p. 85)

Galton most certainly did not deny the existence of special capacities or their potential importance. He cited instances in which memory, musical ability, and artistic and literary talent ran within several members of the same family. Home environment or family tradition could not explain all of such facts, e.g., "prodigies of memory." However, his studies in the main had convinced him ". . . in how small a degree intellectual eminence can be considered as due to purely special powers" (Burt, 1955, p. 85).

As to the measurement of both general and special abilities, Galton suggested that individual differences in both are distributed in accordance with the normal curve, much as other human characteristics, such as size or height, are distributed. He printed a tabular classification of frequencies which he held ". . . may apply to special just as truly as to general ability" (Burt, 1955, p. 85). Thus we see the beginnings of psychometric assessment of both general ability and specific abilities.

On the continent, the laboratories and associationistic traditions of Wilhelm Wundt also spurred a number of German investigators onto the trail of cognitive assessment. About 1880, the German psychiatrist Kraeplin, trained in Wundt's laboratories, suggested the experimental use of different tests to assess higher cognitive functions (Guilford, 1967). His testing interests were directed to such processes as general memory, specific memory, attention (concentration against distraction), ability to adapt to a task, gain with practice, etc. (1901). His student, Ohern (1895), developed tests along similar lines.

There was considerable indecision and debate in the new field of mental measurement concerning which direction to take in assessing intellectual ability or abilities—in particular, whether to attempt to assess simple processes, e.g., as expressed in sensory-motor activities, or to attempt the evaluation of higher and more complex ones. James McKeen Cattell, who first formulated the term "mental tests," rejected the notion of assessing higher cognitive abilities, because these seemed impossible to precisely assess. Cattell's outlook befitted a man who was trained in Wundt's laboratories, with an apprenticeship, of sorts, with Galton. His "simple" tests, as we all know, did not prove to be useful.

In Italy, de Sanctis was not so reluctant as Cattell in attacking the realms of higher cognitive functioning. He published a series of six texts designed to identify feebleminded children. These included memory for colors, recognition of forms, sustained attention, reasoning involving relations, following instructions, and thinking. Could he have gone on to great things? We do not know. His work was quickly eclipsed by that of Alfred Binet who, together with associates Henri, and then Simon, created the first practical means of assessing intelligence.

Binet was interested in higher cognitive functions throughout his career. Earlier, he had been interested in the phenomena of hypnosis and the thought activities of chess masters. Even as he was devising his famous tests for the Paris school system, he was carrying out research on the thinking processes of his two daughters, Marguerite and Armande. The processes he investigated with the two girls were very much in the tradition of faculty psychology; they included abstraction, ideation, imagination, attention, and memory.

Binet carried his interest in higher processes into his work of developing mental tests for use in Paris schools. He and his associates criticized tests of the Galton type as being too simple, too sensory-motor, and overly dependent on associationistic dogma. They expressed their own preference for the study of complex cognitive functions, proposing that ten categories be explored by mental tests: (1) memory, (2) imagery, (3) imagination, (4) attention, (5) comprehension, (6) suggestibility, (7) aesthetic appreciation, (8) moral sentiment, (9) muscular force, force of will, and motor skill, and (10) judgment of visual space. Within these categories of traits they proposed the testing of still more specific functions (Guilford, 1967). It was all rather reminiscent of Reid and Stewart, Gall and Spurzheim, and it is clear that, at least in his original formulations, Binet did, indeed, postulate cognition as constituted out of a number of separate and distinct abilities or powers. His own statements clearly established his position in this respect:

. . . the mental faculties of each subject are independent and unequal; with a little memory there may be associated much judgment. . . . Our mental tests always special in their scope are each appropriate to the analysis of a single faculty. (Guilford, 1967, p. 12)

In his later work (1905), Binet was to talk about tests of memory, intelligence, and, still later, of the "four functions," which are primordial within intelligence—comprehension, invention, direction, and censorship. After such repeated expressions of faith in separate faculties, Binet's use of a single score from his test results to represent general intelligence was, according to Spearman, "inconceivably illogical" (Spearman, 1927).

If Spearman complained about Binet's profferment of a single score of general ability to sum up the results from his tests, when the Frenchman believed in various specific abilities, Guilford was in turn to chide him because he ". . . did not carry his conception of independent faculties to the logical conclusion in terms of measurement," his "single score" being an obvious contradiction to his own convictions.

Were such criticisms fair? Not necessarily. Binet, like Galton, believed in both general and partial aptitudes. He was also, in a sense, a Spencerian Cartesian. Like Descartes, he believed in the unity of the soul, in the face of the diversity of its manifestations. Thus he would speak of the faculties of speech, memory, imagination, and judgment as mental functions operative in the acts of intelligence and state that "Intelligence considered independently of the phenomena of sensibility, emotion, and will is above all a *faculty* of apprehension. . . ." But he also noted "The mind is unitary despite the multiplicity of its faculties" (Klein, 1970, p. 665).

Having given Descartes his due, Binet also paid homage to Spencer. There was, Binet said, a "hierarchy among the diverse manifestations of intelligence," and the more complex and specialized of these mature at later stages and in a progressive order that is relatively fixed (Burt, 1955, p. 87). And he believed that throughout all the manifestations of diverse functions is expressed a fundamental general faculty.

> Nearly all the phenomena with which psychology is concerned are phenomena of intelligence—sensation, perception as much as reasoning. . . . And it would seem that in the phenomena of intelligence there is a fundamental faculty, deficiency in which is of the utmost for practical life. This faculty is variously described as common sense, judgment, the capacity of adapting oneself to circumstances. (Burt, 1955, p. 86)

Since intelligence enters into every cognitive process, tests of any process might in theory be used to assess it. "It is neither necessary or possible to test all the child's psychological processes" to obtain its measure.

So Binet was not so inconsistent after all.[6] There are specific faculties but also a unity that binds them all and the same general fundamental faculty expressed in all. Assessing the highest levels of any particular

---

[6] But inconsistent enough, as we shall see in the second part of this book.

faculty can be used to provide an estimate of the general ability that is experienced in the various special faculties.

Why didn't Binet go further and also evaluate those partial aptitudes of which Galton had originally spoken and to which he, too, was so much inclined? He was on "the firing line" (as educational and psychological academics sometimes condescendingly refer to their brothers who are functioning in the workaday world). He had a job to do—it was not to pursue his interests in separate faculties or the question as to whether they were genetically determined (as he believed) or whether they could be improved (as he also believed), but rather it was to help the Parisian school authorities make practical decisions. A single score, the mental age, representing a child's adaptation to mental tasks, enabled one to do that. And that is what Binet claimed to get from his tests. When he died, he had achieved much; had he lived longer, he surely would have achieved more.

FACULTIES AND FACTOR ANALYSIS

The hypothesis postulated by Galton and by Binet, too—that there was both a general ability and a number of specific special or partial aptitudes—seemed to many pedagogues and psychologists to introduce redundancy into matters of the mind. Why assume two types of capacity when one would do? Writers on applied psychology in the late nineteenth century and the early twentieth, particularly those who were compilers of the more popular educational and psychiatric texts, usually rejected the notion of general ability as an unnecessary philosophical abstraction. They contended that a collection of special abilities or faculties best explained the constitution of the mind according to their practical experiences.

On the other hand, writers on the subject of pure psychology were prone to treat any doctrine of special abilities as one more manifestation of obsolescent faculty psychology. There was, they said, only one form of cognitive activity, though they disagreed among themselves as to its nature. Older associationists, such as Mill and his followers, held that it was association. Younger associationists were prone to regard it as sensory discrimination. Neo-Kantian philosophers and Herbartian psychologists argued that apperception or attention is what essentially characterizes "mind." Some theorists wished to reduce differences in ability to conative rather than cognitive status and insisted that apparent variations in intelligence are nothing more than differences in will. How was one to choose?

What appeared to be a way of rigorously deciding among rival views was suggested by two novel techniques that Galton himself had devised: The obvious plan for attacking the many-sided issues of mental functioning was (1) to devise and apply suitable tests for the various mental activities and (2) to calculate the correlations between the tests' results. Burt described his reasoning, saying that if, for example, there was no

".... organized structure in the mind—no ground for classifying mental performances under one or more broad headings, no basis for inferring efficiency in one type of activity from efficiency in another," then we should expect *all the intercorrelations to be zero* or at least non-significant. If, on the other hand, the mind consists of a number of specialized faculties or abilities such as "observation" (assessed by tests of sensory capacity) or "practical ability" (assessed by tests of motor capacity), then we should expect that all the intercorrelations between the sensory tests would be positive and similarly that *all the intercorrelations between the one group and the other would be approximately zero.*
.... Lastly, if there were no specific faculties at all, but only a single cognitive activity . . . then we should expect the entire table of correlations to exhibit what Spearman called "a perfect hierarchical order" or "a rank of one." (Burt, 1955a, pp. 163, 164)

Cattell was the first to plan a systematic research on these premises. He collected much data by testing freshmen entering Columbia University. Then Clarke Wissler, one of his research students, used those data in the first of the long series of inquiries in which correlational techniques were applied to test results. His primary object was ". . . to find a means whereby the fundamental elements of general and specific ability could be isolated and valued" (Burt, 1955b, p. 87).

The results of such early inquiries using the above approach revealed, almost without exception, positive and significant correlations between every form of cognitive activity. Wissler's results suggested:

Whatever it is that makes for correlation in class standing seems to hold good generally. (Burt, 1955b, p. 87)

Further, when the sample was large and sampling errors were small, there were nearly always well-marked clusters of augmented correlations confined to similar forms of cognitive tests, which left significant residuals after general factors were removed. Thus it would appear that both a general factor and specific group of (broad) factors were at work. Later, factorial investigators such as Brown, Thomson, and Thurstone were to argue that accepting the existence of such group factors or primary abilities (as Thurstone came to call them), one could dispose of the hypothesis of a general factor by assuming that group factors artifactually created it through their overlap; though some of them later begrudgingly admitted the possibilities of the general factor.[7] On the other side, Spearman only belatedly admitted the existence of group factors, and then with the greatest of qualifications, preferring to stick with g (general)[8] and s factors, i.e., those revealed through specific tests. It is to Spearman that we owe the term "factor."

A full-blown discussion of factor analysis is certainly not within the scope of this chapter. Rather, we are here concerned with the relationships of factor analysis to faculty psychology, for the first in many of its manifestations appears to be a variant of the second. We can, in fact, find almost any type of representation of classical cognitive theory represented within factor themes. That of the dominance of the *res cogitans,* the unitary soul or mind, is represented in g theory. Those of extreme specificity find place in Thomson's theories, in which he posited individual neural tracks for every individual correlation in ways suggestive of Hume and Cabanis. Then there are the theories of broad, independent primary abilities, which are very much like those of traditional faculty psychology.

But what is a factor? Or better still, what does it represent? Vernon has described it as ". . . a formal scheme for classifying and interpreting test performances . . . [that] should not be considered as a means to identify the basic abilities of human beings" (Vernon, 1969, p. 22). Cyril Burt, in his lengthy treatise on the "Factors of the Mind" (1940), suggested that factors are most validly valued for their classification utility and stated:

The logical presuppositions of factor analysis afford no prima facie grounds for treating the resulting factors as causal entities . . . their primary use is descriptive merely. (Burt, 1940, p. 7)

. . . factors as such are only statistical abstractions, . . . not concrete entities . . . The primary value of . . . factors lies in their utility for purposes of systematized description . . . and orderly simplification (Burt, 1940, pp. 249, 250).

Mathematically, a factor is simply an average—usually a weighted average—of certain measurements empirically obtained. Logically, it is simply a principle of classification—a principle by which both tests (or traits) and the persons tested may be classified. . . We use factors in psychology as we use rectangular co-ordinates in other sciences, not because we believe that the phenomena investigated are necessarily dependent upon a few, isolated, independent causal agencies, which operate in the mind or brain . . . but merely because such simplified descriptions enable us to organize our facts into a more logical

[7] Partly because Lashley's work on mass action of the brain appeared to demand a general cognitive factor.
[8] Nor was g to be identified as intelligence, a concept which Spearman regarded as hopelessly bemuddled. It was basically a type of mental (neural) energy.

system and help us to state our inductive arguments more cogently, and so endow our predictions with higher probabilities. (Burt, 1940, p. 249)

Strictly speaking, the scientist can never really measure mental capacities as entities in themselves, for there is no ground that such abilities can have any real existence apart from the behavior by which they are displayed or the organism that displays them. What we call an ability is simply a convenient name for designating a set of potential reactions on the part of the individual tested. (Burt, 1940, p. 218)

Burt clearly saw the danger of factors becoming latter-day faculties.

If our mental factors as such can claim no necessary concrete existence, still less can we endow them with effective causal powers. . . . In psychology concepts of this kind appear little more than relics of the old-fashioned faculties. . . . Nearly all psychologists are nowadays agreed in repudiating mental faculties, or at any rate the name; but their reason for this rejection seems rather that there is little or no objective evidence for any set of faculties that has hitherto been proposed, and not that the whole idea of faculties springs from a crude and obsolescent notion of scientific explanation. Factor-analysis, I believe, owes much of its present confusion to the fact that most psychologists still tacitly assume that, if faculties do not exist, mental factors must be invoked to fulfill their explanatory functions. (Burt, 1940, pp. 218, 219)

And so Burt repeated his warnings which, alas still require reiteration some 28 years or so following his reiterations:

Rigorously speaking, factors cannot be regarded as substances, or as parts of a substance, or even as causal attributes inhering in a substance. They are not separate "organs" or isolated "properties" of the mind; they are not "primary abilities," "unitary traits," "mental powers or energies." They are principles of classification described by selective operators. (Burt, 1940, p. 227)

I have quoted Burt at length and continue to quote him because I find much wisdom in his words. However, most factor analysts were not, and still are not, satisfied with such weak tea as he offered them. Eysenck, later, while eulogizing him (1972), criticized Burt's views:

I believe that this insistence on factors as principles of classification led Burt (and factor analysis in general) into a wilderness from which there is no escape. (Das, Kirby & Jarman, 1975, p. 88)

The truth of it is that stopping at classification, as Burt suggested,[9]

---

[9] Burt's later position regarding reality factors seemed to change to the close of his life, at least this was the conclusion that resulted from the author's reading of Burt's *The Structure of the Mind* (1967). Factors in this article seem to be accorded some reality. It should also be noted that Burt's disregard of his own advice on statistics, which recommended that they be considered at all times artifactual, became his postmortem undoing. He came to describe intelligence as innate cognitive efficiency anchored in the structure of the nervous system

was not likely to be very satisfying to vigorous minds, which most faculty psychologists certainly possess. Early factor analysts were fond of quoting Mill's remarks:

> Whatever phenomenon varies in any manner, whenever another phenomenon varies in some particular manner, is either a cause or an effect of that phenomenon, or else connected with it through some fact of causation. (Burt, 1940, p. 3)

And so with test results and test factors. The urge to reify and deify factors was and is strong within the bosom of factor analysts.

> The student of factor-analysis in psychology is tempted to reify the factors named, and to visualize a logical analysis as a physical separation, tacitly assuming that, if distinct abilities are ever to be discovered, they will be concrete and separable "organs," like the heart or the lungs, and that the "mental mechanisms" which form them will be localized in separate brain-centres or critical areas.

> No doubt, this causal language, which we all to some extent favour, arises partly from the irrepressible disposition of the human mind to reify and even to personify whatever it can—to picture inferred reasons as realities and to endow those realities with an active force. . . . It is still further strengthened by the phraseology of most statisticians, who have nearly always discussed probability in terms of hypothetical "causes." From Laplace onwards, scientific writers on the theory of probability have regularly represented it as a procedure for "inferring events from causes" or inversely for "ascending from events to their causes." (Burt, 1940, p. 66)

Thus, most factor analysts insisted upon the reality of their factors. They believed that factors had superior predictive powers:

> . . . not only because they are tacitly assumed to possess a more concrete and more permanent nature than overt actions or behavior, but also because they are held to be the true producers of the performances we observe and of the correlations between them. The latter are but outward and visible effects: the factors (in Spearman's phrase) are the "hidden underlying causes." (Burt, 1940, p. 66)[10]

Spearman's aim was to ". . . discover the causal mechanism of the mind and the general laws which they obey" (Burt, 1940, p. 13).

Cattell argued that factors are "psychological powers which can be measured," like the power of a muscle and are ". . . eventually expressible in terms of energy transactions" (Burt, 1940, p. 67).

---

and inheritable in nature. His pursuit of this latter thesis has cast considerable doubt upon his reliability as a scientist. Let no one doubt, however, that he was a most formidable scholar.

[10] More precisely, Spearman said:

> . . . the system of correlation proposed by Galton and elaborated by Pearson may be conceived as expressing the hidden underlying cause of the variations investigated. (Burt, 1940, p. 4)

Alexander declared, "We . . . seek psychological entities; our purpose is to resolve abilities into their true psychological factors." Stephenson contended, "A factor must be a real and tangible entity, defined in terms of psychological needs, not a mere statistical artifact." Thompson described the purpose of factor analysis as that of measuring the "factors of the mind" (Burt, 1940, p. 212).

Thurstone spoke of factors as primary and fundamental abilities, Kelly often termed them elementary unitary traits, and Guilford referred to them as the fundamental dimensions of the mind and then the structure of the intellect (Burt, 1940, p. 212).

Spearman was at first loathe to identify his factors with faculties and discussed them as "organs" or "fundamental functions" of the mind. But Thurstone came right out and said it: "The aspect of factor analysis is to discover the mental faculties." Burt sadly commented:

> Few if any explain . . . what makes one ability more "fundamental" or more "elementary" than others, how to distinguish "true psychological factors" from the rest, or the "causal" from the merely "descriptive." Nevertheless, nearly all appear agreed that the factors sought by the factorists are at once real and causal. (Burt, 1940, p. 212)

But factor analysts have not been satisfied to merely seek psychological reality for their factors. They have also sought to place them on a neurological basis.

Thompson discussed the physical basis of factors as ". . . on the physiological side an intricate network of possibilities of intercommunication" (Burt, 1940, p. 10). Spearman described his general factor as a form of energy, and the specific factors as nervous mechanisms or engines. Warren, in his *Dictionary of Psychology*, described factors as "a psychoneural element or determiner which is fundamental to all correlated abilities for the same individual." Almost every factor analyst in the early wave of the movement went along with similar speculations. Even Cyril Burt anchored his factors in the nervous system toward the close of his life, for those who eschew causal explanations nevertheless still yearn for them!

In closing, it appears clear that factors can become faculties without too much exercise of the imagination or logic. This is something that current psychoeducational enthusiasts, who so often justify their own theories and practices in light of those of factor analysis, should at least be aware of.

FURTHER PROCESS DEVELOPMENTS WITHIN TESTING

Faculty doctrine was also to appear within other formulations of the testing movement. We turn to consider these developments briefly.

Much of the early testing movement, as we have seen, was directed to the assessment of sensory and motor processes. When efforts were made to assess specific higher processes, they were usually limited to the simpler ones of memory and imagery which appeared to Galton, Cattell, Kraeplin, Wissler, and other earlier investigators to be reducible to simple measures. We have seen that Binet successfully attacked the problems of assessing higher cognitive processes in a test that was directed to producing a measure of general ability rather than specific abilities. With his work, the engines of the age of measurement truly set to work. Binet's achievement inspired a wide variety of subsequent efforts to measure general ability, including that most successful one of all, the Terman-Binet Scale and its later versions. Though Thorndike fumed about the reducibility of the general factor to "connections," his CAVD scale, which assessed educational aptitudes,[11] did poorly in competition with those tests which sought to reduce that mysterious deity, intelligence, to measurable, and manageable, proportions. The road toward assessment of processes that Binet had opened up was to be trodden by many.

Particularly fruitful approaches toward the assessment of processes emerged in the United States during World War I. These were via the U.S. Army mental tests, the first used for classification on a large scale. Because of the large number of men assessed by the army who were illiterate, of foreign origin, or otherwise incapable of dealing with the written verbiage of the original Army Scale Alpha, a nonverbal group test called the Beta was devised. This had within it many of the tests that we now associate with performance scales, including maze, cube analysis, digit symbol, pictorial completion, and geometrical construction tests. And for those recruits who made low scores on either the Alpha or Beta scales, there were individual examinations, which further emphasized nonverbal performances: puzzles, manikin and feature profile constructions, cube imitation and cube construction, a form board, designs to be copied, mazes, picture arrangements, and picture completion tests (Freeman, 1939), all of which are now familiar friends.

Similar nonlanguage and performance items were to appear later in both group and individual tests used with children, e.g., the Arthur Point Scale, the Cornell-Coxe Performance Ability Scale, and the Pintner-Patterson Performance Scale.

From these developments in performance testing emerged one of the most practical types of all cognitive process distinctions, i.e., verbal/nonverbal. It is a gross distinction, but perhaps because of its grossness has stood the test of time and research very well. Admittedly, it is ambiguous because many verbal test items tap processes other than the

---

[11] Which despite his anti-faculty posture sounded faintly like faculties themselves.

verbal, and because nonverbal ones so often have major verbal components. Nevertheless, this distinction (on which we shall not elaborate
further here) has, in fact, shown itself to have useful diagnostic and
predictive implications, as Reitan would surely assert. It has been most
effectively used when not too belabored in the service of some hidden
faculty agenda, and has proved its value when employed to make broad
distinctions in academic performance, the diagnosis of brain injury, and
the like.

Another important development in the direction of process assessment via tests was the development of aptitude tests, which Freeman
once defined as

> . . . the ability or collection of abilities required to perform a specified
> practical activity. . . . The essential characteristic of an aptitude is that it exists
> prior to training or education in the special field of activity to which it is applied,
> and is not dependent on such training. The aptitude may or may not be native or
> inherited, but at least it is not the product of special training . . . it may consist of
> a primary or elementary ability, or in a combination of several. (Freeman, 1939,
> pp. 182, 183)

Aptitude testing has flourished over the past decades. We find
mechanical aptitude tests, those for art, music, clerical areas, and a
variety of academic areas. The verbal/arithmetic aptitude distinction has
been a particularly useful one in academic prediction. Aptitudes and
aptitude tests, too, are the children of faculty psychology, though harking
back to the rather broad faculties that Reid and Gall suggested, rather
than to those of antiquity or scholasticism.

Then, of course, there came the tests of special abilities, tests that are
particularly popular on the current special education scene. Freeman
could say back in 1939 that

> There is no general agreement as to what special abilities exist or indeed
> whether special abilities exist at all in the sense in which the term is ordinarily
> used. (Freeman, 1939, p. 194)

Such lack of agreement as to special abilities did not prevent people from
trying to measure them. Their tests were directed along the lines first
established by Galton and Cattell to simpler functions. Pillsbury,
Seashore, Yerkes, and Watson brought forth a number of sensory tests in
1906. A variety of specific motor ability assessments were prominent in
the years subsequent to World War I, e.g., those developed by Perrin,
Miles, Schulz, Crockett and others. The descendants of such sensory and
motor process tests have been legion.

As to the more popular "special abilities" of today, the idea of testing
perception has always been popular. Many tests originally devised for
sensory-motor assessment, as well as those of card sorting and cancella-

tion of letters, were also used for perceptual assessment in the early years of the twentieth century. We are presumably blessed with better ones today.

Profile tests have almost always warmed the hearts of psychoeducational test enthusiasts. They tell you which process is weak, which is strong. A variety of people claimed credit for instituting or popularizing the procedure, including Burt. Certain psychometric elites took exception, to be sure, including Spearman. But it was a good idea.

Yerkes, Bridges, and Hardwick proposed a profile approach back in 1915, suggesting four major divisions of their point scale into receptivity, imagination (including memory), affectivity (or feeling), and thought; each of these large divisions contained subordinate divisions. Rossolimo was one of the first, if not the first, to develop an elaborate profile test dedicated to analytic measures of the constituents of ability. He reported that the idea first came to him in 1909. By 1926 he had published *Das Psychologische Profil,* which addressed itself to a variety of tests measuring attention, perceptual ability (both auditory and visual), retention, comprehension, combining ability, cleverness, imagination, and power of observation, among other things.

In the 1930s, the Detroit Tests of Learning Aptitude by Baker and Leland were developed to serve in the diagnosis of "specific mental faculties." The California Test of Mental Maturity also, was originally intended to measure visual acuity, auditory acuity, motor coordination, memory, spatial relations, and reasoning. Thurstone's factor-based tests were designed to measure primary mental abilities. *Und so weiter!* In much of today's psychoeducational measurement, particularly in that employed in the learning disability movement, we find faculty psychology redux in test profiles.

FACULTIES ELSEWHERE

Elsewhere in psychology, faculty doctrine was to make its comeback during the twentieth century, after a long period of rejection by scientific and academic psychology, although it had never been denied in popular psychology. Even the behaviorists found it useful after a while to introduce "cognitive" variables in their behavioristic formulae. Tolman's 1930 intervening variable, which subsumed such niceties as cognitive maps and purposes, soon found itself with a younger sibling called hypothetical constructs (MacCorquodale & Meehl, 1948), which helped processes achieve new levels of behavioral respectability following World War II. During the 1950s and the 1960s, cognitive psychology inundated the readers of psychology journals with a variety of new faculties. One has only to examine a recent book, *The Nature of Intelligence* (Resnick, 1976), to see the orgy of process speculations that the most reputable of psychological and educational scientists are likely to indulge in nowadays. Many of the latter issue proper warnings against repeating faculty psychology's faults while repeating them. Some do not bother with qualifiers. Others are quite willing to use the term "faculty" itself in their formulations.

It is true that the modern faculties are many more in number than they were of yore, that they often bear unfamiliar names, sounding of computerese and system analysis analogues, or of the world of business, and are often presented in models and schematics. It is true, too, that process theorists try to give their processes dynamic and nonsubstantive qualities. But look behind the facade of most of their terms and you will find the faculty house that Aristotle and company built as being still very much in business—and accepting new lodgers all the time.

10

Cerebral Localization Up to the Present

THE TRIUMPH OF LOCALIZATION DOCTRINES

There is but one more stage required to bring our narrative of processes to proper currency. And it concerns, once again, the doctrine of cerebral localization.

We have already observed that a variety of clinical neurologists continued to support Gall's thesis of cerebral localization, even in the darkest years of its discreditation, and that after that time, there was sporadic, but mounting evidence—clinical and experimental—to support the premises of cerebral localization.

Bouillaud (1796–1881) argued as early as 1835 that special organs in the brain controlled distinct movements; in particular, that speech was ". . . regulated by a special cerebral centre, distinct and independent" (Young, 1970, p. 137).[1] But by 1861, when Bouillaud became the Doyen of the Faculty, Membre de l'Institut, and head of Le Charité in Paris, the issues of cerebral localization were ready to pass into the hands of a new generation of disputants. (Young, 1970)

The Société d'Anthropologie was to serve as one of the first platforms for their debates. Its founder and First Secretary was Paul Broca (1824–1880). A primitive skull had been presented to the Société for its initial session. It was intended to serve as the subject for a discussion on the significance of brain volume. That debate, however, quickly expanded

---

[1] Unlike Gall, whom he criticized as having "announced rather than demonstrated the facts of localization," Bouillaud decried techniques of relating behaviors to cranial configurations and insisted upon the direct demonstration of clinical brain relationships.

to include the related issue of whether the brain functioned as a whole or was composed, rather, of a number of more or less independent organs or centers. Gratiolet, who had presented the skull to the Société, stated:

> In a general manner I agree with M. Flourens that the intelligence is one, that the brain is one, that is acts above all as a whole; but this does not exclude the idea that certain faculties of the mind stand in special relation, although not exclusively, with certain cerebral regions. (Head, 1926a, p. 16)

Ernst Auburtin, Bouillaud's pupil and son-in-law, also argued for cerebral localization, praising Gall's work, which he said, ". . . has been . . . the point of departure for all the discoveries of our century on the physiology of the brain." (Head, 1926a, p. 18)[2]

The Société's second meeting of April 4 was opened by Auburtin in a similar vein. He presented case reports drawn in large part from Bouillaud's writings that supported brain localization and defended the value of pathological observations in its determination, as against physiological experimentation. In particular, he upheld his father-in-law's localization of speech in the anterior lobes of the brain, arguing that the localization of even a single faculty sufficed to validate the entire hypothesis of cerebral localization. It was in the emotionally charged atmosphere of the discussions following Auburtin's presentation that Broca proposed a patient of his known as "Tan" (real name, Leborgne) be accepted as a test case of the hypothesis.

Tan had died shortly after admission to Broca's surgical service at Bicetré from gangrenous cellulitis of the left leg. He had been a patient at the Bicetré ever since he had lost his speech 21 years earlier. On April 5, Broca demonstrated Tan's brain to the Société d'Anthropologie. There were lesions in it, in what later came to be known as Broca's area. Broca's demonstration clearly supported Bouillaud and Auburtin's views on localization. However, as his statements on the matter were soft-toned, they did not arouse the opposition of antilocalizationists present at the viewing.

Broca's complete account of the case and his contention that the center for articulate speech was located in the third left frontal convolution, were presented to the Société at a later date. By 1863, Broca and his colleagues had collected 20 such cases. All showed pathological alteration in the left half of the brain; in 19 of the group the alteration was in the third frontal convolution.

Head, considerably later, described the aftermaths of Broca's discoveries:

> These communications produced the greatest excitement in the medical

---

[2] He rejected craniology, however.

world of Paris. . . . Localization of speech became a political question; the older Conservative School, haunted by the bogey of phrenology, clung to the conception that the brain "acted as a whole"; whilst the younger Liberals and Republicans passionately favoured the view that different functions were exercised by the various portions of the cerebral hemispheres. During the next few years every medical authority took one side or the other in the discussion. (Head, 1926a, p. 25)

There are two aspects of Broca's approach to the problems of cerebral localization that require special comment:

1. His methodology represented the final and complete rejection of cranioscopy as a technique for establishing cerebral localizations. Bouillaud's insistence upon clinicopathological correlation had won the day.
2. Broca insisted that a precise cerebral nomenclature be used to direct subsequent efforts at localization. Gall and his followers had neglected the study of the cerebral convolutions "far too much." Their researches, he said

. . . were dominated by the old prejudice that the cerebral convolutions are in no way fixed, that they are simply pleats made by chance, comparable to the disorderly flexions of the intestinal loops. (Head, 1926a, p. 59)

But the fundamental convolutions were, of course, constant and could be studied to provide precise cerebral landmarks that could guide localization efforts. Broca told his readers:

We have to investigate not only in what parts of the brain are situated the regions of aphemia, but we also have to designate by their name and by their rank the diseased convolutions and the degree of alterations of each of them. (Head, 1926a, p. 72)

Broca localized speech in a region somewhat different from that suggested by Bouillaud, yet both agreed that his work was confirmatory of Bouillaud's localizations. However, Bouillaud localized the muscular movements involved in speech. On this point, Broca was not quite sure. Discussing the question as to whether speech was an intellectual function or a motor function, Broca noted that:

In the first hypothesis this would be a superior faculty, and aphemia would be an intellectual disturbance. In the second hypothesis, this would be a faculty of much less elevated order and the aphemia would be only a disturbance of locomotion.

He then distinguished between the "thinking part of the brain," i.e., the cortex and the "motor centers of the central nervous system," (Broca, 1861, p. 54) pointing out that:

. . . it is generally admitted that all faculties, called intellectual, have their seat in this part of the brain [the cortex] and it seems therefore very probable, that all faculties that reside in the cerebral convolutions are of the intellectual nature. (Broca, 1861, p. 57).

In discussing the viscissitudes of his patient, Tan, Broca further exploited the distinction between cerebral "thinking" functions and lower motor ones. Tan, ten years after becoming aphasic, had developed progressive left–right paralysis. Broca ruled out a search for the cause of the paralysis within Tan's cerebrum.

Everybody knows that the cerebral convolutions are not motor organs . . . The corpus striatum of the left hemisphere is of all the attacked organs the only one where one could look for the cause of the paralysis of the two right extremities. (Broca, 1861, p. 70)

Broca's almost superstitious insistence that the cerebrum was uninvolved in motor functions but rather activated the motor apparatus of lower centers reflected the continuing influence of the belief that the cerebrum was an organ of exalted higher powers. It was to earn him later criticism and scorn from the camp of experimental neurology.

Broca's "discoveries" were monumental ones. They created shock waves throughout the scientific community. And yet, why? The conception of a faculty of "articulate" language and its location in the frontal region of the brain was not new. Bouillaud and a variety of other clinical workers, as we have seen, had formulated similar hypotheses. While it might be argued that Broca was the first to confirm such localizations, a number of his observations and localizations were off the mark. It was, then, more likely the spirit of his era that made his observations appear so important when he announced them. At the time, a spirit of analysis and specification that was coming into prominence in a variety of scientific circles.

The cell theory, originated by Schleiden and oriented toward minute specificities, was extremely influential within anatomical and physiological circles. Virchow, Professor of Anatomy in Berlin (1858), had described the organism as a "cell state," consisting of units that are primary carriers of all its properties.

Every animal (he wrote) is a sum of vital units, each of which possesses the full characteristics of life. . . . The composition of the major organism, the so-called individual, must be likened to a kind of social arrangement or society, in which a number of separate existences are dependent upon one another, in such a way, however, that each individual possesses its own peculiar activity and carries out its own powers. (Tizard, 1959, p. 138)

Virchow attempted to combat the belief in the unity of functioning as it concerned the whole organism. He believed that such unity was not to be found in anatomical structures, that it was rather an epiphenomenon of consciousness. As to the treatment of disease, he stated: "The localizing principle is the basic principle of modern Medicine" (Riese, 1949, p. 118).

W. Riese, a modern neurological historian observed:

> In no branch the regional factor seemed to be more powerful than in the doctrine of nervous disease. . . . Though localizing efforts were very old, it was not by chance that the century which produced Rudolph Virchow and cellular pathology, saw at the same time the rise of the doctrine of cerebral localization. (Riese, 1949, p. 118)

The late nineteenth century then, was a time to be analytical and to search for specifics; Broca's work was in tune with it. The fact that he avoided phrenological excesses also made his arguments more palatable to neurologists who had been offended by the successes of earlier localizationists.[3]

Broca's work, however, did not fully turn the tide in favor of cerebral localization. The results of clinical neurology were suspect in the laboratories of "scientific" neurology, as those of the correlationist and clinician are usually suspect to their experimental brethren. Fritsch and Hitzig complained that clinical neurological research suffered from "the faultiness and the difficult interpretations of postmortems" as compared with "the simplicity and clearness of vivisections" (Fritsch & Hitzig, 1870, p. 78). Ferrier reduced clinical results to the role of confirming laboratory research rather than answering neurological questions directly; he cautioned against ". . . the facts furnished by the experiments of disease in man" (Ferrier, 1886, p. 222). It would take more than Broca's clinical demonstrations of cerebral localization to convince experimental neurology that the latter was a valid thesis.

In 1870, Gustav Fritsch and Eduard Hitzig published a paper, "The Electrical Excitability of the Cerebrum." Their experiments had demonstrated that

> A part of the convexity of the hemisphere of the brain of the dog is motor . . . another part is not motor. The motor part, in general, is more in front, the non-motor part more behind. By electrical stimulation of the motor part, one obtains combined muscular contractions of the opposite side of the body. (Fritsch & Hitzig, 1870, p. 81)

Their study truly constituted an *experimentum crucis*. It was an

---

[3] His work has been described by Young as a "propaganda victory rather than an original discovery" at a time when the world was ready to be convinced about the merits of cerebral localization (Young, 1970, p. 137).

epochal work that was to change conceptions of neurophysiology evermore. With it, a number of Flourens's major theses of cerebral functioning were dethroned. Stimulating the cerebral cortex of the dog, and ablating parts thereof, they found specific movements related to constant loci within the cerebrum. There was a cerebral "center" for movements of the neck, another for the extensors and adductors of the anterior leg, still another for the flexion and rotation of the same leg, a fourth for the posterior leg, and a fifth for the facial nerve. Demonstrated for the first time was a precise correspondence between specific cerebral centers and specific behavior. (Young, 1970)

Why had Fritsch and Hitzig succeeded where others had either failed or come up with disconfirming conclusions? For one, they were able to rely upon a standard nomenclature of cerebral areas, which we will remember had been so strongly urged by Broca; it had been provided by Richard Owen's *On the Anatomy of the Vertebrates* (1868). Second, they paid meticulous attention to operative conditions in their research and achieved experimental precision at a level not previously achieved in experimental research into localization.[4] When they remarked, "Methods give results," they were repeating a statement that Flourens had made when he demolished Gall's claims. If methods give results, new methods give new results; it has ever thus been so, and so with their new methods, Fritsch and Hitzig demolished Flourens's antilocalizationist arguments.

But it was more than Fritsch and Hitzig's methods that gave them their results. It was also their willingness to reject the old assumption that the cerebral cortex lacked motor components, a time-honored doctrine and deeply imbedded belief, as we know by now in this book, that had seriously impeded cerebral research.

We have already reviewed the reluctance of earlier workers to locate the neurological substrata of sensory and motor processes within the cerebrum. Even into the nineteenth century, the thalami were generally conceived of as being the terminus of specific sensory tracts and the corpus striatum as terminus of the motor tracts. The cerebrum remained the sensorium commune where the soul was seated. It received signals from its lower afferent communication systems and directed motor functions by playing upon the lower motor centers.

As the doctrines of sensationalistic associationism, e.g., those of Hartley, Mills, and Herbart, became ever more popular and dominant in psychology, the notion that the cerebrum might have specific sensory

---

[4] Fritsch and Hitzig used techniques that Flourens had pioneered, cerebral stimulation and ablation. But they reduced the shock factor and contamination by blood and otherwise carried out their work more precisely. Much had been learned between 1870, when they worked, and the years when Flourens had applied his crude technologies.

functions became increasingly acceptable in neurological circles. Thus the
eventual factual demonstration of these centers in the 1870s did not
arouse any extraordinary upheaval. Resistance to the idea of motor
functions being located in the cerebrum, however, was far more pervasive
and detrimental within neurological circles. It was almost a matter of holy
belief that there was discontinuity in the representation of motor functions
within the nervous system.[5]

This reluctance to place motor functions in the brain was so strong
that it persisted even in the work of Hughlings Jackson, who, as we know,
had applied Spencer's sensory-motor paradigm to the entire CNS. In
Jackson's work, prior to Fritsch and Hitzig, we find frequent references to
the corpus striatum as "the highest part of the motor tract . . . through
which we are able to direct our *limbs* voluntarily" (Jackson, 1931b, pp.
122, 123). And even when Jackson did allow for the cerebrum's role in
motor functioning, he was extremely cautious in so doing, speaking of the
movements of the limbs being "represented in *each* part near the corpus
striatum" and elsewhere of the convolutions as the "highest centres of
movement" (Jackson, 1931b, pp. 240, 241). It was only after Fritsch and
Hitzig's work that Jackson would speak out unequivocally as to the role
of the "motor" cortex and discuss its convolutions as representing "over
again, but in new and more complex combinations, the very movements
which are represented in the corpus striatum" (Jackson, 1931a, pp. 114,
115).[6]

When almost simultaneously with Fritsch and Hitzig's research,
Betz, a Kievan anatomist, discovered the giant pyramidal cells of the
anterior central gyrus in the cerebral cortex—the presence of which
clearly distinguished the structure of the motor cortex from that of the
post central cortex[7]—the case for motoric representation in the cortex
clearly appeared to be won. It would take the favorable reviews of Fritsch
and Hitzig's work by commissions of noted physiologists and additional
tests of their hypotheses, however, before the objections of many of the
older neurological workers to the notion of a "motor" cortex would be
overcome.

[5] Anatomical knowledge that should have clearly demonstrated that motor tracts pass
through what is called the corpus striatum into the cortex was overlooked or misinterpreted.
Opponents of motor representation in the cortex were prone to point out that stimulation of
the corpus striatum produces muscular movement, disregarding the fact that stimulation of
the corticospinal tract at any level will do so. They were also able to observe that electrical
stimulation of the cerebrum did not consistently produce motor reactions—i.e., up to Fritsch
and Hitzig's work.
[6] Even Fritsch and Hitzig were at first reluctant to accept the full implications of their results
for cerebral localization and hedged slightly as to their full import.
[7] Later determined to have sensory functions.

Ferrier's experiments, first published in 1873, were the first and most important of the tests confirming Fritsch and Hitzig's discoveries. Where Fritsch and Hitzig had found but five localized centers for movement in the dog, in his monkey subjects, Ferrier found some 15 different areas, electrical stimulation of which resulted in specific movements. Ferrier also carried out ablation work, suppressing or eliminating specific motor functions so as to confirm the results of his stimulation experiments. It is to Ferrier that the credit belongs for clearly demonstrating the wide extensivity of motor representation within the cortex in incontrovertible fashion.[8]

Experimental demonstrations of the cortex's sensory functions lagged somewhat behind proof of its motor aspects. This was somewhat surprising since, as we have noted, philosophical resistance to the notion was never as strong or negative as it had been to that of motor attributes, and earlier neurophysiologists such as Bell, Mueller and, perhaps, even Flourens had played with the notion.

In particular, a strong case for specific cortical sensory centers had been made in Johannes Mueller's doctrine of specific nerve energies, with the publication of the edition of his *Handbuch* (1833–1840). Earlier, Bonnet, largely on the basis of speculation, then Bell, on the basis of his researches, suggested that each sensory nerve carries one kind of sensory experience, i.e., visual nerves carry visual impressions, auditory ones, auditory impressions. Mueller was to express this notion in an explicit doctrine, i.e., to the effect that the various qualities of experience arrive in one's mind only because of the specific qualities or energies of the nerves carrying those experiences. Each of the five types of sensory nerves are specific for their functions, the different qualities of experience that they carry being due to the physical qualities intrinsic in their tissues.

In developing this doctrine, Mueller speculated that the differences in sensory experience might possibly be caused by the different terminations of the various sensory nerve termini in the brain, i.e., by the differential functions of specific brain structures, rather than by the nature of the nerves themselves. He was, however, too much Cartesian to proceed far in this direction. So he finally allowed that the mind, through its sensorium, the cortex, has a direct influence upon sensations, "imparting to them intensity" (Boring, 1950, p. 89), but insisted that differences in the nature of sensations are due specifically to the differences in the nerves themselves. When, by the 1870s, the philosophical notion of sensory

---

[8] Ferrier was exceedingly gracious in acknowledging the influence of a mentor Jackson. "To Hughlings Jackson belongs the credit of having first indicated the motor functions of certain regions of the cortex" (Ferrier, 1878, p. 14). He, however, only begrudgingly acknowledged the antecedent work of Fritsch and Hitzig and had to be chided by the Royal Society before he would give them any more than perfunctory credit in his statements.

centers in the brain had become acceptable, Mueller's doctrine could be reinterpreted in accordance with the age's new insights. The notion of specific cerebral centers replaced that of specific nerve qualities as accounting for the varieties of sensory experience.[9]

The first sense to be experimentally tracked down to its cerebral lair was that of vision. Evidence to the effect that nerve fibers from the two retinas were projected on the sensorium of the brain dates back, at least, to Galen. And anatomical evidence for the semidecussation of the optic nerves at the chiasma had provided grounds, even in medieval days, for believing that the fibers from the left halves of both retinas led to a common locus in the left side of the brain and those from the right halves of the retinas to the right side. Once Mueller's philosophical blinders had been removed from the eyes of neurological science, what had always been observed could now be seen. The senses "projected," as it were, on the cortex.

It was Ferrier who first fixed the "visual center" in the occipital lobes, finding that a monkey with an occipital lobe removed was subject to abnormal eye movements and acted as if blind in the eye opposite to the side of the ablation.[10] Then Munk, in 1881, made such findings more precise by showing that removal of an occipital lobe produced meiopia, the blindness of half of the vision in each eye rather than total blindness. Later, tactile sensitivity was located by Ferrier and Schafer in the angular gyrus, though Hitzig and Munk localized it coextensively with movement in the motor area. Hearing was located in the temporal lobe. And so it went, rightly or wrongly, till all the senses had cerebral homes, though they have repeatedly moved or acquired additional residences since.

The sensory-motor paradigm was at last in a position of primacy as an explanatory principle for cerebral localization. The principles of sensory-motor associationism could be used to explain both the composition of the brain and behavior. Both brain and behavior were to be decomposed into elementary sensory and motor bits and then recomposed (associated) into structures that would explain it all. Now for the bolder of the neurological associationists, the brain was no longer to be regarded as the organ of the mind, i.e., the structure and structures through which the mind or soul expressed itself. The mind, instead, was to be understood as being created by the brain. Ferrier's writings expressed this type of psychophysical reductionism over the years with increasingly greater conviction—and carelessness.

He was initially hopeful but cautious. His researches, he said (1873),

---

[9] The notion that there is some type of topographical correspondence between arrangements of sensory structures in (or on) the body and their representation within the brain.

[10] Ferrier's localization of the visual cortex was badly off the mark, probably due to inaccurate cutting of neural fibers and faulty ablations.

led him to believe that all movements and sensations in higher animals are created by specific parts of the brain. From which findings he held out the hope that

> We may ultimately be enabled to translate into their psychological significa-tion and localize phrenologically the organic centres of various mental endow-ments. (Ferrier, 1874, p. 76)

Bolder conclusions followed from his pen in 1876:

> It must follow from the experimental data that mental operations in the last analysis must be merely the subjective side of sensory and motor substrata. (Ferrier, 1876, pp. 256–257)

And some ten years later, in 1886, he stated unequivocally:

> . . . the cerebral hemispheres consist only of centres related respectively to the sensory and motor tracts which connect them with the periphery and with each other. (Ferrier, 1886, p. 426)

In the crowning statement of his expositions, Ferrier proclaimed:

> Intelligence and will have no local habitation distinct from the sensory and motor substrata of the cortex generally. There are centres for special forms of sensation and ideation, and centres for special motor activities and acquisitions, in response to and in association with the activity of sensory centres; and these in their respective cohesions, actions, and interactions form the substrata of mental operations in all their aspects and all their range. (Ferrier, 1886, p. 436)

And since the mind was to be explained by what went on in the brain, in what was now called the "new phrenology," its higher cognitive functions, as well as its lower ones, were all to be expressed in and explained by the principles of sensory-motor associationism. Ideas, Fer-rier said, are revived associations of sensations and movements, thought is internal speech, and intellectual attention was ideal vision. The will (or, more precisely, purposive behavior) reduces to ". . . muscular actions . . . animals make in carrying out their desires and purposes" (Ferrier, 1874, p. 118). All functions are reducible to sensation, motion, and association.[11] Young points out that the Bell-Magendie paradigm, extended to the highest level of the neuraxis and the cerebrum, was intended by Ferrier to be used as an all-embracing explanatory conception in both physiology and psy-chology (Young, 1970).

---

[11] Ferrier's conceptual leaps required the attribution of psychological significance to the rather simple phenomena he had obtained through stimulation and ablation. The muscular contractions that he and other investigators elicited on stimulation, for example, were interpreted as coordinated purposive actions. The latter, in turn, were interpreted as man-ifestations of complex psychological functions. He was not deterred by doubts.

THE DIAGRAM MAKERS

Such views of sensory-motor associationism guided most of the steps of the florid period of brain localization that flourished in the latter part of the nineteenth century. As Tizard described the scene for what has been called the splendid seventies (i.e., the 1870s) of brain localization,

> The hypothesis generally held in the seventies . . . was that the cortex is the surface of projection for every muscle and every sensitive point in the body. These different cortical cells were held to represent the elementary ideas of sensation and motion of which all mental processes are composed. The fibres between the cells represent the association between ideas, hence there was thought to be a complete and neat parallelism between the brain processes and mental processes. (Tizard, 1959, p. 138)

The mind could be reduced to sensations and motor responses, the ideas created by their activities, and their associations. The frontal lobes were usually selected for the location of centers for "higher" cognitive processes on the basis that they held "silent" areas, those not directly engaged in sensory and motor processes. Flechsig, one of the major proponents of this view, proposed that the brain's various silent areas "associated" the impressions received from the adjacent sensory and motor areas, or combined the perceptions and memories from sensory stimulation.

Some of the old faculty conceptions of localization persisted, i.e., of distinct specific powers (or processes or traits) being localized in distinct loci within the brain, but by and large they were replaced within the "new phrenology" by the explanations of associationist psychology, which could explain the most complex of functions as merely the result of interactions between many simple functions localized within centers of neural networks in various parts of the brain. The very makeup of the neurons, e.g., their axonal and dendritic pathways, encouraged associationistic interpretations.

During the late nineteenth century, there was a veritable orgy of brain localization efforts. The literature on the topic became so voluminous after 1874 that contemporary reviewers contented themselves with simply listing references. Major experimental neurologists partaking in such research during the period were: Hitzig, Munk, Francois-Frank, Luiciani, Beevor, Schafer, Horsley, and Ferrier (Young, 1970).

The clinicians were not be left behind. Approximately ten years after Broca's demonstrations, Wernicke described a case wherein a lesion of the posterior third of the superior temporal gyrus of the left hemisphere disturbed speech comprehension. On its basis, he concluded that "the sensory images of speech" (note the associationist language) are localized in a zone of the cortex of the left hemisphere. Wernicke's area is almost as well known now as Broca's area. His discovery, coming on the decade-old heels of Broca's work, prompted other clinicians to seek centers and depots of the different mental processes. They correlated lesions in circumscribed areas of the cerebral cortex with singular or specific forms of mental defects, often on the basis of casual or careless pathological clinical observations. And they concluded that if a lesion to a particular area of the brain caused a disturbance in some kind of function, the cortical area wherein the lesion was found is the center of that function; the cells of the area are "depots" of highly specialized "memory images." Centers were found for all sorts of processes on the basis of such reasoning.

Cell and tissue studies of the cortex like those carried out by Campbell (1905), Brodmann (1909), and Vogts (1919) supported these localization efforts, as the differentiated structure of the cortex clearly manifested itself. Vogts, father of modern cytoarchitectonics, concluded on the basis of his work that the brain was composed of small organs, each the seat of a particular faculty. Clearly, the revealed structures of the brain supported the labors of the localizationists. Process maps became a popular feature of psychology, psychiatry, and neurology books.

There were a host of diagram makers, as Head contemptuously called them, at work during the late nineteenth and twentieth centuries, Wilhelm Wundt among them. Their "functional maps"

. . . as it seemed to them, finally settled the problem of the functional structure of the brain as the organ of mental activity once and for all. (Luria, 1973, p. 23)

William James critiqued their activities in perceptive fashion:

If we make a symbolic diagram on the blackboard of the laws of association between ideas, we are inevitably led to draw circles, or closed figures of some kind, and to connect them by lines. When we hear that the nerve centres contain cells which send off fibres, we say that Nature has realised our diagram for us, and that the mechanical substratum of thought is plain. In some way, it is true our diagram must be realised in the brain, but surely in no such visible and palpable way as we at first suppose. . . . (Tizard, 1959, p. 140)

The processes localized became ever more complex. Number sense, counting, orientation in space, reading, active ideation, and volitional action were precisely located in the brain. As for personality processes, there were places somewhere on the cerebral convolutions for them, too. When the German psychiatrist, Kleist (1934), who analyzed a large number of gunshot wounds resulting from World War I, established a topographical model localizing complex brain functions, he did not hesitate to cortically locate (and with great precision) such functions as "the body psyche," "the understanding of phrases," "constructive actions,'' "moods," and even "personal and social ego" (Luria, 1973). The American neurologist, Nielson, in 1936, followed in a similar vein, and even distinguished "centres for the perception of living objects" from other cerebral areas where, in his opinion, the perception of nonliving objects was localized. Some of these moves toward the localization of increasingly complex processes were accompanied by a return to trait process constructs, much like those Gall once used. It is difficult, after all, to reduce "personal and social ego" to simple S-R terms—though behaviorists try.

HOLISTIC AND NOETIC OBJECTIONS TO LOCALIZATION DOCTRINES

Nature is rarely as nice as theory. Precise localizations of the late nineteenth and early twentieth centuries were often the result of capricious interpretation of data, disregard of contradictory evidence, unwillingness to entertain alternative explanations of the phenomena explored, and simple wish fulfillment. To many who maintained a critical outlook, it became apparent that circumscribed localization of specific functions was too simplistic to be true. Fritsch and Hitzig reaffirmed Flourens's statement that method creates results. Most certainly! Did one experimentally study brain functions by electrical stimulation, electroencephalograms, coagulation techniques, ablation, or by the correlation of clinical syndromes with pathological anatomical data? One then often found different localizations. If stimulation of specific cortical "motor centers" could elicit certain specific movements, so would stimulation of the motor nerve tracts and lower structures of the brain. If so, what was located where? If a lesion destroyed a particular brain center for a particular function, why did the function often reappear at a later date? How many specific clinical phenomena associated with brain lesions were caused by general, rather than specific, neurological trauma? Which specific clinical symptoms represented stages of the recovery process from a general neurological disease, rather than specific lesions? Why did experimental ablations often yield different "localizations" from clinical lesions? Why did replicated experimental ablations sometimes create different deficits? Why did lesions in the same locations result at times in different deficits? How about all those negative cases where the centers for a so-called function were utterly destroyed and the function still went on? It was a puzzlement; it was a confusion.

Thus while the announcements of new cortical centers continued at a rapid pace, new voices spoke up in opposition to its fatuities. Hughlings Jackson was one of them. Jackson had been a pioneer in brain localization research. He had made several important anatomical discoveries in this area, among them the demonstration of the importance of the right parietal lobe for perceptual awareness and orientation in space and (together with Beevor) the significance of the temporal lobe for visceral and psychic functions. But he scoffed at efforts at precise structural localization of functions. Functions had, he insisted, complex vertical organization and were represented at different levels of the nervous system, rather than being properties of narrowly circumscribed groups of cells. Localization of symptoms, he also insisted, was not the same as localization of functions. They might be based on entirely different neurological foci.

Goltz, who favored holistic interpretations of brain function, looked at the lurid claims made for localization and stated (1888):

> The hypothesis of circumscribed centres for special functions is untenable, and there is no area of the cortex exclusively concerned with sights, hearing, smell, taste, touch . . . or the higher functions. (Tizard, 1959, p. 128)

Talking about brain processes, Finkelburg (1870) described speech as a complex symbolic and nonlocalizable function. Kussmaul (1885) also denied special depots in the cerebral cortex where images and ideas lie "neatly arranged on the shelves" and remarked, "We good-humoredly reject all naive attempts to localize speech in one or the other convolution of the brain" (Luria, 1966, p. 18).

So by the turn of the twentieth century, the numbers in opposition to precise brain localization theory began to grow. Their ranks further swelled as the result of the revival of idealistic philosophy and psychology. To members of the noetic school of psychologists and neurologists, the notions of simple sensory-motor associationism and precise brain localization could not explain the broad issues of human behavior.

The philosopher Henri Bergson was in the forefront of this movement, suggesting that active dynamic schemes of mental function replace those of simple associationism. He insisted upon a flexible relationship of neurological structure and mental function. A given mental state is related to a given cerebral state, he said, but not vice versa; it was not possible to derive from a given cerebral state a corresponding mental state. A number of mental states fit the same cerebral state, etc. (Riese & Hoff, 1950).

The psychological research of the Wurtzburg school further struck out at the elementarisms of associationistic theory. For its members, higher mental states were not reducible to simple associationistic elements. A number of prominent neurologists agreed, Pierre Marie (1906), van Woerom (1925), Bouman (1934) among them. The nature of a process, they said, was not a matter of S-R connections or cerebral centers. Rather

> . . . the principal form of the mental process is "symbolic activity," put into operation as "abstract" schemes, and that every disease of the brain is man-

ifested, not so much by a loss of the ability to carry out specialized processes as by a depression of this symbolic function or abstract orientation. (Luria, 1966, p. 19)

In practice, the neurological investigation instigated or stimulated by these neurologists once again directed itself to the functioning of the brain as a single entity and attempted to understand disturbances of higher mental processes according to the size of the brain lesion, rather than to specifically localized processes.

The field concepts of modern physics and then of psychology, i.e., the Gestalt school, also supported antilocalizationist attitudes. Noetic neurologists like Goldstein were affected by them. Also influenced was psychologist Carl Lashley (1927), who interpreted brain functioning in terms of "cortical dynamics" and offered the latter to counter the doctrines of associationism and localization. Lashley was following in the footsteps of a distinguished predecessor, psychologist Franz Ivory Shephard, who in the early years of the twentieth century had also taken a strong antilocalizationist stand. Shephard, in 1907, utilized the methods evolved by experimental psychology—specifically, those of Thorndike—to assess the effects of ablation in ten monkeys and cats. His conclusions, e.g., that recently acquired ability to escape from the puzzle box was lost after ablation but could be relearned in about as many trials as the first learning contraindicated localization specificities. Most important, he provided a basic paradigm for experimentally studying brain functions, i.e., the use of objective tests quantitatively scored, the procedure of training-operating-retraining, and the use of experimental controls.

Lashley improved on Shephard's methodology by using enough animals to permit statistical analysis in ablation studies and by determining the extent of the ablations by postmortem examination. Running 50 rats through mazes before and after cortical lesions, Lashley found that their performance was impaired in rough proportion to the extent of the cerebral lesions they had received and that the same degree of impairment was produced by equal amounts of destruction in any of the principal regions of the cortex. From such findings, he deduced that particular types of learning deficits could not be ascribed to defects in specific areas of the brain; but rather that the mass of brain tissue removed critically bears upon performance and that different areas of the cerebral cortex are equipotential as concerns complex cerebral functions. He did not deny cerebral localization as is so often believed, but rather concluded that its extent and significance vary from one performance to another, i.e., being precise, for example, in pattern discrimination for example, but not in brightness discrimination; and that there was no evidence that any specific cortical area was critical to learning. Criticism of Lashley's work by Hunter and Pavlov followed. They suggested different interpretations of his results. His principle of mass action, for example, could be explained by the fact that if one sensory center was destroyed, the rats could use others in learning so that no specific lesion would destroy a maze-running habit altogether, but the habit, rather, would be diminished roughly in proportion to the amount of cerebral tissue destroyed, since this would result in fewer sensory cues. Pavlov also criticized Lashley for using crude psychological concepts to interpret extirpation results. Lashley's work, however, was generally accepted among psychologists and was, for a while, regarded as stemming the tide of brain localization doctrine (Tizard, 1959, Luria, 1966).

Among the neurologists, the work of Monakow (1814), Head (1925), and Goldstein (1927) was influential in fostering antilocalizationist views and espousing noetic notions, while at the same time recognizing the legitimacy of at least some of the localizationist principles. A leading authority on the cerebral localization of elementary neurological symbols and signs was von Monakow. He, however, refused to adopt the same principle in his analysis of the cerebral basis of disturbed symbolic activity which he called "asemia." He attributed many of the deficits that had been attributed to specific focal lesions to generalized brain trauma, and the altering and recovering functions that characterized the process of *diachesis*, i.e., the stages of recovery from brain injury. Head had established a sure niche in neurological history in respect to specificities of function on the basis of his investigations of sensation. But he ascribed individual differences in speech disturbance to lesions of large area of the cortex and called upon a general factor of "vigilance" to serve as an explanatory principle of neurological functioning. Goldstein agreed upon cerebral localization of elementary neurological processes, but relied upon the noetic ideas when explaining the complex mental processes involved in abstract or categorical behavior. According to his interpretation of neurological phenomena, the periphery of the cortex, which was responsible for specific sensory and motor functions, operated according to the laws of cerebral localization. The central part of the cortex, which was responsible for abstract orientation and categorical behavior, operated on the basis of the principle of equipotentiality and the creation of "dynamic structures" against some form of "dynamic background" (Luria, 1966, 1973).

A LOOK AT THE CURRENT STATUS OF "LOCALIZATION"

The development of increasingly precise and innovative technologies and methods of inquiry into neurological phenomena, since the days of dispute that we have just reviewed, leave little doubt currently as to the validity of "localization" as a concept. Penfield has elicited from the cortical stimulation of his patients surprisingly complex sensory and cognitive phenomena and movements. There have been sleep centers discovered (Hess), centers related to obesity (Brobeck), and centers for reward and punishment (Olds and Milner). Affective centers have also been found for rage (Bard) and for fear (Masserman). We are able to introduce selective losses of skill in visual discrimination by small ventromedial lesions of the temporal lobe. Performance on delayed alteration tests have been affected by destruction of selected parts of the cortex (Jasper, 1960). Teuber and his associates have shown that the patterns of sensory loss produced by patterns of unilateral brain wounds are not entirely the same on each side of the body. And we are regularly provided with new accounts of specific agraphias, speech disturbances, and the like (Geschwind, 1965).

Particularly impressive support for localization theory came to us in the post–World War II years from work relative to the differentiated functioning of the two cerebral hemispheres (in particular, from the inspired work of Roger Sperry and his associates, who carried out research with a small group of patients in whom the main interhemispheric commisures had been severed for the purpose of treating their epileptic conditions). In a number of remarkable investigations, Sperry et al. restricted various sensory inputs and motor outputs to one or the other of the hemispheres, and by so doing demonstrated contrasting specializations of the two hemispheres. On the basis of their work, they have concluded that two brains appear to be operating within any individual, a left brain and a right brain. And for that matter "two minds," for which there are to be found distinct differences in functions (Sperry, 1967a, 1968, 1972, 1974; Gazzaniga, Bogen, & Sperry, 1967).

Studies of intact nervous systems through dichotic listening procedures, putting left and right sides of normal brains in competition with each other, have also revealed left-side–right-side asymmetries in functioning (Broadbent, 1974), to mention but one other approach to the differentiation of hemispheric functions.[12]

And yet the notion that processes, simple or complex, are specifically, unequivocally, and invariantly associated with specific brain structures, cerebral or otherwise, is not tenable. The so-called projection systems for sensory functions are found to overlap ". . . at all levels and . . . cannot be related to specific functions, nor confined to limited areas" (Jasper, 1960, p. 97). Penfield, responsible for some of the most sophisticated of localization investigations and theories, himself argued for unity of functioning in face of the diversity of "functions" his work appeared to

---

[12] Though Broadbent has cautioned lest there be overspecified interpretation of neurological functioning on the basis of his data.

reveal. Speaking of memory mechanisms in 1952, he offered the following cautions:

> The circuits of this system run out into the various functional areas of the cortex and back again. In a very real sense there is no "higher" and no "lower" in this system. The place of understanding is not walled up in a cell or in a centre of gray matter. It is to be sought in the perfect functioning of all these converging circuits. (Jasper, 1960, p. 107)

The Russian localizationists have also spoken of *functional systems* and made it ". . . abundantly clear that this [a functional system] cannot be understood as the function of a particular tissue" (Luria, 1973, p. 27). A process, whether it is of digestion or thought, is carried out, not as a simple function, but as a complete system embodying many components, the elements of which may be interchangeable because the same result, i.e., the outcome of the functional system, can be achieved by totally different components and methods:

> Naturally all mental processes such as perception and memorizing, gnosis and praxis, speech and thinking, writing, reading and arithmetic, cannot be regarded as isolated or even indivisible faculties . . . presume to be the direct function of limited cell groups or to be "localized" in particular areas of the brain. (Luria, 1973, p. 20)

> They are social, their origin hierarchical in structure and ". . . all based on a complex system of methods and means" (Luria, 1973, p. 30)

More recently John and Schwartz, quite clearly committed to specific neurological process conceptions, but in ways quite contrary to both associationistic and precise neurological localization conceptions, warned:

> . . . . reassuring theoretical and experimental arguments for a localizationist approach to brain function must be critically reevaluated. To a certain extent . . . reductionistic positions have been internalized by many workers in the neurosciences, and the difficult but necessary step of facing the complexity entailed by a global or statistical point of view has been avoided (John & Schwartz, 1978, p. 7)

As Flourens used "new technology" to devastate Gall's arguments, and Fritsch and Hitzig used still newer forms to demolish his, so does each advance in scientific methodology cast doubt upon yesterday's conclusions concerning cerebral localization. Easy answers to the difficult problems posed in this area will almost inevitably prove to be wrong ones in the future.

11

Some Afterthoughts on Processes and Their Localization

It is difficult to conclude from our review that, in the ultimate analysis, processes are anything more than ways of attempting to explain categorized behavior by the labels affixed to such categorized behavior. Categorizing—classifying—behavior is a major activity of rational man and of inductive science. But the use of classificatory terms as explanatory processes can easily become a venture into superstition and magic; at its most benign, it is a convenience, personal or scientific.

It is difficult to stop using process terms, just as it is difficult to stop eating peanuts. Put them before us and we may not like them, but there we go again. Processes are verbal amenities, facilitating conversation and communication. They also serve as advance and post-organizers for our thinking, so that we find ourselves hardly able to do without them. Convenient fictions! We cannot quite recall who so defined processes, but it is as good a description as any.

Are there not activities or structures within us, i.e., internal processes, that are causative of behavior? Well what is meant by within and internal, and why should there be anything of the kind to cause behavior, except in a figurative sense? There are other ways of explaining behavior: ask Herbart, ask Skinner. Yet we persist in believing that there must be inner causes, interior explanations for what we do. Because we are all creatures of religion—the most avowed atheists among us—and practicing lay metaphysicians, to boot; we reach beyond our data to answer our whys and hows. And so we all postulate, all but the truly most stubbornly negative of behaviorists, that something within us causes that which we do.

However, postulate as we will—process this or process that—there is no way of ultimately proving the existence of process this or process that. Operationalize processes you may, anchor them in observables, place them in bondage within stimulus-response chains, yet the belief in your processes or mine remains an act of metaphysical faith. And if they were real, we still could not observe them, but would remain, rather, like Plato's people of the cave, speculating from the shadows of our data.

But do away with processes, banish them from our psychological sciences and educational theories and we have taken a good deal of the fun out of the game, a good deal of romance out of our work and, besides, we have made it difficult to make common sense out of our work. Behaviorists still struggle now and then to kick the process habit. But such efforts sound clumsy, lack communicative conviction for the reader, and leave one with the feeling of not fully knowing what is going on or why. Black boxes are not attractive boxes.

The temptation to banish processes is, nevertheless, quite strong when one reads statements such as those in a recent article extolling process research wherein the authors remark in passing:

. . . one could state that although the abilities may restrict the processes to a certain extent, as the bowl restricts the soup, we can still have a variety of processes within the confines of any ability. (Das, Kirby & Jarman, 1975).

What are the authors talking about? Do they intend to be metaphorical? Let them heed Turbayne's *Myth of the Metaphor*:

Every metaphor contains a wealth of connotations, each connotation has the potential for manifold implications. . . . While metaphors are ordinarily used by people to facilitate communications, the peril is always at hand that people may be used by metaphors. (Sarbin, 1967, p. 447)

Do they believe that they really can distinguish this or that process from another or a process from an ability? Then let them heed Ebel:

Part of the difficulty with the term *higher mental processes* is in seeing the difference between higher and lower mental processes. Is recall a lower mental process? When I leave the office and try to recall where my car was parked the last time I left it, in Lot D, H, M, or P, and where in the lot, it seems that I am using about all the mental processes, high and low, that I possess. Further, because we do not really know what a mental process is, may it not be premature to try to differentiate higher and lower mental processes? (Ebel, 1974, p. 487)

And yet Das and associates are among the more sophisticated of those who reify and deify processes. One need not read extensively in psychology or education to see that many of our finest minds still persist in acting as if their processes are real, even as they protest that they are aware of their hypothetical status. Man thinks in terms of things and causes, and the nature of our language encourages the reification of our concepts. Noun forms become noun things, become real as we talk or think of them. It was so with the Hellenes. It is so now.

Is there any way we can live intelligently with processes, to get their benefits while avoiding their pitfalls? Yes, by constantly maintaining an awareness of their hypothetical status and reiterating it, if not to our sophisticated selves, then to the many of our friends and students who walk about believing that "intelligence," "perception," and all those other wonderful things inside us explain what we are and why we do. But one must remain pessimistic of our chances of success when similar efforts at reform have always failed in the past, with even the reformers failing to reform themselves. Fortunately, this book is a history and has the task of recording rather than solving epistemological problems.

If psychological processes are hypothetical (and they are), why should we be concerned with their localization within the brain? The reason is that the behaviors processes represent are real enough to justify an attempt to understand them in terms of the parameters of brain functioning with which they are associated. We do, after all, hear, see, talk, discriminate aesthetically, love, and otherwise experience and emit behaviors that fall under the rubrics of our various process terms. Why should we not try to understand the physical side of such?

One of the problems in brain localization efforts is the variability of the behaviors that process terms represent. We can be sure that the most precise match of our hypothetical processes to behavior is extremely imperfect, with imperfection increasing as we move to more complex levels of experiencing and behaving. One man's solution of a problem on an intelligence test via a higher cognitive process is another man's solution of the same problem, to the same criterion level, utilizing a lower cognitive process. Analysis of variance to the rescue—perhaps. Certain behaviors and traits that appear to be the enduring property of the organism turn out to be situational when more closely examined. Stages of behavior and development turn out to be stages of development relative to specific methods of inquiry and not to others.

If we cannot assuredly identify the behaviors whose neurological correlates we seek, the success of our localization quest is prelimited in the answers it can provide for our questions. To be sure, there would appear to be clearly identifiable behaviors that are specific enough to permit a precise search for their specific neural substrata. But are there? Is success in the repetition of digit based upon the same subbehavior systems in all the emittents? Does failure in the repetition of digits represent the same type of behavioral deficiencies in one case of failure as in another? Perhaps, perhaps not; efforts to precisely localize the imprecise must be regarded with considerable caution.

A corollary to the behavioral uncertainties we face when we deal with cerebral localization (or localization anywhere else, for that matter) is the imperfection of the labels we attach to our behaviors. What does the word memory really represent—50 stages of storage, the active search for and retrieval of information, the matching of the information to present stimuli, or the active encoding of that information? True, our cognitive psychologists have done us the service of making distinctions between varieties of memory. But even in their most finite subprocess forms, attempts to localize "memory" within the brain presume a veridicality between processes and the names we give them that assuredly does not hold. As to perception, language, love, and Raymond B. Catell's *dysthurgia*—how do we expect to precisely localize the processes identified by labels such as these within the brain, despite their most careful operationalizations?

Nevertheless, there has been great success in discovering the neurological correlates of certain types of behaviors, some quite complex in their nature. There surely is brain localization. But localization of what? Does the elicitation of a motor act or a visual experience through stimulation mean that we have found the center for these? Does the discovery of more than one point of elicitation mean "multiple centers" for such processes? Does turning on the lights with the press of a finger mean that the light switch is the center for the illumination that follows? Surely a point of elicitation does not necessarily mean the center of anything, but rather a point of elicitation.

If lesions or ablations cause the disappearance of certain behaviors, does that mean that we have then located the behavior in the tissues that have been removed or damaged? We have, of course, localized a place within the nervous system where tissue removal or damage interferes with the behavior. The determination of a neurological area where defects impair specific types of behavior no more localizes that behavior—or the processes presumed to cause it—than does its elicitation through electrical stimulation. Nor will the electroencephalographic readings or any other type of indirect measure tell us where this or that process is located, no matter how heated our inferences drawn from them may be. Left brain, right brain? Two minds? Why not a third?

No, one will simply not be able to directly locate processes or the behaviors they "cause" within the brain; neither will one be able to fully explain behavior or processes by the brain. Plato's ratiocinations in *The Republic* would not be understood a wit more by examining his frontal lobes. The transposition of keys in the final bars of the Bolero would not be better grasped by examining Ravel's temporal ones, or Velasquez's visual insights by a view into his occipital cortex.[1] For behaviors are still the

---

[1] William McDougall was fond of speaking in this vein.

behaviors of an entire organism, operating integrally even when disturbed, even when damaged, no matter how stimulated. It is one thing to examine the participation of various neurological components or "brain systems" (to use Luria's term) in behavior; to determine which ones are associated with various behaviors (as specifically defined as possible); to discover the points and places where and how lesions disrupt or change such behaviors; or to study the tempero-spatial electrical phenomena in the brain associated with them. These are legitimate localization goals. It is quite another to attempt to localize psychological processes in the brain. Attempting to do so is to wander off into metaphysics and to join Descartes in his search for the seat of the *res cogitans* and its faculties.

PART II

Process Training in Its Developmental Stages

12
The Beginnings of Process Training

INTRODUCTION

Process is so intimately associated with the essence of man, or at least with what that essence is conceived to be, that it has always been front and center in his concerns. And so, too, has process training continuously characterized man's efforts to prepare himself and his progeny for the tasks of life. The history of such process training efforts is most important to a historical understanding of education and, in particular, the education of exceptional children.

It might be hoped that our earlier discussions of process could provide a consistent basis from which to approach the concerns of process training. Unfortunately this is not the case. The conceptions of process held by theology, philosophy, medicine and psychology down through the ages have often been at odds within themselves as well as with each other. They did not, they do not, provide a uniform set of principles for education to utilize in its process training endeavors. Not that education hasn't borrowed freely from them. However, its borrowings have not been consistent and great varieties of distortions have been introduced in the borrowing. Very often, too, education's processes have simply been reifications of everyday parlance or activities that educators saw their charges engaged in. This is not to say that some agreement did not eventually emerge in educational theory and practice. By the nineteenth century, as will be demonstrated in the later chapters of this book, there was considerable uniformity of conception and practice in respect to process training. Nevertheless, inconsistencies and discontinuities will continue to be found in our intra- and inter-author reviews. There is no need, certainly, for any reader to feel puzzled if the processes they encounter in the succeeding chapters are not congruent with others they have read about in previous ones. Process theorists were creative people on the whole and not to be bugabooed by the hobgoblin Consistency.

THE GREEKS AND PROCESS TRAINING

It is difficult to determine whether the Greeks should receive priority as having first espoused process training, for all peoples, even primitive ones, have sought to strengthen that ultimate process, the soul, and all have sought to develop and nurture reified abstractions such as courage, justice, virtue, wisdom—hypothetical process constructs used to explain behavior—and then trained to improve that behavior. But since Western education truly begins with the Greeks, it is with them that we also begin our tale of process training.

Process training in the broad sense of character training was a fundamental aspect of Greek education. For the Athenians, education was

. . . the art of developing each individual into an integrated whole exercising all basic human functions—family, civic, aesthetic, physical, intellectual, religious, and moral—in relation to the whole man. To be a perfect man would involve balancing all potentialities and powers within the individual, blending into a harmonious personality intellectual and physical powers, individual and social tendencies, aesthetic and moral qualities, and so forth. (Nakosteen, 1965, p. 78)

The ideals of Athenian education emphasized the training of both the body and the soul. Plato emphasized that the training of the former also had within it the possibilities of training of the latter. In *The Republic* we read:

Neither are the two arts of music and gymnastics really designed, as is often supposed, the one for the training of the soul, the other for the training of the body. What, then, is the real object of them? I believe, I said, that the teachers of both have in view chiefly the improvement of the soul. (Nakosteen, 1965, p. 79)

The value of curriculum for shaping the mind or soul in correspondence with inherent cognitive laws seems to have suggested itself relatively early to the Greeks (Brubacher, 1966, p. 743). Both the *trivium,* i.e., grammar didactics, and rhetoric, and the *quadrivium,* the other section of the Greek curriculum, composed of arithmetic, geometry, astronomy and music, were prized for their cognitive training values.

Socrates and Plato and other idealists were avowed cognitive trainers and sought to prepare their students for dealing with eternal verities, seeking to develop within them ". . . the highest elements in the hierarchy of human nature, namely the faculty of theoretical reason and contemplation . . ." for ". . . knowledge, properly speaking, is acquired only by those whose intellect, or reason, has been able to cast off the shadows and shackles created by sense, experience and opinion" (Butts, 1955, pp. 48–49). Since true knowledge comes from the spiritual world and is innate within the immortal soul, such ultimate knowledge can only be achieved ". . . by a process of reminiscence by which the intellect remembers what it knew before its association with an imperfect body" (Butts, 1955, p. 49). To remember properly, the intellect had to be trained so that it could, on one hand, resist the blandishment of misinformation coming through sensory channels and, on the other hand, direct itself to contemplate eternal truths. Thus said Socrates and Plato, amidst recommending that intellectual discipline, i.e., mental training of the strictest type, was required. And process training began its trip through history.

As noted by Monroe, both Socrates and Plato were interested in ". . . process as a process, and in the power developed by its use" (Monroe, 1905, p. 129). These notions were clearly expressed by Plato in *Theatetus* wherein he had Socrates ask:

> . . . is not physical health . . . preserved largely by exercise and motion. . . . So too with the condition of the soul. The soul acquires information and is kept alive and improved by learning and practice—two forms of motion; whereas through inactivity . . . it learns nothing and forgets what it has learned. (Warrington, 1961, p. 80)

Elsewhere, Plato, distinguished between knowledge (innate ideas) and processes. The latter are susceptible to training. Thus in *The Republic*

> . . . what are commonly called excellences of the mind perhaps resemble those of the body, in that they are . . . implanted by subsequent training and practice . . . (Lee, 1974, p. 322).[1]

Process oriented as they were, Plato and Socrates (as we know him through Plato's writing) generally decried training directed toward the acquisition of specific types of knowledge, particularly those that had utilitarian purposes (military ones excepted). In a later section of *The Republic*, Socrates states that "all the useful arts were reckoned mean." Physically, they could lead to distortion of the body away from Greek ideals, e.g., fat bottoms on scribes, hunched shoulders on shoemakers, squints in jewelry workers. Cognitively, they directed the mind to the inferior knowledge of the marketplace and away from the eternal verities

---

[1] The equation of body and mind repeatedly by Plato reveals quite clearly the importance of physical conditioning to the Greeks, as well as the idea that both the physical and mental spheres of man will respond to the same types of regimens.

which Socrates and Plato wanted their students to reach for. Socrates and Plato also resisted attempts to introduce sciences into the curriculum on the grounds that these studies, too, led the mind into mean pursuits. Of them, only astronomy was acceptable, and then only on the grounds that it would be used for cognitive training purposes.

While training in "the useful arts" was certainly appropriate for the lesser people of Plato's *Republic*, it was, beneath the dignity of the Platonic elite—and it was for these, above all, that Plato spun his educational theories in this particular treatise.

The major goal of Socratic-Platonic education—the training of the rational soul—was to be addressed early in life. Even nursery rhymes were to be carefully selected so as to fashion the mind. From the very beginnings of an infants nurture, cognitive training was to be given precedence.[2] (Rusk, 1969)

Musical education was held to be important both spiritually and for cognitive stylistic purposes. It creates harmony and rhythm in the student's soul. It is ". . . the counterpart," Plato said, ". . . of gymnastic," and trains ". . . students, by harmony making them harmonious, by rhythm rhythmical" (Jowett, 1875, p. 522). Music was to assist the Greek elite in turning themselves into living counterparts of their ideal of manhood, by helping them make of themselves works of art.

As that elite matured, it was to be trained through the avenues of philosophy and mathematics. Dialectics was the particular type of philosophical instruction favored by Plato, assisting his pupils, as it did, toward more effective reminiscence. That is, recall of innate ideas that are the human soul's inheritance. Mathematics and geometry were favored avenues of instruction because they develop the mind's powers of abstraction, enabling it more easily to understand and contemplate spiritual "universals, the ultimate truths towards which all higher education aims." Arithmetic, Plato said

. . . is a study which leads naturally to reflection. . . . Arithmetic has a very great and elevating effect, compelling the soul to reason about abstract number. . . . (Monroe, 1971, p. 145)

Plato chided those who sought to teach mathematics toward utilitarian ends:

. . . we must endeavour to persuade those who are to be the principal men of our state to go and learn arithmetic, not as amateurs, but they must carry on the study until they see the nature of numbers with the mind only; nor again, like merchants or retail traders, with a view to buying or selling, but for the sake of their military use, and of the soul herself; and because this will be the easiest way for her to pass from becoming to and being. (Jowett, 1875, p. 525)

[2] In this way Socrates and Plato differed from Aristotle, who accorded body and affective education precedence.

Those who used mathematics for applied purposes were always speaking in "a narrow and ridiculous manner, of squaring and extending and applying and the like" (Jowett, 1875, p. 527).

Plato also foresaw or (more modestly) speculated as to the possibilities of process remediation through mathematics and geometry, asking and responding in *Republic* and *Laws*

Have you further observed, that those who have a natural talent for calculation are generally quick at every other kind of knowledge; and even the dull, if they have had an arithmetical training, although they may derive no other advantage from it, always become much quicker than they would otherwise have been? (Jowett, 1875, p. 526)

Arithmetic stirs up him who is by nature sleepy and dull, and makes him quick to learn, retentive, shrewd, and aided by art divine he makes progress quite beyond his natural powers. (Jowett, 1875, p. 747)

In all departments of knowledge, as experience proves, any one who has studied geometry is infinitely quicker of apprehension than one who has not. (Jowett, 1875, p. 752)

Astronomy can improve reasoning powers. As with mathematics and geometry, Plato insisted that it be employed for its cognitive values rather than for its practical worth:

I am amused at your fear of the world, which makes you guard against the appearance of insisting upon useless studies; and I quite admit the difficulty of believing that in every man there is an eye of the soul which, when by other pursuits lost and dimmed, is by these purified and re-illumined; and is more precious far than ten thousand bodily eyes, for by it alone is truth seen. Then in astronomy, as in geometry, we should employ problems, and let the heavens alone if we would approach the subject in the right way and so make the natural gift of reason to be of any real use. (Jowett, 1875, p. 530)

Plato emerges out of our review as the father of cognitive training, and specifically of formal discipline.[3] The mind, like the body, is trained through exercise. Specific mental functions are trained by the mind's application to specific areas of endeavor. Such training is best accomplished by using curriculum and materials that do not have utilitarian purposes. Training of a particular psychic function in one area prepares it for operations in other, unrelated areas.

Plato's remarks concern the value of calculation exercises for training the mind ("you will not early find a more difficult subject and not many as difficult") (Jowett, 1875, p. 747), further anticipates the doctrine of formal discipline by suggesting that the more difficult or painful the

---

[3] Formal discipline—later mental discipline—intends training of the mind's forms or formative education of the mind, as opposed to instruction for the purpose of imparting information or knowledge.

training, the greater the benefits to be derived from it. And so, the harder the pupil has to work on his lessons, the more they strengthen his cognitive processes. It is on such grounds that the theory of formal discipline has frequently been criticized as advocating the training of illusory mental muscles.

It appears that Plato's later life experiences aroused some occasional doubts concerning such recommendations. Thus, in *Laws*, written when he was an old man, he wrote:

For you surely would not regard the skilled mathematician as a dialectician? Assuredly not . . . I have hardly ever known a mathematician who was capable of reasoning. (Jowett, 1875, p. 531)

This qualification has been offered by some apologists as acquitting Plato of the onus of having initiated process training, but it appears to have been a remark born of a passing exasperation, rather than a genuine renunciation.

Aristotle agreed with Plato that "man is a rational animal" and that "cultivation of the intellect" is his supreme goal. He did distinctly differ from Plato, however, in his acceptance of the values of sense experience for learning and of scientific induction as a useful approach to cognitive training. He also emphasized training in practical skills (so that conventional decisions could be made), as well as training of the reason which is the highest virtue to be achieved in education.

Conceiving of education along process lines, Aristotle's recommendations were to carry out that training in stages hierarchically in the order of the priority that the body, then the irrational soul, and finally, the rational soul make their appearances, though the ultimate goal always to be kept in mind was the training of the rational soul. Hence, his statement:

. . . reason and mind are the end towards which nature strives, so that the . . . discipline of the citizen ought to be ordered with a view to them. And as the body is prior in order of generation to the soul, so the irrational is prior to the rational. Wherefore, the care of the body ought to precede that of the soul, and the training of the appetitive part should follow. None the less our care of it must be for the sake of the reason, and our care of the body for the sake of the soul. (Boyd & King, 1973, pp. 37, 38)

THE ROMANS AND PROCESS TRAINING

The Romans translated much of Greek educational precept and practice into forms suitable for their own pragmatic purposes. They seem to have accepted, without distinctive alterations, the Greek notions of process training. But they valued the practical outcomes of such training more than did their Greek antecedents. Thus at the upper levels of education the trivium and quadrivium were prized for their values in cognitive training, but rhetoric, while taught because of its formative values, was also cherished because of the leverage it provided a would-be achiever in the political world. At lower educational levels, cognitive training was expected to prepare students for the scholarly achievements that would advance their careers.

Quintilian, the most famous of Roman educators (35–95 A.D.), recommended oral reading for his younger pupils, since this would give them a sense of timing, rhythm, animation, and modulation in thought as well as in voice. As for grammar, he said:

> . . . those who enter the inner shrine . . . of this sanctuary will come into the presence of many mysteries fitted not merely to sharpen the wits of boys but to give scope for the exercise of the profoundest erudition and knowledge (Black, Lottich & Seckinger, 1972, p. 210)

Mathematics, too, was found by Quintilian to have valuable process-strengthening powers. It exercised a student's perceptive powers, offered him training in deductive reasoning, and, like grammar, generally "sharpened his wits."

Above all processes, the Roman educational greats urged cultivation of that so easily confused, so quick-to-fail faculty, the memory.[4] Plutarch admonished:

> Above all it is important to exercise and train the memory of the young, since it is the storehouse of education. (Beck, 1965, p. 52)

The major way the Romans trained memory was to overload students with tasks that required memorization, which they were expected to bring off letter perfect. Quintilian recommended memorization of poetry and the utterances of great men for this purpose. Memory training was a not altogether unreasonable demand for the time, considering that the average Roman's accessibility to information and knowledge depended almost entirely upon that memory. Writing materials and books were expensive and scarce; one's library was often confined to the few scribblings that remained from his school days and his own powers of recall.

EARLY CHRISTIANS AND PROCESS TRAINING

Among the early Christian fathers, intellectual ability and achievement were not of any great concern. The Christian's goal was to attain heaven, rather than to achieve cognitive insights, and formal education in

---

[4] Also recognized as the essential process for learning by the Hebrews and Greeks.

general suffered. Process training of the early Christian period was cona-
tively and affectively austere. Its aim was to direct the soul, the ultimate
process, away from the demands of the flesh and the material world and to
prepare it for the world hereafter.

As the Church increasingly came to recognize its need for cognitively
competent and knowing parishioners, it came to embrace Latin models of
training and education and, with them, Roman process concepts. Augustine (354–430 A.D.) subscribed to the doctrine of faculties and advocated
process training along the lines of his Roman educational predecessors,
though he too kept salvation rather than education in the foreground of his
educational philosophy.

Augustine showed, however, a particular interest in the will. The
will, or willpower, is a special force that he described in most vivid theological terms.[5] It is a fleshy, sly, self-aggrandizing faculty that has to be
subdued through prayer, self-abnegation, and training to be obedient and
directed to God's purposes. Will, however, can be construed in other than
theological or affective terms. It can be conceptualized as a faculty or
power through which the mind activates the body's motor apparatus. And
it was in this sense that it came to assume such an important role in later
psychological–medical theory. Its training, then, was not always a matter
of controlling one's appetites; it came also to be a means by which the mind
and its higher faculties could learn to direct the body in its activities, i.e.,
through voluntary action.

THE SCHOLASTICS

Platonic conceptions of the human soul and mind were ascendant
during the early Christian years and the beginning centuries of the Middle
Ages. Then, thanks in large part to the sponsorship of Albertus Magnus
and St. Thomas Aquinas, Aristotelean theories triumphed and—within
them—Aristotelean notions of process. According to Aristotle and then the
Scholastics, the primary characteristic of the soul is *activity*. The soul has
natural potentials for activity. Instruction is to emphasize the exercise of
those natural potentials. (Brubacher, 1966)

St. Thomas accepted the Aristotelean premise that the soul requires
sense experiences in order to begin performing its functions and that it is
the higher cognitive powers that are responsible for the ultimate translation of the raw sensory data so obtained into forms that are meaningful
and useful to the soul. A major thrust of Scholastic education was to
develop acuteness in the thinking of its charges; this was to enable them to
penetrate to the ultimate truths that belonged to Catholic Christianity. It

[5] Despite his insistance upon the soul's unity.

was also necessary to develop a student's cognitive powers so that he could construct theses leading to proofs of the Christian religion from any evidential or inferential starting point. Here St. Thomas was inclined to take what appeared to him to be a reasonable developmental point of view. Much as many present-day special educators confuse their hierarchies of instructional objectives with the hierarchy of developmental processes within the students they teach, so did he believe that these syllogisms reflected the cognitive structures that created them; ergo, train the mind, syllogistically constructed as it is, through training in syllogistic reasoning! Nor did he or the other Scholastic perceptors forget to train memory by making the student memorize.

The Scholastics generally adapted the formalistic educational techniques of their Latin predecessors for the cognitive training of their pupils. They believed that the mind should be trained to think syllogistically rather than worrying about the validity of the syllogism. They believed in training the memory rather than assuring that it had meaningful things to recall. The idea of disciplining the mind appealed greatly to medieval Christians—at all times, force it to struggle under conditions of great discomfort and to carry heavy burdens, so that it might become strong, ascetic, and properly prepared to bear the burdens of religious commitment.

THE HUMANISTS

The advent of humanism proffered some hope of relief from the dreariness of Scholastic training for the pupils of medieval Europe. But since humanism adopted the educational forms and practices of the past, particularly those of the Romans, it also meant, eventually, adaptation of the ancients' less-than-benign process training and practices, rendered even more unpalatable by the use of classical (ancient) Latin to achieve their purposes in an age when Latin no longer served as a means of ordinary human communication.

Humanistic education degenerated into formalistic preparation of students as opposed to instruction intended to impart useful knowledge. In particular, it was perfection in expressing one's self in Latin, both orally and in written form, that humanistic mentors insisted upon. This did not at all mean self-expression by the student in Latin, but rather the slavish verbatim imitation of famous Latin predecessors, among whom Cicero, in particular, was admired and imitated.[6] Since it was verbatim reproduction of ancient means of expression that the humanists prized, so

---

[6] Hence the name Ciceroism was affixed to the educational philosophy and practices of those who insisted that exact training in Latin forms was essential to education.

were their charges subjected to the most odious efforts to improve their memory. Pupils were overwhelmed with masses of Latin grammar, poems, slogans, and literary tracts, which they were expected to memorize to the point of exact reproduction. It is sad to see even the most sympathetic of humanistic educators, such as Vittorino (1378–1446), insisting upon such courses of memory training, while even Vives (1492–1540), striking out for a vitalization of humanistic educational practices, also believed memory training was an essential instructional practice.

For the humanists, as for the Romans, memory training was to begin at the earliest time for, following in Quintilian's footsteps, they were afraid lest a child's earliest, freshest years be lost in wanton play. Thomas Elyot (1490–1546), a most eminent and influential educator in his day, wrote in his *The Boke Named the Governour*:

> The memory should be exercised in early youth, since practice develops it, and we should therefore take care to practice it as much as possible. Now, in youth, the labor is not felt, and thus the memory develops without any trouble and becomes very retentive. (Eby, 1952, p. 189)

It was Elyot's premise and that of Erasmus and other humanistic lights that the young mind took intellectual abuse somehow with less pain than did an older one (harking back to Quintilian). It was, therefore, quite proper to overload the young pupil with tasks that made older and more mature ones groan.

With humanism, process training began to receive formalized educational expression. Elyot, in addition to his recommendations for memory training, advised the use of logic, rhetoric, and oratory to train pupils' rational faculties. Richard Mulcaster (1530–1611), an educational iconoclast in many ways, readily subscribed to both faculty psychology and faculty training. He was concerned with his pupils' inherent "abilities" and recommended careful psychological analyses of their "wit to take (perception), memory to keep and discretion to discern (reason) prior to instruction" (Graves, 1919, p. 252). "The end of education," he stated, ". . . was the training of the pupils' faculties . . . to help nature to her perfection, which is, when all her abilities be perfected in their habit" (Graves, 1919, p. 251). He prescribed various exercises for the purpose, many of a physical nature.

Doctrinaires of various sorts espoused process training. Even the opponents of humanistic education accepted the legitimacy of its process training principles. Michel de Montaigne (1533–1592), who severely criticized humanism's formalism, nonetheless believed that education of mind, as of body, was achieved by the exercise of its inborn faculties, among which were reason, judgment, memory, and understanding (Mulhearn, 1959). Francis Bacon (1561–1621), who sought through inductive reasoning to destroy false idols of the mind, among which were the preconceptions of Scholastic and humanistic thinkers, also spoke of ". . . training the mind to a free and appropriate use of its faculties" (Monroe, 1905). Like Plato, Bacon believed that mathematics could be particularly used to remediate process deficiencies, for example, in attention:

> For instance, if a boy has a light, inattentive inconstant spirit, so that he is easily diverted, and his attention cannot be readily fixed, he will find advantage in mathematics, in which a demonstration must be commenced anew whenever the thought wanders even for a moment. (Monroe, 1905, p. 28)

Humanism dominated the European educational scene for a considerable while. Much of its strength lay in its elitism. Training in the vernacular, learning a profession, developing skills useful for commerce, these were considered to be beneath the dignity of the upper classes of Western Europe. Latin, the major training vehicle of humanism, was the language of the clergy and of the nobility; its acquisition, the mark of the educated man. Its precise utilization and knowledge of the Latin classics (and, to a lesser degree, of Greek classics) distinguished the truly consequential citizen from the inconsequential masses.

But things change, do they not? With the Reformation, Latin ceased to be the sole language used by the clergy. With the ascendancy of France in matters of war and culture, French replaced Latin as the language of diplomacy and courts. With the extensive development of vernacular literature, classics written in ancient languages could no longer be regarded as the mainstay of culture and the humanities. So there began a long and gradual but ever more serious decline in the use of classical languages in schools and universities.

That was all well and good for the course of human knowledge, one might say. But what was to happen to all those teachers of Latin syntax and poesy, those teachers of Ovid and Cicero and Caesar's campaigns, of Aristotle and Plato, and Xenophon, while all this was going on? Clearly, their stock in trade was seriously devalued if classical studies no longer constituted the *via regia* to success. It was not likely that many students would voluntarily seek to pursue classical Latin or Greek in light of the agony associated with their learning. Clearly, then, something was required to justify the perpetuation of humanist education.

Some of the arguments[7] that had been used earlier by Scholastic education to defend itself against the aggressions of Renaissance humanism now were used by the humanists themselves against the pragmatics of vernacular education. As they were forced onto the defensive, it

---

[7] That is, that Scholastic training methods had particular spiritual and mental training values.

became obvious to them, as it had been earlier to their Scholastic predecessors, that the training of the mind and its faculties should be the major goal of education: the essence of their position was:

> . . . the important thing in education was not the thing learned but the process of learning. (Monroe, 1905, p. 506)

And what was most useful in training processes, i.e., faculties? Not too surprisingly, it was, above all, the study of classical languages—Latin primarily, Greek secondarily, while mathematics was also extolled for its cognitive training powers. These were to be the mainstays of education for those who truly mattered—the elites of the nation. For the common man, training in the vernacular and applied curricula would suffice.

Classical instruction was extolled for the purpose of training the human faculties on a variety of grounds. Latin and mathematics curricula were systematically arranged and clearly organized and could be taught along the lines of general principles; their methods were already perfected. They were thus valuable for the purpose of systematically developing the mind and making it capable, not only of dealing with academics, but also of applying itself to a variety of specific, practical purposes. Classical curricula were particularly adapted to the training of those faculties most critical to success in later life—at least for the upper classes—the faculties of memory and reason.

Further, Latin and mathematics, as taught at the time in the proper schools, were tedious subjects, without any clear practical application. Their boring nature made them particularly useful in training the mind, which might be distracted by interesting or utilitarian information.

Finally, both subjects were difficult, and it was by laboring with the difficult that the mind and its faculties could best become strengthened. As recently as the middle of the nineteenth century, Tarver was to extoll the study of Latin on the grounds that it was difficult:

> My claim for Latin, as an Englishman and a foster parent (teacher), is simply that it would be impossible to devise for English boys a better teaching instrument. . . . The acquisition of a language is educationally of no importance; what is important is the process of acquiring it. . . . The one great merit of Latin as a teaching instrument is its tremendous difficulty. (Monroe, 1971, p. 511)

This "new technology" for training the mind through the application of specific curricula came to be known as formal discipline. It is a doctrine that recommends the use of curricular training and experiences to develop and improve the mind's powers and abilities, i.e., its forms. Train the mind and its faculties properly, the disciplinarians would say, and it would be prepared to engage itself successfully in any task or area of endeavor, even those far removed from the original training circumstances. Training in Latin was preparation for medicine, engineering or a military career; the properly prepared mind was prepared to function anywhere properly. So were the practices (and practitioners) of humanism, i.e., classical scholarship (and teachers of the classics), to be saved from unemployment lines.

THE BEGINNING OF THE MODERN PERIOD

Let us pause for a moment and observe the inauguration of the modern period of process training during a particular century—the seventeenth. There is hardly a distinct passage to be noted. The current of events was continuous. The seventeenth century extended the past so that we hesitate to call it a watershed. Yet during the seventeenth century, the various trends that culminated in today's process training efforts became clearly delineated, extending back into the past though they might, requiring elaboration in the future though they would.

Not surprisingly, they are identified with the major forces that shaped European education. These forces were described in 1888 by Oscar Browning in his *Aspects of Education*. The first was *humanism,* out of which grew modern formal discipline. The second was *realism*, based on the study of things instead of words, the education of the mind through the eye and the hand. The third was *naturalism,* described by Monroe as ". . . not in the first instance study at all. It is an attempt to build up the whole nature of man . . ." (Monroe, 1905, pp. 1, 2). The process training practices of the first were directed initially to the so-called higher cognitive processes—memory, reasoning, and the like—and carried out through curriculum. Those of the second and third were to emphasize the training of the mind through the senses and physical activity, and were directed, initially, to the so-called lower cognitive processes, i.e., the modalities.

Process training, as carried out within the early frameworks of formal discipline, can be considered as developmental in its nature, albeit of a rigidly fixed and elitist nature.[8] Formal disciplinarians expected their charges to respond to their training or to remove themselves from consideration as worthy of education. The process training efforts associated with sense realism and naturalism, on the other hand, were both developmental and remedial.[9] They came to be increasingly identified with

[8] Developmental from the standpoint of developing the mind and its faculties, rather than from the standpoint of applying knowledge or theories of human development to the purposes of instruction.

[9] Developmental from the standpoint of developing processes, but also from that of guiding instruction on the basis of the psychology of human development.

the education of the common man and with the purposes of remedial and special education. Seeking the seventeenth century founders of these traditions, we would choose to identify John Locke with that of formal discipline and Comenius with those of realism and naturalism.

We are in great danger of oversimplification of events, however, if we seek to establish precise delineations in respect to the above. In truth, John Locke, despite his clear identification as the modern-day founder of formal discipline, was a leader in the sense realism movement, espoused many of the principles of naturalistic education, and despised the mental disciplinary efforts of the humanists, who so often were to invoke his prestige to justify their endeavors. Comenius, on the other hand, used the principles of mental discipline in his work and attempted to improve Latin instruction. In later centuries, formal disciplinarians made claims to sensory-motor improvements while the process trainers emerging out of the sense-realism-naturalistic traditions oriented themselves to curricula, using disciplinary notions.

Our distinctions, admittedly arbitrary and regrettably shaky, are nonetheless useful in permitting us to organize our narrative in ways that cast light upon the process training practices of the past. Let us now proceed into the modern age of process training. We will begin in the following chapter with a consideration of formal discipline, as it evolved into a coherent educational philosophy.

13
The Rise of Formal Discipline

JOHN LOCKE AND ENGLISH FORMAL DISCIPLINE

John Locke is usually acknowledged as the father of formal discipline. He occupies, however, an ambiguous place relative to the doctrine—quite justifiably so as we shall see—so that his true role in its history is hard to assess. There are those who would excuse him from anything except happenstantial association with the doctrine his name is so often associated with, particularly as he opposed scholasticism, humanism, and faculty psychology. Rusk (1969), for example, calls attention to Plato's role in formulating mental discipline and the general popularity of its practices prior to Locke's arrival on the scene.[1] Yet, there are others (Boyd and King, 1973) who insist that he intended what he said.

Locke was inconsistently inconsistent and consistently self-contradictory.[2] There are, for example, his ambivalencies concerning mental faculties, those mainstays of formal discipline. Locke's broad conception of the mind, the tabula rasa at birth, was intended to sweep away notions of innate ideas and cognitive structures. The mind, Locke said, is acquired from without, through the senses. Nevertheless, he could not altogether do without inherent cognitive faculties or powers, needing

---

[1] Thus in John Milton's tract *Of Education* the term is already in evidence. "These are studies wherein our noble and gentle youth ought to bestow their time in a disciplinary way" (Rusk, 1969, p. 150).

[2] Laslett notes, "Locke is, perhaps, the least consistent of all great philosophers, and pointing out the contradictions either within any of his works or between them is no great task . . ." (Laslett, 1960, p. 82).

135

them to organize the incoming impressions impinging on his tabula rasa to reflect on those impressions, compare, discriminate, organize, and generalize from them. His cognitive powers are "internal" counterparts of the external senses. "Internal senses"? Where have we heard that notion before? Faculties, no? Faculties, yes.

And so it is with Locke's writings on mental discipline. Depending upon where you read and to a considerable degree upon your willingness to interpret this way or that, John Locke emerges as a formal disciplinarian or an antidisciplinarian. Since he is so important to our history of process training, let us examine his writings from both points of view.

In *Of the Conduct of the Understanding* (1706), Locke addresses the basic philosophy of formal discipline:

> The business of education is not to make the young perfect in any one of the sciences, but so to open and dispose their minds as may best make them capable of any, when they shall apply themselves to it. . . . It is therefore to give them this freedom that I think they should be made to look into all sorts of knowledge and exercise their understanding in so wide a variety or stock of knowledge but a variety and freedom of thinking; as an increase of the powers and activities of the mind, not as an enlargement of its possessions. (Monroe, 1905, pp. 518, 519)

Locke proceeds further in this treatise to expound the notion that education should be directed to the formation of habits of thought through exercise of the mind and its faculties:

> The faculties of our souls are improved and made useful to us just after the same manner as our bodies are. Would you have a man write or paint, dance or fence well, or perform any other manual operation dexterously and with ease, let him have ever so much vigor and activity, suppleness and address naturally, yet nobody expects this from him unless he has been used to it, and has employed time and pains in fashioning and forming his hand or outward parts to these motions. Just so it is in the mind; would you have a man reason well, you must use him to it betimes, *exercise his mind*[3] in observing the connection of ideas and following them in train. (Monroe, 1905, p. 519)

His approach to such training broadly followed the plan suggested by Aristotle: the pupil's body, the character, and his intellect were to be trained. A strong ascetic streak is revealed in Locke's recommendations for body and character training, one that, at times, verges on Reikian sadomasochism. Learning to take punishment, deprivation, and even abuse, was good for the soul, taught it to put up with adversity and to direct itself toward ultimate goals at the cost of personal discomfort.

For physical disciplining, for example, he recommended that the child be brought up with ". . . the head and feet kept cold and the feet

---

[3] Italics are mine.

often used to cold water and exposed to wet." (Quick, 1895, p. 30) To achieve properly wet feet, he recommended that a youth was ". . . to have his shoes made to leak water" (Quick, 1895, p. 7). Regarding such procedures, Herbert Spencer was later to remark that thanks to it, "Not a few were 'hardened' out of the world; and those who survive permanently suffer either in growth or constitution" (Rusk, 1969, p. 141).

Speaking of personality development, Locke observed the values of punishment and physical deprivation for the strengthening of the character:

. . . the way to harden and fortify Children against Fear and Danger is to accustom them to suffer Pain . . . I would not have Children much beaten for their Faults, because I would not have them think bodily Pain the greatest Punishment. And I would have them, when they do well, be sometimes put in Pain, for the same Reason, that they might be accuston'd to bear it . . . inuring Children gently to suffer some Degrees of Pain without shrinking, is a way to gain Firmness to their Minds and lay a Foundation for Courage and Resolution in the future Part of their lives. (Monroe, 1905, p. 517)

Locke's concern that children learn to endure hardships expressed itself relative to their cognitive training as well; mental training as discipline stands out in his views, this in *Some Thoughts Concerning Education* (1693):

As the strength of the Body lies chiefly in being able to endure Hardships, so also does that of the Mind, and the great Principle and Foundation of all Virtue and Worth is placed in this: That a Man is able to *deny himself* his own desires, cross his own inclinations and purely follow that Reason directs as best tho' the appetite lean the other way. . . . It seems plain to me that the Principle of all Virtue and Excellence lies in the Power of denying ourselves the Satisfaction of our own Desires, where Reason does not authorize them. This Power is to be got and improved by Custom, made easy and familiar by an early Practice. . . . The first thing they (children) should know should be that they were not to have anything because it pleased them, but because it was thought fit for them." (Monroe, 1905, pp. 515, 516)

Such were the statements that were to appeal to clerical instructors of a later year seeking to asceticize the souls of their pupils and to the not-so-latent sadism that lay in the bosom of lay pedagogues. Hardships strengthen the mind (and soul) and develop its cognitive powers to their fullest, making them fit for the widest applications. Instruction should not be easy, since ease negates its disciplinary values. Instruction is to drill, since in this way the use of the mind's powers become "easy and familiar." Instruction is not to be interesting or pleasurable because virtue, worth, and excellence develops out of denying oneself the pleasurable.

The Abbé Galiani, a formal disciplinarian, writing some 70 years after Locke (1770), said:

Education is the same thing for man and for beast. It can be reduced to two principles, to learn to put up with injustice, to learn to endure ennui. What does one do when one breaks in a horse? Left to himself, the horse ambles, trots, gallops, walks, but does it when it wishes, as he pleases. We teach him to move thus or thus, contrary to his own desire, against his own instinct—there is the injustice: we make him keep on at it for a couple of hours—there is the ennui. It is the same thing when we make a child learn Latin or Greek or French. The intrinsic utility of it is not the main point. The aim is that he should habituate himself to obey another person's will. . . . All pleasant methods of teaching children necessary knowledge are false and ridiculous. It is not a question of learning geography or geometry: it is a question of learning of work, of learning the weariness of concentrating one's attention on the matter in hand. (Bennett & Bristol, 1906, pp. 11, 12, 23, 24, 26)

Locke had a particular predilection for mathematics as a means of cognitive training. In his discussion of its values, he brought up a major principle of formal discipline—that of transfer of training:

Nothing does this better than mathematics, which therefore I think should be taught all those who have the time and opportunity, not so much to make them mathematicians, as to make them reasonable creatures; for though we call ourselves so, because we are born to it if we please, yet we may truly say nature gives us but the seeds of it. We are born to be, if we please, rational creatures, but it is use and exercise that makes us so, and we are indeed so no further than industry and application has carried us. . . . I have mentioned mathematics as a way to settle in the mind a habit of reasoning closely and in train; not that I think it necessary that all men should be deep mathematicians but that having got the way of reasoning, which that study necessarily brings the mind to, they might be able to *transfer*[4] it to other parts of knowledge as they shall have occasion. (Monroe, 1905, pp. 518, 519)

Thus spoke John Locke, formal disciplinarian. He *did* say what later formal disciplinarians lauded him for saying. He did appear to be reflecting and reinforcing the positions of faculty psychology and the training of specific innate cognitive processes.

There was, however, another John Locke, who emerges from his writings as an antidisciplinarian—in the same writings within which his disciplinary recommendations appear. This John Locke is one of the fathers of sense realism, a man who described the mind as a tabula rasa at birth, insisting that whatever is learned comes into the mind through its senses; a man seeking to discard, on this basis, the concept of innate ideas and faculties and of learning being the development of innate potentials or faculties.

This John Locke, too, despite having elsewhere recommended phys-

[4] Italics are mine.

ical and mental deprivations and even punishment for the development of spiritual and mental faculties, spoke against the common practice of corporal punishment in his day, remarking that, "Beating is the worst, and therefore the last means to be used in the correction of children" (Boyd & King, 1975, p. 275). He also recommended attention to individual differences, something that was anathema to traditional formal discipline, noting that "Each mind has some peculiarity . . . the forming of . . . minds and manners requiring constant attention, and particular application to every single boy" (Boyd & King, 1973, p. 276). He even suggested using rewards to reinforce learning and that instruction be adjusted to a student's "disposition" and when he was "in tune" with learning.

The antidisciplinarian John Locke also spoke about the value of utilitarian education—again, anathema to formal discipline. Here he advised: "The busy inclination of children being always to be directed to something that may be useful to them" (Boyd and King, 1973, p. 278).

Finally, the John Locke of sense realism, one who spoke against faculties and innate predispositions, cast general doubt on the fundamental principles of formal discipline—the notion that the mind could be trained or that transfer of training could be accomplished.

> I hear it is said that children should be employed in getting things by heart, to exercise and improve their memories. I could wish this were said with as much authority of reason as it is with forwardness of assurance, and that this practice were established upon good observation more than old custom; for it is evident that strength of memory is owing to an happy constitution, and not to any habitual improvement got by exercise. . . . But the learning pages of Latin by heart no more fits the memory for retention of anything else than the graving of one sentence in lead makes it the more capable of retaining firmly any other characters. If such a sort of exercise of the memory were able to give it strength, and improve our parts, players of all other people must needs have the best memories and be the best company. But whether the scraps that have got into their heads this way make them remember other things the better; and whether their parts be improved proportionately to the pains they have taken in getting by heart others' sayings, experience will show. Memory is so necessary to all parts and conditions of life, and so little is to be done without it, that we are not to fear it should grow dull and useless for want of exercise, if exercise would make it grow stronger. But I fear this faculty of the kind is not capable of much help and amendment in general by any exercise or endeavour of ours, at least not by that used upon this pretence in Grammar Schools. . . . (Quick, 1895, p. 94)

The antidisciplinarian John Locke was particularly scornful of the values of Latin (that favorite tool of formal disciplinarians) being useful for anything other than learning Latin itself.

The older of our readers (I along with them) still remember well our schools' insistence that the study of Latin would assist students in the learning of correct English usage (and of foreign languages). To this he responded:

> The manner of expressing one's self is so very different from ours (the English) that to be perfect in that would very little improve the purity and facility of his English style. (Quick, 1895, p. 172)

Does instruction in syntax truly train the mind? Asking rhetorically, "To whom should grammar be taught?" he responded that he did not find it any use for training in ordinary oral communication. It is, of course, useful to those who wish to improve their written usage of language, and then, only when it is studied directly, i.e., English syntax for English, French syntax for French, etc. In a similar vein, he spoke of providing instruction in mathematics specifically for the purposes of deploying mathematical skills in utilitarian pursuits. As to logic and rhetoric, those favorites of early cognitive training, ". . . he would limit instruction therein . . . because of the little advantage that young people receive from them." (Quick, 1895, p. 188)

The broadest thesis within the conceptual armamentarium of formal discipline was the notion that the development of specific cognitive powers made them transferable and applicable to all sorts of situations. Thus a student's perception, memory, and sagacity, once trained properly, could be applied to politics, medicine, or solving the problems of one's personal finances. On such promises Locke also cast a jaundiced eye in his *Of the Conduct of the Understanding*:

> We see men frequently dextrous and skilled enough making a bargain and who, if you reason with them about matters of religion, appear perfectly stupid. (Fowler, 1901, p. 20)

Then he, in another more general statement of this point, later said

> The mistake is that he that is found reasonable in one thing is concluded to be so in all, and to think or say otherwise is thought so unjust an affront, and so senseless a censure, that nobody ventures to do it. (Fowler, 1901, p. 20)

Thus we have John Locke, accused and pardoned by his own writings on the issue of being a proponent of process training. While writers in our own day seem prone to emphasize his antidisciplinary position, those of his immediate time more often hailed him as the patron saint of formal discipline and justified some of its worst practices on the basis that he sanctioned them.

The appeal of formal discipline was powerful, and the movement was supported by many factions. The Church found it particularly congenial. The notion of chastising unruly students and of bending their minds to the will of authority appealed to both Catholic and Protestant churchmen, as did the faculty psychology implications of such training. Humanistic bureaucracies found within the tenets of formal discipline the justification for their talents (teaching Latin) and the salvation of their jobs. Individual teachers liked the simplicity and concreteness of the goals implicit within it. Training their students' minds, they could avoid the bewilderment of having to put up with the curricular innovations required by a world of rapidly changing values of learning, i.e., how to teach new-fangled, vulgar, and ephemeral technologies of science and commerce. Parents felt reassured that their children were being taught basics.

The students who were the recipients of formal discipline, alas, were subject to the same type of instruction that the humanist and medievalist educator of old had insisted upon: classical curriculum, drill, drill, drill, and regurgitate—and drill again. The study of utilitarian subjects was for those common folks and inept learners who did not respond to disciplinary training, not for those whose minds were to be primed and prepared through comprehensive mental, physical, and spiritual education for the better things in life.

Individual differences were denied by the formal disciplinarians, as a general rule. Formal discipline was a developmental approach to training the mind, and the adaptation of its techniques to individual differences or the notion of remedial training was extraneous to its goals. It was, after all, developed in a time when education was construed by most educators—in its broadest and most fulfilling sense—for the elite members of the clerical, noble, or "upper" classes and, on occasion, for the intellectually superior of the lesser classes. Those who could not manage the rigors of its training were expected to take their brains elsewhere. They were reduced to purely vernacular training: the mathematics of the marketplace, the technologies of the trades, with perhaps a minimum of Latin to keep them reputable. Unfit for formal discipline, they were unfit for "true" education.

The formal disciplinary movement, as might be expected on the basis of John Locke's elevation to the position of its patron saint, received ready acceptance within the British Isles, wherein it assisted the English social-caste system to separate the upper—who were to be truly educated—from the lower classes, for whom lesser, utilitarian education was to suffice for their learning to worship God and meet their working needs; to learn the rules and regulations that would make them take their proper (lower) station in life; to learn how to properly behave in the presence of their betters.

The lower classes were, from one standpoint, blessed by their educational denigration. Those who were worthy of true education—and formal discipline—attended English grammar schools or public schools and were subjected to physical, moral, and mental harassment and punishment. John Locke's disciplinary writings were used, for example, to support all sorts of corporal and psychic brutality. The slightest offense or deficiency on the part of a pupil brought a whipping. Younger children served in degraded menial subservience to older children in the English fagging system—justified on the grounds that it fortified the personality. And on the intellectual side, elementary and secondary education were subverted to the purposes of intellectual form. Long years of training in Latin and Greek syntax composition and the writing of verse were required from students, little of which was employable in adult life.[5] Some schools even rejected mathematics as not being a worthy disciplinary tool. Eton was to accept it about the middle of the eighteenth century, while only gradually thereafter allowing the introduction of other curricula—all of which had to be justified on disciplinary terms.

In English higher education, similar attitudes and circumstances prevailed. The fact that none of the great English scientists of the nineteenth century were trained or did their work in universities attests to the exclusion of sciences in the name of formal discipline by English universities. In Oxford and Cambridge, classics and mathematics made up the bulwark of the curricula. And up to 1850 at Oxford and 1851 at Cambridge, the subjects for entrance examination were chosen only from the classics.

British schools persisted well into this century in their disciplinary notions. Parents kept sending their children to secondary schools to form character, improve their mind, and develop social grace, rather than for purposes of developing practical skills. Even science, when taught, was in the form of formal exercises to train the mind rather than for purposes of practical application (Mulhearn, 1959, p. 516).

DISCIPLINARY PURSUITS ON THE CONTINENT

Within French circles, too, the doctrines of formal discipline received wide acceptance following Locke's espousal of them. Even for many of the French sensationalists, the doctrine appeared a credible one, undoubtedly in part because of its association with Locke's revered name. So we find Condillac, who was ready to reduce most of man's mind to the products of sensation, calling for mental training. The mind, he said, is a sensing substance comparable to the eye, and the sight of the mind is like that of the body. The efficient functioning of both require exercise.

---

[5] The emphasis upon classical studies (or brutality) surely was not what Locke had intended. On the positive side, English belief that schools were responsible for character building and English emphasis on games and sports for physical and emotional education—received inspiration from Locke.

The French rationalists, too, e.g., Voltaire (1694–1778) and Diderot (1713–1784), also attempted to apply the doctrines of sensationalism and mental discipline to the shaping of pupils' minds. They adopted many of the cognitive training approaches of their scorned predecessors—the humanists. The rationalists were trying to develop an intellectual elite which could challenge the authority of France's ecclesiastical and noble classes. Well-trained minds could only be expected to do this. Formal discipline was a means of achieving well-trained minds.

In Germany, the *gymnasium*, the representative secondary school of the nation, epitomized humanistic cognitive, formal disciplinarian values. The very term "gymnasium" bespeaks dedication to exercise, though of the mind, rather than of the body.

German scholars generally extolled the values of disciplinary education. Christian Wolff made particular and most positive comments about Locke's recommendation that mathematics be used to train pupils' reasoning powers. While Gedike, one of Wolff's followers and a staunch advocate of formal discipline, did much to promote the movement within Berlin's educational circles during the eighteenth century. The content of studies, said Gedike, a rector of a prominent Berlin school, is commonly forgotten, even by those who have achieved great success in their chosen spheres of learning. The time and effort spent in studying is, however, never wasted; that is, if one observes humanistic disciplinary precepts. For even if the Greek and Latin one learned may in time be forgotten ". . . you still have the advantage of having given your mind a training and discipline that will go with you into your future occupation" (Russell, 1907, p. 74).

Disciplinary practices in Germany went unchallenged until the beginning of the nineteenth century. At this turning, the new humanism of Germany began to turn the use of classical literature to different purposes in its schools than mental training. The aim became that of developing German national spirit through the study of and identification with the ancient greats of antiquity as they appeared in Greek and Latin literature. There was also a great surge of interest in scientific and technical education as a militant Prussia began to flex its muscles and aspire toward ideas of military and economic hegemony in Europe.

Following the unsuccessful Prussian revolution of the nineteenth century, the reaction against popular ideas led to a reemphasis on disciplinary ideas, now seen as a bulwark of authority in German education. Paulsen, a distinguished German scholar, writing at the close of the nineteenth century (1897) extolled the gymnastics of the mental faculties. Their purpose was, he explained

. . . the development of all the faculties in every possible direction. To this end, a study of the ancient languages is regarded of the utmost importance; for, by cultivating the Greek and Roman languages, we acquire skill in all mental operations. . . . The study of mathematics ranks next in importance and also furnishes excellent training to the faculties. The new era despises the utilitarian and encyclopedic attainments so highly valued by the preceding epoch. True human culture, and not utility is its aim. (Woody, 1951, pp. 198, 199)

Overemphasis on disciplinary education in a united Germany (under Prussian domination) led to the counter concern that a powerful Germany needed more than minds trained in Latin and Greek. In 1892, the German emperor expressed his alarm at the disciplinary movement in German higher schools:

If any one enters into a discussion with these gentlemen (the supporters of the rigid classical gymnasium) on this point, and attempts to show them that a young man ought to be prepared, to some extent, at least, for life and its manifold problems, they will tell him that such is not the function of the school, its principal aim being the discipline or the gymnastic of the mind, and that if this gymnastic were properly conducted the young man would be capable of doing all that is necessary in life. I am of the opinion that we can no longer be guided by this doctrine. (Monroe, 1905, pp. 528, 529)

Suffice it to observe that German minds were not to do without the advantages of either cognitive discipline or technical training. As the world was to learn on all sorts of occasions, perhaps there was too much technical training, too much discipline.

FORMAL DISCIPLINE IN THE UNITED STATES

In the Americas, formal discipline was readily accepted in the colonies, a natural development, considering both their English inheritances and the nature of the Puritans who did so much to shape early American education. By 1650, mastery of Greek and Latin was required for entrance into the hallowed halls of Harvard University. An applicant to Harvard was expected to

. . . make and speak true Latin in verse and prose . . . and decline perfectly the paradigms of Nouns and Verbs in the Greek tongue, let him then, and not before, be capable of admission into the College. (Frost, 1973, p. 291)

The name of Benjamin Franklin is prominent among early Americans who espoused formal discipline. Though Franklin had failed arithmetic as a student, he taught it to himself independently, proceeding then to self-instruction in geometry, navigation, and mechanics. Later, Franklin's Academy was to teach "the several branches of mathematics" with a disciplinary bent. Franklin explained:

Mathematical demonstrations are a logic . . . serving to a just formation of the mind, enlarging its capacity, and strengthening it so as to render the same capable of exact reasoning, and discerning truth from falsehood in all occurrences, even subjects not mathematical. (Woody, 1951, p. 201)

By the nineteenth century, formal discipline of the classical variety was given priority in almost all institutions of higher learning within the United States. Classical languages, particularly Latin, and mathematics were the essentials of such training. Witness a statement from the University of Pennsylvania in 1824 as to its educational purposes:

Liberal education must rest for its basis on an accurate and extensive knowledge of the learned languages, when the acquisition of them has cultivated the taste, strengthened the memory and stored the mind with terms and the capacity to analyze them. Adapted to every brand of knowledge, an introduction of the precise science of mathematics and the art of reasoning is peculiarly seasonable. (Mulhearn, 1933, p. 321)

If there were any doubts that "true" education was not to be vulgarized for the purposes of developing mere professional or vocational competency, the University of Pennsylvania, five years later cleared them up nicely:

It (a liberal education) is not designed . . . to qualify the student in a special manner for any particular profession or pursuit . . . but to aid in the development of all his faculties in their proportions; and by discipline and instruction, to furnish him with those general qualifications, which are useful and ornamental in every profession. . . . (Mulhearn, 1933, p. 321)

Would Yale University have any less? Of course not. Its formulations in 1827 made it clear that the Yalies of the time were attending their Ivy League alma mater primarily for purposes of having their processes polished as befitted gentlemen–scholars. Yale's formulations (1827) proceeded thusly:

The two great points to be gained in intellectual culture are the *discipline* and the *furniture* of the mind; expanding its powers, and storing it with knowledge. The former of these is, perhaps, the more important of the two. (Woody, 1951, p. 202)

Collegiate courses were to be directed, consequently, to "daily and vigorous exercise" of "the faculties of the student."

Nor were women's colleges to be outdone in their support of formal discipline. Graves of Mary Sharp College forcefully announced that the role of teachers was to prepare minds, not teach skills. In 1893, she announced:

> We do not aim to train a woman for a sphere, profession or calling. . . .
> When men complete the college curriculum they rarely have definite ideas of what
> course they will pursue. Why should women be expected to have definite plans?
> All must await developments and whatever . . . [they] may be the college bred
> woman is better equipped to meet them. (McCabe, 1893, p. 4)

In this vein, John Todd, who was a proponent of higher education for
women at a time when many men thought it an unnecessary waste,
recommended that women undergo the rigors of formal discipline in their
college training. The goal of their disciplinary training was to train the
power of attention, i.e., the ability to apply the mind to a task "as long as
is necessary," to further strengthen their memories, develop balanced
judgment, cultivate taste and endurance.

Almira Hart Phelps indulged herself with profuse botanical metaphors in her hymn to mental discipline. Writing *Lectures to Young
Ladies* in 1833, she explained that there was to be harmonious, even
lock-step training of all cognitive and affective faculties, lest uneven and
improper development result:

> We may now consider the human mind as a garden laid out before us; he who
> created this garden, planted in it the seeds of various faculties; these do indeed
> spring up of themselves, but without education, they will be stinted in their
> growth, choked with weeds, and never attain that strength and evaluation of
> which they are susceptible. In one part of our garden the germ of reason is seen to
> unfold itself, in another that of judgment, until all the faculties of the intellect are
> in their full progress of development. The emotions and passions are mingled with
> powers of slower growth; while the intellectual gardener cultivates the latter with
> assiduous care, he knows that the passions need his most vigilant attention; that if
> they grow rank and unpruned, they will poison and destroy the vital principle of
> virtue, and root out the moral harmony on which the beauty of the whole depends.
> Leaving the passions and emotions to be hereafter considered, our concern now is
> with those mental germs which belong to the intellectual department. The skillful
> gardener knows that his roses require one mode of culture, his tulips another, and
> his geraniums another; and that attention to one of these, will not bring forward
> the other. So ought the mental cultivator to understand that the germs of the
> various faculties should be simultaneously brought forward. This truth seems not
> to have been understood by those, who, bending all their efforts towards the
> cultivation of the memory, neglected the other powers of the mind. (Phelps, 1833,
> p. 69)

Mathematics, perhaps because of its "masculine" identifications appears to have been urged upon women's institutions of higher learning. So
Emma Willard praised it as the chief cause of ". . . that stronger intellectual power American women have now shown . . . (Woody, 1929, p.
405). And Almira Hart Phelps extolled it for the many duties it carried out in
strengthening her students' faculties:

The study of mathematics has, by philosophers, been considered the most direct way of controlling the imagination, perfecting reason and judgment, and inducing a habit of method and love of order. . . . Mathematics is peculiarly a science of comparisons; these comparisons are always exact and may be made manifest to the senses. . . . Suppose of two young persons of equal talents, and who have devoted equal time to study, the one is a geometrician, and the other has given her time more to other branches of knowledge—suppose these two commencing together some new science, botany, chemistry, or mental philosophy, we shall soon perceive the great advantage which the knowledge and practice of mathematical reasoning gives the one, over the other, in the mode of arranging facts, of developing truth, and performing such mental analyses as are necessary to disentangle, and bring to light the most complicated subjects. (Bolzau, 1936, p. 279)

Even though a proper formal disciplinarian held to the classics and mathematics as the tools of his trade, there were other educators who believed that any subject properly taught could have disciplinary value. By this means, the meanest of instructional tasks could be dignified. By this means, those educators outside the pale of classical instruction could also claim their place in the disciplinary sun. The exclusivity of classical formal discipline was to be repeatedly challenged from such quarters. This we shall clearly see in later chapters.

14

The Changing Fortunes of Formal Discipline

THE DEFENSE OF THE CLASSICISTS

Throughout the nineteenth century and well into the twentieth, the teachers of classical languages saw themselves as the guardians of disciplinarian traditions. In this role (and from the standpoint of their livelihoods) they were repeatedly threatened by the emergence of new curricular contenders.

The classicists attempted to confound their challengers by claiming that the study of classical languages, most particularly Latin, is both the sine qua non and ne plus ultra of cognitive training. They did so on a number of grounds. One was that knowledge of the great minds of the past will improve the minds of the present. Another was that classical writing provides a model of thinking for current minds, which, if imitated, can train those minds to think in model fashion—specifically that the clear and logical structure of classical languages is conducive to the development of a clear and logical mind. Still another reason was that classical studies are of such great difficulty as to have great exercise potential for the mind and its faculties. In that vein Latin and (secondarily) Greek, as we have noted earlier, were particularly extolled on the basis of their tediousness and lack of utility; they are not likely to distract the mind from its "exercises" with frivolous diversions.

Tarver, sadly observing the encroachment of newer curricula in the midst of the eighteenth century, saw it to be a sign of a general decline in the intellectual rigor of his England, for he found nowhere ". . . the smallest trace of enthusiasm for sound intellectual training . . . (Woody,

148

1951, p. 205), and he continued to make his case for Latin and Greek. He admitted their general lack of utility, but they are but means to an end. If the "mere acquisition" of a language is to be considered an end to itself, then Tarver agreed that the importance of classical languages should most assuredly be deemphasized. But the least important aspect of learning Greek and Latin is the acquisition of these languages. It is the *process* of acquiring the languages that is of importance to a student. Why? "The one great merit of Latin . . ." he explained, ". . . is its difficulty" (Woody, 1951, p. 207). It was largely on this basis that he could say in 1897

My claim for Latin, from the point of view of an Englishman, is simply that it would be impossible to devise for English boys a better teaching instrument. There may be as good, but I have not come across better. (Monroe, 1905, p. 511)

Classical scholars, including the famed Catholic scholar Cardinal Newman, continued to defend the study of classical languages on the basis of their difficulty well into the twentieth century. Bennett and Bristol recommended Latin translation as a particularly "severe exercise."[1] Paul Shorey, making "The Case for Classics" in the *School Review* of 1910, expressed disciplinary virtues of the classics in unequivocal terms:

Information, knowledge, culture, originality, eloquence, genius may exist without classical training; the critical sense and a sound feeling for the relativity of meaning rarely, if ever . . . the law is the only discipline comparable to the classics in this regard. (Colvin, 1911, p. 247)

Shorey further asserted that "The critical interpretation or translation of classical languages supplied the simplest and most effective all around discipline of the greatest number of faculties." In this respect, "Latin is a necessity in anything but an elementary or purely technical education. Greek is not in this sense a necessity. It is the first of the luxuries" (Colvin, 1911, p. 247).

THE CHALLENGE OF SCIENCE

By such arguments, the classicists sought to keep "upstart" curricula in their proper place, most particularly out of institutions of higher learning. It was thus that the advanced study of science was restricted, for the longest time in the British Isles, to technical institutes. For

---

[1] They proposed another major reason for the study of Latin, one that is still popular today: Latin was to provide training that would improve one's learning and expression of the English language.

it was science, in all its branches, that was a particular bugaboo to the classicists, who sought to deny it any conspicuous disciplinary value.

Science, they said, is utilitarian and vulgar. It is not sufficiently arduous as to effectively train the mind and its faculties. It doesn't make the same rigorous demands on them as do classical studies. The very fact that sciences are interesting and useful mitigates against their value as training vehicles for one's cognitive processes.

But science found powerful voices speaking out in its behalf as a disciplinary arm of education—Herbert Spencer in his book *Education: Intellectual, Moral and Physical* (1861) and Thomas Huxley in *Science and Education* (1868).

Spencer's book is a collection of essays. In the first of these, he exalted the role that science could play in education, asking his readers "... what knowledge is of more worth?" And responding for them he answered, "Science." Asking further what subject was of the greatest value for disciplining the mind, he concluded:

. . . that for discipline, science is of chiefest value. In all its effects, learning the meanings of things, is better than learning the meanings of words. Whether for intellectual, moral or religious training, the study of surrounding phenomena is immensely superior to the study of grammars and lexicons. (Spencer, 1860, p. 84)

It is the very fact of their utility, their "worth . . . for purposes of guidance" that make the sciences immensely superior to the classical studies for cognitive training.

We may be quite sure that the acquirement of those classes of facts which are most useful for regulating conduct, involves a mental exercise best fitted for strengthening the faculties. . . . Everywhere throughout creation we find faculties developed through the performance of those functions which it is their office to perform; not through the performance of artificial exercises devised to fit them for these functions. (Spencer, 1860, p. 74)

Spencer attacked classical studies on the very grounds that science could better train those very faculties that classical studies were professed to train best:

One advantage claimed for that devotion to language-learning which forms so prominent a feature in the ordinary *curriculum,* is, that, the memory is thereby strengthened. And it is apparently assumed that this is an advantage peculiar to the study of words. But the truth is that the sciences afford far wider fields for the exercises of memory. . . . So vast is the accumulation of facts which men of science have before them, that only by dividing and subdividing their labours can they deal with it. . . . Surely, then, science, cultivated even to a very modest extent, affords adequate training for memory. To say the very least, it involves quite as good training for this faculty as language does. (Spencer, 1860, pp. 75–77)

More than that, science has an "immense superiority" over languages in the nature of its cultivation of memory. Unlike language learning, wherein the associations mastered may be of a fortuitous nature

. . . the relations which science presents are causal relations; and, when properly taught, are understood as such. Instead of being practically accidental, they are necessary; and as such, give exercise to the reasoning faculties. While language familiarizes with non-rational relations, science familiarizes with rational relations. While the one exercises memory only, the other exercises both memory and understanding. (Spencer, 1860, pp. 77, 78)

The next "great superiority" that science holds over language as a means of discipline is that it cultivates judgment.

No extent of acquaintance with the meanings of words, can give the power of forming correct inferences respecting causes and effects. The constant habit of drawing conclusions from data, and then of verifying those conclusions by observation and experiment, can alone give the power of judging correctly. And that it necessitates this habit is one of the immense advantages of science. (Spencer, 1860, pp. 78, 79)

And if all that were not enough to establish the primacy of science as a disciplinary force, it also is "best" for "moral discipline" and "religious culture."

Huxley strongly supported Spencer's views. He, too, saw science as the major tool with which to forge mental discipline. Unlike the "liberal" education of classical studies suggested by the humanist scholars, an education that would turn a student into a "stunted ascetic," the training provided by ". . . the great and fundamental truths of nature and of the law of her operations . . . is full of life and fire . . ." (Mulhearn, 1959, p. 513). And it would result in the preparation of a new type of cognitive elite through a new type of liberal education.

That man, I think has had a liberal education who has been so trained in youth that his body is the ready servant of his will, and does with ease and pleasure all the work that, as a mechanism it is capable of; whose intellect is a clear cold logic engine, with all its parts of equal strength, and in smooth working order; ready, like a steam engine to be turned to any kind of work. . . . (Huxley, 1879, p. 34)

The arguments of classicists that science was too interesting to permit it full disciplinary value were answered by Huxley, with tongue in cheek. With proper effort, he proposed, it could be made as dull as Latin and Greek—for example, paleontology:

It is wonderful how close a parallel to classical training could be made out of that paleontology to which I refer. In the first place I could get up an osteological primer so arid, so pedantic in its terminology, so altogether distasteful to the youthful mind, as to beat the recent famous production of the head-masters out of the field in all these excellences. Next, I could exercise my boys upon easy fossils, and bring out all their powers of memory and all their ingenuity in the application of myosteogrammatical rules to the interpretation, or construing, of these fragments. To those who had reached the higher classes, I might supply odd bones to be built up into animals, giving great honor and reward to him who succeeded in fabricating monsters most entirely in accordance with the rules. That would answer to the verse-making and essay writing in the dead languages. (Huxley, 1902, p. 90)

Fouillée, a classicist, countered such attacks by contrasting the classics as mind builders, with science as an information or knowledge base. The former are obviously superior on the grounds of the types of cognitive training they provide:

Huxley proposes to make the natural and physical sciences the basis of education. Spencer, in his turn, by a kind of idolatry of science which is widespread in these days makes of positive science almost exclusively the subject for youth, under the pretext that, in this life, geometry is necessary for the construction of bridges and railways, and that in every definite trade, even in poetry, we must have knowledge. How conclusive is poetry as an instance? Is a Virgil or a Racine made by learning rules of versification? The scientific man is not made by teaching him science, for true science, like poetry, is invention. We can learn to build a railway by rule of thumb, but those who invented railways did so only by the force of the intellectual power they had acquired, and not by the force of the mere knowledge they had received; it is therefore intellectual force that we must aim at developing. And then returns the question: Is the best means of strengthening and developing the intellect of our youth, to load the memory with the results of modern science, or is it to teach them to reason, to imagine, to combine, to divine, to know beforehand what ought to be true from an innate sense of order and harmony, of the simple and the fruitful—a sense near akin to that of the beautiful? And besides, are youths educated to be engineers or poets? Education is not an apprenticeship to a trade, it is the culture of moral and intellectual forces in the individual and in the race." (Monroe, 1905, p. 510)

Such arguments stemmed but did not stop the tide of science. If the proof of the pudding was in the eating, the scientific mind trained through science appeared certainly as disciplined as that of the humanist. And the scientist was making the engines of the industrial revolution hum in England and everywhere else.

BASIC EDUCATION AND UTILITARIANISM

While science was breeching the walls of classicism in higher education during the nineteenth century, serious attacks were also being launched against the latter on the level of basic education. The traditional means of disciplining the mind were being questioned. This was particularly true in the United States, where Latin, Greek, and advanced mathematics hardly seemed to help the farmer, or the laborer who had come to a new land.

There were voices raised in all corners of the new country in favor of job-directed, tasks-of-living–oriented training. There were ever-intensified calls for the nation's public schools to provide their pupils with useful skills rather than cognitively "disciplined" minds. Americans on the grange called for education that would improve farming practices and domestic management. Those in the city, industrialists seeking cheap well-trained labor and immigrants needing job skills to survive in the land of opportunity, wanted the schools to address the needs of the shop, the factory, and commerce.

Horace Greeley, writing in the *Pennsylvania School Journal* (1857), stated his concerns in unequivocal terms:

> . . . mind is disciplined best by its own proper work; and not by making this discipline the great end. I would say to the farmer's son, poring over Greek verbs and Hebrew roots and accents, to the damsel of sixteen, wasting her sweetness on algebra and geometry, what do you propose to do with this . . . ? If you propose to turn it to some practical account, very well; but if you only acquire it with an eye to mental discipline, then I protest against it as a waste of time and energy. (Greeley, 1857, p. 158)

It was not that Greeley, himself, doubted that classical studies trained the mind. He rather felt that many, if not most, of the students of his acquaintance would find other studies more useful and yet equally as valuable (as the classics) for "mental discipline and growth." He was speaking with the times and for the times, in any case. Classicists would continue to insist that the classics are the ultimate means of training the mind, but to many professional and lay practitioners and observers, it made increasing sense to regard all curricula as having, when properly applied, disciplinary value. Since it was hardly likely that classicism could hold out against the realities of a world exploding, as it were, into technology, the assignment of disciplinary values to studies other than the classics and mathematics was to significantly extend formal discipline's life. New curricula approved for disciplinary purposes created new supporters for disciplinary ideas among the teachers who taught those curricula. Formal discipline was an elitist conception and most teachers of humble subjects enjoyed their newfound acceptance within it's ranks. The refurbishing of formal discipline also allowed it to fit right into the educational psychology, of the late nineteenth, early twentieth century, which was usually a faculty psychology.

The pressure upon schools to become utilitarian had actually been going on for quite a while prior to Greeley's call for functional instruction. This was true even in the educational bastions of the privileged. In 1789, the Boston Latin School offered Latin, Greek, and a wee bit of English instruction to its students over their four years of attendance there. Between 1824 and 1828, the school's curriculum expanded rapidly; and at the end of that period, it was offering arithmetic, geometry, trigonometry, algebra, geography, reading, declamation, English grammar, English composition, forensic discussion, history, chronology, and constitutions of both the United States and Massachusetts. In later years, as institutions of public learning were created to cope with the educational needs of the common man, curricula became ever more diversified. The time span 1860–1900 found 40 high schools offering a total of 74 different course offerings.

At the college level, the inroads of utilitarianism were also clearly in evidence during the nineteenth century. The elective principle was first applied at the University of Virginia in 1825. It received its imprimatur proper when Harvard decided in favor of electives in 1869, after which the movement toward electives was clearly an appropriate one for other institutions of higher learning to join.

The Report of the Committee of Ten on Secondary School Studies of the National Educational Association (1893) shed disciplinary grace upon almost any conceivable form of study, while trying at the same time to reassure classical scholars of their primacy in the disciplinary game: It recognized the concern of disciplinary traditionalists, noting that ". . . many teachers and directors of education felt no confidence in . . ." the newcomers ". . . as disciplinary material" (NEA, 1894, p. 72).

The Report noted that Latin had ". . . been more successfully employed in England, Germany, and France . . . than with us 'as an instrument for training the mind to habits of intellectual conscientiousness, patience, discrimination, accuracy, and thoroughness—in a word, to habits of clear and sound thinking' . . ." as more time was given to it in those European countries. It was recommended for continuation as a diciplinary study in American schools, with the added stipulations that its study should not begin later than age 14, it should not continue less than four years, and it should be taught for five 45-minute periods a week for best disciplinary results.

The Committee reaffirmed the values of mathematics for cognitive training. Geometry's chief claims for cognitive training lay in its ". . . discipline in complete, exact and logical statement." In arithmetic "simple calculation" and "concrete problems" were commended for their exercise value, but the Committee cautioned that certain matters be omitted in arithmetic which ". . . perplex and exhaust the pupil without affording any really valuable discipline" (NEA, 1894, p. 12).

The Committee of Ten recommended, further, that English in the secondary schools ". . . be made the equal of any other study in disciplinary or developing power. . . . The study of formal grammar is valuable as training in thought" (NEA, 1894, pp. 21, 89, 210).

Modern languages, that is German and French, were also argued for in terms of their disciplinary contributions. The Committee stated that modern language study

. . . will train their (the pupils') memory and develop their sense of accuracy; it will quicken and strengthen their reasoning powers by offering them, at every step, problems that must be immediately solved by the correct applications of the results of their own observation. (NEA, 1894, p. 49)

The conference held by the Committee on history, government, and political economy observed that the disciplinary value of these subjects was still "imperfectly apprehended." The Committee's members were confident, nevertheless, concerning ". . . the efficiency of these studies in training the judgment." The mind was to be chiefly developed in three ways: by cultivating its powers of discriminating observation; by strengthening its logical faculty, i.e., ability to follow an argument from point to point; and by improving its judgment, i.e., its processes of comparison. Since the ". . . principal end of all education is training (of such powers) . . ." history, though having different values in this respect from language, mathematics, and science, is ". . . in no way inferior to . . . these subjects in respect to the mental training it afforded" (NEA, 1894, pp. 28, 168).

As studies in language and in the natural sciences are best adapted to cultivate the habits of observation; as mathematics are the traditional training of the reasoning faculties; so history and its allied branches are better adapted than any other studies to promote the invaluable mental power which we call the judgment. (NEA, 1894, p. 168)

The Committee of Ten then proceeded to formulate an egalitarian principle of formal discipline for secondary schools. Everything taught, they said, could be regarded as having essentially "equal value" in preparing a youth for college (the aim of all this), for they could:

. . . all be used for training the powers of observation, memory, expression, and reasoning. . . . Every youth who entered college would have spent four years in studying a few subjects thoroughly; and, on the theory that all the subjects are to be considered equivalent in educational rank for the purposes of admission into college, it would make no difference which subjects he had chosen from the programme—he would have had four years of strong and effective mental training. (NEA, 1894, p. 52)

When the Report of the Committee of Ten was accepted and endorsed by the Committee on College Entrance Requirements of the National Education Association, the principle of egalitarianism for school subjects was convincingly reaffirmed.

The way appeared clear for subject matter of any kind and at any level of education to be accepted as having disciplinary value if properly taught. It was a matter, now, of rationalizing a subject area in terms of formal discipline rather than qualifying it in terms of its unique constitutional characteristics. Properly taught, needlework could develop logical powers, just as did classical studies.

The sloyd system of manual training,[2] became popular after 1883 and was held in high esteem for cognitive training, after it had been favorably described in the Annual Report of the Massachusetts Board of Education. Its popularity as a system of formal disciplinary training demonstrated that the humblest of pursuits could aspire to the heights once held only by the classics and mathematics. Hoffman, writing of the sloyd system in 1892, made its disciplinary features the salient ones, favoring it over other competing systems of industrial arts, for sloyd went well beyond the preparation of a student for the purposes of making a living. He described its virtues as follows:

> Primarily, sloyd is to be used as a means of formal education as opposed to material. A material education seeks to impart a definite knowledge of things for their own sake. A formal education seeks chiefly to develop the innate mental powers, and selects and imparts knowledge in order to strengthen character, will-power, memory, perception.
>
> Sloyd has for its aims, as a means of formal instruction: to instill a love for work in general; to create a respect for rough honest labor; to develop self-reliance and independence; to train to habits of order, exactness, cleanliness and neatness; to teach habits of attention, industry and perseverance; to promote the development of the physical powers; to train the eye to the sense of form, and to cultivate the dexterity of the hand. (Parker, 1912, p. 464)

If manualism was to be considered a formal discipline, could other subject areas be far behind? Home economics, commercial studies, agriculture, art, music, physical education, and the three Rs all lined up for admission into the once-exclusive club whose portals had been guarded by the classicists.

To that end, their proponents had to prove that they were based on a suitable foundation of educational science and theory and taught in a "formal" way that developed a pupil's cognitive, moral, and affective powers. The most mundane of studies had to be organized in a formal logical manner; this made for good syllabi, even if students' brain powers were not appreciably improved. And, surprisingly, in the later years of

---

[2] Sloyd originated in Finland, inspired by Froebel's theories of manual expression.

formal discipline's decline, these lower realms of instruction were to prove themselves among the staunchest bastions of the old faith. For at a time when, except in the most hard-headed circles, colleges and universities had abandoned the "doctrine of discipline," teachers in the elementary schools were still to be found emphasizing drill and memorization in "basics" as ways to improve their students' faculties.

But that decline was still a time away. For the moment, let us consider why the doctrines of formal discipline were able to survive the decline of classical studies, with whose fortunes they had been so long inextricably involved. The reasons lie elsewhere than in formal discipline proper. They are to be found in the sense–realist and naturalist movements, which were, together with humanist education, to become major forces in determining the course of European and American education. Within these movements, process training also was emphasized as a major educational goal. Even though the principles of sense–realism and naturalism were in many ways antithetical to those of classical formal discipline, in the end, they were to reinforce them. This will become clear in the following chapter, in which we consider these movements and the names of those so intimately associated with them—Comenius, Rousseau, Pestalozzi, and Froebel.

15
Educational Realism and Naturalism—The Beginnings

INTRODUCTION

We are ready now to begin our examination of those two other great movements within European education, out of which were to emerge the mainstreams of modern-day process training—educational realism and educational naturalism.

There are many and extensive dimensions to these movements. I do not intend to review them all in this chapter, that being the appropriate task of general histories of education. Instead, my goal will be to distinguish and discuss within these movements components that directly impinge upon process training.

THE REALIST MOVEMENT

Let us direct our attention first to the realist movement. It is one that, in its educational aspects,[1] was directed to instruction on the basis of experience with real things as opposed to verbal learning. Verbal learning had been emphasized by medieval and humanist educators. The medieval educators sought to train their pupils through the literature of Christianity, the humanist educators, through the classical languages of the past, usually Latin. As humanist education came to dominate the Euro-

---

[1] Within educational realism, this book will most directly concern itself with those aspects usually deemed as "sense–realism." This will be clearly evidenced in later pages.

pean scene, the forms of Latin and of mathematics, rather than their content, became important as vehicles for disciplining and training minds. Utilitarian education trained students in the vernacular, the mathematics of the marketplace and commerce, and the skills of trades and professions. But such training was regarded as less valuable than formal training and consequently assigned to the lower regions of educational practice.

It was against these earlier ivory tower conceptions of what education should be about that the forces of realism mounted their challenges.

The realist movement expressed itself in philosophy, art, medicine, and even broad social movements. Within education, it made the practical and utilitarian respectable: studies in the vernacular; vocational skill preparation; the teaching of foreign languages for purposes of travel and commerce; the study of history, politics, and science. Above all else, however, realism stressed learning with real things rather than through and by bookish education.[2] One of the realist movement's catch phrases was "things above words" (Good & Teller, 1969). It was the movement's emphasis upon things, rather than words, as legitimate objects of study, that was to revolutionize later education.

A corollary of and sequitur to the emphasis upon things above words that characterized the realist movement was its other catch phrase "everything through the senses." This was opposed to theories that learning is based upon inner, predetermined cognitive structures and ideas. Out of this vein of sense–realism was to emerge the great modality training conceptions of later special education.

The realist movement had many forefathers: the Greek sophists, who insisted upon experience as the only teacher and Aristotle, who wrote of the empirical nature of knowledge. Later, there was St. Thomas Aquinas who stressed the priority of the senses in learning, and the Spanish scholar Juan Luis Vives (1492–1540), who urged the study of nature and "accepted the principles of utility and practical application as criteria for judging education and life" (Good & Teller, 1969, p. 167). Then, too, there was Richard Mulcaster, whose emphasis upon games and physical education as means of developing cognitive powers was to be later echoed in the work of Séguin and followers of the *education nouvelle*. Also, Wolfgang Ratke (1571–1635) who wrote that the senses are our first

---

[2] Despite the agreement within several medieval and humanist circles as to the importance of sensory learning, they rarely deviated from adherence to written texts as the major if not the sole means of instruction. For the Christian educator saw the soul as separate and distinct from the body and its organs—sensory and otherwise—and therefore to be taught by symbol rather than substance. The humanist was so enthralled by the stylistic perfection of the ancients as expressed in classical literature that he saw no greater value in education than its emulation; and, of course, such education peculiarly fitted the requirements of formal discipline—laboriousness, ennui, and irrelevance.

teachers, sight being first among them; Ratke otherwise stressed the humanist traditions of process training, with memory drill, alas, foremost among these; for which we forgive him in light of the striking insights he had into human psychology and the learning process. Less often recognized is the work of Thomas Campenall (1568–1639), who in his book *City of the Sun* recommended extensive experiential learning and the use of elaborate visual displays to stimulate and promote the learning process. August Hermann Francke (1663–1727) is a more well-known member of the realist avant-garde. His pupil Julius Hecker, who formed a *Realschule* in Berlin in 1747, demonstrated in the very name of his school—a real school—as well as in its tenets, the realist principles of his mentor. Of particular importance to the "scientific" age that blossomed forth in the seventeenth century was an earlier theorist, Francis Bacon (1561–1621), whose *Novum Organum* presented observation and inductive reasoning as the roads to true knowledge. The development of new seventeenth century technologies such as the telescope and microscope (and the information that they revealed) magnified his message for all to read.

When the British empiricists presented their message of "all knowledge through the senses," the times were ripe! One might have expected the most prominent of the empiricists, John Locke, to have been the one to lead the realist movement of education onto its future paths. But as we have seen earlier, this was not to be. While Locke did not neglect the value of experiential learning in his musings on education, he did not himself concretely contribute much to education's movement in a sensory direction. Although his later influence upon it was enormous, Locke was too much the speculative philosopher and metaphysician to crowd his mind with the day to day problems of teaching. The sensory training traditions of modern education were to begin with Comenius.

COMENIUS

Johann Amos Comenius (1592–1670) (née Komensky) was one of the great reformers in educational history. No less from the standpoint of processes and process training, than from the standpoint of his pansophic theory of education, which sought to assemble all the knowledge of the world and to instruct all mankind according to it.

Comenius was a great egalitarian. He believed that the potential for growth—intellectually and spiritually—existed in everyone, regardless of station in life, to an almost unlimited degree, if only they could be stimulated and directed appropriately. All it took was the right philosophy (his), the correct methods (his), and appropriate attention to the developmental needs of the child (as he conceived them) and the school could become a "forging place or manufactory of humanity" wherein the faculties of man could be improved to perfection (Eby, 1934, p. 183). So he advised:

> The seeds of knowledge, of virtue, and of piety are . . . naturally implanted . . . but the actual knowledge . . . not so given. These must be acquired by prayer, by education and by action. . . . . For all faculties do but exist potentially and need development. (Cole, 1950, p. 341)

Comenius confidently declared that there was a new day aborning within education, when the painful methods of the past would be quite replaced by easeful, fail-safe methods:

> As soon as we have succeeded in finding the proper method, it will be no harder to teach schoolboys, in any number desired, than with the help of the printing press, to cover a thousand sheets daily with the neatest writing. . . . It will be as pleasant to see education carried out on my plan as to look at an automatic machine of this kind, and the process will be as free from failure as are these mechanical contrivances, when skillfully made (Keatinge, 1931, pp. 50–51)[3]

The confident assertions of his age that technology and science would solve every problem had clearly affected the great Moravian scholar. All seemed possible if a scientific approach to educational management and instruction were taken. We have in his work an uncanny presagement of management by objectives; one almost seems to hear whispered suggestions of performance contracting.

Comenius accepted, without question, the faculty theories that had come down through the Church fathers; he was, after all, a bishop. The faculty doctrines that he adhered to are the ones that are familiar to us from the formulations of St. Thomas Aquinas. He was to take these formulations and to utilize them instructionally within a developmental framework.[4] For example, he advised

> Let our maxim be to follow the lead of nature in all things, to observe how the faculties develop one after the other, and to base our method on this principle of succession. (Keatinge, 1896, p. 409)

His "principle of succession," or of developmental training, was expressed variously by him, as were the tenets of sense–realism:

> The correct order of instruction is followed if boys be made to exercise, first

---

[3] Comenius utilized mechanical metaphors to assist his conceptualizations of instruction. He also used botanical ones: seeds, growths, cultivation, and the like, from an earlier age, which were to be brought to particularly fulgent expression by Froebel. At times, he also employed musical metaphors: a teacher striking a child for an error was likened to a musician striking his instrument because it played a wrong note. The teacher, like the musician, was advised to look to his own skills to obtain better results.

[4] Aristotle had also conceived of process training as proceeding in a developmental sequence. The powers of the body were to be trained first, followed by training directed to the affective powers, followed by training of the cognitive powers.

the senses (for this is the easiest), then the memory, next the understanding, and finally the judgment. For knowledge begins with sense, and passes into memory through imagination, then the understanding of universals is reached by induction from particulars; and finally comes judgment on the facts of understanding, leading to the establishment of knowledge. (Lucas, 1972, p. 320)

The processes have to be trained in appropriate developmental sequence:

To attempt to cultivate the will before the intellect, or the intellect before the imagination, or the imagination before the faculty of sense perception is a mere waste of time. (Keatinge, 1896, p. 409)

The developmental stages conceived by Comenius are, for all his admiration of Bacon and the inductive method, quite a priori and largely deductive in terms of their elaboration. The child's development proceeds in distinct discrete stages, and his training is to keep afoot with and appropriate to the unfolding of his powers at each stage. In keeping with his level of development and his stage-specific needs. Comenius divided his school system into four levels, with each level consisting of six years.[5] For infancy, there was the mother's knee (*Schola materna*); for childhood, the vernacular school (*Schola vernacula*); for boyhood, the Latin school (*Schola Latina*); and for youth, the university and travel. To each was designated responsibility for the emergence and maturation of specific faculties; to each and for each, there was special training. Education could be successful and easy, he pointed out, if . . .

. . . the intellect be forced to nothing to which its natural bent does not incline it, in accordance with its age, and with the right method. (Ulich, 1968, p. 194)

The *Schola materna* had as its goals early social and religious training and the exercise of the external senses. Vernacular school training included the commonplaces of basic education, though in more extensive and deeper draughts than we expect children 6 to 12 to inbibe these days. Pupils in the *Schola vernacula* received instruction in their mother tongue—the speaking, reading, and writing of it. They also were instructed in mechanical arts, singing, religion, history, geography, and politics. It was also the place where special attention was to be given in training the ". . . internal senses, the imagination and memory in combination with their cognate organs" (Eby, 1934, p. 187). In the Latin school (Schola Latina) or gymnasium, which was for all boys "who aspire higher than the workshop," the higher cognitive powers were at last to

---

[5] We are talking now of his projected school system, not the actualities with which Comenius dealt.

receive their due. Pupils attending the Latin school were to be trained in logic, grammar, rhetoric, and the sciences and art, all of which exercised the rational powers so favored by formal discipline, since they ". . . are based on principles of causation" (Eby, 1934, p. 187). In the final stage of school, the faculty to be trained was that of the will. "To the University . . ." Comenius wrote ". . . belong those subjects that have special relation to the will" (Eby, 1934, p. 188). It was, therefore, not only a cognitive elite pupil body that was to pass on to the halls of higher learning, but one also characterized by distinct moral superiority.

Comenius recommended that the precise order of instruction at all stages of a pupil's academic career be structured in accordance with the laws of nature. By this he intended nature as it relates to the natural world, rather than to the pupil's psychological or physical constitution. The principles by which nature operated, those that were to guide instruction, were his very own combinations of observations, inferences, and phantasmagorical meanderings.

Nature observes a suitable time. The birds hatch their eggs and the gardener plants his seeds in the spring, thus by analogy education should begin in the "springtime of life." Since nature prepares material before giving it form, things and language should be taught together rather than the latter prior to the former. Since development is from within in all of nature's operations, a subject should be understood by a child before he memorizes any material from it. Because nature, in its formative processes, proceeds from the universal and ends with the particular, large simple general elements should come first in instruction; details are to be delegated to its later stages. Because nature makes no leaps, but rather proceeds step by step, so should all studies be carefully graded by minute steps. And, finally, since nature compels nothing to advance that is not propelled forward by its own strength,

Nothing should be taught to the young, unless it is not only permitted but actually demanded by their age and mental strength. (Keatinge, 1896, p. 230)

As for education, so for corrective education:

If we wish to find a remedy for the defects of nature, it is in nature itself that we must look for it, since it is certain that art can do nothing unless it imitates nature. (Keatinge, 1834, p. 52)

So much for some of the wisdom of Comenius, a great deal of unnecessary and tendentious analogy, but also containing much insight into the learning process. Such insight, however, was not particularly novel for his age and not of enough consequence to have earned him his place in educational history, were he not responsible for much more. His contributions included the developmental approach to process training discussed earlier and, more importantly, the first comprehensive statement of sensory training for the modern age.

Comenius appears to have been the first educator to have systematically applied the principles of sense–realism to education. He had predecessors, of course, and we have discussed a number of them. In particular, Comenius appears to have been excited and inspired by the writings of Bacon, who wrote ". . . the mind derives the material for all its thoughts from sense" (Lucas, 1972, p. 320). He also appears to have been influenced by Ratke, who holds priority over Comenius in recommending that instruction follow the course of nature, proceeding from concrete experiences to abstract ideas, and under the guidance of the principle *per inductionem et experimentum omnia*. But as Brubacher observed:

> . . . it is nevertheless to his credit that he was the earliest to contrive specific methods for instruction wherein bodily organs would be brought to the aid of the intellect. (Brubacher, 1966, p. 199)

Comenius, in his *Didactica magna,* laid down for the first time the broad principle that everything should be taught through the medium of the senses. It was only this way, he said, that effective learning could be accomplished. He made the following points:

> To the rational soul, that dwells within us, organs of sense have been supplied. . . . These are sight, hearing, smell, sound, and touch, and there is nothing whatever that can escape their notice. For, since there is nothing in the visible universe which cannot be seen, *things;* and by the term I mean determinate, real, and useful things that can make an impression on the senses and the imagination. . . .[6]
>
> From this a golden rule for teachers may be derived. Everything should, as far as possible, be placed before the senses. The commencement of knowledge must always come from the senses (for the understanding possesses nothing that it has not first derived from the senses). (Keatinge, 1896, pp. 336–337)[7]

It is hard to understand the vehemence of these exhortations from our own vantage point of the last quarter of the twentieth century, but it was common practice in Comenius's day for scholars to undertake the study of physics entirely on the basis of texts that had been written by Aristotle and without any exposure to practical experiences. Surgeons often entered into practice with perhaps no more than one opportunity to observe the dissection of a human cadaver and often no prior practical

---

[6] Interpreted here as the faculty that recalls past sensations.

[7] Comenius was not altogether consistent here, since he also accepted the concept of innate ideas and of knowledge derived from the operations of understanding (interpret the reasoning faculty) upon these.

experience. Pupils were forced to memorize Latin without understanding the contents of what they labored with, and so on. The mind (soul) was addressed as separate from the body, and hence, learning on its own apart from that body. What might appear as hyperbole on Comenius's part was, in fact, an essential admonition to instructors who had forgotten that the children they were teaching were flesh-and-blood creatures.

Comenius went beyond sense training to recommend multisensory training. And in this, he clearly stood alone in his manifest formulations of the principles thereof:

> The sense of hearing should always be conjoined with that of sight, and the tongue should be trained in combination with the hand. The subjects that are taught should not merely be taught orally, and thus appeal to the ear alone, but should be pictorially illustrated, and thus develop the imagination by the help of the eye. . . . (Keatinge, 1896, p. 291)

Or as more succinctly stated: "Let every sense be engaged in the perception . . . of objects" (Keatinge, 1896, p. 291).

If the reader, accustomed to a different type of perceptual training these days, is somewhat puzzled, let him not be. Comenius was, in fact, not talking about giving his students ditto sheets with figure-ground exercises to improve their perceptual skills. Rather, he was talking of developing their senses through exposure to the natural environment or representations of the things therein, as opposed to swamping their minds with words. But he was also speaking of providing natural sensory encounters with "things" and the use of audiovisual aids, as opposed to arbitrary perceptual exercises (for the latter we shall have to wait until Pestalozzi). The most successful and revolutionary application of Commenian sensory training theories is to be found in his *Orbis Pictus* (world in pictures) the first textbook to employ illustrations as a teaching device.

Along with exposure to sensory information, Commenius advised upon activity as a major avenue of instruction; again, the obvious for us must be interpreted in terms of the bookish preoccupations of his age:

> What is to be done must be learned by practice. . . . In schools, therefore, let the students learn to write by writing, to talk by talking, to sing by singing, and to reason by reasoning. (Keatinge, 1896, p. 347)

This principle of activity would be later expressed in a motor variety of educational theories, some very dear to the hearts of special educators.

Comenius brought to the educational world its first precise conceptions of sensory training and developmental process training. However while hailed in the latter part of the nineteenth century, and in our own, as a great force in education, he was by and large neglected in his own century and subsequent times, except for his *Orbis Pictus* which was simply too good an idea to overlook. Various reasons have been given for this neglect, including the fact that he was a member of an oppressed religious sect. Perhaps it was, too, that his theories were too radical, too extravagant to draw a ready following. Whatever the reason, his great didactic did not translate into much practical application. Itard was to later invoke the names of Locke and Condillac when he applied sensory training principles to the training of Victor. Nor did Comenius's sophisticated plans for school reorganization and educational management influence to any appreciable degree the schools of the normal in the century after his death. Belated recognition of his genius he has received in full, including his contributions to process training.

NATURALISM AND JEAN-JACQUES ROUSSEAU

Naturalism, as a movement in education, was a response to the excessive formalism that had come to dominate the society of the early eighteenth century (Monroe, 1905). Religious orthodoxy was still powerful, stifling innovations in philosophical thought, politics, and educational practice. The Enlightenment,[8] exemplified by Hume and Gibbon in England, and Voltaire and the Diderot in France, had challenged this orthodoxy. They rejected the Catholic church's traditions as superstitious and oppressive, glorifying the operations of the intellect—rational thought in particular, in their stead. The Enlightenment, however, did not become a liberating force for mankind. Its various members sought rather to replace the authoritarianism of Church and aristocracy with another based on ability and money. The common man had no place in all of this. The *homme moyen* was still regarded as scarcely human by the likes of John Locke in England, barely rational by the intellectual *haute* of France. Monroe has observed:

> The general conception of civilization held by Voltaire and his associates . . . permitted the populace no rights; had no sympathy with the masses; erected a polished intellectual society—that was rational enough to be sure, but that, through its artificiality, had lost all approach to a natural mode of living. . . . This

---

[8] This movement of eighteenth century thinkers, largely French, relied only on sense perception and reason, as a basis for knowledge, abandoning all belief in revelation. The *Philosophes,* led by Diderot and Condillac, expressed their philosophy in which the traditional faculty of reason is joined together with empiricism suchly:

> We know truth only by our reason. That reason is enlightened only by our senses. What they do not tell us we cannot know, and it is mere folly to waste time in conjecturing. Imagination and feeling are blind leaders of the blind. All men who pretend to supernatural revelation or inspiration are swindlers, and those who believe them are dupes (Lowell, 1892, p. 61)

stilted wisdom and affected superiority of the learned class, now shunning simplicity as a mark of vulgarity, and naturalness as a mark of irrationality, developed into a formalism that was no less repressive to the masses and no less distasteful to many. . . . The later eighteenth century, weary of the formalism of both (clericalism and the Enlightenment) became, under the leadership of Rousseau, directed to a new purpose. (Monroe, 1905, p. 542)

This "new purpose" was the ". . . liberation of the common man" (Monroe, 1905, p. 547). And since the rule of reason and the primacy of the senses had come to be used to justify power and privilege for the newly privileged, they, too, were to be challenged by Rousseau and other members of the naturalist movement. The senses were to be shown as fallible, reason as not always rational. The emotions or inner sentiments were to take their places as chief arbiters of right and wrong. They, rather than cognitive processes, were to be followed as guides to just and proper conduct, though cognitive processes, as we shall see, were certainly to have their proper due. Jean-Jacques Rousseau (1712–1778), who led the movement was himself too much a child of the rational age for it to be otherwise.

Rousseau saw society, along with its acculturating educational agencies, as responsible for most of man's woes, through its corruption of man's natural state. Primitive man, as conceived by Rousseau, was indeed a creature of unequal powers, physical and mental, one man to another. These inequalities were givens. Nevertheless, under the conditions of natural primitive life, they did not reveal themselves to any great degree and, therefore, did not much affect man's potential for success and happiness. Nor did negative emotional states exist, since man, not knowing what was good or bad, could not be vicious. Man's primitive virtue— pity—served as the major acculturating force of primitive society, serving as a benign prototype of later customs and manners.

As society developed, inequalities among men became accentuated and began to play a significant role in the dominance and exploitation of certain men by others. Environmental opportunities and differential influences played a significant role in this. The development of private property rights preserved the social inequalities that resulted; these in turn were protected by political power. To remedy the downgrading of the great majority of mankind that resulted from such processes was the theme of much of Rousseau's writings.

Beyond the social inequities that he saw created by the society of his day, Rousseau was appalled by the violence that this society wrought upon its children, both privileged and poor. The privileged child was perhaps to be more pitied than the underprivileged or the starveling in this respect, for he was forced into the mold of an adult from the time he began to walk. It meant his being stuffed into the types of clothes that the adults of his age wore. It meant being forced into modes and lengths of study far beyond his maturity. It meant that the fact of his childhood, with its own natural interests and activities, was overlooked or even denied by parents, educators and society, from an early age. It was against the dreadful artificiality of the child rearing practices of his day that Rousseau proposed his naturalistic doctrines of care and education. The opening statement of his book on education, *Émile*, presents the fundamental premise that guided his thinking:

> . . . everything is good as it comes from the hand of nature; but everything degenerates in the hands of man. (Monroe, 1905, p. 553)

Rousseau believed that education should proceed according to the precepts of nature and that nature clearly showed the way toward the proper preparation and instruction of the individual. This view was completely antithetical to the prevailing opinions held by the "correct" society of the 18th century, a society which, almost without exception, saw the purpose of education as that of subduing the child, repressing his natural instincts, and of forcing his behavior into the molds of preconceived proprieties.[9]

What was Rousseau's concept of nature? From one standpoint, he was referring to natural endowment and the individual differences to be found in it from person to person. Nature establishes the inherited dispositions and capacities of the individual prior to their being influenced by the environment. In this sense, nature is beyond man's control. Education based on this insight is a matter of development from within rather than the accretion of experiences from without. It is the result of the expression and expansion of the natural powers and various abilities of the individual, on the basis of maturation rather than through didactic acculturation.

Society, and its educational institutions, said Rousseau, is an artificial product which makes the good things of nature "degenerate" in man's hands. It was on these grounds that Rousseau recommended a "negative" (i.e., slow and relatively hands-off) education in the early part of the child's growth, lest opportunities for the child's internal potentials to freely and properly express themselves and develop be thwarted.

Another connotation of nature in Rousseau's writings is that the nature of the universe is governed by a divine providence that makes it "right," so that to live by nature's rules is to live according to reason and accord-

---

[9] Education, in the ordinary sense, may have been seen as an evil by Rousseau, but as a necessary evil. He warned: "Things would be worse without this education . . . a man left to himself from birth would be more a monster than the rest. . . . When I want to train a natural man, I do not want to make him a savage . . . it is enough that he should not be carried away by the passions and prejudices of men" (Rousseau, 1911, p. 5).

ing to the divine will. Comenius had seen things, we will recall, in a somewhat similar light. Rousseau spoke vehemently about this "rightness" of nature and the wrongness of thwarting her.

Watch nature carefully and follow the paths she traces out for you. She gives children continual exercise; she strengthens their constitution by ordeals of every kind; she teaches them early what pain and trouble mean . . . the law of nature.[10] Why do you oppose her? Do you not see that in thinking to correct her you destroy her work and counteract the effect of all her cares? (Mayer, 1966, pp. 232, 233)

For Rousseau to think of the development of the child without and within education, was for him to think in terms of the development and training of the child's faculties, for faculty psychology was still the psychology of the day. The expression of one's faculties was the assertion of life itself as Rousseau observed:

To live is not merely to breathe, it is to act. It is to make use of our organs, of our senses, of our faculties, of all the powers which bear witness to us of our own existence. (Mayer, 1966, p. 228)

Rousseau definitely associated the development and fortunes of cognitive and affective processes with those of the physical body.[11] On this basis alone, he assumes major importance for a historical understanding of special education. For Rousseau, as with Plato, it was ". . . the body for the sake of the soul."

A feeble body makes a feeble mind. All wickedness comes from weakness. Would you cultivate your pupil's intelligence, cultivate the strength it is meant to control? Give his body constant exercise, make it strong and healthy, in order to make him good and wise; let him work, let him do things, let him run and shout, let him be always on the go; make a man of him in strength, and he will soon be a man of reason. As he grows in health and strength he grows in wisdom and discernment. This is the way to attain to what is generally incompatible, strength of body and strength of mind, the reason of the philosopher and the vigor of the athlete. (Rousseau, 1892, pp. 21, 33, 82, 84)

Rousseau, like Comenius before him and Aristotle still earlier, perceived a child's development as proceeding through stages. His theories were considerably more complicated than those of his predecessors,

[10] Following the creation of Newtonian science, nature was seen as a mechanism that functioned according to its own intrinsic and ordered patterns. Man, as a microcosm within the macrocosm of the universe, also could be conceived as developing and functioning according to nature's immutable laws. The latter were to be used as the basis for explaining the development of man and the rules of his behavior. Psychologists still keep seeking these laws and educators still justify their instruction by them.
[11] Comenius had emphasized the importance of activity in learning, but not physical movement as such.

however. For one, his developmental musings encompassed a recapitulation theory, wherein a child, progressing from birth to maturity, is conceived as living through (recapitulating) the epochs through which the human race passed in its movement to civilization. He begins as an animal, then turns into a savage, subsequently achieves rationality, and, finally, becomes a social human being (Eby, 1934).[12]

Rousseau was also the first to introduce the saltatory theory of development. He saw the stages of development as being sharply marked off, one from the other, with special characteristics and new functions suddenly emerging at later stages that had not previously been in operation in earlier ones. The reader, I am sure, need not be told that these stages and their functions were to play an important part in Rousseau's educational programming.[13]

For each of the stages—birth to 5, 5 to 12, 12 to 15, 15 to 20 and adulthood—there are certain appropriate modes of activity—educational and otherwise. If the developing organism is provided with them, a healthy, satisfactory, and complete maturation of abilities can be expected, a harmonious development of faculties conducive to successful adult life. If, on the other hand, activities suitable to later stages are forced upon the child prematurely, damaging consequences may result.[14]

Rousseau made his arguments for appropriate activities at each stage on both sentimental and psychological grounds. As to the first, he reminded his readers that most of their pupils would not reach adulthood. Was it right, then, to deprive them of the joys that should be theirs as children? As to the second, he appealed to the "laws" of nature:

> Nature would have children be children before men. If we wish to pervert this order we shall produce precocious fruits which will have neither maturity nor flavor, and will speedily deteriorate. . . . Childhood has its own way of seeing, thinking, and feeling, and nothing is more foolish than to substitute our own for them. (Payne, 1892, p. 121)

The physical and psychological givens of the child's original nature mature according to their own inner organismic schedule. Nature (the child's nature) is to be allowed to determine the order, manner and degree by which and to which the child's processes develop and are active at the

---

[12] The recapitulation theory was to later be enthusiastically supported by advocates of Darwinian evolution. Spencer believed in it. G. Stanley Hall based his psychologies of childhood and adolescence on it. There were even attempts to explain mental retardation on its basis (Groszman, 1917).

[13] Any more than he has to be reminded that they anticipate the stages of another great—later—Swiss epistemologist.

[14] Rousseau was talking in all of this of a presumably well-endowed but not extraordinarily gifted individual, one without any special intellectual or physical deficiencies. His theories are of general rather than special education.

various stages of his development. The role of society (parents, teachers, etc.) is to nourish the growth of these processes and provide them the stimulation and exercise they need; to support their development, rather than to actively seek their training or education. Rousseau clearly distinguished between this aspect (developmental) of process education and the later training provided within formal education and through experiential learning.

. . . education comes to us from nature, from men, and from things. The inner growth of our organs and faculties is the education of nature; the use we make of this growth is the education of men, what we gain by our experience of our surroundings is the education of things. (Rousseau, 1911, p. 6)

Rousseau's famous book *Émile* presents the education of a boy according to his theories. Rousseau's training of *Émile* is discussed within five books, each dedicated to a particular period of his development.

In the first book, which deals with Émile's infancy, the child's main desire is for physical activity, this is to be permitted under conditions in which he is close to nature and within which only those minimal restraints and precautions absolutely required to preserve life are exercised.

Surely, never before was the value of movement so extolled, so exalted as by Rousseau in *Émile*. It is so throughout the five books. But the flavor particularly comes through in the pages of this first book on the training of infancy. Here he castigates those who limit the movements of infants as causing deformities and resulting in "patched up men." The case for allowing freedom of activity to the infant is clear and unequivocal:

[In the heart of the child] activity is abundant and extends itself outward. . . . Whether he makes or unmakes is not; it suffices that he changes the state of things and every change is an action. (Rousseau, 1892, p. 32)

The importance of motor activity is also expressed in Rousseau's exposition of sensory development, another major aspect of the first stage of Émile's development. Rousseau clearly relates perception to motor activity and establishes both as fundi for the development of higher cognitive structures. In the following statement about Émile's education during infancy—a statement in which Rousseau's *stage specific* concepts of process development are clearly on view—sensory-motor processes are clearly accorded primacy. Memory, imagination, and understanding are not yet active.

In this onset of life (infancy), while memory and imagination are still inactive, the child pays attention only to what actually affects his senses. The first materials of his knowledge are his sensations. If, therefore, these are presented to him in suitable order, his memory can hereafter present them to his understanding in the same order. But as he attends to sensations only, it will at first suffice to show him very clearly the connection between these sensations and the objects which give rise to them. He is eager to touch everything, to handle everything. Do not thwart this restless desire; it suggests to him a very necessary apprenticeship. It is thus he learns to feel the heat and coldness, hardness and softness, heaviness and lightness of bodies; to judge of their size, their shape, and all their sensible qualities, by looking, listening; above all by comparing the results of sight with those of touch, estimating with the eye, the sensation a thing produces upon the fingers.

By movement alone we learn the existence of things which are not ourselves; and it is by our own movements alone that we gain the idea of extention. . . . (Mayer, 1966, p. 236)

Lo, we have just read a statement of the principles of sensory-motor education, multi-sensory learning and also a clear anticipation of what special education pioneers such as Itard, Séguin, Montessori (to name but several) were to later say. Rousseau's principles of sensory-motor training and those of training the higher cognitive powers through or in association with it were presented in his second book on Émile's education. Émile, during the second stage of his education (age 5 to 12 years), was to leave home and live under the tutelage of a personal tutor, being exposed to the concrete experiences provided by nature, i.e., natural, nonurban surroundings. Here the boy's tutor is admonished to "exercise the body, the organs, the senses and powers, but keep the soul lying fallow as long as you can" (Monroe, 1905, p. 561). This statement renders, in still another translation, "Keep his organs, his senses, his physical body busy, but, as long as possible, keep his mind inactive" (Mayer, 1966, p. 247).

In both of the preceding renderings, as elsewhere in his writings, Rousseau was essentially recommending that sensory and motor, rather than intellectual, development, be the aim of education between the ages of 5 and 12. He even recommended for all young pupils: "They must do nothing with their soul until it has all its faculties (Cole, 1931, p. 237).

Rousseau seemed to be proceeding with such statements on the basis of the developmental premise that the higher of man's faculties, emerge only after the—lower—ones have been developed.[15] This developmental hypothesis is explicit in another of his statements concerning the second stage of Émile's educational career, to the effect that "Childhood is the

---

[15] There are several ways in which hierarchical theories of faculty psychology conceived the relationships of higher to lower processes. In some, higher processes are potentials that emerge in later years. In others, they are present but dormant in earlier years. In still others they are active in early forms from the beginning of life. Higher cognitive processes could be conceptualized as developing independently from lower processes, as being based on them, as emerging from them, as being part of them.

sleep of reason. . . . Of all the faculties of man, reason . . . is developed with the most difficulty and latest" (Eby, 1934, p. 353), and in still another, "The senses are the first faculties to take form and attain perfection, and consequently should be the first to be cultivated" (Boyd & King, 1973, p. 299).

Yet elsewhere Rousseau clearly indicated that the higher cognitive powers are to be developed, even trained, through or along with the instrumentalities of perceptual and motor functioning. Discussing Émile's education during the second developmental stage, he advised: "Our first teachers of philosophy are our feet, our hands, and our eyes" (Cole, 1931, pp. 239, 240). "To learn to think, we must exercise the limbs, senses and organs which are the instrument of intellect" (Boyd and King, 1973, p. 229).

Furthermore, Rousseau made it clear that the very activities that are intended for the training of limbs, organs, and senses are also conducive to the development of the child's higher cognitive powers. Émile, between the ages of 5 and 12, was to undergo a physical-hardening process (like that recommended by Locke). He was also to learn to swim, practice high and long jumps, leap walls, scale rocks, etc. But at the same time he was to exercise his reasoning powers through natural problems in weighing, measuring, estimating, etc. In the statement below we see Rousseau combining motor, perceptual, and higher cognitive power (judgment, reasoning, etc.) within such "motor" activities.

. . . do not exercise the child's strength alone, but call into exercise all the senses which direct it. . . . Measure, count, weigh, compare, and do not employ force until after having estimated the resistance (Rousseau, 1892, p. 97)

Additionally Rousseau appeared to be making a distinction between two types of reasoning, one having to do with the concrete and trained through sensory and motor experiences (like those discussed above), the other dealing with the abstract and trained with symbols and ideas. There are several statements concerning Émile's education during its second stage suggesting that Rousseau placed great store on reasoning in the concrete.

. . . on the other hand he [Émile] judges, foresees, and reasons on everything which is directly related to him. He does not prate but he acts. . . . As he is incessantly active, he is forced to observe many things and to know many effects. (Rousseau, 1892, p. 85)

I am very far from thinking, however, that children are incapable of any kind of reasoning. On the contrary, I see that they reason very well on whatever they know, and on whatever is related to their present and obvious interest (Rousseau, 1892, p. 71)

Even géometry could effectively be taught, Rousseau believed, on the basis of simple concrete rationality:[16]

Draw exact figures, combine them, superimpose them, and examine their relations. You will find the whole of elementary geometry by advancing from one observation to another, without the need of definitions, problems, or of any other form of demonstration than simple superposition. (Rousseau, 1892, p. 110)

Rousseau's second stage education for Émile is directed toward the optimal development of the child's perceptual and perceptual-motor abilities through a variety of natural experiences.

He had been most impressed by stories of how the blind had acutely increased tactile powers, and of how Indians were able to forego the use of hunting dogs because of the accentuation of their own sense of smell. The life he recommended for Émile during his second stage of education was one admirably suited, he believed, to a similar training of perceptual powers. He was also partial to drawing as a means of training both visual perception and hand–eye coordination.

I would have my pupil cultivate this art, not exactly for the art itself, but for rendering the eye accurate and the hand flexible. (Cole, 1931, p. 241)

I am aware that . . . he will scrawl for a long time without making anything that is recognizable; that he will be late in catching the elegance of contours (etc.) . . . but by way of compensation he will certainly contract a juster glance of the eye, a steadier hand, a knowledge of the true relations of volume and form . . . and the more ready use of the play of perspective. (Rousseau, 1892, p. 108)

Rousseau was insistent that perception be trained in its own right, without too hasty a transition from training the senses as senses to using the latter as a means of training higher cognitive processes or to gain verbal and symbolic knowledge;[17] though in keeping with his sensationalistic progenitors he identified ideas as products of sensation, and the acquisition of sensations as necessary to achieve ideas.

Let us transform our sensations into ideas, but let us not jump abruptly from sensible objects to intellectual objects; for it is through the first that we are to reach the second. In the first movement of the mind, let the senses be the guides. (Monroe, 1905, pp. 576, 577)

Rousseau also advised against overloading a young child's memory by excessively committing it to things it could not master. He accorded memory a position of great importance. So he spoke in the second book of Émile of a natural development of memory based upon a child becoming

---

[16] The divisions between the thinking in the concrete and thinking in the abstract have a frequent echo in psychology and education, as we know all too well.

[17] Rousseau decried early training in reading and suggested putting it (reading) off to adolescence.

conscious of his "own being," wherein "Memory extends this feeling of personal identity to every moment of his existence . . ." whereby ". . . he becomes really one, the same one . . ." (Mayer, 1966, p. 242). However he was adamantly against the traditional memory training for which formal discipline was so justly infamous. In particular, he was against excessive commitment of bookish information to memory. For all instances of where memorization was required, he called for an understanding of the material to be memorized prior to its memorization. In this way, true memory may be accomplished. While Comenius and many others prior to him had said much the same, Rousseau's recommendations differed in one important way—the others had seen in the child's very youth a plasticity that made memory easy, so that memory training should begin at an early age. Rousseau admitted the plasticity but saw in it great danger:

> The apparent facility with which children learn is the cause of their ruin. We do not see that this facility is proof that they are learning nothing. Their smooth and polished brain reflects like a mirror the objects that are presented to it; but nothing remains, nothing penetrates. . . . No, if nature gives to a child's brain that plasticity which renders it capable of receiving all sorts of impressions, it is not for the purpose of engraving on it . . . all those words without meaning for his age, and without utility for any age whatever with which his sad and barren infancy is harassed; but it is in order that all the ideas which he can conceive and are useful to him . . . may be traced there. . . . (Rousseau, 1892, p. 79)

He contrasted the disservice done a child's mind by traditional memory drill with the benefits that might be achieved by the child being able to understand the subjects of his retention efforts:

> When the understanding fully masters a thing before entrusting it to memory, what it afterwards draws therefrom is in reality its own. But if we load the memory with matters the understanding has not mastered, we run the risk of never finding anything there that belongs to it. (Mayer, 1966, p. 247)

Thus by Rousseau's precepts and in contradiction to the accepted practices of his and prior times, memory is not to be trained at an early age. It is not only to wait upon the development of the child's sensory and motor processes, but also upon that of the reasoning processes as well. Its training is most certainly no longer to be considered a prime instructional desideratum for young school children. [18]

If Rousseau was reluctant to accord memory early attention, he was also quite willing to let language development proceed at a languid pace, on much the same basis that he deferred memory. It was language's association with bookishness that he so hated. He saw a child, if developing language skills early, as being drawn away from the rightful develop-

---

[18] Memory in its broadest definition was something else. Rousseau expected that his pupil would learn from experience, which certainly required memory. The discussion above relates to memory as a faculty artificially distinguished for training purposes.

ment of his mind and character by natural experiences into a preoccupation with words and verbalism. Verbal learning of a formal nature was to be deferred to a later stage of a pupil's instruction and, even then, to be maintained at a level where words would not overwhelm experience. There was certainly no equivocation by Rousseau on this point for the educational period he circumscribed between ages 5 and 12. Rousseau expected that within this age range a pupil's language powers would be developed in the normal course of events—by conversations with his tutor, by learning to discriminate the phenomena of nature, and through singing; training in harmony would in particular improve the pupil's auditory discrimination powers. But the formalistic oral and written and reading training that was traditional in the schools of his day was to be resisted at all costs. Rousseau told Émile's fictitious tutor: "Do not give your pupil any sort of lesson verbally" (Mayer, 1966, p. 245). The consequences for Émile?

> His ideas are few but precise, he knows nothing by rote but much by experience. If he reads our books worse than other children, he reads far better in the book of nature; his thoughts are not in his tongue but in his brain . . . he can only speak one language[19] but he understands what he is saying, and if his speech is not so good as that of other children his deeds are better. (Foxley, 1925, pp. 124–126)

The age period between 12 and 15 was described by Rousseau as the "age of reason." The emergence of rational judgment in terms of its highest meaning is the signal characteristic of this period (Eby, 1934).

Rousseau, when he had broken with the Enlightenment, had done so in part on the basis of its excessive emphasis on reason as the arbiter of man's affairs. But a systematic program of education, even one as revolutionary as that he planned for Émile, could not ignore the role played by higher cognitive processes. We have already seen the faculty of reason at work in Rousseau's theories. It was to make a frequent appearance. His conception of *Reason*, however, represented a distinct departure from the traditional faculty psychology and sense perception traditions of his day. Reason is not an original innate principle as the rationalists of his day believed; nor does it arise from sensation as a thorough-going empiricist would have it. Rather, it is a natural accessory faculty that has its origin in the emotional life of the child.[20] (Eby, 1934)

The following description of Émile's school career up to 15 years of age appears to summarize this conception:

---

[19] Remember that Latin was taught at an early age to the children of the privileged and otherwise elite.

[20] Only when the child reaches the age of 12 does reason, in its abstract-symbolic forms, begin to function and its period for uninterrupted development is quite short (Eby, 1934). As we have seen earlier in our discussion of Rousseau's theories, he did allow for certain expressions of higher cognitive faculties within concrete activities at earlier ages.

After exercising his body and his senses we have exercised his mind and judgment. Finally we have joined together the use of his limbs and his faculties. We have made him a worker and a thinker; we have now to make him loving and tenderhearted, to perfect reason through feelings. (Rousseau, 1911, p. 170)

What accounts for reason's increased manifestations after the age of 12? Rousseau explained it in rather innovative terms. The inner life of the child, he believed, is conditioned by the relation of his needs to the strength of the powers required to satisfy them. In the earlier years of his life, a child's strength is feeble compared to the needs it has to fulfill. In later years, there is a surplus of this strength:

At the age of twelve or thirteen the strength of the child is developed much more rapidly than his needs. . . . He whose strength exceeds his desires has some power to spare. (Rousseau, 1911, pp. 133–137)

This prepubertal increase in strength is muscular but it also has psychic components. Thus reason rises into eminence. It is a necessary faculty, required to guide the behavior of the preadolescent (or adolescent), which would be excessive if it were directed solely by his energies, powers, and desires. Rousseau explained the complicated affair:

In proportion as a sensitive being becomes active, he acquires a discernment proportional to his powers; and it is only with the power which is in excess of what is needed for self-conservation that there comes to be developed in him the speculative faculty suited for employing that excess of power for other uses. If then you would cultivate the intelligence of your pupil, cultivate the power which it is to govern. . . . Let him be a man in vigor, and soon he will be such by force of reason. (Rousseau, 1911, p. 84)

Once again, we should observe in the above statement the importance of the body for the development of the intellect. Even an advanced faculty, reason, must rely on physical development for its own development.

Up to this stage (that of the emergence of reason as a major faculty), Rousseau's pupil is largely to be educated in terms of his own nature, his own activities, and his encounters with the world about him. The primary rule of this education is that the child is to be stimulated and guided but not interfered with by either parents or tutor. Within this new (3rd) stage of development, between the ages 12 and 15, the age of rationality, formal education finally begins in earnest. It is ". . . the period of labor, of instruction, and of study." For now reason, guided by curiosity and foresight, can project the future of the child, and direct the other faculties toward academic interests.

What . . . shall our pupil do with that surplus of faculties and powers which he has on hand at present but which he will stand in need of at a subsequent period of life. . . . He will project into the future, so to speak, that which is superfluous for the time being. (Rousseau, 1911, p. 133)

Reason, then, was allowed by Rousseau to assume a planning function, a management function. However, Rousseau was still too hostile to the Enlightenment which sought to enthrone reason above all. Thus he would not accord its favorite faculty the ultimate controlling power over other faculties. Rather, he said, reason develops later than the emotions, and as it emerges from them, it is subordinate to them! Rousseau saw a wiser guide to behavior than rational thought, ". . . the divine voice of man's heart and his inner conscience alone are the infallible guides and capable of bringing him happiness" (Eby, 1934, p. 355).

Hampered by its subservience to emotion and by the short time span (between ages 12 and 15) that Rousseau allotted to it for its task of directing a growing pupil's faculties and powers towards formal academic learning, what is reason expected to achieve?

Unlike formal disciplinarians, Rousseau emphasized that reason should put its efforts into utilitarian pursuits. He regarded book learning as an anathema even for the 12 to 15-year-old. Only *Robinson Crusoe* was permitted to Émile since it is a naturalistic novel, expresses some of Rousseau's theories, and shows how an individual, by himself, can master his environment and his life. However education, even formal education, can proceed nicely without books, thought Rousseau. Making his own instruments, Émile is expected to learn the phenomena of nature, the fundamentals of geography, astronomy, the principles of physics. For later employability and manual dexterity the art of cabinetmaking is advised. It is all learning for use, rather than for knowledge—the concrete rather than the symbolic, the experience rather than the word. The pupil is to be given a taste for knowledge and the means of acquiring it, rather than knowledge itself of any particular area. All in all, enough room is allowed reason, thusly, to exercise its guiding functions.

A particularly active and abhorrent faculty, ages 12–15, is imagination (in the sense of invention and fantasy rather than recreation of sensory impressions). It is this faculty, above all others, that Rousseau regarded as responsible for man's ills. Imagination creates artificial, unnecessary, and often vicious needs. It inflames the passions and is responsible for vice and competition. It is to be discouraged.

The result of Émile's education (including the exercise of his faculties), at age 15, is the creation of a boy, full of physical endurance and courage and possessing a tempered, well-modulated mind:

> [He] has every virtue which is related to himself. In order to have the social virtues also, all he lacks is to know the relations that exact them. . . . He has no faults, and no vices. He has a sound body, agile limbs, a just unprejudiced mind, and a heart that is free and without passion. (Rousseau, 1911, pp. 190, 191)

The fourth stage or development (15–20) sees the inauguration of a new life for Émile. At 15 years of age, adolescent and pubescent Émile is on the threshold of great things. Rousseau put it dramatically, "We are born twice, once for existing and again for living; once for the species and again for sex" (Rousseau, 1911, p. 192).

For at 15 years of age there is the birth of the soul. Whereas before, life has been at the animal level, now human sentiments truly emerge. Since, however, our interest in Émile is in cognition rather than his tumescence, we need give his education from age 15 to 20 scant attention. The youth now has to learn to control his passions (pubescence-based) by acquiring social sentiments. At 18, he studies men as they appeared in history and makes his acquaintance with the abstractions of religion. Books are finally allowed.

With stage 5 arriving, Émile at 20 enters society and learns the skills needed for social relations from great literature (especially the classics). He then meets the ideal woman[21] and travels widely to broaden his knowledge and learn about politics. He finally marries and his education is complete (Boyd and King, 1973).

Rousseau's influence on society and education was enormous. Emile was, say Boyd and King ". . . perhaps the most considerable book ever written on education" (1973, p. 301). Parents tried to raise their children by it. Émile-based schools sprang up—and texts to teach within them—all over Europe; Johann Bernard Basedow's efforts (1723–1790) and replicas thereof being prime examples. More importantly, for our history, Rousseau's theories and convictions strongly influenced, positively and negatively, such important figures in the history of process training as Pestalozzi, Herbart, and Froebel.

As to Rousseau's own distinct contributions to process training, they have been abundantly apparent, have they not? His own particular theory of process development—stage-specific emergents, primacy of sensory and motor processes in the developmental sequence, the dominance of cognitive by affective processes. Perhaps most important, from the standpoint of later developments, was his emphasis upon motor behavior. It influenced many other later theories, as did his emphasis on naturalistic activities as means of training processes. This latter was to be generally "lost" in later school-bound, classroom-restricted, paper-and-pencil and trampoline-mitigated process training times.

---

[21] About whom Rousseau could have known little. For the most part it was that naughty faculty imagination which, in lieu of personal experience with women, appears to have provided the basis for his theories about them, their roles, and their sexual manners.

16
Educational Realism and Naturalism—Expansion of Theories

PESTALOZZI

Johann Heinrich Pestalozzi (1747–1827) is the third of our major contributors to process training within the frameworks of sense-realism and naturalism. Whereas Comenius's influence was essentially limited to innovations in textbooks, and while Rousseau's theories remained for others to apply, Pestalozzi was to directly and personally affect the events of day-to-day educational practice.

Whatever sins the Enlightenment had been guilty of, including those of intellectual hubris, it was in great degree thanks to its efforts that the world came to be viewed as a place where rational direction could make a difference and that the gloom of earlier theological pessimism concerning the nature of man was lifted. Despite the pernicious wars that wracked Europe at the beginning of Pestalozzi's career, there was still hope for a better tomorrow.

The climate of Pestalozzi's times was also one in which the universe and all in it could be interpreted as being governed by certain immutable natural laws.[1] Discover the nature of these natural laws and the environment can be controlled. Teach according to these natural laws and man can be raised to new heights of perfection. Who could resist the notion that they were proceeding in their pursuits according to natural law? Most certainly not Pestalozzi.

---

[1] On the basis of the influence his writings had upon the development of special education, Sir Isaac Newton (1642–1727) should be recognized as one of its pioneers.

180

While nature could be interpreted scientifically, it might also be interpreted in a romantic mystical way as having special beneficient powers. The natural development of children could be explained from both standpoints, as was done by Rousseau who wielded a major, probably the major influence upon Pestalozzi. Pestalozzi described his experiences upon reading *Émile* in ecstatic terms ". . . my visionary and highly speculative mind was enthusiastically seized by this visionary and highly speculative book" (Gutek, 1968, p. 11). Émile was to turn Pestalozzi's life around, determine his career, exert an ever-present effect on his thinking. From Rousseau, Pestalozzi appears to have derived many of his beliefs: that man is fundamentally good but that society has a corrupting influence on him; that education can help to block and even undo the distortions created by society and help a child achieve the positive potentials that are inherent in his nature; that human growth proceeds through well-defined stages; that sensations and concrete experiences, rather than book learning, are the correct ways to proceed in education; that the natural environment is a source of educational experiences.

Pestalozzi did not, however, reject society's teachings as severely as did Rousseau or completely accept his doctrine of pan-naturalism. He was most distinctly not an atheist or a deist, perhaps best was described as a "naturalist Christian humanist" (Gutek, 1968). As a consequence of his combination of the traditions of reformed Christianity with the natural religion of Rousseau and the intellectualism of the age, he came to view the training and education of children as a responsibility under the laws of human development, the deity, and man himself. The following statement is in this vein:

Education, instead of merely considering what is to be imparted to children, ought to consider first what they may be said already to possess. If not as a developed, at least as an involved faculty capable of development. Or, if, instead of speaking thus in the abstract, we will but recollect that it is to the great Author of life that man owes the possession, and is responsible for the use, of his innate faculties, education should not only decide what is to be made of a child, but rather inquire, what is a child qualified for . . . what are his faculties as a rational and moral being; what are the means pointed out for their perfection, and the end held out as the highest object of their efforts? They embrace the rightful claims of all classes to a general diffusion of useful knowledge, a careful development of the intellect, and judicious attention to all the faculties of man, physical, intellectual and moral. (Holman, 1908, p. 170)

It was process rather than product that Pestalozzi opted for, in education, as did Rousseau and Comenius before him, and so he stated:

It is a principle of ours that the teacher should aim at increasing the powers of his pupil than at increasing his knowledge. (Green, 1913, pp. 348)

His choice of process training, over imparting content, was in some degree based on his belief that the traditional methods of teaching of his day, and what was taught through them, burdened a pupil's mind with superfluities of information a child could not understand, digest, or act upon; that they created an impression of culture and knowledge, when the true state was ignorance; that, as a consequence of traditional instruction, a pupil's powers failed to develop, victims of disuse or misuse.

Pestalozzi's choice of process over product was also a sequitur of his developmental theory—based on Rousseau's—whose major premise was that proper development of psychological processes should take precedence over the teaching of content and would eventually facilitate learning of the latter. And Pestalozzi was an elementary school pedagogue, whose work encompassed the ages wherein Rousseau had urged almost full attention to the development of processes and the exclusion of formal academic instruction.

If process training it was to be for Pestalozzi, that training was to take place in accordance with the laws of human nature. Nature holds the answers to the development of man's faculties:

> Nature develops all the forces of humanity by exercising them; they increase with use. The exercise of a man's faculty, to be profitable, just follows the course laid down by Nature. . . . (Mayer, 1960, p. 272)

Moreover, a teacher must regard himself as an auxiliary in such exercise:

> Man can, at best, do no more than assist the child's nature in the effort which it makes for its own development: and to do this, so that the impressions made upon the child may always be commensurate, and in harmony, with the measure and character of the powers already unfolded in him is the great secret of education. . . . (Holman, 1908, p. 172)

The phrase "development of the faculties" was to become a byword among Pestalozzi's followers in future years. Another catch phrase was to be the "harmonious development of the faculties." But what did it mean when he said, "Education . . . involves the harmonious balance of all a man's powers, and this involves the natural development of each and all" (Holman, 1908, p. 170)?

Pestalozzi was, in fact, very much a traditional faculty psychologist. He certainly accepted the view that the traditional powers of the mind, were to be developed and exercised; he never fully forsook the doctrines of formal discipline.

Pestalozzi, however, chose to categorize faculties in his own special way as falling under three aspects of man's unitary nature, i.e., "the head, the hand, and the heart."[2] Each develops in its own characteristic

---

[2] Corresponding roughly to Kant's three major categories of faculties.

way and is governed by ascertainable laws (Eby, 1934). It was the task of Pestalozzi guided education to find these laws and guide its practices by them.

While being distinct, the powers of the head, hand, and heart, i.e., the child's intellectual, constructive, executive, and ethical powers, are intended to function together and to be developed in unison. Pestalozzi was emphatic on this issue:

> Only that is truly and naturally educative which appeals to the whole of our being, heart, head, and hand together. . . . To consider any one capacity exclusively is to undermine and destroy man's native equilibrium. (Eby, 1934, p. 444)

Whenever one of these three elements of human nature is overemphasized or neglected, the organism's unity is disrupted, a normal life is no longer possible and the individual's adjustment to society is imperiled.

> Perhaps the most fearful gift that a fiendish spirit has made to this age is *knowledge without power of doing and insight without power of execution or of overcoming* that makes it possible and easy for our life to be in harmony with our inmost nature. Man! needing much, and desiring all, thou must to satisfy thy wants and needs *know* and *think*, but for this thou must also (and can) *do*. Knowing and doing are so closely connected that if one cease the other cease with it. (Pestalozzi, 1894, p. 173)

So Pestalozzi expressed himself (rather inarticulately) concerning the dangers of an inharmonious development of the faculties. The result of a harmonious development is a complete personality, able to live amicably with others and fulfilling his duties to the Supreme Being, as well as making a proper living. That this harmonious development is not all that easy we shall find in our later reading. There is no doubt, however, that the term "harmonious" was a most felicitous one, to be repeatedly used by later process trainers in warning their less cautious colleagues against overtraining specific faculties.

The education that Pestalozzi recommended to assure harmonious development of the faculties (according to his nature-determined developmental model) used botanical metaphors of human development, which were juicily capitalized on later by Froebel. Man and his powers grow in ways like unto a tree. Education is to stimulate and foster their growth, rather than attempt to control them.

In his first writing, *The Evening Hour of a Hermit,* Pestalozzi constantly returned to the analogy of a child's development as corresponding to a plant's natural growth. For example

> Sound education stands before me symbolized by a tree planted near fertilizing waters. A little seed, which contains the design of the tree, its form and proportions, is placed into the soil. See how it germinates and expands into trunk, branches, leaves, flowers, and fruit. The whole tree is an uninterrupted chain of

organic parts, the plan of which existed in its seed and root. Man is similar to the tree. In the new-born child are hidden those faculties which are to unfold during life. The individual and separate organs of his being form themselves gradually into unison, and build up humanity in the image of God. (Graves, 1913, p. 137)

For a child's instructional activities, botanical metaphors were again used:

It is like the art of the gardener under whose care a thousand trees blossom and grow. He contributes nothing to their actual growth; the principle of growth lies in the trees themselves. He plants and waters, but God gives the increase . . . so with the educator: he imparts no single power to men. He only watches lest any external force should injure or disturb. He takes care that development runs its course in accordance with its own law. (Green, 1912, p. 195)

From the first of our botanical quotes, we learn that Pestalozzi did not adapt a saltatory position concerning the development of human processes. There are, it is true, stages of development, but the individual moves from one stage to another slowly and gradually, almost impercep- tibly. His teacher is to be guided by the principle, Pestalozzi admonished:

[That] the knowledge to which the child is to be led by instruction must . . . be subjected to a certain order of succession, the beginning of which is adapted to his first unfolding of his powers, and the development kept exactly parallel to that of his development. (Graves, 1913, p. 137)

It is partly a matter of readiness, something Rousseau had also cautioned about. Pestallozi believed that attempts to force progress can be injurious, may disrupt the harmonious development of the faculties, and cause irreversible damage to a growing child. Hence, just as the gardener should attend the slowly emerging growth of the tree or plant, so should a teacher grade his student's work ". . . according to the degree of the growing power of the child" (Eby, 1934, p. 447).

Try to make in every act, graduated steps of knowedge, in which each new idea is only a small, scarcely perceptible addition to that which is already known. . . . Everything which the child has to learn must be proportioned to his strength, getting more complicated and difficult in the same degree as his powers of attention, of judgment and thought increase. (Green, 1912, pp. 174–175)

Such gradation is a matter of mastery. Each step depends on the one before and must be perfectly acquired before the pupil proceeds. Accu- rate assessment is needed to determine when the pupil has mastered a step and when he is ready to proceed to the next one, to proceed from the simple to the complex. Pestalozzi had developed a system of management by objectives. Well, perhaps he did not quite go that far in his "physico- mechanical" (the words are his) instructional system, but almost.

From the second of our botanical quotes above, we derive a picture of instructor passivity that does not match the pictures we have obtained concerning Pestalozzi's teaching activities. By personality makeup alone, he does not appear to have been able to let nature take its course, despite his recommendations along these lines. From the standpoint of the student population that he and his early followers worked with, it does not appear that he would have been allowed to assume a caretaker–gardener role. He was dealing with the culturally deprived, the delinquent, the emotionally disturbed, and the retarded—under less than optimal conditions. Theory was one thing, practice another. And we have enough examples of what he did to indicate to us that his human botany specimens had their growth urged along—with the laws of nature observed perhaps, but with active assists along the way.

Pestalozzi spoke both of mechanizing education and of psychologizing it. The mechanization aspects appear to be reflected in the Pestalozzian method of analyzing each subject into its ABCs or simplest elements, and moving through those subjects in a systematic fashion, which would eventually, Pestalozzi felt, reduce the expense of instruction to a tenth of its traditional cost. He was, remember, an elementary school educator, and management by objectives has always been easiest, at least in appearance, at the lower levels of educational accession.

The psychologizing aspects of Pestalozzi's system appear in his commitment to the training of the pupil in accordance with the laws of human development, his giving process (faculty) training priority over subject matter, his individualizing instruction according to the level and state of the pupil's powers (at least, theoretically), his training of the pupil by and through his senses. Not very different from the methods of Rousseau and Comenius, this teaching through the senses, say you? In fact, Pestalozzi's method was considerably different from those of his predecessors. He was the first of the true perceptual trainers. (There are some qualifications that will be apparent concerning this statement as we proceed to further explore its implications, but I believe it will be borne out by our further examination of his work.)

Pestalozzi, like so many before him, called attention to the role of sense learning in human knowledge and made it the keystone of instruction. He did so from the nature standpoint that was his heritage from Rousseau.

Sense impression of Nature is the only foundation of human instruction, because it is the only true foundation of human knowledge. (Pestalozzi, 1894, p. 200)

Very well and good so far, but it is essentially what Rousseau had said. And yet Pestalozzi was prompted, in summarizing his achievements, to declare:

When I now look back and ask myself: What have I specially done for the very being of education? I find I have fixed the highest, supreme principle of instruction in the recognition of *sense–impression as the absolute foundation of all knowledge*. (Pestalozzi, 1894, p. 139)

And, despite the fact that the doctrine of sense–impression was commonplace when he wrote, the educational world was to essentially agree with his self-encomium of the above statement. Why? Because Pestalozzi was the first to recommend the systematic training of the senses. Locke and most of the empiricists had seen the mind as being a receptive vessel to be filled by sensory information. Comenius and Basedow had used objects, largely pictures, to assist pupils in learning their academics. Rousseau had seen the child as naturally responding to the world about him and learning from his encounters with it, with a minimum of instructional guidance, until the time for formal academic instruction was reached. Besides, Rousseau's motor orientation to learning was too strong for him to let the senses—as senses—predominate in instruction.

Pestalozzi went beyond them all: first, in insisting that perceptual experiences were to be first and foremost in all instruction; second, in conceiving of sense experience as an active process of the mind in which the child begins to discriminate, analyze, and abstract the qualities of objects; and finally, in the systematic program of perceptual training in which he engaged his students within all areas of cognitive acquisition. Herbart was to say of the Pestalozzian method:

Its peculiar merit consists in having laid hold more boldly and more zealously than any former method of the duty of building up the child's mind, of constructing in it a definite experience in the light of clear sense–perception, not acting as if the child had already an experience but taking care that he gets one. . . . (Herbart 1903, p. 61)

In this development of perceptual training theory, that of *Anschauung,* Pestalozzi proceeded on the basis of his actual instructional experiences on the firing line of instruction, as befits a practicing pedagogue. His teaching of children and his writings on how children should be taught grew out of his constant concern that they learn directly from objects.

In one of his earlier books, *Leonard and Gertrude* (1781), he extolled the role of the family in training their children on the basis of what later came to be known in the period of Pestalozzianism following his death as "object lessons":

The instruction (Gertrude) gave them in the rudiments of arithmetic was intimately connected with the realities of life. She taught them to count the number of steps from one end of the room to the other; and two of the rows of five panes each in one of the windows gave her an opportunity to unfold the decimal relations of numbers. She also made them count their threads while spinning, and the number of turns on the reel, when they wound the yarn into skeins. Above all, in every occupation of life she taught them an accurate and intelligent observation of common objects and the forces of nature. (Pestalozzi, 1906, p. 130)

Pestalozzi's insistence upon the primacy of sense–impression is even more clearly manifested in what he intended as a language lesson. One of his pupils reported on the experience:

The language exercises were the best thing we had, especially those on the wall-paper of the schoolroom, which were real practice in sense impression. We spent hours before this old and torn paper, occupied in examining the number, form, position, and color of the different designs, holes, and rents, and expressing our ideas in more and more enlarged sentences. Thus he would ask: "Boys, what do you see? . . ."
Answer: A hole in the paper.
Pestalozzi: Very well, say after me:
I see a hole in the paper.
I see a long hole in the paper.
Through the hole I see the wall.
Through the long narrow hole I see the wall.
I see figures on the paper.
I see black figures on the paper.
I see round black figures on the paper.
I see a square yellow figure on the paper.
By the side of the square yellow figure I see a round black one.
The square figure is joined to the round figure by a large black stripe, etc.
(DeGuimps, 1901, p. 181)

The unsettled nature of the times and the unstable nature of Pestalozzi's personality were such as to require his moving from educational facility to facility several times.[3] However, his educational concepts, such as those revealed in the preceding passages, kept systematically evolving the while. Pestalozzi, describing his own efforts, wrote that he:

. . . sought by every means to bring the elements of reading and arithmetic to the greatest simplicity, and by grouping them psychologically, enable the child to pass easily and surely from the first step to the second and from the second to the third, and so on. (Graves, 1912, p. 131)

Among his "sense" innovations was the invention of large movable

---

[3] A writer who documented his career wrote of Pestalozzi: ". . . he had everything against him; thick indistinct speech, bad writing, ignorance of drawing, scorn of grammatical learning . . . (Graves, 1912, p. 130).

letters for teaching children to read. He developed a "table of units," devising boards that were divided into squares upon which dots or lines were placed which concretely represented each unit up to a hundred; by this means he sought to give his pupils a concrete understanding of the meaning of digits. To even further concretize their experience of numerosity, Pestalozzi had his pupils count their fingers, beans, pebbles, and other objects. These were major steps forward for his day in the teaching of arithmetic. Geometry, he taught through the drawing of angles, lines, curves, etc. Out of such experiences, the Pestalozzian theory of *Anschauung* was formulated.

Immanuel Kant, in his *Critique of Pure Reason* had earlier formulated a theory of *Anschauung*.[4] Kant had written:

> All thought . . . must directly or indirectly go back to *Anschauungen*. . . . Whatever the process and the means may be by which knowledge refers to its objects, there is one that refers to them directly, and forms the ultimate material of all thought, namely *die Anschauungen*. (Rusk, 1969, p. 215)

Pestalozzi's theory of *Anschauung* was influenced by those of Kant—apparently, however, in indirect form, which may account for his own version, idiosyncratic, easily misunderstood, and often misinterpreted.

Pestalozzi's *Anschauung* has been described as a "multifunctional" term, while at the same time conceived as a "unitary operational process" (Gutek, 1968). He saw it as the source of all human cognition. It appears to have been understood by him as both a transactional process—with the environment—through which the mind employed its various faculties in order to extract meaning from and assign meaning to objects, situations, and events, and at the same time as a power in its own right. He believed that his discovery of the *Anschauung* principle was his greatest contribution to educational theory. As stated earlier, it was to be a source of much confusion as to what was intended by it, thanks in a great measure to his own uncertain exposition on the subject.

Curtis and Boutwood (1953, pp. 340–341) discuss *Anschauung* as the fundamental processes of the mind in all and any stages of concept formation:

> Sometimes it is the process of reception by the mind of a sense–impression and the resultant production of an idea—an idea of softness, of prickliness, of warmth, of dullness—independent of a knowledge of the appropriate word used to describe it. Sometimes it is the process of idea-formation through a combination of sense–impression and observation—the latter term implying intellectual aware-

---

[4] A term that does not have any precise English equivalent but which generally implies a perceptual awareness of objects and situations.

ness or attention. Sometimes it is the immediate mental realization of an idea without the intervention of external things. These three versions of *Anschauung* explain its translation as "sense–impression" or "observation" or "intuition."

The preceding quotation suggests that Pestalozzi saw the formation of thought as proceeding through three basic phases, i.e., of sensation, perception, and cognition. The mind first receives the chaotic and confused qualities of objects. Through the process of *Anschauung* it recognizes the forms underlying the superficial sense data and accordingly organizes those data into informational structures of a perceptual nature. From perception, the mind proceeds to validation, which results in the formation of accurate concepts (Gutek, 1969).

Pestalozzi's process of *Anschauung* requires the operation of a host of mental faculties such as memory, imagination, thought, understanding, judgment, and reasoning. His "perceptual" theories differed sharply from those of the empiricists. Pestalozzian faculties are innate properties and principles of the mind, not mere products of sensory experience as Hume and Hartley, for example, would have proposed.[5]

The art of sense–impression (as the training of *Anschauung* was often referred to, making clear its perceptual nature) is procedurally quite rigid and requires lessons specifically created for its purposes. The pupil is first to be exposed to objects that possess the most essential characteristic of the classes of which they were members. This is to establish the primacy of the objects' essential natures as opposed to their accidental properties, so that the latter can be properly subordinated to the former. To proceed therefrom to clear conceptualizations, three operations have to be carried out by the pupil: (1) The pupil must recognize the number of objects; (2) he must recognize their forms or structures; (3) he must identify the objects through speech. Thus the famous Pestalozzian object lesson which was based on the teaching of number, form, and language. Pestalozzi enunciated it all rather nicely:

> When a confused conglomeration of objects is brought before our eyes, and we wish to dissect it and gradually make it clear to ourselves, we have to consider three things: (1) how many things and how many kinds there are before our eyes, i.e., their number; (2) what they are like, i.e., their form; (3) what they are called, i.e., their names. (Power, 1962, p. 492)

This is the process he saw a cultivated man going through to make things clear to himself. Consequently, instruction of children should proceed along the same lines:

> . . . thought, number, form and language are, together, the elementary

---

[5] Condillac, though an empiricist, came close to Pestalozzi's notions. We shall examine his concepts further in our discussion on Itard.

means of instruction, because the whole sum of the external properties of any object is comprised in its outline and its number, and is brought home to my consciousness through language. It must then be an immutable law of the technique of instruction to start from and work within this threefold principle:

(i)   To teach children to look upon every object that is brought before them as a unit, that is, as separated from those with which it is connected.

(ii) To teach them the form of every object, that is, its size and proportions.

(iii) As soon as possible to make them acquainted with all the words and names descriptive of objects known to them.

And as the instruction of children should proceed from these three elementary points, it is evident that the first efforts of the technique of instruction should be directed to the primary faculties of counting, measuring, and speaking, which lie at the basis of all accurate knowledge of objects of sense. We should cultivate them with strictest psychological technique of instruction, endeavor to strengthen and make them strong and to bring them, as a means of development of simplicity, consistency and harmony. (Pestalozzi, 1894, pp. 86-88)

It is obvious by now that Pestalozzi's sensory–impression theories and procedures are rather different from those which usually come to mind when we think of "perception," and yet, they have many of the characteristics that characterize current perceptual thinking. Perception is developmental and develops from sensation into concept: It has a number of distinct aspects: It can and should be trained; it is essential that it be trained for proper cognitive learning to take place. The procedures of training (as we shall see) are finite and incremental. Very much within current practice, Pestalozzi even gave form and figure–ground relations (number) priority in visual perception at a time when many theorists assigned primacy to color identification. In his use of language as a process to anchor perception, he anticipated Pavlov and Luria.

It was on the basis of number, form, and language that Pestalozzi sought to create his *Anschauung* curriculum for intellectual development. It included object lessons, always accompanied by language, since perception—even visual perception—and language are mutually dependent. Arithmetic, both written and oral, was deemed important, not only because of its role in *Anschauung* but because it fosters clear and accurate thinking. The development of form was to come through the study of nature, including geography, and also through the study of objects of manufacture and art. More directly related to current interests in perceptual training is the fact that Pestalozzi insisted that form be developed through drawing, interest in colors and modeling, and through exercises in geometry. Language training was to begin with exercises in vocalization and extend upward into written language and content subject areas. Let us examine some aspects of the Pestalozzian curriculum, as they have implications for the training of cognitive processes in greater detail.

We have already reviewed Pestalozzi's methods relative to number. Beyond the mental disciplinary aspects of his work in arithmetic, he brought the teaching of arithmetic down into the first grade; previously children had not been taught arithmetic until they were ten years of age. He made the subject accessible to the young. His principle in teaching arithmetic was:

Arithmetic arises entirely from simply putting together and separating several units. Its basis is essentially this: "One and one is two. One from two leaves one." Any number whatever is only an abbreviation of processes which are fundamental in all numeration. (Boyd and King, 1973)

We have already seen this concretizing of number in our earlier review of Pestalozzi's work and our bucolic quotation from his book *Leonard and Gertrude,* in which the child learns number from the steps he takes, the number of plies in the thread he is weaving, etc.

Pestalozzi's fundamental contention in respect to teaching arithmetic was that the mental processes involved are more important than the actual content, an emphasis consistent with his general position. By this he intended both the special mental operations involved in working out particular arithmetic problems and the general mental processes that he was also insistent on training, e.g., of judgment and reasoning. To eliminate the old emphasis on "ciphering" according to rule, he had all written arithmetic postponed until a child had achieved considerable understanding of arithmetical processes. With Pestalozzi originated what was called "mental" or "intellectual"—what we now know as oral—arithmetic. In keeping with the *Anschauung* principle, early Pestalozzian arithmetic training also emphasized form, so that elementary number combinations could be learned through arranging, grouping, and the use of charts and concrete objects, instead of commitment to memory as was traditional. Further in keeping with the *Anschauung* principle was the Pestalozzian emphasis on incidental language during number work, the pupil being requested by the instructor to elaborate on various number arrangements. For example, the teacher would arrange some beans on his desk while the children looked away—I present a brief quote from an interminable exchange:

What change do you see in the position of the beans?
They are further apart.
Is there any change in the number?
There are eight beans as before.
What other change do you see?
They lie in a crooked row.
Any other change?
The beans are on the right side. (DeGuimps, 1901, p. 181)

And so on. It is obvious why his method was criticized as being too much language and not enough arithmetic, but it was consistent, as we know, with his principles.

The teaching of form, the second of the *Anschauung* three Rs, led Pestalozzi to give drawing an important place in the curriculum. He was the first in modern times to establish it as a regular part of the elementary curriculum. Pestalozzi saw drawing as being intimately connected with the perception of form and as training a child in accuracy of observation, thus laying the foundation for clearness and precision in thought. He, alas, was a rather poor draftsman himself and had to rely upon an assistant to create the actual lesson plans for drawing. However, his enthusiasm over the potential of drawing was very much in the current perceptual training mode. Pestalozzi was convinced that:

> . . . by exercises in lines, angles and curves, a readiness in gaining sense impressions of all kinds is produced in children, as well as skill of hand, of which the effect will be to make everything that comes within the sphere of their observation gradually clear and plain. (Pestalozzi, 1894, p. 51)

This "alphabet of form," as he called it, was recommended by Pestalozzi as the first step in elementary instruction. He was the progenitor of all those tedious drudging exercises that have rolled off countless ditto and duplicating machines these many years in the name of perceptual training. Rousseau had also recommended drawing as a means of developing eye and hand coordination. But his was the graphics of what was real. Pestalozzi's approach was the reduction of drawing to what has been called Pestalozzian formalism. (Parker, 1912)

This formalism saw a series of consecutive exercises devised by Buss, one of Pestalozzi's assistants, on the premise of developing basic elements in visual perception that could be built into wholes through interminable repetitions. Objects such as sticks or pencils were placed in different directions and the lines representing them had then to be drawn; such exercises were elaborated upon until all "elementary" forms, straight or curved, were mastered. These forms were then combined. It was a pedagogy of lines, angles, and curves, moving upward and onward into higher complexities that led, expectedly, to mastery of form. Models from life were eschewed. Pestalozzi was sensitive to possible criticisms of this syllabus of form on grounds of its artificiality, and he protested against those who thought he was concentrating too much on the means of his training to the devastation of the intended aims of his training, saying:

> Nature gives the child no lines, she only gives him things, and lines must be given him only in order that he may perceive things rightly. The things must not be taken from him in order that he may see only lines. (Holland, 1894, p. 69)

He also angrily responded to criticism regarding the danger of rejecting nature for the sake of his technology of reductionism:

God forbid that I should overwhelm the human mind and harden it against natural sense–impressions, for the sake of these lines and of the technique of instruction, as idolatrous priests have overwhelmed it with superstitious teaching, and hardened it against natural sense–impressions. (Holland, 1894, p. 69)

But he did, or at least his followers did. N. A. Calkin's *Primary Object Lessons* (1861), one of the best of the object lesson books of the Pestalozzian movement in the United States, had the elements of form occupy some 60 pages of her treatise. There was instruction on every geometric form possible, including the square, rhomb, parallelogram, pyramid, prism, cube, cone, sphere, cylinder.

Pestalozzi regarded drawing as an essential precursor to handwriting, saying, ". . . to teach writing, I found I must begin by teaching drawing" (Graves, 1912, p. 141). Writing was thus deferred until the pupil knew how to draw at least up to the level of initial mastery. The subsequent teaching of handwriting was then divided into two stages: In the first, the child became cognizant of the various letter shapes and letter combinations prior to writing them with a pen. He studied the letter forms and practiced them on a slate, proceeding from simpler to more complex forms and then to combinations of several letters, finally progressing to the writing of words. Only after he was able to write letters perfectly upon his slate did the pupil proceed to exercises with a pen. Writing lessons were later integrated with reading and grammar exercises, serving to reinforce them.

Such practice in writing seems commonplace to us now. It is important to recognize that it was, from Pestalozzi's standpoint and time in history, regarded by him as a revolutionary step representing the application of perceptual principles, as indeed it was. His use of handwriting to reinforce reading was, it should be observed, anticipatory of Montessori's approach to reading (Gutek, 1968).

Constructive geometry was also taught by Pestalozzi on a perceptual basis. It was in considerable part taught, like handwriting, through drawing. Pestalozzi's pupils learned to distinguish every possible position of line (and to identify them by name), proceeding from vertical to horizontal, on to oblique and then to parallel lines, the various types of angles, etc. To make geometry even more concrete Pestalozzi had his pupils cut out figures from cardboard and make geometric models. Thus the association of geometry with drawing that we see in Calkin's primary books on object lessons.

With Pestalozzi, we see language clearly treated as a process in its own right—or, perhaps more appropriately, a series of processes, becoming ever more complex and intertwined with perceptual processes. Believing, like Rousseau, that man recapitulates the history of race, Pestalozzi established language as the first means of gaining knowledge after the perceptual grasp of things was established. Oral language was particularly important—indeed, Pestalozzi insisted that his pupils master it prior to learning to read, which was an innovation for his time. Pestalozzi saw oral language, through the "power of sound" (Gutek, 1968), as being the means through which confused sense impressions become clear and as a way of making them lasting and communicable by anchoring them to words. The extremely complex roles played by language in learning were thus understood by Pestalozzi in a way that is distinctly modern, despite all the errors of his conceptualization of them and their often faulty applications within instruction.

The "perceptual" aspect of language,[6] one of his trio in *Anschauung*, is clearly manifested in one of his statements on the matter:

> The speech of my race was long only a power of mimicry and of making sounds that imitated the tones of living and lifeless nature. From mimicry and sound-making they came to hieroglyphics and separate words, and for long they gave special objects special names.
>
> From this point speech gradually went further. Men first observed the striking differences in the objects they named. Then they came to name properties; and then to name the differences in the actions and forces of objects. Much later the art developed of making single words mean much, unity, plurality, size, many or few, form and number, and at last to express clearly all variations and properties of an object, which were produced by changes of time and place, by modifying the form and by joining words together. (Pestalozzi, 1894, p. 150)

Given as he was to dividing his processes into their basic elements, Pestalozzi approached language instruction (including reading and written language) in three graduated phases. First, there was sound teaching, in which the pupil's speech organs were to be developed and trained. This was followed by instruction in words, through which the child learned to identify single objects by their names. Then came language teaching, in which the pupil learned to accurately describe and discuss the objects he had experienced. There are more than several language training programs currently promoted within general and special education that have their parentage clearly visible in Pestalozzi's work, even though it is unacknowledged. Let us look at these three phases of his process training in these three spheres more closely.

During the first phase of language instruction, Pestalozzi sought to teach sounds via spoken and sung avenues. He emphasized the importance of having the pupil exposed to spoken language as early as possible. Formal instruction in sounds was to begin with vowels and proceed to consonants, one after another alphabetically. These were to be committed irrevocably to memory by repetition. Simple sounds such as ma, ma, da,

---

[6] As well as his recapitulation theory of language.

da, la, la developed auditory acuity. Sung sounds served to sophisticate language processes, as well as to prepare the pupil to sing songs.

Pestalozzi initially approached reading through syllabaries. These joined the five vowels, in succession, to the different consonants, "ab, eb, ib, ob, ub," and so on, all through the consonants. He also constructed long lists of nonsense syllables that the pupils were required to repeat until mastered, to make them comfortable with the sounds of words. For Pestalozzi, moving from the simple to the complex in reading meant moving from mastery of letters to that of syllables, words, phrases, and, finally, sentences. The meaning of it all was quite neglected by this approach despite his stated goal of making learning meaningful.

Proceeding into the second phase of language training, Pestalozzi's instructional manual still observed the principles of moving from the sensory into the conceptual and from the simple through to the complex. The pupil, now that his speech organs had physiologically matured and his auditory perception had been prepared through sound exercises, was supposed to be ready to learn words as symbols of objects. Having become conscious of the perceptual qualities of objects, he was also expected to feel the need to name them. The names of objects, in addition to being learned to facilitate language development, served the additional purpose of facilitating the perception of these objects, i.e., by enriching them with meaning and helping in their classification, e.g., according to genus and species. It was on this latter basis that Pestalozzi expected his pupils to commit long lists of names from all divisions of nature and human intercourse to memory, i.e., of important objects found in nature, history, geography, occupations, and social relations. Quite in disregard, this all was, of his own sense–perception principles, i.e., since the pupils were not actually being exposed to the things and situations these names designated. Pestalozzi justified this practice on the basis that it would facilitate later perception and understanding and, to boot, improve oral and written instruction. He was, however, really preaching the old memoriter principles that he himself decried in his theories of instruction.

The third phase of Pestalozzian language training, that of instruction in language usage, combined both the sound and name stages of early instruction in still more complex types of operation. Remember, language, as Pestalozzi viewed it, has a major perceptual responsibility. It assists in transforming obscure, unclear sense impressions into clear, meaningful concepts. The methodology of this later stage of Pestalozzian language lessons is roughly as follows: There was to be recognition of a specific object as separate and distinct from others and its identification by a particular name. Following this, there was to be gradual learning of the object's essential characteristics and the names of these characteristics. Then the pupil was to be required to develop skill in defining these characteristics by the use of verbs and adverbs. He was further to learn how to verbally distinguish the basic characteristics of the objects from those that were situationally or accidentally present in or about them, and then to distinguish their essential qualities from adventitious ones. There is an intimate relationship between language and perception in Pestalozzian theory.

Pestalozzi's methods of employing language to clarify perception have already been illustrated in our earlier quotation concerning his wallpaper language lesson. They were to be broadly and persistently applied by him to acquaint his pupils with the whole of man's experiences. For language, to Pestalozzi, encompassed natural science, history, geography, etc.

I believe that our review has been comprehensive enough for the reader to grasp the basic principles of Pestalozzi's cognitive training programs. What then of the hand and the heart that were to be trained in conjunction with the head?

As to the first, it is important to note that Pestalozzi contributed much to the principles of industrial education and that he was a firm believer in physical education. By the hand, he meant more than fine motor coordination, which was dealt with in his drawing and geometric exercises—and handwriting too—all "head" activities. He was looking beyond these in his intended hand training program to the achievement of what he called *Fertigkeit,* which means skill or capacity for production. *Fertigkeit* meant for Pestalozzi the achievement of practical power by an individual, which would enable him to master the ordinary activities of living. Pestalozzi's pupils were the poor of the land. They had to learn to express themselves, to develop themselves through means of physical expression; and to support themselves—again—by physical means.

Pestalozzi had hoped to create an appropriate curriculum to develop this broad power and the faculties associated with it. Alas, he did not get very far. He admitted his inability to develop an ABC of skill for it in any comprehensive form. But he did have some suggestions as to how the training might at least commence and to what it might lead.

Such training is to begin, he said, perhaps within the child's home itself, with the expression of the simplest of physical powers, elements which, combined, make up the most complicated practical expressions of man. These elements include striking, carrying, swinging, throwing, drawing, turning, etc. Graduated exercises are to achieve mastery in their use and to then lead to graduated mastery of broader movements. The broader movements, in time, are to be merged into practical applied activities that will result in physical mastery of the environment. It would remain, however, for his followers to develop this aspect of his educational program. Pestalozzi, himself, was not up to its completion.

As to his training of the heart, which he described as the "keystone of my whole system" (Eby, 1934), it was a matter of moral-religious education, which is not a keystone of our treatise.

Have I made too much of Pestalozzi, devoted too much space to him? I think not, for his place in process training has been generally overlooked. Much of what the process-obsessed educational psychology and educational texts of the later nineteenth century and the early twentieth century expressed was an extension of his philosophies. That it was process rather than product that he was concerned with is attested to by a report of the Board of Education of Oswego County, New York, who in reviewing Pestalozzian practices, so popular for a while in the United States, praised his approach thusly:

> He sought to develop and strengthen the faculties of the child. He wished that the art of observing should be acquired. He thought the thing perceived of less importance than the cultivation of the perceptive powers. (Parker, 1912, p. 278)

"As a consequence . . . " remarked this Samuel Chester Parker, ". . . was established the dreary grind of sense training" (Parker, 1912). There is no mention in Parker's book *The History of Modern Elementary Education* of Itard, Séguin, Binet, or, for that matter, of Montessori either, for general education took its leads in sense–perception from Pestalozzi rather than from these aforementioned worthies. Sense perception and perceptual training were as popular within general education for a good time, thanks to Pestalozzi and his disciples, as they are now within special education.

Should opinions be ventured concerning the value of Pestalozzi's philosophies or methods? I have made some in passing. Perhaps a few reiterations and additional comments are due. The perceptualization of learning that he is responsible for stands now, in retrospect, as anticipating the present, as it was a reaction in his time against the past. Perception is inextricably involved in all our experiences, all our learning. Surely, he made that point better than anyone else prior to his day. That language is an inextricable part of our thought processes and is in its own right perceptual is another modernity for which we are indebted to Pestalozzi. That there is internal structure as well as perceptual flow in our cognition is not his, but he said it again so well.

Pestalozzi also stands forth clearly as a preeminent among those who early sought to make instruction scientific, providing harbingers of instructional objectives and management of instruction by them—along with a flawed confusion of instructional procedures with developmental processes—just like today! He deduced the way children learned, not from his observations but from his theoretical predilections. Thus he taught children not according to their psychological sequences but according to his hypothetical deductive theorems. How utterly dreary his work sounds at times, and how familiar, too, in our age when so many instructional manuals, based presumably on the fundamentals of human development, are generated instead on the basis of a priori supposition. At least Pestalozzi developed his ideas on the basis of personal experiences with children.

Faculty psychologist though he was, Pestalozzi cannot be blamed for being a man of his times, and so we can forgive his attempts to train memory and the other faculties. Less forgivable are the attempts he made to systematize *Anschauung* in a way that would eventually lead to the formalization of perceptual training through ritualized exercises of the sort that are so commonplace today. One shudders to think what he might have done had he had access to high speed mimeograph or ditto facilities. Certainly a graded training series on wallpaper (and accompanying holes) discrimination would have been forthcoming.

But let us recognize at the same time Pestalozzi's awareness of the need for methodical, precise instruction for the cognitively less able (for that is with whom he by and large worked). His attempt to train processes developmentally, his recognition of the importance of auditory training, and all those other innovations of his, stripped of their antiquarian elements, lead us very much into our own modern day of special education.

FROEBEL

There were many Pestalozzians to follow in the master's footsteps. Herbart and Froebel (1782–1852) were the most famous of these. Herbart's path was to eventuate in an antifaculty, antiprocess training position. The path trod upon by Froebel is one that extended Pestalozzi's vision. Froebel, among other things, was to take Pestalozzi's conception of a curriculum for the hand and make it into an instructional reality. However, while Froebel's work was in many respects an extension of Pestalozzi's work, it also expressed influences from a variety of other sources that require examination if we are to fully understand its implications for process training. Froebel's educational principles and instructional methodologies cannot be understood without an understanding of the philosophical atmosphere and influences of his times.

Friedrich Froebel, for one thing, had come under the sway of the philosophical idealism that had been initiated by Kant and extended by the writings of such German philosophers as Fichte, Schelling, Hegel, and Krause. It was not necessarily through formal study of their work that he had come to know of their ideas. "The intercourse of university life" at the University of Jena, which he attended, was largely responsible and, as he later wrote in his autobiography, provided him with ". . . a many-sided intellectual impulse."

Kant had raised a philosophical problem, the resolution of which was to be critical to Froebel's conceptualization of the educational process. It was a distinction between phenomenal and noumenal worlds. The phenomenal world is the world of space, time, substance, cause, etc. It is a world that operates according to the laws of science. The noumenal world implies forms of experience other than those of the phenomenal, material one. It is a sphere of existence within which such principles as the existence of God, the immortality and freedom of the human soul, morality, etc., achieve validity. Attempts to apply the rules of one world to the other result in antinomies, conclusions that conflict despite their being based on apparently logical deductions (Rusk, 1969). For Kant, the resolution of antinomies was in the separation of the two worlds. Man's phenomenal existence is governed by the conception of cause; his noumenal existence is an ethical one characterized by freedom of choice.

Kant's dualism was not altogether satisfactory and his successors set about to resolve it, one way or the other. Various naturalistic and realistic interpreters of Kantian doctrine emphasized the verities of the phenomenal world and sought to reduce the principles and events of the noumenal world to the status of fictions. Others, such as the German philosopher Fichte, proceeded in the other direction, emphasizing the reality of the noumenal world to the point that the phenomenal one was reduced to the status of mere appearance or illusion.

The German philosopher Schelling offered a compromise solution: His theory of transcendental idealism reconciled the two worlds created by Kant by insisting on their essential unity. According to Schelling the Absolute manifests itself equally in nature and in spirit. Intelligence can be found in both. There can be no doubt that Schelling's writings strongly influenced Froebel's thinking. In his autobiography, Froebel acknowledged his indebtedness to the philosopher who, he observed

> . . . seeks . . . a principle which shall reduce the whole of nature to unity. This principle must not be sought in any transcendental, supernatural region . . . but in nature itself . . . in a conception of matter as a unity of opposing forces . . . the single principle of a force that always manifests itself in opposite directions. Accordingly nature must no longer be divided up into separate groups of phenomena, with a special force for each . . . but in all must be seen the same force in various forms, the same unity in duality . . . practically identical with the idea of nature as an external process or manifestation of self-activity. (Froebel, 1886, p. 40)

What relation does this have with processes? A great deal,

because Froebel's theories of process training were based upon such theories as those of Schelling. Belief in the unity of nature resulted in Froebel's conceiving of cognitive training as proceeding through physical as well as intellectual means. It also resulted in his conceiving of the simplest of labors as manifestations of the highest of cognitive powers and as ways to train higher cognitive processes. Belief in the principle of self-activity, one governing in and at all levels of nature, was to become a keystone of Froebel's educational theories; man is more than a passive register of sensations, he creates from within and molds the environment as well as being molded by it. It is simply impossible to understand Froebel's theories of process training without understanding the philosophies that undergird them.

Hegel was another German philosopher whose thinking strongly influenced Froebel, albeit perhaps indirectly. He came up with a solution to Kant's antinomies that was well suited to the direction which Froebel's thinking was to take him.

Instead of two realms, the natural (phenomenal) and the spiritual (noumenal), as with Kant, there was for Hegel only one form of reality. It was the spiritual, which comprises within it the natural. "The real is the rational . . . " Hegel said and ". . . the rational is the real. . . . The Absolute is Mind . . . and to grasp its meaning and burthen is . . . the ultimate purpose of all education and all philosophy" (Wallace, 1894, p. 11).

Froebel's dedication of his book *The Education of Man* loosely expresses Hegel's Absolute:

> The whole world—the All, the Universe, is a single great organism in which an external uniformity expresses itself as much in external nature as in spirit. Life is the union of the spiritual with the material. . . . Every creature, every object is matter informed by spirit. . . . God is the presupposition, the condition of their existence. (Froebel, 1909, p. 1)

For Hegel, the truth is the whole. Mind or the Absolute cannot be contained within any particular fragmentary form of existence and seeks, instead, to actualize itself by successive stages, according to a definite pattern, a dialectical movement. The impasses that Kant found in attempting to apply the categories from either phenomenal or noumenal worlds to the other (his antinomies) are resolvable. For Hegel saw the conflict of contradictions, the clash of opposites, as characteristics of all thought. "Collisions . . .," he said, "belong to the nature of thought, the nature of consciousness and its dialectic" (Dyde, 1896, p. 211)—thus the Hegelian "law of opposites," in which opposite propositions achieve significance by their resolution within a broader, higher, unity. The triadic structure of Hegel's dialectic is familiar to most of us: thesis, which necessarily calls forth its opposite antithesis, and the reconciliation and resolution of these within the broader, more comprehensive synthesis.[7]

Froebel relied heavily upon this triadic structure, both theoretically and practically. In *The Education of Man*, he stated:

> Everything and every being comes to be known only as it is connected with the opposite of its kind, and as its unity, its agreement with its opposite, is discovered. (Froebel, 1909, p. 42)

Thus a child is a child of nature (thesis); it is also a human child (antithesis); but then (synthesis) a child of God. The contradiction manifest between religion and practical efficiency is resolved in morality. Even in selecting manipulatives, the dialectic triad is to be observed:

> The sphere and the cube are pure opposites. They stand to each other in the relation of unity and plurality, but especially of movement and rest, of round and straight. The law of connection demands for these two objects of play a connecting one, which is the cylinder. It combines unity complete in itself in the round surface, and plurality in the two straight ones. (Froebel, 1905, p. 204)

Another major influence upon Froebel was his lesser-known contemporary K. C. F. Krause, a philosopher with whom Froebel maintained correspondence and whom Froebel regarded as being particularly successful in harmonizing disparate philosophical theories and contemporary scientific knowledge. Krause's philosophy has been described as being one of pantheism (Eby, 1934), for it postulated that everything existed within God. Reason and nature are the "highest hemispheres" of the world. Man is a unity of the two and the most glorious expression of their harmony.

Writing at a time when ideas of evolution were making themselves felt in every intellectual quarter, Krause developed a concept of organismic unity and development called *Gliedganzes* (part-whole).[8] It nicely fit the other philosophical notions we have been talking about and was extremely compatible with the direction in which Froebel's thinking had been taking him. Let us give expression to what *Gliedganzes* was all about.

A finger can be conceived of as a unity, of and by itself; it is, however, part of a hand. A hand is a unity in itself, but is also part of an arm. Everything in the universe has these dual aspects. The universe is a living organism with many diversities which are also parts of a greater whole—God. How well this all fitted in with Froebel's personal biases and theoretical predilections!

---

[7] Also expressed by Fichte and Schelling, though in less compelling terms.
[8] Glied also being interpretable and interpreted as a member of the body.

The evolutionary side of Krause's theories, with which Froebel was in accord, maintained a deistic orientation. Every object, nonliving as well as living, all the events of the world, every facet of human development, was supposed to evolve in keeping with God's purposes. Even the formations of inorganic crystals showed this sort of evolution, an organic development toward higher goals, in keeping with God's purposes.[9]

The principle of organic development was most often expressed by Froebel in botanical metaphors for which he is notorious. He was not original, as we know, in his choice of plants as analogues for humans. Kant had earlier said:

There are many germs lying undeveloped in man. It is for us to make these germs grow, by developing his natural gifts in their due proportions, and to see that he fulfills his destiny. (Monroe, 1905, p. 595)

Pestalozzi, too, had been extremely fond of botanical metaphors; in fact, one can find the latter strewn through psychological, educational, and medical literature back into antiquity. But surely no one prior to Froebel belabored them in the manner of Froebel, who spoke of the child almost literally as a human plant—a human plant created by God, to be tended by family and teachers as an emerging seedling and cultivated until a fully branched, sturdy-trunked specimen evolved.

For Froebel, the growth of man, God's special plant, intended more, however, than just a growth of an infant into a child and then into an adult, with an appropriate burgeoning of powers. That growth was viewed by Froebel as the expression of unseen forces that develop the structures of the plant (botanical or human) out of matter absorbed from nature; forces governed by a special inner law, orderly in nature, evolutionary in principle, and operating in accordance with the Almighty's universal scheme. Let us keep this in mind as we directly examine Froebel's "botany" of human development:

Man, as a child, resembles the flower on the plant, the blossom on the tree, as these are in relation to the tree, so is the child in relation to humanity—a young bud, a fresh blossom, and as such, it bears, includes, and proclaims the ceaseless reappearance of human life.

---

[9] Froebel had studied the formation of crystals at the University of Berlin, under the direction of Professor Christian S. Weiss, whose influence is reflected in Froebel's statement:

What I had recognized in things great or noble, in the life of man and in the ways of God, as serving towards the development of the human race, I found I could here recognize also in the smallest of these fixed forms which nature alone had shaped. . . . And thereafter my rocks and crystals served me as a mirror wherein I might discern mankind, and man's development and history. (Graves, 1912, pp. 198–199)

As the flower bud of the tree—connected with twig, branch, and trunk, with the whole ramification of root and crown, and through this double ramification, with earth and heaven—stands in united coherence and reciprocal exchange with the whole universe for the development and vivification of its being, so stands man also, in all-sided developing life exchange with nature, with humanity, and with all spiritual efforts and influences—with the universal life. (Mayer, 1966, p. 368)

Each individual thing which is attained, however small and simple, or however large and complex it may be, is therefore always a self-contained whole, and so resembles a bud or a kernel of corn, from which manifold new developments can be called forth, which again converge into a higher unity. (Mayer, 1966, p. 376)

All the child is ever to be and become lies, however slightly indicated, in the child, and can be attained only through development from within outward. . . . The tree germ bears within itself the nature of the whole tree . . . the development and formation of the whole future life of each being is contained in the beginning of its existence. (Froebel, 1909, p. 68)

Even God is bound to observe and abide by the rules of man's growth according to botanical ordinations. Froebel conceived of Him as a master gardener:

God never grafts in the world of nature, nor is the soul of man to be grafted. God *develops* the most minute and imperfect elements, through everlasting stages, according to a law eternally founded in itself, and ever unfolding out of its own nature. (Graves, 1912, p. 209)

It is apparent, this time, that Froebel's appellation, kindergarten, was not intended as simply another propagandizing name for early childhood education. He was quite serious in his intentions that children be nurtured and cultivated in accordance with the principles of botanical growth, which he saw as expressing those immutable and inexorable laws that we reviewed earlier. The plant and the human grow from within. They externalize their true natures according to predetermined principles, i.e., they make external what was originally internal. However—as the obverse to this—they also make the external internal in growing. The plant takes in nutrients from the soil and utilizes sunlight and water. The human absorbs sensory information and experiences from his environmental encounters. How nicely it all fits with Froebel's theoretical conception of spiritual and natural worlds being one, despite their apparent contradictions. How nicely it expresses the "law of opposites," with the seeming contradictions of internal and external synthetically reconciled in the unity of the organism. How far a cry it was from the tabula rasa of the empiricists and sensationalists when Froebel proclaimed:

. . . all knowledge and comprehension of life are connected with making the internal external, the external internal, and with perceiving the harmony and accord of both. (Froebel, 1905, p. 174)

We have earlier discussed the influence of German philosophers and of Pestalozzi upon Froebel, all of which are very important indeed. That of still another progenitor must be acknowledged, another very important one indeed, one whose principles Froebel responded to directly, as well as through their influences on others such as Kant and Pestalozzi. It is Jean-Jacques Rousseau of whom we speak. Of Rousseau's importance relative to Froebel's work, Eby has remarked:

The likeness of their principles and methods warrants the conclusion that Froebel was a Teutonic Jean-Jacques. (Eby, 1934, p. 501)

The above statement is perhaps excessive. For Froebel was, as we have seen, influenced by a variety of forces and was, also, very much his own man, his own philosopher, in the long run. Nevertheless, there is much of Rousseau to be found in Froebel, and even Froebel's disagreements with Rousseau are contributory to his (Froebel's) theories. Let us examine several examples of Froebel's agreements and disagreements with Rousseau's tenets. Others will be apparent as we further extend our examination of Froebel's work.

Froebel was in agreement with Rousseau's theories of developmental recapitulation. Like Rousseau, he believed that the life of the individual recapitulates that of the history of man; specifically, the history of the particular race to which the individual belongs. He also agreed that there are distinct stages in human development: infancy, childhood, boyhood, youth, and maturity. Further, he concurred that each of these stages should be comprehensively exploited educationally and that the expectations for successful development at one stage are dependent upon the successful developments of prior ones:

The vigorous and complete development and culture of each successive stage depends on the vigorous, complete and characteristic development of each and all preceding stages. (Froebel, 1892, pp. 28–29)

Each stage is equally important in "its time and place." There is, thus, not to be made any precipitous or accelerated efforts in attempting to further a child's development, training, or education:

. . . this hurrying (from the germ to the fruit, from the wish directly to the fulfillment . . . springing over all the necessary conditions which should be previously fulfilled) has had the saddest and most pernicious results. (Froebel, 1909, p. 10)

So said Froebel, and so far Rousseau. However, the former disagreed with the latter on several points of human development. First, Froebel did not accept Rousseau's so-called saltatory theory of development. He did not believe in stages of development that are sharply distinct one from the other. These are contrary to the particular ways in which the Almighty manages the universe. The laws of the latter govern the unfolding of each organism in a gradual and continuous way that manifest an overriding unity, even in diversity. Froebel was unequivocal on this point:

> It is highly pernicious to consider the stages of human development . . . as really distinct, and not, as life shows them, as continuous in themselves in unbroken transitions . . . The child should be viewed and treated with reference to all stages of development and age, without breaks and omissions. (Graves, 1912, p. 210)

Froebel also disagreed with Rousseau in not allowing distinct and inviolable characteristics for each given stage. He, rather, postulated a central tendency that characterized each stage.[10]

Further in contradiction to Rousseau's tenets, Froebel insisted upon the regulation of human development from without, to a far greater degree than Rousseau admitted as permissible. He did so in part on the basis of his belief that human development is governed by the external laws of nature as well as by inner preordinations. He also believed the first are more critical than the second in respect to directing instruction. Froebel cautioned:

> Instruction is conducted not so much in accordance with the nature of man as in accordance with the fixed, definite, clear *laws* in the nature of things, and more particularly the laws to which man and things are equally subject. It is conducted in accordance with fixed and definite conditions lying outside the human being. (Froebel, 1909, pp. 94, 95)

Froebel was probably just too Germanic, as well, to be philosophically comfortable with the freedom of expression that Rousseau sought for Émile, though "self-expression" (intended here in a permissive sense) in schools was later to be justified in his name.

Perhaps the two most important positive influences Rousseau wielded over Froebel were in respect to self-activity and physical activity.[11] Self-activity and physical activity, of course, are what much of Émile is about—learning by doing, based on the child's own impulses and interests; physical expression as a means of self-development and

---

[10] The education provided a child at each stage was to be generally based on this central tendency.

[11] The German philosophers who influenced Froebel also emphasized what constituted, in one form or another, self-activity; in part because of Rousseau's influences upon them. Froebel's work was also influenced by the educational writings of one Johann H. G. Heusinger whose book, *On the Utilization of the Powerful Impulse in Children to Activity,* put the ideas of Rousseau and Basedow to work. Froebel was well acquainted with Heusinger's writings. (Eby, 1934)

learning. The heart of Froebel's process training conceptions are these two, as we shall see.

We are, at last, ready to proceed to a direct examination of Froebel's process theories and his process training approaches. The two are closely intertwined and require interpretation within the philosophical frameworks we earlier reviewed.

First, Froebel's educational intentions were, above and beyond all else, a matter of process development. Such was a necessary sequitur to the mystical-religious manner in which he approached education.

> The representation of the infinite in the finite, of the eternal in the temporal, of the celestial in the terrestrial, of the divine in and through man, in the life of man by the *nursing* of his originally divine nature, confronts us unmistakably on every side as the only object, the only aim of all education, in all instruction and training. (Froebel, 1909, pp. 4–5)

An insistence upon process is to be found throughout Froebel's educational writings. Even when the requirements of a properly rounded education (according to Froebelian tenets) necessitates a shift in instructional emphasis from process to product, the shift is to be carried out on the premise that the proper expression of product also means that process, too, is served. Even man's attempts to obtain for himself the basics of survival (products) requires their subordination to the spiritual (process) aspects of his life.

> The debasing illusion that man works, produces, creates in order to preserve his body, in order to secure food, clothing, shelter, may have to be endured, but should not be diffused and propagated. Primarily and in truth man works only that his spiritual, divine essence may assume outward form, and thus he may be enabled to recognize his own spiritual divine nature and the innermost being of God. Whatever food, clothing, and shelter he obtains thereby comes to him as an insignificant surplus. (Froebel, 1909, p. 16)

That principle of unity, which was so important to Froebel, governed his conception of the interrelatedness of the organism's faculties and their functions within the human manifold. True, there are diverse bodily organs, senses, and faculties. But the nature of their functioning must be interpreted in terms of the unity of the organism of which they are parts. The faculties of the human spirit—perception, memory, reasoning, feeling, will etc.—all participate with each other in human activity and with and through the senses, muscles, and nervous system of the physical organism.

> That he may fulfill and attain his destiny, man is endowed on the one hand with senses, the organs by which he can make the external internal; on the other hand with bodily strength and limbs by which he can represent his inner nature outwardly, therefore always by material means; finally that he may comprehend spiritual unity, the nature of man appears as an anticipating and individual soul,

because this nature is in itself a perceptive and uniting spirit. (Graves, 1912, p. 210)

It was because of his conception of the oneness of organism and organismic experience that Froebel came to postulate sensory-motor activity, play, and other expressive activities, as so important to psychological development.

The spiritual and the physical (the noumenal and phenomenal) were, for Froebel, simply aspects of the basic unity that is man, and from this followed his thesis that the training of the senses and the body is entirely compatible with the intentions of psychological or spiritual (process) training. For the latter is a matter both of externalizing the internal (the spiritual) through physical expression, and internalizing the external (the physical) through the senses:

> The inner essence of things is recognized by the innermost spirit of man through outer manifestations, and all education, all instruction, start from the outer manifestations of man and things, and proceeding from the outer, act upon the inner, and form its judgments concerning the inner. (Graves, 1912, p. 209)[12]

Froebel was somewhat contradictory concerning the instructor's role in training and education. Like Rousseau and in accordance with his own view of human development as an unfolding of human potential, he adhered to the principle of the instructor being a guardian of human growth rather than its active promoter. Thus the statement:

> The purpose of teaching and instruction is to bring more *out* of man rather than to put more and more *into* man. . . . All he is ever to be and become, lies in the child. . . . (Froebel, 1909, pp. 20, 61)

This particular position is based on the premise that human nature is inherently good and that under perfect conditions man develops ". . . from within, self-active and free." It leads to the recommendation of a "hands-off" policy for the instructor over much of a child's formative years, as Rousseau had also advised. Thus Froebel made diagnostic but nonprescriptive recommendations:

> Therefore, education in instruction and training, originally and in its first principles, should necessarily be *passive, following* (only guarding and protecting), not *prescriptive, categorical, interfering.* (Froebel, 1909, p. 7)

However, while he agreed with Rousseau that man's original nature was good—indeed, divine—he also recognized that in this less-than-perfect world, the unmarred soon becomes marred and so, despite the ideal of free, self-directed activity for a pupil, there has to be direction

---

[12] We see the "law of opposites" at work here, too.

from without for that pupil; in any case, Froebel was too Teutonic-compulsive to let things proceed untended. Hence his statement of a second position concerning human development:

> All true education in training and instruction should, therefore, at every moment, in every demand and regulation, be simultaneously double-sided, giving and taking, uniting and dividing, prescribing and following . . . between educator and pupil, between request and obedience, there should invisibly rule a third something, to which educator and pupil are equally subject. This third something is the *right*, the best. (Froebel, 1909, p. 14)

From this position, Froebel then moved to taking a very modern stance in his appreciation of instruction and the instructor's role.

> For the purpose of a living, life-giving, and life-stirring instruction, it is most important to note the moment, the proper place, for the introduction of a new branch of instruction. The distinctive character of a natural and rational . . . system of instruction lies in the finding and fixing of this point. . . . (Froebel, 1909, p. 279)

Froebel thus was willing, despite contradictions of his own philosophical position, to take an active role within instruction. In fact, he was particularly insistent upon aggressive intervention when psychological development went awry. His remedial strategy in such cases harkened back to the idea of man's original "good nature." The remedial method he recommended was to restore a function (i.e., process or faculty) to its original pristine state and then to build upon it in a re-education process to bring it to proper fulfillment.

> . . . a good tendency . . . lies originally at the bottom of every shortcoming in man. Hence the only infallible remedy for counteracting any shortcoming . . . is to find the original good source . . . and then to foster, build up, and properly guide this good side. (Froebel, 1909, pp. 121–122)

At all levels of training, but particularly in the earlier ones, Froebel called for active parental participation. The role of the home and the duties of the parents, particularly of the mother, were called sacred responsibilities by Froebel. Hence his famous cri de coeur "Come let us live with our children." Froebel's process orientation is, again, clearly on stage in his admonition to parents as to their responsibilities:

> The aim and object of parental care, in the domestic and family circle, is to awaken and develop, to quicken all the powers and natural gifts of the child, to enable the members and organs of man to fulfill the requirements of the child's powers and gifts. (Mayer, 1960, p. 287)

We are now ready to more precisely discuss Froebel's contributions to process training. They will be approached in conjunction with his theories of developmental (and educational) stages. The reader should be reminded that these coincide, generally speaking, with those proposed by Rousseau, although the types of experiences and the training recommended for the various stages by Froebel do not necessarily correspond with those of Émile's author.

The first stage of development for man is that of infancy. Infancy extends to three years of life. Its primary considerations in training are sensory and motor. Among the senses, those of vision and hearing are to receive predominant attention, since they have most to do with the acquisition of knowledge and higher spiritual nature. For a time, hearing must have precedence over vision because of its intimate association with language; for without language there can be no development of a spiritual sort. The child is still spiritually and emotionally one with his parents, just as the living shoot growing out of a branch is a unity with that branch.

The stage of childhood begins at three years of age and ends at about six or seven. In infancy, the child was still one with its parents. Now there is a clear and distinct emergence of "self"—in this second stage.

As soon as the activity of the senses, of the body, and the limbs is developed to such a degree that the child begins self-activity to represent the internal outwardly, the stage of infancy in human development ceases and the stage of childhood begins. (Froebel, 1909, p. 49)

Froebel proclaimed childhood as the most important of educational opportunities.[13] This is the period in which the child's fundamental instincts awaken. They must be provided assistance in their unfolding and growth, in keeping both with the inner principles of the child's nature and the external laws of Nature. (Froebel's particular interest in childhood was to eventually result in his creation of the kindergarten, an idealized [by him] institution, which was to cultivate the growing powers of the young child.)

Froebel regarded childhood as being particularly distinguished from infancy by the emergence of language. It is, he pointed out, ". . . preeminently the period of development of the faculty of speech" (Eby, 1934, p. 518). As did Pestalozzi, Froebel placed a great deal of emphasis upon language development. For one thing, it is the earliest means by which the human being expresses his feelings; speech and language training can assist him in so doing. Language is further important because it generally awakens the human mind and its potentials, lifting them above the animal world. It also anchors in the mind the impressions it receives from the natural world and social relations.

Froebel's speech and language training efforts took their lead from

[13] This, despite having said (earlier) that all stages of development are equally important.

Pestalozzi. Each object, he said, is to be given its proper name and each word uttered clearly and distinctly. Much of Pestalozzi's tedious name-calling exercises were justified by Froebel on the grounds that a name is the same as the thing for the child and that it creates the thing for the child. On similar grounds the child was to learn about nature and life by memorizing short poems about objects and incidents of living.

Froebel's emphasis upon play as a means of self-expression and child development has given his kindergarten its greatest renown. He invested a great deal of effort into making it a major instructional vehicle. It is here that the philosophies of Rousseau shine through Froebel's work most brightly. It is here, where perhaps above all else, Froebel's conceptions are most lucidly expressed.

Learning by doing, Froebel pointed out, is the *via regia* to knowledge.

. . . to learn a thing in life and through doing is much more developing, cultivating, and strengthening than to learn it merely through verbal communication of ideas. Similarly, plastic material representation in life and through doing, united with thought and speech, is by far more developing and cultivating than merely verbal representation. (Froebel, 1909, p. 279)

And play, play above all else, is the means by which a child learns to do. Its virtues are repeatedly extolled by Froebel in his books *The Education of Man* and *The Pedagogics of the Kindergarten*.

Play is the first means of development of the human mind, its first effort to make acquaintance with the outward world, to collect original experiences from things and facts, and to exercise the powers of the body and mind. The child indeed recognizes no purpose in it, and knows nothing, in the beginning, of any end which is to be reached when it imitates the play it sees around it, but it expresses its own nature, and that is nature in its playful activity. (Marenholz-Bülow, 1895)

Play is the highest phase of child development of human development . . . for it is *self-active representation of the inner from inner necessity and impulse*. Play is the purest, most spiritual activity of man at this stage. . . . It gives joy, freedom, contentment, inner and outer rest, peace with the world. A child that plays thoroughly, with self-active determination, persevering until physical fatigue forbids, will surely be a thorough determined man, capable of self-sacrifice for the promotion of the welfare of himself and others. . . . The spontaneous play of the child discloses the future inner life of the man. The plays of childhood are the germinal leaves of all later life. (Froebel, 1909, pp. 54–55)

Play, as Froebel construed it, really must be viewed in terms of the broader implications of motor education. It is through motor expression that the human organism best expresses itself and learns. It was on this basis that Froebel believed training in rhythmics to be important. Among other things, it serves as a basis for the development of language and of the moral faculties (including firmness, moderation, and control).

Froebel also recommended (as did Pestalozzi in a less-systematic fashion) that mothers early direct the attention of their children to the members of their bodies, which learning would create self-consciousness (or what we today would call body image or ego). It was on this basis, too, that his curriculum included drawing, which, like Pestalozzi, he believed to be of great training worth.

The faculty of drawing is[14] . . . as much innate in a child, as is the faculty of speech, and demands its development and cultivation as imperatively as the latter. (Froebel, 1909, p. 79)

Exercise of the drawing faculty improves motor functioning and sharpens perception; it also increases the child's understanding, all leading to a greater mastery of his environment. On a higher cognitive level, it develops judgment and reflection and facilitates growth of the ability to think abstractly. There is a later gain in academics to be expected from drawing since it exercises the faculty of visual perception. For example, visual perception is the way the developing pupil originally begins his ascent to a knowledge of number, and this is the beginning of mathematics, in which Froebel placed great store as a formative influence in the development of the mind and its contents—all a matter of essential genetic development.

The contradiction between Froebel's repeated emphasis upon free activity and his calls for control upon it lest it go astray has been pointed out twice earlier. It is expressed in his attitude toward motor expression and play, as well. On these counts, he is reported to have said:

Without rational, conscious guidance, childish activity degenerates into aimless play instead of preparing for those tasks of life for which it is destined. . . . Without law-abiding guidance there is no free development. (Marenholz-Bülow, 1895, pp. 67–68)

It was on this basis that he invented a variety of systematic apparatuses to channel children's activities within the kindergarten, an anticipation of Montessori in this respect; thus, his famous gifts and occupations.

Froebel's distinction between gifts and occupations is rather arbitrary. They are actually quite closely connected in use. The occupations represent activities, however, while the gifts furnish ideas for activities.

[14] Froebel's discussion of a faculty of drawing expresses a common fault to be found in most faculty psychologists. To do something means that one has the "power," "ability" or "faculty", etc., to do it. The act of drawing requires the faculty of drawing.

The gifts combine and rearrange specific types of objects. The occupations modify and transform materials. Both are manifestations of Froebel's efforts to make play constructive. Both are rich in sensory and motor implications. Both are also rich in terms of broad cognitive implications.

Froebel appears to have placed greater store in the importance of his gifts because of their symbolic implications. They were called gifts because they are divinely given to meet the needs of the child. The first gift is the ball, "the most universal plaything of children." The ball "gift" consists of a box of six woolen balls of different colors, which are to be rolled about in play to develop ideas of color, form, material, motion, and direction, and to train muscular sensibility as well. The ball was of unique and mystical importance to Froebel, for, in addition to being a "universal plaything," it symbolizes the world and is representative of all things.

Froebel's second gift consists of a ball, a cube, and a cylinder. These three objects, when used jointly, symbolize the dialectic process. There is a known factor in the round sphere of the ball and an unknown one in the cube. The child compares the stability of the cube with the movability of the ball. The two are harmonized in the cylinder which is imbued with the characteristics and powers of both. Thesis, antithesis, and synthesis are thus provided to the child and, presumably, understood by him.

The third gift is a large wooden cube divided into eight equal cubes, which teach the relations of the parts to the whole and to one another. They also make it possible to build things such as chairs, doorways, steps, monuments—in short, to do what children have always done with blocks.

The three subsequent gifts divided the cube in different ways so as to make solid bodies of different types and sizes. They create an interest in number, relation, and form and prepare the way into geometry, algebra, and artistic constructions as well. Together with the first three gifts, they make up Froebel's basic package of six.

Froebel added auxiliary gifts to the above: tablets, sticks, and rings, constituting gifts seven to nine. Through these the child is introduced to surfaces, lines, and points which contrast with the solids of the first six gifts. They serve, together, to create an understanding of relations of area, outline, and circumference to volume. They also provide a great deal of opportunity to develop and appreciate symmetrical patterns and artistic types of design.

Froebel's recommendations for the use of his gifts constitute a scheme of elaborate, systematic education. The gifts are arranged so as to lead from the properties and activities of one to the other and to repeat and extend old impressions while introducing new ones. Froebel recommended that each new gift be used alternately with a previous one to make play with the earlier one more flexible and meaningful.

All in all, gift training constitutes an extensive scheme of process training, extending from the very simple elements of sense and motor experience up through the exercise of higher cognitive powers to the development of the entire (unitary) soul. Froebel's expectations that a child could understand and benefit from the manifold symbolic and abstract meanings of his gifts, as well as from the sensory and motor experiences they provided, verges on the absurd. But this does not detract from the useful modality and motor training that these gifts might have provided his charges.

Froebel's "occupations" are a rather more relaxed affair than his gifts. They are intended to provide a child opportunities to practice what he has learned through his training with the gifts; they are old familiars to the modern kindergarten scene. Froebel's occupations comprise an extended list of constructive activities—clay modeling, paper cutting, coloring of pictures, sand-pile play, simple drawing, cardboard work, sewing, weaving, bead threading, paper pricking, etc. Such occupations can be grouped to correspond with the gifts, but this correspondence has been generally overlooked in practice. In any event, a child, through the occupations, is exposed to a massive set of opportunities for sensory-motor training and (Froebel believed) the exercise of higher mental faculties as well. Froebel's directions for the use of the occupations are mercifully free from the excess baggage of philosophy that encumber the gifts.

There is a considerable shift in Froebel's theories from process to product for the pupil passing from childhood into boyhood. Whereas childhood is a period in which the emphasis is upon making the internal external, boyhood is a time for making the external internal. In other words, there is a definitive shift from earlier play and self-expression to the formal training of the pupil,[15] with the intention that this formal training will result in the creation of products. Froebel stated:

> What formerly the child did only *for the sake of the activity,* the boy now does *for the sake of the result* or product of his activity; the child's instinct of activity has in the boy become a *formative instinct.* (Froebel, 1909, p. 520)

However, even in this period, process is really not neglected. The products of the boy are to be seen as ways through which his processes are expressed, mature, and are channeled. (The principle of "unity" which governed Froebel's thinking must be kept in mind.) The human spirit is really one with the physical work in which it engages. Processes create products. Processes are expressed as products. We may even speak of product as process—all because of that participation in the unity of the universal.

---

[15] Rousseau put off formal training to a later time of life.

God creates and works productively in uninterrupted continuity. Each thought of God is a work, a deed, a product, and each thought of God continues to work with creative power . . . *man should create and bring forth like God . . .* the spirit of man should hover over the shapeless, and move it that it may take shape and form[16] . . . This is the high meaning, the deep significance, and great purpose of work and industry, of productive and creative activity. We become truly godlike . . . in working and doing. . . . (Froebel, 1909, p. 30)

Man works, only that his spiritual divine essence may assume outward form (Froebel, 1909, p. 32)

Before we more closely examine the important notion of process as product as it was exemplified in Froebel's recommendations for constructive activity, let us quickly examine the remainder of his curriculum that is of interest to us vis-à-vis process. Froebel emphasized nature study, being almost as passionately committed to it as Rousseau and seeing it, as he did almost all activities, not merely as an activity valuable in itself, but as preparatory for higher stages of development. Nature study is, among others, a means of training sense perception. It also leads into the sciences, and the science of mathematics, the highest of all, is a means of ". . . the expression of life as such." Nature study has other benefits. Memorization of poetic descriptions of nature develops language proficiency and singing potential.

Froebel was less suspicious of book knowledge than were his predecessors, Pestalozzi and Rousseau. Stories, myths, legends, and fairy tales, particularly, received a high educational ranking from him. He believed proper tales, properly told, develop a sense of time and history in a pupil. More important was the role they played in developing the mind's powers:

Mind breathes mind; power feels power and absorbs it as it were. The telling of stories refreshes the mind as a bath refreshes the body; it gives exercise to the intellect and its powers; it tests the judgment and the feelings. (Froebel, 1909, p. 307)

While Froebel did not forget to recommend play during the boyhood stage, he also believed it should be carried out on a more mature level, as befits an older child with different and more sophisticated needs. He recommended that every town have a common playground for boys and regular gaming. The most important results of "play" in boyhood may be seen in the development of social characteristics and moral qualities.

Let us now review some of the constructive activities that Froebel

---

[16] Froebel believed that the mathematical insight of the human mind corresponded to the mathematical construction of the universe and that both are the result of the same evolutionary law.

advised during boyhood, ones that perhaps most of all justify the statement that he developed Pestalozzi's curriculum of the hand into a working reality. Keep in mind the notion of process expressed through product as we proceed.

First, the child, now a boy, is, within the third stage of Froebel's process-developmental educational system, to be engaged in a variety of activities that model upon the activity of his elders. The boy (remember the age for which he wrote) in the period of education he set for him, i.e., between the ages of 6 and 10, was to be exposed to a variety of adult activities. Whereas the younger child was to model his behavior on the basis of his observations of domestic activities, the boy now is to carry out activities which are renditions of the adult occupations he sees about him in his extended environment, but these activities are intended to develop his faculties, rather than for utilitarian purposes. Second, the boy is expected to apply himself manually:[17]

> . . . daily, at least one or two hours to some serious activity in the production of some definite external piece of work . . . (lest) a vast amount of human power . . . remains undeveloped and is lost. (Froebel, 1909, pp. 236–237)

Is it somewhat difficult to encompass what Froebel means by this? Hailmann, one of his translators, gives us an idea:

> Froebel proposed to devote the forenoon to instruction in the current subjects of school study, and the afternoon to work in the field, the garden, the forest, in and around the house. His list of occupations comprised the preparation of wood for the kitchen and furnace; the making of simple wooden kitchen utensils, the weaving and binding of mats, for the table and for the floor; the binding of books and the ruling of slates and practice-paper; the making of a variety of collections of objects of nature and art, and of suitable boxes for these objects . . . the care of pigeons, chickens, ducks, etc.; the preparation of artistic and geometrical forms with paper in folding, cutting, and mounting, pricking, weaving, interlacing, etc.; the use of pasteboard in the making of stars, wheels, boxes, napkin rings, car baskets, lamp shades, etc.; play with splints, tablets, sticks and peas; the whittling of boats, windmills, waterwheels, etc.; the making of chains and baskets from flexible wire; modeling with clay; drawing and painting; and many other things. (Froebel, 1909, p. 38)

Froebel was the patron saint of manual tradition, the first complete motor messiah.[18] A classic German aphorism is that *Arbeit macht das Leben süss* (Work makes life sweet). If so, a Froebelian curriculum would be enough to make anyone ecstatic, and it was primarily for spiritual development, not crass materialistic benefits; process training most of all,

---

[17] The adolescent and adult as well. For the child, the gifts and occupations and play serve the purposes of manual expression.

[18] To use one of Cratty's terms.

even when products were expressed. And among the processes trained, most especially was that of will:

> To give firmness to the will, to quicken it, and to make it pure, strong, and enduring . . . is the chief concern, the main object in the guidance of a boy, in instruction and the school. (Froebel, 1909, p. 96)

Froebel did not complete *The Education of Man*. He never went on to tell how adolescents should be taught or the young man cultured. His beloved kindergarten had come to occupy the greater part of his attention. But certainly if he had continued his elaboration of education for the later years, it would have continued in the vein we have seen developed to this point, so we need not conjecture too much as to what he might have written. Let us instead discuss some aspects of his process approach that significantly influenced later education.

Froebel's insistence upon an organismic evolutionary model of process development had its corollary in the biological-psychological evolutionary theories of Spencer, Jackson, etc. He was subject to some of the same evolutionary influences as they, though Lamarck rather than Charles Darwin influenced the intellectual circles that, in turn, influenced him. Froebel helped give an evolutionary cast to later conceptions of mental development.

Froebel's botanical metaphor of human psychological development was to be a most potent influence in later faculty psychology and mental discipline circles. It became de rigueur to write of cultivating the faculties; books were written in which faculties were discussed as branches on a parent cognitive-affective-conative tree.

The manual training movement looked to Froebel for inspiration. And manual training came to be used in disciplinary ways, i.e., as a means of training the mind and its powers, rather than as a technology of developing utilitarian skills. We have already discussed sloyd in our previous chapter. Let us examine it now more closely. The manual training movement in schools began in earnest in Finland, when Uno Cygnaeus, an admirer of Froebel, succeeded in introducing courses in basket making, wood carving, and metal work into the schools. Sweden innovated by adding woodworking to its curriculum, while also within Sweden, Otto Saloman became a prophet of manualism as the road to spiritualism. A schoolboy's creation of such things as penholders, bucket handles, and soup ladles were viewed as a means of developing his basic cognitive skills to a degree that would allow him to viably participate in all subsequent work activities, as well as improving his judgment, moral fiber, and all other good things. Nor was the United States much different for a long while, until someone decided that there could be more useful effects obtained from such utilitarian training.

Certainly, the justification of all sorts of handiwork in the name of formal discipline was based on Froebel's insistence that manipulation and manipulatives expressed the mind as well as the body, that product, properly produced, expresses process.

Play as a means of training the mind, as well as the body, has a long and honored history, but certainly no one made it quite as plain as Froebel. The same holds true for motor expression. Rousseau philosophized, Froebel practiced. Froebelians used to say "no impression without expression"—motor expression, that is to say. Colonel Francis W. Parker (1837–1902), a champion of Froebel's work in the United States, described expression thusly:

Expression may be generally defined as the manifestation of thought through the body by means of physical agents. The modes of expression are: (1) Gesture, (2) Voice, (3) Speech, (4) Music, (5) Making, (6) Modeling, (7) Painting, (8) Drawing, (9) Writing. (Parke, 1894, p. 227)

In other words, "doing" was the thing for a pupil to do.[19]

Thanks to Froebel, "free expression" became a popular recommendation for instruction with the young, and hyperkinesia, a phenomenon to be welcomed rather than medicated. His emphasis upon motor expression even made William James somewhat nervous so that he warned against forgetting the values of verbal recitation and "reproduction." Even Edward Thorndike became alarmed at the motor excesses within the education of his day.

The head is intellectual king even in the muscular system . . . muscular contraction, the expression of mental life, is not synonymous with movement. A great part of muscular activity serves to prevent movement. These inhibitory activities are indeed the ones most concerned in mental life. The mind may almost be said to be what the body does not do. (Thorndike, 1903, p. 50)

However, we should not blame Froebel for all the emphasis upon motor expression. Once motor functions were allowed in the cerebrum, the result of epochal events related in the first half of this book, it seemed quite right to talk about the motor aspects of the mind. M. F. Washburn (1908) built up a theory of motor consciousness in the United States. E. B. Holt (1915) suggested that consciousness is just a name for a specific type of sensory-motor adjustment to an object (Murphy & Kovach, 1972). Féré and Ribot in France, Ferrier in Brittania—to name but a few additional supporters of motor-determined thinking—also contributed to the

---

[19] Dewey, who believed in doing for oneself, acknowledged Froebel's precedence for significant aspects of his own work.

idea that motor behavior is thinking behavior, not to mention Watson with his subvert speech movements constituting thinking.[20]

Nevertheless, it was Froebel who plunked it all down in classrooms and created the gardens within which motorized children were to grow. He was responsible for making toys and games forevermore a part of the educational scene, which brings us to consider a possible oversight in our acknowledged heritage in special education. Froebel's name crops up here and there in special education texts that take a historical departure, but not too often. And he is not usually acknowledged for the goods and bads of the manualism that has characterized special education for much of its formal—institutional—history. We are inclined to think that the manual activities of special education's bygone years—the basket weaving, potholder making, birdhouse building, and plasticene molding that constituted the curriculum of the handicapped in lieu of reading, writing, and arithmetic are somebody else's fault. Didn't these things start with Itard, or at least with Séguin? Surely Montessori was also responsible? Well yes, but to a great degree, no. They appear to also be the unrecognized products of Froebelism, as are the more currently accepted activities that seek to develop the mind through hand and eye and bodily expression.[21]

AN APPRAISAL

I have written of four great educational pioneers in this chapter from the standpoint of their contributions to process theory and process training. My discussion of their work is hardly comprehensive. I fear for the historical scholar of education that my reviews are on the flimsy side. On the other hand, for those less concerned with the historical antecedents of their practices, I am sure that I will have proceeded too far and too long. But Comenius, Rousseau, Pestalozzi, and Froebel are important to anyone who wishes to understand the place of process within educational practice. So acquaintance or reacquaintance with them should be worth the reader's time and patience, whether scholar, practitioner, or novice.

Let us ask ourselves now just where these four giants fit in the process scheme of things, the answer to which is not necessarily forthcoming in our earlier review of their work.

[20] Anticipated by James Rush's *Brief Outline of an Analysis of the Human Intellect* (1860) which expressed a motor theory of behavior and suggested that vocal muscles are important to thinking.

[21] Still based on such ideas as Froebel expressed: ". . . human work . . . can only become intellectual when the occupation of the hand is at the same time the occupation of the mind" (Monroe, 1905, p. 664).

Comenius? His work, as discussed earlier, suffered general eclipse after his death. The first of the true sense trainers of modern time, it was his picture books rather than his educational ideas on process training that influenced most later generations. By the time his insights and innovations were recognized, they had already been put into practice by others without recognition of his precedence. But at least he should be honored—again and again.

Rousseau? The man's influence has been so broad and overwhelming that it becomes difficult to avoid overattributing developments and events in education and special education to that influence: developmental theory, sensory-motor development, the training of higher cognitive processes through lower tones. We know the important role his work played in the later conceptualizations of Pestalozzi and Froebel, and hence in the work of Pestalozzians and Froebelians who were for a long time so influential in schools. But did he affect Itard? Rousseau's birth antecedes Itard's by over 50 years and he even wrote about wild children.[22] Certainly, then, an affinity should have existed between the two men. But in France, despite Rousseau's influences on thought and attitude, his influence on education was relatively slight. The *ancien régime* was too threatened by his egalitarianism to allow it much play in practice. In England, too, where Rousseau's social ideas drew many converts, there wasn't enough of an organized school network to allow rapid dissemination of his educational novelties. In any case, John Locke's disciplinary ideas were more popular, and since Locke recommended his own brand of naturalism, Rousseau's educational philosophy did not necessarily appear all that innovative to the English. It was the Germans and Swiss who responded to Rousseau's ideas most directly in their school reforms: Basedow, Salzman, Campe, Froebel, Pestalozzi, to name some. But Itard's thinking was responsive to that of Englishmen and Frenchmen, not to the Swiss or the Germans. Locke and Condillac, rather than Rousseau, particularly impressed him with their brands of sense–realism.

As to Séguin, certainly his manualism and jumping about owes much to Rousseau? But Séguin's acknowledged masters were Itard and Pereire, that secretive teacher of the deaf. Rousseau must have influenced Séguin. Their direct linkage is hard to discern; their indirect linkage is an easier matter. Jean often visited Pereire's school, is reported as having been a good friend of the Jewish Portuguese instructor of the deaf, and to have incorporated some of his ideas in his own Émile. And Séguin was profoundly impressed by Pereire's work (though Itard was not), so there is a link between Rousseau and Séguin.

---

[22] *The Wild Boy of Aveyron* was used by some of Rousseau's critics as evidence of the fallacy of his "nature's nobleman" thesis for untutored, therefore unspoiled, man.

In any case, by the time that the *education nouvelle* was well under way in the twentieth century, Rousseau's theories were clearly acknowledged by some of Itard and Séguin's successors, and just about everyone else. Decroly and Descoeudres were to justify many of their recommended activities for normals and retardates on the basis of the Swiss master's imprimaturs.

Pestalozzi, another Swiss, does not seem to fit anywhere directly in the continuum of special education process training history, even though he worked with children who by current educational, psychological, neurological, or psychiatric standards would be called "special." But by his time, the line of special education development had been operating conceptually in the process realm pretty well along French lines. Also, Pestalozzi's theories required—or at least seemed to require—generally more intact types of functioning than was the expectation for "idiots," the prime focus of special education process training in his day. Pestalozzi had a most formidable effect upon process training within general education, particularly at the elementary school level, but we do not find him directly influencing process training of the handicapped.

Froebel's influence within special education I have already touched upon. Descoeudres gives him mention, too, in her oeuvre on training the mentally retarded. We suspect that his influence has been much wider within special education than his reputation for it. Like Pestalozzi, he was profoundly influential in respect to the process training of the normal child. The notion of kindergarten is one of preparing processes. Whether Froebel should have been grouped as a sense–realist is a question that I feel somewhat insecure about. And about Pestalozzi, I feel the same way. Should they perhaps be classified as naturalists or as both? Monroe calls Froebel and Pestalozzi psychologizers of education, rather than naturalists or sense–realists. Yet they were also systematizers and promulgators of the doctrines of sense–realism and naturalism, so that, certainly, we cannot be too far wrong if we associate their names with these doctrines.

Within general education's process training theories and practices, Froebel, like Pestalozzi, looms large. His name, like that of Pestalozzi, was to be frequently invoked to justify an extraordinary number of practices as being valuable for their cognitive and spiritual training purposes. The educational psychology of the late nineteenth and early twentieth centuries is redolent of Froebelism. Psychic trees were described in a variety of texts, their processes to be tended by thoughtful teachers. Not even the hostilities of eminent critics such as Herbart were enough to staunch the march of process training theory and practice across the educational practices of the late nineteenth and early twentieth centuries—not when the passionate voice of Froebel was joined to the pleas of formal disciplinarians. Though it was not likely that a teacher of either classical languages or advanced science was thrilled at the notion of having his "discipline" equated psychologically with block play in the kindergarten or manual labor in the shops. Froebel was certainly in great part responsible, then, for the fact that the simplest action of a child and the grossest labors of the illiterate were allowed to take their part in the panorama of process training along with Greek, Latin, mathematics, and the sciences, and for making the body and its appendages co-equals with the mind, even in the training of that mind. Let us keep this in mind when we later examine developments in process training that might give the impression of entirely different and even opposing forces at work.

17
Phrenology and Process Training

The giants, whose work we have reviewed in the previous chapter, spoke and wrote of individualizing instruction to meet the needs of individual pupils. However, their systems of instruction were a priori in nature, and the pupils who participated therein were expected, de facto, to proceed pretty well in lockstep, theoretically and methodologically. It is not at all clear to whom we can attribute the first true individualization in process management and training. What is certain is that a most definite claim in this respect can be registered for phrenology and phrenologists.

The reader will recall, from this book's earlier concern with phrenology, that Gall created his phrenological doctrines partly in protest against the abstract faculties of the philosophers, which he criticized, in considerable part, on the basis that they did not explain individual propensities. His own, he believed, did that. Interindividual and intraindividual differences in behavior could be explained on the basis of differing degrees of development of the various brain structures. Or to be more precise about it, interindividual and intraindividual differences in the strength and weakness of the various faculties, and the powers associated with them, could be explained on the basis of individualized differentiation of brain structures—all of which accounted for differences in behavior. So said Gall, and generations of phrenologists after him. Their beliefs encouraged the study of individual differences in processes, and their work, despite its excesses, deserves an honored place in the annals of process assessment, training, and remediation. We will find it difficult to deny it this place, as we read in future chapters of more modern and more rational efforts in these realms. Long after the ghost of phrenology was presumably put to rest, its influences will be found to have lingered on and to have affected education and the management of human behavior. Within the present chapter, we shall try to sketch some of the more important developments and misdevelopments within phrenology as they relate to these.

Again, let me emphasize the most important aspects of phrenology as seen from the perspectives of modern-day process practices: first, they were directed toward the empirical analyses of mental and personological processes; second, phrenological knowledge of individual differences was used both for psychological and educational guidance and as a basis from which one could proceed to intervene for the purposes of human betterment.

The first of these aspects was attested to by the insistence of the phrenologists that the study of faculties be essentially directed toward the explanation of individual differences. We have already seen Gall's views on this matter. Similar ones were expressed by phrenologist George Combe, who, in offering himself as a candidate (in 1837) for the vacated chair of logic at the University of Edinburgh, suggested that he was more qualified than other contenders for the position on the basis of their commitment to classical (pre-Gall) faculty doctrine, which, he said

. . . gave no account of the obvious fact of different individuals possessing the faculties in different degrees of endowment which fit them for different pursuits. (Bakan, 1966, p. 210)

While this statement was not entirely fair (Christian Wolff, for one, having most certainly acknowledged individual differences in faculty development), it is nevertheless true that the phrenologists were to take account of "the faculties in different degrees of endowment" in an unprecedented way. As Bakan has observed about phrenology:

. . . one of its major claims is to have specified an extremely comprehensive scheme of presumably uncorrelated functions for the assessment of individuals, with great pains being taken to define the different functions rather precisely and exhaustively. (Bakan, 1966, p. 210)[1]

And these functions, or faculties,[2] the two terms often being used interchangeably by phrenologists, were not idealized processes, like those

---

[1] Bakan also claimed that the faculties that emerged from phrenology, based as they were on observed correlations (fanciful though they might have been) between specific types of behavior and specific sections of the skull (and the brain organs beneath) represented the results of a primitive sort of factor analysis.

[2] Bakan observed, as did K. M. Dallenbach in his study of the antecedents of function, that: "At its root, the very concept of 'function' for mental functioning is phrenological" (1966, p. 215).

of the earlier faculty psychologists, but rather traits, attributes, abilities, etc., with specific survival purposes, ones that might be specifically modifiable by external events.

The phrenologists' attempts to assess these new-fangled faculties their "science" had discovered was to result in the creation of the first formal psychological assessment procedures. In fact, Joseph Rodes Buchanan, one of the most prolific (and fanciful) of those who attempted to popularize phrenology—alas, for the purpose of commercial exploitation—used the term "psychometric" for his evaluations. He also went beyond skull measurements in addressing general issues of assessment, claiming (1849) that the product of any action an individual engaged in can be used as a basis for his assessment since the individual expressed himself in every action and ". . . man, in every act, leaves the impression, or daguerreotype of his mental being . . ." (Bakan, 1966, p. 212). Thus was established a basic premise of modern-day psychological examination.

Fowler and Wells, who were the most influential (one hesitates to use the term greatest) of phrenological popularizers in the United States and who founded the *American Phrenological Journal* in 1838, actualized Buchanan's "psychometrics" in grand style. They created printed rating scales which delineated the 37-odd faculties or functions that they chose to assess through skull readings. Each of these functions was to be noted as to the extent of its development on the basis of either three or nine points, with pluses and minuses to also be employed where extra precision might be required. They even allowed some spaces where the phrenologists were to check, *cultivate*, or *restrain*; such were the diagnostic prescriptives of their day.

In order to assist in the interpretation of their scales Fowler and Wells provided a pamphlet, giving a comprehensive explanation of the purposes of phrenological examination and interpretation, of the results obtained through it. For those clients who took their test profiles with them, there were page references in the scales that allowed the phrenologized customer the leisure of referring to their texts so as to make their own analyses.

Fowler and Wells, family and friends, were indeed the Psychological Corporation of their era. They supplied all the equipment necessary for one to set himself up in business as a practicing phrenologist. Charts, models (of a head, with the various faculties charted upon it), and measuring devices could be obtained from them. At one time they claimed to have the largest mail-order business in New York City, their headquarters (McCord, 1969). They even made phrenological readings from photographs. Employers came to insist that job applicants undergo aptitude examinations in consultation with Fowler and Wells. Horace Greeley demanded these examinations for railroad crews. A classic Fowler-Wells advertisement reads as follows:

A correct Phrenological examination will teach, with SCIENTIFIC CERTAINTY, that most useful of all knowledge—YOURSELF; YOUR DEFECTS, and how to obviate them; your EXCELLENCES and how to make the most of them; your NATURAL TALENTS, and thereby in what spheres and pursuits you can best succeed; show wherein you are liable to imperfections, errors, and excesses; direct you SPECIFICALLY, what mental faculties and functions you require especially to cultivate and restrain; give all needed advice touching self-improvement, and the preservation and restoration of health; show, THROUGHOUT, how to DEVELOP, PERFECT, and make the VERY MOST POSSIBLE out of YOUR OWN SELF; disclose to parents their children's INNATE CAPABILITIES, natural callings, dispositions, defects, means of improvement, the mode of government especially adapted to each, predispositions to disease, together with preventives, etc., etc.—nor can as little be spent on them profitably as in learning their Phrenologies and Physiologies—it will enable business men to choose reliable partners and customers; merchants, confidential clerks; mechanics, apprentices having natural GIFTS adapted to particular branches; shipmasters, good crews; the friendly desirable associates; guide matrimonial candidates in selecting CONGENIAL life companions, especially adapted to each other; show the married what in each other to allow for and conciliate; and can be made the VERY best instrumentality for PERSONAL DEVELOPMENT, IMPROVEMENT, AND HAPPINESS.

SELF-PERFECTION should be life's FIRST AND GREATEST business. This involves that very self-knowledge which a phrenological examination, with a chart, furnishes. Surely, it will point out, and show how to obviate, at least *one* fault, and cultivate *one* virtue, besides reinvigorating health—the value of which ASTOR'S MILLIONS can not equal! Shall, then, the trifling examination fee prevent what is thus INFINITELY valuable? Will you allow this to intercept your MENTAL progress, especially if just starting in life? In no other way can you even obtain for your self, at such a trifle, as much good—as great a luxury. You can, by following it, make it the means and the beginning of a COMPLETE PHYSIOLOGICAL AND MENTAL REGENERATION!—especially, if you have EVERY WORD of the description WRITTEN DOWN in full, just as it falls fresh from the examiner's lips. This spreads before yourself, friends, descendants, (and what would you not give for such a mental portrait of parents or ancestors?) every minute shading and ramification of character he describes; perpetuates every word of advice he utters, so that every perusal reimpresses it; fastens his answer to all your questions; and furnishes, in black and white, fit for printing, a complete *mental* daguerreotype of yourself. 'All this you can obtain, at moderate cost, from those who have devoted their entire lives to this study and practice, and understand it perfectly, by calling at our Rooms.'

FOWLER AND WELLS, Phrenologists

(Bakan, 1960, p. 200)

How could one resist such blandishments? The promise and the glory of psychoeducational assessment, psychological counseling, vocational guidance, and process remediation. Colleges and institutes offering training in phrenology came and went as demand for services waxed and waned. The many imitators and competitors of Fowler and Wells, oft equipped with their materials, stormed carnivals and church fairs and kept many a store front rented. Various lotions were sold to be rubbed on the head to promote growth of selective parts of the brain and improve the faculties associated with them. Special hats were devised that were supposed to provide pressure over those parts of the skull that marked the brain organs subserving the less desirable faculties or those that were improperly overdeveloped. The hats were loosely fitted on those places on the skull where one wished to promote the growth of specific brain organs. There was even a vacuum hat (pump included) that was supposed to promote the growth of hair but might also be employed for brain development (McCord, 1969).[3]

Such was the low road that phrenology took. But there was also a high road, traveled by many sober and eminent men of science and education who saw in phrenology a powerful means of improving society. We have already seen that Bain and Spencer were at one time among these, though later they were apostates to the cause. If they defected, there were still others who rallied to the cause or remained loyal to it, particularly since phrenology allied itself with reform movements in education and human services and because it insisted upon (as well as seemd to provide) a scientific basis for the study and improvement of man, one based upon physical observations rather than metaphysical speculations, one insisting upon observable facts.

In Philadelphia, William Elder, a noted physician and economist, writing in the *American Phrenological Journal* in 1850, attributed the evils of society to the failure of education to develop the physical, intellectual, and moral qualities of man in harmony with nature. A system of education based on phrenology could correct such evils and ultimately reform the world.

Books on the application of phrenology to education flourished. There was Spurzheim's *Education, Its Elementary Principles Founded on the Nature of Man,* George Combe's *Lectures on Popular Education*, and Orson Fowler's *Education and Self-Improvement,* to name a few. Children were to be raised and educated on the basis of phrenological principles.

[3] The early nineteenth century had arrived at the conclusion that the brain was a "plastic" organ with the capacity for dramatic modifications and, potentially, susceptible to dramatic improvements. Many of the positive claims made concerning the cure of mental illness or retardation were based on this belief. Phrenology obviously took part in all this.

Not all the recommendations were unsound. Since the mind cannot function without the brain and the brain is part of the body, a healthy body improves both the brain and mind. Thus phrenologists recommended a healthy life with plenty of physical exercise and play for children. A young child was not to be excessively trained lest he permanently damage his brain. Knowledge of a child's phrenological makeup would allow a teacher to understand the individual child and to reinforce desired actions through rewards which in turn would strengthen the brain organs responsible for such behavior. Studies should be practical and concrete rather than abstract and irrelevant. The use of classical languages such as Greek and Latin might be justified perhaps on the basis of training the brain, if the brain were a single mental organ. However, since it consisted of congeries of organs, differing aptitudes were to be exercised individually. The whole child was to be trained through the harmonious exercise of his specific brain organs. Properly exercised, the brain organs associated with them would grow and the skulls might be expected to swell (but not necessarily).

Phrenology was a natural tool for those who believed that common man should be upwardly mobile. Training of his faculties could make his brain an elite organ, equal to that of his social betters. Phrenologists were against capital punishment and physical punishment in all forms. By modifying behavior in respect to inhibiting undesirable behavior and encouraging positive behavior, a delinquent or criminal person's basic functions could be so altered (physiologically as well as psychologically) as to make reform a truly organic affair.

As Fowler and Wells had convinced the American masses, Spurzheim and Combe influenced the learned in the country. Combe, in particular, appears to have impressed a good share of the leadership of this country.[4] Horace Mann was so impressed that, besides basing his theories of mental and moral improvement on phrenology, he named a son after Combe. Samuel Gridley Howe, one of the true American greats in special education, firmly believed in phrenological doctrines. During his work as the first superintendent of the new Boston School for the Blind, he was so converted to the new doctrine that he had been introduced to by Combe that he had an outline of Combe's writings printed in raised type calling it ". . . the most valuable addition yet made to the library of the blind in any language." Howe attributed all his success in training blind pupils to his knowledge of phrenology. Hence his statement:

Before I knew phrenology, I was groping my way in the dark as blind as my pupils; I derived very little satisfaction from labors, and fear I gave but little to

---

[4] Remarks to his audience such as "My eyes never rested on such a collection of excellent brains" did his cause no harm.

others. . . . Some of our teachers are persons of considerable intellectual attainments, and all of them adopted the new philosophy since they joined the institution . . . because their duties led them to examine all the theories of mental philosophy, and the new system recommended itself most forcibly to their understanding, and appeared more susceptible of practical application. (Hinsdale, 1898, p. 95)

Howe practiced remedial phrenology. He had perceived through his use of phrenology that an ungovernable blind pupil had an overdeveloped propensity for destructiveness, so he put him to sawing wood and working out in the gymnasium before school hours, with a complete abatement of all difficulties, disciplinary and otherwise. Howe also used to train his students' organs of propriety by never allowing them to appear undressed within vision of each other—even though they could not see. Howe's phrenology was used to guide the education of Laura Bridgeman, the Helen Keller of her time, thought to be hopeless because she was a blind deaf-mute. Her response to treatment was considerable and was credited in large part to phrenological principles. Combe, who followed Howe's progress in the case, was very enthusiastic since it justified his optimism that phrenology would lead the way into a new age of education. The new science, he wrote:

. . . leads us to understand that in this child, Laura Bridgeman, the moral and intellectual powers exist in great vigour and activity, and that all that is wanting to her successful education is the means of conveying knowledge to them. (Hinsdale, 1898, p. 95)

Howe became such a believer on the basis of his work with Laura, that he once stated in an official report that even oysters would be capable of improvement through the application of phrenological principles. Upon hearing reports that James Simpson, an Edinburgh phrenologist, had succeeded in educating an idiot boy, he investigated the incident, which may have encouraged him to start the first school for mental defectives in Boston in 1848.

Other special educators also joined Howe in his enthusiasm for phrenology. Thomas Hopkins Gallaudet, first principal of the Hartford School for the Deaf and Dumb, became a subscriber to its doctrines. Silas Jones, prior to his appointment as head of the New York Asylum for the Blind in 1838, was a traveling lecturer in phrenology.

Phrenology gave special educators such as these the belief that, despite the negative experiences of the past, the handicapped could be educated. What it took, as Howe said, was:

. . . a knowledge of physiology, of human and comparative anatomy, and of *educability* in its widest sense . . . requisite for a phrenologist. (Bakan, 1966, p. 214)

Indeed, tributes were offered to phrenology from all corners of America's educational establishment. Perhaps the most convincing was the attempt to introduce phrenology into the schools as a subject to be taught the pupils. Mrs. Lorenzo Fowler wrote a series of simple question-answer books on phrenology, hygiene, and astronomy for school adoption. The Albany Phrenological Society arranged for an edition of Combe's *The Constitution of Man* for similar purposes, The Cincinnati high schools and the Boston School for Moral Discipline offered secondary-level courses in phrenology. Parental guidance books recommending the use of phrenology for the understanding of one's children were also written. There was one, for example, by William A. Crandal entitled *Three Hours School a Day: A Talk with Parents* advising them to learn the foundations of the "Science of Education" represented by Combe's writings (Davies, 1971).

Things went so far as to see one of the editors of the *American Phrenological Journal*, B. J. Gray, purchase a building at Eatonville, New Jersey, in 1846, for a school to be run on strict phrenological principles; however, it never came off.

Were the phrenologists influenced by the great process trainers who were discussed in the previous chapter? Davies, from whose book *Phrenology, Fad and Science* I have so liberally borrowed, makes the following comment:

The parallelism between certain phrenological educational theories—the education of the child through his own voluntary activity, the development of inborn faculties by arousing interest and exercise—and the theories of Pestalozzi and Froebel is evident. Since the phrenologists never cited these great Europeans, obviously the assimilation was indirect, unconscious, and a result of "spirit of the times." (Davies, 1971, pp. 81–82)

To which I would like to append "A zeitgeist is a zeitgeist," and it is difficult to imagine that such searching and fertile minds as possessed by the phrenologists would not have been influenced by the Pestalozzian and Froebelian movements in the United States and Europe. They were, above all else, shrewd capitalizers on information and exploitive of what they learned.

As could be expected, phrenology ran its course. Its decline had its share of mourners. There were those who discerned the gold amidst its dross. Among these was Albert Russell Wallace, a prominent and distinguished biologist. In 1899, Wallace published a book, *The Wonderful Century*, which reviewed the great progress the nineteenth century, just then passing into the twentieth, had made. Wallace wrote that the neglect of phrenology was one of the nineteenth century's great failures. For this he blamed the narrowness and biases of scientists who, he believed, had, in the large, approached phrenology with closed minds. The triumph of this science, he believed, was nevertheless inevitable; the twentieth century would make good the nineteenth century's failures to recognize and capitalize upon the importance of phrenology:

> . . . in the coming century phrenology will assuredly attain general acceptance. It will prove itself to be the true science of the mind. Its practical uses in education, in self-discipline, in the reformatory treatment of the insane, will give it one of the highest places in the hierarchy of the sciences. (Wallace, 1899, p. 193)

More to the purposes of our book, its influences were and continue to be major ones in the realm of process. The correspondence of brain structures and behavioral functions and the influence of one by the other were persistent themes in the faculty psychology of the late nineteenth and early twentieth centuries. We shall still find these themes operating within the developments discussed in the following chapters, and they continue to persist in modern attempts to link education and neurology. Even Hebb's cell assemblies represent a realization of Gall's idea that practice makes neurology. Or, how about recent calls to teach the right brain to make it even "righter" by creating a greater condition of equality for it with the left brain? Does neurology make practice? Of that we have no doubts these days, even if we still don't quite know how.

PART III

Process Training in Education and Special Education

18
Faculty Psychology in the Schools

INTRODUCTION

In this and several subsequent chapters we shall examine some representative texts in education and educational psychology (oft the two were synonymous) of the nineteenth and early twentieth centuries, as they addressed the issues of process training. The reader will encounter considerable similitudes in moving through this review, from one author to another. Clearly the suspicion is justified that in those days, as in our own, authors were freely borrowing from each other.[1] Two points will rapidly be revealed by our review: (1) Process training was a major pursuit of educationists during the nineteenth and early twentieth century; (2) the training of the mind and its faculties was considered as important, if not more important, than the imparting of knowledge—at least from the standpoint of educational and psychological theory.

By and large, faculty psychology and formal discipline were partners in the enterprise of such previous process training. Mature faculty theory, properly developmentalized after Rousseau and Froebel had gotten through with it, recognized a hierarchy of cognitive, affective and conative processes. Educational psychology texts usually recommended that the training of processes begin with attention to perception and its various sub-faculties, progress through imagination into memory, or from memory into imagination (the order depending on how one conceptualized the operations of these faculties or the variety of functions

---

[1] Though unlike our own day they rarely justified their borrowings by references.

assigned to the sub-faculties which they commanded),[2] upward to encompass reason and the cognitive powers or faculties associated with it; then, finally concluding with the training of the will.[3] Affective processes were also to be trained. Motor processes sometimes were considered apart from the others, but in most instances I have examined, trained as subordinate components to other faculties in lower grades, higher cognitive processes in higher grades. Some theorists, like Harris, objected to this arrangement—as we shall see; but it generally held. Will and will-power were often a matter of higher education, e.g., at the college level.[4]

The doctrines of classical formal discipline were still very influential; in particular, the idea that curriculum should be used to train processes. However, the spread of popular education and the influences wielded by sense-realist and naturalist movements resulted (we have observed in earlier chapters) in a variety of approaches becoming acceptable as means of training the mind—even though some heavy rationalization had to be indulged in at times to justify their acceptability as "disciplines." Gradually the term "discipline" came to be interchangeable with or replaced by appellations of a less rigorous sort, e.g., mental culture, mental cultivation, mental training—at least in the lower grades. There was general agreement, in any case, that the mind and its powers could only be improved through use, i.e., exercise. E. B. Wickersham, Superintendant of Schools in Pennsylvania, during the middle years of the nineteenth century, wrote:

> No means are known whereby the faculties of the mind can be developed but by exercising them. By the potent spell of the magic word Exercise, is evoked all human power. The proof of this proposition is found in multitudes of facts. The senses grow more acute by using them. The memory is improved by remembering, the reason by reasoning, the imagination by imagining. All these powers, too, become weak if not used. These facts may be learned from each person's own experience, or from observation upon others. The law inferred from them is fixed and universal. (Bode, 1940, p. 85)

While the idea that exercise was essential to accomplish such training continued to be a sine qua non of cognitive education, after the work of such men as Rousseau and Froebel, the notion that the goals of such training could only be accomplished when its means induced ennui went

---

[2] Some process trainers believed that memory training should precede the training of imagination (depending upon idiosyncratic interpretations of how these two "faculties" worked, and their precedences).

[3] The Will was interpretable both in cognitive as well as conative and affective terms. We owe this facility of usage to St. Thomas Aquinas, whose theories brought reason and faith together so as to satisfy both Aristotle and church authorities.

[4] We often forget that moral training was as much a responsibility of our colleges and universities as cognitive training or knowledge (Jenks and Riesman, 1968).

pretty much by the board. More and more we read in the process training texts of the nineteenth and early twentieth centuries of the need to elicit the pupil's interests in order to make process training effective; though to be sure the methods recommended for the elicitation hardly seem conducive to this goal.

An important point: Whereas faculty psychology and formal discipline were typically seen as essential copartners in cognitive training theory, this was not necessarily the case as time went on. One could conceive of faculties as being trained entirely without a curricular framework. One could also conceptualize formal discipline as directed to improving the activities of a unitary mind, rather than as training specific cognitive processes.[5] In the years of formal discipline's decline, its proponents often tried to salvage its doctrines by disavowing faculty theory, which had become odious in many scientific circles.

There are other issues that should be kept in mind as we review process training efforts in this chapter. First, the theories that sustained them evolved with the times; we shall see this even more clearly in later chapters when we take up the cause of process training within special education. As new theories and new psychological and educational information appeared on the scene, process trainers picked them up and used them. The idea of instinct thus is to be found frequently in their writings, in association with and sometimes as explanation for faculties—a most proper association. Gall had, in fact, adapted the conception of Pierre Jean George Cabanis (1757–1808) that the organism is equipped by nature with basic reaction tendencies in its nervous system that assist it in its adjustments; that is what Gall's faculties were intended to do. Thomas Reid had also spoken about instinctive tendencies. Bain, whose writings, *The Senses and the Intellect* (1855) and *The Emotions and the Will* (1859), were exceedingly prominent works in their day, was quite concerned with innate dispositions to actions. His writings did not go unheeded by facultists. Above all else, there were theories of evolution. Charles Darwin's *The Origin of the Species* (1858), *The Descent of Man* (1871), etc., could not be ignored by au courant process trainers, especially when Spencer was hovering about. Since habit is closely associated with instinct it too began to appear regularly in process trainers' theories and methods. Bain, in particular, appears to deserve credit for this. His treatment of learning and habit (elaborated from some of Spencer's suggestions) influenced

[5] The "new" phrenology, e.g., emerging from the work of Fritz and Hirtzig, Fernier, Broca. The "diagram makers" and other localizers were regarded by some disciplinarians as mounting a new threat to formal discipline. This was on the grounds that formal discipline was intended to address a unitary mind (or soul) functioning through its faculties rather than as a horde of disparate localized brain functions.

many important theorists, including William James. It also influenced the maxims of process training.[6]

NEUROLOGY IN EDUCATION TEXTS

Of particular importance to nineteenth and early twentieth century process trainers was the nature of processes they trained. If their books addressed "mind" and mental powers, what were the origins of it and them? Originally, educators could look to philosophers for the answers. After the neurological revolution created by Gall and the later "new phrenology," they felt compelled, most of them, to at least acknowledge the nervous sytem in their accounts of mental process. It is instructive to follow some of the ways our process trainers of the past came to grips with the CNS.

Addressing a select sample of books,[7] my observation for the mid-nineteenth century is that educational process trainers of that time did not feel compelled to consider neurological functions. Warren Burton's book, *The Culture of the Observing Faculties* (1865), did not concern itself with neurons, nor appreciably with any other parts of the body. However, during the latter decades of the nineteenth century, neurology had to be addressed by faculty trainers, since they sought to base their training practices on the science of psychology, and this psychology, at least in such important quarters as those inhabited by Bain, Spencer, Ribot, and certainly Wundt, was decidedly physiological-psychological.

N. A. Calkins, in his *Manual of Object-Teaching* (1882), a Pestalozzian manifesto for Americans, recognized the brain as ". . . the chief organ of the mind" though, he cautioned ". . . precisely how the mind acts through the brain and nerves and various organs of sense, no man can fully explain." Nevertheless, training the mind means altering the brain, which was regarded as "plastic," readily altered by experience, and compared to the musculature in the changes it undergoes through exercise.

The great means of improving any power, physical or mental, is exercise . . . the first effect of an exercise on a muscle is to occasion the destruction of a portion of the material that composes it, and this leads to an increased flow of nutritious

[6] To be sure, habit was a commonplace term across the centuries. Aristotle and Froebel both shared interest in it.
[7] Using what might be called a random-walk sampling procedure, I walked through the stacks at the University of Pennsylvania's library rather randomly and picked what books I could that seemed to address the topic of faculty training. My walk was random. I doubt that my selection of books could be called the same; it was, however, decidedly unbiased; I took whatever I found on a particular day.

material to restore that part. In this way the repeated exercise of a muscle enlarges its size and gives it increased strength and power.

In like manner, the exercise of any of our mental powers, while causing the destruction[8] of a portion of the nerve material of the brain, causes also an additional flow of nutritious material to that part, and thus the mind is improved and strengthened by the increased volume and strength imparted to the organ of the mind—the brain. (Calkins, 1882, p. 297)

Louisa Parsons Hopkins, in her *Educational Psychology: A Treatise for Parents and Educators* (1886), gave a stern admonition to her readers:

The teacher must have a knowledge of his material; he must understand the nature and laws of the human mind and body, . . . prepared to train and develop them . . . he must have learned the science of the body which is physiology, and the science of the mind and soul, which is psychology, or he is in no degree fitted to assume the office of teacher. (Hopkins, 1886, p. 3)

She does warn, in her book, of the limitations of physiological study:

The brain is not the mind. . . . The nervous accompaniment of a mental phenomenon does not account for that phenomenon, it is only its medium. The difference between the two is one of kind. "No sound psychology" . . ., "is possible which does not keep in view this fundamental disparity of the physical and psychical, and the consequent limits of the physiological explanation of mental facts." (Hopkins, 1886, p. 8)

Hopkins, however, adhered to the phrenological conception that training improves the brain:

The brain structure of each individual will naturally progress according to the law of race development; yet training is an important factor in that development, and may determine, to a great extent, its conformity or nonconformity to heredity, and create individual independence of growth and structure. (Hopkins, 1886, p. 31)

In some of her discussions, we appear to be in the presence of opinions that were molded by the evolutionary ideas of Spencer and Jackson, and of neurological S-R associationism:

From the physiological point of view, the voluntary motor act which emanates from the brain is only the repercussions more or less immediate of a sensory impression. It may not be a simple and purely reflex phenomenon, but a complex one that lays various zones of the brain under contribution and resumes in itself the different elements, so that the unity at last represents personality; it is sensibility multiplied by all the cerebral activities in agitation, and becomes the

---

[8] The conception of nervous matter requiring "destruction" and nutrition to be developed to a higher level of functioning or to improve in efficiency was faulty neurology, based on analogies to the musculature.

conscious human personality which reveals itself in this coordinated series of activities. (Hopkins, 1886, pp. 31,32)

Hopkins's book was developed from a course of lectures which she gave to the "Normal Class of the Swain Free School." It was, therefore, based upon lectures given to a relatively unsophisticated group of teachers in preparation. That neurology was considered essential for a basic understanding of education by novices is testimony to the "neurologizing" spirit of Hopkins's day and of the increasing reliance of process trainers upon the nervous system as a rationalizer of their procedures.

Joseph Baldwin, Professor of Pedagogy at the University of Texas (ca. 1896), was a particularly fluent exponent for both the psychology and education of his times. We find a relatively brief amount of direct attention paid to the CNS in his book *Psychology Applied to the Art of Teaching* (1896). How does this fit with my claims that process trainers of his day were prone to neurologize? A ready answer is to be found. Baldwin was also author of *Elementary Psychology*. His students could turn to that for necessary knowledge about the nervous system, and then to his book on process training for the meat and potatoes of training that nervous system.

However, *Psychology Applied to the Art of Teaching* does touch on nervous functioning and in a most charming way that deserves re-recitation. Baldwin speaks of a Sensorium and a Motorium through which the self receives and sends messages. As the physiologist studies the body from the standpoint of it being an "animal organism," the psychologist (faculty psychologist, here) must restudy the body from the standpoint of self and ask:

What is the plan of the human body? How may it be made the fittest instrument of self? (Baldwin, 1896, p. 18)

Baldwin wrote about making the nervous system an ally; however, he, like Hopkins, warned against confusing it with mental activity and self.

So blended are mental activity and brain activity that self is sometimes confounded with his physical organism. But a self-conscious physical organism is not even conceivable. With sensory excitation in the sensor-cerebral-ganglia the series of physical forces terminates. Self initiates a *new series*. Mental acts are occasioned but not caused. Self does these acts; self is the cause. To establish the theory of one substance and one series the votaries of materialism are forced to sacrifice self, God, immortality. They think of mind as mere fleeting phenomena, a succession of nervous shocks, a secretion of brain. Materialism is a cruel master, annihilating even hope. (Baldwin, 1896, p. 24)

Baldwin was thus a dualist, in the Descartian tradition. The self, that is to say the soul, used the brain but was not *it*. Baldwin's further comments on the issue of unconscious thought underline this point:

> Unconscious cerebration is a vicious expression, implying that a brain thinks. . . . This notion is one of a nest of vipers that prey upon the vitals of a true psychology. . . . Self, not organism does all mental acts. . . . A brain is merely a physical organism in connection with which self, in some unknown way, thinks, feels and wills. (Baldwin, 1896, p. 24)

If Baldwin was niggardly in his appreciation of the role of the CNS in mental functioning, Reuben Post Halleck, in *Psychology and Psychic Culture* (1895) and *The Education of the Central Nervous System: A Study of Foundations, Especially of Sensory and Motor Training* (1897), was to effusively extol it.[9]

> Marvelous as are the mind's achievements, we must note that it is as completely dependent upon the nervous system as is a plant upon sun, rain, and air. (Halleck, 1895, pp. 9,10)

Both of Halleck's books devote a considerable number of pages to neurological functioning and its importance to mental functioning.

Halleck's treatment of the nervous system is rather didactic in *Psychology and Psychic Culture*. One chapter sufficed: "The Nervous Mechanism at the Disposal of the Mind." Its connection with the process training chapters that followed is rather tenuous. A much more vigorous treatment of the nervous sytem and its cultivation through training is to be found in *The Education of the Central Nervous System*, wherein we find chapter titles clearly showing Halleck's neurological biases.

Chapter I.   The Central Nervous System
Chapter II.   Fatalistic Aspects [referring here to views that the CNS could not be modified by training]
Chapter III. The Possible Modifications of the Brain
Chapter IV.   Attention, Nutrition, and Fatigue in Their Relations to the Central Nervous System

[9] There is some uncertainty in my mind as to the actual dates of Halleck's books. *The Education of the Central Nervous System* was first printed in 1896 and reprinted in 1897, which is the version I am using for this presentation. However, Halleck, in his credits for *Psychology and Psychic Culture*, apparently printed in 1895, lists the 1897 book, which according to its printing date had not yet seen the light of day—obviously. However, two different publishers were used and this might explain the riddle of publication dates. It would seem that *The Education of the Central Nervous System* did have priority, in light of its greater emphasis on neurology and its lesser emphasis on process training. But it is a matter for speculation. He also wrote a book on psychology, which preceded *The Education of the Central Nervous System*.

Chapter IX.   Cerebral Development by the Formation of Images
Chapter XII. The Central Nervous System and Enjoyment

Halleck's theories of brain training were based on the premises of the new phrenology. There are specific areas of the brain, he said, related to and underlying specific mental and behavioral functions:

> When we speak of developing certain parts of the brain or of lack of develop-ment in certain tracts because of deficiency in early training, we may be said to assume the theory of definite brain localization. . . . The fact that the body is a unit and that the same blood courses to all parts of it, must not cause us to shut our eyes to these undoubted facts of localization of function. We know that special exercise develops special muscles. We also know that, if the sense of sight is trained, while hearing receives no education, the brain tract correlated with hearing will not be proportionately developed. (Halleck, 1896, pp. 2,3)

Halleck took issue with those who claimed that the brain could not be modified, for example, on the basis that the number of brain cells is determined at birth, ". . . and that no training will increase this number."

> We, however, fail to see why it is necessary to increase them. We might as well argue that it is hopeless for any one desirous of becoming a runner to exercise the muscles in his legs because the number of his legs is absolutely determined at birth. . . . There are between one and two thousand million cells in the brain, and there was probably never a person who did not have several million undeveloped ones. (Halleck, 1896, pp. 42,43)

There are three different ways, he explained, by which the brain is developed. (1) The sensory brain tracts are modified by incoming currents from the nerves leading to the different senses and motor areas of the brain by the organism initiating new muscular movements or repeating old ones, (2) the "fibers of association" of the brain are developed by the complex activities of the organism which involve "associations." (3) The more psychological associations formed between modalities and functions lo-cated in different parts of the brain, the more are developed the association fibers, which ". . . are, of course, as important to a brain as good wagon roads, canals, and railroads are in the development of a country (Halleck, 1896, p. 55).

This was the way of the diagram makers of the 1880s and the way much of process training in the future would take for a great many years. The faculties are created by associations. This was the way of the "new" phrenology. But certain echoes from the "old" phrenology will surely strike the reader's ear in Halleck's enthusiastic anticipations for the sci-ence of neurology.

If we could examine the developing motor region with a microscope of sufficient magnifying power, it is conceivable that we might learn wherein the modification due to exercise consists. We might also, under such conditions, be able to say, "This is the motor region of a piano player. The modifications here correspond precisely to those necessary for controlling such movements of the hand"; or, "This is the motor tract of a blacksmith; this of an engraver, and these must be cells which govern the vocal organs of an orator." (Halleck, 1896, p. 55)

Halleck did not intend to wait upon such improvements in microscopic technology to proceed on his course of cerebral development. The facts were clear as he saw them:

Every time the song of a bird is heard, a flower is seen, a rose is smelled, a door knob is touched, a fruit is tasted, a pound weight is lifted, the corresponding sensory brain tract is thereby modified. Whenever the fingers are flexed, an arm extended, the muscles of a leg moved, the body bent, the expression of the face changed, or a word spoken, there is a corresponding motor modification in the brain. (Halleck, 1896, p. 60)

A rather ambivalent attitude toward mind-faculty-brain relationships was demonstrated by T. F. G. Dexter and S. H. Garlick in their book *Psychology in the Schoolroom,* which went through a number of editions between 1898 and 1902. The spirit of Wundt is to be seen in many of their pages, despite the book's being largely directed toward process training of a sort that Wundt would scarcely have approved. Thus they define psychology as "the science of consciousness," and the role of the psychologist that of dissecting ". . . mental phenomena into elementary states of consciousness" (Dexter & Garlick, 1902, p. 2). As to mind–body relationships, it would seem that they read a bit of Descartes and Leibnitz.

The terms *soul, spirit, ego, self, subject,* are sometimes used as synonymous with mind. Mind is contrasted with matter. Matter occupies space; its special quality is *Extension.* Mind does not occupy space. It is *unextended. . . .* Matter is outside us; it is *objective.* Mind is something within us; it is *subjective.* Mind has reference to the ego, to the self. Matter has reference to the non-ego, to the not-self. . . . Through the body the mind acts upon the outside world; through the body the outside world acts upon the mind. . . . Between mind and body there is an intimate though mysterious interdependence. (Dexter & Garlick, 1902, pp. 6–7)

The way the authors deal with the issues of localization are suggestive of Flourens's diffuse assignment of functions to the cerebrum; unlike Halleck, Dexter and Garlick were relatively unresponsive to the glamour of more precise brain localization theories.

The part of the body most intimately connected with the mind is the brain. The brain is the chief part of the nervous system. Even a brief study of the nervous system will do something to help us understand the working of the mind. (Dexter & Garlick, 1902, p. 7)

Speaking of the "functions of central, end and connecting organs," Dexter and Garlick used the terms of the past:

The sensory organ is especially fitted to receive certain impressions of the outer world . . . generally conveyed to the end organ in the form of *vibrations*, which the *End Organ* transmits to the *Afferent Central Organ* . . . [which] interprets these vibrations and sends vibrations along the *Efferent Nerve* to the other *End Organ*, which is set into action in some special way by these vibrations (Dexter & Garlick, 1902, p. 10)

The cerebrum is the seat of *sensation, reasoning, emotion and volition*. These powers would seem to reside in the grey matter. (Dexter & Garlick, 1902, p. 12)

So much for those readers who thought process trainers had to keep up with the latest developments, theories, and research in neurology. Our two authors, perhaps made nervous by their awareness of Wundt's antifaculty position and his psychophysical parallelism, were quite content to adhere to the mind–brain relationships proposed at a much earlier time, which did not commit them strongly to any particular current position. Nor does their exposition of process training, the bulk of their book, depend upon neurological explanations. The mind and its powers were to do quite well in their own independent spiritual atmosphere.

W. T. Harris is our next facultist to be considered. One of the most influential men of his period in education, and one who was responsible for many school reforms. Harris was disturbed by the assaults made upon the psyche by materialism. His book *Psychologic Foundations of Education* (1910), subtitled *An Attempt to Show the Genesis of the Higher Faculties of the Mind,* was an effort to reestablish spiritual values within education. He leaned heavily upon Kant's a priori forms (categories) and Hegel's dialectics in so doing. The book, erudite and mystical, seems more intended for philosophers than for teachers. But Harris saw philosophy and education as inextricably interdependent (Cremin, 1961).

Writing at a time when brain localization of psychological processes was generally accepted though still argued about, Harris provides his readers with a rather sophisticated discussion of brain localization history, theory, and problems for his time, as well as a description of neurological and sensory functioning.

However, Hegelian that he was, Harris, was not inclined, despite his recognition of the importance of neurological research, to believe that mind and its higher spiritual powers would be found lurking in the plies and pleats of the brain. He was clearly a dualist:

It is evident . . . that there is some connection with the soul and the body. . . . We use the body in two ways: we perceive the external world by means of it, and we use the body as an instrument in order to produce changes on the world that we see. Here we have inward movement and outward movement through nerves. . . . In both we have what may be explained as mechanical action. It may be so explained, but it is not as yet so explained. Mechanical action borrows all its energy from another—it merely transmits it and does not originate it. Vital action is self-activity[10] in combination with mechanical action; it originates activity and guides it . . . the origination of motion before the nerves receive it is certainly self-activity. The spiritual individuality of the soul builds its body and uses it in interaction with the world, in perception and volition. (Harris, 1910, pp. 91–92)

The dualism that Harris espoused, one of mind–body separation but interaction, allowed him to acknowledge the importance of neurological knowledge and yet ignore it, in his formulation of a "psychologic" theory of education.[11] It was the higher faculties that Harris was concerned about, and these were not to be explained on any physical basis. Discussing the localization of brain functions he made the point distinctly that mind is not reducible to matter:

When interpreted by introspective psychology and compared with its results, we do not discover any grounds for distrusting the spiritual theory of the soul, nor do we see in these researches much that throws any light on the real nature of the mind itself. (Harris, 1910, p. 112)

The mind–body distinction is again made by Harris in his discussion of the eternal or universal nature of the soul as against the ephemeral, unstable matter that is the nervous system.

The matter of the brain and nerves is constantly changing . . . the body is organic; the soul is not organic, but a higher form of being—namely, a pure self-activity which makes its product (that is to say, its organism) for the sake of self-revelation. (Harris, 1910, pp. 113, 114)

There is a precipitous decline in references to neurological functioning in the texts that I have observed in succeeding years of the twentieth century insofar as process formulations are concerned—texts by Colvin

---

[10] Self-activity is a cardinal Hegelian thesis. It was used heavily by Froebel and it was a major point of departure for Harris.

[11] He was somewhat approving of Gall's observations which he found "original and of some value." However, he did not think much of Spurzheim, because the latter was imprecise and unoriginal in his formulations and omitted the ". . . higher intellectual powers," because he (Spurzheim) ". . . possessed them feebly and had no power to observe them" (Harris, 1910, pp. 100–101).

(1914), Norsworthy and Whitley (1920), Drever (1922), Sawrey and Telford (1964), and Garrison, Kingston and McDonald (1964), contain
scarcely any traces of reference to the CNS. One reason for this could be
the increasing specialization which was found in psychology texts, so that
"ed psych" books no longer had to carry the major burden of providing
teachers with an understanding of psychology. Second, neurology appears to have been most in favor with facultists at a time when psychology
was basically of an "armchair" variety, i.e., based on speculation. Even
William James's "Principles" were of the "armchair" variety. Under
such circumstances, process psychology chose to use neurology as its
base of hard data. Once psychology moved into research, however,
process psychology had entirely new sources of "evidence" to support its
postulations. Psychological data and psychological theory (even when not
supported by data) became the foundations of process theory as formulated for teachers. The biological references in Colvin's book were to
reflex–action, instinct, and habit, not to brain centers. Norsworthy's
book *The Psychology of Childhood* presented developmental data. Drever's book *The Psychology of Education,* talked of instinct and emotion,
not of sensory and motor tracts. Sawrey and Telford considered developmental data and heredity, but afforded no attention to any type of
brain functions. Garrison, Kingston, and McDonald did the same. Psychological and educational tests, measurements, and experiments basically became the basis of process, where and when process was speculated.

Factor analysts have always had a yearning to locate their factors
(faculties) within neural tissue, though I will not provide a litany of their
names and claims here. In recent years, within the field of learning
disabilities there have been those who still insist upon anchoring their
"abilities" a la neurone, while others talk of processes in terms of
correlated disabilities, and still others talk of no processes at all.

THE SENSE ORGANS IN EDUCATIONAL TEXTS

We would be amiss if, in preparation for our examination of latter-
day faculty training positions, we did not also call to your attention the
assiduous discussions that facultists of the late nineteenth and early
twentieth centuries also assigned to the senses. These were concerned
with the anatomy and physiology of the sense organs, as well as their
functions relative to process training. For our latter-day faculty trainers
were the products of the sense–realist movement examined in the previous chapters. Perception was the key to process training at all levels for a
great many of them, at least until the influences of Pestalozzi and Froebel

abated sufficiently to allow the scientific psychology of the future to become present. But then that was sensory in large part, too, was it not, and so, sense organs to the fore, ever again, until, at last they, like the CNS, were relegated by educational psychology and education to other texts as time passed. Musculature, too, I might mention in passing, suffered a similar fate.[12]

---

[12] Passing references to anatomy and physiology are, however, still to be found in some educational psychology books written well into the twentieth century.

19
Process Training in the Schools—The Beginnings

INTRODUCTION

We are ready to approach the training of faculties within the classrooms of the late nineteenth and early twentieth century. Much of it will be on the basis of the texts we have already reviewed in the previous chapter. The faculties of education, as I have said elsewhere in this text, have not always been identical with those of philosophy, psychology or neurology. In some cases, the term "faculty" was employed by educators purely as an instructional reification. If a pupil was able to do something, he was described as having the faculty of doing it. From this standpoint, one could, and did, speak of pupils having a faculty of two column addition, dotting i's, or writing impassioned poems. It is not always clear whether *faculty* thus used was intended by its author as a figure of speech or as *process*. From my reading of texts in which this was common, it appears that there are regular shifts from one type of meaning to another.

In other cases, the faculties educators addressed are the traditional ones of philosophy and psychology. Aristotelean, Scholastic and—quite popular—Kantian models were used by this or that writer on classroom processes, often with individual variations of the author's own creation. As the modern age of experimental and correlation psychology matured, the processes educators spoke about sounded increasingly like those of our own age. Quite naturally, in the sense that their data, like ours, was that of the experiment or correlational study. There were also efforts to reinterpret traditional faculties in more modern garb that would allow them to survive their critics. Not all facultists chose such latter-day

246

means of accommodation, but chose, as we shall see in later chapters, to call a faculty a faculty and live with its conceptualizations in ways that would have made Christian Wolff proud. But most moved with the times, whatever those times. Keepers of the flame they were, nevertheless, even though they managed their lights, at different times, with whale oil, gas, or copper wires, rather than with tallow. It was, and is, this adaptability of faculty psychology that has enabled it to survive the attacks of the mighty and the righteous scorn of the elite. What does it matter, however, if a faculty is forced to change its conceptual shape from deus ex machina to homunculus, to hydrolics, to the headache-conquering machinery of over-the-counter drug advertisements, to—more recently—television-type schematics, and—most recently of all—computer-speak? As long as it survives. And as far as faculty training goes, that has even managed to endure by disavowing that faculties exist at all, but proceeding ahead, nevertheless, to train pupils in proper habits of perceiving, attending, remembering, reasoning, willing, etc.—by a process of unreification, if you please, which still preserves the implications of the original reifications intact. Keep this in mind for all the chapters that follow.

Most important to keep in mind as we proceed, is that this review of process training has now reached a post-Rousseau, post-Pestalozzi, post-Froebel age. Whereas classical formal discipline had concerned itself with the use of traditional curricula to train the mind, later educators were attempting to train cognitive processes directly. Whereas classical formal discipline had sought, above all, to train the memory, later faculty trainers were much more concerned with perception. Whereas bookish instruction had been stressed by classical formal disciplinarians for its value in cognitive training, the educator whose mind had been shaped by the theories of Rousseau, Pestalozzi, and Froebel was likely to emphasize experience as the great trainer.

BURTON

The first of the books that we shall examine in this chapter, *The Culture of the Observing Faculties* (1865), by Warren Burton, is clearly in the Pestalozzian tradition. The term "observing faculties," in fact, is a translated version of our old friend *Anschauung*. And while Rousseau also speaks to us from the pages of Burton's books, it is Pestalozzi who dominates its pages. Anticipations of Froebel are there also, to be sure.

Burton wrote of the infant's self-culture of his faculties—though with assistance from members of the family—as he ". . . creeps about the room . . . for the pleasure of muscular action . . . hunting for prey to his awakened and craving perceptions'' (Burton, 1865, p. 11). In the process:

> The several perceptive powers then come into action: finding out the various qualities—figure, color, size, weight. (Burton, 1865, p. 12)

Things, rather than books, are to be the major vehicles of instruction for the schoolchild in Burton's object-lesson classroom:

> Let our primary-schoolrooms, and, indeed, the higher schoolrooms, be well provided with shelves and boxes. Let these be filled with all sorts of productions of nature and art; specimens of all sorts of wood and metal; all kinds of cloth and leather, or any other fabric—indeed, with everything which can well be brought into a school, and put in some proper receptacle. Let each one of these objects be a subject for examination by classes in convenient order, under the direction of the teacher. (Burton, 1965, p. 17)

Burton wrote of training the individualizing faculty[1] as soon as a child learns to talk and learn names (Pestalozzi at work here). It is the most important of the "perceptive" faculties, and differs constitutionally in strength, one individual to another. Through it the individual learns to distinguish various properties in objects. Despite innate differences in strength, it is subject to training. A child's success ". . . at such perception is a matter of discipline and use" (Burton, 1865, p. 34).

Following his learning to individualize, the pupil is to proceed to learn the discrimination of form, size, measurement, weight, and color. Are these faculties? Yes and no, depending where you read of them, for they are also described by Burton as qualities. Thus there is "the quality of weight." Its training proceeds by providing the child with scales and letting him weigh various commodities. The teacher is advised:

> Do not make a task of the matter, but rather a pastime which you may join in yourselves. In the first place, let each one present take the commodity in hand, and lift it up and down, and guess how much it weighs, or rather try to form an accurate judgment about it. Then put it onto the scale and see who comes nearest to the fact. Thus the little company, parents and children, not only receive entertainment, but gain knowledge, and a special faculty is disciplined for future and valuable use in the affairs of life. (Burton, 1865, p. 39)

Reflecting the strong influence of Rousseau, whether directly or through the medium of Pestalozzi, Burton recommended that nature be used to train the perceptive faculties. Flowers, grains, trees, leaves, minerals, animals, insect curiosities, fishes and shells, local geography, etc., all are means of developing ever more fine and precise discriminations.

---

[1] Borrowed from phrenology.

Some families have on hand a great variety of shells. It would be a pretty exercise for the children, on a winter's day, to sort out these flowers of the sea according to species, size, or some other rule. Thus several of the observing faculties would be cultivated, together with pleasant occupation. (Burton, 1865, p. 57)[2]

This emphasis upon nature or—more broadly conceptualized—environment as both medium and method of training faculties is to be found throughout Burton's book. Ignorance of nature's phenomena he observed all about him, even in the best-educated children. He was writing at a time when Latin and Greek were still of more importance than science within proper academic circles and when the idea that natural phenomena were worthy objects of knowledge was still being contested. Burton's complaint that a young girl of his acquaintance thought that rain was the result of holes being torn in "big bags in the sky" was followed by his vehement protest:

But was she not at a grand boarding-school, learning great, great words in big books, and at high expense? Was she not getting a fashionable education? What more could the world ask of her? (Burton, 1865, p. 59)

Thus the study of nature—is not simply for the need of acquiring useful knowledge but to properly train the observing faculties, to make a child:

. . . a more accurate as well as far reaching observor. Train him to notice every distinct object within the scope of his eye; all the inequalities of the surface, all varying tints of the vegetation between the first tender green of the spring and the russet of the autumn. Every rock, every little hillock and bush, or whatever else may make a distinctly observable thing, should be a lesson to his eye . . . unspeakably more profitable than the dry, hard description of textbooks, as they have generally been forced upon poor learners, or rather word-getters . . . even some . . . minutiae of the land's surface are important indications to the eye of science; and would you not be glad to have your son look upon nature with such an eye. Wherever he shall ramble or travel, would you not have him exercise a keen, detective, sight, instead of a vacant gaze. (Burton, 1965, p. 66)

The study of nature was also thought to be productive in cultivating the higher powers.

Nature is . . . performing operations continually. . . . The child observes many of them . . . and he may ask, "Why is this or that? what makes it do so?"

---

[2] To remind the reader: The emphasis on pleasure and interest, increasingly found in faculty training texts and reflecting a severe departure from traditional disciplinarian emphasis, is a clear indication of the impact that Rousseau and later Pestalozzi and Froebel were having on faculty training procedures. The child was to be enticed into faculty training, rather than whipped into it.

The loftier reflective faculties are now beginning to operate. . . . The reflective faculty—the causality more than any other—prompts to questions. (Burton, 1865, p. 57)

We might digress a bit at this point to observe that perceptual training in many educational texts into the twentieth century was based upon the notion of experiential, even sensory, deprivation. Studies were carried out by such eminents as G. S. Hall in the United States and E. Meumann in Germany showing that city children were unaware of or unresponsive to the phenomena of nature because of their tenement-bounded existences; and that rural children, conversely, were ignorant of urban phenomena. These deficiencies were often considered perceptual, since perceptual is whatever one defines it to be. In such cases, the senses were to be trained through appropriate environmental exposure, with verbal labeling and explanations of the phenomena encountered.

Returning to Burton, we find that he listed among the more important of the perceptual powers to be trained "the central and leading perceptive power" (Burton, 1865, p. 87), i.e., the power of eventuality, one he adapted from the phrenologists. It is ". . . a distinct operation of the intellect . . ." having the function of observing action, and to watch for what shall be done next, a ". . . distinct faculty . . ." (Burton, 1865, p. 95). Not to be neglected, either, "the faculty of time," defects in which may be due to "constitutional deformity" (Burton, 1865, p. 135). And particularly important:

> . . . a special mental faculty which takes cognizance of order. It gives to the individual the ability to notice and appreciate it in things around, and also the ability to do things, and keep things himself, according to the same rule. (Burton, 1865, p. 139)

The perceptual faculties are the basis for the development of all higher faculties. Thus recollection and memory (facultists often distinguished between the two) require effective cultivation of perception:

> The memory, as a general rule, performs its office well or ill, just in proportion as the original perceptions are disciplined and developed. (Burton, 1865, p. 154)

Effective judgment, too, depends upon the effective discipline and development of perception. If the latter is properly trained, effective judgment can be expected. In fact, if an individual has had proper perceptual training, failures in his judgment can only be attributed to poor character. Burton wrote his book at the time of the American Civil War when issues of cost effectiveness, budget overrides, and the like were major problems:

> Millions of money are lost to the nation through the ignorance of commissaries, quartermasters, contractors, and other providers for our armies, through

the lack of that early and continued education of observing faculties which has now been advised. If the loss, for the most part, comes from any other cause, it must be from a criminal dishonesty, deserving the punishment of a penitentiary from a cheated country. (Burton, 1865, p. 153)

Did Burton have a place for learning disabilities in his scheme of things? It would seem so, for he repeatedly expressed concern about uneven endowment in the various observing faculties and remarked about their implications. In speaking about disciplining the "special mental faculty which takes cognizance of order," he recommended preparation in systematic habits of dressing, taking care of belongings, repeatedly ordering objects in prescribed places, and systematic training in domestic and vocational activities. However, there will inevitably be those who do not accommodate easily to such training:

Indeed, how many there are who, as to a systematic disposition of things, are about as much to be calculated on as the dust blown and tossed by the wind: They cannot calculate on themselves. They are disturbed by tendencies which have crept into their natures from some progenitor: so these tendencies impel them to and fro, up and down, evermore, because no educating hand came in good season to the rescue.

Such being the contingencies of poor human nature, they should be looked after without fail, and right early. The educator should understand the child's native mark of ability to appreciate order and conform to its laws. . . . Be the faculty stronger or weaker, it should be put to its use, and consequently under discipline, the same as the other intellectual powers. The . . . loving heart . . . together with a quickening conscience will prompt to perseverance and insure success in the more difficult case. (Burton, 1965, p. 141)

If Burton was responsive to learning disabilities, he was also cognizant of the implications of giftedness. The latter, in his estimation, is usually a state due to inherited qualities. It might also be a consequence of being spared the debilitations of traditional academic training:

The histories of many distinguished persons show that a culture quite independent of prescribed educational forms made them useful and eminent. Among the extraordinary men of our own country are those whose literary advantages were exceedingly limited. They simply exercised their faculties on whatever came before them, or lay in any providential line of duty. They might have had some one power, like individuality or eventuality, in uncommon strength. This, spontaneously leading the way, might have brought concomitant powers into action and increasing ability. All the faculties were employed on the objects, the events, the realities of the present world and state of things, while their privileged contemporaries were engaged in abstract books and chapters, sentences and words. (Burton, 1865, p. 155)

CALKINS

N. A. Calkins's books on object teaching were among the most prominent and influential in the American Pestalozzian movement. *Primary Object Lessons,* first published in 1861, was an exemplar of its day and was printed in some 40 or so editions. It is very much Pestalozzi as transmitted through English Pestalozzians, being derived from a work called *Lessons on Objects* written by an Englishwoman, Elizabeth Mayo (1830). Calkins's later book, *Manual of Object-Teaching* (1881) is both a supplement and expansion of the author's original treatise. It is on this later book, which seems to reflect Froebel as well as Pestalozzi, that our discussion of Calkins's work is based. It should provide us with an understanding of object lessons, at the height of a mature exposition, as they related to the training of cognitive processes; we are not otherwise concerned with object lessons and object teaching.

In a discussion of the "Principles of Education" within Calkins's latter-day book, the reader is told:

> Education is the cultivation of all the native powers of the child by exercising them in accordance with the laws of his being with a view to development and growth. Repeated exercises of bodily organs give ease of action, and produce habits. Proper exercise of the mental powers gives clearness of perception and certainty of knowledge. Proper exercise of any bodily organ, or mental or moral power, increases its strength. (Calkins, 1881, p. 348)

The ideas that we have read about in our chapter on the sense–realist—educational–naturalists are reiterated by Calkins. Learning begins through sensation, which is elaborated into perception and conception. Action and reaction between external objects and the mind's inherent powers constitute the process of "natural education."

The pupil should be an "active doer" learning directly from "things and acts," while the teacher's role is that of a ". . . *stimulator and guide of the learner's work*" (Calkins, 1881, p. 348).

> A child may be surrounded with a thousand objects, and these may act on the organs of sense, but *until the mind voluntarily occupies itself with one or more of these sensations there can be no mental acquisition or culture*. Education, then, does not depend on the number of objects . . . or subjects . . . employed by the teacher but upon those only which the mind looks at, observes, and thinks about. (Calkins, 1881, p. 358)

Calkins's powers and faculties are either perceptually derived, perceptually dependent, or inextricably committed to furthering perceptual purposes. The first to operate is the power of perceptiveness. After sensations are transmitted from the sense organs to the brain "over the nerves,'' the faculty of perceptiveness gives ''notice'' to them. Perceptiveness is the power of doing this; perception is the act.

> *Perceptiveness* is that power, or natural tendency of the mind, to act in perceiving whenever the occasion for action occurs. *Perception* is the action of *perceptiveness*. When its action ceases, perception ceases: but *perceptiveness* is a permanent power, or tendency of the mind, which is always ready to act whenever the appropriate excitement affects it. (Calkins, 1881, p. 366)

The next power in Calkins's panoply is *conception* which after ''. . . mere perception ceases . . .'' takes the ''impressions'' and the ''mental residua'' that *perceptiveness* has created and organizes them in such a way ''that the image, or knowledge, may be retained and recalled without the presence of the object . . .'' (Calkins, 1881, p. 366).

Calkins's exposition of the relationship of conception and perceptiveness is hardly clear. They somehow seem to be subpowers within another, broader, power in which their functions are combined or unified:

> *This mental power of receiving and retaining* the mental elements of knowledge of objects, whether called *conception,*[3] or *intuition,* or *apprehension,* or *perceptive faculties* or by some other name, is the *primary knowledge-gatherer* of the mind. It collects elements of knowledge that aid in other mental operations. It furnishes the means of recognizing the same objects when they come again under notice. (Calkins, 1881, pp. 366–367)

Does this particular mental power, described above, constitute *Anschauung*? The answer appears to be that it shares in *Anschauung* with other processes, as we shall soon see. For the moment, let us try to understand Calkins's distinction between *perceptiveness* and *perceptive faculties*. The first would appear to be a designation for faculties associated with the operation of single sense modality. The second appears to be a broader multimodality process. At least this interpretation suggests itself from the manner in which Calkins approached its cultivation:

> This faculty, or mental power, depends for its development and strength upon the activity and acuteness of *the several senses*. Whatever will render the perceptions through the eye more clear, keen, and certain, and those through the ear more acute and quick, will greatly increase the intellectual strength of the faculty of perceptiveness. . . .
>
> Therefore, to cultivate this power of *perceptiveness* in a right manner, means should be devised for such exercises as will attract the attention of the perceptive powers, and lead to careful observation of properties and qualities of objects. (Calkins, 1881, p. 375)

---

[3] Calkins's use of conception here is particularly confusing. Perhaps it was a cognitive ''typo'' on his part.

Thus sense training is essential, both to train the powers of the individual modalities and for the more global perceptive faculties. Teachers were enjoined by Calkins to "devise suitable exercises for increasing . . . facilities of action" for each of the modalities (Calkins, 1881, p. 367). The eye, since it is "the intellectual sense" is to receive priority. It is to be cultivated by observing the physical properties of objects, such as form, color, number, surface, size, position, distance, motion, rest, solidity, and their various combinations and uses. Hearing is to be trained through distinguishing "sounds of various kinds" and by proper speech habits. "The organ of touch," whose greatest power is centered in the finger tips, is to be trained by being exposed to such properties as hardness, softness, smoothness, roughness, heat, cold, and ". . . all those minute sensations which come to us through the tips of the fingers" (Calkins, 1881, p. 372). The muscular sense is also to be trained:

That which is known as the *muscular sense* is intimately connected with *feeling*, and is the peculiar manifestation of the sense of touch which takes cognizance of resistance, and enables the mind to obtain ideas of size, distance, position, form and weight.

The cultivation of the muscular sense is important, not only because this is the organ of force, but because it is also necessary to bring the muscles under the complete control of the mind, so that their movements may be made with facility and precision, and thus contribute to skill of workmanship and manual execution in any trade, art, or occupation. It may be cultivated by observing those sensations which arise from *resistance* and *pressure*, such as weight, strength, toughness, and elasticity, or from a push, a prick, or a blow. (Calkins, 1881, p. 372)

Smell and taste also require training, the first essentially as an "aid in the preservation of life . . . as to distinguish between smells that are simply disagreeable and those that indicate miasma and disease"; the second ". . . to cultivate a desire for those kinds of foods . . . conducive to health . . . and to increase a dislike for those things which . . . pleasant to the taste, are nevertheless known to be injurious to health" (Calkins, 1881, p. 373).

In all instances, concrete sensory experiences, Calkins recommended, should constitute "the chief lessons of childhood."

The knowledge a child acquires by the exercise of his own senses penetrates the intellect more deeply and pervades it more completely than any other: for it is the impression which Nature herself makes upon the mind by direct contact, whilst all other media of instruction are but representations, more or less imperfect, of nature. The originals and types of all erudition must be thus stored by direct sense perception, for without it words would have no significance. (Calkins, 1881, p. 377)

Whereas the perceptive powers are the means by which "the elements of knowledge are gained and ideas formed" (Calkins, 1881, p. 379), there is another higher set of faculties. These loosely correspond, it seems, to the "inner senses" of medieval facultists:

> The term *Powers of Mental Acquisition* is here used to designate that class of faculties, or powers, which causes those active operations that take place at the several gate-ways of knowledge, and transmit information to the mind from the outward world; and those also which aid to combine, arrange, classify, and retain this information, so that it may become permanent knowledge. These powers are manifested in the mind's ability to gain a knowledge of form, color, number, size, position, distance, order, weight, sound, time, etc., and in the ability to compare, combine, construct, classify and arrange. (Calkins, 1881, p. 379)

It is somewhat difficult to determine, from the above description, how the powers of mental acquisition differ muchly from the powers of perceptiveness. However, further discussion by Calkins suggests that they subsume the powers of perceptiveness and include the former with higher cognitive operations such as attention.

> Our powers of mental acquisition may be cultivated by attentively observing likeness and unlikeness or resemblances and differences, in whatever comes within the range of the senses. It is by such an exercise of the senses as will impart to them activity, acuteness, accuracy, facility, and strength that the desired cultivation must be accomplished. Appropriate exercises of the organs of sense will add these qualities to the several powers of the mind. (Calkins, 1882, p. 379)

The powers of mental acquisition participate in *Anschauung* which in Anglo-American terminology is discussed by Calkins as observation.[4]

> This is not a faculty of the mind, but rather a common term used to express the results of the action of several mental powers, prominent among which are those of perceptiveness, conception and attention. Inasmuch as in the practical exercises of education the combined action of these powers of mental acquisition is chiefly considered rather than their individual qualities, I shall here treat of them in this united capacity under the name of *Observation*. (Calkins, 1882, p. 380)

It is, when all is said and done, this observation, a matter of broad perception with affective accompaniments focalized through attention:

> To observe is not merely to see, and hear, and feel, but *to see, and hear, and feel with such attention as to perceive clearly and accurately*. The more the observation is thus employed, the more will be brought into the view of the mind by sensations and perceptions. (Calkins, 1882, p. 380)

The training of observation is critical to the development of later

---

[4] Observation training, has implications far beyond the perceptual realm.

understanding. ". . . the memory and judgment are [thus] directly cultivated," and ". . . it strengthens and rouses the energy of the mind . . ."
(Calkins, 1882, p. 382).

If training of the perceptual powers and those of *observation* constitutes a first stage of process training for Calkins, language training is the
second.

Sensations, perceptions, and conceptions may exist, impressions may be
taken into the mind, and these may blend into ideas of objects, all without the aid
of language. But we come to a point, in the development of the human mind,
where a new development is required . . . which will enable the mind to embody
its ideas in *signs* external to ourselves, so that it can safely store them away with
the certainty of finding them again when wanted; and also making them known to
others. This element is supplied by language. . . . Although we *perceive* the
world by means of the senses it is through the forms of language that we comprehend it. (Calkins, 1882, pp. 384–385)[5]

Language serves to energize and clarify perception's products, to
stabilize and organize them, to condense and symbolize them in abstract
forms. That is the substance of the preceding quotation. That is why it
plays such an important role in object lessons:[6]

A fine exercise for perceptiveness, and for making distinct perception a habit,
is to take pupils to parks, gardens, groves, workshops, manufactories, etc., and
afterwards to get them to write out descriptions of all they saw and heard that
came to their knowledge through each or all organs of sense. (Calkins, 1881, p.
377)

Calkins recommended language training along Pestalozzian lines.
The child is to gradually and systematically learn to name and describe
objects from an early age, clear articulation being emphasized. And if
perceptual progress is to be accelerated through the use of language, the
converse, too, holds true.

The instructor (as the child enters formal schooling) should employ every
means . . . to guard his pupils against using obscure terms or words without
definite ideas attached to them. . . . The introduction of a new expression should
be preceded by the perception of the thing signified, or the illustration of the fact
which it serves to designate. (Calkins, 1882, p. 388)[7]

Things the most familiar, circumstances the most trivial, may give rise to
instructive and interesting observations, and to the highest contemplations. Any

[5] Calkins sounds very much like Luria in his discussions of language as thought. One might
even detect anticipations of Pavlov's "second signal system" within his writings.
[6] Pestalozzi's views, of course.
[7] Description of things, conversation about things, whether spontaneously expressed by the
pupil or directed by the teacher, all improve language, which requires anchoring in perceptual
experience for its proper maturation.

object in the house, in the street, a toy—anything which is within reach or view —all that nature has produced, or art has modified, can be made a subject of observation. . . . The more numerous the facts which children collect . . . the more clear and extensive will be their knowledge of words. (Calkins, 1882, pp. 389–390)[8]

Frequently ply them [pupils] with questions which will lead them to tell what they know of the objects that they see, and the sounds which they hear; and cause them also to gain ability to answer, by observing carefully those things about which the questions relate. (Calkins, 1882, p. 389)

After language, according to Calkins, it is memory that is to engage the process trainer's attention. Memory is a ". . . combination of several powers. . . ." The major principle governing effective memory is ". . . *order and system in blending, classifying and associating our ideas*" (Calkins, 1882, p. 393).

The principles of association must be observed in developing memory: ". . . to fix important truths and principles indelibly in the mind of a pupil" so that he is able to readily recall them, it is necessary to establish ". . . connections between them and *other ideas already existing in his mind.*"[9] Language plays an important role in memory.

Association of ideas alone produces but involuntary memory. The sight of an object, a sound, an odor, a taste, or a feeling, may each recall ideas which have been previously associated with them; but the mind has not the power to recall at will, unaided by the presence of the associated object or quality, ideas that have not been symbolized with words or signs. (Calkins, 1882, p. 395)

But language, to be effective in memory, must, in turn, be based on training the powers of observation.

. . . in cultivating the memory through the aid of language, care must be taken to secure the ideas which the words symbolize by means of classification, also by associating them with the words, and the words with the things represented. . . . If the perceptive faculties be clear and active, the observation quick and accurate, the power of attention steady and strong, and habits of classifying and associating ideas carefully formed, the memory will firmly hold and readily reproduce the ideas and words which have been duly acquired. Therefore, by cultivating the powers of mental acquisition, the foundation for a retentive and ready memory will be laid. (Calkins, 1882, pp. 395–396)

Further in the vein of perceptualism, Calkins recommended multisensory training as a means of ensuring effective memory.

Employ as many of the senses in the acquisition of knowledge as possible, for each one will convey its peculiar form of impressions to the mind, and the

---

[8] Calkins was quoting from C. Marcels's book *Language as a Means of Mental Culture*.
[9] Herbart's influences are to be detected here, the principle of apperception at work.

blending of these . . . furnish a great number of links by which knowledge may be connected and recalled at will. If an object be examined by sight, then by touch, and the ideas which are thus gained of it be clearly stated in words, the mind will receive a third and new impression through the sense of hearing. Here, then, will be three distinct classes of impressions, derived by means of the senses of seeing, feeling, and hearing, to unite in forming a complete idea of the object, and also at the same time furnishing three classes of links by which it may be remembered. (Calkins, 1882, p. 401)

"Attention is a mental phenomenon indicating a most important power of the mind," according to Calkins (1882, p. 402). It was not classified by him, however, as belonging ". . . to that class of powers which are usually called 'faculties' " (Calkins, 1882, p. 402). It rather exerts its influence (whatever it is) through and by the other faculties, rather than of itself; it originates nothing, it teaches nothing, but it is essential to the operation of the other faculties:

. . . since the several faculties would become so deficient in the ability of continued action without it, that even natural acuteness could accomplish but little, and we should be destitute of those mental characteristics and steady habits which contribute so largely to success in life. (Calkins, 1882, p. 402)

Calkins's definitions of attention, are, as are all other cognitive processes, associated with perception. In a sense, attention is a qualitative state of perception, and part of the observation process.

The force of attention is simply the perceptiveness of the mind adjusting itself perfectly to the objects it contemplates, so that they may produce their full effect upon it. Until this adjustment is effected, the impression of the objects must necessarily be confused and imperfect. . . . (Calkins, 1882, pp. 402–403)

It is critical that attention be brought under control of the will as early in life as possible.

. . . for when this power has become subject to the *will,* the foundation is laid for every degree of mental culture which circumstance will permit. (Calkins, 1882, p. 403)

The culture of attention is not, however, a matter of training it as much as it is one of creating attitudes in the pupil that will promote its proper habits. Rather than compulsion being used to command a pupil's attention, he is to be drawn into its exercise through his curiosity, love of activity, and his interest in what he is doing. A pupil's preferences for specific elective courses of study are to be encouraged on the basis that he will learn to attend to less interesting courses of study at a later time.

The next in the parade of powers dealt with by Calkins is *imagination*.

The mind has the power . . . of recombining at will parts of the simple elements of many ideas into new images of the mind's own ideal creation. These powers of simple analysis and synthesis are called imagination. (Calkins, 1882, p. 408)

Imagination was described as being, at its core, perceptual. We would expect, at this point of our review, nothing less from Calkins.

It is a law of the mind that *the imagination can deal only with ideas of sensible objects*, with concepts derived from something seen, or heard, or felt, or tasted or smelled. *It has nothing to do with abstract ideas and truths, or with feelings wholly separated from sensible forms.* Whatever imagination deals with it represents in such conditions and clothes in such forms and colors, as come within the cognizance of the senses. Ideas derived from sensible objects, therefore, constitute the groundwork of its operations. (Calkins, 1882, pp. 408–409)

Imagination manifests itself in all sorts of activities: in children's play, the artist's creations, the philosopher's axioms, the scientist's discoveries. It builds upon memory's products and collaborates with higher faculties:

In the process of reasoning imagination goes beyond the known and forms conceptions of something in the unknown, to which reason extends its powers of rigid examination. (Calkins, 1882, p. 410)

Calkins bemoaned the fact that the cultivation of the imagination was ". . . almost totally neglected in the usual processes of education . . ." and that it was often viewed in its displays as being a waste of time on a pupil's part. He consequently warned:

If we do not cultivate the imagination in such a manner that the child may delight itself in forming natural combinations and useful mental creations, the mind will run riot in folly and idle musings. . . . (Calkins, 1882, p. 410)

The proper means of cultivating the imagination are through language and pictorial illustrations forming word pictures in the child's mind. Lessons in geography allow children to be "transported in imagination" to different locales. History lessons can help the child imagine colorful events of the past, the study of biographies permits mental identification with great personages.

The pleasure which young children derive from a narration of the simplest history is due to the liveliness of the pictures in their minds. The images which are conjured up within them are, perhaps, more brilliant and highly wrought than real objects would be. (Calkins, 1882, p. 411)

There are other ways, too: "Fables, riddles, conundrums, puzzles . . . furnish means for exercising this faculty" (Calkins, 1882, p. 414).

Nor should the teacher forget to use these vehicles to impart practical maxims and moral truths.

The exercise of imagination prepares the mind for cultural appreciation and imagination is, in turn, exercised by exposure to the treasures of culture, for ". . . every work of the imagination appeals to the imagination of the observer, and . . . develops the faculty . . . (Calkins, 1882, p. 415). Nature, however, is imagination's great teacher, and keeps it reality-oriented.

The study of nature . . . is the most successful mode of developing the highest powers of this faculty. The science of astronomy furnishes an excellent means of exercising the imagination in a manner that will strengthen the intellectual and moral powers, and prevent the development of those fancies which, while they can never be realized, tend to weaken these powers, and to create a dislike for science and the realities of life. (Calkins, 1882, p. 415)

Calkins's discussion of the powers of human reason lists three major processes: comparison, judgment, and reasoning. It is not clear whether these are three independent faculties, since the author speaks of them as powers, or operations (a term he also uses frequently), of the basic faculty of reasoning.

The development of these powers is a matter of a progression from the sensory and the concrete to the abstract and symbolic. Their training, as of all other powers, must be grounded on sound perceptual preparation.

It will . . . readily be perceived that accuracy of judgment must depend upon habits of correct observation. Here we see again the great importance of thoroughly training the *Powers of Mental Acquisition;* for, unless these be thoroughly cultivated, much of the labor bestowed upon the other powers of the mind will be in vain, and it will be impossible to attain accuracy in reasoning. (Calkins, 1882, pp. 421–422)

The cultivation of comparison powers is founded on the law of similarity, which ". . . exists in the mind before any educational processes can be applied to shape it." Its habits are acquired by exercises in the discrimination of likenesses and differences in a progression from the concrete to the abstract.

. . . the familiar objects of nature should first claim our attention, and their physical parts and properties be considered earlier than their abstract qualities.

The child's earliest perceptions being those of color, form, size . . . motion, given . . . by sight, he should be led to notice resemblance of one object to another . . . in respect to these perceptions. Thus the dog is set beside the cat, the sheep beside the goat, the horse beside the ox . . . the grape with the plum; while comparisons are made in respect to form, color, size, manner of motion, etc. The covering of the sheep may be compared with that of the dog, the overlapping feathers of birds with the shingles or tiles on a roof.

Subsequently this process of comparison may be extended to objects of which one is absent and inaccessible; thus it becomes the means of enabling the imagination to form conceptions of things beyond the range of our senses. In this manner the formation of the claw of the tiger may be understood from comparison with that of the cat; the contour and characteristics of a wolf from those of a dog. . . . Indeed the field is boundless for the exercise of comparison. . . . (Calkins, 1882, pp. 417–418)

After training to compare on the basis of other senses than the visual, the pupil is to move into considerations of likenesses and differences in various areas of school work, e.g., through classification into genus and species of various objects. At still higher levels of training, he is to compare relations, e.g., by studying analogies.

Comparison leads to judgment, does it not? Training the mind in the operations of comparison also trains it to judge.

During the exercises of comparison and classification the mind is constantly forming divisions as to the likeness and unlikeness, resemblances and differences of objects and qualities, and these decisions are called *judgments*. . . .

By this exercise of considering various things with reference to each other there is laid a foundation for accuracy in discrimination and soundness of judgment. (Calkins, 1882, p. 421)

Calkins's definition of judgment, which he occasionally equates with understanding, leaves us somewhat uncertain as to what this particular power, operation, or form of "activity" really is. We do know that is important and that it plays an essential role in determining the operations of the reasoning faculty.

There is . . . that higher form of mental activity, which determines the result of reasoning, that is called judgment. This term is also applied to the final decisions of the mind, attained through the process of reasoning. The mental activity, known as judgment and its processes, is so intimately connected with the operations of other mental powers, and their special educational influences are so inseparable, that it will not be profitable to dwell longer on the separate consideration of judgment in this connection. (Calkins, 1882, p. 422)

Perhaps, because of its rather uncertain status as a separate and distinct faculty, Calkins was not about to offer any specific training program directed to the improvement of judgment qua judgment. It was to be trained in conjunction with comparison, and as a subprocess within reasoning.

Plato had enthroned reason as the highest and noblest of cognitive faculties and the one of greatest spirituality; reason is that faculty that partakes in the universal. Few psychologists, physicians or philosophers disagreed with Plato's exaltation of reason, not even Freud. To Calkins, too, it was the noblest of cognitive processes.

Calkins observed that while the exercise of comparison and judgment "in the discriminating processes of classification" (Calkins, 1882, p. 423), "definiteness and exactness" to thought, something more was needed to complete the processes of thinking:

> . . . there appears to be a still higher mental power which enables the mind to search deeply and scrutinize closely even the obscure or doubtful in our mental accumulations, till everything is brought into light, the false separated from the true, and our conscious knowledge rendered positive. This highest mental power is called *reason*. This power of the mind differs from all others in its capacity for dealing with a multiplicity of objects and ideas at once, and drawing general results out of a whole.
>
> Reasoning is a mental process by which unknown truths are determined, or learned, by means of those that are known. We see some things to be true in consequence of having seen other things to be true. This mode of seeing is called *reasoning*.[10] If we observe what the mind does—what its successive acts are when it sees a thing to be true because it has previously seen another thing to be true—we shall observe the process of reasoning. (Calkins, 1882, p. 423)

Calkins then distinguished between mathematical reasoning which is a process whereby the mind ". . . determines unknown mathematical truths by means of those that are known . . ." and moral reasoning which ". . . deals with things in the concrete. . .," placing its reliance upon testimony in contrast to mathematical reasoning in which ". . . all terms are exactly defined and limited" (Calkins, 1882, p. 424).

Reason is the truth organ of the mind, which furnishes the answer to the hows as well as to the whats of existence. It can go back into the past to find causes, and it anticipates their effects in the future. It apprehends the relations of the universe.

> It is by this faculty that these relations, in all their complexity can be known or apprehended, and the great law of intelligence exhibited in its highest form. (Calkins, 1882, p. 426)

But in the end, this most far-reaching of faculties is assigned very much the same type of training as lower ones—at least in the beginning stages, when reasoning is a matter of observing relationships in dealing with ". . . present objects and present acts" (Calkins, 1882, p. 426).

> *The reasoning of children consists chiefly in making simple deductions or inferences from palpable facts, or from the comparison of two objects, one or two being present.* (Calkins, 1882, p. 426)

[10] Calkins could not resist the perceptual implications of anything whatsoever.

Later on, as the child matures (between 12 and 15 years of age), his reasoning powers are trained in the ways of methodical thinking, investigating relations of abstract ideas, but also (never forget perception) in ". . . dealing with facts established by experience and observation" (Calkins, 1882, p. 427).

Whatever will add clearness, directness, conciseness, and a natural order to the habits of thinking and speaking, of readily perceiving and inferring all the relations of a subject, and deriving therefrom the proper conclusions, will strengthen the power of reasoning. (Calkins, 1882, p. 427)

Calkins, however, generally neglected the training of the higher faculties. The Pestalozzian tradition he was working in was one in which the concerns of secondary education were quite secondary. He was at home with the young, training them how to observe and to describe their observations, and so the higher powers were to be trained along and by means of the lower powers or through the traditional means of formal discipline. But the lower powers, ah yes the lower powers! Certainly no one reads Calkins's book need have any fear that children exposed to object lessons did not receive their full measure of perceptual training.[11]

HOPKINS

Louisa Parson Hopkins was a prolific author. She was also a Pestalozzian, having written her very own *Observations Lessons in the Primary Schools;* the naturalistic tradition was strong within her. Other of her books were: *The Handbook of the Earth,* a book about "natural methods" in geography; *Natural History Plays;* and *Breath of the Field and Shore.* The sanctification of mother nurturance by Pestalozzi found its echo in her book *Motherhood.* Pestalozzi's insistence upon the scientific method in education was emulated in her *Practical Pedagogy,* subtitled *The Science of Teaching.* Her physiological orientation to education is demonstrated in her *Psychology in Education* and her *Educational Psychology: A Treatise for Parents and Educators* (1886), strongly influenced by physiological psychology as well as by Pestalozzi and Froebel. The latter book is worthy of our attention, in that it demonstrates the sort of faculty wisdom that "experts" of the day believed was appropriate for normal school teachers and parent audiences.

To Hopkins, psychology was faculty psychology; though her defini-

---

[11] Once again, the reader should be reminded that our treatise deals with cognitive powers. Faculty trainers, Calkins among them, also placed great store on training the moral powers, particularly that of the will, and the emotions, too.

tion seems to take Wundt as well as Pestalozzi and Froebel into consideration:

> Psychology gives us the knowledge of the nature and order of the faculties of the mind and soul; it reveals the laws of activity and growth of the mental and moral powers. . . . It is the science of the immortal part of man. . . . It is a descriptive science, taking the mental and moral constitution of man as the field of its observation. It is founded on the introverted subjective observation of the mature mind, the analysis of experience, and upon the objective observation of the activities and growth of childhood. It was studied experimentally in this latter way by Pestalozzi and Froebel, among educators; by metaphysicians it has been studied subjectively. (Hopkins, 1886, p. 4)

Hopkins's discussion of process development pretty well parallels that of Froebel's spiritual accounts. Her faculties, despite the fact that the brain is ". . . the mind's only organ in this life . . ." are spiritual, since the brain, as well as other parts of the body ". . . is but the tool and the servant of the mind, and not an essential part of it" (Hopkins, 1886, p. 15).

The spiritual nature of cognition was further emphasized by Hopkins when she assured her readers that the validity of sensory information (upon which every good Pestalozzian and Froebelian must build) is vouchsafed by the Creator.

> The certainty of knowledge is assumed by reason of our belief in the integrity of the Creator, who could not deceive or mislead his creatures by the faculties which he has given them, or play them false through the only means with which they have been endowed for learning the truth. (Hopkins, 1886, p. 15)[12]

Hopkins's list of "activities or faculties of the mind" is a classical one. In the order of their natural development, they are: sense perception, memory, imagination, judgment and reason, and taste (the aesthetic faculty). As to sense perception, Hopkin's writings present us with a now-familiar party line:

> The most simple, most obvious, most universal, and earliest developed activity of the mind is sense perception. It is the fundamental source of objective knowledge. In childhood it is the only source of knowledge, and the senses are the only avenue to the intelligence. (Hopkins, 1886, p. 33)

Thus begins Hopkins's chapter on sense perception.

Hopkins warned against seeking the secrets of perception in the sense organs, the nerves or the brain, which is ". . . but an instrument or medium for the operations of the mind so fine as to be often mistaken for

[12] Descartes had made a similar point. The validity of our knowledge about the external world is vouchsafed for by the self-evident truth that God is not a "deceiver." Berkley offered a similar explanation.

the mind itself'' (Hopkins, 1886, pp. 34–35). For ''. . . we cannot understand the intellectual part of an act of knowledge . . .'' from the standpoint of a physical act (Hopkins, 1886, p. 35). She was clearly a mind–body dualist.

Perceptual training? But of course. ''All faculties grow by exercise. Simple exercise builds up the power for higher'' (Hopkins, 1886, p. 35). Effective exercise of the mind is dependent upon attention, which concentrates nervous energy upon particular groups of brain cells. In young children, natural exercise through spontaneous activity provides perceptual development. In their application to objects of investigation, the senses assist each other. ''Knowledge is best attained by the combined exercise of all the organs of sense'' (Hopkins, 1886, p. 37).

> It is the duty of the teacher to exercise and strengthen the organs of sense and to make the sense perception as accurate and as complicated as possible; to train the mind to perfect attention to the impressions made on the brain through the senses. (Hopkins, 1886, p. 38)

To a great degree, this is accomplished by allowing nature to give perceptual training. ''The forester makes his sight keen by living in the forest. . .'' (Hopkins, 1886, p. 39). However, the eye and the ear should also be assisted to expand their range of perceptual functioning by artificial aids such as the microscope and telescope for sight and ''other scientific instruments'' (unspecified) for hearing.

In sense perception, Hopkins noted that we exploit the other cognitive processes.

> In the act of sense perception we constantly exercise the faculties of apprehension, of comparison, and of judgment, thereby developing the reasoning powers; by the accumulation of facts we exercise the memory, and by the orderly arrangement, the powers of analysis and generalization; also by the perception of the beauty and harmony of the universe we develop the taste and the soul. It is by this great function of sense perception that we make all our connections with nature and our fellow-men, and through the mental activity to which they give rise we reach the development of our whole mind and spirit, and the establishment of our relationships with the universe and its Creator. (Hopkins, 1886, pp. 42–43)

Hopkins also discussed the possibilities of perceptual disability. Proper perception depends upon the soundness of the sense organs involved, an adequate nervous system, a properly ordered mind, and effectively directed attention.

> If the organ of sense is perfectly sound, but the nerve defective, or *vice versa,* the act of perception is defective; and if the nerve and organ are both sound, but the mind disordered or absorbed, so that attention is imperfect, then perception is defective. (Hopkins, 1886, p. 35)

In latter-day use, imagination as a faculty came more and more to be defined in terms of the elaborations that it carried out with stored information, rather than simply as a power that provided the higher processes with *simaculacra* of perceptions. Memory came to be increasingly assigned the job of storing and producing images and often moved up to second place (following perception) operationally, in the *seriatim* of cognitive functioning.

From this followed Hopkins's statement: "In the natural order of mental development memory follows sense perception" (Hopkins, 1886, p. 44). Memory which ". . . primarily means the retentive power of the mind . . ." is to be distinguished from recollection which is ". . . a power of calling . . . knowledge into consciousness, or recollecting the information or experience," which ". . . completes the function of the mind called memory" (Hopkins, 1886, p. 44).

The faculty of sense perception would be as useless without the faculty of memory, as either would be without the faculty of recollection, yet they are each distinct faculties. (Hopkins, 1886, p. 45)

Memory, like the other faculties, was to be "strengthened and trained."

Habits of concentrated attention to objects of memory, of association of ideas, of analyzing trains of thought, improve and develop the power of the memory and recollection. (Hopkins, 1886, p. 49)

Multisensory experiences, learning under conditions of positive emotional attitudes, and increasing the number of associations with which they (memory and recollection) may operate, also "improve and develop" their power:

It will be easier to commit words to memory if repeated aloud or frequently copied or said in concert, thus multiplying the means of mental impression. It will be easier to retain ideas acquired under pleasurable excitement. . . . The memory will be quickened by a complicated association of ideas and strengthened by constant exercise. (Hopkins, 1885, p. 52)

The importance of memory was emphasized by Hopkins from several standpoints. Besides retaining knowledge, it also develops automaticity of behavior through "permanent changes" in the nervous system. Additionally, in keeping with Spencer's theories of evolutionary psychology, she believed that the memories of the individual gradually become the "instincts" of his race:

In view of all this . . . how important is the training and nourishment of the memory. That such facts and images shall be put within its grasp as are worthy never to be forgotten, such as may enter into the very organic structure of the mind and build up the immortal intellect and character; that no habits of thought shall be begun and consummated by the teacher which cannot be woven into the very tissue of the understanding—this is the great aim of the education of the memory. If sense perception takes in the mind's nourishment and food, the memory digests and assimilates it and thus builds up individual and race characteristics. (Hopkins, 1886, p. 55)

Imagination, the third of Hopkins's major faculties, was allowed by her its ancient role of reproducing images, though dependent upon memory for this purpose. Imagination, Hopkins said, is the "faculty of reproducing the impressions made on the memory" and the "power of complete and active revivability and reproduction" (Hopkins, 1886, p. 56). She then made the traditional distinction between the aspect of imagination that reproduces images and its more active transforming side. Respecting the reproduction aspect of imagination, she explained:

(The) mental conception, or image, is a pattern which memory gives . . . for imitation. . . . If we have observed a material object in its totality of impression on the sense perception; if we have so retained it in the mind . . . that we are able to reproduce it in all its entirety, so that it stands before the mind's eye as if the senses again perceived it—then we produce it not merely by memory, but by imagination. (Hopkins, 1886, p. 57)

This sort of imagination should be exercised "in the vivid and thorough recollection of what has been presented to sense perception." It requires prior cultivation of the "faculty of complete observation and the acuteness of sense perception . . . so as to provide the mind with clear facts it may reproduce" (Hopkins, 1886, p. 59). Means of providing imagery training include "drawing, moulding, building, singing, acting, and coloring," feeding the imagination "through well-chosen stories or fancies, by pictures, by demanding . . . original effort . . . in talking and writing" (Hopkins, 1886, p. 60).

The other aspect of imagination, "the power of reconstruction" which results in "an original combination or organization of revived facts of memory" was identified by Hopkins as "productive or creative imagination" (Hopkins, 1886, p. 61).

Poetry, painting, sculpture, architecture, musical composition, dramatic acting, mechanical invention, and even the higher mathematics and the sciences, are all fields for the exercise of this power. (Hopkins, 1886, p. 63)

Properly cultivated imagination of this second sort is particularly important to mankind. It connects itself with the moral faculties. "If allowed to construct ideals of degradation, or revel in visions of vice or horror" imagination can debilitate the soul. But imagination can also conceive of "ideals of beauty, of harmony, of goodness, of truth" which nourish the soul (Hopkins, 1886, pp. 66–67). Constant exercise, within proper channels, is recommended:

> The imagination easily yields to the law of habit or automatic tendency; it grows by exercise; it submits to control; and is more effective under the influence of systematic training. . . . Constant effort and labor, training and study, are essential to the best exercise of even the productive imagination. . . . The greatest genius imposes the greatest amount of arduous labor in its possessor, and requires persistent practice and intense efforts of will for its accomplishments. (Hopkins, 1886, p. 65)

Judgment and reason are the highest of the faculties in Hopkins's hierarchy and the last that we shall study in her book. Very much like Binet was to say later (and, for that matter, many other process trainers), Hopkins described judgment as an omnipresent, omnioperative faculty:

> In the processes of the mind involved in sense perception,[13] memory and imagination, we find evidence of a pervading faculty essential to them all, which we call judgment. The function of this faculty is to analyze and compare the facts of apprehension, and draw a conclusion from this analysis and comparison. Every act of sense perception is to some extent a judgment,[14] and involves comparison and generalization, a balancing of associated sensations, and a determining apprehension of their relations. (Hopkins, 1886, p. 71)

The child exercises his faculty of judgment[15] when he gains facts. He observes things, compares them according to degree and kind, and on the basis of such comparisons forms his judgments.

> . . . by this judgment he analyzes, compares, generalizes, and arranges the results of observation which he holds before his mind for this purpose. Judgment, therefore, includes apprehension, abstraction, analysis, comparison, generalization. It lays a foundation for memory and imagination by grouping or classifying facts in the mind according to every variety of association, so that these faculties may have their material assorted and ready for use. (Hopkins, 1886, p. 72)

Training of this most pervasive, most important faculty is obviously essential:

> The faculty of judgment is susceptible of constant and careful culture. It should be called into exercise at every step of education. It will lead the child to

---

[13] Hopkins also discusses "taste" or the "sense for beauty," but it isn't clear as to whether she considered it a separate faculty; so we have gratefully omitted it from further consideration.

[14] Aristotle similarly called perception an act of judgment.

[15] Judgment is partly identified with "common sense," since it is a "rectifier of individual peculiarities of judgment."

intellectual and moral results which shall be final, to decisions which he need never again question. (Hopkins, 1886, p. 73)

The highest of Hopkins's cognitive faculties is reason, which proceeds beyond judgment to determine the verity of propositions and observations. "Every conclusion reached by reasoning must go back to axioms" (Hopkins, 1886, p. 77).

Reason, like the other faculties, is susceptible to training, which resolves itself, in considerable part, to a matter of teaching the pupil to reason inductively.

Modern education proceeds by the methods of inductive reasoning, which are the natural methods of the developing mind. (Hopkins, 1886, p. 81)

The pupil is to be taught to draw his own intellectual and moral inferences correctly so as to reach "true conclusions." He is to be trained to move from fact to opinion, and from experience to principles, and to establish cause and effect relationships when and where possible.

Hopkins's little treatise on educational psychology was an exemplar of the guides that were provided to budding teachers for work in the fields of cognitive development during the later years of the nineteenth century. Armchair psychology was still the psychology of the age. Pestalozzi and Froebel could be compatible with Spencer. It all had to fit rationally; empirical evidence was not required. Historical examples and common sense observations justified the system. It was with complete assurance in the correctness of her approach that Hopkins offered her pupils a summing up of her philosophy of process training:

Let me once more call attention to the insensible gradation of the faculties of the body, mind, and soul, and their indissoluble connection and order of precedence, passing through incomprehensible steps of transition from lower to higher, each serving its superior, and feeding and nourishing the higher functions of the complex unity of man. (Hopkins, 1886, p. 70)

BALDWIN

Joseph Baldwin was a prominent and prolific educator–psychologist who wrote a variety of texts, including one on *Elementary Psychology* and another on the *Art of School Management*. His *Psychology Applied to the Art of Teaching* (1892) is essentially a treatise on process training. The contents of the book quickly make this apparent. Part I was dedicated to the "Education of the Perceptive Powers"; Part II dealt with "Education of the Representative Powers"; Part III moved up into the higher cognitive range and proposed "Education of the Thought-Powers"; Part

IV was concerned with "Education of the Emotions"; and Part V addressed itself to "Education of the Will-Powers." Finally, in Part VI of the book, a bare 27 pages out of a total 371, the author took up "The Art of Teaching."

Baldwin was an effusive, hyperbolic, but systematic faculty psychologist. He had read them all, he said, from Plato to Herbart and beyond and, with the aid of successive classes of his pupils, whom he had engaged as helpmates, had developed a process training system approaching the ultimate, even if imperfect about the edges. Modesty did not become him. He did not stoop to it.

Baldwin defined psychology as the science of self, which breaks down into Kantian categories of "I know, I feel, I will." This self lives and works in a physical organism. Baldwin described its mental relationships:

> My sensorium and motorium give me direct connection with the universe. I have my headquarters for life in my cerebrum. In some unknown way I think, love, and decide through my cerebral ganglia and their connections. I cannot comprehend it; this knowledge is too high for me; but I know that self is generated with the body, lives in it, works through it, and leaves it at death. (Baldwin, 1892, p. 5)

Baldin defined his faculties in rather dynamic terms:

> I find that I have capabilities to know, feel, and will in distinct ways. I learn to call these energies my powers, my faculties, my capabilities. My faculties are simply my capabilities of knowing, feeling, and willing. (Baldwin, 1882, p. 5)

> The native energies of self are termed capabilities, power, faculties. I do acts different in kind. I perceive, I admire, I determine. I learn to call my energies to do acts different in kind from my powers, my faculties, my capabilities. The name by which I learn to designate each of my capabilities indicates its office in my mental economy. (Baldwin, 1892, p. 7)

Elsewhere, Baldwin indicated that faculties are really acts of a unitary organism and, still again elsewhere, offers what amounts to an operational definition of a faculty:

> Our faculties are simply our capabilities to do acts different in kind. A faculty is merely a distinct native energy of self. (Baldwin, 1892, p. 201)

If the reader suspects a bit of hedging, or pussyfooting, on the part of Baldwin in the above definitions, he is most probably right. Baldwin was a committed faculty psychologist, but he was writing in an age when the respectability of faculty doctrine was generally at low ebb—something on the order of illicit sex: many practitioners, but few boasters. Herbart had thundered forth his disapproval. Wundt was dissecting consciousness and had little time for traditional faculties. Baldwin wanted desperately to be scientific. At the same time, he was writing a text on educational psychology, from which, if one took away faculties, there was not too much left to talk about.

Whatever he sought to define them as, to avoid accusations of not having read his Herbart, Baldwin clearly and boldly defended the concept of basic independent processes, whose cooperative working together at times obscured the separate and distinct nature of each. This will be obvious in the narrative to come.

Baldwin emerges in his writings as a facultist of Froebelian persuasion, but with strong currents of traditional formal discipline still to be found throughout his thinking. Let us observe some of the more obvious Froebelian trends in his approach to processes.

Baldwin's discussion of processes presents them as botanicallike growths. (See cover.) We are presented everywhere in his book with graphic representations of mental, affective, and conative powers, appearing as leaves, stems, twiglets and branches on the fundamental *tree of self*. Baldwin described human development very much in the tradition of Froebel:

> The bud develops into the rose; the egg develops into the eagle; the child develops into the man. The process is termed *evolution*. . . . The process of the child-self developing into the man-self is called education and is *self-evolution*. The germ-self becomes the man-self. (Baldwin, 1892, p. 12)

Still further in the manner of Froebel, Baldwin wrote about self-effort, which is nothing else than the self-activity which the German philosophes and Froebel prized so much.

> Self-Effort educates. Nothing else does. The germ-tree in the acorn spontaneously appropriates the elements necessary for its growth. . . . The child-self spontaneously makes the efforts necessary to its growth. . . . The child makes efforts to remember; somehow its memory becomes more and more vigorous. The youth thinks; somehow his capabilities to think become more and more powerful. Self-effort develops power. . . . (Baldwin, 1892, p. 12)

Baldwin also insisted upon directed growth, again in the Froebelian tradition:

> Lawful Effort educates. Well-directed effort develops capability. The uniform ways in which self *must* act in order to grow are educational laws. Self-effort, conforming to the laws of growth, educates. . . . The science of education states the laws of self-growth in general terms as, "Well-directed effort develops faculty." (Baldwin, 1892, p. 12)

The term "culture" is often synonymous with education in the writings of bygone faculty psychologists, an inheritance from you know whom. No less so with Baldwin, who distinguished between the values of various studies for the mental culture they provide and their immediate content values." To wit:

> Studies are valuable for two things: for the *culture* they afford, and for the *use* that can be made of them. By culture here is meant the entire effect of knowledge on the mind, both in acquisition and possession. (Baldwin, 1892, p. 49)

What may be used for culture? Baldwin tells us this, too.

> A grindstone is a means of sharpening an axe and a plow is a means of cultivating the soil. Mathematics is a means of educating judgment and reason. Art is a means of cultivating imagination. In general, whatever tends to call forth normal mental activity may become a means for culture. (Baldwin, 1892, p. 49)

The teacher is to rely upon applied psychology to guide him in his efforts to culture his pupils' minds and powers.

> *Applied Psychology Is a Priceless Boon to the Teacher*. The teacher works in the light. He studies each mental power and discovers its nature and relations, its periods of growth, its laws of growth. Now he forms a map of childhood, a map of youth, a map of manhood. He beholds in one view the entire mental economy of the boy, of the youth, of the man. Here he discovers three fundamental principles: (1) *All the mental powers supplement and reinforce each other* so that educating one power incidentally educates in some degree all the powers. (2) *Each capability is susceptible of and requires distinct and specific culture.* As each stroke of the artist's brush tends to perfect the painting, so each lesson has its specific culture value. Teaching educates. (3) *The faculties develop in a definite order.* Educational maps attempt to show the order, and the teacher finds that a method of teaching is simply a systematic, persistent, efficient, plan of work adapted to a growing mind. (Baldwin, 1892, pp. 14–15)

By this time, I am sure the reader is aware that we are, with Baldwin's presence, in the company of a man who intended to be systematic in his approach to process training. His very conception of processes is one that organized them for this purpose. Baldwin's faculties, conveniently arrayed in a neat hierarchical order despite the complexities of their synchronies, allowed themselves to be precisely separated for purposes of training.

> As gravity is the fundamental physical force, so perception is the fundamental psychical energy. Sense-perception is the base of the cognitive pyramid and reason the crown. As we ascend we find that each capability rests on and is chronologically and psychologically dependent on all the capabilities below it; as, for example, imagination could not act but for perception and memory. This psychological insight is confirmed by practical experience, as the practice of all educators proves. . . . The claim that these powers are not elemental, but mere eddies in the stream of thought, forms of consciousness, modes of analysis and

synthesis, is based, I think, on the failure to discern clearly the co-operative nature of the mental economy. When we once gain the insight that each capability of self supplements and re-enforces all his other powers it is not difficult to gain the deeper insight that the stream of thought and assimilation and analysis and synthesis and apperception are in reality *resultant* co-operative processes. Each capability is a native energy of self, and is elemental in the mental economy. (Baldwin, 1892, p. 154)

Let us first of all review Baldwin's overall schema for process training. Then we will comprehensively review its application to sense–perception and selectively review its applications in the culture of the other faculties.

Baldwin first of all defined his terms for the faculties he intended to train. Then he provided his readers with a discussion of the importance of such training, e.g., the importance of sense–perception culture. This was followed by a discussion of the "growth" of the faculty (with an accompanying diagram charting it), describing the faculty's emergence at birth, its maturation and its eventual fate in old age. The *laws* of "growth" for the faculty were next in consideration.

A law is a uniform way in which an energy acts. Physical laws are uniform ways in which physical forces act—as, for instance, the laws of falling bodies. A mental law is a uniform way in which a mental energy acts, as a law of association. An educational law is a uniform way in which a mind must act in order to grow. Some educational laws are common to all our mental powers, and hence are called general laws. Other laws of mental growth are peculiar to certain mental energies and are termed specific laws. (Baldwin, 1892, pp. 47–48)

What are the general laws? There are three: the law of effort, the law of means, and the law of method. The observance of these three laws is predicated on the fundamental premise that "education is the development of capability by exercise" (Baldwin, 1892, p. 48)

Among the various educational principles lying at the foundation of all true teaching, no one is so universally accepted as this. (Baldwin, 1892, p. 48)

The law of effort calls for "well-directed effort" to educate a particular faculty. It is this kind of effort that develops "power" and strengthens "capability." The law of means states that any activity that calls a faculty into "vigorous activity" is the means for its "culture." The opportunity must be available for the faculty's exercise. The faculty must be actively called into operation as well. The law of method, the final of the three general laws of education, calls for "systematic, persistent and efficient" plans of work in order to educate the faculties; it is "orderly, continued and vigorous" efforts alone that truly develop "power."

What are the special laws? They vary from faculty to faculty, though there is some replication. Besides recommending his own special laws to govern the training of specific faculties, Baldwin recommended that his readers attempt to develop their own.

> You will discover other laws. . . . When you realize that all good comes from working in harmony with law, you will search for laws like diamonds. (Baldwin, 1892, p. 49)

As to the means of "educating" the faculties, Baldwin provided recommendations for each stage of life, preschool through high school, and sometimes beyond. He provided "tables of educational values" to assist in this education. These tables (one for each of the faculties to be trained) provided ratings by experts (including himself), on a scale of 1–10, for a variety of school subjects, as to their effectiveness in educating, training, cultivating, culturing—or what have you—the various faculties. In addition, the reader was asked to make his own ratings of these subjects and to "average" these with those of the experts. The rating "averages" were to provide a scientific basis from which to proceed in process training. For example, kindergarten and object lesson activities received ratings of "ten" from both Baldwin and an unidentified guest rater, a certain Dr. Brooks, for their values in training perception; while objective arithmetic and objective geometry received scores of eight and six, respectively (the lowest ratings in Baldwin's table of educational values for perceptual culture).[16]

Baldwin's comprehensive text on process training also reviewed the various causes of process deficiencies and defects these included: (1) *society mistakes*, for example, poor facilities and the "employment of incompetent teachers"; (2) *hygienic mistakes*, which might impede the development of the sense organs or impair their functioning; (3) *teaching mistakes*, the consequence of the violation of educational principles or their "injudicious or unskillful application"; (4) and *psychological mistakes*, which result from a "want of knowledge" concerning the nature of the various faculties and their laws of "growth."

Finally, Baldwin provided his readers with suggestive study hints so that they might best pursue excellence in the training and utilization of their pupils' faculties.

The reader, at this point, should have a good general grasp of Baldwin's approach to process training. We are now ready to view his agenda at work within specific applications.

The first of these, naturally, are those that broadly constitute "percep-

---

[16] Baldwin deliberately omitted school subjects which had low training values from his tables. Hence, there was a narrow range of scores in his ratings. He also warned his readers that the value of a particular subject for process training depended as heavily, if not more, upon the methods used to teach it as on the content of the subject.

tion" a term which Baldwin chose to identify as intuition,[17] since it (perception) provides "direct insight" into things. Baldwin also chose to distinguish between several different types of perception, as might be expected from an educator–psychologist steeped in German philosophy. There is sense–perception, which is "self perceiving external objects. It is direct insight into the matter world" (Baldwin, 1892, p. 28). There are, however, other types of perception (which we shall not consider in any great detail), which also provide "direct insight." Thus self-perception is "the power of direct insight into the mind world" (Baldwin, 1892, p. 30). It is also called self-intuition, conscious perception, and self-consciousness. Self-perception "*is self perceiving himself knowing, feeling, willing. . . .* It is the power of introspection" (Baldwin, 1892, p. 31). Thus too a power called by Baldwin necessary perception, which is "the power of direct insight into the world of necessary realities" (Baldwin, 1892, p. 34). "*Necessary perception is self perceiving necessary realities . . .* the realities that *must* be, that things *may* be" (Baldwin, 1892, p. 34). These include necessary elements, necessary conditions, necessary relations—all gained through necessary percepts.

There is also "perceptive knowing," which is a matter of "gaining a direct elementary knowledge of self and his environments . . ." (Baldwin, 1892, p. 38).

In exercising all of the perceptual processes enumerated, various general principles are to be observed. The learner must actually do the perceiving; his knowing must not be secondhand; imagination must not take the place of experience. Habits of exact observation, whether in sense perception or self-perception, are essential. "The habit of exact observation of *noumena* as well as *phenomena* is highly important" (Baldwin, 1892, p. 87). There must be assimilation of "present with . . . previous acquisitions" and these acquisitions must be made ". . . an organic whole. . ."[18]

Of Baldwin's programs of perceptual training, we shall, in these pages, only review those that deal with sense–perception. Those that are concerned with the other types of "intuition" with which Baldwin concerned himself are too alien to our current perspectives to warrent further attention. Baldwin's assiduous attempts to develop sense–perception should provide a clear enough picture, for our purposes, of his views of perceptual culture.

The first general law of process training, applied to sense–perception training, is the *law of effort*.

---

[17] Not uncommonly done by philosophers concerned with the definition of perception.
[18] This particular statement is not only one of perception but also of apperception; Baldwin was properly attuned to both Herbart and Kant.

Well-directed effort in gaining sense–percepts educates sense perception. Such effort develops power. Directed exercise strengthens capability. Endeavors to master the world of material things promotes the growth of sense–intuition (perception). (Baldwin, 1892, p. 48)

The second general law is the *law of means*:

Whatever calls sense–perception into vigorous activity is a means for its culture. We gain sense–ideas in the presence of sense–objects. . . . Sense–experience is the basis of all mental activity. Acquiring such experience by means of objective work educates sense–perception. (Baldwin, 1892, p. 48)

The final general law is the *law of method*:

Systematic, persistent, and efficient plans of work, in mastering the matter-world, educate sense–perception. Orderly, continued, and vigorous efforts develop power. (Baldwin, 1892, p. 48)

The special laws of process training, applied to perceptual culture, include:

1. *The law of conditions:* "A sound sensorium favors sense–perception growth" and "physical improvement underlies" mental improvement and sound perception. Practical hygiene is important in the classroom.
2. *The law of attention:* "Interested attention to material things accelerates perception growth." If the child is distracted his sense–perceptions become blurred, "and no attention means no percepts."
3. *The law of ascent:* There is a natural progression in training sense–perception. "The child perceives the object; gains the idea, and embodies the idea in a word.[19] (Baldwin, 1892, p. 49)

Teachers were advised, in addition to applying these special laws, to search for their own special laws, a search, if you remember from an earlier quote, was one that Baldwin saw as a search for "diamonds."

The importance of sense–perception culture was repeated everywhere in his book by Baldwin.

The foundation for all forms of mental growth must be laid in sense–activity. Sense–ideas underlie all other ideas; sense–intuition (perception) is fundamental in the mental economy. (Baldwin, 1892, p. 43)

Sense–perception's growth and culture were conceived of as a lifetime affair by Baldwin. Despite the primacy of the senses in mental economy during the early years of life, the powers of sense–perception do

---

[19] Pestalozzi and Froebel proceeded in a similar way, generally speaking.

not reach full maturity until approximately age 22. They can even continue to further develop into old age or at least be kept vigorous during this period by constant exercise.

Sense–perception is kept vigorous by use even in old age. The eye may grow dim and the ear dull, but the power to interpret sensations may grow more and more powerful. (Baldwin, 1892, p. 47)

For each period of the developing human organism, there is to be a distinct focus in sense–perception culture, as for the other faculties. Guiding this culture, or education, are general developmental principles. The period from age three to six is the kindergarten period.

During this period the growth of sense–perception is wonderful. The foundation of future achievement is now laid in sense–experience. Not the culture of the senses,[20] but of the power to gain sense notions, is the aim. (Baldwin, 1892, p. 47)

From six to ten is the primary period, during which the child is trained to observe closely and to gain and express clear sense–ideas; from ten to 14 is the intermediate period, during which the pupil's perceptual powers are now fully active. "Boys and girls gain a deeper insight into things having properties," they develop "clean-cut" sense percepts and are able to develop them into concepts and judgments. From 14 to 18, the high school period, sense–perception becomes a matter of scientific observation and "Sense–perception, the power to gain accurate sense-knowledge, is at its best" (Baldwin, 1892, p. 47). From 18 to 22, the college period, a gradual sharpening of sense–perception continues. "Observation is now penetrating, exact, and exhaustive" (Baldwin, 1892, p. 47).

Baldwin offered generalized prescriptions for each of the stages we have just reviewed:

For kindergarten, he suggested the following:

1. Trying things educates sense–perception: The child becomes acquainted with things by "testing" them through his senses.
2. Doing educates sense–perception: The child is led into doing things purposively. "It speaks, sings, draws, molds, handles, measures, makes, exercises, combines, builds" (Baldwin, 1892, p. 52). Such "intimate and active" contact with things trains his perceptual powers.
3. Observing educates sense–perception: The child learns to discriminate more sharply, distinguishes parts from wholes, develops "fuller and clearer notions."

[20] For example, the improvement of sensory functioning.

At the time of primary education, when children fall between the ages of six to ten, "Sensation is now at its best . . . the children have been busy, heretofore, exploring the wonder-world about them" (Baldwin, 1892, p. 53). All children have acquired a great store of sense-perceptions, even those from deprived circumstances. Those, however, who have had exposure to the kindergarten are at least two years advanced in the sense–perception progress they have made over those who have not had this particular "head-start" experience. Some of the prescriptions of the kindergarten are to be carried over to primary education, but with elaborations.

Here are the rules that Baldwin suggested be followed for primary education:

1. *Acquiring sense–intuitions educates sense–perception:* At six the child's sensory powers are almost equal to those of an adult but his "capability to interpret sensations and make exact percepts" is still relatively weak; thus he requires a storing of his mind "with ideas of things in land, sea, and sky" (Baldwin, 1892, p. 54).

2. *Objective experimental work develops sense–perception:* The child continually experiments through sense–tests and discovers the properties of objects therefrom "he discriminates the properties of objects and assimilates these into notions" (Baldwin, 1892, p. 54).

3. *Doing educates sense–perceptions:* The child should be doing in such a way as to engage in "*handling, combining, separating, weighing, measuring*" (Baldwin, 1892, p. 54).

4. *Teaching primary arithmetic, primary geography, primary reading, and primary language lessons educates sense–perception.* However, academic instruction must be carried out on a concrete experiential basis in order to be effective for perceptual training purposes. "The child . . . out of its own experiences . . . makes its numbers notions, and its geography notions, and its notions used in reading and language . . ." Baldwin, 1892, p. 54). The child builds on the "rock" of its sense experiences. "It learns how to see and hear and taste and smell and touch, so as to gain clear and full notions of things" (Baldwin, 1892, p. 55).

At the intermediate level of instruction, "book instruction" supplements the earlier oral type. "Semi-science takes the place of miscellaneous object-lessons" (Baldwin, 1892, p. 55). At this level of instruction, Baldwin's precepts in perceptual training recommend:

1. *Observing critically educates sense–perception:* The pupil examines things minutely and with "penetrating scrutiny" so as to "gain clear

and exhaustive sense–notions, and greatly strengthens sense–intuition'' (Baldwin, 1892, p. 55).

2. *Analyzing and synthesizing material things cultivates sense perception;* ''. . . they [the pupils] gain exact knowledge and deeper insight'' (Baldwin, 1892, p. 55).

3. *The study of objective science develops sense–perception:* The pupil is given a ''solid foundation'' in the concrete aspects, the ''objective side,'' of geography, botany, zoology, etc.

4. *Manual training educates sense–perception:* The intermediate-level pupil clearly should be learning to use tools and ''make things''; such ''doing'' educates perception because of the interest it awakens and the attention it fosters.

5. *Good methods of teaching reading, language, vocal music, drawing, geography, botany, zoology, educate sense–perception:* Apropos of these, Baldwin told his readers that ''each word in the reading or language lesson becomes a jewel glittering with meaning'' (Baldwin, 1892, p. 56), though it was not explained how such jewels train perception. For the sciences, he recommended, grandiosely, ''The pupils need no book except the book of nature,'' though he did recommend a syllabus for the teacher (Baldwin, 1892, p. 56).

At the high school level, Baldwin does not recommend any systematic procedures for the training or cultivation of the powers of sense-perception. Perceptual considerations, he said, ''are incidental in the high-school, since thought culture should predominate at this level . . .'' (Baldwin, 1892, p. 57). Nevertheless, the study of science provides excellent opportunities for the pupil to further develop his perceptive powers, albeit indirectly, while pursuing his assignments.

The exact and penetrating observation demanded by science gives the highest culture to sense–perception. Botany, zoology, geology, and chemistry are the best studies for this culture. Books are now used, but the student must still build on his own experience . . . to verify conclusions the student needs constantly to go back to sensations; then to make advances, he must make new and closer observations. Thus the power to gain sense–knowledge is not only kept vigorous, but is steadily improved. (Baldwin, 1892, p. 57)

You will remember our discussion of Baldwin's ''Tables of Educational Values,'' which were to be used to guide the utilization of curricula and other educational technology for faculty culture in the schools. We shall now examine the particular table that Baldwin recommended (once the teacher's own judgments were averaged in) to provide ''. . . the comparative values for perception–culture of the leading studies preceding college work'' (Baldwin, 1892, p. 50).

Following are the various subjects as listed in order of ranking by Baldwin, and their scores, assigned by Brooks and himself:

1. Kindergarten work and general object lessons—10, 10
2. Botany, zoology, geology, chemistry, geography—10, 10
3. Manual artwork, penmanship, drawing, molding—8, 9
4. Reading, spelling, language lessons, vocal music—8, 9
5. Physiology, physics, astronomy—7, 8
6. Objective arithmetic, objective geometry—6, 8

Subjects deemed low in their perceptual training possibilities, such as mathematics and Latin history, were not rated at all.

As to educational and psychological mistakes that bear upon mal-development of the perceptual faculty, under the first category we find:

1. *Poor school facilities*, and employment of incompetent teachers who "neither understand child-nature nor the nature of the subjects to be taught." (Baldwin, 1892, p. 58)
2. *Hygienic mistakes*, whereby pupils are not trained in proper hygienic habits; they injure their eyes, develop poor posture, neglect invigorating exercise—"perfect health conditions perfect sensations; perfect sensations condition perfect sense-percepts." (Baldwin, 1892, p. 59)
3. *Teaching mistakes*, in which there are violations of educational principles or their improper application, including bookwork before oral work, words before ideas, and concepts before percepts.

Mistakes of the second kind are the consequence of errors that "result from a want of knowledge of the nature of sense–perception and its laws of growth" (Baldwin, 1892, p. 59). These errors result in:

1. *The teacher's reliance on second-hand work*, which "does not develop perception. . . . Children must gain sense–ideas directly."
2. *Too much hurry:* "There must be time for a permanent unification or the perception will not be complete. . ."
3. *Failure to discriminate and assimilate*, when the teacher forgets that "objects . . . presented to the senses as to stimulate a perception of differences are the proper external occasions of perception."
4. *Appealing to a single sense.* Baldwin was a great proponent of multisensory education, and he believed that "much of the poverty of school work" was the result of overreliance upon one sense, particularly hearing. "Young children need to test things by several of the senses . . . in teaching children perfectly endowed (with all senses) we must appeal to all senses" (Baldwin, 1892, pp. 60–61).

The representative powers were next in Baldwin's itinerary of cognitive process training. They are defined as:

. . . capabilities to make our acquisitions present again in old and new forms. They are our native energies to modify as well as to revive our experiences. (Baldwin, 1892, p. 95)

The representative powers include memory, fantasy, and imagination. Culture of the representative powers means "the development of our capabilities to represent our experiences in *old* and *new* forms" (Baldwin, 1892, p. 143).

Memory was defined by Baldwin in greater detail as "the native energy of self to reproduce his acquisitions" (Baldwin, 1892, p. 96). It enters into all our "knowing, feeling and willing." It depends upon association (and proceeds according to the laws of association) "but interest, attention, systematic efforts widen and deepen" the association network upon which it depends (Baldwin, 1892). It is more an issue at the elementary school level than at the secondary. However its exercise (as Alexander Bain pointed out) makes greater demands upon nervous energies than on more creative or constructive activities. A good memory is one that discriminates so that "it receives and holds important facts and truths, while it rejects those which are unimportant" (Baldwin, 1892, p. 151). The functions of memory were broadly conceived by Baldwin, so that this faculty "includes association, suggestion, reproduction, and recognition," all directed to the recalling of past experiences (Baldwin, 1892, p. 110).

As for perception, so for memory. There are certain laws, general and specific, that are to be observed to promote its growth.

Among the general laws applicable to memory culture, the Law of effort states that: "Well-directed effort in associating and recalling our ideas educates memory. We assimilate and associate our new and old experiences" (Baldwin, 1892, p. 110). The law of means proposes:

Studies which call memory into constant and vigorous activity have a high memory–culture value. The study of history is an excellent means for improving memory. The study of algebra is not a good means for memory–culture. (Baldwin, 1892, p. 110)

The law of method, as applied to memory, simply calls for plans of work which "call memory into lawful, systematic, vigorous, and persistent activity" to develop its power (Baldwin, 1892, p. 110).

The special laws of memory are many, and Baldwin contented himself with listing but a few:

1. *Law of the brain:* A healthy brain conditions a good memory. This law emphasizes the importance of good school hygiene. Pupils who study in crowded rooms, exercise little, and do not receive enough exposure to fresh air, suffer from poor memory. "Boys who smoke

. . . and girls who chew gum nearly always complain of poor memories" (Baldwin, 1892, p. 111).

2. *Law of association:* "Vigor of *mind,* interested *attention,* rational *order,* and *repetition* strengthen association . . . the key to good memory."

3. *Law of interest:* "Delight in study marvelously strengthens association and suggestion" (Baldwin, 1892, p. 110). We rarely forget what interests us or gives us enjoyment.

4. *Law of determination:* Systematic efforts to retain and reproduce what we have learned that strengthens our memory. "I will remember is almost invincible" (Baldwin, 1892, p. 110).

5. *Law of retentive memory:* "In general we treasure what we understand. . .," and while we must sometimes commit to memory what is not understood, "to crowd memory with unmeaning words, as the Chinese do, is a fundamental educational error" (Baldwin, 1892, p. 111).

6. *Law of time:* Keeping a topic "before the mind" for an extended period of time or reviewing it regularly will firmly fix it in the mind; "knowledge not recalled soon fades into forgetfulness" (Baldwin, 1892, p. 111).

Training in memory is to observe the "stages of growth," in similar fashion to that for perception, though the stages are somewhat different. Baldwin notes that infant memory, that of the first three years of life, is "feeble, though the child will be able to remember both objects and their names when but a few months old." Childhood memories are those from the third to the tenth year, and are "fresh and active," but comparatively weak. There is objective memory and the ability to associate words with objects and with other words; stories and pictures can now be remembered. Memory in boyhood and girlhood (10 to 14) is objective memory in full activity, with abstract memory becoming active. Language and semiscience are a "delight" for children at this stage. Memory in youth (14 to 18) is extremely vigorous. "All forms of knowledge are now easily remembered. Impressions are lasting" (Baldwin, 1892, p. 109). Memory in manhood becomes more and more "commanding" up to the "meridian of life." It is still capable of improvement well into maturity. Memory in old age tends to become feeble "when the old cease to make new conquests," but can remain intact in vigorous individuals who are still active in their lives (Baldwin, 1892, p. 110).

Memory training, Baldwin recommended, is to take into cognizance the needs and limitations of the various ages of man, proceed roughly according to a pupil's school career, and be guided by an appropriate table of educational values.

For kindergarten, the method is to give the child a broad and free exposure to experiences:

> Its sense–experiences become sense–ideas. These it embodies in words, which become signs of the ideas. New experiences and old are assimilated and associated. The child . . . is trained to recall often and accurately its few experiences. As its world becomes larger, its memory grows stronger. (Baldwin, 1892, p. 114).

During the primary period, memory of words as signs of objects is at its best. This is the golden period for object lessons. The child is learning to speak, read, and write.

> Stories, hymns, precepts and memory gems which touch child experience educate child memory. Leading children to find out and tell about the earth and the animals and the plants develops memory. . . . The effort of the child to remember and *act* good manners and morals strengthens memory. (Baldwin, 1892, p. 114)

Intermediate methods for the cultivation of memory can rely on the fact that objective and verbal memory are highly active, and memory of the abstract is beginning to be active. The rules suggested for this period to assist in the improvement of memory are as follows:

1. *Lead your pupils to study science.* These studies elicit deep interest and command close attention. "The experience gained is assimilated, associated, and constantly recalled. There is no better way of improving memory" (Baldwin, 1892, p. 115).
2. *Lead your pupils to study history and literature.* Everything in such reading is to "connect with the pupil's experience." The teacher is to lead ". . . his pupils to *understand, assimilate, associate,* and *recall*" (Baldwin, 1892, p. 115). Since the pupil's interest is intense and his attention "complete," his memory "grows strong."
3. *Reading, language, music, manners, and morals* must to taught so as to "educate memory." "The learner will remember because he knows" (Baldwin, 1892, p. 115).
4. *Doing educates memory.* What the pupil does, he seldom forgets. Show him a map of a continent and talk to him about it, and he soon forgets; have him mold that continent and draw it and he remembers.

High school methods for educating memory can rely upon the fact that memory, in all its forms, is highly active during this period, peaking about the 18th year. The student is aided in memory by his ability to "think his knowledge into system" and his ability to logically associate his experiences. The rules for memory training at this level are as follows:

1. *Lead the student to master botany and zoology.* "For memory cul-

ture these studies are among the best. . . . Memory is called into constant and vigorous use" (Baldwin, 1892, p. 116).

2. *Lead the student to master the Latin language and Greek and Latin literature.* No other work will develop a more vigorous memory (Baldwin, 1892, p. 116).
3. *Lead the student to study properly history and literature.* "Facts are grouped and associated by their cause relations. . . . Such studies grandly educate memory" (Baldwin, 1892, p. 116).
4. *Lead the student to cultivate a discriminating memory.* "To forget is as important as to retain. . . . Selection is the basis of good memory, and forgetfulness its partner" (Baldwin, 1892, p. 116). The learner should gradually be trained to select the important things for retention.
5. *Train the student to organize his knowledge.* Through organization, mastery of materials is achieved. "Organization means numerous associations; and the more numerous the associations the greater the power of recalling" (Baldwin, 1892, p. 117).

The teacher's responsibilities in guiding the direction his pupils' memories will take in their formation was repeatedly emphasized by Baldwin. The teacher should be systematic, use illustrations which "intensely interest, deeply impress and secure system" (Baldwin, 1892, p. 118) and, assure that the physical conditions of the room are conducive to learning.

Baldwin warned against "mistakes in educating memory."

1. Examinations and reviews for which the pupil has to prepare cause "much waste time" in education; Baldwin preferred review and "testing" during each lesson.
2. The Chinese method, i.e., memorizing words without ideas; he exclaimed, "No wonder China has made little progress for two thousand years" (Baldwin, 1892, p. 119).
3. Memory before experience.
4. Books rather than nature.
5. Indiscriminate remembering, which ". . . crowds the mind with rubbish and tends to weaken memory" (Baldwin, 1892, p. 120).

Along with the above, Baldwin offered various and sundry hints for improving memory, both through classroom instruction and self-training.

Fantasy is a power that Baldwin defined as "the native energy of self to represent his experiences as fancies" and as "undirected imagination" (Baldwin, 1892, p. 122). It is the "play faculty of the soul." Characteristic of it is that fancies seem to be reality. Fantasy dissociates and recombines old experiences in new forms (Baldwin, 1892, p. 122). It expresses itself normally in play and imaginative activities such as identifying with the characters and actions in fairy stories. It also enters into fantasies, illusions, and dreams. Respecting dreams, Baldwin sees them as a possible source of cognitive disturbance, especially when arising out of a bedtime after ". . . a sour stomach, overwork, and a troubled conscience" (Baldwin, 1892). He recommended that teachers and pupils alike rarely tell their dreams lest they remember them too well, for "No one desires to retain his dreams" (Baldwin, 1892, p. 123).

Fantasy is to be distinguished from imagination. "Phantasy makes our fancies; imagination our ideals" (Baldwin, 1882, p. 124). It is not to be educated as such but rather studied and treated "so as to make its activity wholesome" (Baldwin, 1892, p. 124).

Imagination, on the other hand, is a faculty deserving of royal treatment in Baldwin's estimation. Its education is the "development of our ideal making power" (Baldwin, 1892, p. 125). It is a "master power . . . commanding all our other capabilities . . . the master-builder and our other powers are the co-operating workmen" (Baldwin, 1892, pp. 125,126). These workmen include memory, which provides imagination with materials and associates and recalls its products; will, which contributes purpose and concentrated effort; emotion which gives imagination wings; thought which "contributes discretion and law" (Baldwin, 1892, p. 125).

Baldwin believed that training of the imagination was critical, not only to assist pupils to develop ideals that can effectively guide their lives but because it also ". . . leads the way in high achievement . . . *stimulates mental energy . . . inspires effort . . . adds immeasurably to our joys . . . is the fountain of perceptual youth*" (Baldwin, 1892, p. 128).

Baldwin's general laws of education applied to "imagination-growth," find the law of effort engaged in "Well-directed effort in creating ideals . . . determined effort under guidance" (Baldwin, 1892, pp. 130–131). The law of means calls for the pupil's undertaking studies which "demand constant and vigorous imaginative effort" (Baldwin, 1892, p. 131) with literature and art ranking highest among these. The law of method insists that imagination be exercised in "plans of work" that call imagination into "lawful, vigorous and persistent" activity. "Roaming fancy free does not educate" (Baldwin, 1892, p. 131).

The special laws for training the imagination emphasize that:

1. *"Imagination is educated by illustrating the abstract* . . . Imagination seeks a particular instance; it furnishes examples" (Baldwin, 1892, p. 131).
2. *Efforts to realize ideals educate imagination:* "The sculptor toils to embody his ideal. . ." (Baldwin, 1892, p. 131).

As for imagination in and at the different stages of development, it is a matter of increasing activity and power:

> *In childhood imagination is moderately active.* Much of what seems to be imagination is in reality phantasy. . . . The child-imagination is feeble, and its ideals crude. . . . *In girlhood and boyhood imagination is quite active* . . . You will note a marvelous growth of imagination. . . . *In youth imagination is marvelously active.* . . . About the fourteenth year imagination bursts into wonderful activity and becomes more and more vigorous as the years go by. (Baldwin, 1892, pp. 129, 130)

There are, of course, curricular priorities for imagination culture at each developmental stage: For kindergarten, Baldwin recommended that the child be "led to make new combinations of blocks and sticks and lines" (Baldwin, 1892, p. 133) and to develop new arrangements in stories, pictures, and plays. The child is to be encouraged in imaginative play.

Primary methods of educating imagination should observe the following precepts:

1. *Lead the child to make new combinations.* The child should creatively utilize the methods and materials of "drawing, molding, object-lessons, and language lessons" to develop original forms therefrom (Baldwin, 1892, p. 134).
2. *Lead the child to image what it reads.*
3. *Lead the child to construct.*
4. *Lead the child to drink in the beautiful.* "Make the surroundings as beautiful as you can . . . lead the child to draw . . . and . . . produce beautiful objects" (Baldwin, 1892, p. 135).
5. *Lead the child to drink in child literature.* Biographical stories and histories, as well as the classics, strengthen the imagination.

Intermediate methods of training imagination must take into account the fact that pupils at this level ". . . are incapable of sustained flights of imagination" (Baldwin, 1892, p. 136). They require assistance in developing their imaginations according to the following precepts:

1. *Lead the pupil to write original compositions.*
2. *Lead the pupil to construct his geography world.* Using charts, globes, maps, etc., the pupil is to construct his own models. "The pupil has never seen a mountain. He has seen hills of various heights; out of his hill experiences he must construct a mountain" (Baldwin, 1892, p. 136).
3. *Interest the pupil in juvenile literature.*
4. *Lead the pupil to create his history world.* "Lead them to construct in imagination the geography, the people, the scenes. It will become

almost as real to them as if they were actors. In connection with the studies in literature and history you may impress every noble trait" (Baldwin, 1892, p. 137).

5. *Lead the pupil to teach.* "Nothing is better to awaken interest and strengthen imagination" (Baldwin, 1892, p. 137). The pupils are to make up their own definitions and rules and invent their own illustrations.

6. *Lead the pupil to idealize character.* This is a process whereby the pupil develops empathetic identifications with various characters in books and plays.

Advanced methods of imagination culture were also suggested by Baldwin who believed that a high school pupil's need to develop his imagination is no less important than his need to develop his reasoning powers. Recommended:

1. *Lead the student to construct science.* The student is to develop idealized images of objects he works with in science: "The learner sees, feels, touches, tastes, and smells the plant. He analyzes and synthesizes it. He compares it with other plants. In imagination he constructs the typical plant and associates it with a name" (Baldwin, 1892, p. 138).

2. *Lead the student to construct history.* He is to place himself, in imagination, in the scenes of ancient times, to participate in the Trojan wars, for example, fighting beside Ajax or Achilles.

3. *Lead the student at every step to make the abstract concrete.* Such homilies as "Honesty is the best policy . . . need to be illustrated. Mr. Jones . . . has been known for integrity. Everyone respects and trusts him. He has gradually accumulated a competence and is happy." (Baldwin, 1892, p. 139). The abstract notion is imaginatively translated into a concrete exemplification.

4. *Lead the student to study art from the standpoint of the artist.* The artist created ideals; the pupil, by creating them over again, educates imagination.

5. *Lead the student to form and try to realize an ideal character.* "From the lives of the grand and great of all ages we construct an ideal life, our highest conception of a grand manhood. Now we think and feel and will to realize in ourselves the ideal" (Baldwin, 1892, p. 139).

Baldwin's "Table of Educational Values" for imagination culture (in which he was again assisted by Dr. Brooks in making ratings) rated language composition and literature as highest in respect to awakening and educating imagination. Of second rank is art, i.e., drawing, molding, music, and elocution. Geography and history come next. Mathematics, i.e., arithmetic, algebra, geometry, rank lowest, though Baldwin believed that, properly employed, they can be extremely valuable. "Imagination is only second to reason in the right study of geometry" (Baldwin, 1892, p. 133).

Baldwin called attention to errors in educating imagination of which he scolded: "No feature of our educational world is now in greater need of reform" (Baldwin, 1892, p. 140). These errors include:

1. *Repeating instead of memorizing.* Excessive repetition "weakens inventiveness and makes plodders rather than originators" (Baldwin, 1892, p. 140).
2. *Drudgery instead of mastery.* This is the ". . . dominant educational sin of our times. The student is weighted down with facts" (Baldwin, 1892, p. 140).
3. *Too much explaining.* This leaves nothing to the imagination, since the mind doesn't have much stimulus to "wrestle with problems."
4. *Saying instead of doing.*
5. *Leaving imagination to roam fancy-free.* The student needs to learn to distinguish between the reals and ideals. "Thus may be prevented a dreamy, stickly, sentimental life" (Baldwin, 1892, p. 141).
6. *Cherishing or even tolerating low ideals.* "Boys and girls saturated with low literature form low ideals, and will likely live low lives" (Baldwin, 1892, p. 141).
7. *Neglect of imagination culture.* Baldwin bemoaned the fact that "The culture of imagination seems to be more uniformly neglected than that of any other faculty" (Baldwin, 1892, p. 141). He found students generally unable to "represent" scenes, persons, or stories to themselves on the basis of verbal descriptions. In history, geography, or astronomy, there were few able to "form any distinct and true" pictures in their minds of what they had described to them. Fewer still were able to "create ideal personages and scenes." Pupils, he said, must receive more training of their imagination ". . . not only in capacity to receive but in power to create" (Baldwin, 1892, p. 141).

We have at last arrived at the education of the thought-powers as promulgated by Baldwin, who offered the following definition of thinking in his introduction to the training of higher cognitive processes:

> Thinking is discerning relations. The relations between things are as real as the things themselves. Our thought-powers are our capabilities to discern these relations. Self as thought discerns relations and assimilate his experiences into thought-unity. Thinking is the crowning act of knowing. (Baldwin, 1892, p. 155)

What are the "thought-powers"? Again, let us hear from his definitions of what are, by now, familiar terms:

We discover that some things are related to other things by common properties; we discern these group relations and think individuals into classes; our
capability to do this is termed *conception*. We discover that our notions agree or
disagree; that they are related as true or false; we discern truth relations and think
our notions into truths; our capability to do this is termed *judgment*. Finally, we
discover that the universe is a cause-unit; we discover cause relations and think
truths into reasons and systems; our power to do this is termed *reason*. (Baldwin,
1892, p. 156)

Psychology provides insights into the nature of the thought processes, asking "What does self do when he thinks." Logic gives insight
into the laws and forms of thought, asking" How may we so think to reach
truth?"

The approach to training the higher faculties, a la Baldwin, is similar
to the one he developed for the lower ones. We shall review Baldwin's
conceptions concerning these higher faculties in the order of their ascent
into the rarified heights of cognition. We shall not, however, be as assiduous as we were with the lower processes in examining the various facets of
their education.

Baldwin, in clarifying the role of conception notes that it is the source
of "general notions" or "class-notions." When we think of percepts we
think of particular notions, and when we think of concepts we think of
general notions. Perceptions relate to individual objects and result in
images. "*A conception is not a mental picture.* Conceptions relate to
general classes or abstractions" (Baldwin, 1892, p. 159).

The steps by which conceptions are reached are "*experience, comparison, abstraction, generalization, classification, and naming*"
(Baldwin, 1892, p. 161). Conception is dependent upon perception
for the materials it works upon. It is further dependent upon memory
to recall "particular notions" and on imagination to conjure up specific
images from the past—or imaginary ones, so as to obtain further material
for its operations. Conception, in turn, provides the "general notions to
be appropriated by judgment and reason" for purposes of their operations. Its culture is important, because it is the initial or portal faculty of
the higher processes. Its culture also greatly increases mental vigor, since
those who deal with concepts are characterized by "broad and vigorous"
thinking. Its culture, too, conserves "mental energy," since "Percepts
not crystallized into concepts are squandered. . . . Concepts are more
precious than fine gold" (Baldwin, 1892, p. 174). Its culture, finally,
makes science possible. "Persons whose classifying power is undeveloped neither make nor understand science" (Baldwin, 1892, p. 174).
Science is classified knowledge, and concepts, of course, classify.

The general educational laws applied to conception make the case for
strongly energized self-activity on the part of the pupil.

1. *The law of effort* requires that the student do his own classifying and discerning of relations. "Individuals must be thought into groups," and concepts must be incorporated into the mental life (Baldwin, 1892, p. 176).
2. *The law of means* requires that the student be exposed to studies which ". . . call conception into the most vigorous and constant activity" (Baldwin, 1892, p. 176). Zoology and botany rank high in this respect.
3. *The law of method* requires that "Plans of work which lead the pupils to put forth, in the best ways, their best efforts in acquiring and using concepts to educate conception" (Baldwin, 1892, p. 176).

Baldwin's special laws of conception growth, directed toward strengthening the "grouping faculty," are nothing more than banal. One suspects a temporary flagging of energy or interest on his part in their exposition. There are but two special laws:

1. *Ascending through percepts to concepts educates conception.* It is the learner who is to make the ascent, not his instructor for him.
2. *Organizing particular notions into general notions educates conception.* "Object-lessons which stop with percepts are wasted labor . . . to save its particular notions the child must be led to assimilate them into general notions" (Baldwin, 1892, p. 176).

The growth of conception, as it moves through the various developmental stages is gradual, and parallels that of the other faculties. During the early years of life, the kindergarten period, the child is already able to "crystalize . . . sense percepts into sense-concepts" (Baldwin, 1892, p. 174). In fact, the infant is able to group things before the end of the first year of life.

The primary period, from age six to ten, when verbal memory is active and objective conception moderately operative, is the time when the child can classify items of both a concrete and verbal nature. The intermediate period is a time when ". . . boys and girls take delight in objective analysis and synthesis and in discovering group notions" (Baldwin, 1892, p. 175). During the high school period, conception reaches a still higher level and the classifications of science find a ready audience. The college period is ". . . preeminently the period for its (conception's) vigorous use and systematic culture" (Baldwin, 1892, p. 175). The student's classifications become "philosophical and exhaustive." Conception can then improve beyond college and be kept young and vigorous "by pushing our researches into new realms" (Baldwin, 1892, p. 175).

Baldwin's recommendations for the education of the conceptual faculty begin, as is to be expected, from a sensory basis. But we find, as we move along into higher strata of educational endeavor, a strong emphasis upon language and the abstract.

For the primary approach to conceptual training, Baldwin recommends that the child's chief work up to the age of six be in respect to forming an acquaintance with sense objects and learning to roughly group them. From six to ten, the child is supposed to advance to "objective classifications" The following recommendations are offered to guide training:

1. *Lead the child to detect resemblances and group common objects.* "Take chairs, knives, doors, windows, fruits, parts of the body, colors, and so on" (Baldwin, 1892, p. 178).
2. *Lead the pupil to group geometrical forms and construct tables of weights and measures.* Baldwin describes this sort of activity as easy and interesting work.
3. *By easy steps lead the learner through percepts to concepts.* "Resemblances must be obvious, the classifications must be bold and picturesque, and names of concepts must be easy" (Baldwin, 1892, p. 179).

Intermediate methods for conception training, Baldwin complained, were far inferior to those at the primary and high school level in the "best schools."

This stage of development does not seem to be grasped by the great body of our teachers. The precious years of girlhood and boyhood are largely squandered. This is the semi-scientific period . . . [when] the foundation for science work and language work should be deeply laid in experience. (Baldwin, 1892, p. 180)

Recommendations for conception culture at the intermediate level include the following:

1. *Lead the learner to make bold but accurate classifications.* Boys and girls take delight in objective classification and synthesis and like to find out classifications on their own.
2. *Lead the learner to find out the classifications of science.* Botany, zoology, and geography are particularly useful for developing concepts. Pupils ". . . observe that plants and animals are related by resemblances. Through these common characteristics they think animals and plants into classes" (Baldwin, 1892, p. 180).
3. *Lead the learner to make outlines and definitions.* The pupils are to be given all the possible visual aids they need in addition to objects themselves.

Lead the learner to discover relations between concepts and make the outlines, as of parts of speech, classes of vertebrates, etc. Concepts must now be defined. Children define percepts by describing objects, but boys and girls define objective concepts by referring the notion defined to a higher class and giving the characteristic difference. (Baldwin, 1892, pp. 180–181)

4. *Lead the learner to make tables of weights and measures.* "The pupils weigh and measure, and thus gain the percepts which they think into concepts. Reform is needed, and we should hasten the domination of the metric system" (Baldwin, 1892, p. 181).

As to high school methods of conceptual training, Baldwin felt this is "pre-eminently the period to master classified knowledge" (Baldwin, 1892, p. 181). Conception is now full active, and memory is at its best. In high school, science is the best way to approach conception culture:

1. *Lead the student to rediscover the classifications of science.* He should learn them from the vicarious experiences of others in books, but must always return to nature to "rediscover and verify for himself." His percepts and concepts must be his own.
2. *Logical diagraming educates conception.* It helps the student to more clearly discern class limits as well as class relations—but the pupil must do the diagraming on his own to benefit from it.
3. *Giving logical definitions educates conception.* The student learns to use concepts with exactness, and words that represent concept develop meaning; the student thinks clearly. Again, there must be self-activity. The pupil must make his own definitions. Those that are not of his making do not develop conception.
4. *Conceiving and using clear-cut self-concepts educates conception.* A pupil needs to explore "the mind world as well as the matter world [and] make his *self-concepts* out of his own *self-percepts*" (Baldwin, 1892, p. 182). Thus a feeling of gratitude generated at different times (self-percepts) must be developed into a generalized feeling (self-concept).
5. *Stating clearly and using logically necessary concepts educates conception.* "Necessary concepts must be thought out of intuitions of necessary realities" (Baldwin, 1892, p. 183). Again, it is a matter of taking specifics and generalizing on their basis, but at a conceptual level. Out of feelings of beauty develops the general notion of beauty. "Out of . . . duty percepts I make the concept *duty*. I think my intuitions of particular space into the general notion *space*" (Baldwin, 1892, p. 183).

As to errors in conception culture, there are five. The first is that of placing concepts before percepts:

This group of errors is most common and most baneful. The law of ascent is palpably violated. . . . This hurtful error pervades the old education. This blunder may be said to characterize the work of teachers ignorant of child-nature and ignorant of the laws of growth. (Baldwin, 1892, p. 184)

The second error is stopping with percepts:

Particular notions are of little value except as they lead up to general notions. Percepts are scaffolding; concepts are completed structures. (Baldwin, 1892, p. 184)

The third error is exclusive book work, as a result of which the student learns "meaningless words because they are not rooted in experience" (Baldwin, 1892, p. 185). The fourth results from the teacher providing the learner with definitions, classifications, and diagrams. Baldwin was once again emphasizing pupil activity, as he advised, "Eat the pupil's dinner for him if you will, but I beg of you to let him do his own thinking" (Baldwin, 1892, p. 185).

The fifth error in conception culture, said Baldwin is its neglect, a neglect that characterizes training in all aspects of thinking, of which conception (classification) is but the first step. An impassioned plea for reform was voiced by this formidable pedagogue:

Few really take this step, few really think. One person in a thousand thinks up to the truth. Is it strange? Do our schools teach pupils to think? Do our churches? Do political parties? It need not surprise you to find the unthinking masses drifting along in grooves made by their predecessors. A revolution is demanded. The school-room is the place to begin. The great want of the world is *thinking teachers* capable of educating a *race of thinkers*. (Baldwin, 1892, p. 185)

Judgment is next in the ascending order of the higher cognitive faculties. Judgment is the power to discern truth, Baldwin told his readers. "The agreement and disagreement of our notions of things are realities. Self as judgment discerns and asserts. . ." the various agreements and disagreements (Baldwin, 1892, p. 187). Our judgments are true when they correspond with reality; they are false when they do not accord with it. "A sound judgment is the ability to see things in their proper relations." (Baldwin, 1892, p. 187). Self as judgment thinks percepts and concepts into "truths." "To think is to judge."

Judgment's place in one's mental economy is, in considerable part, dictated by its relations to the other powers of the mind. It is obviously related to perception and conception. It is highly dependent on memory, which provides it with material upon which to operate. Memory also plays the role of storing ". . . truths as our most precious treasures. Truths, like ideas, are assimilated, associated, and recalled" (Baldwin, 1892, p. 189). Judgment also maintains relations with reason.

Reason takes ready-made judgments for premises and discerns their ground relations. Conclusions are simply inferred judgments. Reason contributes largely to the work of judgment-making (Baldwin, 1892, p. 189).

Judgment is also intimately related to the emotions, "Truths discerned occasion truth emotions" (Baldwin, 1892, p. 189). Many of life's deepest joys are the result of discovering new truths. In turn, the love of truth inspires research.

The culture of judgment is important: "For nothing should one be more thankful than for a *sound* judgment" (Baldwin, 1892, p. 190). Its cultivation is urged on the grounds that it is, as discussed earlier, our "truth-discerning power" because it enters into our various experiences. *"Judgment is the stuff out of which reasons are made"* (Baldwin, 1892, p. 190).

Baldwin's general laws of education applied to judgment growth emphasize well-directed effort, vigorous self-activity and systematic and persistent efforts in applying judgment. Baldwin's special laws of culture recommended:

1. *We ascend through percepts and concepts to judgments.*
2. *Sentence-making develops judgment:* "A sentence is an expressed judgment. All sentence-making consists in discerning and expressing truth-relations, and hence promotes the growth of this faculty" (Baldwin, 1892, p. 193).
3. *Perceiving judgments as true cultivates the "truth-discerning power."* This because "Belief is assent to the truth of a judgment" (Baldwin, 1892, p. 193). Hence the practice of making judgments and accepting them as true strengthens our capability in respect to making judgments.

In making his recommendations as to methods of educating judgment, Baldwin combined kindergarten and primary methods. The child in the earlier grade is able to discern truth relations of things that are "objective and obtrusive." He is also able to use easy concrete sentences. He moves from using percepts as the basis of his judgments to simple concepts. Training of judgment at these tender stages (kindergarten and primary grades) must be adapted to the child's limitations:

1. *Lead the child to form his own judgments.* But do not hurry about it. Allow easy and simple concepts and judgments to be formed. "Lead the child to discern and express obvious truths" (Baldwin, 1892, p. 195).
2. *Lead the child to prize the truth and form the truth habit.* "Judgment must express actual relations. Is the apple really sour? Did I in reality recite well?" (Baldwin, 1892, p. 195).

3. *Be certain that the child judges.* "Babbling is not thinking. . . . Lead the child through percepts to grasp the concepts. . ." (Baldwin, 1892, p. 195).

Intermediate methods, for 10- to 14-year-olds, rely upon the fact that ". . . boys and girls delight in forming and using judgments." (Baldwin, 1892, p. 196). There are three major recommendations for this period:

1. *Lead the learner to construct and analyze sentences.* Baldwin made the following observations concerning the use of written language in developmental judgmental processes:

I count composition and analysis of the English sentence of great educational value, disciplinary and practical. Each step is based on the learner's experience. Truth-relations are discerned and expressed. These sentences are expressed judgments. This is the period to master the English sentence. The old-time manner of parsing hinders, and does not help; indeed, in our time, it is avoided during this period by the wise teacher. (Baldwin, 1892, p. 1960)

2. *Lead the learner to study things in their relations.* "Each step is a judgment, and, when the work is properly adjusted, the pupil may be led to take successive steps for himself" (Baldwin, 1892, p. 196).
3. *Lead the learner to classify and define.* "A concept is a condensed judgment and may be expanded into a sentence. A logical definition is a judgment. . ." (Baldwin, 1892, p. 196). Geography, botany, and zoology are of the highest value in respect to developing logical definitions.

The high school level, from 14 to 18, when "judgment is wonderfully active and becomes more and more penetrating and reliable" is the time for the "highest culture" of judgment (Baldwin, 1892, p. 196). The three precepts of training for this period are:

1. *Lead the learner to judge for himself.* "Stimulate to the utmost independent effort. At any cost manage to have the learner master problems for himself" (Baldwin, 1892, p. 197).
2. *Stimulate vigorous judging.* "Only sturdy effort develops power. . . . Vigorous endeavor gives the penetrating judgment and develops power" (Baldwin, 1892, p. 197).
3. *Develop a thirst for truth.* "Happy the student who hungers and thirsts for truth. He longs to become acquainted with things in their proper relations" (Baldwin, 1892, p. 197). He seeks to conform his judgments to realities. He hates untruth as he despises sin.

What are the errors made in educating judgment? There are cardinal ones.

1. *Memory is crowded and judgment neglected.* As a consequence, what is learned is often a "crude jumble," a "heterogeneous mass."
2. *Children are dragged through difficult abstract work.* This results in confusion and discouragement and, as a result, the pupil is "dwarfed" rather than educated. Truth relations must be understood with "sunlight clearness," if study is to develop judgment.
3. *Youths are fed with spoons.* Teachers coddle the older pupils and don't give them the opportunity to vigorously exercise their judgment.
4. *The laws of descent and ascent are violated.* "With many teachers judgments in the form of definitions and rules come before percepts and concepts" (Baldwin, 1892, p. 198).
5. *Hasty judgments are assented to as true.* Opinions of others are too easily accepted as true without examination. Prejudices stop us from discerning the truth. We have to, therefore, cultivate honesty and thoroughness in judgment-making and discriminate sharply between opinions and truths.
6. *Pupils take the statements of teachers and books without thinking.* This frequently results in "feebleness of judgment." The learner must be led to "judge at every step."

Reason is the last of the cognitive faculties that Baldwin attended to. Reason is the faculty that "crowns the intellectual pyramid" (Baldwin, 1892, p. 200). "Self as reason" commands all the other intellectual powers. It, of course, builds upon the activities of the powers lower in the hierarchy of cognitive faculties for its operations, but it serves, as well as commands them. It ". . . assists in the formation of percepts and concepts and judgments and ideals (the products of imagination)" (Baldwin, 1892, p. 201).

What is reason? It is a many-splendored thing. It is the capability to *"discern new truths through related truths"*; it is *"discerning ground-relations"*, i.e., inferring conclusions; it is inferring premises (Baldwin, 1892, p. 201). It, perhaps, can be most clearly defined in terms of its place within thinking:

> Thinking is discerning relations. When we conceive we discern class-relations; as, *animal, vegetable.* When we judge we discern truth-relations; as *God is love.* When we reason we discern cause-relations; *as, we are happy because we are good.* We conceive, judge, and reason; thus we elaborate crude notions into science. (Baldwin, 1892, p. 200)

While all the faculties grow together, some reach maturity later than others. Reason is the "latest" to reach full vigor. Its cultivation at all levels of development is important, however.

Not to educate reason is to limit one's knowledge to his perceptions, and leave him to grope his way in a sea of inexplicable mystery. (Baldwin, 1892, p. 202)

Baldwin set forth specific reasons for reason culture. A cultured reason provides one's mind with a "rational universe." Things assume proportion and harmony and ". . . all things fall into system, and make for us the music of the spheres." The education of reason gives independence in thinking:

The student acquires power, to investigate . . . to discover truth for himself. . . . He becomes a self-helper, an independent thinker, an original worker. He finds out the relation of the facts of history, discerns the logic of mathematics, and penetrates the secrets of cause and effect in the natural sciences. (Baldwin, 1892, p. 202)

Educated reason also gives "mastery" and multiplies the values of "remembrances." As a consequence, it is able to project the future.

The general laws of process training hold for reasoning. The law of effort states that well-directed effort in discerning cause relations will educate reason.

From generals we infer particulars, through particular truths we discern general truths. Thus we think up to laws and create science. (Baldwin, 1892, p. 204)

The law of means calls for the use of studies that exercise reasoning. Psychology, logic, philosophy, history, political economy, and sociology are particularly beneficial in this respect. The law of method calls for well-ordered self-activity of the pupil in investigating under the leadership of the teacher.

There are two basic *special laws* to be observed in the training of reasoning.

1. *Law of ascent.* The mind ascends through particulars to generals. It ascends through intuitions to concepts, through concepts to judgments, through related judgments to conclusions.
2. *Law of descent.* The mind descends from generals to particulars. It descends from reasons to judgments, from judgments to concepts, from concepts to intuitions. It descends from aggregates to elements, from the complex to the simple, from the vague to the definite.

Working in harmony with the laws of ascent and descent educates reason. Such work calls into wise activity all the intellectual powers and tends to their harmonious development. (Baldwin, 1892, p. 205)

Though Baldwin believed that all the faculties are present from the inception of life, he recommended that the training of the reasoning faculty only begins at the elementary level. His proposals for training at this level follow a now familiar path. It is a matter of making the obvious somewhat more obvious:

1. *Lead the child to make easy inference.* While reason is still feeble at the elementary level, training can prepare it for better things later on. "Dimly the child discerns simple cause-relations in its narrow world; hence it may be led to make easy inferences and thus strengthen reason" (Baldwin, 1892, p. 207).

2. *Be satisfied with obvious inferences.* "Abstract reasoning and committing logical formularies are very much out of place in this period" (Baldwin, 1892, p. 207). The teacher should lead the child to make "bold and apparent" inferences.

3. *Lead the pupil to find out.* "Boys and girls are trained to tell *why,* and say *because*" (Baldwin, 1892, p. 208).

In arithmetic they give a reason for each step. In history they are led to discover cause-relations between events. In language-lessons they are trained to think and analyze thought. In botany and zoology they are led to infer for themselves. (Baldwin, 1892, p. 208)

Advanced methods of training reason were recommended for students who are 14 years of age and beyond, with no particular academic level specified, though high school appears to be what Baldwin had in mind.

From the fourteenth year upward the student investigates and finds out for himself. Before this period his questions were: "What is it?" and "How is it?" Now he asks also: "Why is it?" "Whence is it?" and "What can I do with it?" Self as reason seeks answers to these questions, and systematic and vigorous endeavor to find answers develops the thinking powers. (Baldwin, 1892, p. 208)

Baldwin offered six advanced methods for developing reason at this higher level.

1. *Lead the student to investigate:*

You incite a burning desire to know. You lead the learner to form habits of effective penetrating thought. You train him to discriminate and assimilate; to analyze and synthesize; to induce, deduce, and reduce; to descend from aggregates to elements and ascend from elements to systems. (Baldwin, 1892, p. 208)

2. *Lead the learner to discuss.* Both written and oral discussion develops "penetrating and sturdy reason." "Ideas fight. Iron sharpens iron. Conflict of minds develops power" (Baldwin, 1892, p. 208).

3. *Lead the student to study mathematics as to develop reason.* It is a superior subject for reason culture. It treats of ". . . related truths. Each intelligent step necessitates reasoning" (Baldwin, 1892, p. 209).

4. *Lead the student to study science as to educate reason.* "Each one for himself gains elementary experience by direct insight into the sense-world, the self-world and the world of necessary realities" (Baldwin, 1892, p. 209).

> Finally, he discerns through related truths cause-relations and infers conclusions. Through particular truths he thinks more general truths, and from general truths he infers particular truths. (Baldwin, 1892, p. 210)

5. *Lead the student to so study language, literature, and history as to educate reason.* History records causes and effects. Constructing a "rational history . . . requires a tremendous effort of reason and gives scope and vigor to this power. The investigation method of studying history, language, and literature, all require constant and vigorous exercise of *reason*, thus are means of cultivating it" (Baldwin, 1892, p. 210).
6. *The investigation method of studying psychology, logic, and philosophy educates reason.* "High thinking" is required for their mastery. They demand "penetrating and long-sustained" thought.

Mistakes in reason culture? Alas they were pervasive, Baldwin, found:

> The unthinking masses: This is the exclamation of all the ages. Individuals think, but millions drift. . . . Why this dearth of thinkers? The answers come slowly and sadly. Our schools fail to develop the art and habit of high thinking. (Baldwin, 1892, p. 210)

The errors are correctable if teachers will take the time but to correct. What are the errors?

1. *Crowding memory while neglecting reason;* Baldwin recommends *"fewer facts and more mental force"* (Baldwin, 1892, p. 211).
2. *Allowing feeble thinking on the part of the pupil.* The teacher does all the work, lecturing while the pupils recline on "downy beds of ease."
3. *Misty thinking*, induced in the pupils by the teacher's own misty thinking.
4. *An overemphasis on mathematics:* ". . . when it assumes to cover all the ground it is time to protest" (Baldwin, 1892, p. 211).
5. *Tediousness*. This is the great "sin of instruction." It causes distraction.
6. *Failure to think knowledge into system.* Things out of their relation are worthless. ". . . concepts not assimilated into truths are of little value . . . truths not thought into systems are squandered (Baldwin, 1892, p. 213).

My account of Baldwin's training of cognitive powers is at an end.

Exhaustive it may appear, but it is, in truth, brief in terms of the sample it provides of his thinking. He was also to provide within his book recommendations for education of the emotions and education of the willpower. These are beyond the purview of our intended survey of processes, i.e., one limited to those directly specified as cognitive powers. It will, however, be useful for us to tarry a bit longer with Professor Baldwin to at least examine the emotions and willpower he dealt with in his further process training efforts.

Regarding the former, Baldwin writes of educating:

1. the self-emotions
2. the altruistic emotions
3. the truth emotions
4. the aesthetic emotions
5. the conscience "or the ethical emotions"

Regarding the education of the willpower, Baldwin writes of educating:

1. attention,[21] or "self-concentration"
2. choice or "self-determination"
3. executive volition or "self-action"
4. culture of the willpower

It is important to remember, in respect, particularly, to the willpower, that faculty trainers were quite sensitive to charges that they might be neglecting the "whole" child. The training of the emotions and willpower was the "affective" education of the day. Baldwin's inclusion of attention among the willpowers is logical, though it was considered under cognitive operations by a host of other process trainers.[22]

---

[21] "Will is voluntary and purposed effort. . . . Self *selects* a special field and devotes himself to it: this is will as attention" (Baldwin, 1892, p. 293). It is also defined as the "power to devote ourselves wholly to one subject" (Baldwin, 1892, p. 293).

[22] The will or willpower, could also, of itself be conceptualized and trained as a cognitive faculty. I have treated it otherwise in this book.

20

Process Training in the Schools—Theories Expanded

INTRODUCTION

Whereas Baldwin in his writings on process training had paid proper obeisance to the new neurologies and psychologies of his age, he was really very little indebteded to them in his thinking. His neurology was essentially a "yea-saying" to the belief that the central nervous system was integrally involved in learning; it was otherwise given very little consideration. Baldwin's psychology was rooted in earlier times. Froebel, Herbart, Immanuel Kant—even the Scholastic fathers—influenced him more than the "experimental psychology" that Wundt had birthed amidst those of the speculative variety. It was James whom Baldwin acknowledged the most in his writings on process training. And James, like Baldwin, was essentially an armchair psychologist. A number of other prominent faculty trainers were to follow Baldwin's speculative route, including W. T. Harris and W. T. White (to be discussed later). However, there were still other process trainers emerging during the late nineteenth century, who insisted upon keeping their process theories au courant and rationalized as to the latest in neurology and psychology, thus beginning a trend that has proven to be long-lived. We shall encounter it repeatedly in the later pages of this book, wherein we will find special education and remedial education process trainers constantly rationalizing their claims and methods on the basis of "tests and measurement" and "research."

HALLECK

Reuben P. Halleck was one of these. His two books on the subject, *Psychology and Psychic Culture (1895)* and *The Education of the Central Nervous System* (1897), constantly refer to Wundt, Külpe, etc., on one hand and the new "facts" of brain localization on the other. While his books were most definitely speculative—at times downright fanciful—he was always referring his theories and practices back to the "evidence" that he found self-evident in neurology and psychology.

Halleck's *The Education of the Central Nervous System* is essentially concerned with the physical side of process training and is a more traditional faculty psychology training text than his first book. It is also heavily committed to sensory processes and imagery, which were prime topics for experimental psychology in his day. We shall thus consider it again, to a considerable degree, in a later chapter within this book which will concern some specific questions about modality training and imagery. Certainly, the title for Halleck's Chapter X, "How Shakespere's Senses Were Trained," should whet the reader's appetite for this chapter to be. But for the nonce, we are more concerned with *The Education of the Central Nervous System* for what it has to tell us about Halleck's conceptions of how that nervous system could be educated.

The preface to Halleck's book begins with the statement:

> The old theory that education consists solely in modifications in an immaterial entity has worked untold damage. It was argued that the immaterial never grew old, and that it could be trained as well at one time as at another. (Halleck, 1896, p. vii)

Not so, warned Halleck, not so at all!

> Education may be something more, as the writer believes, than modifications in the central nervous system, but it is also true that without these modifications no mortal can be educated. (Halleck, 1896, p. vii)

And then Halleck raised an alarm at laggard efforts ". . . to prescribe . . . at the proper time the special kinds of exercise, sensory, motor and ideational, demanded for full development" . . . of that "complex central nervous system." (Halleck, 1896, p. viii). There are critical times for that training, when the brain is "plastic" and impressionable. If the training takes place beyond that time, it cannot be as effective.[1]

---

[1] Plasticity of the brain was a repeated theme in nineteenth century speculations on the nervous system.

If brain cells are allowed to pass the plastic stage without being subjected to proper training, they will never fully develop. The majority of adults have many undeveloped spots in their brains. (Halleck, 1896, p. vii)

This book calls attention to the importance of early purposive training of the central nervous system while its brief morning of plasticity lasts. Then, and only then, can the nerve cells be made lifelong friends, who will take upon themselves the duty of pronouncing correctly, of speaking grammatically, of making habitually correct responses to the thousand and one demands of life. . . . No human being knows a more relentless enemy than motor nerve cells which have been wrongly trained early in life. Such a man may be worth a million, but the bad grammar will continue to flow automatically from the motor mechanism of speech, and to mortify him in good society. (Halleck, 1896, p. viii)

Halleck was openly a supporter of brain localization theory. He deployed the associationistic localization doctrines that we reviewed in the first part of the book with ease and sureness. There is sensory localization. There is motor localization and ". . . a third kind . . . as important as either the motor or the sensory type . . . *associational* localization" (Halleck, 1896, p. 21). Is there any doubt that training does not specifically affect specific parts of the brain? Halleck did not believe that the notion could be seriously entertained, in light of the facts available at the time he was writing. Specific training causing specific neural alterations simply made sense.

We know that special exercise develops special muscles. We also know that, if the sense of sight is trained, while hearing receives no education, the brain tract correlated with hearing will not be proportionately developed. (Halleck, 1896, p. 3)

Halleck assured his readers that all aspects of cognition have a physical basis, e.g., ". . . all forms of mental exercise produce a rise of cerebral temperature" (Halleck, 1896, p. 25). Brain work's physical side is clearly demonstrated by the fact that it requires "more nourishing food" than manual labor.

During a portion of the period of writing a book, an author was at a summer resort where the food was poor and scanty. The part written there was so feeble in comparison with the other chapters, that he rewrote it in the autumn when he had better food. (Halleck, 1896, p. 26)

Halleck was disturbed about those who were fatalistic about the possibilities of improving the nervous system through training and who made ". . . assertions . . . that we are as powerless to improve the quality of our nerve cells as a tree is to change the character of its leaves. . ." (Halleck, 1896, p. 28). These fatalists lamentably regarded the nervous system as "a machine bound to develop in accordance with its native potential capacities" (Halleck, 1896, p. 28). The old and ever-fresh argument over nature and nurture was going on then as it went on earlier, goes on now, and will forevermore. In contrast, Halleck described himself as a "freedomist," who, while accepting certain immutables about the nervous system and the behavior it mediates, believed that it is extraordinarily susceptible to improvement under training, though he did admit that nervous functioning takes on machinelike and unalterable characteristics more and more as the organism moves into later life.

Writing in an age when heredity was given priority over environment by most scholars as well as by the laity, Halleck made his case for the values of environmental intervention. Its effects may be relatively small compared to the constraints of genetics, but they are powerful, nevertheless.

Halleck knew his Galton, as he knew other psychologists and neurologists. So he was willing to admit to hereditary limitations concerning what nurture can accomplish, though he was ever insistent upon the possibilities of neurological improvement.

No human being can defy the laws of his existence and organization; but although the circle of his freedom is small, it is large enough to require several lifetimes to develop to the fullest extent all his natural capacities. Along his own line, he can become a better or worse man. (Halleck, 1896, p. 37)

Halleck provided an illustrious example to support his intervention theories. Remember now, that he was not simply concerned with changes in behavior induced by experience or education. It was changes in the nervous system about which he was insistent upon convincing his audience.

Probably Mozart was born with a remarkable auditory brain tract, with nerve cells of exquisite sensitiveness and complexity of interlacement. All the practice in the world would not make fifth-grade musicians out of some people, who are born without natural capacity. The truth must also be emphasized that if Mozart's parents had sternly refused to allow him to have the proper musical training early in life, he would have failed to develop his temporal lobes to the limits of their capacity, and later in life he would have been compelled to work with a far less plastic brain. Thus, if the requisite means for training and developing the nervous system are not forthcoming early in life, even the possible genius may never develop a fraction of his earliest possibilities. In the same way, a person who might have been ordinarily successful in the walks of life may shrivel up into a nonentity because his latent capacities were not developed at the proper time. (Halleck, 1896, pp. 37,38)

We are all familiar with such statements, albeit in altered form, in these days of early childhood intervention, head start, Benjamin Bloom,

Milwaukee projects, and the like. At the time Halleck was writing, it was hardly *de nouveau,* but required reiteration because of the strong antienvironmentalist biases (and racism) that flourished during the latter years of the nineteenth century. Yes, there are limitations biologically. No, there are no reasons that improvements can not be achieved within limitations.[2]

> It is an old saying that one cannot make a silk purse out of a sow's ear. Another proverb supplementary to this ought to become current—that both the quality of the sow and of her ear may be improved. (Halleck, 1896, p. 44)

There are three ways in which exercise affects the brain:

1. The sensory brain tracts are modified by "incoming currents" from the various senses.
2. The motor areas change as a result of initiating new motor movements or repeating old ones.
3. There is modification of the association tracts which mediate higher functioning, as consequence of their serving to associate various sensations and motor functions.

Halleck's exposition is rather unclear as to how the higher cognitive powers benefit from such exercise formulae. At certain places in his book he described the higher processes as depending upon the exercise of lower sensory, motor, and association ones, in the sense that training of the latter processes helps to establish those automatic behaviors in the human organism that allow its ". . . intellectual powers . . . [to be] free to devote their entire energies to weightier matters" (Halleck, 1896, p. viii). At other times, however, Halleck described the higher cognitive processes as products created by the lower ones—in keeping with the associationist tenets of his times.

What is patently clear in Halleck's accounts of how all psychological processes are formed and function is that physiological association and anatomical association fibers are pan explanatory.

> We now come to the third class, the association fibres, the most important for the psychologist. These fibres connect different convolutions in the same hemisphere. Were it not for the existence of these fibres, perception, memory, and thought would be impossible . . . We see no reason for disagreeing with Dr. Flatau, who says: "The main function of the association fibres is probably psychical. They appear the most fitted to form the anatomical basis for the association processes of perception, thought, and will. (Halleck, 1896, pp. 24–25)

---

[2] The improvability of brain states and functioning and along with these human thinking and behavior—was thought by many neurologists and psychologists to be almost limitless during the early part of the nineteenth century. The latter part saw much more pessimism concerning such prospects.

The Education of the Central Nervous System considers in detail the effects of physical and environmental conditions on the growth of cognitive processes (and the neural tissue underlying them), and goes on to repeatedly insist that:

> It may be true, as we believe it to be, that education consists in developing a mind as well as mere brain cells; but the mind, for its materials, is completely at the mercy of the nervous system. A well-trained nervous system is the greatest friend that the mind can have. An ill-trained nervous system is a relentless enemy to the higher mental powers. It follows its victims and thwarts their aims until the pitying grave stops it. (Halleck, 1896, p. 95)

I have quoted a similar statement earlier in my account of Halleck's work; similar statements are common in his book. For the struggle was then still going on between those who insisted upon a mind beyond the body and those who insisted that the mind was the body or dependent on the body. Halleck, though trying to be materialistic in his approach, wavered (as we see in the preceding quotation and elsewhere) in his convictions and came out recanting his materialism in a feeble sort of mind-body dualism, which allowed him to keep on insisting that education had to educate neurons as well as minds, even though minds might be different from neurons.

Halleck's sensory training emphasis was not particularly original by the lights of his day; a great variety of educational and psychological texts were making similar recommendations. Neither was Halleck's emphasis upon cerebral development by the formation of images novel in its recommendations that the imagining or image-making faculty be trained. Halleck's language and concepts, however, couched as they are in the jargon of the "new" experimental psychology do distinguish his approach from those of other process theorists such as Baldwin. His commitment to motor training is also something that I find "novel" for the period in which he was writing. Halleck approached motor training as motor training instead of as a means of training the higher faculties of the soul. It was Wundt rather than Froebel who was guiding him; and rather than manualism, he was concerned with the training of motor cells and motor tracts. Again, we see a reflection of the psychology and neurology of the day. Cognitive motors were important aspects of both. And the sensory and motor were regarded as working in association with one another. Several quotations from Halleck's book reveal the importance of motor functioning and the sensory-motor paradigm (Bell-Magendie ride again!) in his conceptions:

> Brain exercise of all kinds is accompanied with motor elements. . . When a sensation pours into a nerve cell, the energy from this sensorial stream is not swallowed up and lost. A part of this energy is absorbed in modifying the cell, and a

part tends to flow out in motor action. A sensation, which gave rise to no motor element, was never experienced. . . . If the proper associative nerve fibers in the brain are not developed by fitting nurture and training, there must be both motor and sensory deficiency. When we see a flying bird, raise our guns and shoot it; when we see various piano keys and dextrously touch them . . . it is plain that there must be connection between the various sensory and motor nerve cells. . . . Strictly speaking, one can study neither sensory nor motor action by itself, for every sensation has its motor accompaniment. (Halleck, pp. 210–211)

Halleck recommended that the training of motor habits begin as early as possible (compatible with his general insistence upon early training of processes) but also in a way so as to make them automatic and operative without the intervention or even the surveillance of higher cognitive processes. Respecting this latter point he remarked:

Those children are specially fortunate who are compelled to acquire certain proper motor reactions before the reasons for them are understood. Such children will find out later that they have a wonderful mechanism properly fashioned to their hand. When the workings of the central nervous system are more widely known, there will be a reaction in favour of blind authoritative training early in life; that is if fit parents and teachers can be found to apply such training. (Halleck, 1896, p. 229)

The results of neurophysiology had led him to the same conclusions that Froebel, Rousseau, and other educational psychologists had arrived at from different departure points. "Education. . ." Halleck insisted ". . . should consist in doing" (Halleck, 1896, p. 235).

The act of doing results in changed physiological disposition. It is of little use for one to be told, or to read, how anything is done, unless he follows this with the appropriate actions . . . the learner, under the proper guidance . . . made to perform the necessary actions . . . is on the royal road leading to the desired result. (Halleck, 1896, p. 235)

Halleck's other book that we have under review in this chapter is in a more traditional vein. *Psychology and Psychic Culture,* though it takes up the nervous system and other essentials of "physiological psychology," and also ". . . aims to present the latest ascertained facts of . . . introspective psychology" (Halleck, 1895, p. 6), is essentially cast in the mold of traditional speculative faculty psychology. An examination of its table of contents is instructive in this respect. We note the headings of the various chapters:

I.   The Nervous Mechanism at the Disposal of the Mind
II. Consciousness and Attention
III. Presentation
IV. The Cultivation of Perception

Taking the tripartite road clearly pointed out by Kant and adhered to by generations of psychologists, Halleck made ``. . . a three-fold classification of [the mind's] . . . major functions into *intellect, feeling* or *emotion,* and *will''* (Halleck, 1895, p. 50).

I have said that Halleck was writing in the traditional faculty tradition and that statement stands; however, as was pointed out earlier, Halleck was also very much determined to keep his conceptions rationalized in terms of the latest developments in neurology and psychology. A great deal of devastation had been wrought amongst faculty ranks by the time he wrote his book. Herbart had spoken out earlier in a loud and harsh voice against faculties and against their training. Wundt and the other introspectionists had been strongly critical, too. But Halleck found, as process trainers have always found, that one could rename his faculties and have them, too. So instead of hard-and-fast faculty reifications, we find in his writing what amounts to operational definitions.[3]

> Intellectual action is mental energy expended in perceiving, remembering, imagining, and thinking. In emotional action, the mind is mainly occupied with feeling pleasure or pain. In willing, the mind is busied with acting or refraining from action. (Halleck, 1895, p. 51)

Nor was Halleck going to expose himself to the criticism that he believed the ``mind'' or ``consciousness'' to be anything other than a unity. Facultists had gotten in trouble on this count as well. So he spoke of the different faculties as aspects of mental classification (as Wundt would have wanted him to do).

> We have seen that intellectual action is one of the three sides of mental action. Now intellectual action itself has three different sides, according as we are busy *perceiving, remembering or imagining,* or *thinking.* In actual practice these all go together like an apple and its color. (Halleck, 1895, p. 51)

The unity of experience, so nicely expressed in our times within the catch phrase of ``teaching the whole child,'' was nicely violated by Halleck

---

[3] We have found this before; we shall find it again. Similarly, statements are repeatedly made about the fundamental unity of the mind or soul or the fictive ``as if'' status of faculties.

in the next quotation I have seized from his book, which shows clearly that behind the nonsubstantial, unitized nature of the mind he was writing about, are the good old familiar faculties that we have by now come to know and love, being called in this instance "powers."

All the mental powers are factors in a complete mental act. We are constantly busied with things which bring into play all the powers of the mind. A boy looks into a garden and sees a tree laden with fruit. This mental activity is chiefly *perception.* The tree is at some little distance, and he is puzzled to decide whether the branches are laden with apples or quinces. He calls up by the *representative power* mental images of former quinces that he has seen. Next, he proceeds to compare the fruit before him with this image, and he decides that both the color and the shape differ somewhat from those of the quince. In this activity he is *thinking.* He is pleased with the juicy-looking fruit. Memories come to him of the pleasure experienced in eating other apples, and with those memories comes *emotion.* But still he stands there. The mental state is incomplete. The more he looks at the apples the more he wants them, the stronger becomes his emotion. But he soon finds out that to want and to feel do not bring the apples to him. A high fence is between him and them. Finally his *will* causes him to act. He climbs the fence, plucks the fruit, and begins to eat. This boy has now brought every mental power into play. He has perceived, remembered, thought, felt, acted; and he is now in consequence, eating the fruit. (Halleck, 1895, pp. 51–52)

The unity of experience, in face of the diverse factors (faculties) taking part in it, was elsewhere emphasized by Halleck, while at the same time he indicated the importance of dissecting it for purposes of study (and training, which will be discussed later).

All Knowledge is a Resultant of All the Mental Powers. . . . The mental powers may not appear in the order in which we have named them. They may never appear singly, for we cannot have even a simple sensation without also having an emotional element and discrimination connected with it; nor can we remember without comparing a present sensation with a past one. Yet it will aid us, in study, to isolate each of the processes, in the same way we may consider the form of a house apart from its color. But all the mental powers are, at the same time, weavers at the loom of knowledge, and the product is a web so closely woven that it is often very difficult to pick out the separate threads. (Halleck, 1895, pp. 58–59)

Halleck saw all actions as expressing the various faculties in different aspects or stages thereof.[4]

The simplest knowledge is the result of complex processes . . . "I simply use my eyes and see the apple," would be a common unthinking expression, and yet

---

[4] An observation that Binet was to use to justify his use of different types of test items to obtain an overall assessment of intelligence or judgment. We have observed similar remarks in earlier process trainers such as that perception requires comparison and judgment for its effective operations.

every power at the disposal of the mind is woven into the process that enables us
to make the statement. (Halleck, 1895, p. 56)

The powers to which Halleck gave most of his attention in *Psychology and Psychic Culture* are familiar ones. The new era of experimental
psychology, however, toned his observations and his inferences.

Thus in his discussion of perception, two-point limens are used to
explicate the mind's interpretation of local tactile sensations, Halleck also
used tactile and kinesthetic inferences in ways that smack of familiarity
with the laboratories of introspective psychology. Thus he told his readers
that "Muscular and tactile perception is . . . a process of translating the
external world into greater or smaller masses in terms of our body" (Halleck, 1895, p. 71) and that ". . . the blending of our muscular and tactile
sensations . . . allows perception . . . to translate the combined data into far
more definite knowledge" (Halleck, 1875, p. 70). Visual perception was
explained by the muscular movements of the eyes as well as the sensations
they receive. Distance and depth perception were discussed in some detail,
particularly when he wrote of "How Perception Constructs a Field of
Vision." Similarly, Halleck explained the use of the ear vis-à-vis pitch,
intensity quality, harmony, and localization of space.

Halleck also wrote of "transferred perceptions." "A transferred
perception is one that takes data from one sense in order to draw a
conclusion that primarily depends on data furnished by another sense"
(Halleck, 1895, p. 81). Here, then, he appears to have been thinking of
cross-modality transfer, something that has been of considerable interest
within special education circles for some years now.

Halleck also emphasized apperception, loosely interpreted by him in
keeping with earlier Germanic interpretations as ". . . perception of
things in relation to the ideas which we already possess" (Halleck, 1895,
p. 84). We have met apperception, before; we will meet it again as a
cognitive power or faculty, even though Herbart tried to use it as an
antifaculty when he made the concept popular.

I did say earlier that Halleck was writing in the traditional faculty
training mold, despite his responsiveness to the newer facts and findings
of neurology and experimental psychology. This is most clearly in view
when we find him approaching the training of his "powers." Since we
have begun with perception, let us examine this bent relative to perception. Halleck talks about the evils of overdependence upon books in
education as a consequence of which ". . . perception threatens to become a lost art" (Halleck, 1895, p. 91). Training in perception is essential.
It is ". . . one of the factors that enables a person to survive in competition, which grows fiercer every year. . . ."; defects in perception ". . .
claim as their special victims those whose perceptive powers are
deficient" (Halleck, 1895, p. 95). He provided examples of successes and

failures in life that were due to perception. The Indian is a prime example of the value of good perceptual powers. A woman is defrauded in buying a cheap lace collar of poor quality at inflated price because the salesman saw she could not discriminate ". . . between a fine and a coarse grade, or a machine and a handmade article, so he kept making new discoveries in his stock and raising the price each time" (Halleck, 1895, p. 90). Improvement in perception is to be gained by training the pupil to observe and discriminate with particular attention to details. Concentrated attention is important in this respect.[5] The natural sciences aided by graphic efforts on the pupil's part are the best teachers of perception.

All the natural sciences afford unusual opportunity for using the senses. Among these sciences may be mentioned physics, geology, ornithology, entomology, botany. They all require the most searching use of the perceptive faculties. In connection with them, drawing should be taught. If any one wishes to find out how imperfectly he has perceived anything, let him undertake to draw it. In order to draw well, one must perceive well. (Halleck, 1895, p. 97)

Halleck also made a number of recommendations for games that improve rapidity of perception, such as walking rapidly by a shop window and then writing down as many articles displayed as possible or throwing a number of articles up into the air and allowing the observer to identify them before or after they fall from view behind a screen, in a basket, etc. Training in rapidity of perception is important because:

This age of the world wants persons who can do things not only well but quickly. Those who cannot combine both qualities will be pushed to the rear in the struggle for existence. (Halleck, 1895, p. 100)[6]

Despite the importance of perception for survival in school, hunting, and lace collar purchases, Halleck warned against its overcultivation, which might have as its consequence the enfeeblement of growth of other, higher cognitive processes. Similar concerns were expressed by a variety of other faculty trainers, including Harris, whose book (we shall soon see) warned vehemently against overtraining of *all* processes subservient to the rational faculties, lest such training subvert the latter. Plato had expressed a similar concern in his day.

After perception, memory is elaborately discussed in terms of its

[5] Halleck did not define attention as a faculty in its own right. Rather it is discussed as a "focusing of consciousness" or as "detention" in consciousness. There are two kinds of attention as concerns direction; one upon mental objects; the other nonexternal objects. From the point of view of effort involved, there is to be distinguished reflex and voluntary attention, etc.

[6] Thus the spirit of social Darwinism is expressed even for perception. Survival of the fittest seemed only reasonable and right to many psychologists following Charles Darwin's monumental theories of evolution.

physical basis within the nervous system and as a ". . . special case of imaginative representation" (Halleck, 1895, p. 106),[7] with proper hello and adieu to auditory, visual, tactile, and other sense-related memory systems. In remembering, several distinct subpowers can be distinguished:

In order to remember anything, the mind must have the power (1) of retention, (2) of reproduction, (3) of recognition, and (4) of referring an object to a certain more or less definite place and time. (Halleck, 1895, p. 109)

The physical basis for the different memories is to be found in "different brain tracts." The laws governing memory are those essentially of association, the primary and secondary laws familiar to all beginning students of psychology, and a few other laws and regulations that appear to be Halleck's own personalized contributions.

Can the memory be trained? This question has plagued wise men (and fools) down through the centuries. And almost every generation of philosophers, physicians, psychologists, educators, and religious orders have struggled with attempts to answer this question in a positive vein.[8] It was to be on the issue of memory training (failure therein) that William James was to take a negative stance on transfer of training effects (as we shall see in the following chapter). Halleck was most positive on the subject:

For lasting memory, perception must cause a permanent change in the brain cells. Since physiological psychology has demonstrated this, it has been possible to proceed more intelligently in cultivating the memory. . . . That men should differ in brain power is no stranger than that they should differ in muscular power. Without training, John L. Sullivan could have overpowered several ordinary men at one time. He was naturally endowed with unusually strong muscles. We may grant all these physiological facts and native differences, and yet insist on the great importance of memory culture. If the muscles of an arm are naturally weak and flabby, there is all the more reason for exercising it. Even a Sullivan improves his strong arms by exercise. Had he kept one in a sling, that arm would soon have become weak. To keep either muscle or brain tissue from becoming weak we must obey certain laws. (Halleck, 1895, p. 132)

Those familiar with Ebbinghouse's masterpiece on memory will have no problem in recommending some of Halleck's suggestions for strengthening the memory. Repetition is, of course, one way in which one may remember better ". . . new and similar sensations . . ." being

---

[7] ". . . there are no absolute demarcations between the images of so-called memory and of the imaginative power. Both are products of this latter power" (Halleck, 1895, p. 106).
[8] Extensive writings on mnemonics to aid faltering or insecure memories have been published since antiquity; they are still proffered to the public.

required to ". . . renew this [a particular impression] disposition in the course of time . . ." lest ". . . it imperceptibly lose its ability and be finally obliterated" (Halleck, 1895, p. 133). The formation of clear-cut images facilitates memory. Drawing assists in this particular. Obey the law of correlation, the law of emotional preference, make sure that you attend what you wish to remember. Avoid mnemonics, which make the memory excessively dependent upon external crutches. The rule of improvement is through ". . . proper and methodical exercise" (Halleck, 1895, p. 149).

How about remedial training for a weak or faltering memory? Halleck prescribed confidently for a condition he calls mind wandering.

A sure cure for mind wandering is to make an abstract from memory of sermons, speeches, or books. If one is reading a work on history, let him, after finishing a page, close the book and repeat to himself the substance of that page. If he cannot do so with one reading, let him reread until he can. . . . The mind may wander at first . . . but as soon as the mind feels that it will surely be called upon to reproduce what has been read, its energy will be doubled. It will soon cease the lazy habit of merely allowing impressions to come in to meet it; it will reach out to meet the impression. The author knows of a case of mind wandering cured by the oral recital and making of a written abstract of . . . an English history, John Stuart Mill's *Political Economy,* and a text-book on psychology, (Halleck, 1895, p. 148)

Imagination as defined by Halleck is merely another aspect of the "representative power at work," another aspect of memory through which "Things which have been once presented are presented again . . . in a more or less new way" (Halleck, 1895, p. 150). Both memory and imagination, partners in the "representative power," deal with images. But whereas memory requires association as a first step, imagination requires disassociation for its step ". . . preparatory to combining [images] in different ways" (Halleck, 1895, p. 152). Then there is recombination in different ways, ranging from the "approximately literal" to the downright chimerical. There is a distinction, in this latter respect, between mechanical and constructive imagination, the first joining "images in any order," as in dreams, without altering them and the second characterized by "*a definite purpose,*" which is selective, aided by the "thinking power." Like Baldwin, Halleck regarded constructive imagination as a basis of progress, "The constructive imagination of primeval man, aided by thought, began to conquer the world" (Halleck, 1895, p. 166).

Halleck, like many faculty psychologists of his day, decried the attempts to denigrate imagination.

It was once thought that the imagination should be repressed, not cultivated, that it was in the human mind like weeds in a garden . . . the reverse is true . . .

there is no mental power that stands in need of more cultivation than the imagination. So practical are its results that a man without it cannot possibly be a good plumber. . . . (Halleck, 1895, p. 166)

The cultivation of imagination depends upon "abundant perceptional material," including perception developed from the internal perceptions that result from reading good descriptive literature. Clear-cut images assist in its cultivation, as they do in that of reproductive memory. "Pictorial interpretations" and "oral descriptions" are also of major value, as is creative writing.

As soon as knowledge is acquired, it should be used in as many different combinations as possible. No one should gather a mass of materials without attempting original composition. Above all, every person should write something imaginative, not necessarily for publication, but as a matter of cultivation. . . . The writing of poetry furnishes the finest imaginative exercise. (Halleck, 1895, p. 171)

Forecasting the plot of a partially read novel or completing an unfinished story were also recommended by Halleck as means of training the imagination. Through all of this, the cultivatee is to attempt to form his own images rather than relying upon the images formulated by others.

If we let another do all the lifting for us, and take all the exercise, we shall get no muscular development. If we take all our images ready made from other people, we shall never have much imaginative power. (Halleck, 1895, p. 173)

There is more training provided to the imagination by one's own creative efforts than by effort expended in participating in the imaginative creations of others; though this latter also can cultivate the imagination, as we have seen. Think by images, rather than through abstractions. Wherever possible, formulate ideals. Thus, too, is imagination to be developed.

Imagination, of course, can be abused. The common practices of "daydreaming" and "castle building" are morally and physically unhealthy. Castle builders ". . . after reveling in . . . imaginative sweets" . . . find the "dry bread of actual toil . . . exceedingly distasteful" (Halleck, 1895, p. 178)

Not infrequently these castle-builders abandon effort in an actual world. Success comes too slow for them. They become speculators or gamblers, and in spite of all their grand castles, gradually sink into utter nonentities in the world of action. (Halleck, 1895, p. 178)

It is thus that the reading of too much fiction should be discouraged.

The reading of too much fiction is dangerous. The impossible stories that have been sown broadcast over the land have wrecked many a young life. (Halleck, 1895, p. 179)

The power of thought is the last of the cognitive processes that Halleck considered. It is present at the inception of life. In discussing this point, Halleck exemplified the changes in faculty theory (and training) that had evolved. When he was writing, faculties were no longer necessarily considered distinct and discrete. There was a tendency to see all processes as represented from the beginning of life itself, though some as weaker than others. This was part of the heritage of the sense realist movement, which saw mind arising out of sensation. It was also an inheritance from Froebelism and its Germanic philosophical origins, which viewed all of man's powers as being present in germinal form within the infant. Thus Halleck's statement:

The Thinking Power Active From the First. It was formerly supposed that human beings did not think early in life; that then they perceived and remembered; that after they had seen and treasured up a great deal, they began to think. These processes were considered to be as sharply marked off from each other. . . . We now know that no one can perceive without thinking at the same time. In perceiving . . . we are constantly discriminating . . . in remembering, we must think, in order to discriminate. This power of discrimination is due to thought. . . . In imaginative productions that amount to anything, thought must work vigorously. (Halleck, 1895, p. 195)

The steps in thinking that Halleck delineated are all too familiar to us by now:

1. Conception based upon presentation of materials, i.e., perception, comparing, abstraction, generalization, denomination, i.e., affixing a name to a particular class of objects
2. Judgment ". . . the power revolutionizing the world" (Halleck, 1895, p. 194)
3. Reasoning, both inductive and deductive

There are three primary (positive) laws of thought which the mind ". . . must obey in thinking correctly" (Halleck, 1895, p. 200).
There is the law of identity, which holds that the same quality or thing remains such no matter how different the conditions in which it occurs. There is the law of contradiction, which states that no thing ". . . can at the same time and place both be and not be" (Halleck, 1895, p. 201). And, finally, there is the law of excluded middle, which states: "Everything must either be or not be; there is no alternative or middle course." (Halleck, 1895, p. 201). Does all this sound foolish? Read some of the definitions in recent psychology texts. But I will spare the reader further discourse on the nature of thought processes as elucidated by Halleck, as we hurry on to consider their cultivation.
Reminding his readers that the cultivation of perception, memory, and imagination also dealt with the cultivation of thought, it being ". . .

impossible to train one mental power correctly without cultivating others at the same time'' (Halleck, 1895, p. 222),[9] he went on to make specific recommendations for the cultivation of thinking.

> The first practical rule for the cultivation of the thinking powers is: Be ever on the hunt for relations. The only way in which the world can advance is by finding out new relations between things. (Halleck, 1895, p. 233)

The dire results of overlooking relations were vividly presented by an alert Halleck, who was never one to let a moral homily of cognitive sorts get by him, when and if it could be avoided:

> Some capitalists built a street-car line in a certain town without sufficiently considering the number that would probably travel each day and comparing that number with the daily expenses, without reflecting on the sources of the town's growth and direction that its expansion would take. After a struggle the company failed. It is well for the learner to note the precise grounds of failure, to realize that it was due to the lack of fully thinking out things *in their relation to other things.* There was no failure in building the line. That was perfectly feasible. Street-car lines had been built again and again. Horses or electricity could draw the cars; conductors could be found. But the expense of building and running the line did not stand in the proper relation to the number of people who would ride, nor was the direction of the line properly related to the suburban growth of the place. (Halleck, 1895, pp. 223–224)

Hence Halleck's warning to all would-be thinkers:

> Whenever one learns a new thing, apparently unrelated to any other part of his knowledge, he should make haste to form connections. In doing this, he will think. (Halleck, 1895, p. 224)

Various advice was offered by Halleck to improve one's thinking: Accuracy of concepts is important, as is comparison developed through skillful classifications. The search for analogies is still another.

Halleck offered his readers certain cautions about thought culture. First, there must be an emphasis upon "breadth of thought." It is dangerous to neglect breadth of thinking early in age for "If a broad foundation is not laid early, it will never be obtained. . . . We shall then think in ruts" (Halleck, 1895, p. 231). Woe to him who has overspecialized in thinking in his tender years. He may be permitted to ". . . think on foundations already laid, but . . . allowed to build no new ones" (Halleck, 1895, p. 231). Second, there must be an effort to prevent "fickleness," or being rattlebrained. Stability of character is erected on ". . . a foundation of definite thought. . . ." (Halleck, 1895, p. 233).

---

[9] A point of wisdom unfortunately overlooked by too many of today's process trainers.

Fickleness is the great enemy of thought culture and of knowledge of self. The ideas in the minds of many change so often that they have no consecutive and determined self. (Halleck, 1895, p. 233)

Third, there must be an avoidance of excessive novel reading.

For proper nutrition, it is necessary that food should remain a certain length of time in the stomach. Digestion, mental or physical, takes time. Ideas must be kept in the mind until their relations to other ideas can be thought out. . . . The rapid devouring of novels is fatal to thought. No idea is allowed to linger; the mind rushes on from one exciting scene to another in as quick a succession as possible ever calling for more excitement. One novel is finished and another begun. No time is left for perfect digestion. The circulation of many general libraries averages eighty percent of fiction. They deserve to be known as aiders and abettors in killing thought. The minds of inveterate novel readers are apt soon to become so unsuited to severe thought, that they regard it with as much aversion as a rheumatic person does a foot race. (Halleck, 1895, p. 233)

Fortunately for those who like to "curl up with a good novel" but might have apprehensions about debauching their thinking powers, Halleck provided a way out.

Since fiction is certain to be widely read, it is important to know how it may be made to cultivate the thinking powers. If persons would read a novel with the same care as a history, as much mental discipline might result. (Halleck, 1895, p. 234)

There were a number of ways of accomplishing this. For one, "every move" of the fictional character the reader was indulging his mental appetites with was to be compared to actions "in real life."

The principle of *comparison* between the fictional and the real may be brought in at every step. Thought consists essentially in comparing, in noting likenesses and differences; and it cannot be repeated too often that all mental exercise of this sort tends to cultivate thought in the only true way. (Halleck, 1895, p. 234)

Another way to cultivate higher cognitive functioning through fiction is to have the reader, after reading one chapter, forecast the following one. When the hero or heroine is "plunged into difficulties," the reader should "lay down his book," and attempt to seek solutions to their problems on his own.

By so doing, he will develop the power of constructive thought. This practice would serve him in good stead in the actual difficulties of his own life. He would think his way out of trouble quicker. When he found himself in a corner, his nimble-witted mind might suggest several alternatives of escape, while one who had not thus trained his thinking power might see no way out until too late. Many a lawyer, doctor, business man has said to himself: "If only I had seen that other alternative before the case was lost, the patient dead, the enterprise ruined." (Halleck, 1895, p. 235)

Also recommended was the study of the more esteemed authors such as Scott, Dickens, Reade, and Collins, whose writings provide insight into human nature as well as a variety of ingenious plots. Their work provides for the exercise of "constructive thought." For purposes of increasing the reader's ability to systematically develop his train of thoughts, on the other hand, Halleck suggested the novels of Thackeray, Hawthorne, and Eliot.

After finishing *Romola,* let him trace the growth of the differing emotions in the leading characters and institute close comparison between them, noting the likenesses and the differences. If studied as we have indicated, fiction will, in its own way, be as serviceable as mathematics for training thought. (Halleck, 1895, p. 235)

Good fiction, then, if properly studied, will serve to train thought as well as that particularly favored cognitive trainer of the ancients and formal disciplinarians—mathematics—that is, if the student approaches it with the purpose of improving his mind and ". . . is careful to form accurate concepts of every term, to link these logically together, and to note all points of attachment of new knowledge to old" (Halleck, 1895, p. 237).

The reader most certainly has a good sampling of Halleck's ideas about thought culture, memory culture, perceptual culture, etc. (Remember that we are omitting, as is our policy in this book, the culture of the emotions and feelings, which were always mainstays of mental training texts; affective education is hardly new.)[10] I would like to think that the reader has been touched, as well as amused, by Halleck's approach to processes and process training. There is something charming about it— also much that has a utilitarian ring to it that is still appealing after all these many years.

DEXTER AND GARLICK

F. C. Dexter and A. H. Garlick's *Psychology in the Schoolroom* was a most popular text in its day, going through several editions and a number of printings from 1898 through 1902. The book was dedicated to helping teachers apply the general principles of psychology to the "art" of

---

[10] We have also chosen to ignore his discussion of sensation, to which he gave considerable attention as well, which we might expect from such a good S-R theorist as he was.

teaching, ". . . to apply the laws of Mental and Moral Science to school work—to take the elements of Psychology into the Schoolroom." Psychology, as defined by Dexter and Garlick, is "The Science dealing with the working of the *Mind* . . ." or, more accurately, ". . . the Science of Consciousness . . ." and ". . . the Science which describes, classifies and explains our mental operations" (Dexter & Garlick, 1902, p. 2).

What we find in all this, as espoused by Dexter and Garlick, is a melange of Wundtian introspection, a good deal of Ribot, and even a great deal more of Froebel. The book *Psychology in the Schoolroom* represents a most interesting advance in sophistication, albeit armchair rather than empirical, over the previous authors whose work we have perused. At the same time, it is steeped in the romantic conceptions of facultists gone by and shows a strong Victorian righteousness, which was certainly not lacking in some of the earlier books we have examined, but is more curious here in light of the latter-day scientism Dexter & Garlick espoused.

The faculties were referred to as operations in Dexter and Garlick's tome. There are three leading states of consciousness:

1. *Feeling or Emotion,* which includes all pleasurable or painful conditions of mind, e.g., *thirst, sight, love, anger.*
2. *Knowing or Intellect,* which includes all operations connected with the discrimination of one state of consciousness from another, e.g., *memory, imagination, reasoning.*
3. *Willing or Volition,* which includes all mental operations leading or tending to lead to action, e.g., *attention, impulse, resolution.* (Dexter & Garlick, 1902, p. 19)

The old familiar tripartite division of the soul we meet again through Dexter and Garlick, as we did through so many of their predecessors. (What Immanuel Kant had split asunder, let no faculty psychologist join their parts.) Do we have faculties in these operations of the mind or states of consciousness? We do. Of course, but they were qualified, modified, so that if the spectre of Herbart were still about, it would not scowl too severely and proper introspectionists might not be angered at seeing their consciousness split up too broadly. And so for the Kantian three:

Sometimes they are spoken of as *Functions* of the mind, i.e., as certain operations which the mind performs. More frequently they are regarded as *Faculties* of the mind.

A mental faculty is the power the mind has of acting on "objects" and discriminating them from one another.

Feeling, knowing, willing are not different parts of the mind, but merely different *Phases* or forms of activity of one and the same mind. (Dexter & Garlick, 1902, p. 19)

The three broad basic faculties or major operations of the mind are "connected." Two examples are given:

(a)   A boy falls down in the playground and hurts himself. I am sorry for him *(Feeling)*; I look at the injured part and see that it should be bound up *(Knowing)*; and I proceed to do it *(Willing)*.

(b)   I hear that a friend has passed a difficult examination *(Knowing)*; I rejoice at his success *(Feeling)*; and hasten to send him a congratulatory telegram *(Willing)*. (Dexter & Garlick, 1902, pp. 19–20)

The authors attempted to placate the ghost of Herbart and the neo-Herbartians all about them by making the proper obeisances to the conceptual or nominal aspects of the faculties they wrote about—as opposed to their reality. It is, they apologized, easier to reason about one thing at a time rather than three; that is why the three faculties or states of consciousness are to be spoken of as if they are distinct entities, when in fact they are not. So Dexter and Garlick qualified:

The constant use of the terms employed in classifying various phases of mental activity (e.g., memory, attention, etc.) has led some to the erroneous view that the mind is an organism consisting of component parts (memory, attention, etc.), just as the body is an organism consisting of head, trunk, limbs, etc. (Dexter & Garlick, 1902, p. 21)

They, nevertheless, subsequently went on to talk about the three major Kantian faculties as faculties. They are indeed "indissolubly" connected. One state grows out of another. We can't separate them. In the simplest of mental operations, many may be represented. However, they are also opposed to each other. Feeling, based on afferent nervous impulses, is a passive state (largely). Willing, giving rise to efferent impulses, is mainly active. Knowing oscillates between the two poles; it is both passive and active. Had not Plato said the same, and Aristotle? Why not Dexter and Garlick? The three states are "constantly striving for mastery." All minds predominate in one state or the other so we have a typology among men: There is the emotional man, the intellectual man, and the strong-willed man. He with a "perfectly balanced mind" will have all three faculties developed to the same proportions. A well-rounded education rounds out the faculties as well as filling in the lacunae of· knowledge within pupils' minds.

We have seen that Dexter and Garlick essentially adopted a faculty position, even though their faculties are alternately discussed as functions, states of consciousness, operations, etc. Their discussion of the various cognitive faculties, which follows, was also very much in the traditional vein. I shall attempt to extract from their book those aspects that will help us (1) understand the continuity of faculty tradition in educational psychology as we begin to move into the twentieth century and (2) pay specific attention to particular points that may not have been stressed sufficiently by the earlier authors we have reviewed.[11]

An awareness of the physical basis of mental processes and, specifically, the faculties, is never much out of the reader's focus as he proceeds through Dexter and Garlick's book, with its chapter after chapter of cognitive training. We do not have the theme of matter under mind hammered into our consciousness as incessantly as was the case with Halleck, but the presence of the body was always—and clearly— acknowledged by the authors. Thus sensation was provided a chapter of its own, with considerable discussion given to the sense organs and the "facts" of sensory operations.

Perception was treated in this chapter very much in the "modern" sense.[12] For example, in the case of vision, the vibration of ether[13] transmitted from the object to the optic nerve of the eye is then conveyed to the brain, which allows the mind to "interpret" and distinguish these vibrations from other impressions transmitted through the other sense organs.

Dexter and Garlick divided the "process of perception" into two "well-marked" stages. There is (1) the prehensive part of the process, which involves the discrimination and identification of sense impressions, and (2) the apprehensive part of the process, "perception proper," which was defined as:

> The conjunction of these present sense impressions with reproduced images of past sense impressions, and the projection of the whole group of present and past impressions into some external object. (Dexter & Garlick, 1902, pp. 59–60).

Perception, as conceived by Dexter and Garlick is a very complex process, involving sensation, reproductive imagination, memory conception (the reproduced image being a concept), reasoning (in assimilation and discrimination), and belief (in the reality of the external world).

[11] We might observe that Dexter and Garlick, while also considering attention as an operation of the will, also applied it in broader terms. Thus they defined attention as an "intensified form of consciousness," as a direction of the mind at any given time. They also make the following point:

> Attention can hardly be called a faculty of the mind. It is rather a *condition* of intellectual operations. *Clear* thoughts, *distinct* feelings, *deliberate* volitions are impossible without attention. (Dexter & Garlick, 1902, p. 29)

We have already remarked about the uncertain status of attention as a faculty at earlier points in this book. This uncertainty continued into the future as well.

[12] Following Reid's distinction of sensation from perception, this was common.

[13] The ether theory of visual sensation is a most interesting one; it was one of the dominant explanations of "how we see" for quite a while.

The first of the modalities Dexter and Garlick took up are the "sense of touch and the muscular sense." The involvement of these two senses and the perceptions resulting from them, they argued are fundamental to the operations of the other modalities.[14] The premise seems sound, but their reasoning supporting it is somewhat specious, as we see in the following quotations:

> The other senses may be considered as modifications and developments of it. Sapid substances must *touch* the tongue, odiferous particles must *touch* the nose, air waves must *touch* the ear, ether waves must *touch* the eye, before tasting, smelling, hearing or seeing is possible. (Dexter & Garlick, p. 63)

> The other senses depend upon it for assistance or confirmation. We prove or disprove our visual and auditory perceptions by our tactual ones. We might see "ghosts," we might hear them; if we could *touch* them our skepticism in these apparitions would be considerably shaken. (Dexter & Garlick, 1902, p. 63)

Nevertheless, the attention given to touch and muscular sensations by Dexter and Garlick is commendable for a faculty psychology text. It goes beyond the attention called to these senses by Froebelism. The authors drew upon the knowledge founts of experimental psychology to study the tactile and kinesthetic senses. The importance of tactile and kinesthetic percepts to the "perception of bodily self" is also clearly in the ball park of psychoanalytic theory. Freud, after all, insisted that the ego is first and foremost a "body" ego, and psychoanalysts have always been aware of the critical role played by perceptions emanating from the body, as well as those of the distal variety.

All this notwithstanding, Dexter and Garlick still ranked vision and hearing first among the intellectual senses and advised that in particular,

> . . . the eye must be awarded the palm as the intellectual sense organ. Our memories are chiefly visual ones. Our visual images are more numerous and admit of more easy recall than our auditory images. (Dexter & Garlick, 1902, p. 79)[15]

Perceptual training, as recommended by Dexter and Garlick, is to proceed through "observation." We should not forget how powerful an influence Pestalozzism was for so long, both directly and through its influence on other theories and methodologies such as those of Froebel. In this vein, the authors recommended testing a child's powers of observation by having him draw objects from memory; some of the pages of their text could have emanated from Florence Goodenough (including DAP illustrations), though the authors did not have an adequate appreciation of the developmental factors contributing to the makeup of children's

[14] A notion made particularly popular by Condillac.
[15] We shall discuss imagery in greater detail in a later chapter.

drawings. Drawing errors were attributed essentially to "errors" of observation and execution.

Training the powers of observation trained the powers of perception and attention.[16] Hurrah, then, for object lessons—though science, geography, grammar, history, and writing were also means of training these powers. (Remember Baldwin in these respects.)

Should the senses be trained? Most certainly. The authors decried the efforts made by other facultists (usually traditional mental disciplinarians) to bypass sense training on the grounds that it was unimportant or inferior in importance. They regarded these efforts as misguided and commented:

> Misled by erroneous notions of human dignity, older pedagodic methods have endeavored to overleap the first stage of nature's culture, and to give a training of *con*ceptions before, and in place of, that of *per*ceptions. (Dexter & Garlick, 1902, p. 99)

The training of the senses, however, is a necessary preliminary to the training of the higher cognitive powers. The teacher who tries to train the powers of judgment and reasoning based upon incomplete and inaccurate sense–perceptions is building his edifice of education upon sand. The first responsibility of the teacher of the young is to train the senses.

> By the Training of the Senses is meant the regular and systematic exercise of the organs of sense with a view to making the sense–percepts thereby acquired the efficient instruments of reasoning. (Dexter & Garlick, 1902, p. 99)

The senses are to be trained in the order of their development:

1. Touch and the muscular sense first
2. Sight, which, while sometimes shown on the day of birth, doesn't effectively operate till later
3. Hearing, which is "comparatively slow in development"
4. Taste, which, while regarded by some as the first sense to develop, matures slowly and is relatively unimportant educationally
5. Smell, which appears to develop last of all and has but "small potentiality" for development.

The exclusive training of a single faculty, however, is impossible. When one trains touch, he usually also trains the eye and engages the "higher faculties" of judgment and reasoning. It is a matter of special attention to a particular sense when we speak of training that sense, rather than excluding other senses. In teaching, as many senses should be appealed to as possible:

---

[16] Even though the authors had already denied attention to faculty or "power" status.

Bunyan says that the town of Man-soul has five gates—ear-gate, eye-gate, etc. Too many teachers approach one gate only. . . . Other teachers "knock" at as many "gates" as possible. (Dexter & Garlick, 1902, p. 101)

Another dictum of Dexter and Garlick's regimen for sense training is that the senses be trained "in proportion" to their "intellectual proportions." Here accolades were accorded sight and touch, the intellectual senses par excellence. Earlier in their discourse hearing was ranked as the "intellectual sense" second only in importance to vision. Some qualifications are in order. Dexter and Garlick regarded sight and hearing as the major intellectual senses in adulthood. In childhood, and in childhood training, however touch takes precedence over hearing in terms of importance.

The eye should be appealed to whenever possible. A child remembers what he sees much better than what he hears. The impressions gained through sight should be corrected by those gained through touch. A child, who, on being told to look at a brick and tell the number of its sides, answers that there are four, should be made to *handle* the brick and count the sides. (Dexter & Garlick, 1902, p. 101)

Activity is another dictum of sense training. Here Dexter and Garlick acknowledged Froebel and his insistence that we "learn by doing."

Children should always be kept doing *something*. "Doing nothing" should not be tolerated. . . . Exercise strengthens any faculty, provided that exercise is neither too excessive nor too prolonged. (Dexter & Garlick, 1902, p. 102)

In their recommendations for the culture of visual perception, the authors emphasized training in color and form perception, with reliance on drawing, reading, and writing as major means of exercising the visual modality in these respects. Geography was also recommended on grounds that it employs models, diagrams, and maps. There is also to be training in perception of distance. Touch is to be trained through handling objects such as Froebel's kindergarten gifts. Drawing and writing are excellent means of training the muscular sense. Clay modeling and paper folding are further means, as are all forms of manual training. Object lessons, properly constituted, to allow distinctions of hardness from softness, rough from smooth, and weight estimations, have their place as well.

As to the training of hearing, reading provides ample opportunities to develop a "nice discrimination" of auditory impressions. The teacher should exaggerate his or her emphasis on words in initial auditory training. A less-exaggerated style may be adapted once the hearing faculty has been properly sensitized to discriminate finer differences. Singing is another means of developing auditory perception.

Dexter and Garlick placed little store on the training of either smell or taste and indicated that there is "little opportunity," in any case, for their training in school. They did, however, suggest that children be allowed to smell and taste objects that have distinct smells and tastes during object lessons and that chemistry experiments may provide considerable opportunity for the cultivation of the sense of smell, but that instruction in this subject comes too late to improve it.''

The authors, while lauding the importance of sense–perception training, recognized possible dangers resulting from abuses in it. Since the intent of sense training is to prepare the mind for the proper development of the higher cognitive faculties, overspecialization in sense training holds real dangers.

It is not our business to make our children embryo artists, or musicians, or mechanics, or chemists, but men and women of good perceptive power and sound judgment. (Dexter & Garlick, 1902, p. 107)

Another abuse of sense training may result from its being too prolonged. Excessive sense training makes the expression of the senses automatic so that there is little call upon the higher faculties in their exercise. What is valuable for a young child may be useless for an older one. Sense training that exercises the mind at a young age may be merely distracting at an older age.

Still another problem that may arise out of improperly directed sense training is that it can be too exclusive. The perceptive powers may "employ the whole energy of the mind," as a result of which the child may not learn to ". . . see the universal which underlies the particular." (Dexter & Garlick, 1902, p. 107).

Yet another admonition to be observed in sense training follows from the one discussed above. There is the "possible defect" in sense training that the pupil concentrates too exclusively upon "individual notions," and not enough upon general ones. Thus the child only develops limited powers of generalization. He may be further restricted in his reasoning to rudimentary ways.

. . . care must be taken to give *simple* exercises in the higher mental faculties as well as good training in sense–perception. Sense training lessons are not an *end* in education, they are but a *means* of rising higher. (Dexter & Garlick, 1902, p. 107)

Dexter and Garlick's chapter "The Development and Training of the Senses" concludes, as do the others in *Psychology in the Schoolroom,* with a series of questions that aspiring teachers were expected to respond to after exposure to the authors' ideas on perceptual training. These questions are produced below verbatim in order to provide a fuller appreciation of the importance of perceptual training around the turn of our century.

Questions

1. What do you understand by training the senses? State concisely the advantages secured by it; are any of these obtainable in other ways?

2. How would you set about the training of the senses with a view to secure a wide range as well as minute accuracy of observation.

3. What can be done in school to make hearing more sensitive and exact, or to improve the voice?

4. "Some of the senses are more precocious, and others more tardy, in their development, and besides, the senses are of unequal importance, and not rendering the same services do not deserve the same attention." Comment on this and illustrate your statement. Deduce practical considerations as to the times and ways of training the senses in school.

5. Define precisely what you understand by training the senses of a child. Illustrate how you would seek to carry out such training.

6. What is meant by the training of the senses? What are the proper place and value of this training in general education? Examine the assertions (a) that the senses do not need training, and (b) that they can be overtrained.

7. Take one of the three senses: sight, hearing, touch, and classify the sensations we receive by it; also show in what ways exercise improves the capacity of the sense, illustrating by a reference to elementary processes of instruction.

8. It is said that the senses do not give us knowledge, but only the materials out of which knowledge is built up by the mind. Explain what is meant, and bring out by reference to an object lesson the bearing of this point on the proper method of object teaching.

9. Explain psychologically the function of the senses in the growth of knowledge, assigning as accurately as you can the proper place of exercise and improvement of the senses in intellectual education.

10. How far does your knowledge of the sense of sight support the principle of Froebel that a nice perception of form is best gained in connection with the device of manual reproduction?

11. What seems to you the specific excellences of sense–perception? How far and in what ways may these be obtained through systematic training?

12. Bring out the meaning of the principle "Exercise strengthens faculty," and show its bearing on education. Do all kinds of exercise develop the faculties?

13. Explain why a teacher should begin a course of instruction with an exercise of the senses. What senses is it most important to exercise in connection with the work of teaching?

14. What is meant by exercising the senses? Discuss the question whether a high degree of sense-discrimination should be made a chief aim in education.
15. Discuss the use of sense-training, and explain the methods of training the observation through sight and touch, singly, or in coordination with each other.

The redundancies of the above questions and their designation by various initials, e.g., E.D., C.P., suggests that the participants in a Dexter-and-Garlick-guided course were not forced to submit to all of the inquiries posed, or that some were intended for class discussion, others for individual homework. No matter; it is obvious that our authors gave a great deal of thought to the issues, promises, and problems of sense training and that they wished their students to pay some attention to these as well. Would that as much care were exercised in current examinations on the value of perceptual training, at least some of the ones of which I am cognizant. Similar attention was paid to the training of other of the faculties in subsequent chapters of their book. Such were the beliefs and expectations of the day before Thorndike forever shook the foundations in the belief that faculties (1) existed and (2) could be trained in the schools of America (though it is obvious, on the basis of current practices in American schools, that forever is a relative affair at best).

Let us proceed to the matter of memory a la Dexter and Garlick. They clearly distinguish between percepts and images and give a number of rules by which their teacher audiences may also distinguish them. An image is defined as a "revived" percept or a revived group of percepts. It is a "re-presentative element" in consciousness.

Dexter and Garlick discuss the processing of percepts prior to their becoming images and make the point that not all percepts develop into the imagery that constitutes the material of memory. The three stages of percept into image when it occurs are, (1) apprehension—the *fixing* in memory; (2) retention—the keeping in memory; and (3) reproduction—the bringing into memory. Passive memory in which there is little or no effort involved—remembering—is distinguished from active memory, which is recollection. The authors also allowed for subconscious memory. There is more Herbart than Freud here: they did not speak of an "unconscious."

Conditions of reproduction were described by Dexter and Garlick as dependent upon the force and frequency of stimulus repetition and the individual's degree of mental vigor at the time impressions are registered. The traditional laws of association explain memory, and the laws of similarity, contrast, and contiguity are duly active.[17]

[17] They also explain the process of apprehension.

The aims in the "culture of the memory" are twofold: (1) to acquire as much knowledge as possible; (2) to strengthen and develop the memory to make it an "efficient instrument" for the acquisition of more knowledge. This second aim is the more important of the two.

The proverb, "Knowledge is power," has been responsible for much bad teaching. Theories which will not reduce to practice are the general result. What or how much information is acquired is of less consequence than *how* that information is acquired. Mere knowledge is not power; it is the *ability* to use knowledge which is power. We are "too apt to *furnish* the memory; we forget to form it." (Dexter & Garlick, 1902, p. 132)

Thus the call of authors who disclaimed identity with the formal disciplinarians of old, but who embraced their doctrines, in this statement at least, with a fervor that our old friend Tarver would certainly have applauded.

There are various rules to be observed in memory formation. They do not strike the reader as exciting or innovative. Important facts should be carefully discriminated from unimportant ones in presenting material within memory lessons.

The teacher should go over any memory exercise with the child, he should draw his special attention to the leading points and show how the less important ones centre around it. In this way memory is economized. (Dexter & Garlick, 1902, pp. 132–133)

Facts should be classified and arranged in order to facilitate memory. And the teacher should always remember that memory work "takes time."

There is a distinction to be made between learning by rote and learning by heart. The latter requires that facts be remembered according to the sequence of ideas as well as of words. It is a process of verbal association; more precisely a case of association by "contiguity." In learning by rote, the sequence of words alone is taken into consideration; that of ideas is disregarded. Learning by heart, the authors stated, fell into disrepute because it became confused with learning by rote. Proper learning by heart, if it includes an "appeal to the intelligence" is of great educational value. Among the things that should be learned by heart are important dates in history, important data in geography, the spelling of irregular words, and foreign vocabularies. Also "beautiful passages in literature," various formulae in mathematics, and definitions. These things can be learned to advantage even if the child has not effectively developed his reasoning powers. "The fuller, deeper richer meaning will come later on" (Dexter & Garlick, 1902, p. 135).

If we deferred the teaching of things until they were thoroughly understood, many of the grandest truths would never be taught at all. We teach, and rightly teach, little children that "God is Love," yet how many children, nay more, how many *men* realize its full meaning? (Dexter & Garlick, 1902, p. 135)

Some things that should not be learned by heart are lists of exceptions to rules in grammar and the minutiae of geographical data.

The general rule to be adhered to in assisting children to learn by heart is to proceed from the concrete and material to the abstract and logical. Thus there should first be observation of particular cases, their classification, deduction of the rule or law governing the classification, and the memorizing of the rule or law; that is, when the child is mature enough to proceed thusly.

Dexter and Garlick discussed the growth and development of memory in "stage theory" fashion:

1. In infant life there is a rudimentary memory that by the age of three achieves some degree of mastery.
2. In early childhood, i.e., the fourth to ninth years, the memory is at work storing the impressions created by the senses. Because the mind is so easily impressed during this time, it has been designated the plastic period of memory. The memory processes are generally passive and operate according to the laws of contiguity. Toward the close of the period, the reasoning powers may be "cautiously stimulated" and a more active and orderly memory may be encouraged.
3. In later childhood, tenth to sixteenth years, the memory becomes active as the reasoning powers assert themselves more. There is a search for connections between things prior to committing them to memory. "The law of similarity asserts its superiority over that of contiguity and the foundations of a *Logical Memory* are laid" (Dexter & Garlick, 1902, pp. 137–138).

Imagination was divided by our two authors between reproductive and constructive imagination. It involves two processes: (1) *the isolating process,* which picks and chooses amongst the products of imagery and (2) *the combining process,* in which parts and whole of revived percepts are joined with the isolated percepts obtained by the first process.

Dexter and Garlick defended the value of imagination as did most of our faculty trainers. They recognized that uncontrolled imagination may have pernicious effects, but

It may at times be wise to moderate a child's fancy, it cannot but be unwise to endeavor to crush it. The person who tries to stifle a child's imagination may be strangling an embryo artist, or poet or inventor. (Dexter and Garlick, 1902, p. 145)

Fairy tales and other stories encourage imagination. History and geography also appeal to it, though care should be taken that the use of these subjects to encourage imagination should be based upon actual objects and physical experiences when the child is young and dependent upon sense impressions for his images. Contrary to the warnings of Halleck, the authors advised the use of literature in later years, since the novel may supply ". . . many persons with the only material upon which they exercise their imagination" (Dexter & Garlick, 1902, p. 146).

Dexter and Garlick finally arrived at the higher cognitive powers: conception, judgment, reasoning, and apperception. They nicely defined conception as ". . . a mental process which results in a concept" (Dexter & Garlick, 1902, p. 150). They elaborated on this definition: "Conception is the power to think individuals into classes"—the power "to think the many into the one" (Dexter & Garlick, 1902, p. 151).

The stages in conception are (1) observation, involving percepts or images; (2) comparison; (3) abstraction; (4) generalization. The mark of good concepts is that they are founded on concrete examples and a wide base of experience and are definite. The mark of poor concepts is their lack of distinctiveness, which results from indistinct percepts, faulty or inadequate observation, imperfect abstractions, looseness of language, imperfections in memory, etc.

We are told that, as concerns its growth and development, "Conception comes late and its true progress is slow" (Dexter & Garlick, 1902, p. 157); that it gradually matures with age, greatly abetted by the development of language (if there is a Froebelian, can a Pestalozzian be far behind?) and, in later childhood, that language turns from the part of a "servant" to conception to "enact the role of master"; that, at all times, "the basis of full and accurate conception is full and accurate perception" (Dexter & Garlick, 1902, p. 158); and that conception moves from the concrete to the abstract in later years.

The importance of conception cultivation was stressed by the authors on the basis of its general and specific roles within mental operations:

1. Its culture increases the strength and number of mental operations, since there are many important (though unidentified) mental faculties involved in any given act of conception.
2. Conception economizes "mental force," preventing the mind from being overburdened with too many particulars.
3. Conception makes judgment and reasoning possible; it also makes science possible, since science is based on generalities derived from particulars.

In training conception, we find Dexter and Garlick anything but innovative. They recommended object lessons and science with as much pupil "self-activity" as possible; and, in the later years, composition, since

Sentence-making is a great aid in training conception, provided the teacher see that clear concepts do actually lie behind the . . . words. . . . No word should be admitted to use unless some definite meaning is attached to it. (Dexter and Garlick, 1902, p. 160)

Dexter and Garlick's definition of judgment is twofold: to assert agreement or disagreement between two ideas, to discover the relationship between two ideas. It consists of two parts (1) comparison and (2) decision.

Judgment is founded on perception, memory, and conception. It also partakes of these and all other mental processes. For example, in perception we compare and contrast the things we are observing and come to a decision about them. Judgment can be easily separated into two classes. One is the intuitive, which involves judgments arrived at immediately. The other is the deliberative and involves judgments that are arrived at after more or less prolonged deliberation.

Judgment can also be classified in terms of being analytic, i.e., expressions of previously formed judgments, and synthetic, i.e., judgments used for the first time and the results of new experience. The latter adds to our knowledge, the former makes our knowledge clearer.

Developmentally approached, we find the young child exercising his judgment from the beginning of his life. "The essential of any mental operation is differentiation. But differentiation implies comparison and decision. Hence the earliest mental operations involve judgments" (Dexter & Garlick, 1902, p. 168).

Kindergarten provides ample training for judgment because of the opportunities it provides for comparison and decision. Language is a useful gauge to the development of judgment in the earlier years. In later years, it is the "outward and visible" sign of judgment and a valuable adjunct in its training.

Inadequate judgment is due to the lack of clear ideas, lack of time to examine ideas, accepting without "due examination" other people's words, and the biases induced by emotions.

The importance of training judgment is apparent to all.

As we have seen, judging enters into every department of our mental life, and in many mental operations it is a most important factor. No system of training can be complete which does not provide for the education of the judgment. (Dexter & Garlick, 1902, p. 167)

School subjects "especially serviceable" in the training of judgment include writing and drawing. In comparing his handwriting and drawing efforts to models, the child has to make comparisons and come to decisions. Manual training exercises, including paper folding, paper cutting, clay modeling, woodwork, etc., also develop judgment. Sentence making is a particularly valuable adjunct:

The child should be compelled to give his answers, not in disjointed words, but in complete sentences, and should be rigorously cross-examined with the idea of discovering whether the corresponding judgments do lie behind the sentences which he has made. (Dexter & Garlick, 1902, p. 168)

Parsing and analysis, if taught in relation to sentence making, are valuable training tools for judgment. Arithmetic, particularly when taught via "problems" is among "the finest school exercises for training the judging faculty" (Dexter & Garlick, 1902, p. 169). Games should not be overlooked, either. Since they require "a nice appreciation" of the effort (muscular) needed to obtain a particular result, they call upon the mind to practice comparisons and make decisions, hence judgment is exercised.

What are the pitfalls of judgment training? They are simple enough: overreliance upon memory, which is easier to "load" than is the training of judgment; the failure to provide precedence to percepts and concepts (the child being told the judgment by the teacher and then led to discover the percepts and concepts upon which the judgment is founded); and the blind acceptance of statements in textbooks.

Reasoning, the final of Dexter and Garlick's cognitive faculties, is defined as perceiving relations among judgments ". . . much in the same way as judging is perceiving relations among concepts" (Dexter & Garlick, 1902, p. 173). Inductive and deductive reasoning are to be differentiated. Their principles are to be used to guide education and instruction, just as education and instruction are to be used to develop them. Induction is the method of education, deduction that of instruction. Induction is slow, requiring that knowledge be acquired first hand by particular observations. Deduction is quicker, since the child uses knowledge acquired by others. Induction is a natural method, since the child proceeds in the "true" order (developmentally) from percepts to concepts, to judgments, and then to reasoning. Deduction is not a natural method, since in deduction judgments are put before concepts, concepts have priority over percepts, and theories have priorities over facts. Induction is a "sure method," arriving at general laws "little by little," achieving meanings that can be well grasped and applied to new cases. Deduction is not a sure method, since general laws may be too difficult for a child to grasp, resulting in "faulty application" of the laws to new cases. Induction is a method fostering self-reliance in children, leading them to depend on their own acts of perception, conception, and judgment. Deduction, on the other hand, encourages dependence on others.

The greatest values to be achieved in reason culture arise when both inductive and deductive (despite its flaws) reasoning[18] are exercised in what may be called the complete method. This should be followed whenever possible, because the authors say "True Education is a training

[18] There is yet another component of *reasoning: reasoning by analogy*. However, we shall not review its training here.

of the whole of a child's faculty" (Dexter & Garlick, 1902, p. 178), and the complete method appeals to the whole child. (Even then, educators were writing about educating the "whole" child.)

Apperception is the last of Dexter and Garlick's cognitive line, however, it is straight out of Herbart, with a few modern embellishments. Apperception is of interest to us from the standpoint of it's representing a process in the sense of process as an ongoing activity, rather than a reified organismic activity producer. Its discussion was carried out in nonfaculty terms by Dexter and Garlick; undoubtedly, because it was Herbart's process. Dexter and Garlick define apperception as follows:

. . . that form of mental activity under which percepts are brought into relation with our previous intellectual and emotional states and assimilated with them. (Dexter & Garlick, 1902, p. 184)[19]

Apperception is also defined as the "process" of mentally "taking in" things into the mind and giving them "position and meaning" and as the "bringing to bear" of past experiences in such a manner as to interpret or specially weight the new experience.

But does this talking of apperception as an activity rather than a faculty have any meaning outside of my cognitive nit-picking? Yes, for nowhere in their chapter on apperception do we find that Dexter and Garlick talk about training it. And since they do not engage themselves in training it, they devote their time and efforts to the application of apperception to teaching (one of their chapter's subsections). Apperception is used as a principle to guide teaching, not a thing to be cultivated, cultured, trained, remediated, etc. May we all take a lesson from their self-discipline in dealing with apperception. 'Tis a pity they did not manage themselves similarly while dealing with the other "faculties."[20]

HARRIS

William Torrey Harris was a towering figure among the school men of the post–Civil War era. He distinguished himself as the superintendant of the St. Louis public schools (1868–1880) and, later, as United States Commissioner of Education (1889–1906). He was also a major educational psychologist and theorist, and it is in this latter role that he interests us

[19] For other aspects of the pupil, such as his feelings, e.g., the egoistic feelings, the social feelings, the aesthetic sentiment, his will, habits, and character, as discussed by Dexter and Garlick, also have intellective aspects. Indeed, the authors even devoted a chapter to the *"Intellectual Sentiment,"* which is a ". . . special class of feelings which more or less accompany the pursuit of knowledge" (Dexter & Garlick, 1902, p. 251).

[20] Though, to be sure, they showed relative restraint compared to other authors.

here. This man, who ". . . ultimately rationalized the institution of the public school" (Cremins, 1961, p. 15), was also intensely fascinated with the abstruse writings of Hegel whose logic he struggled with for many years. We see some of the fruits of this struggle in his book *Psychologic Foundations of Education,* first published in 1898. The subtitle of this book, *An Attempt to Show the Genesis of the Higher Faculties of the Mind,* shows us where his concerns with faculties lie—or the "so-called faculties" as he often referred to them. It is well to keep Hegel and Froebel in mind as we attempt to understand Harris, whose efforts are of particular interest as a counteraction against the excessive perceptual emphasis of process training in his day. Others made similar protests, we know, but few as vehemently as he.

In his preface he quickly attempted to separate himself from traditional faculty psychology, which, he complained, was too narrow and simplistic in its purview.

> It has been assumed that education has to do with "cultivating the faculties." Perhaps the analogy of the body has been taken as valid for the soul, and, inasmuch as we can train this or that muscle, it is inferred that we can cultivate this or that faculty. The defect of this mode of view is that it leaves out of sight the genesis of the higher faculties from the lower ones. Muscles are not consecutive, the one growing out of another and taking its place, but they are co-ordinate and side by side in space, whereas in mind the higher faculties take the place of the lower faculties and in some sort absorb them. Conception, instead of existing side by side with perception, like the wheels of a clock, contains the latter in a more complete form of activity. Sense–perception, according to the definition, should apprehend individual things, and conception should take note of classes or species. But conception really transforms perception into a seeing of each object as a member of a class, so that the line between perception and conception has vanished, and we can not find in consciousness a mere perception of an individual object, but only that kind of perception which sees the object in its process of production. (Harris, 1892, p. vi)

Certainly, Froebel's plant here—but a more sophisticated version, emerging out of Harris's deep study of Hegel's theories, on the basis of which he conceived the mind's proper development to be an ever-moving thrust forward to achieve identification with and participation in the universal. On these grounds, Harris objected to excessive fractionation in respect to developing the mind. He regarded this as one of faculty psychology's severest faults.

> It is the source of a long train of . . . evils, for it arrests the investigation [of the mind] at the stage of isolated details, and makes impossible any insight into the genesis of the higher faculties of the mind. (Harris, 1898, pp. vi–vii)

Harris feared that education's conception of the mind as composed of independently operating, separate, and distinct faculties (though cooperating one with the others) and its excessive commitments to perceptualism would have negative consequences.

Education can not be wisely administered except from the high ground of the spirit of civilization. The child is to be brought most expeditiously into a correct understanding of his relation to the race and into a helpful activity within civilization. Unless the psychology of civilization is understood by a teacher, he will quite likely be harmed by learning a list of the so-called faculties. He will suppose, for example, that his business is to bring about a "harmony among these faculties," and develop them all symmetrically. Being ignorant of the way in which higher faculties re-inforce the lower, he will attempt to cultivate them isolatedly, and he will generally produce arrested development of the mind in the lower stages of its activities or faculties, and prevent the further intellectual growth of his pupils during their lives; for it happens that the fundamental categories of the different faculties or activities are radically opposed, and to harmonize them is to stultify the mind. . . . The highest faculty contains the solution of the contradictions of the lower ones. The solution of immature activities is to be found in growth out of immaturity. (Harris, 1898, pp. viii–ix)

The faculties are involved in a dialogue, it would appear that Harris was trying to tell his reader. The contradictions found in the operations of faculties at lower levels are resolved in syntheses within the operations of faculties at the higher levels.

The most important end of "intellectual education" Harris tells us is to take the pupil safely through the stages of sense–perception and other lower levels of the manifestation of the human spirit up to the summit of self-actualization through participation in the highest reaches of the spirit:

The highest thought of the understanding is that of negative unity wherein all individuality is swallowed up, as a sea swallows up its waves. (Harris, 1898, p. xxiii)

Harris's book is difficult to digest, just as are Hegel's writings. Hegelianism dictated Harris's psychology and his orientation toward process training. Fortunately, our experience in an earlier chapter with Froebel prepares us for some of Harris's *appercus*; unfortunately, not quite enough to allow an easy presentation of them.

Perhaps the easiest approach to Harris's theories lies in a quick perusal and accompanying comment concerning his chapter titles. Let us, then, proceed via his chapter titles.

The first chapter, the introduction, is intended ". . . to show the usefulness of psychology in education" (Harris, 1898, p. xl). The greatest assistance psychology gives the teacher is to provide him with a knowledge of the three stages of thought and the three different views of the world that arise out of them:

(a) All objects independent and real-sense–perception; (b) all things and events dependent on environment, all is relative (i.e., an understanding of objects through their relationships); (c) all dependent being presupposes an independent being, which is self-active; true being is self-active and exists as will and intellect—a personality. (Harris, 1898, p. xl)

The first part of Harris's book, following his preface and introduction, is entitled "The Psychologic Method"; it addresses the methods of rational psychology, methods which arrive at psychological truths that transcend empiricism and experimental investigation. These methods, Harris believed, are the only way we can arrive at an understanding of self-activity as the explanation of "life and mind."

The first chapter of this first part of Harris's book is entitled "What Is Meant by Educational Psychology" and deals with the internal, or mental, side of man, the psychology of how he feels, knows, and wills. Educational psychology must investigate the "inner reactions of man that accompany his manifold activities."

Educational psychology deals with all phases of action and reaction of the mind by itself or in the presence of objects, by which the mind develops or unfolds, or is arrested or degenerates. . . . Education is interested especially in methods of mental development, and in the ideals of perfection that can be attained. . . . The science of education has to draw from psychology . . . the theory of developing the mind. (Harris, 1898, p. 15)

The second chapter, entitled "What Is Introspection?", establishes "consciousness of the inward activity of the mind" as essential to understanding all observation, including that of "self activity . . . in the life of plants and animals" (Harris, 1890, p. xii). External observation can only perceive phenomena; internal observation can also perceive noumena. The latter is critical to the evolutionary development of the mind (and race).

In the view of evolution there is a goal toward which relatively lower orders are progressing, and the facts, forces, and laws are seen as parts of a great world-process which explains all. (Harris, 1898, p. 19)

Harris's third chapter is "What Is Self-Activity?", and it reveals a much broader concept than that which we discussed in conjunction with Froebel's process theories. It is a most difficult concept (as Harris agreed, along with its critics), one burdened with a great deal of philosophical baggage, which makes it a difficult concept, far more difficult than the following quote and my simplified narrative suggest.

Mental pictures of self-activity impossible . . . motion, change and energy unpicturable [but since]. . . . Assimilation,[21] sensation, volition, thought are forms of self-activity and its denial makes both physiology and psychology impossible. (Harris, 1898, p. xii)

[21] Plants have assimilation. Higher organisms have the other attributes of self-activity.

Harris's insistence upon the "activity of the mind," it should be observed, prevents his text from emerging as a traditional faculty psychology tome. For much of the way throughout, the author managed to keep a perspective upon processes as processes, i.e., activities of the organism as opposed to reified cognitive organs, though he did not consistently avoid the pitfalls of reification.

The fourth chapter in Harris's text, "The Three Stages of Thought," takes up in greater detail that which he regarded as "the most important discovery ever made in psychology" (Harris, 1898, p. 32). It is out of Plato. The lowest stage of thought is that of sense–perception,[22] which results in objects being conceived as being "all independent," one from another. Each is "self-existent" and a "solid reality" by itself. While things (objects) may be seen in relation, relations appear to be arbitrary or contrived—and unessential at this stage.

The intermediate stage of thought nearest allied to sense–perception is understanding. It is the result of "A little development of the thought of power . . ." which ". . . produces . . . the consciousness that some relations, at least, are the essential elements of our experience" (Harris, 1898, p. 37). The mind at this stage is able to deal with the "category of relativity" and recognizes that: "Each thing is relative to every other, and there is reciprocal or mutual dependence" (Harris, 1898, p. 33).

The third stage in the ascending steps of thought development that Harris laid out for us is relativity, an ambiguous concept as the author presented it.

Relativity presupposes self-relation. Self-relation is the category of the *reason,* just as relativity is the category of the *understanding,* or non-relativity (atomism) the category of *sense–perception.* . . . Reflection discovers relativity or dependence. (Harris, 1898, p. 35)

. It is the highest level of thinking, though not directly identified as a faculty but rather as a level at which the reasoning faculty functions at its highest. As a consequence of cognitive operations at this level, the interrelatedness of things and events are discovered through reflection.

Reflection discovers relativity or dependence, and hence unites beings into systems. Deepest reflection discovers total systems and the self-determining principles which originate systems of dependent being. The reason looks for complete, independent, or total beings. (Harris, 1898, p. 35)

Chapter V of Harris's *Psychologic Foundations of Education* is entitled "A Concept Not a Mental Picture." It does not take up the issue of imageless thought, however, being, rather, an attempt to establish concepts as examples of ideational universals, in the mode of the Platonic

---

[22] Which Plato detested, seeing it as the major source of error in thinking.

thinking so congenial to Harris. A concept is essentially a definition, of which percepts and images are particular examples. Contrary to the empiricism of Hume and the image-symbolism of Spencer, it is concepts, rather than percepts, that are the building blocks of the mind.

To us the images are far less true than our concepts. The images stand for fleeing or evanescent forms, while the concepts state the eternal and abiding laws, the causal energies that constitute the essence of all phenomena." (Harris, 1898, p. 41)

Harris's Chapter VI, "Time, Space and Causality—Three Ideas That Make Experience Possible," is a primer and an imprimateur dedicated to Immanuel Kant. Kant's doctrine of the structure of the mind, no less than Guilford's SOT explains how we mentate. To Harris, the Kantian a priori's made experience possible.[23]

Chapters VII and VIII show Harris's deep commitment to philosophy as the basis for both psychology and education. Their titles are "Causality and the Absolute," and "The Psychological Meaning of the Infinite and the Absolute."

The true ideas of infinitude and first cause lie at the basis of educational psychology, because they make possible the higher orders of knowing; without them the ideas of education (God, freedom and immortality) are not possible. (Harris, 1898, p. xiv)

With Chapters IX and X, we reach the boundaries of traditional faculty psychology (in the late nineteenth century). They deal with sense–perception. Harris's approach was, however, hardly of whole cloth with that of his colleagues. The titles of these two chapters make this clear: Chapter IX—"The Logic of Sense-Perception. What Figure of the Syllogism Apperception Uses"; Chapter X—"How Sense–Perception Uses the First Figure of the Syllogism to Re-inforce Its First Act Which Takes Place in the Second Figure." How his poor readers must have strained in those days, those underpaid, underprivileged graduates of normal schools who, in addition to attempting to rule the unruly, had to struggle with Hegelian dialectics in their accreditation courses. A sparkling cynosure his book may have appeared to Harris; to the teachers reading it—hardly! Even perception, which had been made conceptually easy by most other trainers, was now to be approached, the Harris way, via the hard high road of logic. But Harris would have it no other way. How else could even the simplest of processes be understood, unless in terms of Platonic universals, Kantian imperatives, Hegelian dialectic? And beyond such, Harris was

---

[23] The commercialization possibilities that open up for training programs based upon Kantian imperatives are enormous—*Dingansich* process training, to accompany a prepackaged set of Froebelian gifts.

attempting to make another major point in his approach to perception, one that is not unfamiliar to us at this stage of our book, i.e., that even at the simplest levels of cognition or the most primitive interactions with the environment, the highest cognitive powers still express themselves.

The exposition of the structure of the mind, of its forms used in sense–perception or reasoning, belongs to psychology. Hence formal logic is a part of psychology, and a very important one.[24] A consideration of its significance will throw light on the structure of sense–perception. Sense–perception is not a simple act that can be no further analyzed. In its most elementary forms one may readily find the entire structure of reason. The difference between the higher and lower forms of intelligence consists not in the presence or absence of phases of thought, but in the degree of completeness of the consciousness of them—the whole is present, but is not consciously perceived to be present, in the lower forms. The whole structure of reason functions not only in every act of mind, no matter how low in the scale—even in the animal intelligence—nay, more, in the life of the plant which has not yet reached the plane of intellect—yes, even in the movement of inorganic matter: in the laws of celestial gravitation there is manifested the structural framework of reason. (Harris, 1898, pp. 62–63)

And since the structure of reason is revealed in logic, logic is a part of psychology; it is "rational psychology." And since reason is present in perception, there is logic expressed in perception. An act of perception is a series of "acts of predication or judgment." And one can approach perception through syllogisms, which Harris did.

The point of all this is that Harris regarded the training of perception as more than a simple matter of providing the senses with sufficient information to absorb or of perceptual exercises. It is to be a matter of verifying one's observations, by setting up in the mind ". . . myriad anticipations of experience which test and cross-question observation at every turn." (Harris, 1898, p. 75). Formal logic may be useful in these respects—". . . as a science of the spiritual structure of cognition—a science of the forms of perception—it is not contemptible" (Harris, 1898, p. 75).

In the two chapters discussed above, which are expressly dedicated to sense–perception, we do not read of training perception. Harris's interest in the utilization of formal logic by the cognitive processes, however, led him to discuss, in his Chapter XI, the derivation of general concepts out of perception via the mind's logical operations. Its title: "How General Concepts Arise. How Sense–Perception Uses the Third Figure of the Syllogism to Store Up Its Experience in General Terms." The title of this chapter also indicates that out of syllogism comes memory, or at least mnemonics.

---

[24] Since the mind functions according to a priori principles.

Chapters XII though XIV deal with physiological psychology, the body–mind relationship, the brain centers of "sensation and motion," and the localization of functions of the brain. However wondrous all of this might be, said Harris, it is more a matter of interesting correspondences between bodily function on one hand and mental or spiritual operations on the other. Thus in concluding his survey of recent research into brain localization he stated:

> . . . a word must be added as to its results. When interpreted by introspective psychology and compared with its results, we do not find any new grounds for distrusting the spiritual theory of the soul, nor do we see in these researches much that throws any light on the real nature of the mind itself . . . while the body is organic, the soul is not organic, but a higher form of being—namely, a pure self-activity . . . (Harris, 1898, pp. 112-114)

Harris's lack of interest in the physiological substrata of cognitive processes is further manifest in his Chapter XV, "The Will," in which he made the point that while physiological pathology explains disorders in this basic faculty, physiology does not explain its operations which ". . . relate to universal conditions of being and thereby transcend all organs" (Harris, 1898, p. xvii).

Harris's general epistemology, rather than his theories on process, was expressed in Chapters XVI and XVII which are entitled, respectively, "The Fallacy of the Doctrine That the Strongest Motive Governs the Will, and Therefore the Will is Not Free," and "Freedom versus Fate." These chapters interest us tangentially, in that they reveal Harris's philosophical obsessions as having been so strong as to overwhelm his perceptions of teachers' instructional needs, although remember, he was a practicing educator for quite a while, and a most successful one in developing the modern public school system. Perhaps the explanation lies in the fact that this book, *Psychologic Foundations of Education,* was a product of his later years, when one is more inclined to meander amidst the metaphysical. This impression is enforced by the final chapter in the first part of this treatise, "Old and New Psychologies Compared as to Their Provinces and Their Results for Education," a chapter that defends rational psychologies, the study of the structure of the mind, and the nature of its operations through introspection and speculation.

The second part of Harris's book, which is entitled *Psychologic System* (the first part being *Psychologic Method*), is, in a general sense, a recapitulation of his theories and their expansion into practice. We now move more directly into the traditional domains of faculty psychology in this rather unorthodox book. His chapter "Method and System in Psychology" (XIX) discusses his favorite themes, e.g., self-activity, the infinite, the absolute, figures of the syllogism, as applied to "produce a system." The two following chapters, XX, "The Individuality of Inorganic and Organic Beings,'' and XXI, ''Psychologic Functions of Plants and Animals,'' are delays in his march into faculty territory while he attempted to make distinctions between the structure and animal, vegetable, and mineral. But at last with Chapter XXII, ''Feeling and Emotions,'' he properly entered process land. In keeping with the principle of unity in diversity, Harris refused to allow feelings (emotions being a synonym) to be divigated from the other broad Kantian faculties. Feeling is a type of intellect and will in an ''unconscious form.'' Within intellectual ''unconscious form,'' there are the feelings that are passive—sensation, emotions, and affections. On the side of will, there are instincts, appetites, and desires.

On the one side the feelings look towards the intellect, and tend to become conscious and pass over into cognitions, motives and reflections. On the other side, the feelings tend to rise into conscious volition, and become deliberate and responsible. (Harris, 1898, p. 162)

Continuing to proceed in the vein sketched above, Harris also refused to disassociate affective education from that of other aspects of the individual's education. ''How to educate the feelings,'' he asked. It cannot be done directly, because feelings are ''immediate'' and do not remain about long enough to be trained. Good feelings, however, can be strengthened and evil ones repressed by ''correct intellectual views'' and by adopting ''proper motives,'' while instinctive actions ''according to bad motives'' can be inhibited by the will and ''correct habitual action'' substituted for them through proper actions of the will.

Harris's negative attitude toward sense training is exemplified by the cursory treatment he gave ''The Five Senses'' (Chapter XXIII), with under five pages being dedicated to their discussion. While there is self-activity expressed in sensory activities, the latter are of the lowest rank cognitively and, therefore, not of much interest to Harris. His favorite senses were hearing and the ''sense of sight,'' and this on the basis of metaphysical qualities. Thus the lowest sense and the next low sense, are, respectively, taste and hearing. This because they perceive objects in the process of ''dissolution.'' Hearing, however, is a ''. . . manifestation of resistance to dissolution. The cohesion of the body is attacked and resists . . . '' (Harris, 1898, p. 168).[25] It is thus a higher ''far more ideal'' sense. The sense of sight is ''the most ideal.'' Whereas taste and smell perceive an object in a state of dissolution, prior to attack, and hearing engages in active resistance to the object's attack, sight maintains its independence.

Sight is therefore the most ideal sense, inasmuch as it is farthest from the real process of assimilation, in which one energy destroys the product of another energy and extends its sway over it. It is the altruistic sense, because it perceives

---

[25] This resistance setting up vibrations which are perceived by the sense of hearing.

the existence-for-itself of the object, and not merely its existence-for-others or its existence-for-me. (Harris, 1898, p. 169)

Touch was not discussed in terms of the fine terms Harris deployed above; however, he was most impressed with it as a substitute for other senses, since he believed that it contained all higher senses ''in potentiality.'' Thus if the higher senses do not develop or were damaged or destroyed, touch can substitute. It can respond to the ''vibrations of sound and light.'' Nor is it to be disregarded as a supernumerary in respect to taste and smell, since it may detect the ''slighter modifications'' resulting from stimulation in these realms.

Harris was not prone to recommend perceptual training in copious amounts. Harris, in fact, did not recommend any perceptual cultivation at all in the book we are reviewing. His negative attitude toward it was based on the belief that excessive training of the lower faculties inhibited the development of the higher ones. We have touched on this before; we shall examine his position hereon in greater detail later.

If disdainful of the senses and their training, Harris was far more respectful of that favorite faculty of the ancients, memory, whose training had been considerably discredited by the sense–realists. With Chapter XXIV of the *Psychologic Foundations of Education,* ''Recollection and Memory,'' we find a great deal of thought and deliberation given to the processes involved in recall, and to their training as well. As suggested by the title of this chapter, the author distinguished between recollection and memory. While dismissing perception as ''mere sensation'' that acts only in the presence of objects, both recognition and memory proper were accorded membership by Harris among the higher cognitive processes.

. . . the faculty of recollection is a higher form of self-activity (or reaction against surrounding conditions), because it can recall, at its own pleasure, the ideal object. Here is the beginning of emancipation from the limitations of time. (Harris, 1898, pp. 170–171)

If recollection escaped the grime of lower process status, memory proper was accorded still higher cognitive status.[26]

We may distinguish memory from mere recollection by letting it denote systematized recollection—recollection organized into wholes of experience— relative wholes which are called *events.* Memory may thus be regarded as the grouping faculty by whose aid sense–perception becomes a perceiver of species as well as individuals. . . . It contains the stores of experience by which the present

[26] Though recollection (or representation) can become memory if it is used by the soul not only to recall objects and events but also to ''. . . compare the present with the past and identify or distinguish between the two'' (Harris, 1898, p. 171)—in short, utilizing reasoning in its operations.

object is explained and interpreted. . . . It . . . uses general or class ideas. It has already become conscious in its act of recollection that it can call up at will the past perceptions. Human sense–perception is nearly always not simple sense–perception, but complex, being united to memory in such a way that objects perceived are identified . . . or apperceived as specimens of classes.[27] This makes possible language; for language can not be used unless the special object of the senses can be expressed in general terms already become familiar in remembered experience. (Harris, 1898, p. 172)

The activity through which the mind "ascends" from sense–perception to memory is the "activity of introspection," actually an "unconscious act of attention. Attention itself was defined as a habit which is ". . . to be the first step in intellectual activity," not just attention that means focusing upon an object, as a cat might on a mouse, but ". . . attention which arrives at the results of abstraction . . . the distinguishing characteristic of educative beings . . ." (Harris, 1898, p. 174).

While Harris was not interested in training sense–perception as sense–perception, he was decidedly intent upon seeing that memory be properly cultivated. This was a necessity, since memory contributed to the development of the "power of rational thinking." But memory training, he cautioned, had to be selective and that which contributed to mere recall without meaning, e.g., by merely improving one's ability to "associate" ideas, was to be condemned. On the other hand:

Necessary connection enables the mind to make deductions, and thus it acquires a sort of generative memory, so to speak, a memory which can deduce or develop from given data the other data that stand in relation to it . . . an . . . important question to determine is the proper amount of memory culture. The Chinese education fills the memory with the maxims of Confucius and Mencius, and the individual follows these because there is so little else in his mind: their lines are graven so deep that nothing else seems important. The antidote for this baleful effect of memory is to be sought in a method of training that associates effects with causes, and individuals with species; that associates one idea with another through its essential relations, and not by its accidental properties. One must put thought into the act of memory. (Harris, 1898, pp. 176–182)

As to techniques of training for the memory, Harris reverted very much to the position of classic formal disciplinarians. His reversion was undoubtedly due to his distrust of sense–perception. Language being the medium of higher processes, it was the major route of memory training that he recommended his readers take.

---

[27] We will remember that Harris conceived the higher powers as being present and operative at all stages of life and as being expressed in lower powers.

The memory of days, names, or words in general can and should be cultivated without attempting association of any kind but sequence.[28] The committing to memory of fine passages from poets and literary prose writers certainly cultivates a memory for words without detriment to thought. A memorized list of proper names, names of persons of historic note or characters in great literary works of art . . . serve the double purpose of being . . . useful and a means of arousing into activity the faculty of remembering proper names. . . . Also the memorizing of paradigms in the study of language has the effect to cultivate this memory of words and isolated items . . . committing to memory new masterpieces of poetry and prose, or . . . the words of a new language . . . is profit . . . to the thinking powers as well as to the memory. . . . (Harris, 1898, p. 177)

Harris's sympathy for formal discipline of the classic variety is further demonstrated in his defense of the *memoriter* techniques, which proponents of modern education were constantly attacking.

Certainly they are right in opposing the extremes of the old pedagogy which obliged the pupils to memorize page after page of the contents of a grammar "verbatim et literatim et punctuatim. . . ." But is there not a middle ground? Is there not a minimum of details of dates and names which must and should be memorized. . . . The simile of a magnet is to the point here. Load it today with iron filings, and tomorrow it will support a few more. The memory, if only strong enough to retain a single item with effort, will grow stronger by the effort, and will soon retain two items, and finally others in vast numbers and without effort. (Harris, 1898, pp. 178–182)

Despite being disdainful of attempts to reduce the mind to physiology, Harris was convinced of a basic tenet held by phrenology. Training the mind would improve the brain.

If the discovery of Broca, generally recognized as the beginning of physiological psychology on the new basis, is to be understood in the sense that a certain convolution near the base of the brain is used by the mind in recalling words and associating them with ideas, it would seem that a cultivation of the memory of words should be undertaken in later life by all people who have an incipient tendency to aphasia. If a person finds himself forgetful of names, it is a health-giving process to take a certain portion of time in committing to memory words. . . . Doubtless the cultivation of verbal memory, building up as it does a certain convolution in the brain, has a tendency to prevent atrophy in that organ. . . . The tendency is to neglect childish faculties and allow them to become torpid. But if this is liable to weaken certain portions of the brain in such a way as to induce hemorrhage, ending in softening of the brain, certainly the memory should be cultivated if only for the health of the brain. . . . This is a question for the educational pathologist. (Harris, 1898, pp. 177,178)

---

[28] By this, Harris intended that the memory be directed toward meaning, rather than to rote commitments, though his methods have much of the rote about them.

As to improving specific memory weaknesses, Harris proposed specificity in training. "The true method of cultivating and strengthening a defective memory is to practice it on the kinds of items that it easily forgets." (Harris, 1898, p. 183).

Thus if you have trouble remembering dates, you practice by remembering dates, adding more and more to your list as your mind becomes accustomed to the practice and strengthened in the process of remembering.

A list with fifty items thus memorized will suffice to develop a habit of attention to such items and a power of recalling them which will grow steadily with such exercise as circumstances bring occasion for . . . and correct the weak faculty. . . . A list of a hundred proper names learned in their order, as kings of France and England and the emperors of Rome . . . or, indeed, a list half as large, will so discipline the memory for names as to permanently remove all embarrassment from this source. (Harris, 1898, p. 184)

Some faculty psychologists (Halleck certainly among them) believed that strengthening the body strengthened the mind. Not at all, said Harris:

. . . we are not able to cure an ordinary case of ailing memory except by pure psychological means—namely, by attention, mental association, and repetition—doubtlessly affecting the brain thereby, but through free acts of the will. We can affect the brain through the effort of the will on the memory, but we can not as yet develop the memory through body-culture. (Harris, 1898, p. 185)[29]

Despite his concern about memory (and there is a great deal of additional theory and opinion in his book on the topic), Harris also emphasized that as the mind developed in its higher stages, the memory (and other lower faculties) was less and less to be cultivated, except in terms of improving brain health.

Memory is . . . not a faculty of the soul which is to be desired on all accounts and cultivated always with assiduity. With the growth of culture of the higher powers it will occupy less and less place compared with the whole mind. (Harris, 1898, p. 188)

Chapter XXV, "From Perception to Conception: Each Object Seen in Its Class," is a gateway chapter, discussing the development of conception and the role that the processes of perception, recollection, memory and imagination play in providing the mind with materials for the higher mental processes to operate upon, those higher processes that allow the mind to seek universals and lead to abstract "freedom." Chapter XXVI "Language as the Distinguishing Characteristic of the Human Being,"

[29] For those interested in medical views on memory training, I recommend the reading of famed early-American psychiatrist Benjamin Rush.

proceeds in the same direction. For language "fixes" our knowledge of things in terms of universals:

> No being can use language, much less create language, unless it has learned to see all objects as individuals belonging to classes, and incidentally recognized its own individuality. (Harris, 1898, p. 199)[30]

Language is the sign which denotes arrival at a stage of mental development on the way to full realization of the soul, i.e., "complete self-activity." It is an indication that mental processes have proceeded beyond concrete perceptual stages and that there is "recognition of classes," of species and genera—". . . the universal processes underlying the existence of the particular."

In Chapters XXVII and XXVIII, Harris takes us at last into the rarified realms of the "high" cognitive processes. The first of these chapters is "Thinking as the Activity of the Understanding, including 'Common Sense' and Reflection," and the second is bluntly entitled "The Reason." Much of Harris's writing in these two chapters constitutes a discourse on metaphysics rather than psychology or education, though he obviously believed that without such a metaphysical background as the one he presents, teachers could neither understand higher mental processes nor utilize them in education.[31]

The lower levels of the highest of the high cognitive processes (remember that memory, conception, and language also claim membership in the advanced ranks of Harris's hierarchy of mental faculties) are occupied by the two faculties of understanding (activities, phases, and stages are also used to describe them). The first of these is common sense, a "naive and dogmatical" phase of understanding that deals with the phenomenal world. The common sense (here used in the ancient Greek frame of reference) is an inner sense that takes sense data and their products and organizes them for the still higher faculties of the mind to act upon. It ". . . looks upon the sense-world as composed of real, independent things" (Harris, 1898, p. 214). It deals with objects as isolated entities possessing meaning and importance in and of themselves. The second of the stages (or faculties) composing understanding is that of reflection, which is "enlightened and skeptical." It seeks relationships and makes sense out of the products of sense information in terms of their

---

[30] Harris, very much in a modern vein, our modern vein, allowed gesture as part of language, and to participate in abstract thinking.

> Even deaf and dumb human beings invent and use gestures as words, each gesture denoting a class with a possible infinite number of special applications. (Harris, 1898, p. 198)

[31] I am only able to present a gross oversimplification of Harris's writings on these matters.

relativity, i.e., relationships. It seeks the noumena behind the phenomena and interprets the second in terms of the first. It is engaged with a "deeper and more conscious" knowing—a grasp of abstractions rather than of particulars, a reaching toward the ideal universals that constitute true thought.

> This stage of reflection, with its doctrine of abstract ideals, or of negative powers or forces, finally becomes convinced of the essential unity of all processes and all forces. (Harris, 1898, p. 211)

Understanding, however, in both of its phases of operation, common sense and reflection, still deals with the concrete and "finite." Thus, like all cognitive operations based on sense information, it is prone to error and faulty conclusions:

> In the first stage (common-sense) it mistakes the phenomenal for the noumenal, taking perishable things for imperishable; the second stage (reflection) mistaking the noumenal for the phenomenal, and taking even the absolute for the relative. (Harris, 1898, p. 214)

Thus the mind, through its operations of understanding, can only arrive at "fragmentary realizations" of the truth that lies behind things—the truth that can only be grasped at, or properly sought, by that highest faculty of all, reason. Whereas understanding is the highest level of operations on concrete levels of thinking, reason is the final standpoint" of the intellect. It deals with the abstract and the absolute. It leads to an understanding of a "Personal Creator, who makes it the theatre of the development of conscious beings in his image" (Harris, 1898, p. 227). It is the stage of true insight and ". . . the only form which is consistent with a true theory of education and leads into participation in the synthesis, resolving the contradictions of individuality, that is *race*."

> Each individual should ascend by education into participation—*conscious* participation—in the life of the species. Institutions—family, society, state, Church—all are instrumentalities by which the humble individual may avail himself of the help of the race, and live over in himself its life. The highest stage of thinking is the stage of insight. It sees the world as explained by the principle of Absolute Person. It finds the world of institutions a world in harmony with such a principle. (Harris, 1898, p. 227)

In Chapter XXIX of *Psychologic Foundations of Education*, "A Review of the Psychology of the Intellect," Harris presented the growth of the mind, the development of its processes, as a "progressive realization" or unfolding of a principle inherent in the theories he (and Froebel before him) had inherited from Hegel, but also Fichte, Kant, etc., in which man pursues his ". . . ideal of culture which it is his destiny or vocation to achieve" (Harris, 1898, p. 235).

In Chapter XXX, Harris made it clear that it is not mere knowing as self-knowing, that enables man to achieve such an ideal but rather that it is a knowing ". . . beyond the world or in its innermost," that is responsible.[32] And in this chapter, "The Will and the Intellect," he asserted that it is necessary that the will combine with the intellect to "produce the highest orders of knowing." The will is first unified with the intellect when it focuses perception in such a way that order is created out of the "chaos of sense–impressions," through the exercise of attention. It also unites with the intellect, in fact is necessary to its operations for such purposes, to produce ". . . analysis, synthesis, reflection, and insight" (Harris, 1898, p. 244). The highest realm of thinking, "theistic knowing," is achieved when:

> . . . the self as will perceives will, or a self, as the fundamental being and final explanation of things. It is only this kind of knowing (which may be called theistic knowing) that can recognise truly what is involved in freedom and responsibility. (Harris, 1898, p. 247)

The third part of Harris's book, called "Psychologic Foundations," is an effort to apply his principles of psychology to actual instruction, an attempt to deal with "the mental coefficient" in education. It is not a treatise on process training.[33] Rather, it was expected of Harris's readers that they would be able to understand the matters he wrote about because they understood and accepted his process theories. His psychological constructs were applied broadly and boldly, via a grand educational *weltanschauung,* as can be seen from Chapters XXXI–XXXIX: "The Psychology of Social Science; The Institutions That Educate. The Psychology of Nations; Reactions Against the Social Order—Crime and Play; The Psychology of Infancy; Psychology of the Course of Study in Schools—Elementary, Secondary, and Higher; The Psychology of Quantity; The Psychology of Art and Literature; and the Psychology of Science and Philosophy."

While I have said that Harris was not concerned with process training in any of these chapters save one, he was most certainly concerned with cognitive processes from the standpoint of emphasizing the importance of assuring the regnancy of reason in cognitive functioning and its unimpedance by excessive operations of other, lower, faculties. This was to be accomplished through a form of negative education.

The idea of negative education had been popularized by Rousseau. But his intention, and that of those who emulated him, was to encourage

---

[32] If the reader detects the firm foundations of racism being established in much of the above, he is, of course, absolutely correct. Nazism, for one, clearly had its roots in such thinking.

[33] Except for the chapter on infancy, which takes its leads from Froebel, even if not fully agreeing with all of his precepts.

the growth of processes through a posture of noninterference on the part of the instructor. Harris's version had other objectives in mind. He was concerned lest the effective operations of the highest of cognitive processes, reason, be hampered or delayed by developing lower ones.[34] Reason, which represents the highest level of man's existence, and anything that would contribute to its culture, was beyond reproach to Harris. But other processes—and their cultivation—were not. Let us examine some of Harris's criticisms. He was anything but ambiguous in his expression of them. We read, in the statement following, his belief that the schools of his day were neglectful of the higher cognitive processes because of their overattention to the lower ones.

It is believed that the arrested development of the higher mental and moral faculties is caused in many cases by the school. The habit of teaching with too much thoroughness and too-long continued drill, the semi-mechanical branches of study, such as arithmetic, spelling, the discrimination of colours, the observation of surface and solid forms, and even the distinctions of formal grammar, often leaves the pupil fixed in lower stages of growth and unable to exercise the higher functions of thought. . . . It is necessary to ascertain the effect of every sort of training or method of instruction upon the further growth of the child. For instance, do methods of teaching arithmetic by the use of blocks, objects, and other illustrative materials advance the child or retard him in his ability to master the higher branches of mathematics? . . . Does a careful training in discriminating fine shades of colour and in naming them, continued for twenty weeks to a half a year in the primary school, permanently set the mind of the pupil towards the mischievous habit of observing tints of colour to such an extent as to make the mind oblivious of differences in form or shape, and especially inattentive to relations which arise from the interaction of one object upon another? (Harris, 1898, p. 7)[35]

Elsewhere, Harris stated:

We must be able to recognize what activity tends to fix the soul in a lower order of thought and action, and what exercise will tend to lift it to a higher order. (Harris, 1898, p. 140)

[34] I have written of this concern earlier in our review of Harris's work.
[35] Harris was writing at a time when scientific education was at a fever pitch in the United States. Thus he remarked that questions such as the above, and cases of "arrested development" in terms of cognitive growth, be determined by "careful experimental study." He hoped that the laboratories being established by psychology would assist in this study. However, understanding of "rational psychology," his brand of Hegelianism, would be necessary to augment the schools' techniques of "child study." Otherwise teachers might be ill equipped to

> . . . undertake the careful and delicate observations which explain why certain children stop growing at various points in different studies and require patient and persistent effort on the part of the teacher to help them overcome their mental difficulties. . . (Harris, 1898, p. 8)

Dangers of fixing the soul in lower process functions, to the detriment of higher ones, were ever present.

> A severe drill in mechanical habits of memorizing or calculating, any over-cultivation of sense-perception in tender years, may so arrest the development of the soul in a mechanical method of thinking as to prevent further growth into spiritual insight.[36] Especially on the second plane of thought which follows that of sense–perception and the mechanical relations and of classifying by mere likeness or difference, or even the search for causal relations, there is much danger of this arrested development . . . absorption of the gaze upon adjustments within the machine prevents us from seeing the machine as a whole. The attention to details of colouring and drawing may prevent one from seeing the significance of the great work of art. . . . The question is, then, where to stop and change to other and higher branches in time to preserve the full momentum of progress that the child has made. (Harris, 1898, pp. 142,143)

Memory, for Harris, above all other faculties, was the one he recommended training, but even memory is to be cautiously approached in its culture, the author warned, lest it fix the mind in "habit."

> "Memory is indispensable in all intellectual processes, and therefore must be trained and developed." Yes, but it is liable to prove destructive to the other faculties (so called) and supplant them; hence it must be restrained within its proper limits, and made auxilliary to the other faculties, and not allowed to assume the chief role. It is a matter of everyday comment that much memorization deadens the power of thought, verbal or statistical memory being "mechanical." But it is also true that memory may train the powers of sense–perception, imagination, and will. (Harris, 1898, pp. 180,181)

Harris, however, was most concerned with the overtraining in sense–perception that had resulted in American education, largely as a result of the Pestalozzian movement. He believed that the Pestalozzians overlooked the pernicious effects created by excessive cultivation of lower powers. They also overlooked the fact that the higher cognitive powers, if they are properly developed will incorporate the functions of the lower ones, a matter of thesis, antithesis, and synthesis. The higher powers first assume a negative position (antithetical as they are to the thesis of the lower powers), but then synthesize the important aspects of the lower powers within themselves.

> The Pestalozzians who speak so often of the importance of cultivating sense–perception in the school do not seem to have ever considered the relation of

---

[36] One of the examples of this arrested development was expressed vis-á-vis *sloyd* according to Harris. The educational effects of manual training (as process training) are destroyed by having pupils prepare in technical skills that have marketable values. "It turns the attention towards the training in skill, and the educational effect which comes of first insight is afterwards neglected" (Harris, 1898, p. 143)

perception to memory, for they make no mention of this radical difference of activity, nor do they proceed to show how the higher faculty may be made to assist the lower. A similar mistake is made by those writers on psychology who do not discriminate the higher from the lower faculties, but treat them all alike. They hold that the higher are built up out of the lower, as though perceptions would grow into thoughts when they become sufficiently numerous.[37] They have no insight into the primary fact of psychology, namely, that every higher faculty is an activity which is negative to the lower activities, although it preserves in a transfigured shape what was valid in the lower. (Harris, 1898, p. 180)

We have finished with T. H. Harris, an unusual man, feet rooted in public education, mind grappling with the metaphysical questions of man's place on earth, purpose in life, participation in the universal scheme of things. A reading, or re-reading of his writings is truly an exercise of one's highest faculties, as well as an introduction to German philosophy as expressed within American educational thought. While Harris was a most important figure within American education, it is questionable as to how much effect his particular "psychology" had upon actual classroom practice. Froebel's transmutations of German philosophy, in its end products, were essentially usable by the practicing educator. Harris's brand of process psychology appears to have been too abstruse to have had any extensive effects in an age and country when and where "doing" was becoming ever more important than "knowing." The next theorist of the process movement we will consider (and the last of our major considerations in this chapter) was much more influential in terms of classroom adoptions and adaptations.

WHITE

Emerson E. White's book, *The Art of Teaching,* represents a culmination of formal disciplinarian and faculty doctrines, expressed within a framework of practical classroom applications. Certainly, a most influential work, read, and presumably observed by many teachers, a book that is a testimony to the vigor of the cognitive training movement at the beginning of the twentieth century.

White admitted to the excesses of the so-called dogma of formal discipline, ". . . which in its extreme form . . . is largely a product of imagination. It certainly has a small acceptance as a theory of mental discipline" (White, 1901, p. 40). He forsook, as well, any listing (with appropriate training activities) of the various faculties, which he redubbed

---

[37] Reference is being made here obviously to the sense–realist and, particularly, the empiricist-sensationalist-associationistic doctrines of Locke, Hume. Hartley, Condillac, etc.

powers, tendencies, habits, and skills—with a preference for power.[38] Nevertheless, facultist he was, disciplinarian he was.

> Every normal act of the mind leaves as an enduring result an increased power to act and a tendency to act again in like manner. Power and tendency are the resultants of all mental action. The power and tendency of the mind to observe are increased by observing; to imagine by imagining; to judge by judging, to reason by reasoning. . . . (White, 1901, p. 39)

As to whether process or product should receive prime attention by educators, White was clearly on the side of the angels.

> . . . there are . . . practical reasons for the making of the training of power the leading aim in teaching knowledge. Mental power is not only more abiding than knowledge, but is of greater practical utility. While knowledge is a necessary guide in human effort, mental power, gives acumen, grasp, strength, inspiration, and these are the winners of success in all the activities and conflicts of life. Even so-called practical knowledge, to be of real utility for guidance, must be thought out and applied by an intelligent mind. The superficial empiricist is liable to blunder in every new application of his knowledge . . . if my mind were a tablet and with a sponge I should erase every fact learned in school and college, and not applied at the time in some art, I should not be intellectually very poor, but were I to lose the mental power gained in the mastery of these facts, so many of which were long since happily forgotten, I should be poor indeed. The abiding practical result of my school and college training, such as it was, is *soul power*. This is believed to be the experience of all who have lived long enough to test fully the practical value of their school training.
> It is thus seen that in education the act of acquiring knowledge is more important than the knowledge acquired. (White, 1901, pp. 42,43)

White was willing to allow disciplinary studies to have practical values; and one suspects that he believed his permissiveness on this issue spared him culpability on the score of being a classic formal disciplinarian. Nevertheless, his bending here did not negate his belief concerning the necessity of teachers giving priority to process over product in their instructional schemes:

> No intelligent person questions the value of practical knowledge or the importance of properly including such knowledge in school courses, and certainly few modern educators hold that the practical worth of knowledge lessens its value

---

[38] Just when and where the term "formal discipline" gave way to that of "mental discipline" has escaped my perusal. Most likely it happened because the first term became excessively identified with earlier classical training procedures. As to the distinction between discipline and training, we do have at least one antecedent referent. Simon Laurie, well-known educator and writer, and Professor of Education at the University of Edinburgh (1876–1903), based the distinction upon another distinction—between that of power and facility. Formal or mental discipline develops mental resourcefulness, initiative and power. Mental training develops facility in mental operations (Drever, 1922).

as a means of mental discipline. The one result to be secured in teaching knowledge, *whatever may be its nature,* is the effective power to acquire and express it. To this end it must be taught and acquired by methods that put the developing of power before knowledge. (White, 1901, p. 45)

White allowed that exercise of any of the mind's powers could have a general energizing effect on the entire mind and the "whole mental life." Nevertheless, the correct training of a power was the specific training of that power.

The teacher must have in mind the special power to be developed, or, what may be clearer, the special direction in which mental power is to be helpful. There is little helpful guidance in the vague notion that the purpose of a teaching exercise is to develop mental strength or bigness. A training exercise must be guided by an aim more definite than this. Indefinite activity does not give definite power. (White, 1901, p. 29)

White offered his readers what, indeed, amounts to a classic statement of disciplinarian doctrine, in his concern that they not stray into paths other than that of specific training for specific purposes.

The several powers are trained only by occasioning their appropriate activity of another power. It follows from these principles that analytic power is trained only by analytic activity and synthetic power only by synthetic activity. (White, 1902, p. 221)

From this followed his criticism of those process trainers who believed that all curricula at all instructional levels, if properly applied, would have equal value in exercising the mind's powers.[39] This he categorically denied. Specific powers require specific training. Specific training requires specific curricula.

The elementary studies, for example, do not equally train the power of observation, even when taught by an "observational method," nor is an observation method equally applicable to all elementary studies. No one study affords equally effective training in all directions, and certainly all studies do not give equally valuable training in any one direction. There is no ground for the claim that all studies have equal value, either as discipline or as knowledge. (White, 1901, p. 42)

One way of assuring that all of the mind's powers are being properly trained within schools is to see that all possible course offerings be made available to the student; that way the chances are that no particular faculty (power) will be overlooked in training and that somewhere there will be a proper "match" of curricula with faculties:[40]

[39] Something that Joseph Bruner, in more recent years, was notoriously prone to say.
[40] White was writing at a time when electives were being freely chosen. The egalitarian views of cognitive training taken by the Committee of Ten had seen all manner and shape of curricular offerings being made in the name of mental discipline.

A course of school training should clearly include at least the elements of knowledge in all fundamental branches. This is necessary for the acquisition of higher knowledge, as well as for the harmonious development of the mental powers. All children who are not mentally defective are capable of receiving this necessary training. (White, 1901, p. 42)

However, the rules of developmental psychology are to be observed in the child's education. In his stance on this issue, White is more clearly identified with Froebel than with traditional formal disciplinarians. The child is not the man. Various processes are more active at one stage of life than another.[41]

. . . the mind of the child differs from the mind of the adult, not simply in strength but in the *relative* activity and energy of the several mental powers, the perceptive powers, for example, being more active in infancy than the thought powers. The mental condition of pupils as they advance from the kindergarten to the high school is characterized by changes in the relative activity of the several mental powers. (White, 1901, pp. 17,18)

White had reached the conclusions of many factor analysts in the above statement without a single rotation. And since the nature and activity of processes differ from age to age, so must instruction follow their indications. His position on this is quite familiar to us by now.

. . . *there is a natural order in which the powers of the mind should be exercised and the corresponding kinds of knowledge taught.* The natural movement of the mind in the earlier processes of knowing is from sense perception through representative activity to reason, that is *from sense activity to reason through the activity of the intermediate powers.* (White, 1901, p. 31)

White took issue with those critics of mental discipline who questioned transfer of training and who claimed:

. . . the power of the mind developed by a given activity is not available in other activities; that there are as many kinds of mental discipline as there are different "spheres" of mental action, and that the mental power developed in a given sphere is available only in that sphere. (White, 1901, p. 41)[42]

To the contrary, there are clear transfer effects to be obtained through disciplinarian means:

---

[41] The original idea behind faculties, if we recall, was that all faculties are present at birth. Some of the earlier writers in this chapter still held to this premise. Another original concept supporting faculty training was that all faculties were of equal strength at birth; this was no longer tenable after the work of such as Froebel.

[42] Just whom he was referring to is not clear from statements like this and the one that follows. Thorndike had not yet made disciplinarians quake with fear; nor was it likely that he was acquainted with William James's negative conclusions (see next chapter). More likely, he was responding to the attacks of the Herbartians who sneered at both faculty psychology and formal discipline.

The analytic power developed by the solution of arithmetical problems is helpful in the analysis of sentences in grammar; the study of Latin shows itself in the easier mastery of natural science; the observation of plant life helps in the observation of animal life. (White, 1901, p. 41)

It is true, White observed that there are some restrictions on the possibilities of transfer. The latter is to be expected when the nature of the activity in which the power is to be expressed resembles, in some fashion, the nature of the training activity. Only thus can one be sure that the same power(s) is at work; even then, a diminishment of that power's force in the transfer may be expected since activity II most likely will express the workings of powers other than that trained in activity I.

. . . all experience shows that while mental power developed by a special activity may not be available in a totally different activity, it is available, though not, it may be, in equal degree, *in all related activities,* that is in all spheres that involve, though not exclusively the action of the same mental powers. (White, 1901, p. 41)

A more elaborate explanation as to what his position was concerning transfer of training was offered by White, in which he explained, as well, that there may be negative transfer effects as well as positive ones.

It is not claimed, let it be noted, that mental power gained in one sphere of activity is *equally* available in all related activities. The power of observation acquired in the study of plants is not equally available in the observation of animal life, much less of chemical phenomena. The powers of the mind are most facile in the directions in which they have been exercised, especially in which *habits* of action have been formed. Indeed, long and absorbing observation of one kind of phenomena may result in a mental habit which may be a hindrance in the observation of other phenomena. But these facts do not show that the mental power developed by a given activity is *limited* to that special activity and is not available in other activities. Nor do they show that power developed by a given activity may not energize the mind as a whole, or if preferred, may not energize the whole mental life.

The dogma of formal discipline is one extreme, and the doctrine that mental power is available only in the special activity that has developed it is another extreme. The truth lies in neither of these extremes. All experience shows that mental power developed in any sphere of activity is available, in greater or less degree, in all related activities. (White, 1902, p. 221)

White provided the readers of *The Art of Teaching* with the fundamental tenets of process training, as he conceived them to be, goals and methods, etc. He was particularly concerned that teachers systematically conceptualize and execute their teaching exercises. He was very much a methods man, and he was very sure that he knew where and how to go.

While there are many special directions in which power may be trained in a teaching exercise, there are three directions of fundamental importance. These are (1) the acquisition of knowledge, by observation and thought; (2) the expression of knowledge by language, drawing, etc.; and (3) its application or use. So far as the training of power is related to knowledge, it takes the direction of *acquisition* or *expression* or *application*. A given teaching exercise may in its progress take all three of these directions, and will usually take the first two, but one should be the leading or central aim. (White, 1901, p. 29)

As he offered a trinity of goals for the teacher to aspire to in her lessons, he also offered a trinity of instructional techniques for "The Lesson." This has three aspects, if we wish to proceed a la White. The first is instruction, wherein the pupil receives knowledge and has his cognitive powers strengthened in its acquisition. Second is drilling, which is essential if one seeks to make knowledge permanent and to effectively strengthen the cognitive powers engaged in acquisition, expression, and application of that knowledge. So great is the importance of drill, that White believed it should engage three-fourths of instructional time. White's statement below on the importance of drill echoes what formal disciplinarians, stretching back to antiquity, have claimed:

. . . the principles that underlie the acquisition of skill in any art are clearly and fully stated. It remains to apply these principles to the conduct of the drill when skill is its special end . . . it must be kept in mind that power and skill are trained only by action; that every act of the soul increases the power to act, and leaves a tendency to act again in a like manner. This is not only true of psychical activity, but, within certain limits, it holds true of bodily activity, and especially of the activity of the senses; as the eye, the ear, the touch, etc. What is true of a first action is true also of its repetition. Every repetition of an act increases both power and tendency, and thus through repetition an act may "repeat itself," that is become automatic (White, 1901, p. 81)

The third aspect is testing. Testing is critical to determine the results of instruction and drilling. "The test . . ." said White, ". . . is the eye of teaching; the guide and inspirer of teacher and pupil" (White, 1901, p. 53). It arouses interest and draws attention, and adds "energy and persistence" to the pupil's efforts. It also informs the teacher as to what was being accomplished through teaching. The three aspects of teaching— instruction, drilling, and testing are really parts of the same exercise or lesson, with the testing subordinate to the first two. All three exercise the faculties, though no specifics are given by White as to their precise manner of doing so.

Thus spoke Emerson E. White in his *Art of Teaching* upon which serried rows of early twentieth century teachers cut their instructional teeth. He was writing on the eve of formal discipline's disastrous decline, though he did not know it. Of that, more in the following chapter; we will not discuss it in detail in the present one. The only reason I bring it to the reader's attention now is that it must be kept in mind as we discuss and bring to a close the later days of faculty training, to which we now proceed.

AFTERMATH

Following severe attacks and extended debates upon faculty psychology and formal discipline, the doctrines of both were left in general disarray as the twentieth century began. It was more than these, however, that led to the decline of these dogmas. Other things, too, were responsible. The "new" psychologies were not congenial to these hoary workmates—not that the old faculties were entirely neglected. Colvin's superb book, *The Learning Process* (1914), still addressed perception, memory, attention, and the higher thought processes, and still pondered their improvement through training and education. However there is a quality of dereification, if I may neologize, in his writing. He talks about products and events, for example, about perceptions and perceiving, about thoughts and thinking. Not about perception and reason.

Books like the *Psychology of Childhood* of Norsworthy and Whitley (1920) represent a regression relative to works such as Colvin's. We hear familiar terms couched in familiar ways—perception (and the "necessity of training" it), memory and a call for "memory work," and the "power to think." Nevertheless, this book, too, shows the inroads of a new way of looking at cognition—Thorndike's way, and of a new way of training people and their processes—Dewey's way. The influence of both these men is exemplified in Norsworthy and Whitley's discussion of perceptual training.

In all this training, it must be constantly borne in mind that there is no faculty of observation or perception that can be trained for usefulness by an arbitrarily arranged material. If observation of people is needed, training in that line must be given; if of nature, the training must be of that material . . . in each case the training must be definite and particular. . . . Every bit of development acquired comes as the result of some definite activity. (Norsworthy & Whitley, 1920, p. 128)

Dewey says ". . . No training of sense organs in school, introduced for the sake of training, can begin to compete with the alertness and fullness of sense–life that comes through daily intimacy and interest in familiar occupations." No matter where the child is living, material is there—living, vital material, to which the child is constantly reacting. It is the duty of the teacher to take these life situations, and in connection with the reactions which naturally take place to develop perceptions which are clear, correct, adequate, to see to it that they are as numerous and rich as possible, and to supply material or motive when either is lacking; for upon the material gathered from sense perception will depend all future growth and development. (Norsworthy & Whitley, 1920, pp. 128,129)

In James Drever's book *An Introduction to the Psychology of Education* (1922), a further decline in faculty psychology's fortunes is to be observed. Drever talks of mental development, general tendencies, of "capacities, general and specific"; he even talks about "sense, imagination, and thought," those mighty faculties of old. But he is not considering any of these in faculty terms. They are, rather, topics that gather together behavioral data and organize them. What used to be the faculties, powers, capacities of old are redefined in behavioral ways:

> . . . with reference to the response or behavior of the organism, as playing part in that behavior, and possibly as a phase of behavior. (Drever, 1922, p. 183)

No reified cognitive engines here, but rather responses that have been learned in the presence of specific stimulus situations. No mental training here, either, unless specific types of learning improved by practice are intended. Transfer of training? Certainly, but of skills learned in one situation that may be applied to others because of communalities in both, skills acquired according to the laws of learning, not broad muscular faculties strengthened through exercise. Drever's definition of imagination will provide a clearer understanding of his behavioral approach:

> . . . to give some account of ideal representation or imagination . . . it must be noted that these are merely names given to conscious process when, and so far as, the organism is active in a certain definite way, and do not designate a certain entity, the producing case of certain phenomena of inner life. At this time of day there is no need to dwell on such a point. (Drever, 1922, p. 190)

In discussing the possibilities of perceptual training, particularly as popularized by Montessori, Drever observed the following:

> "Sensory gymnastics" would seem to convey the suggestion that we should seek to develop sensory discrimination for its own sake, and part from any response to a real world. Such "sensory gymnastics," at its best can have but a limited value. (Drever, 1922, p. 189)

And so continued the decline of interest in faculties and their training within educational psychology texts. Perusing the *Educational Psychology* of Garrison, Kingston, and McDonald (1964), there is not a single chapter dedicated as such to the familiar names of sense–perception, imagination, memory, reasoning, or will, nor of cultivating them. There is attention to learning for retention and transfer, the acquisition of skills, knowledge, understanding, creative thinking, problem solving, and character education—new names and ways for new times. In an even more recent book by Gage and Berliner, *Educational Psychology* (1975), there are topics on learning theory, the improvement of transfer of training, individual differences, etc., but not a single unit, chapter, or topic on the faculties as we have discussed them; not even one on sense–perception, as if the Frostig revolution had passed the authors by—though they do write about intelligence (our now sturdiest of faculties), and talk about "perceptions and cognitions" and various types of "learning processes"—all very behavioral, all very much tied to data. As I said, new names and ways for new times and new means for processes to express themselves.[43]

So now, within educational psychology we work with topics such as imagery, and memory, creativity and perception, rather than with faculties of such. Alas, the topics, or the behaviors the topics represent, become reified into new variants of old faculties all too easily. Unavoidable, it would seem, as long as we are cognitively conduced to create things out of words, as we always have been in the past and most likely will be in the future.

---

[43] For an interesting and most informative approach to processes, including critiques of factor analytic and cognitive psychology approaches to processes, see Sternberg's recent book (1977), though it will not provide anything of utility to process training.

21
The Once and Future Formal Discipline

INTRODUCTION

In the previous chapter we observed the training of traditional cognitive faculties at its zenith. We also observed in that chapter, and in earlier ones as well, the travails of such training, and in the first part of this book, the vicissitudes of faculty doctrine. In the current chapter, we shall examine more closely some of the events that brought the golden age (perhaps I should say golden ages or stages) of process training to a close within regular education.[1] For that purpose, we shall have to retrace our steps briefly.

Formal discipline and formal disciplinarians were repeatedly challenged over the centuries: among the ancient Greeks; by the Sophists, who emphasized utilitarian training against the cognitive training espoused by Socrates and Plato; and, later, by John Locke, who, while credited as the spiritual founder of modern formal discipline, was scornful of the earlier efforts at mental training made by the Scholastics and humanists, who forced classical studies upon the hapless pupils of yore. Similar attacks were endured by the doctrine, as we know, over the course of the years subsequent to those of John Locke's theoretical hegemony. They struck, however, at the periphery rather than the core of formal discipline, as much as classicists such as Tarver would have disagreed. Much more serious were the assaults made upon the notion of

---

[1] It was to continue quite a while longer within special and remedial education, as we shall see in later chapters.

a mind with specific faculties or powers that existed to be trained and, later, those upon its corollary that powers or faculties once trained under one set of circumstances can be transferred to effectively operate under others. Again, we have touched upon these issues in earlier pages of this treatise. Let us review them in greater thoroughness now, beginning with the work of Herbart.[2]

HERBART

George Friederich Herbart (1774–1841) has been accused of formulating a psychology without a soul. Actually, he allowed for a soul (mind), but did not allow his soul faculties.[3] It has, he said, ". . . no innate tendencies nor faculties. . . . It is a grievous ". . . error to look upon the human soul as an aggregate of all sorts of faculties" (Rusk, 1969, p. 232). These presumed faculties, i.e., broad mental powers, are really apperceptive masses, i.e., individual mental contents bound together in a framework of *apperception*[4] to form particular conglomerates of ideas. They are the results of activities rather than their causes. Speaking about the so-called faculty of feeling, Herbart stated: "Feeling is not a separate independent faculty of the soul, but only a consequence of the mutual interaction of ideas" (Rusk, 1969, pp. 234–235).

Beyond his reductio ad finitum of faculties, Herbart was also intent upon dismissing formal discipline from its role within education:

> Those, however, who have no true psychological insight, rarely understand anything of education. They may cherish the obsolete opinion that there reside in the human soul certain powers or faculties which have to be trained in one way or another. These people seemingly have in mind gymnastic exercises which strengthen the muscles, for man has only one kind of muscles. Indeed in each single apperceptive mass or group of ideas are contained so-called fantasy, memory and intelligence, but they are not equally distributed. Rather in one and the same person a certain mass of apperception may be of more intellectual, imaginative, or of reproductive character; another with an atmosphere of coolness, etc. Therefore what educators call formal discipline (Formelle Bildung) would be an absurdity if it meant the training of mental faculties which exist only in some people's imagination. (Ulich, 1947, p. 511)

Herbart was clearly a product person. His view of education was one in which the instructor provides his pupils with organized and controlled

[2] I refer the reader to Chapter 11 for a review of Herbart's position on faculty psychology.
[3] He allowed his soul organizing privileges and powers that are, to some degree, equivalents of the traditional faculties, though he tried to "externalize" them.
[4] Which later facultists (see earlier and later chapters) were to appropriate as a faculty in its own right.

streams of ideas, which those pupils can associate and correlate, synthesize, and analyze. In all of this, the teacher need not concern himself with nonexistent mental powers. There are none that exist to be trained. The role of instruction is to provide specifics the pupil may apprehend and apperceive. Latin is to be taught for its own sake or for its cultural-historical values, not because of the discipline it might provide the mind. And the same holds true for all the other cherished disciplinary studies of would-be mental trainers.

For what is at stake and what must be trained are not abstract powers or faculties but masses of ideas and their gradual formation. . . . (Ulich, 1947, pp. 511–512)

So spoke the associationist and promoter of educational contents. One learned what he was taught and did not strengthen his cognitive powers whatsoever in the learning. Similar views were expressed by Herbart regarding other subjects as applied in formal discipline.

Another instance of erroneous ideas about formal discipline is the frequent recommendation of mathematics as a special instrument for intellectual training. No wonder that most educators try to attain this end by a shorter method. Why all these figures and formulae if the ancient languages, which have to be learned anyway, serve the same purpose? Just study grammar; this will sharpen the intellect even more than mathematics, because, as some people believe, they have discovered that even poor intellects can acquire skill in figuring. But is it better not to ask whether the grammarians surpass the mathematicians and excel as great statesmen or generals or in other areas.

Grammatical thinking remains within grammar; and mathematical thinking remains within mathematics; the reasoning within each discipline of thought forms itself in accordance with the discipline. But if grammatical or mathematical notions enter by any chance and even through distant channels into the sphere of a general or a statesman, he will reproduce what he has learnt and it will assist him in all his actions.

Hence grammar and mathematics cannot be substituted for one another, but each holds value in its own sphere. Nor can grammar be used as a pattern for learning logic, though there exists some relationship, consequently also some educational interaction. The same holds true for logic and mathematics. But, alas, if somebody who needs logic to master the higher spheres of philosophy relied on his previous studies in grammar and mathematics! Neither grammar, nor mathematics, nor logic makes the metaphysician, although he cannot make any progress without logic and mathematics. (Ulich, 1947, pp. 512–513)

Since Herbart was a predominant psychological and educational figure, both during his life and posthumously, his antifaculty and antidisciplinary postures were to seriously affect the credibility of faculties and efforts to train them. For quite a while thereafter, it became unpopular to appear an avowed facultist in proper circles, or a disciplinary mind polisher. The baiting of faculty psychology and formal discipline became a common pastime for many. Bain, who had enough process skeletons hidden in his own conceptual closets to have remained silent about these matters, spoke out negatively about formal discipline. He proclaimed in 1879:

(There) is a discipline that we learn from everything that we have to do; it is not a prerogative of any one study or occupation, and it does not necessarily extend itself beyond the special subject. (Bain, 1879, p. 142)[5]

W. Rein, one of Herbart's disciples wrote in his *Outlines of Pedagogics* (1895) to the effect that formal discipline was a fiction, that "In general, there is no such education at all . . ."; rather, that there are ". . . as many kinds of formal education as there are essentially different spheres of intellectual employment" (Rein, 1895, p. 61).

John Adams in his hymn to Herbart, *The Herbartian Psychology Applied to Education* (1897), triumphantly proclaimed the victory of content over process, thanks to the influence of Herbart's doctrines:

Teachers used to have, and ignorant people still have, a pretty theory that we ought to learn pieces of poetry to cultivate the memory. This venerable, this ludicrous fallacy has long been exploded. . . . The point of view is entirely changed. Pupils learn poetry now not for the sake of memory, but for the sake of poetry. (Adams, 1897, p. 134)

Not that the proponents of formal discipline were routed by any of this. As we have seen in the previous chapter, there were ways to have one's formal discipline and one's Herbart too—or to think that you were getting away with it, as Baldwin manifestly did, or to simply go blithely along pointing to Pestalozzi and Froebel and, later, Montessori to justify what you were doing, or, at the very least, get the chance to get into print taking pros or cons on the issue of cognitive training. Brown, in "How is Formal Culture Possible?" published in *The Public School Journal,* December 1883, tried to save the baby, while allowing some of the bath water to be spilt away. He criticized the doctrine of formal discipline for its broader claims, yet he urged that a variety of mental attitudes and affective orientations, including voluntary attention, methodical habits, self-confidence, and even love of truth be trained through disciplinary methods. On the other hand, Hinsdale, writing on "The Dogma of Formal Discipline" in the 1894 *Proceedings of The N.E.A.,* vigorously attacked formal discipline on a general front, asserting, that ". . . the power generated by any mental activity is far more special than general" (Colvin, 1914, p. 229). It was just this sort of statement that was to become the

---

[5] On the other hand, the great scientist Hermann Ludwig Helmholz (1821–1894) was a firm believer in the basic premises of formal discipline and valued particular studies for their value in taxing ". . . equally all the intellectual powers" (Colvin, 1914, p. 213).

center of dispute concerning the viability of formal discipline. It posed the central question concerning transfer of training. Does training have specific or general transfer effects?

Transfer of training is taken for granted nowadays. It is only questions concerning the whats and hows of that transfer, the conditions under which it takes place, what facilitates it, what hinders it, etc., that we now debate. Transfer of training is a fundamental topic in psychology and education. It was then, too, in the latter years of the nineteenth century and the early decades of the twentieth.

Teachers usually teach for transfer. Rarely do they intend that a learner perform precisely the same task, under the same conditions wherein he was originally taught that task, or that he learn a specific content specifically for its precise repetition at a later date. Teachers teach for transfer, obviously. If what they teach cannot transfer from the instructional task and the instructional medium to broader areas within school and life, what good is their teaching? Not much, obviously. It was the same in the days of formal discipline. The value of the latter rested on the presumption that cognitive, affective, conative, and whatever other powers (faculties, abilities, etc.) there were could be trained under conditions of formal discipline so as to transfer to still other conditions. That was, indeed, what formal discipline was all about.

Early research studies appeared to support such transfer, making disciplinarians secure, regardless of what Herbart had said. In a number of early studies in German experimental laboratories (1858) the evidence for transfer seemed to be clearly established. Volkmann, investigating spatial discrimination, found that practice with the fingertips of the left hand improved discrimination with the fingertips of the right hand. Practice with the third phalanx improved fineness of discrimination with the first phalanx. Urbantschisch found training in sound discrimination improved a subject's sensitivity to visual, gustatory, olfactory, and tactile stimuli. Epstein found transfer from sound discrimination to visual discrimination. Vogt demonstrated that habituation to distractions in one situation could be carried over to yet another.

In American psychological laboratories, similar types of evidence emerged from studies carried out by E. W. Scripture's group, reported in publications released in 1894, 1898, and 1900. Work by T. L. Smith, Emily M. Brown, and Walter W. Davis all supported transfer of training principles. Their experiments found that muscular steadiness in inserting a needle in a very small hole transferred to the left hand after training with the right, a finding that Scripture attributed to the training of attention rather than of specific motor skills. Practice intended to specifically increase the muscular power of the right hand also resulted in an increase in the power of the left. Training subjects to improve their rapidity in tapping a telegraph key with one hand showed improvement in the rapidity with which such tapping was carried out by their other members. Experiments in lunging at a target with a fencer's foil with the right hand improved lunging with the left, etc. Davis interpreted such results as showing not only that the effects of exercise could be transferred but that also ". . . will power and attention are educated by physical training, and that when trained by a special act they are developed for all other acts" (Colvin, 1914, p. 226).[6]

All well and good, such studies, for the doctrine of formal discipline—or so it seemed. Alas for such expectations. Transfer of training was to be seriously challenged—and in such a way that would permanently weaken the cause of formal discipline. The attack upon its premises was to be led by two of America's foremost psychologists, William James and Edward L. Thorndike.

JAMES

William James was essentially an armchair psychologist, proceeding on observation and speculation rather than experimental research. He did, however, venture into the experimental arena to determine whether memory could, as faculty psychologists claimed, be improved through cultivation or training.

On eight successive days, James learned 150 lines of Victor Hugo's *Satyr*. He then worked 20 minutes daily to learn the entire first book of *Paradise Lost*, taking 38 consecutive days in the process. Afterward, when James returned to learn more of *Satyr*, he found that whereas he had initially been able to memorize Hugo's poetry at the rate of one line in fifty seconds, he was now able to only manage one line in 57 seconds. If there was a memory muscle of some sort, he had clearly not exercised it well through training via Milton's epic. James did admit that by the time he had gotten around to attempting Hugo for the second time he was rather fatigued, as well he might be; it is hard enough to wade through *Paradise Lost* without attempting to memorize it; he didn't consider negative transfer effects.

Later, James found slight positive transfer effects in similar experiments he carried out with his students under more positive conditions for such transfer. But his jury of one came back with a negative report on memory training in any case. In the chapter "Memory" in *Principles of Psychology* (1890), he concluded that memory, good or bad, is attributable to the state of one's brain tissues. What is construed as improvement

---

[6] Somehow it appears to have escaped these investigators that they were training a person rather than the isolated use of a limb or other part of his body.

of the memory faculty through training really is the improvement of one's habitual methods of recording what one learns. Mnemonics may "improve" memory, but memory cannot be trained.

This ipse dixit by James made the cheeks of formal disciplinarians pale.[7] Their favorite faculty had not shown itself to be improvable by America's most renowned psychologist. But worse was to come a little more than a decade later, this time, inaugurated by the research of Edward L. Thorndike and Robert S. Woodworth, who published several papers on transfer of training in the *Psychological Review* of 1901. It was a time when the mental measurement movement was well on its way, and there was a considerably more sophisticated appreciation of the scientific method in psychology than when James had carried out his crude researches.

THORNDIKE

The object of the Thorndike-Woodworth experiments was to determine the effects of training in certain functions on closely similar ones, as shown by the general title of their researches, "The Influence of Improvement in One Mental Function Upon the Efficiency of Other Functions." Studied was the influence of training in the estimation of weights of one type on the ability to estimate the weight of miscellaneous items; the influence of practice in cancellation of words containing certain letters on the ability to pick out words containing other letters, and the identification of misspelled words; etc. There was, to be sure, some improvement in the "transfer" from one task to another, in certain instances. But some transfers produced negative results, and others near-zero results. The authors' summary of their work produced the statement: "Spread of practice occurs only where identical elements are concerned in the influencing and influenced functions" (Thorndike & Woodworth, 1901, p. 250).

It was the functioning of identical elements in the practice series and in the final test series that accounted for what improvement was to be found through so-called mental training or disciplinary exercises, rather than any ". . . mysterious transfer of practice, to an unanalyzable property of mental functions." This is what Thorndike said in a later paper (1902). Improvements due to transfer of training can be explained on the basis of *identical elements* in both training and transfer situations rather than on the basis of cognitive abilities improved in the former and

---

[7] Halleck scorned his conclusions on the basis that they violated common sense observations.

applied in the latter; and these improvements are restricted, in the main, to activities that closely resemble each other.

Like so many psychometric theorists, then and later, Thorndike appealed to the nervous system to explain his elements. His identical elements were identified as ". . . those mental processes which have the same cell action in the brain as their physical correlates," he said (Thorndike, 1913, p. 359). Rather than the mind being made up of broad faculties there are ". . . thousands of particular independent capacities each of which must be developed by itself" (Thorndike, 1913, p. 359). These are created on the basis of *neural grooves,* along which reactions in the nervous system occur under practice, the nerve cells therein changing to *fix* memories for transfer purposes. Thorndike proposed:

. . . one ability is improved by the exercise of another only when the neurons whose action the former represents are actually altered in the course of the exercise of the latter. (Thorndike, 1913, p. 359)[8]

None of this boded well for the proposition of formal disciplinarians that training of the mind's powers would dramatically improve those powers in a broad pervasive sense—not when the mind consisted of countless elements to be bonded together:

Training the mind means the development of thousands of particular independent capacities, the formation of countless particular habits, for the working of any mental capacity depends upon the concrete data with which it works. Improvement of any one mental function or activity will improve others only insofar as they possess elements common to it also. The amount of identical elements in different mental functions and the amount of general influence from special training are much less than common opinion supposes. (Thorndike, 1906, p. 246)

Thus spoke Thorndike in his *Educational Psychology* (1913).

As per Thorndike, that transfer of training was a matter of identical elements in trained-in and trained-to situations. They, and they alone, explain what transfer there is to be found. Identical elements are of two sorts and between them account for transfer of content and form. The first depends on an identity of substance, i.e., identity of objective elements. The second rests on an identity of procedure, i.e., an identity of subjective aspects and results in broader transfer than the first. It includes a wide range of general methods and techniques in learning, and of attitudes and

[8] Brain centers of various sorts were quite in vogue when he was writing, so Thorndike was not averse to different types of identical elements, e.g., of a visual or auditory sort. They were not, however, to be construed as constituting traditional faculties. Thorndike also came to categorize test results in terms of "group factors," e.g., verbal, mathematical, mechanical, and suggested that cognitive functioning might be construed in terms of a "few big abilities" (Cattell, 1971). Again this is not to be construed as the construction of reified faculties on his part.

dispositions; all of which are very much dependent on the nature of the learner and his interests and purposes. In his later years, Thorndike allowed for considerably increased transfer possibilities on the basis of this second kind of identity, and he showed considerable softening of his original scornful posture concerning meaningful transfer. In an article written with A. I. Gates in 1929, we find the following admission:

> Studies of the transfer of training . . . have shown that the methods used in guiding pupil's learning activities have marked effect upon the degree of transfer. The more clearly the crucial elements or fact or *principle* in a situation is brought to the pupil's attention the more readily the same element or fact or *principle* may be identified in another situation. . . . If a child observes, *despite many differences in details* in a new mechanical puzzle, that the vital *principle* is the same as in puzzles previously solved, the solution is more likely to be achieved than when the *common principle* is not identified. (Orata, 1945, p. 269)[9]

But I fear, at this point, that my encapsulations of Thorndike's writings may be diluting the reader's appreciation of his original negative position on the subject of transfer of training, which was so critical to the misfortunes of formal discipline. So let us retrace a bit and consider some of his early, vehement, antitransfer statements. Thus again a quote from his 1901 study with Woodworth:

> Improvement in any single mental function need not improve the ability in functions commonly called by the same name. It may injure it. Improvement in any single mental function rarely brings about equal improvement in any other function, no matter how similar, for the working of every mental function-group is conditioned by the nature of the data in each particular case. . . . There is no inner necessity for improvement of one function to improve others closely similar to it, due to definite factors, the operation of which training may or may not secure. (Sawrey and Telford, 1964, p. 242)

Another statement in *Educational Psychology*, which was carrying Thorndike's gospel to teachers, made the case for identical elements in everyday educational activities. It asserted that there are specific elements to be learned in school (and to be transferred) rather than faculties to be trained.

> . . . a change in one function alters any other only insofar as the two functions have as factors identical elements. The change in the second function is in amount that is due to the change in the elements common to it and the first. The change is simply the necessary result upon the second function of the alteration of those of its factors which were elements of the first function, and so were altered

---

[9] This was after considerable research had been generated supporting transfer of training, which we shall shortly review. Thorndike was never one, however, for cognitive training and his later, more positive position on transfer was oriented to educational training, i.e., school activities, rather than to process training.

by its training. To take a concrete example, improvement in addition will alter one's ability in multiplication because addition is absolutely identical with a part of multiplication and because certain other processes, e.g., eye movements and the inhibition of all save arithmetical impulses, are in part common to the two functions. (Thorndike, 1913, pp. 268–269)

Such statements led Thorndike's readers to interpret his position as being one of extreme specificity as regards the outcome of training. And though, as we have seen Thorndike previously allowed for broader phenomena of transfer, he seems to have largely encouraged an identification of his position with a stance of severe specificity, even as evidence positively supporting broader interpretations of training, including his own, mounted. Why?

It would appear that Thorndike was engaged in a tidy bit of conceptual bear-baiting in all of this. He was after the "sick men" of psychology and education—faculty psychology and formal discipline. These two were beaten about, harried, and discredited, but persevered all the same. Spearman later expressed his astonishment at the tenacity of these weary dogmas, and even expressed admiration at their ability to restore themselves and make their claims on theory and practice still another time. Antaean in their recuperative powers, or bad pennies psychology and education somehow could not lose—depending upon one's perspective. Thorndike was seeking, once and for all, a final end to both.

In the midst of the devastation he sought to wreak on them, Thorndike would trot out what he regarded were the ridiculous claims made for the cognitive training potentials of this and that method of instruction or curriculum. In his *Education: A First Book* (1912) he quoted from a number of unidentified authors, who, he said ". . . represent fairly this now discredited notion of very great general mental discipline by the improvement of one or another ability" (Thorndike, 1912, p. 115).

The pursuit of mathematics gives command of the attention. . . . The man or woman who has been drilled by means of mathematics is the better able to select from a number of possible lines which may be suggested that which is easiest or most direct to attain a desired end. The second purpose of this study is . . . the strengthening and training of the reasoning powers.

By means of experimental and observational work in science . . . his attention will be excited, the power of observation . . . much strengthened, and the senses exercised and disciplined.

Correct use of the foreign language . . . makes *concentration* imperative and serves in an eminent degree as the discipline of the will. . . . Practice in the use of a foreign language cultivates the imagination.

The capability of concentrating attention on a certain point in question, in whatever field it is acquired, will show itself efficacious in all fields.

Will-power and attention are educated by physical training. When developed by any special act, they are developed for all acts. (Thorndike, 1912, p. 115)

In his book *Educational Psychology,* Thorndike identified some of the disciplinarian culprits he sought to chastise:

It is as a means of training the faculties or perception and generalization that the study of such a language as Latin in comparison with English is so valuable. (C. L. Morgan, *Psychology for Teachers,* p. 186)

Arithmetic, if judiciously taught, forms in the pupil habits of mental attention, argumentative sequence, absolute accuracy, and satisfaction in truth as a result, that do not seem to spring equally from the study of any other subject suitable to the elementary stage of instruction. (Joseph Payne, *Lectures on Education,* Vol. 1, p. 260)

Let us examine in detail the advantages which a person who has taken the ordinary Bachelor's degree has derived from the study of classics. Aside from the discipline of the will, which comes from any hard work, we find the following: (1) His memory for facts has been strengthened by committing paradigms and learning a new vocabulary. (2) He has been obliged to formulate pretty distinctly a regular system of classified facts—the facts which form the material of the grammar—classified in due form under chapter, section, subsection, and so on. This means that he has learned to remember things by their relations—a power which can hardly be acquired without practice informing or using such classified systems. (3) He has had his judgment broadened and strengthened by constant calls upon it to account for things which cannot be accounted for without its exercise. (E. H. Babbitt, *Methods of Teaching the Modern Languages,* p. 126)

The visual, mental, and manual powers are cultivated in combination, the eye being trained to see clearly and judge accurately, the mind to think, and the hand to record the appearance of the object seen, or the conceptions formed in the mind. Facility and skill in handicraft, and delicacy of manipulation, all depend largely upon the extent to which this hand and eye training has been fostered. The inventive and imaginative faculties are stimulated and exercised in design, and the graphic memory is strengthened by practice in memory drawing, the aesthetic judgment is brought into use, the power of discerning beauty, congruity, proportion, symmetry, is made stronger; and the love of the beautiful, inherent more or less in mankind, is greatly increased. (J. H. Morris, *Teaching and Organization* [edited by P. A. Barnett], pp. 63–64 (Thorndike, 1913,b, pp. 269–271)

Statements such as the above were sitting ducks per Thorndike, ready to be discredited. He did not miss his opportunity.

Norsworthy, writing on "Formal Training" in the *New York Teachers Monograph* in 1902 paraphrased Thorndike's position in unequivocal terms. It was specificity over generality all the way.

It seems probable that certain functions which are of importance in school work, such as quickness in arithmetic, accuracy in spelling, attention to forms, etc., are highly specialized and not secondary results of some general function. That just as there is no such thing as general memory, so there is no such thing as general quickness or accuracy or observation. . . . Accuracy in spelling is independent of accuracy in multiplication, and quickness in arithmetic is not found with quickness in marking misspelled words; ability to pick out the word "boy" on a printed page is no guarantee that the child will be able to pick out a geometrical form with as great ease and accuracy. (Norsworthy, 1902, p. 25)

This pejorative on general transfer, emerging out of Thorndike's camp following the dawn of his theories, made it clear: Faculty psychology and formal discipline were dead. Viva identical elements and specificity of training.

Statements such as Norsworthy's were the beginning shots in what came to be the great transfer-of-training wars and there was a flood of papers on transfer of training taking positions for and against it; a splendid opportunity it was, too, for doctoral students to complete their research requirements.

Nor were all the victories to be won by Thorndike forces, though much of the research generated on the topic of transfer emerged from his laboratories or, at least, was created in Columbia's Teachers College, whereon he cast a giant shadow. Even at Columbia, where most of the studies clearly supported Thorndike's contentions, there were those who insisted upon giving quarter to formal discipline. Blair, examining practice curves obtained in studies on the acquisition of skills, concluded:

Any bit of special training helps us find ourselves. It gives us a method of orientation which leaves us in our reactions, not entirely at the mercy of chance even in unfamiliar situations. The experience which we get from special training gives us a general power to meet an entirely new situation with a more favorable response than had we not had this special training. (Colvin, 1914, p. 218)

Bennett, also at Columbia's Teachers College, studied the effects of training in discriminating shades of one color on the discrimination of others and found transfer effects also. So it wasn't all Thorndike, even in his own haunts.

However, there was a general tendency for quite a while to interpret at Columbia, and elsewhere, whatever transfer-of-training effects were found in terms of the doctrine of identical elements rather than those of broad transfers of power. For example, Coover and Angell (1911) carried out investigations into cross-modality transfer and broad-task transfer. In one study they trained pupils to discriminate sound intensities and tested for improvement in the pupils' discrimination of shades of gray. In another, they studied the effects of training in card sorting on a test series of typewriter reactions. They found some improvements but did not regard them as truly indicative of skill transfer. Rather the improvements were interpreted as due to the pupils' ". . . divesting the essential process of the unessential factors. There is a greater habituation and more economical adaptation of attention" (Colvin, 1914, p. 219).

Foster, also at Teachers College, studied transfer effects in the area of visualization with a munificent sum of three pupils, and concluded from his results that it was Thorndike all the way. He commented that their training did not make them

. . . noticeably better observers or memorizers in general or given them any habits of observing closely or reporting correctly, or furnished any ability to meet better any situations generally met with. . . . Specific practice is demanded for best results. . . . (Colvin, 1914, pp. 218–219)

Countering such conclusions were studies by Fracker at the University of Iowa (1907). Using a training series requiring the memorizing of four auditory tones in order, he found improvement in test series that covered a diverse lot of memory items. Improvement in memory was found for: poetry; the order of four shades of gray; the order of nine tones; the order of nine shades of gray; the order of nine geometrical figures; the extent of arm movement; etc.—not everywhere, but enough to suggest that positive transfer effects could result in an area where James had concluded there were no useful ones to be found.

The camps of the formal disciplinarians, rightly suspecting that their cause depended upon the proofs of transfer, carried out studies that showed high correlations between studies of foreign language and success in such subjects as mathematics, e.g., Rietz and Shade (1908). These correlations proved transfer—they supposed. They were, however, rather a testimony to the fact that pupils who do well in one area of study often do well in others. Bright is bright! Thorndike kept reminding people of this fact. In his writings on mental discipline in high schools (1924), he explained the apparent transfer effects from study in foreign languages on the basis of bright students participating, i.e., who did well across studies because they were bright rather than due to any mental training that foreign language study provided.

The cause was clearly being won by Thorndike's camp through much of the early controversy, until two doughty champions appeared on the scene, whose efforts still serve as beacons to the present for explaining transfer of training and justifying efforts to create transfer effects. What was needed were ideas supporting transfer of training, not mere results. Charles H. Judd and William C. Bagley were able to provide them.

JUDD AND BAGLEY—TRANSFER OF TRAINING

Judd's theory of transfer was one of generalization. Rather than the mere transference of identical elements from one situation to another, it was generalization from experiences on the basis of understood principles that could explain positive transfer of training results. So said Judd, on the basis of some famous experiments (1902, 1908), still discussed in modern educational psychology textbooks. In Judd's research, experimental subjects were instructed in the principle of refraction of light, while control subjects did not receive such training. The experimentals did considerably better in tests of ability to strike objects under water, making more adequate adjustments to different depths thereof than did the controls. Had Thorndike said something similar in discussing transfer of identical elements of the second kind? H. A. Carroll, P. Sandiford, and A. A. Douglass thought so:

> The conclusions to which the writer has come is that Judd and Thorndike are fundamentally one with respect to transfer, though each is emphasizing an opposite extreme. (Carroll, 1930, p. 4)

> Judd's generalization of experience . . . resolves itself into nothing more nor less than the formation of specific . . . habits having applicability to situations other than those in which they were learned. (Sandiford, 1928, p. 298)

> In the minds of many psychologists a theory of transfer based on the process of generalization is not opposed to one which conceives of transfer as occurring through identical elements. (Douglass, 1927, p. 352)

But what Judd did was provide a philosophical support for those who wanted to teach for transfer, while Thorndike was advising against it. Formal discipline was at stake. Judd's position appeared to support it, and gave its adherents new hope.

William Bagley also appeared as a champion of formal discipline, on much the same type of grounds as did Judd. Judd was a psychologist of prominence; Bagley was an educator of importance. Judd spoke about generalization, a good concept for a psychology that was increasingly becoming experimental and behavioral in orientation. Bagley spoke about educational goals, specifically, those of conscious ideals. Generalization explained transfer effects; so could conscious ideals.

Bagley carried out experiments with children while at Montana State Normal College (1907). He specifically attempted ". . . to determine whether the habit of producing neat papers in arithmetic will function with reference to neat written work in other studies." The immediate answer from his research into the question was a resounding "no." Thorndike seemed to be right after all. There was improvement in subsequent arithmetic papers through training in neatness on previous arithmetic papers. But there was ". . . also a failure to show the slightest improvement in language and spelling papers." (Colvin, 1914, pp. 221–222)

Bagley's results were not quite what he had hoped to arrive at. So he concluded that his failure to find transfer-of-training effects was due to the fact that the habit of neatness had not become a "conscious ideal" in the minds of his subjects. Would improvements under the influence of conscious ideals developed in one situation and transferred to another type really constitute transfer of training? And if they did would they be anything other than identical elements of the second class, as proposed by Thorndike? If one wishes to be ultra precise, one might quibble, as one might also quibble at Judd's generalization principles; and yet "organizers," advance or retrospective, do help to create transfer effects. So take the broad view, particularly since formal discipline is at stake. Use a good idea. Bagley did. All he needed was some substantiating evidence.

FURTHER SUPPORT FOR TRANSFER OF TRAINING

This substantiating evidence was convincingly provided by W. C. Ruediger (1908) in a study called Improvement of Mental Functions Through Ideals (1908). The study was quite massive for its time. Seventh-grade students from a number of different schools were trained and studied over an eight-week period. Ruediger's experimental group, in addition to training for neatness on a particular subject, was also given training to raise the habit of neatness into consciousness as an "ideal" of neatness. So carried out, Ruediger's study showed positive transfer of neatness from one type of study to others quite removed in nature. Neatness in geography "transferred" to neatness in arithmetic, grammar, and history.

Ruger, working on a more molecular basis, provided even broader support for Bagley's theory, working to determine whether transfer effects could be achieved from training on one type of complicated puzzle to performance on another. His results came down on the side of Bagley's conclusions.[10] Subjects who developed a general formula in solving one form of puzzle were then able to successfully "transfer" special abilities or habits developed from their experiences with that form to help them more effectively solve others. Those who didn't develop a "general ideal of procedure" failed to show much in the way of transfer. Ruger's conclusions were: "In general, the value of specific habits under a change of conditions depended directly on the presence of a general idea which would serve for their control" (Colvin, 1914, p. 221).

Extensive experiments at the University of Illinois by Colvin (with up to 1,500 pupils) also found positive transfer effects, as predicted by Bagley, when the proper conditions prevailed—at least partly. Colvin had his pupils first mark the letter X on sheets of paper marked off in squares. He divided his subjects, one group receiving ". . . work . . ." which emphasized ". . . the factor of exactness and hence raised it to the level of clear consciousness in the minds of the pupils" (Colvin, 1914, p. 223).

---

[10] Also on the side of Judd's conclusions.

The result was a positive transfer in accuracy by those who had their factors of exactness raised into clear consciousness—but at the cost of a loss in speed. Was Bagley justified? Had Bagley, in any case, said anything more than Thorndike and Woodworth, who had said that the ". . . acquisition of definite ideas. . ." played an important part as to ". . . influence of improvement in one function on the efficiency of others" (Colvin, 1914, p. 223). Some people didn't seem to think so, as we saw earlier. Colvin apparently did.

With champions for and against transfer of training as grounds for substantiating claims made for mental training, the research went on, producing contradictory results. Saucier complained in 1927 that, "The results are so conflicting as to prove only that something is wrong somewhere" (Saucier, 1927, p. 50).

To help organize and synthesize the masses of data that the struggle left in its wake, various review articles appeared. They generally supported the positive in respect to transfer of training. Betz reported for mathematics in 1930; Ruggs (1916), and Whipple (1928) from a broader perspective.

Sandiford's 1941 review firmly supported transfer of training but the author believed that the positive results he generally found in no way vitiated observations that

> . . . it is safer for educators to depend on specific training and practice than to expect results at second hand through transfer of training. (Woody, 1951, pp. 216–217)

Orata, a supporter of formal discipline (in modern clothing) reviewed "all" studies from 1890, first to 1927 and then to 1935. There was no doubt in his mind that if one taught for transfer, one would get transfer, and that was what modern mental discipline was all about. Speaking about "all" of the transfer literature he had examined of an "objective" sort, a total of "no less" than 167 research investigations, Orata gave his conclusions:

> . . . assuming that they possess a fair degree of validity and reliability, we may, with confidence make the following generalization: 47 or nearly 30% show considerable *transfer*, 80 or nearly 50% show *appreciable* transfer, 15 or less than 10% show *little* transfer, 6 or less than 4% show *no* transfer, and the rest which comprise less than 10% show both *transference* and *interference*. And since interference is indicative of transfer of a negative character, it is safe to conclude that all doubts with reference to the possibilities of transfer of training may be cast away. (Orata, 1945, pp. 266–267)

Bruner, writing in his *The Process of Education* (1961), reaffirmed the role of transfer of training in learning and its substantiation of the theory of formal discipline (with proper allowances made for the latter's past errors). It was part of the "learning to learn" scene that accompanied the broader panoramas of cognitive psychology.

Virtually all of the evidence of the last two decades on the nature of learning and transfer has indicated that, while the original theory of formal discipline was poorly stated in terms of the training of faculties, it is indeed a fact that massive general transfer can be achieved by appropriate learning, even to the degree that learning properly under optimal conditions leads one to "learn how to learn." These studies have stimulated a renewed interest in complex learning of a kind . . . designed to produce general understanding of the structure of a subject matter. . . . How can [a necessarily limited exposure to materials to be learned] be made to count in (students') thinking for the rest of their lives . . . the answer to his question lies in giving pupils an understanding of the fundamental structure of whatever subjects we choose to teach. This is a minimum requirement for using knowledge, for bringing it to bear on problems and events one encounters outside a classroom, or in . . . one's later training. The teaching and learning of structure, rather than simply the mastery of facts and techniques, is at the center of the classic problem of transfer. (Bruner, 1961, pp. 5–6, 8, 11–12)

Such a statement (by Bruner) is not quite a piece with traditional cognitive training as we have come to know and love it within the forms of formal discipline. Bruner was talking of transfer in the tradition of Judd and Bagley. He was further writing about the structure of the subject matter, rather than the structures of the mind as that which transfer of training was to concern itself with. But in the end, Bruner was one of the leaders in that training of the mind movement introduced by cognitive psychology into education and, as such, takes his place (perhaps) in the successions of the formal disciplinary movement.

One final observer of the transfer-of-training scene remains to be attended to before we move on to other issues relating to formal discipline. We travel some years back from Bruner's statement to consider one by a physiological psychologist, whose opinions were a major influence for many decades upon psychologists' attitudes towards the brain and its functions. I am talking now of Carl Lashley, whose book *Brain Mechanisms and Intelligence* made the case for such concepts as mass action, equipotentiality, and vicarious functioning. Thorndike's extreme specificities and cavalier neurological opinions apparently irritated Lashley, who took a dynamic and gestaltist approach to transfer of training, based on his experiments with rats whose brains were in various stages of ablation or other conditions of violation.

Lashley denied that Thorndike's theories received support from either neurology or physiological psychology. He held that transfer was achieved on the basis of perceptions of relationships achieved through a process (gestaltist in origin) of insight; that the theory of formal discipline was still a viable one, since Thorndike's mechanical bond-formation notions of learning were invalid; and that the limits as to quality and quantity of transfer possible through training remained yet to be determined:

There is no evidence to support . . . belief in the identity of nervous elements. On the contrary, it is very doubtful if the same neurons or synapses are involved even in two similar reactions to the same stimulus. Our data seem to prove that the structural elements are relatively unimportant for integration and that the common elements must be some sort of dynamic patterns, determined by the relations or ratios among the parts of the system and not by the specific neurons activated. If this be true, we cannot, on the basis of our present knowledge of the nervous system, set any limit to the kinds or amount of transfer possible or to the sort of relations which may be directly recognized. . . . The rejection of doctrines of formal discipline seems to have been based far more upon such reasoning [as that of Thorndike's mechanistic explanations of transfer] than upon any convincing experimental evidence. (Lashley, 1929, pp. 172–173)

Transfer of training had triumphed. Why did it not carry along formal discipline with it? In a general sense, it did. In the specific sense of rescuing the traditional doctrine, it did not. Thorndikean propaganda appears to have been very much responsible for this, rather than Thorndikean fact, which could have been interpreted as supporting formal discipline. Perhaps if there had been a Thurstone or Guilford standing by to support faculty interpretations or if there had not been various negative influences, formal discipline might have done better. But as to the validity of formal discipline as a doctrine? Let us go on to the great debates of the early twentieth century—a proper subject, now, after our review of transfer of training, whose validity was part of those debates.

The debates went on upon podium and within book. We shall concern ourselves with but several instances of both, which shall suffice for our purposes. They are those hovering about the close of the first decade of the twentieth century when critics and countercritics in the transfer of training controversy tried to make their points, often at the cost of some concessions to the enemy.

A most distinguished group of psychologists convened to discuss formal discipline in a meeting presented in a symposium held by the Michigan Schoolmaster's Club at Ann Arbor on April 2, 1908 (subsequently published in the *Educational Review*, June of that year).

C. H. Judd, on the basis of his transfer-of-training experiments came out with a point of view that favored formal discipline:

(1) Certain habits gained in the mastery of one study may be appropriately directed in another. (2) They may be slightly modified before such application and still show for their possessor a great gain as compared with the individual who has to start from the beginning. . . . It seems probable that a certain gain in the power to use and sustain attention will accrue from a purposeful and persistent intellectual application. (Colvin, 1914, p. 230)

Judd also spoke of being able to train the mind either in general or specific ways. In fact, all activities can be taught, he said, either for purposes of broad generalizations, or narrowed in respect to specific purposes, greatly dependent upon the teacher's approach to training.

W. B. Pillsbury also came out in favor of a disciplinary approach to education:

Training one part . . . trains related parts and the whole in some degree. . . . So the man with well rounded training is probably better trained for learning in any field than the untrained man, or even the man with a narrow education in any other field. (Colvin, 1914, pp. 230–231)

J. R. Angell was more hesitant, perhaps because he had studied with John Dewey and was exposed to Thorndike's influences. He warned that there was much of an unsettled and unknown nature in transfer and cognitive training and that ". . . dogmatism is wholly impossible in advance of . . . dramatic and exhaustive investigation (Colvin, 1914, p. 230). Judd agreed in principle:

Does nature study train in observation? Does washing of slates train in neatness? Does saying good morning to the principal conduce to good manner on the play ground? If there is any . . . answer given to you when you ask these questions, put it aside. There is no single answer to any one of these questions. (Colvin, 1914, p. 231)

A second symposium on formal discipline was held at Brown University on April 3, 1909, and published in Education, May of that year. Presenting were some of William James's most distinguished students, Delebarre and Henderson.

Delebarre was determined to defend formal discipline, on the basis of its structural values first, on the possiblities of its transfer of information second.

. . . formal elements can be taught . . . one subject unquestionably helps in the learning of others . . . there are disciplinary subjects that are of especial value for this purpose . . . not only does good training in any subject improve methods of learning, of attention, of work, of comprehension, but it is also true that all knowledge possesses some elements in common, and the number of these may be very considerable, even in the case of subjects that appear at first sight little related. (Colvin, 1914, pp. 232–233)

Henderson reviewed experimental studies of transfer of training in his contribution to the symposium and expressed his belief in cognitive training and transfer, while also voicing uncertainty as to whether transfer for form or content was more valuable. In a later book, *Principles of Education* (1910), he was to state his position on formal discipline clearly and concisely:

There is something which may appropriately be called formal discipline. It consists in the establishment of habitual reactions that correspond to the form of situations; these reactions foster adjustments, attitudes and ideas that favor the successful dealing with the energies that arouse them. On the other hand, both the form to deal with it more effectively, and the reactions that we associate with it are definite. There is no general training of the powers or faculties as far as we can determine. (Colvin, 1914, p. 232)

W. C. Ruediger, in his volume the *Principles of Education* took up the cudgel for formal discipline, though he rejected the idea of independent processes being trained or transferred. He also allowed for the possibilities of negative transfer. The evidence, he said,

. . . does not argue for an independence and discreteness of mental functions but for an interdependence and interrelation of such functions. This being true, we should expect not only that one function will assist another somewhat related function but that under different conditions the first would interfere with the second. (Colvin, 1914, p. 233)

He believed that such a position tolerated the continuance of the doctrine of formal discipline, while at the same time allowing Thorndike's identical elements their place, too.

. . . if we have analyzed the doctrine correctly (that of formal discipline), it is evident that its extreme advocates and its extreme opponents are both wrong. Knowledge and training are not merely specific in their application but they also have a general value. (Colvin, 1914, p. 233)

Defenders of formal discipline, such as Henderson and Ruediger, had attempted to salvage the doctrine, by acknowledging and qualifying its more glaring excesses and by attempting to divorce it from the grosser features of faculty psychology, the naiveties of which were becoming increasingly obvious (in their nineteenth century formats) in the bright light of scientific psychology. Still another attempt was made to remove formal discipline from its association with faculty psychology by Meikejohn, a logician, who presented a paper on the subject at a meeting of the New England Association of Colleges and Preparatory Schools at Boston University on October 8, 1908, which was later published in the *Educational Review* of February 1909. Meikejohn, in his paper, was trying to establish process as process, i.e., as ongoing activity rather than fixed substantive faculty or stabilized trait. In order to do so—and rescue formal discipline—he returned to the distinctions that Aristotle sought to make between form and content.

. . . discipline in certain discoverable forms of intellectual activity . . . does not imply the bad psychology of the faculties, it does imply the throughly sound and respectable distinction of form and content, which is made by the logician. (Colvin, 1914, p. 232)

But the critics of formal discipline, who were very powerful and influential, also made their voices heard. In his monograph *Mental Discipline and Educational Values* (1910), Heck announced that formal discipline was a pernicious influence, as well as a faulty doctrine, both theoretically and in practice. He agreed to Thorndike's principles of identical elements, including those of the second type; methodological and attitudinal transfer thus being accepted. But the idea of formal discipline, he believed, could not fully divorce itself from the doctrine of the faculties, which were clearly incompatible with current theories of brain localization. Further, habit training was specific and generalized habits not possible. Finally, there was a need for plain and simple practical training rather than broad mental exercises, for America's pupils. Thus he advised:

. . . the business and professional word relies more and more on the superiority of specialized ability resulting from specialized training, as a backlash to formal discipline with its extreme demands. (Colvin, 1914, p. 234)

It was opinions such as those of Heck's that carried the day over the course of the years that followed, even though the tide of transfer-of-training experiments was to turn against Thorndike's original gloomy position. And even though tried-and-true scholars persisted in defending the basic principles of formal discipline, what Thorndike had undone, no formal disciplinarian could reassemble. This ingenious, productive, hard-driving educational psychologist sought to destroy formal discipline, his science in the service of his politics. At the time, he was powerful enough to influence professional opinion his way, turn others around, and negate or at least dampen the voice of opponents. He had set out to destroy formal discipline as an acceptable doctrine of educational training, and he just about did. It was, when he got through with it, at least in full rout.

There were forces, however, other than those unleashed by Thorndike that were responsible for putting traditional formal discipline to flight. The Zeitgeist of the early decades of the twentieth century was one in which elementarism, structuralism, functionalism, behaviorism, and gestaltism were the "isms" of psychology. None of them, however, were theoretically congenial to faculty psychology,[11] least of all behaviorism, which had as its avowed goal the expunging of mentalism from psychology, once and for all. Faculties were decidedly mental, and formal

---

[11] Though faculty psychology managed to adapt to, borrow from, and contribute to all in its own peculiar chameleon ways. Earlier noted in this text was faculty psychology's precedence to functionalism, and its various alliances with associationism, as well as its being "born again" within test profiles.

discipline could never quite divorce itself from them. So there was less and less psychological support for the principles of formal discipline.[12]

DEWEY

Nor did formal discipline find any support from another dominant figure of early twentieth century education. The nation's teachers were swayed by the writings of John Dewey, and he did not favor disciplinary approaches; they were antithetical to his own brand of "naturalism"—not that Dewey did not believe in training the mind. But such training, as far as he was concerned, was to come out of natural learning experiences and utilitarian goal-oriented study.

Discovery of typical modes of activity, whether play or useful occupations, in which individuals are concerned, in whose outcome they recognize they have something at stake . . . is the remedy . . . the root of the error long prevalent in the conception of training of minds consists in leaving out of account movements of things to future results in which an individual shares. . . . (Dewey, 1916, p. 156)

Dewey did not altogether deny those favorite processes of faculty psychologists—observation, recollection, imagination, memory, reflection, reason, etc. He wrote of "enlisting" them in a pupil's education—however, not via formal discipline.

. . . ability to train thought is not achieved merely by knowledge of the best forms of thought. Possession of this information is no guarantee for ability to think well. Moreover, there are no set exercises in correct thinking whose repeated performance will cause one to be a good thinker. The information and the exercises are both of value. But no individual realizes their value except as he is personally animated by certain dominant attitudes in his own character. . . . Similarly it is highly questionable whether the practice of thinking in accordance with some logical formula results in creation of a general habit of thinking, namely one applicable over a range of subjects. (Dewey, 1933, p. 29)

Dewey's followers, by and large, echoed their master's position against formal discipline. Kilpatrick appears to have gone particularly far in this respect. Also W. A. Saucier, a latter-day Deweyite. Saucier believed that the mind is trained through "doing," directed toward the social goals that are the ultimate aims of education in a democratic society. Thus formal discipline, to him, was a capriciously arbitrary and contrived approach to developing the mind, and it was to be avoided.

[12] Within special education, faculty psychology has rarely had difficulty justifying itself, so that cognitive training of the handicapped had, and continues to have, a fertile theoretical base from which to operate.

When we discard the concept of formal discipline, we cease . . . to place a premium upon abstract or "exact" subjects for the improvement of intelligence. On the contrary we recognize that practice on social problems in the whole school program is essential in the preparation of the individual. . . . If thinking is limited to narrow fields in school, it will probably be limited outside the school. For improvements in habits of thinking, thinking need not be and must not be separated from action or the development of skills. . . . What the pupil needs is to be placed in positions where intelligence will function in the development of skills, as it does in the solution of problems. (Saucier, 1937, pp. 159–160)

FORMAL DISCIPLINE FURTHER DEFENDED AND CHALLENGED

The struggle between process and product tilted in favor of process, and mental training gave way to subject content and information in curriculum texts as the century wore on. W. M. Bobbit (1918, 1924), W. W. Charters (1923), and J. L. Meriam (1920) all wrote curricular treatises that expressed antidisciplinarian biases. There were still a few "last hurrahs" left in the disciplinarian camp, however, even in these respects. Bagley persisted in emphasizing cognitive training. Shorey issued an impassioned plea in its behalf on the basis of "common sense" and opinions offered by "educated and practical men." His 1919 exhortation is worth repeating:

There is no science of psychology, sociology, or pedagogy that can pronounce with any authority on either the aims or methods of education . . . nor provide proof . . . that mental discipline is a myth. . . . There is no authentic deliberance of science . . . to oppose the vast presumption of common-sense and the belief of the majority of educated and practical men. (Shorey, 1910, pp. 598,607,608)

Some major educators like Chapman and Counts, in their *Principles of Education,* tried to salvage formal discipline by disengaging it from faculty psychology and recasting it in modern psychological terms. They were even willing to use Thorndike's theory of connectionism to explain its results.

If the theory of mental discipline depended upon the so called faculty psychology for its validity, it could be given instant dismissal. All psychologists are now agreed that it is not legitimate to regard the mind as an aggregation of various independent faculties, each of which can receive a separate training. Modern investigation shows that the mind is not departmental but unified in its activity. The "memory," "observation," "reasoning," and "imagination" of the faculty psychologists are not separate powers which can be developed in isolation but rather different aspects of the working of a mechanism which always functions as a unit. When the individual reasons, it is not some specialized faculty, analagous to a large muscle, which is in operation, but a host of connections involving a large part of the nervous system. The faculty theory has given way to the modern doctrine of a mind made up of a multitude of connections integrated together to control behavior. But the abandonment of the old faculty psychology does not shatter, as many believe, the theory of mental discipline. Our manner of statement makes it still a tenable theory, even though the faculty psychology is moribund. To restate the question, do not some studies leave behind in the individual pursuing them certain intellectual powers of wide application which are so valuable, and so economically imparted through these studies that, quite apart from any direct and obvious relation of their content to life activities, they should find a place in the curriculum. (Chapman and Counts, 1924, p. 388)

Chapman and Counts were valiantly trying to keep formal discipline afloat. No, they were not concerned with faculties; faculties were moribund. But, of course, there were intellectual powers, habits or procedures to be trained; perish the thought that they should be confused with faculties. Their names suggested otherwise? Inquiry, concentration, persistence, open-mindedness, integrity, disavowal, demonstration, analysis, generalization, application, self-reliance. These were the "more significant" intellectual powers that formal discipline could train; Reid, Gall, and McDougal would have been comfortable with them. As to their training, Chapman and Counts would have none of the "egalitarianism" of curricula that an elective-happy academic world was proposing. Electives, they said, were

. . . too often justified by the erroneous theory that each subject taught by a human teacher is of equal value from the standpoint of training . . . but one isn't fed but merely puffed up by disorganized knowledge. For the quick and sure return which content teaching gives, we must not sacrifice the values accruing from an education which includes procedures of wide range of application in the most important activities of life. (Chapman and Counts, 1924, p. 398)

Chapman and Counts then proposed an approach to curriculum that was of classical formal disciplinary dimensions, even if connectionism was evoked to explain their whys.

With reference to . . . the relative values of different subjects in inculcating sound intellectual habits, it is idle to say that all subjects have equal value from this standpoint. For purposes of exposition these intellectual powers will henceforth be referred to as procedures. As far as the school or college curriculum is concerned today, one may almost venture the statement that the correlation between content values and procedure values is low. In the languages, in mathematics, and in the exact sciences, if loose thinking takes place, the erring student is at once brought to book. If, in German, a wrong case is used, if, in physics, a wrong method is employed, there is scarcely need to bring home to the student the consciousness of his failure to grasp the fundamental principles; his failure is writ large. To produce the same inner conviction of error in the descriptive studies such as English, history, civics, and sociology is quite impossible. In other words, loose thinking can be punished in certain subjects in a more effective way than in others. It is a mere platitude of psychology that the results of undesirable connections must be readily recognizable by the student; likewise when undesirable connections are made they must be apparent. Hence a subject which brings these facts inevitably to the notice of the pupil has a very great pedagogical value. Can it be seriously maintained that all subjects fulfill this fundamental law of learning to the same degree? The student who fails to solve a problem in geometry is cognizant of his own shortcomings—in such clear-cut fields there is no "shuffling." Lax procedure and lax thinking fail to yield the product desired, and nobody is more clearly aware of the fact than the student himself. The student in other subjects, which are more speculative and therefore less exact, indulges in equally loose thinking, but from the very nature of the subject, he is not so painfully conscious of the lacunae in the process. (Chapman and Counts, 1924, pp. 390–391)

It sounds familiar all of this, both within and without a formal disciplinarian framework. It was late afternoon for formal discipline. Nevertheless, scholars continued to speak out in favor of formal discipline well beyond that time.

. . . an intellect properly disciplined, an intellect properly habituated, is an intellect able to operate well in all fields. (Hutchins, 1936, p. 63)

. . . education is the process by which those powers of . . . of men that are susceptible to habituation are perfected by good habits. (Adler, 1942, p. 209)

. . . the original theory of Formal discipline was poorly stated in terms of the training of faculties . . . learning properly under optimum conditions leads one to "learn how to learn" . . . (Bruner, 1961, pp. 5–6)

But formal discipline in its original form needed more than positive results from transfer-of-training experiments or expressions of faith from authorities to survive as it once was. It became declassé because of its associations with a doctrine of processes that, at the time, appeared to most psychologists and educators to be invalid, and because of its commitment to a tradition of instruction that appeared ever more anachronistic to the advances of technology. Besides, people were simply tired of it. The show had to go on, yes; but please, some other show. Progressive education, efficiency movements, all right. Conditioned responses, *habs,* and *pavs,* laws of effect and reinforcement; very well, let us allow a cognitive map for Tolman's sake. But a mind to be strengthened through training? Egad! R.I.P. Formal D.

So, despite the little bands of supporters who held out, for a while we heard little about formal discipline, except as an example of what bad education used to be. However, as classical behaviorism loosened its grip and intervening variables were allowed to keep company with hypothetical constructs, cognitive psychology became respectable again. Cognitive processes could now be spoken about in public, and their training suggested. Even in the most austere circles, there were people teaching pupils to learn how to learn, structures of intellects, different kinds of intelligence. Could curricula with magical mind-enhancing powers be far behind? Read Bloom's taxonomies to see it all long ago, but not so long ago.

Not quite formal discipline, you say? But look at the baby's expression and tell me if you do not see its parents' features aglimmering.

As this book is being completed, calls for more rigorous curricula to create more rigorous minds have received support from very recent events. As institutions of basic and higher learning have loosened standards, allowed more electives, demanded less from students, there has been a decided decline in academic skill areas—and in what appear to be cognitive ability areas as well. Has this decline been due to the failure of the schools to exercise their disciplinary roles? Or is it a matter of not enough, or the wrong, content? Or is it a matter of not enough form and content? We shall not decide in these pages. But read the laments of commentators on America's academic decline, and see their fingers pointing at intellectually pabulumized, overindulged, and undisciplined students. Hear the call that the latter be exposed to the rigors of academic curricula that will develop their logical processes, their intellectual control, their characters. And you will find formal discipline smiling through.

22

The Beginnings of Process Training within Special Education

INTRODUCTION

Herbert Woodrow, writing from the time perspective of his book *Brightness and Dullness in Children* (1919), observed that the major principle guiding special education of the cognitively handicapped—from Itard to his time—was that

> . . . education should deal with the training of mental functions. It clearly implies the existence of mental faculties of powers, and aims directly at the training of these powers. . . . Its excellence is shown by results . . . from the time of Itard down to the present. . . . (Woodrow, 1919, p. 283)

And so it was that most of the efforts of special educators, great and small, European and American, well into the current century were guided by the notion of specific mental abilities, either to be trained, strengthened or corrected when undeveloped or weak or to be taught or relied upon when strong. The ancient doctrines of faculty psychology and formal discipline, battered about though they might be elsewhere, were to receive a warm reception at the hands of those who worked with the mentally retarded or otherwise cognitively disabled—beginning with the work of Jean-Marc-Gaspard Itard (1775–1838).

This began in the face of what appeared to be an almost complete victory at the time for those archenemies of traditional faculty psychologists, the associationists. The revolution in the conception of the mind that the British and French empiricists had wrought was, to be sure, not gainsaid by special education's commitment to the training of faculties. Itard and Séguin, to name two major figures, were both great admirers of

John Locke and of others within the empiricist movement who had struck out violently at the notion of innate powers and innate ideas. But associationism, nee empiricism, which Locke, Hume, Hartley, and their successors espoused, conceived of the mind not as consisting of diverse, broad mental powers that were basic givens, but rather as a complex composition developing out of elementary sensory and motor elements and the products of their associations. These latter, in various primary and secondary constellations, made up all there was to say about the mind, the way it functioned, and what it did. Special education was to be dominated by associationist dogmas from its very earliest years. How then could it also commit itself to what were essentially faculty doctrines, which associationism's credos denied?

There is no unresolvable paradox here—the commitment of special education to both associationism and faculty psychology, despite their fundamental opposition—because at this juncture of our history, such possibilities of the improbable are already familiar to us. We have, in fact, encountered these seemingly noncongenial bedfellows in miscegenational embrace before, have we not? John Locke talked bravely of the mind as a tabula rasa, upon which experiences were to write their tales in the form of mind. But neither he nor most of his predecessors and successors were ever quite able to do entirely without some basic and innate faculties or powers to manage these experiences (though Hume and Hartley gave it a good go). And if such as Locke could not guard the empty slate of experience well enough to permanently bar faculties from scribbling upon it, why should Itard and his successors have worried themselves about theoretical incongruities? They did not, and mixtures of sensory-motor associationism and faculty psychology have ever more dominated special education.[1]

The most direct effort toward the reconciliation of faculty psychology and associationism for purposes of training the cognitively impaired, however, did not come from John Locke. Rather it is Etienne Bonnet de Condillac who is our hero here. He of the statue, equipped with the physical structures of the human body but without sensations or mind, a statue gradually acquiring knowledge with the awakening of its senses, one at a time beginning with touch, and out of such knowledge developing cognitive faculties.

CONDILLAC

Because Condillac (1715–1780) had such a profound influence upon Itard's theories of practices of cognitive training, and those also of Séguin

---

[1] Nor have they done badly within other forms of education.

(though to a lesser degree), and because process training of the cognitively impaired begins with Itard and Séguin, it is fitting that we begin our consideration of specific worthies in this chapter with him. Edward J. Power, in his book *Main Currents in the History of Education,* while, in fact acknowledging Condillac's role in educational history, remarks that his general neglect in most other histories is "no great historical crime" (1962). It might well be in a history of special education and of process training.

Condillac was a more radical sensationalist than Locke, though at first he was at Locke-step with the English philosopher. In his first publication, *Essay on the Origin of Human Knowledge* (1754) he allowed for ideas developed on the basis of reflection, as well as directly from sensory information, in keeping with Locke's distinction. In his later *Treatise on Sensations* (1754), he proceeded to do away with this distinction. In *Treatise,* he sought to show that all ideas, mental operations, and functions could and should be reduced to sensations, stating therein that ". . . in the natural order all knowledge arises from sensations . . ." that "even the knowledge attributed to the higher cognitive processes was a matter of transformed sensations" (Lucas, 1972, p. 339).[2] Isaiah Berlin, in his book *The Age of Enlightenment: The Eighteenth Century Philosophers,* discusses Condillac's position on the role of sensation in the construction of the mind and its contents:[3]

> Condillac undertakes to reconstruct every human experience—the most complex and sophisticated thoughts or "movements of the soul," the most elaborate play of the imagination, the most subtle scientific speculation—out of "simple" ideas, that is, sensations classifiable as being given to one or the other of our normal senses, each of which can, as it were, be pin-pointed and assigned to its rightful place in the stream of sensations. (Berlin, 1956, pp. 266–268)

This lay the groundwork for the programs of sense training that Itard was to later undertake. In fact, Condillac likened the mind to a sense organ, or sensing mechanism, comparable to the eye, and to be developed like the body through exercise. He also discussed the development of the sensory powers (perceptual powers, actually) as proceeding according to an orderly methodological scheme, active, rather than passive, in nature.

---

[2] The reader is referred to the first part of this book to review Condillac's statue as to the manner in which this could be accomplished.

[3] Berlin asserts that Condillac exerted a stronger influence upon European naturalism than usually assumed. It is possible that his thinking played a greater role in that of Rousseau's than he is given credit for. The two men knew each other, and their writings overlapped. Much of his systematic breakdown of the acquisition of perception and his suggestions for the orderly step-by-step training of cognitive processes resemble those of Pestalozzi. His ideas concerning the presence of higher cognitive functions in the operation of lower ones we have encountered in our earlier chapters.

Sensations are to be acquired in an orderly fashion so that the ideas obtained therefrom will be orderly. Perception successively analyzes an object by mentally decomposing it and then recomposing it; thus its essential qualities can be isolated and utilized for higher cognitive purposes. In properly perceiving objects, the subject, Condillac said, (1) observes them, (2) notes their relationships, (3) notes the intervals that exist between them, (4) observes the secondary objects that occupy the intervals between the principal objects being perceived, and (5) compares all of these. Then, after recognizing the objects as being particular and discrete, identifying their forms and situations, and comparing them, a "collective and simultaneous concept" can be formed (Gutek, 1972).

This might suggest that the senses are to be singled out for special training. Condillac, however, refused to separate the senses from the rest of the mind. The operation of the higher cognitive faculties are present in the operation of the senses from their very beginning. The senses do not constitute separate, independent faculties and are not to be trained as senses through specific sensory exercises, but rather through the exercise of "the faculties of understanding," which he observed ". . . are the same in a child as a grown-up man" (Boyd and King, 1969). Reasoning thus, he made the following assertion:

It is proved then, that the faculty of reasoning appears thus as soon as our senses develop; and that we have the use of our senses at an early age, only because we have reasoned at an early age. (Lucas, 1972, p. 339)[4]

In another passage in his treatise, he provides examples of this assertion:

We judge objects by touch, only because we have learned to judge. In effect, since the size of an object depends on its relation to other objects, we must compare it with other objects and judge whether it differs from them by less or more, if we are to form an idea of its size. It is the same with ideas of distance, of shape and of weight. In a word, all the ideas that come to us through touch presuppose comparisons and judgment. (Boyd and King, 1969, p. 289)

So with touch, the most important and primordial of senses to Condillac; so also with the other senses that follow touch in their development. His later book, intended to guide instruction for the Prince of Parma, Louis XV's grandson, the *Course of Instruction* (1775) (totaling some 13 volumes) began by calling for the training of judgment and reasoning, rather than the senses, as the primary goal of education.

We should keep Condillac's thinking in mind when we examine Itard's monumental step forward in the education of the mentally retarded. The higher functions, the higher processes, were to be the ultimate object of his

[4] The association of perceptual functioning and that of the higher cognitive processes from birth is an oft repeated hypothecation from Aristotle on.

training, even though that training began at the sensory level. Within so-called perceptual operations are the operations of the higher cognitive processes. When Séguin complained about Itard's theoretical errors (while making his own) he was alluding to Itard's commitment to Condillac's theories.

ITARD

When Victor, the wild boy of Aveyron, appeared on the Parisian scene at the close of the eighteenth century, Condillac was strongly in vogue in France. Victor appeared, to theorists and public alike, to offer a splendid opportunity for demonstrating in vivo the values of Condillac's theories. However, when initial attempts to train him failed, interest rapidly declined. The boy was pronounced a hopeless idiot by the most distinguished medical authorities and delivered to the hands of Abbé de Sicard to be managed at the National Institute for Deaf Mutes. And Victor's tale probably would not have survived as more than a historical footnote, had it not been for the presence of a young French physician who took more than a passing interest in it. For Jean-Marc-Gaspard Itard (1774–1838), despite expert opinion that Victor was mentally retarded, persisted in perceiving Victor's problems as deriving from a lack of proper sensory experiences, thus providing an opportunity (given enough time) of proving Condillac's theories upon him.

Séguin provides us with a capsule summary of the events leading up to Itard's momentous commitment to Victor's education:

At the time that the wild boy of Aveyron was brought to Paris, people thought they had found Condillac's statue, an animated machine, that only needed to be touched in the right places for it to produce the operations of the mind . . . but the wonderment soon dissipated when confronted with the reality, disgust replaced enthusiasm, and the unhappy boy was abandoned . . . before Doctor Itard laid claim to him. Allied with the philosophers of his time, a philosopher himself as much as anyone, and, moreover, a brilliant theoretician, though guided by the accepted psychology of the period, he put all his originality and his devotion in the service of the *sauvage de l'Aveyron* or, to speak more precisely, in the service of the current Metaphysics. (Lane, 1976, p. 92)

To Itard go many firsts. Those in which we are interested in this volume concern his pioneer efforts in process training, which have been admirably documented by Itard himself and memorably discussed more recently by Harlan Lane (1976).

I have already observed that Itard's efforts with Victor were based on Condillac's particular ideas of "mind" and how it was to be trained. Lane also credits Condillac with influencing Itard on the basis of his shift of educational theory from an emphasis on subject matter to pupil-based and directed ("in strict psychological progression") instruction. Lane contrasts Condillac's educational conceptions with those of other educational revolutionaries of the eighteenth and nineteenth centuries, specifically Rousseau, Comenius, and Pestalozzi. In Lane's analysis, they suffer by comparison because, unlike Condillac's pupil-based orientation toward instruction, theirs were based on "a priori, external principles" (Lane, 1976, p. 93). It was by following in Condillac's theoretical footprints and ". . . by shifting the focus of instruction from material to the learner . . ." that Itard founded a new movement in education (Lane, 1976, p. 95).

Lane's analysis appears to unduly credit Condillac with a "first" in espousing instruction directed to the learner and his characteristics. The history of education presents a variety of other earlier similar espousements. Lane also appears to be guilty of denigrating the pupil orientations of Comenius, Rousseau, and Pestalozzi. Despite their adherence to "a priori, external principles," these worthies were very much concerned with teaching their pupils as individuals, while Condillac, after all, was also guided by a priori principles, i.e., those of empiricism and associationism. That Itard launched, as Lane states, "a new movement in education" is, however, incontrovertible. It is with him that modern efforts at cognitive intervention with the intellectually impaired begins.

Turning back to Itard now, it is to be observed that his training efforts with Victor took place in two stages. During the first, the young physician refused to accept the opinion of experts to the effect that Victor was an incurable idiot. He chose, rather, to view Victor's deficiencies as the consequence of his having been deprived from birth of social companionship and of any form of education. In response to the prevailing prognostications of experts as to the boy's ineducability, Itard proposed (as Lane has observed) that all that was required to restore Victor to the world of men was a program of training that would ". . . teach the boy the distinctions, categories, needs, language and mental processes that were normally the unprogrammed results of socialization" (Lane, 1976, p. 74). He called his approach "medico-psychological" treatment; it was based on the analytic approach to knowledge proposed by Condillac.

A precise observer, Itard provided education with its first detailed records of a pupil's behavior. On the basis of an early analysis of progress achieved with Victor, he decided that the major components of the wild boy's problems were sensory, motivational, and verbal. Treatment was to follow along the lines of this analysis, beginning with sensory activities and moving up to language and abstract thought. Within his general program, Victor's needs were to be used as spurs to engage him in desired behaviors.

After about a year, Itard was forced to admit Victor's fundamental cognitive limitations. Thus commenced a new program, one described by

Séguin as being the result of Itard's ". . . secret consciousness of his error in diagnosis . . ." which ". . . forced him to link his labors to more scientific traditions" (Séguin, 1856, p. 22). It was clearly in the vein of faculty psychology embracing:

1. the development of the senses
2. the development of intellectual faculties, e.g., attention, reflection, and memory
3. The development of affective functions

While the preceding had also been objectives of Itard's earlier training efforts, they were to be addressed now by procedures considerably more precise and systematic.

Itard established priorities for his efforts to train Victor's senses. Hearing was given first consideration (remember Itard also was teacher of the deaf), then vision, followed by touch, smell, and taste. Itard's relative lack of concern with touch is somewhat surprising in light of Condillac's emphasis upon this sense's primacy among the others.

Itard was later to be chided by Séguin for insufficient training of this modality, as well as for his neglect of gross motor training. However, Séguin's criticisms of Itard on these latter two counts may be somewhat unfair. In truth, Victor seemed to be relatively adept in motor activities, fine though gross, as expressed in activities from bean shelling to tree climbing. He was also exposed to manipulative opportunities in the course of his training in the other "modalities."

Smell had a particular low priority in Itard's training schemes:

. . . since the sense of smell is much more closely bound up with the exercise of digestive functions than with the development of intellectual faculties. . . . (Lane, 1976, p. 138)

Victor was, in any case, a sniffer, who relied on his nose as a general guide so that his sense of smell did not suffer too much from his trainer's attitude of benign neglect. The boy's taste was to be improved, as behooved a Frenchman even of savage antecedents, through a widening of his preferences in food and drink.

Itard's aim in sensory training was to both generally stimulate Victor's nervous system (a notion that Séguin was later to particularly latch onto) and to specifically train the individual senses—and the higher cognitive powers through them. His modality training techniques essentially sought to teach the boy to make ever-finer discriminations through his senses. To train Victor to manage distinctions in temperature, to which the boy appeared to be insensitive, he was at first required to discriminate between extreme contrasts of hot and cold; and then, by gradually decreasing temperature differences, helped to develop finer thermal discriminations (Kirk and Johnson, 1951).

To improve his sense of touch, Victor was taught to discriminate objects, again, proceeding from the gross to the fine. He learned to discriminate between a key and coin money; between a stone and a chestnut; up to the differentiation of metal letters such as B and R, I and J, C and G, and between chestnuts and acorns.

In order to improve Victor's auditory powers, the boy was blindfolded and taught to distinguish between various sounds, moving from gross distinctions between those emitted by a bell and a drum to discriminations made between various sounds of the human voice. Victor even managed to learn to distinguish between certain vowels. His excessive emotional reactions, both of frustration and joy, during auditory training limited progress in this sphere (Kirk and Johnson, 1951).

Visual training followed the same teaching principles of contrast, comparison, and discrimination that were used with the other senses. Through training in this modality, Victor was able to progress from simple distinctions between large and small objects to the identification of certain written words, even to the point of "reading" and "writing" them, though he made no great progress with language, either oral or written.

Itard's attempts to teach Victor to speak produced discouraging results. Auditory training, the association of words with objects, and other techniques found successful with the deaf were to no avail with Victor. The boy, except for occasional utterances, remained a mute.

As to higher cognitive processes, Itard, as an associationist strongly influenced by Locke and even more strongly by Condillac, sought to train higher mental powers through the senses (though it might be more correct to say that he viewed the higher cognitive processes as being inevitably drawn into play—and trained—when the senses were trained).

> . . . while I was limiting my efforts to exercising the senses of our savage, the mind took its share of the attention given exclusively to the education of these organs, and followed the same order of development. It is readily understandable that in instructing his senses to perceive and distinguish new objects I forced his attention to fix on them, his judgment to compare them, and his memory to retain them. . . . Everything engaged his mind. Everything put the faculties of his intelligence into play and prepared them for the great work of communicating ideas. (Lane, 1976, p. 134)

Cognitive training also proceeded through training Victor in speech and then in reading. To teach Victor to read, Itard attempted to teach the boy to relate various objects to their printed significates. He found, however, that while Victor could learn to identify a specific object with a printed word, any change in objects requiring generalization, e.g., the substitution of a large knife for a small one, confused the boy. Learning through this avenue, as through others, was extremely limited.

Séguin was to regard Itard's efforts at training the higher cognitive powers as being deficient in both conception and execution, though a "sublime attempt." Itard failed, said the student of his master, since:

> Relying in his studies, as well as in his faith, on the materialism of Locke and Condillac, his teaching sometimes reached the senses of his pupil but never penetrated to his mind and soul; he gave to his senses certain notions of things, he even excited some physical sensibility to the caresses bestowed upon him; but the boy remained destitute of ideas and of social or moral feelings, incapable of labor and, consequently, of independence. (Séguin, 1856, p. 146)

Séguin's criticisms of Itard in the above instance, as well as in others, were always given with full appreciation of his teacher's great achievements and proper priorities in cognitive training. While others, like the French psychiatrist Phillipe Pinel, scorned the total of Itard's accomplishments. Posterity's verdict we know.

SÉGUIN

In the year 1837, Itard was asked by Geursant, Director of the Children's Hospital of Paris, to accept one of the "idiots" in the hospital for language instruction. Itard demurred because of his age, but agreed to direct the efforts of another physician, if one suitable to the task could be found. The eventual choice was Edouard Séguin, who served as a student both to Itard and psychiatrist Jean-Etienne-Dominique Esquirol, a formidable diagnostician. Séguin (1812–1880) was destined to become the formalizer of Itard's notions into what came to be known as physiological education.

Séguin threw himself into his work with first one and then many mentally defective pupils with a fervor and enthusiasm that was to earn for him the title of "Apostle of the Idiots." He did so in the face of established medical opinion which considered idiots "incurable" and "hopeless." Esquirol had expressed the general view of the medical community when he wrote in the second edition of the prestigious *Dictionnaire des Sciences Médicales*, "It is useless to combat idiocy" (Lane, 1976, p. 263).

Séguin, however, was a member of a group of reformers who espoused the revolutionary doctrines, religious and social, of Henri Saint-Simon. This group sought at personal sacrifice, to assist *les miserables* of France. Séguin's choice of unfortunates was, of course, mental defectives; and he was later to be critical of those who studied idiots simply for scientific purposes. His efforts were always clearly guided by humanitarian concerns, though he showed a fair share of personal egotism concerning his contributions to medicine and education.

The results of Séguin's early educational efforts with the mentally retarded were sufficiently promising to even draw encomiums from Esquirol, who was decidedly sour about any attempts to educate idiots. An extended account of Séguin's educational accomplishments is, however, appropriately the topic of a broad history of special education. Our interest within this text is in Séguin's theories and techniques of process training.

In keeping with neurological distinctions between the peripheral and central nervous systems that the physiology of his era clearly stressed, Séguin distinguished two types of feeblemindedness, or idiocy. There is superficial feeblemindedness, in which the central nervous system (CNS) is intact but not properly developing or functioning because a weakened or damaged peripheral nervous system does not effectively transmit information. Then there is profound feeblemindedness, in which the CNS itself is impaired.

In superficial feeblemindedness, since the CNS was considered intact, Séguin's intended training was directed specifically to the peripheral nervous system through sense and muscle, to strengthen it and facilitate its managing of signals to and from the CNS. For the profound condition, the CNS was bombarded through the senses to stimulate its functioning. The actual techniques used for the latter were, however, essentially the same as those used with peripheral defectiveness. The reader will readily recognize Itard's own conceptions within such training stratagems.

Séguin, like Itard, was strongly influenced by the work of the empiricists, particularly by Condillac. He was also influenced directly by faculty psychology; in fact, it appears from some of his writings that he was more than just a closet convert to some of Gall's phrenological views.

Séguin's empiricist convictions are clearly evident in the sensory-motor emphasis of his training methodologies. His adherence to faculty doctrines reveals itself in his interests in higher cognitive faculties (i.e., those processes not directly based on the senses) and in the adaptive purposes to which cognitive processes are directed. These interests led him to seek ways of directly training or remediating the higher faculties and found expression as well in his attempts to develop utilitarian capabilities and skills.

Séguin was neither consistent nor clear in the exposition of his theories; it is often difficult to understand what he intended in his pronouncements. He seems reasonably clear when he discusses the development of the "imperfect sense organs" of the mentally defective through exercise. We are somewhat less sure what he means by his statements that he aimed "to lead the child from the education of the muscular system, to that of the nervous system and the senses . . . from the education of the senses to general notions, from general notions to

abstract thought, from abstract thought to morality'' (Wallin, 1924, p. 17).
Are such statements ones of philosophical position or a curriculum guide?
Did Séguin mean that sensory-motor training would eventually culminate
in the training of higher cognitive processes, or that the two go hand in
hand? We have noted earlier, Séguin was critical of Itard for just such a
"superficial" approach. There are ambiguities enough in Séguin's writing
to engage the interest of a talmudic scholar. Let us fiddle with his ideas
still further.

The conception of the mind and its faculties developing through the
modalities (and within these we must include the muscular system) is
clearly suggested by Séguin's writing:

. . . the senses, and each one in particular, can be submitted to physiological
training by which their primordial capability may be indefinitely intellectualized
. . . our most abstract ideas are comparisons and generalizations by the mind of
what we have perceived through our senses . . . educating the modes of perception is to prepare pabulum for the mind proper . . . sensations are intellectual
functions performed through external apparatus as much as reasoning, imagination, etc., through more internal organs. (Séguin, 1866, pp. 24–25)

The notion of training higher cognitive processes through the modalities is further supported by Séguin's contentions that as a consequence
of the "artificial training" provided by the schools of his day,

. . . the sensorial and intellectual development of children appear quite
disconnected, nay, effectively rendered antagonistic; the overcultivation of one
causing the drooping of the other; the exclusive training of the function impairing
the faculty, the exclusive training of the faculty atrophying the function. Contrar-
ily to this practice, we say, the exercise of each function must give rise to a
corresponding exercise of the complementary faculty . . . and each sense must be
taught as a function, and taught besides as a faculty. (Séguin, 1866, p. 137)

This raises a question, however: What is a function and what is a
faculty? Thomas Ball, in his study of Itard, Séguin, and Kephart (1971)
suggests that Séguin meant the passive aspects of a process by his use of
the term "function," while by "faculty" he meant its active side. Yet
Séguin refers to a variety of "active" functions.[5] Is one to interpret
function as passive when Séguin discussed the "functions" of extending
the arm, grasping "looking . . . raising the spine to the sitting posture
. . . hearing voices . . . reproducing them. . . ." and also described functions
as becoming capabilities. (Séguin, 1866, pp. 87–88).

Wallin (1924) would have us believe that Séguin intended function to
imply the physiological stratum of a process and faculty to represent its
cognitive side. This premise is supported by statements that sensations
become "idealized," i.e., turned into ideas, by the process of comparison
representing the principle of contrast.

[5] And remember his phrenological beliefs.

To contradict this interpretation, however, Séguin in places fleshed his functions out cognitively to a considerable degree. Thus we read about the functions of the "auditory apparatus" which includes "auditing, listening, selecting, and repelling sounds" and of visual functions that involve the perception of color, forms, dimensions, distances, plans, etc. Functions thus described certainly imply more than mere physiological registration.

In some places, it would appear that Séguin intended lower cognitive powers to be assigned to the peripheral nervous system by his use of the term "function," while higher cognitive powers, residing and operating in the central parts of the nervous system, achieved faculty status. His remarks that sensations are "intellectual functions performed through the external apparatus . . . reasoning, imagination, etc. through more internal organs" suggests this interpretation.

So does the distinction that Séguin made between problems induced in learning by the errors of the senses and those of the higher sensorium.

But in reading, as in all intellectual operations which take place immediately through the senses, we have to distinguish for the perfection of the teaching, the function from the faculty. This temporary analysis favors the development of the two aspects of the same capacity.[6] By striving to give at the start correct perceptions through a sense, we insure correct impressions to the sensorium, impressions which will be the premises of sound judgments for the mind. What is called error, scarcely ever depends upon false conclusions of the intellect, but mostly on false premises gotten from incorrect perceptions; so that the faculty of judging is not so often the culprit, as is the function of observation; what is badly seen is wrongly judged of; and our future is too often the stake we pay for the error of our senses." (Séguin, 1866, p. 184)

Have we reached any conclusions as to what is function and faculty? Then they are confounded when we read about "elevating functions to the intellectual excellence of faculties . . . and training faculties . . . as if they were simple functions" (Séguin, 1866, p. 192). When, in talking about memory, he states that it must be trained through ". . . its double aspect of perceiving and expressing . . . impressions . . . at first, as if they were independent functions whose convergence produces later the complete faculty" (Séguin, 1866, p. 194), Séguin might have been suggesting that a faculty is a unit of broad capacity, a function, a particular aspect of it. But do we know?[7]

Small wonder that Binet was somewhat contemptuous and most considerably exasperated by his reading of Séguin's work.

Séguin's work must not be examined too closely; those who praise it have

[6] One presumes he meant reading.

[7] Perhaps Séguin was simply trying to be a good Aristotelean. We find much the same distinction between function and faculty in Aristotle's theories of perception; though Aristotle was not at all interested in the training aspects of such.

certainly not read it. Séguin impresses us as an empiric, endowed with great personal talent, which he has not succeeded in embodying clearly in his works. These contain some pages of good sense, with many obscurities and many absurdities. . . . One might make many criticisms . . . but to what end? We prefer to say of such predecessors what Ingres said to his pupils in the Rubens Gallery at the Louvre, "Salute them, but pay no attention to them." (Kirk and Johnson, 1951, p. 85)

What of Séguin's actual training methods? Motor training, or more properly sensory-motor training, is the first "volume" in his curriculum of physiological education. There are described in it isolated didactic exercises (and equipment) for specific motor and sensory functions, and exercises and plays that are elaborations of ordinary daily activities. There are also gymnastics to engage the pupil's entire body in sequence—from feet to legs, legs to torso, torso to shoulders, and on up to and through the arms, wrists, hands, and finally the fingers. Séguin placed great store on training hands and fingers, particularly in light of their theoretical implications in learning. Remember Condillac's emphasis on touch for cognitive training. The hands and fingers as well as the senses lead the way to one's mind.

Second in priority to motor training to Séguin was the strengthening and remediation of the sensory modalities, he recommended that these be trained both in conjunction with motor training and separately. Unlike his predecessor, Itard, Séguin gave touch priority in modality training. It is the fundamental modality from which Condillac said all other senses were derived. It was also considered the primary sense by Pereire, a successful educator of the deaf, whose work had greatly impressed and influenced Séguin. After touch, came the training of visual, auditory, taste, and smell modalities.

Special rooms or surroundings were recommended for the training of each of the senses. Taste and smell can be exercized in the same room. Hearing requires a specialized room. The "gymnastics of sight" require extended space and have to be carried on outdoors, as well as within, to assure effectiveness.

Séguin's modality training procedures were extensions of Itard's, thus touch is to be trained, a la Séguin, by presenting the child with various shapes, sizes, textures, temperatures, weights, etc. The auditory sense is to be trained to discriminate general sounds, then to recognize musical scales, and then vocal expression. The education of visual abilities includes the discrimination of color, forms, dimensions, distances, and planes. Visual training should often proceed through manipulatives, the importance of the hand as a teacher of the eye being stressed. Language is to be trained through oral speech, reading, and writing.

Séguin had been rather denigratory of Itard's efforts to train higher cognitive processes. He had found his mentor too sense bound and too materialistic. But he himself could not produce much that was new or original to improve upon Itard's work in this respect. He bombarded the senses to reach and stimulate the faculties associated with them and to pass through to higher ones located within the centers of the CNS. He trained the higher powers through various modality approaches. But how was this in any way better than what Itard had done? Except in terms of deeper progressions and greater complications of training and greater involvement of language. Séguin himself at one point rather sadly remarked:

> We can, up to a certain point, oblige the senses to perceive a notion, since the senses are susceptible to environmental control, whereas we do not know how to oblige reasoning to function. (Lane, 1976, pp. 275–276)

And so in the end, Séguin was forced to fall back on the techniques that Itard had first employed to approach the higher processes —exercises in discrimination and concept learning via modality training— though, it is true, with a much greater emphasis upon manipulatives. Since this patently wasn't enough, Séguin also adapted a variant of formal discipline to train higher cognitive processes. It was not Latin or Greek that Séguin had his students learn. Rather, his emphasis was upon basic academics, gymnastics, games and workaday skills. If these did not improve higher cognitive processes, at least some of his pupils learned something of use in their lives; this utilitarian side of his process training efforts was in contrast to the more "formal" process training approaches accepted as proper mental discipline by most cognitive trainers in his day—for which Kilpatrick gave him commendation (1914).

Séguin was more than enthusiastic over the results of his own work. As we shall see, it was to bear much fruit—for example, in the work of Maria Montessori.

MARIA MONTESSORI

Séguin had ambitions beyond the training of idiots for his *methode physiologique*. The preface to his book *Idiocy and Its Treatment Through the Physiologic Method* talks about the method's ". . . fitness for the training of all children." Because of the modifications that he, Séguin, had wrought to it, Itard's program of education was "competent for the training of mankind" (Lane, 1976, p. 276).

Albeit, it was not until the last year of his life that Séguin published a review of the physiological method in which it was applied to normal children. It had a scant circulation. So his, and Itard's work, might have been limited to a restricted pale of operation, i.e., with the mentally defective, had not their oeuvres come to the attention of Maria Montessori (1870–1952), the first woman to receive a medical degree in Italy. Montessori's pedagogic interests initially lay with the mentally handicapped. To expand her knowledge and skills during the two years that she directed a school for orthophrenics, she visited and observed Séguin's programs of education at Bicêtre, France, and read his and Itard's writings. She was later to observe:

> After study of the methods in use throughout Europe, I concluded my experiments upon the deficients of Rome, and taught them through two years. I followed Séguin's book and also derived much help from the remarkable experiments of Itard. Guided by the work of these two men, I manufactured a great deal of didactic material. . . . I myself observed most surprising results through their application. . . . Having through actual experience justified my faith in Séguin's method, I withdrew from active work among the deficient. . . . The man (Séguin) who had studied abnormal children for thirty years expressed the idea that the physiological method which has at its base the individual study of the pupil and which forms to educative methods upon the analyses of physiological and psychological phenomena, must come also to be applied to normal children. This step he believed would show the way to a complete human regeneration. The voice of Séguin seemed to be like the voice of a forerunner crying in the wilderness, and my thoughts were filled with the immensity and importance of a work which should be able to reform school and education. (Montessori, 1912, pp. 41–42)

It would seem that Séguin was to play John the Baptist to Montessori's you know whom.

Montessori returned to the University of Rome, from which she had received her medical degree, to re-enroll in studies of anthropology and psychology that would prepare herself for work with normal children. In 1906 she received the opportunity to apply her ideas when the Roman Association for Good Construction, upon planning a number of low-cost housing projects, decided to equip each one with a special class for the purpose of educating preschool children. Montessori was asked to organize these and thus began the first Casa dei Bambini in 1907 followed by four more similar programs within the year.

Within these schools, Montessori made Séguin's vision a reality. The rationale for her transmutations of Itard and Séguin's methods, and her own extensions thereof, from the mentally defective to young normal children, was based upon analogies.

The mentally defective individual, whose development was arrested, and the normal undeveloped child manifested similar features. These included poor muscular coordination, deficiencies in motor and manual skills and in sensory discrimination, primitive language, brief spans of attention, etc. What worked with one should work with the other.

After approximately four years of Montessori's work at the children's houses, the knowledge of her methods spread throughout Italy, then Europe and America. She soon was giving courses on her method. A model training school for teachers followed. Her book *The Method of Scientific Pedagogy Applied to Childhood Education* became world famous, appearing in English as *The Montessori Method* in 1912. Worldwide dissemination of her techniques, Montessori societies everywhere, and additional books by her and her disciples brought her widespread fame. (Lane 1976).

Was Montessori a faculty psychologist? John Dewey and his disciple John Kilpatrick thought so, and we will shortly see why they had good grounds for that opinion. True, Montessori countered such charges in her book *The Absorbent Mind* (1967), insisting that she in no way intended an atomistic conception of the mind but rather believed that the "mental organism is a dynamic whole, which transforms its structure by active experience obtained from its surroundings" (p. 82). Well and good, and agreed also that many of her training efforts were directed to practical academic and social skill development. The greater part of her program was still concerned with the education of the senses as senses. And most of her elaborately developed didactic materials were intended for this purpose. Thus there is little doubt about where her theoretical predilections lay. They were those of faculty psychology.

Let us examine Montessori's system of sense training. It is her beginning approach to education and occupies a goodly portion of her early writings on "scientific pedagogy" and "auto-education." In *The Montessori Method,* she spoke clearly of "the education of the senses."

It is exactly in the repetition of exercises that the education of the senses consist; their aim is not that the child shall know colors, forms, and the different qualities of objects, but that he refine his senses through an exercise of attention, comparison, of judgment. These exercises are true intellectual gymnastics. Such gymnastics, reasonably directed by means of various devices, aid in the formation of the intellect, just as physical exercises fortify the general health and quicken the growth of the body. (Kilpatrick, 1914, p. 47)

Believing in broad transfer of training, Montessori was convinced that education of the senses

. . . makes men observers, and not only accomplishes the general work of adaptation to the present epoch of civilization, but also prepares them directly for practical life. (Woodrow, 1919, p. 284)

It was on the basis of statements such as this that Dewey and Kilpatrick considered her a faculty psychologist and formal disciplinarian.

For her training of the senses, Montessori emphasized what she called an auto-education or self-teaching approach.[8] To assist in this training, she developed 26 didactic apparatuses providing for the training of all the senses except those of taste and smell. Her methods were

---

[8] Used for all the senses except hearing, which Montessori felt was not possible for the child to exercise himself.

persistent and systematic. Some of the "senses" that she wished to teach have exotic names such as "thermic," "baric," and "stereognostic." What it largely amounted to was an extension of Itard and Séguin's concepts and technology. Perceptual discrimination was at its basis.

To train the visual sense, vis-à-vis Montessori, a child is given wooden cylinders to fit into holes in a solid block of wood. To develop the perception of dimensions, he manipulates objects of various sizes and shapes. The thermic sense is trained by discriminatory immersions in waters of different temperature. Tactile training proceeds through the stroking of alternating strips of sandpaper and smooth paper. The chromatic sense is trained by teaching the child to discriminate a set of 64 spools of eight colors in eight shades. Auditory powers are trained through sound contrasts proceeding from strong to subtle, by shaking small boxes with sand and pebbles, and through "silence" games in which the child is asked to listen to the rustling of tree leaves, the sounds of insects. The baric sense is trained through picking up wooden tablets of the same size but of different weight. The stereognostic sense (in which both tactual and muscular senses are simultaneously involved) undergoes development by having the child distinguish objects of different shapes. (Kirk and Johnson, 1951).

While Montessori also created programs to enhance muscular coordination (through directed gymnastics, games, manual skills) and the "tactile and muscular" senses, she did not place as great a store upon bodily movement as did Séguin; thus it is Séguin rather than Montessori whom Ball puts in lineal relationship to Newell Kephart (1971).

Woodrow (1919) has pointed out a most interesting claim made for the Montessori Method which supported its position as scientific pedagogy. Educators have clung to scientific pedagogy ever since science (as opposed to philosophy as a means of knowledge) became popular. It was based upon the principles of experimental psychology. Montessori, too!

Experimental psychology, to Montessori, was a science that assessed and measured the various senses and other functions. Many of its tests resembled the training technologies of Itard and Séguin with which she was so enamored. The experimental psychologist assayed hearing by determining the smallest perceptible differences between tones in loudness and pitch; color vision by the smallest perceptible differences in the hues of two colors; touch by the smallest possible distance between two points applied to the skin which allowed their discrimination as two rather than one; and so on. Such psychological tests could be classified according to the various mental functions they tested. And what were tests of functions could be modified to train those functions. In fact, as Montessori saw it, to test a function was to also exercise it. And so was inaugurated a tradition of cognitive training that has now become quite popular. Teaching the test!

Now if only what is being tested is important enough to be trained. There was, there still is, the rub of much of what process training is all about.

BINET

The final figure in our pantheon of early special education process trainers is Alfred Binet (1857–1911), an unabashed faculty psychologist, despite his creation of a test of general intelligence. He never gave up his goal of studying the individual faculties that constituted general intelligence or (depending where you read or how you interpret) acted in concert with it. Spearman, a grouch at best when it came to those who challenged his conceptions of g or claimed primacy in formulating theories relative to its general intelligence, was, as we have earlier seen, exasperated by Binet's erratic theories.[9] And not without justification, for Binet (and his associates) seemed to be constantly changing his mind or shifting his theoretical stance from article to article, or even from paragraph to paragraph in the same article.

In one of their later statements about what their tests measured, Binet and Simon stated:

Comprehension, invention, direction and censorship; intelligence lies in these four words. Consequently we can conclude . . . that these four functions, which are primordial, may be considered to have been studied by our method. (Spearman, 1923, p. 9–10)

Primordial would appear to be, well, primordial. But Binet went on to analyze his primordial faculties into more finite ones (which were even more primordial?). On the very same page of their discussion of a "primordial" faculty, reasoning, he and co-worker Theodore Simon break it down into a "crowd of faculties," including "memory, imagination, judgment, and especially language" (Spearman, 1923, p. 10). And so Binet went. Given a little longer to live he might well have proceeded much further down that road toward the testing of multiple faculties that Guilford interpreted him as truly being interested in (1967). As it was, we have clear evidence at all stages of the path that he took with his colleagues in mental measurement that he was interested—always—in specific cognitive processes.

Beyond that, Binet was interested in specific "higher" cognitive processes. True, his tests did not neglect sensory-motor ones; he, Binet, too, after all, was a child of Galton. But the development (and success) of the intelligence test associated with his name was based upon his belief

[9] Spearman claims that Binet did not really create a test of general intelligence but one in which he "pooled" faculties to create an "average" estimate of their presumed operations.

that previous (unsuccessful) intelligence tests had been weighted too heavily in favor of sensory functions and of simple psychological processes. Binet believed that in order to successfully create an instrument to assess intelligence (in a Spencerian manner of speaking) as an adaptive process it would be required to test a variety of higher cognitive abilities. Revision of the Binet-Simon scales moved ever upward in emphasis upon the assessment of complex, and central, mental powers.

It is in his role as a faculty psychologist that Binet appears to us in the garb of a special educator.[10] Further, though it may surprise some, he was firmly convinced of the modifiability of intelligence and provided a chapter on its training in *Les Ideés Modernes sur les Enfants*. This chapter, "The Training of Intelligence," begins with the phrase "After the illness, the remedy" (Kamin, 1974, p. 5). In response to those who claimed "that intelligence is a fixed quantity, a quantity which one cannot augment" he retorted "We must protest and react against this brutal pessimism" (Kamin, 1974, p. 5).

Binet, in his belief that the faculties could be trained through exercise, was continuing the tradition and expectations of formal disciplinarians and faculty process trainers of the past. In his belief that they could be remediated, he was also continuing Séguin's traditions, while often excoriating his predecessor because of the excessive claims he had made concerning the success of his methods. By developing a system intended to increase scores on intelligence tests, Binet was creating a new tradition on his own.

For his particular brand of cognitive training, Binet proposed the terms "mental orthopedics." Just as physical orthopedics strengthen and correct structural physical disabilities, so could mental orthopedics strengthen and correct perception, attention, memory, judgment, the will, and other faculties.

The degree to which Binet's mental orthopedics improved over Séguin's physiological education is questionable. Like Montessori, he appears to have helped himself liberally from Séguin's ideas. For one, while his own interest was generally directed towards higher cognitive processes, he did recognize the importance of sensory and motor training— particularly for retarded children in whom he was convinced that these were major areas of strength.[11]

In several communications, together with Belot and Vaney, students

---

[10] It is certainly of interest that both Frostig and Kirk have repeatedly referred their own work back to the authority of Binet's contributions.

[11] He was talking about children in the higher levels of mental retardation. Binet maintained that special education should only be for "the educable." He was dubious about educating "imbeciles," and completely opposed to educating "idiots" (Wolf, 1973, p. 306). He was fully cognizant of the unequal distribution of abilities in retardates.

of his, and then in *Les Ideés Modernes sur les Enfants*, Binet offered and expanded upon recommendations for mental orthopedics, which he believed would help normal and cognitively impaired alike.

Motor control and agility may be trained through tests of grip and speed of tapping, in which children are encouraged to rival each other. Attention, willpower, and motor control can be trained by having children carry full cups of water from one table to another without spilling a drop. Exercises of this sort require prolonged maintenance of one's attitude. In others with similar training purposes, the pupil is to be required to maintain a straight face while staring at a classmate who, for his part, is grimacing at him. Or he has to remain motionless holding a copybook with a stick of chalk balanced upright upon it. Or, motionless, he holds one foot in one hand while his other hand is placed at the back of his neck. A number of variations on such themes can be improvised (Descoeudres, 1929).

As to improving the higher mental powers, Binet noted that his orthopedics awaken attention in the scatterbrained, improve self-confidence, and encourage a competitive spirit.

Binet was very much interested in the education of memory. One of his training exercises for it (and attention) employs the very brief exposure of a large card on which a number of objects are shown. The pupil is required to attempt to grasp within his attention all the items on the card and then write their names from memory. Binet developed a long series of such cards, with gradually increasing numbers of objects upon them.[12]

But were such orthopedics successful? Like Montessori and Séguin, Binet was sure of his techniques and produced testimonies from teachers to support his own positive observations and test results. It is no wonder modern-day process trainers are so fond of Binet and look back at him as an advocate. We find in his work the beginning of theirs. I, myself, will also confess a fondness for this protean researcher who simply did not have enough lifetime remaining to him to make a final comprehensive statement on the mind and its processes.

---

[12] He claimed that educable retarded children trained on this test were able, after five seconds of exposure, to retain in mind as many as nine objects—and to retain them sufficiently to be able to return to their seats and write out the names; a performance which leaves one slightly incredulous.

23
More about the Modalities

At this late stage of our narrative, it might seem that the modalities, and the roles they played (and continue to play) within process doctrine would not require additional attention. Yet they do because of the unusually prominent role they have assumed over the centuries, both theoretically and practically. So we consider them again in this chapter, though from a somewhat different viewpoint than in previous ones. We will be more concerned with modality products and derivatives than we are with the operation of the modalities directly through that great faculty(ies) perception, though the latter will not be entirely neglected. We will be speaking of imagery and different types of memory, of visiles and audiles, and perhaps of cabbages and kings.

The concepts of sensory psychology being with the Greeks. Though the distinction between sensation and perception remained to be formally made by one of Scotland's associationist faculty psychologists,[1] Aristotle clearly distinguished between what we now call sensory and perceptual functions, and he conceived of images being created from percepts and memories composed of images. Nor was he without precursors. Later, Hobbes and Locke, Hume, Hartley, and French sensationalists such as Condillac, Cabanis, and Helvetius might disagree upon the finer points of how sensation became whatever in and of the mind. But that it was the basis of the mind's contents, in this they were of single accord. We have

---

[1] Thomas Reid (1710–1796).

already examined how such ideas affected the mind-training orientation of sense–realists, naturalists, and most faculty psychologists, except those of the classical position, for whom memory, disembodied from its perceptual bases, was the major process of concern at the lower levels, as was reason at the highest. Nor was the sensory concern of the psychologists without major impression upon neurology, much of whose later history represents an amplification and confirmation of Hartley's theories that vibratiuncles in neural tissue caused by sensations and motor behavior alter the nervous system so as to render learning possible.

The number of senses was a matter of debate. Through most of the centuries subsequent to his death, Aristotle's theory of the five senses held sway, both theoretically and in terms of process training programs. There was vision, hearing, taste, smell, and touch. James Mill (1773–1836) added a muscle sense and one for sensations emanating from the alimentary canal. Other theorists proposed other senses, such as one for innervation, i.e., sensations resulting from moving a nervous impulse into action (to be differentiated from kinesthesis), and a muscle sense that identifies sensations from muscles, tendons, and joints; this latter one was by Wundt, though he later discarded it. There was even a sense proposed for sexual sensations. Now we talk about information processing and the like and our senses no longer look so simple to us, unless we read a lot of learning-disability literature.

IMAGERY IN TRANSITION

From sensation to percept to image was the way the mind moved in most past theories. Images were essential to those theories; they were essential in almost all theories. They are the means by which percepts are retained. Aristotle had in fact spoken of images as being the products of "decaying sense." Images are also the stuff of memory, the regurgitations of recall. And they are the bases of thought. Aristotle's postulate was generally accepted: "There is no thought without image" (Spearman, 1923, p. 179).

To theologians, who insisted that the mind and body were separate and the former beyond the sway of the latter's material processes, the concept of imagery was essential to explain the obvious influences of body on mind. It was agreed that the body, though not being able to directly influence the mind, is capable of providing information for it. It creates sensations which are transformed into images which are employed by the mind in thought. St. Thomas Aquinas used this conceptualization to explain why inebriation made one drunk and why psychosis (which he believed to be a physical affliction) caused mental derangement.

With a great deal less substantiation than St. Thomas produced, the distinguished British psychologist Stout confidently declared (1913): "An idea can no more exist without an image than perception can exist without sensation" (Spearman, 1923, p. 179).

And a distinguished American psychologist rested the case for images upon their essentiality to cognitive theory. To the question as to whether thought could exist without images, Angell responded:

> To suppose that one can occur without the other is utterly to destroy the entire foundation on which rests the theory advocated by most . . . concerning cognitive operations. (Spearman, 1923, p. 180)

Wundt, the founder of the experimental tradition in modern psychology, was very much in the modality camp. He distinguished between three types of mental elements that experimental psychology was to study:

1. Sensations, the ultimate elementary elements of consciousness
2. Images, which do not differ from sensations fundamentally but are also associated with local excitations within the cortex
3. Feelings

Titchner, who adapted Wundt's theories in what has come to be known as structuralism, also regarded mental states as made up of sensations, images, and feelings. And images, Titchner proposed, are the most important of these when one thinks. Cognition hangs on a framework of sentience within which imagery provides its anchorages. Titchner waxed eloquent on the subject:

> It is a fairly complete picture gallery, not of finished paintings, but of impressionist notes. Whenever I read or hear that somebody has done something modestly or gravely, or proudly or humbly, or courteously, I see a visual hint. . . . The stately heroine gives a flash of a tall figure, the only clear part of which is a hand holding up a steely grey skirt. . . . I never sit down to read a book, or to write a paragraph, or to think out a problem, without a musical accompaniment. . . . There are occasions when my voice rings out clearly to the mental ear and my throat feels still as if with much talking. (Spearman, 1923, p. 182)

This was Titchner writing on *Experimental Studies of the Thought Processes*, in 1909. Later, in his *Textbook of Psychology* (1911), he described a very concrete association between abstractions and images. Thus he traced back the process of understanding the word *infinity* to kinesthesis.

The kinesthetic symbol for *infinity* is found in the tendency to prolong the word, this prolongation being accompanied by the distinct impression of projecting it from the mouth, and then following this projected word by definite bodily movements. (Spearman, 1923, p. 177)

Titchner was saying, in the preceding quotation, that the bodily movements involved in forming words somehow created symbolic imagery, which was really giving oral-lingual activities a great deal of credit as to their ability to provide meaning through sensory feedbacks. But that is the sort of game one gets into when one tries to translate cognitive processes into physical ones.[2]

Not only did those in the Wundt-Titchnerian camp believe images were essential for the formation of concepts. They also believed that images steadied the mercurial processes of thinking. Aveling, in his *The Consciousness of the Universal* (1912), clarified imagery's role relative to higher cognitive functioning:

Thought is perpetually in process of becoming, in which process it passes beyond itself. It is unstable. But the image is a relatively stable formation; and as long as it is present in consciousness, its conceptual element will also tend to remain. (Spearman, 1923, p. 187)

What one proposes, another seeks to dispose of. Images are important, essential, inevitable? Some very important men had said so. And what is more, they had experimental evidence to back it up. Introspection clearly showed images as involved in thought—or so it seemed, until some other important men raised the possibility of thought without images.

The term "imageless thought" was apparently first offered by Stout. It is, however, forever identified with the name of Oswald Külpe (1862–1915) and the Würtzburg School. Though a student at the University of Leipzig where Wundt reigned, and his assistant (after Cattell left), Külpe was to enrage his old *patron* by later encouraging a center of opposition to Wundt's theories at Würtzburg. Here Külpe and his students began to distinguish, in their experiments, between thought process and thought content—between the act of thinking and what constituted the material for that act. In addition, they concerned themselves with what might be called "conscious attitudes" (*Bewusstseinlagen*), which involved states of consciousness that could not be reduced to simple sensations, images, or feelings. There was a great deal more they did, but the above sample of their work should be enough to see why Wundt became enraged at the Würtzburgians (Külpe and his followers), and why Titchner attempted to dismiss their work as misguided and erroneous. What they had done, Titchner said, was to confuse logical deductions with psychology, to misidentify interpretations of conscious experiences as descriptions of those

---

[2] Colvin was prone to credit postural kinesthetics for much of imagery-induced meaning (1914).

conscious experiences, and to use faulty methods of introspection—among other mistakes. He particularly called attention to the probability that Külpe and his followers were overlooking the origins of conscious attitudes and thought in kinesthetic sensations and that the imageless attitudes and thoughts they believed they had found, were really vestigial forms of kinesthetic and organic sensations (Murphy and Kovach, 1972).

The "imageless thought" battles and debates were on. Experiments and testimony supported both sides. Discussing *The Distribution and Functions of Mental Imagery* (1909), Martin described the stabilizing values of imagery in respect to memory:

> As a fixation point, the visual image unquestionably gives the memorative experience a more certain foundation, inasmuch as it is maintained with great constancy and is held more continuously in the focus of consciousness. (Spearman, 1923, p. 188)

On the other hand, evidence was produced that controverted such conclusions. Judd and Cowling (1907) found images to be of dubious value in the fixation and recall of complex visual stimuli. M. R. Fernald (1912) disputed the value of simple imagery for memory, through experiments using the Binet Letter Square, in which the letters are arranged in vertical and horizontal fashion so as to create a visual square. Subjects were first asked to develop a complete visual image of the letter square. The letters were then removed and the subjects asked to recall them. Some could do this but became confused and disorganized when asked to "read" them from memory proceeding from lower right-hand corner to the upper right-hand corner vertically, or from right to left horizontally, etc. Obviously, the subjects who had succeeded with the task of recalling the letters (without order being taken into consideration) were relying on other than visual imagery to do so. Perhaps they were aided in recalling individual letters by seeing them in their mind's eye, but surely the letters had not been "seen," i.e., their images recalled, in terms of the square they composed.

The theories offered to explain or controvert imageless thought were various and often ingenious. Woodworth, for one, decided that perceptual experiences could be revived without their original sensory experiences explicit in the mind of the reviver—and that was what constituted imageless thought. We have reviewed the disexplanations from Titchner's side of the controversy previously. So back and forth it went, with both sides producing champions and research supporting their causes. The disagreement among introspectionists gave behaviorists ample ammunition. J. B. Watson would point to the imageless thought controversies as still another example of their incompetencies and move to scrap all their theories of introspectionism and consciousness. The decline of psychology's interest in imagery was a matter of course after that. The revival of interest in it, after decades, another matter of course.

Let us take stock. We have brought our review of imagery, in general terms, far enough for the purposes of this particular book. But what about imagery in the specific, that is to say in regard to individual differences? Let us go back in time for a clearer appreciation of these.

INDIVIDUAL DIFFERENCES IN IMAGERY

Just when individual differences or grades in the modalities first emerged is not altogether clear; presumably by the Renaissance, when degrees of endowment in various cognitive functions had come to be clearly recognized. By the time Christian von Wolff had written his *Psychologica Empirica* (1732), sensory abilities appear to have been clearly recognized as varying from one individual to another. Wolff's book allowed gradations from person to person for all of the faculties, including the powers of sensory perception (Spearman, 1927).

Sensory perception, beyond all the other faculties, appears to have received attention from later process authorities in respect to individual differences. F. E. Beneke, a disciple of Herbart's, developed his master's teachings in terms of their practical applications, and most particularly in terms of individual differences. While Beneke, as might be expected from a Herbartian, tried to dissect the traditional faculties into many part processes and contributed in this fashion to the discreditation of classical faculty doctrine, he nevertheless provided an impetus to the development of modality conceptualizations.

According to Beneke, there are certain ground systems (*Grundsysteme*) which furnish individual differences with their "ultimate basis." Each of these systems is constituted by one of the senses. These are the original Aristotelian five—at first; later Beneke added "vital" senses, including under these (and doing James Mill one better in the adding) senses associated with muscular, digestive, and sexual organs.

From the creation of specific ground systems for modalities, which allow for individual modality differences (or, for that matter, from traditional faculty doctrine adjusted to allow for individual perceptual differences) it was a short step to the differentiation of degrees of imagery associated with the individual modalities. The French neurologist Jean Martin Charcot (1825–1893) boldly instituted the idea of modality types, classifying people according to whether their imagery was predominantly visual, auditory, or kinesthetic. From then on, the world was expected to consider visual or auditory-minded people or those of the kinesthetic type—visiles, audiles, kinesiles. A distinction in these types was made between perception and imagery. One could be quite adequate, for example, in respect to his perceptual processes and yet be deficient in his imagery processes vis-à-vis the same modality; Woodworth, if you recall, had given an explanation. For Charcot, it was somewhat similar, allowing for the differences based upon the first writer being a psychologist, the second a neurologist (the first deriving his observations from "normal" behavior, the second dealing with pathology).

Gustav Theodor Fechner (1801–1887) also discussed different types of imagery in the visual and auditory realms, with attention paid to the role these differences played in the lives of certain individuals.

Francis Galton (1822–1911), with whom we are well acquainted by this time, placed the study of individual differences in imagery on a definitive scientific basis. Galton attempted to use the study of imagery to study the mind in his *Inquiries Into Human Faculty* (1883). His was the first quantitative use of the questionnaire for psychological research. He asked his subjects to respond to inquiries on matters of the imagery relative to type and strength. Images were arranged in serial order from 0 to 100, according to intensity or likeness to sensation. Galton found evidence that some individuals have little or no imagery for certain fields, while others reported images of such vividness as to approach hallucinatory experiences. Galton was prone to see differences in imagery as having a hereditary basis. He also recognized environmental influences. The vividness and effectiveness of an individual's imagery was dependent upon his experiences, training, and general usages. Disuse of a certain type of imagery could result in its atrophy. Bookish philosophers were prone to be deficient in concrete types of imagery, in visual imagery in particular.

Classification of imagery, either as an armchair exercise or as food for experimental investigation, was quite popular in the latter days of the nineteenth century and the early days of the twentieth. Meumann's welter of writings and opinions on the matter were quite influential. He made an important distinction between object and word types of imagery. These he believed, constituted the two main classes of images. Object types include all concrete images created by the senses, including motor ones, in which ideational processes are expressed in imitative movements.[3] Word types of imagery are also related to modality functioning. There are verbal-visual, verbal-acoustic, and verbal-tactile-kinesthetic types of imagery (Colvin, 1914). The difference between the concrete and the verbal types of imagery is that the latter is symbolic, rather than concrete.

Colvin elaborated on Meumann's types of imagery. That which involves reproduction of the form of a word usually engages speech-motor

---

[3] It need not be dwelt on that kinesthesis of this sort can be utilized to explain a great deal of behavior, including that dealt with in current "modeling" theories.

images. Colvin urged that imagery of a postural kinesthetic, or symbolic mimetic nature, receive further attention from educational psychologists in light of its importance in language and thought.

> In thinking in this type of imagery the person does not employ "inner-speech" (thought in speech-motor terms) but rather an inner sign language that carries the meaning often of abstract and colorless modes of thought. (Colvin, 1914, p. 109)

Here, then, lay a behavioral explanation of what was regarded as imageless thought. It was somewhere in the vicinity of Titchner's camp, though Colvin preferred to be identified with James and Dewey.

> . . . the meaning of a situation is after all an attitude, and . . . an attitude must in the final analysis be a motor affair. Thus it is but a step to the conclusion that this general dependence of experience for its significance on motor adjustments has left a deposit or "mind-stuff" that symbolically represents concrete situations, not actually present, but ideally represented. (Colvin, 1914, p. 111)

Even as the interest and research in imagery mounted, there were serious doubts raised as to the validity of clear-cut imagery types. Meumann pointed out that a person might think in terms of concrete visual images in one type of task and utilize acoustic motor imagery for another. Baldwin (1893) believed that he personally thought in "speech-motor and auditory" terms in German and in "visual and hand-motor" terms in French, having learned German conversationally and having acquired French in school through reading and writing exercises. Segal (1908) suggested that individuals tend to have particular types of imagery dominant at different times, rather than being of one particular imagery type for all activities. Most people, he believed, were, in any case, of a mixed type in terms of the imagery they employed. When it appeared that someone was favoring a particular type of imagery, i.e., seemed to be a particular imagery type, it was because of the particular material or activity that was being studied, i.e., one calling more than others for the utilization of imagery associated with a particular modality or function.

Negative evidence as to modality types contributed to the general decline of interest in imagery as the twentieth century proceeded in behavioristic directions. However, the interest of educators in imagery continued in many quarters, and belief that imagery preferences could be utilized educationally persisted along with it. Colvin, knowing of the problems confronting imagery conceptualizations, still could not deny himself the solace of believing that better days lay ahead.

> It is no longer possible, in the light of modern investigations, to hold that any one method of instruction, or plan of procedure in school technique can be applied

with favorable results to all children, not even to all normal children. A method of instruction in reading, for example, which will be effective for the child possessing strong visual imagery, may be of very doubtful merit when used in instructing a child of the motor type. It is to be hoped that the time is not far distant when certain standard tests may be used . . . to the end that instruction may be modified and adapted to suit individual rather than general needs. (Colvin, 1914, p. 21)

Since precise tests for imagery were not yet generally available for school children, brave souls like Barbara Morgan (1914) made recommendations for its determination. One might have a child tell a story and see if sounds or sights prevail in his recollections. If the child lacks the literary "sense" needed for such a test, it might be better to have him tell what comes to mind when he thinks of a "hand organ." If he replies "monkey" or "dancing," he is a visile. If he instead hums "The Wearing of the Green," or says "nice music," he is an audile.

From such were modality preferences determined. There were other methods, too, but not as much fun in the telling. Imagery types, modality preferences, audiles, visiles, all were very exciting to education and educators. In England's fair green land, it all went far enough to have educators enthuse about the possibilities of sectioning their classes so that children could be taught according to their modality types—visiles to be taught visually, audiles to be taught auditorally. But more of this later. For we should at this point turn to the central nervous system to see where it stood during much of the excitement concerning perceptual and imagery research and training. Let us never forget that no matter how disguised or larvated it may be, in the heart of every process trainer there lies the conviction that he is training that nervous system.

MODALITIES AND BRAIN LOCALIZATION

The first part of this book described the struggle of the Bell-Magendie law to reach the cortices of the CNS. Once there, it could be employed, aided and abetted by the doctrines of associationism to explain the faculties of old and to make Gall's dream of localization of function become a respectable reality. May I refer you to a quick review of the "new phrenology" prior to continuing with this chapter. Broca, Fritz, Hitzig, and Ferrier were, you remember, greatly responsible for phrenology's renaissance. The "diagram makers," of whom Head had spoken contemptuously, had a field era in exploiting their breakthroughs. Let us highlight some of these.

Bastian, in 1869, followed Broca's work in localizing articulate language. He was one of the first to use diagrams to illustrate his theoretical conceptions. In addition to determining specific locales in the brain for tongue and hand control, he also localized auditory and visual word centers. Bastian believed that language problems could be divided into two groups. One group is that of comprehension difficulties. These were explained by defects in the brain that affect its sensory centers or the connections (associations) between them and higher centers. The second group of disorders—concerned with those of language expression[4]—he interpreted as due to defects in the connective tissues, i.e., association tracts between "the cortical gray matter and the center for muscular control of the movements of speech" (Wepman, 1951, p. 10).

Following this English contribution to the literature, the German neurologists jumped into the arena with both feet. Notable was the work of Wernicke, who in 1873 described an auditory center residing in the first temporal convolution of the cortex. Out of this grew the distinction between receptive aphasia, due to disturbances in the sensory aspects of language, and expressive aphasia (Broca's aphasia), due to disturbances or defects in the motor areas of the cortex. Lichtheim used Wernicke's data to precisely diagram how defects affected brain function. He was a model builder for the localizationists of his and future times.

Charcot accepted wholeheartedly the conception of brain centers and exploited Broca's work in describing the *"centres . . . corticaux chez homme"* (Wepman, 1951, p. 11). He added centers of his own to the ones previously found, including one for "ideation," which served to integrate the activities of the other centers. Within the center concept, he found neurological footing for his clinical observations on modality types. Apropos of these he observed that a defect in a visual center of the brain would necessarily produce a considerably greater disturbance to the functioning of a visile than to that of an audile. Also, according to Charcot, there may be discriminatory impairment of modality functioning. For example, one's powers of perception may be unimpaired while the imagery for that modality is severely dysfunctional.

The literature of brain location as it concerns modality centers, is too extensive for us to review here. It is enough for us to recognize that it was generally agreed, after the diagram makers made it visibly apparent,[5] that there were centers for modalities and

[4] While leaving comprehension intact.
[5] They were the model makers of their day. It seems that there is a basic belief inherent in the human species that when ignorance about a certain topic exists, drawing schemata somehow provides light to the darkness of that ignorance. Underwood amusingly described the situation in 1975:

> . . . in the last dozen years, the favorite after-class occupation of many college professors has been that of building models of memory. Just what is

modality subfunctions, centers for motor behaviors of all sorts, and association tracts between the centers. Weaknesses somewhere in such nice simple diagrammatic pastiches explained what was wrong with someone and what had to be trained, exercized, or at least acknowledged. The association fibers were particularly friendly areas of the brain to those whose localization theories were challenged. Thus, in 1925, Elizabeth Lord, confronted with negative evidence concerning the pathology of brain centers vis-à-vis defective sensory centers, expressed the following opinion:

> If our conclusions have been correctly drawn, so-called congenital word-blindness is not a pathological condition of a visual memory center for words and letters, but is due to a defect in the association fibers; to insufficient associations between the sense areas and to lack of co-ordination in the motor response to visual and auditory stimuli. (Robinson, 1946, p. 37)

This was a safe conclusion for the time. Who was going to muck about in Broadman's various areas to track down the connections between this cerebral zone and that? And how was one going to prove that they weren't defective, when the victim was participating in his own autopsy?

Since we have observed a quotation about word blindness, it is perhaps appropriate to review the concept briefly at this time. A most popular condition was that of word blindness, later to become more popularly known as alexia, dyslexia, and the like. A related term, "strephosymbolia," which explained similar phenomena on a different basis, never quite became popular in a similar fashion. Orton had overrated the memory span of professionals working with learning problems; there were just too many syllables. Hinschelwood, of course, is the towering figure, in respect to word blindness, defining it as "a condition in which, with normal vision and therefore seeing the letters and words distinctly, an individual is unable to interpret written or printed language" (Wiederholt, 1974, p. 115). To explain the condition, in the Charcot tradition, he found an individual who had no cognitive problems other than loss of memory for the visual aspects of language, and whose problems were attributable (based on autopsy) to destruction of the association fibers in the angular gyrus of the left side of the brain. The deceased patient had *acquired word blindness*. Hinschelwood is perhaps better known for his distinction of *congenital word blindness,* attributable to some defect in an otherwise normal brain (perhaps in

---

responsible for this furious activity is not entirely apparent to me. . . . The fact is that we have models running out of our ears, and there seems to be no surcease.

This may be quite healthy; at least lots of people are getting skilled in drawing boxes, arrows, and circular notes. But all these models cannot be right, or even useful or believable, and evaluation seems to be rather low on the priority list. It seems easier to formulate a new model than test an old one, and one never gets pinned down that way. (Underwood, 1975, p. 128)

the area of the cerebrum which stored visual memories for written language). To "... some congenital deficiency ... of visual memory of words ..." Hinschelwood said, in the case of a young boy whose reading problems he had investigated. In other cases, it was a deficiency of the auditory tract. Neurological paraphrasing of learning problems could explain all, and an autopsy, if possible, rarely disallowed some type of interpretation of learning problems in terms of defective neurological functioning. Particularly as the nomenclature of the brain became more precise, one could sound more erudite, seemingly explain more, and have his claims disallowed less.

Groszman, writing in *The Exceptional Child* (1917), explained the reading problems of three children he had examined. He found that their inability to read was clearly due to the "impassibility" or nonfunctioning of various association tracts within the cerebrum. Paths 5 and 7 weren't conducting correctly. The disturbance of path 5 resulted in a separation of the writing motor center from the speech motor center. The impassibility of path 7 caused a disturbance between optic and acoustic components of the brain. One can only conclude from Dr. Groszman's remarkable delineations that modern day psychoeducational enthusiasts who speak of "pinpointing" learning disabilities are working in a far cruder tradition than once existed.

Explanation abhors a vacuum. Meretricious answers will do, if better ones are not to be had. Often they are more acceptable, because they are more pleasing than the truth. For those who saw the modalities and faculties of the philosopher and educator as unreliable because of their nonsubstantive basis, brain centers and association tracts provided grounds for conversion. How could one deny the validity of the diagrams that the high and the mighty of neurology and psychology spread before them in which every bit of human behavior at last was lodged in, or could be explained by, the nooks and crannies of the human brain? Some protests against oversimplification were heard and sometimes slowed things down a bit. The likes of Jackson, Marie, Monakow, and Head were not to be sneezed at. Head complained over the pseudowonders of diagnosis and explanation that the "diagram makers" had wrought. He found most unfortunate the idea that the mind could be conceived as dissolvable through some cognitive chemolysis to allow the classification of "... clinical phenomena under such categories as 'motor' and 'sensory,' 'auditory' and 'visual,' or some analogous terminology" (Head, 1926, p. 143).

Head further lamented:

An even more disastrous error . . . is the attempt to correlate anatomical changes in definite regions of the brain with "speech," "reading," "writing," and the "memory for words." These are purely verbal descriptions for certain human actions. There is no reason to believe that these convenient terms correspond to any distinct and separable group of psychical or physiological functions. (Head, 1926, pp. 143–144)

Among those who were particularly influential in psychological circles in the antilocalization movement of the post–World War II years was Carl Lashley. As a consequence of his researches, for a considerable time it was unpopular to ascribe higher cognitive functions any specific locales in the cerebrum.

Certainly, the activities of latter-day neurologists-cum-educators proceeded for a while in a more tempered and reasoned fashion concerning localization phenomena. Samuel Torrey Orton, writing about strephosymbolia (1937), avoided some of the pitfalls of naive localization. Neurologist Kurt Goldstein (who did not deny the phenomena resulting from specific cortical defects) kept reminding his readers that, despite the locale or discreteness or severity of brain damage, it was a total organism that was responding to a world with which it had to re-learn to cope. Luria provided a more sophisticated update on how functions were localized—and it was not a matter of discrete tissues responsible for this or that localization, that is until split brains appeared. But enough of neurology. Let us turn back to modalities as they were sensed in education.

MODALITIES IN EDUCATION

Where shall we begin—or resume—our discussion? Certainly, there is no need to take another tenebrous descent into *Anschauung* theory or other previous aspects of perception and perceptual training that we have discussed.

Let us, rather, regard the latter part of the present chapter as a "mopping-up" operation, mopping up in the military sense of attacking some previously unattacked issues in this book, mopping up as it relates to the use of a cleaning utensil, i.e., in an effort to clarify some of the usages of "modality," from under the puddles of misconception and preconception that are so obviously about us now. From these standpoints, I can take the liberty of discussing various aspects of modality without being embarrassed by the lack of continuity that will frequently appear in my narrative. The one coherent string running through the content that follows concerns schools and education. We shall also largely concern ourselves with those modality-based processes which succeed perception, i.e., imagery and memory (the two are often synonymous). This is, in fact, in keeping with the general tenor of the chapter, though an overlap of processes is unavoidable in the telling.

Let us begin first with the role that modalities have played in the acquisition of knowledge. We are speaking of education and training through, rather than of, the modalities. Let us begin with Fernald's account, in her historical introduction to the classic *Remedial Techniques in Basic School Subjects* (1943).

Fernald tells us that the three modalities she regarded as basic to instruction—the visual, auditory, and tactile-kinesthetic—were all given their proper recognition in the years of Greek, Roman, and medieval education. Vision was regarded as the major portal to the soul. Much learning, however, was of an oral nature, so the auditory modality also received its proper due. Further, instructors insisted that pupils learn through tracing; and manipulables provided tactile-kinesthetic training as well. Preoccupied as she was with this latter type of training, Fernald remarked approvingly on Plato's insistence that schoolmasters draw lines and have their pupils "write as the lines direct" (actually, this was common practice in Greek, Roman and, later, medieval schools). Quintilian, the famed pedagogue of Roman history, recommended a grooved board upon whose engraved letters pupils traced to learn their letters and words (again, a common strategem for the day). St. Jerome recommended the use of alphabet letters carved out of ivory for a little girl whose education he guided; for that matter, the Hebrews used alphabets made out of cookies, thus throwing a bit of oral reinforcement into their manipulatives. John Locke recommended that ". . . writing sheets be printed off with red ink . . ." upon which ". . . the pupil had nothing to do but go over with a good pen filled with black ink" (Fernald, 1941, p. 28). How happily Fernald regarded all of this.

Unfortunately, if you believe that kinesthesis is important in education, education tended to become more visual as the centuries progressed. Perhaps it is unfair to blame the visual modality, as Fernald does, for the suppression of auditory and kinesthetic senses. It appears to me that it was a matter of a bookish education being emphasized rather than a truly visual one. Otherwise what were Comenius, Rousseau, and Pestalozzi all complaining about? Perceptual powers were generally neglected by education—not just kinesthesis and audition, but vision as well. Nevertheless, it is true that look-say became a popular way of teaching reading, which may have also been due to the influence of educators of the deaf, for whom auditory means of teaching reading did not hold much promise. But if this is true, why did not those educators of the most kinesthetic of the handicapped, the deaf, emphasize the tactile and the kinesthetic in the influences they purportedly wielded? As the King of Siam told Anna, it is a puzzlement.

Fernald is, however, absolutely correct when she says that the visual sense became the major sense for educational effort. Please read our faculty trainers again, if you do not believe that. Visual processes, specifically visual imagery and memory, were the prime targets of Galton's epochal investigation of imagery. Like Fernald, he was also concerned with neglect and disuse of modalities, and of imagery and memory. Like her, too, he was sure of the value of kinesthesis, but the faculty he found being severely neglected was vision, a neglect he believed bordering on the heinous.

In Galton's *Inquiries into Human Faculty and its Development,* we find an extended discussion concerning the visualizing faculty.[6]

> There can . . . be no doubt as to the utility of the visualizing faculty, when it is duly subordinated to the higher intellectual operations. A visual image in the most perfect form of mental representation wherever the shape, position, and relations of objects in space are concerned. It is of importance in every handicraft and profession where design is required. . . . Strategists, artists of all denominations, physicists who contrive new experiments, and in short all who do not follow routine have need of it. . . . Our bookish and wordy education tends to repress this valuable gift of nature. A faculty that is of importance in all technical and artistic occupations, that gives accuracy to our perceptions, and justness to our generalizations, is starved by lazy disuse, instead of being cultivated judiciously in such a way as will on the whole bring the best return. I believe that a serious study of the best method of developing and utilizing this faculty, without prejudice to the practice of abstract thought in symbols, is one of the many pressing desiderata in the yet unformed science of education.[7] (Galton, 1873, p. 79)

The perceptive reader has undoubtedly perceived that Galton, in his recommendations for training the visualizing faculty, was concerned lest the operations of higher intellectual powers be interfered with or diminished by an overconcern with such training. Galton's studies had shown a limited correlation between "high visualising power" and the "intellectual faculties" (i.e., higher cognitive processes). In the end, it was the latter that he believed were most important. The powers of perception were to serve them, not overwhelm them with their operations.

Galton made a variety of recommendations for improving the visualizing faculty. It is, he said, clearly strengthened by practice. It is also improved by precise application, which results in a "thorough understanding" of the objects observed. Prosthetics can be helpful, for example, the use of marks and lines or dots to suggest a visual image. The use of a doll allows a child to clothe it through imagery with all sorts of

---

[6] Broadly conceived as encompassing perception, imagery, and memory related to the visual modality.

[7] Galton was curiously unresponsive to (or possibly unaware of) the great emphasis on perceptual training encouraged by sense–realist and naturalist movements. We do not read of Rousseau, Pestalozzi, or Froebel in his "Inquiry . . ."

"fantastic attributes" that provide practice in imagery. Memory training, i.e., the recall of images should follow along associationistic lines.

The chief art of strengthening visual, as well as every other form of memory, lies in multiplying associations; the healthiest memory being that in which all the associations are logical, and toward which all the senses concur in their due proportions. It is wonderful how much the vividness of a recollection is increased when two or more lines of association are simultaneously excited. (Galton, 187, p. 75)

Among the specific ways in which one can improve visual memory, we find the following in Galton's recommendations:

A useful faculty, easily developed by practice, is that of retaining a retinal picture. A scene is flashed upon the eye; the memory of it persists, and details, which escaped during the brief time it was actually seen, may be analyzed and studied at leisure in the subsequent vision. (Galton, 1873, p. 74)

Extensive awareness of the possibilities of kinesthetic learning was extant past the midpoint of the nineteenth century as we know from our previous chapters. That kinesthesis (more specifically called the hand-kinesthetic approach by Fernald) might improve learning through other modalities was also known. First let us observe Galton's observations on the matter. He expressed enthusiasm concerning the accomplishments of M. Lecoq de Boisbaudran, who had directed the École Nationale de Dessin in Paris and written a book, *Education de la Mémoire Pittoresque*, in which kinesthetic means were used to develop visual processes:

He trained his pupils with extraordinary success, beginning with the simplest figures. They were made to study the models thoroughly before they began to draw them from memory. One favorite expedient was to associate the sight memory with the muscular memory, by making the pupils follow at a distance the outlines of the figures with a pencil held in their hands. After three of four months their visual memory became greatly strengthened. They had no difficulty in summoning images at will, in holding them steady, and in drawing them. Their copies were executed with marvelous fidelity, as attested by a commission of the Institute, appointed in 1852 to inquire into the matter. (Galton, 1873, pp. 73–74)

Binet also wrote about M. Boisbaudran's accomplishments which caused him to be mentioned by William James, who also told about Boisbaudran's remarkable achievements. Binet observed that tracing letter and word forms accomplished significant improvements in what appeared to be otherwise intractable cases of word blindness. Binet commented:

[They] succeeded in reading in an ingenious roundabout way which they often discover for themselves; it is enough that they should trace the letters with their fingers to understand their sense. (Fernald, 1943, p. 163)

James remarked on the use of eye tracing to improve his own faulty visual memory processes:

> I am a myself a good draftsman, and have a very lively interest in pictures, statues, and architecture and decoration, and a keen sensibility to artistic effects. But I am an extremely poor visualizer and find myself unable to reproduce in my mind's eye pictures which I have most carefully examined . . . and find that I can seldom call to mind even a single letter of the alphabet in purely retinal terms. I must trace the letter by running my mental eyes over its contour in order that the image of it shall have any distinctness at all. (Fernald, 1943, p. 174)

We may turn at this point to a rather expressive, if somewhat over-ripe, discussion of imagery training. Once again it is Reuben Halleck with whom we are concerned—a remarkably neglected pioneer, one whose interests in all aspects of modality[8] (and motor) training have much that is original about them. There is little in current books about process training that cannot be identified with analogues in Halleck's work (if we allow Pestalozzi to provide the paper-and-pencil aspects). His book *The Education of the Central Nervous System* sought to establish a comprehensive curriculum for sensory-motor training in the schools of his day, with a particular emphasis upon the early grades when the nervous system is still plastic. His curriculum was intended ". . . to prescribe for our complex nervous systems the proper kinds of exercise, sensory, motor and ideational, demanded for full development" (Halleck, 1897, p. viii).

Halleck was cognizant of audiles and visiles, but recognized that one sense could create the imagery for another. Certain types of literature, for example, even when presented to the pupil orally "excite the visual tract most strongly" (Halleck, 1897, p. 53). He, like Fernald, was concerned about excessive emphasis upon the visual sense (and on the auditory, to a lesser extent). Unlike many process trainers of his day and later, he believed that all the senses, including taste and smell,[9] were to receive equal cultivation, since all were necessary for the full maturation and effective functioning of the brain. He, like, Galton, Binet, Fernald, etc., recognized the possibilities of using the sense of touch to support the more fundamental modalities deployed in education. Halleck said it had to be effectively trained in order for an individual to use his eyes "intelligently," and he mused over the advantages of having a child be blind the first two years of its life so that it would develop greater responsiveness to tactile sensations.

Of particular interest to us are Halleck's theories of imagery culture, i.e., "recalled images of sense–objects," as an aid in ". . . modifying and developing the sensory cells" (Halleck, 1897, p. ix).

---

[8] Channels and all.

[9] It took a ". . . cultivated olefactory brain tract in order to assimilate the words of the greatest writers" (Halleck, 1897, p. 116).

These "recalled images," he said, are to be distinguished from those impressions immediately remaining after the cessation and as an immediate result of sensory impressions.

> To have the various sensory images pouring into the brain is but one-half of the battle in modifying the central nervous system. In order to render this modification more definite and lasting, images of these various stimuli must be recalled. . . . A successful recall helps to modify the brain in the same way that the original stimulus did. (Halleck, 1897, p. 149)

One major way of providing a pupil training in imagery is to expose him to the best of English writers whose works abound with multivariegated and vivid imagery. Such poets as Milton and Browning are among those ". . . whose sensory and motor tracts must be well developed" (Halleck, 1897, p. 83). This was to be expected as a result of their having dwelt amidst rural settings, wherein they were exposed to the "incomparable stimuli of the country." The imagery of their literature can be used to train imagery in pupils, if this literature is managed for this purpose. And above all writers whose imagery was to be used for such cultivation was Shakespeare (written Shakspere in Halleck's tome). The greatest of poets was also the greatest of image makers. And so we find *the Education of the Central Nervous System* devoting a goodly number of pages to Shakespeare's life and writings. Where else can we find a chapter entitled "How Shakspere's Senses were Trained"? If Halleck devoted so much time to Shakespeare's relationships with modalities, surely we can take a page or two to consider them ourselves.

> . . . in his sensory experience is to be found the foundation of all those imperishable structures given to humanity by his heaven-climbing genius. Two things are true of Shakspere—his senses had magnificent training; the stimuli of nature also had in him a wonderful central nervous system to develop. (Halleck, 1897, p. 171)[10]

Halleck admitted that evidence from Shakespeare's life was sparse as to his education. However, from his products one can tell about his processes! In truth, forsooth, there is much to be said in favor of Halleck's arguments as they wade through Shakespeare's plays and poetry to show the wide ranged use of imagery that the Bard employed. All of which suggests that he received ". . . fine sense training from the field, the forest, and the sky" (Halleck, 1897, p. 205).

Shakespeare was clearly a multimodality person, with a tendency to synesthesia perhaps; really, one can't fault Halleck's evidence for

---

[10] Halleck was concerned with motor processes, too. So he mentioned that not only did Shakespeare have "magnificent" sensory training through his exposure to the environment of his time (not through school), but also because he ". . . made the proper motor responses thereto. . . ."

Shakespeare's heightened sensitivity of senses, perception, and imagery. In one passage (we ignore, in quoting, the original framework of the poetry), Shakespeare appeals to the sense of smell to express the beauty of a piece of music: ". . . the sweet sound that breathes upon a bank of violets, stealing and giving odour." In describing Cleopatra's trip down the Nile, the poet again appeals to smell, this time to heighten the visual imagery of his verse: "Purple the sails, and so perfumed that the winds were lovesick with them" (Halleck, 1897, p. 111).

Taste also has its day in Shakespeare's poetry as Halleck demonstrated: though less abundant and more concrete in its imagery than is the case with smell. Touch too is given its due. For example: "Love's feeling is more soft and sensible than are the tender horns of cockled snails" (Halleck, 1897, p. 120). Kinesthesis, Halleck strained to show, is also there. His book provides a few examples. Thus a speech describing Hamlet's behavior when near Ophelia (*Hamlet,* Act II, Sc. I):

> At last a little shaking of mine arm,
> And thrice his head thus waving up and down,
> He raised a sigh so piteous and profound
> As it did seem to shatter all his bulk
> And end his being.

About this description, Halleck remarked, "It is well to notice that if we form definite images of Hamlet's behavior with Ophelia, as we read these lines, we must appeal to former muscular sensations" (Halleck, 1897, p. 122).

And so on through the lexicon of senses or sensations, not ignoring the "temperature sense," which, Halleck pointed out, recent experiment had shown to be different from those of "touch."

The great poets, like Shakespeare, Browning, and Milton (his favorite examples) Halleck repeatedly pointed out, developed their imagery-laden verse, not only on the basis of superior nervous systems, but also because of superior experiences; they had early and continued exposure to the experiences that broad and varied lives within nature provided. True, he admitted, we cannot expect all children to develop the same highly sensitive and specialized nervous systems without some aid from heredity. Even the most deprived CNS, however, will benefit from proper sensory exposure and proper modality training. For the latter, it is nature and the great writers that will be helpful. But, to be sure, specific types of training programs for specific modalities can also help. Did anyone who is reading this book expect less? Of course, there are things to be touched and seen and heard, and there are thermal experiences to induce different shades of temperature, etc., and images, images, everywhere. Not a sense is to be neglected in this training.

The truth is that man has not a single unnecessary sense, not one that should not be systematically trained. We have become accustomed to class people as those whose images are chiefly those of the visual or auditory type. In many things these two classes of persons are scarcely intelligible to each other, because their ideas do not rest on the same sensory experiences. To the one class, the world is one of sight; to the other, one of sound.

We agree with Binet (*La Psychologie du Raisonnement*) that the normal man is one who can form definite images from all the senses, who can recall amost equally well the odour, colour, and touch of a rose, the taste of whipped custard as well as the sound made in beating it. If this is the right view, many are but sawed-off specimens of human beings. (Halleck, 1897, p. 110)

Of all the training "kits" that Halleck assembled to train imagery we shall only quote his program on *Taste Images for Recall*.

After repeatedly tasting the following named edibles, see how distinctly you can recall the

Taste of chicken	Taste of lemon	Taste of honey
Taste of duck	Taste of strawberry	Taste of sugar
Taste of quail	Taste of raspberry	Taste of molasses
Taste of turkey	Taste of pineapple	Taste of vingegar
Taste of shad	Taste of peach	Taste of castor oil
Taste of salmon	Taste of pear	Taste of turnip
Taste of herring	Taste of sour apple	Taste of celery
Taste of oyster	Taste of sweet apple	Taste of mustard
Taste of veal	Taste of custard	Taste of pepper
Taste of beef	Taste of coffee	Taste of jelly
		Taste of maple syrup

Can you place two taste images side by side and be clearly aware of the difference between them? Compare, for instance, the remembered taste of chicken with turkey, of apple with peach, of cabbage with turnip, of mustard with horseradish.

Can you imagine the taste of a lemon or sour apple so vividly that you can note the resulting effects in the mouth, in perhaps a puckering sensation, or feeling as if the saliva was curdling?

It may be wise to call attention again to the fact that the more interest one feels in the taste and flavour of his food, the slower will he eat, and the better will be his digestion. Many persons eat so fast and so many different things together, that no definite taste images are formed. (Halleck, 1897, pp. 161–162)

Halleck, concerned as he was with the use of literary training and specific modality training to insure development of the sensory-motor centers and tracts of the central nervous system, still, most of all, insisted that natural exposure to the right things of life trained best of all. The world of things, if properly smelled, touched, viewed, heard, provides the best of all sensory-motor culture.

We have seen in previous chapters that the systematic training of the senses is something that perhaps begins with Pestalozzi, or if not with him, certainly with Itard. But much of what sense training was about in the past was really the exercise of those senses upon the world around one. This emphasis upon natural training of the senses was more than a recognition that cognitive processes should be developed. It was also part of a general revolt against bookishness and the blighting of experiential opportunities that appeared to prevail even among the privileged classes. That was what Rousseau had complained about, and much of process training beyond him had Rousseau (manifest or otherwise) on its agendas. Read him again, and read some other process trainers of current day. For that matter read Piaget, not quite classed as a process trainer, and see if you don't see Rousseau.

What I am leading up to is a reminder to the reader that it was nature and nature study and the sciences that were used to train the various senses, as well as boxes of thyme, marjoram, and tasting contests. The scientific age of educational psychology moved into the study of children's perceptions with this in mind, armed with the "educator's friend," the questionnaire.

Colvin stated a basic premise guiding this sort of research.

. . . it happens that at the basis of every developed experience there lies a perception, and it follows further that the more extended the experience of the individual is, both in particular and in general, the wider is his range of perception. (Colvin, 1914, p. 83)

Off they went, psychologist and educator, to study the "range and nature" of children's perceptions. The first of the "experiments" in this area were apparently performed in Berlin under the direction of the Pedagogical Verein, in 1870, with the principal results reported by a Herr Bartholomai. The results indicated that Berlin school children had relatively few and weak perceptions at the time of their entry into school. Nine years later, Karl Lange carried out a similar experiment in Plauen, Germany. Children were asked 14 different questions, e.g., who had seen the sun, stars, moon. He found that city children knew considerably less about natural phemonena than did country children.

In the United States, G. Stanley Hall carried out an investigation to determine "the contents of the minds of children of average intelligence." He interrogated children entering the primary schools of Boston to develop an inventory of those contents. The results surprised him. Hall's report showed what appeared to be an unusual amount of perceptual confusion in children on the threshold of their school careers.

The high rate of ignorance . . . may surprise most persons. . . . Skeins and spools of thread were said to grow on the sheep's back or on bushes, stockings on trees, butter to come from buttercups. . . . Cheese is squeezed butter, the cow says "bow-wow," the pig purrs or burrows, etc. . . . (Colvin, 1914, p. 85)

In what particulars these children's responses were deficient and whether or not they were able to comprehend Hall's questions was not too carefully thought through by this investigator, but the conclusions seemed obvious:

(1) That there is next to nothing of pedagogic value, the knowledge of which is safe to assume at the outset of school life . . . (2) The best preparation parents can give their children for good school training is to make them acquainted with natural objects, especially with the sights and sounds of the country. (Colvin, 1914, p. 85)

It seems to me that Comenius, Rousseau, and other earlier investigators had reached similar conclusions, even without the aid of questionnaires, but they did not have to contend with graduate students seeking thesis topics—so perhaps-hence-their lack of scientific inventiveness.

It was a generally accepted position that Hall enunciated, really. We find Norsworthy and Whitley writing decades later paraphrasing it:

It is the duty of the teacher to take . . . life situations, and in connection with the reactions which naturally take place, to develop sense perceptions which are clear, correct, and adequate, to see to it that they are numerous and rich as possible, and to supply material or motive when either is lacking; for upon material gathered from sense perception will depend all future growth and development. (Norsworthy and Whitley, 1918, p. 129)

These authors were writing with Thorndike and Dewey in the background. It was still a matter, as Galton had suggested, of increasing associations—and still a matter of Rousseau as to what was to be associated. The fresh-air camps for exposing the underprivileged to the wonders of nature owe their heritage to these beliefs. (At least this is true of that part not associated with the idea that fresh air improves one's health, also a reform idea but one with different antecedents.)

Hall's investigations were confirmed in their conclusions by subsequent studies carried out by B. Hartman in 1880–1884 in the schools of Annaberg, Germany, over an unusually long period for that (or any other) time. Hartman also disproved Herbart's thesis that the triangle was the simplest and best known geometric figure, it coming in a poor third in terms of familiarity to the globe (ball) and circle, which occupied first and second place.

Seyffert, Superintendant of Schools in Zwickau, Germany, found that pictorial objects are not nearly as well known as their concrete representations. Olsen in 1896 studied 5600 pupils in Denmark and observed "remarkable" misconceptions on children's part regarding the world about them. He commented:

> Very much that passed under the children's eyes every day was not noticed. School work must be built upon a very poor foundation of clear ideas. The fact that children see objects a hundred times without acquiring consciousness of them suggests that we need to converse with children about the commonest things. (Colvin, 1914, p. 87)

Meumann, that energetic refugee from Wundt's laboratories (who might have saddened his mentor because he chose to put his talents to work in applied rather than experimental psychology) also moved onto the topic. A team of teachers, Dr. Engelsperger and Dr. Zigeler, working under his direction in the *volkschule* in Munich during the school year 1903–1904, studied children with both rural and urban backgrounds. Not surprisingly, they found great differences in the accuracy of their perceptions. The results of this investigation clearly proved, Meumann said, that city children should be taken into the country as often as possible and country children into the city as often as possible; and that instruction of both should proceed on the basis of the instructor's awareness that these two different classes of children were quite different in their stores of ideas.

Other of Meumann's conclusions were that the child knows happenings in his home the best; that things encountered in mere wanderings are known much less exactly; that things the child handles become more familiar to him than those he does not handle; that he knows things he is interested in better than those which hold no interest for him; and that things arousing unpleasant feelings are better known than those which create positive affects.

In general, Meumann concluded that the child of six is generally deficient in perception and that his perceptual knowledge is at best fragmentary, incomplete, and inaccurate. The early use of models and the observation of concrete objects, rather than immersion in books, was the prescription he offered for improving affairs.

By the 1920s, a considerable body of information had accrued concerning children's modality functions through experiment, questionnaire, and test. Books such as Whipple's *Manual of Mental and Physical Tests* guided the assessment of sensory and motor capacities. Sandiford, in *The Mental and Physical Life of School Children*, and the omniactive Meumann's *The Psychology of Learning*, were among the guides to psychologists and educators concerned with learning processes. The results of varied investigations revealed a prevalence of sensory defects in children, particularly among those attending public schools. The development of the powers of perception and imagery was charted.

Different "stages" were found. Under-seven children attend to disconnected items that constitute a "substance" stage, which is succeeded by one involving greater attention to action; girls are more mature in their development through such stages. A ten-year-old begins to report on spatial, temporal, and causal relationships, but his ability to qualitatively analyze objects comes after age 12. Training to observe by different categories such as number, color, and form has an immediate but ephemeral impact if the category used is too advanced for the child's age. So Norsworthy and Whitley summed up the observations of developmental and educational psychologists in the period leading up to their book (Norsworthy and Whitley, 1920).

These coauthors also reviewed the available literature on imagery. The type concept, as we noted earlier, still hung about, though qualified, in their writings. Children, they found, were usually of mixed types in respect to imagery. "This is as true of children as . . . of adults . . . though the greater proportion of visual images in childhood remains a fact" (Norsworthy and Whitley, 1920, p. 150). Children also employ concrete imagery more than adults. Children at a preschool level usually use reproductive imagery and rely on imitation for its expression. From age three upward to seven or eight, there is evidence of the development of creative imagination. Between 10 and 13, children's imagination tends to become more practical and purposive, more "realistic than fanciful." During adolescence, imagery becomes related to the youth and maiden in terms of their "own doings, ambitions, accomplishments, and plans." It is highly subjective. As adolescence passes, the demands of the everyday world press in and the ". . . average adult so pressed by the demands of a practical world that his imagery, to fill his need, must measure up to the requirements of life" (Norsworthy and Whitley, 1920, pp. 155–156).

We need not go further in our review of developmental perception and imagery. The age of research in childhood development, inaugurated by Preyer, Darwin, etc., in Europe and advanced in the United States by such energetic thinkers as G. Stanley Hall, has never since left us. We have charted children's behaviors up and down. Those associated with what we call modalities have never been far out of the limelight in this childhood-preoccupied country of ours.

EARLY RESEARCH INTO MODALITY FUNCTIONING

While I do not intend to comprehensively catalog all early educational research into modality functioning, some of it is worth reviewing to make the point that many communalities existed "way back then" with the sort of work still going on in schools. Research workers, educational and psychological, in the decades closing the eighteenth century and opening the nineteenth, were proceeding on a sensory-motor basis in many of their investigations, which is to be expected. The "facts" upon which they were proceeding were those of the new phrenology, of the introspectionist laboratories, and of the new tests-and-measurement movement, all of which were very sensory-motor. Research moves where its facts and tools lead it. Research in the schools moved in a modality direction.

Alors, we find McLenman and Dewey writing as far back as 1897 on the importance of proper perceptual discrimination and clear percepts to number mastery, and producing research to prove their point. Meumann, to be found everywhere bustling about the halls of school research, produced evidence for muscle memory (along with memories associated with pain, temperature, and just about every other sensory quality he could identify). Presumably, it formed a basis for academic retention and transfer of training (Colvin, 1914). Eckhardt, a German investigator, carried out experiments (1907) into the significance of the modalities in schoolwork. Pupils who visualized well did well in respect to number readiness and arithmetic memory. Visiles were slower but more accurate than those who solved arithmetic problems through other modalities. Lobsen, like his countryman Eckhardt, working in a mathematical frame of reference, arrived at altogether different conclusions. He found that strong auditory processes were basic to arithmetic success in the earlier years that he and Eckhardt were studying; and that there was a negative correlation between visual memory and both oral and written arithmetic (Bronner, 1917). The "I found this even though you found that" paradigm in educational research has a long history.

In spelling research, modalities also led the way. In 1892, Wycoff published an account of results obtained through spelling tests. She gave two series of tests, "one for the eye and one for ear impressions." Her conclusions:

> Knowledge of spelling begins with perception through eye or ear, and ends with the establishment of a train of memories. Somewhere along this line we may find a defective provision. (Hollingsworth, 1918, p. 2)

Lay and Abbott and Kuhlmann (1899–1909) investigated the differences in success found with spelling when modality variations were employed. They compared auditory versus visual presentation of words; they compared loud and soft speaking and the role of hand-kinesthetic reinforcement of spelling lessons. On the whole, it was discrimination of sound and association of visual form with word sounds that appeared to be the basic elements in spelling. Carman (1900–1901), on the other hand, quite likely influenced by Woodworth, ruled more in favor of specific attention to "small differences" in words as being responsible for success in spelling than were factors of visual perception or memory.

Brown (1913–1914) reached similar conclusions. On the other hand, Carman's investigations led him to blame spelling problems on (among other factors) motorial incoordination, sensorial incoordination (accentuating the auditory), and a combination of both motorial and sensorial difficulties (1902). Smedley, to the contrary, found that good spelling had a very limited relationship to visual or auditory factors and concluded that higher processes are at work, i.e., a rational factor, to account for proper spelling accuracy. But these results disagreed with Kline's findings (1912) that learning in spelling is related to imagery type and that both sensory and motor processes are, when faulty, at the basis of poor spelling. Leta Hollingsworth, in her investigation (1918), wrote of spelling errors being due to difficulties in forming cognitive bonds. In spelling, a child is expected to "bind the visual perception of the separate letters with the muscular movements of hand, arm and fingers necessary to copy the words" (Hollingsworth, 1918, p. 80). Bronner decided that poor spelling may be due to problems in "binding" visual symbols with auditory ones (Bronner, 1917). No one can say that these researchers were not trying.

Similar role calls of processes and associations to make them function all together are to be found in the research on other language arts. Meumann (we cannot escape him) told his readers the obvious. Language is a unit, from learning to decode one's native language up to and through the understanding of abstruse contents, acquisition of a foreign language, and learning how to write intelligent compositions. Within this unit, both the words employed and the mental contents conveyed by them, said Meumann, are presented through visual symbols that must be interpreted by the reader. There must be association of visual symbols with sound patterns. There must be memory from the standpoint of recognition and recall. Do not forget motor processes or associations. You now have had reading explained.

MODALITIES IN REMEDIAL EDUCATION

Remedial reading has always had a strong modality bent. Hinschelwood's recommendations for correcting or curing congenital word blindness were based on the notion of modality centers. He suggested three stages in teaching the word-blind child to read. The first was to teach him to store up individual letters of the alphabet in the visual memory part of his brain. The second stage was that of teaching the pupil to read by spelling the words out loud, appealing to auditory memory for retrieval of the whole word. The third stage was a matter of gradual acquisitions of words by the visual memory storage system (Wiederholt, 1974). Visual memory centers were favorite places to point to whenever there were problems in reading, of which Orton remarked (1928):

> No pathological condition of the visual memory centre has yet been demonstrated, and ordinary methods of school instruction may cover a multitude of sins. (Monroe, 1946, p. 38)

The simplicity of explanation that was and is possible in referring reading problems to brain centers, however, continued to draw adherents to the idea, once visual centers had been established in the brain by neurological research. The list of supporters of the notion is extensive, but need not be repeated here. What we are rather concerned with immediately is the paralleling belief (with or without adherence to neurological explanations) that modality problems explained reading problems. Groszman expressed the belief that there are children who, without any other mental defects to explain their poor reading,

> . . . had poor powers of visualization, and impaired visual and aural memory, even when their power of judgment and rational thought appear unaffected. (Groszman, 1917, p. 126)

Remedial language specialists also turned to modalities and modality problems to explain learning problems. If poor visualization did not explain a reading problem, faulty auditorization was there to fall back on. But visual problems were preferred. Gates, in his earlier edition of *The Improvement of Reading* (1927), stated:

> The author believes . . . deficiencies in visual perception and analysis of words to be the most common cause of failure and difficulty in reading. (Fernald, 1943, p. 165)

In a later edition (1935), in which one suspects Gates was influenced by the antiprocess mood of the behavioristic thirties, the modality aspects are reduced in importance. He describes his program as embodying ". . . relatively little exploration of 'auditory perception,' 'visual memory,' etc.," (Fernald, 1943, p. 166). He was willing rather to attribute most reading problems to ". . . failure to acquire techniques that might have been acquired had the right guidance been given at the right time" (Fernald, 1943, p. 166). L. J. Brueckner, writing on remedial education in 1931, almost entirely eschewed mention of any type of cognitive processes. It was depression time and hypothetical constructs were starving too.

Nevertheless, they did persist, and neither Gates nor even Brueckner could do entirely without some modality speculations in their writings, while Marian Monroe in her book *Children Who Cannot Read* (1936) remained true to modalities, emphasizing auditory as well as visual ones. Causes for reading disability included, she said:

> ... defects in discrimination of complex visual patterns, defects in discrimination or orientation and sequence of patterns, lack of precision in discrimination of speech sounds and of the temporal sequence of sounds. (Fernald, 1943, p. 166)

There is a gestalt psychology flavor in such hypothecations. There are also anticipations of the ITPA, for Samuel Kirk was influenced by Monroe (1940). Let us examine the Monroe Reading Aptitude Test, tests that allowed profiles of the testee's aptitudes.

There are a variety of aptitudes it assessed: visual aptitudes: visual orientation, ocular motor control, visual memory; auditory aptitudes: auditory discrimination, auditory sound blending, auditory memory. There are motor aptitudes: motor tapping, motor tracing, and motor writing; aptitudes for articulation: articulation reproduction, articulation speed. Finally, there are language aptitudes: language vocabulary, language classification, and language sentence use.

Both Gates and Monroe recommended the inclusion of kinesthetic technology in remedial education, though to a lesser degree than Fernald and of a sort that Fernald did not fully approve.[11] While recognizing that kinesthesis from whatever source was useful in supporting the imagery and memories resulting from the visual and auditory modalities, Fernald recommended the hand-tracing method as best. The kinesthetic inputs from voicing words, aloud or silently, while reading, the use of a pencil to trace words, were simply not as good as the hand-kinesthetic method. She was somewhat disparaging of the methods recommended by Gates and Monroe on these accounts, despite their kinesthetic components. Some of Gates's recommendations appeared in the 1935 edition of *Visual Study and Writing (Spelling) Method for Non-Readers:*

They included (as described by Fernald):

> (1) Careful observation of the printed word during pronunciation by syllables; (2) attempt to visualize the word with the eyes closed during silent articulation by syllables for the purpose of providing a check on the success of observation; and (3) writing of the word with silent articulation by syllables. (Fernald, 1943, p. 169)

One of Monroe's remedial approaches, based it would appear on the Fernald-Keller method (1921) is described by Monroe in an example:

> The teacher wrote the word to be learned in large handwriting on a piece of paper. She said to the child, "See this word? This word is man. Say man. Now let me see how slowly you can say man, like this, m-a-n. Now I want you to do two things at the same time. Take your pencil and trace over this word while you say

---

[11] Fernald was quite jealous concerning credits concerning tactile-kinesthetic training.

m-a-n, slowly. Be sure to trace quickly enough and speak slowly enough that you will come out just even.'' The sounding consisted simply of articulating the word distinctly and slowly enough for the sequence of sounds to become evident. . . . The tracing united the letters as the pencil was not lifted until the end of the word. (Fernald, 1943, pp. 169–170)

Dolch recommended tests of visual memory in studying reading problems and an emphasis upon visual imagery in training. Hildreth told readers of *Teaching Spelling, A Guide to Principles and Practices* (1955): "Emphasize visual imagery as well as sound if you want pupils to spell accurately and learn readily'' (Otto and McMenemy, 1966, p. 219).

In her book *Learning the Three Rs* (1936), Hildreth made the case for visual imagery in equally strong terms and for visual perception, too. Problems in handwriting, for example are related to

Difficulty in retaining visual impressions . . . faulty perception . . . and faulty imagery . . . (as a result) . . . the pupil's ability to accurately recall letter form models is impaired and the result is inefficient reproduction of letter forms in handwriting (Otto and McMenemy, 1966, pp. 282–283)

Mckee, Durrell, and Kottmeyer made a strong case for auditory training in their recommendations for remediation (not overlooking other processes, however). Hegge and Kirk's methods were strong in auditory and kinesthetic training. Check Spache for the latest in modality considerations in remedial education, but then look back at William Tydiman's recommendations for the teaching of spelling (1917) in which he recommended the pupil try to ''see'' a word with his eyes closed (Brueckner, 1931). There is a long time span between the two men but, conceptually, the distance does not appear that great.

Our sojourn with remedial modality specialists is almost at a close, however, it would not do to part from remediation without a deeper initiation into the thinking of Grace Fernald.[12] Let us begin with her deliberations on memory types:

We find great individual differences in types of recall images. . . . Every student of psychology knows that some people tend to get visual images, that is to picture experiences that they recall; that other people either get no visual images at all or very vague ones. Some of these latter individuals remember things in terms of sound, getting what we call auditory images. . . . Still others would

[12] I have not devoted the space to Fernald that her role in modality training deserves. This is because there is so much already written about her technique, and her book on remediation is still generally available. Let me note, however, that Lewis Terman regarded her book as one of the most significant contributions ever made to "experimental pedagogy." "The value of Dr. Fernald's work goes far beyond the treatment of extreme non-readers," he enthused, "With minor modifications, the same method succeeds with all" (Fernald, 1943, p. ix).

remember things in terms of their own movements. In the case of a word, invididuals in this last group would think of the word in terms of lip and throat movement or the movement of the hand in writing the word. Most people get a combination of all three imagery types, either recalling single objects in all three ways or thinking certain objects in one of the imagery forms and other objects in some other form. (Fernald, 1943, p. 182)

There are several points to be observed relative to Fernald's posture on modalities.[13] That they were of prime consideration in education, in her view, does not require reiteration. She believed in multisensory training and became identified with it, though she was but one of many. She agreed with Galton that the visual sense was the major one in the acquisition and accorded auditory perception its due as second in importance. She believed in individual differences in imagery and in imagery types or dominance, but in her book did not linger on them stating: "The whole matter is too complicated to discuss fully here" (Fernald, 1943, p. 182). She was rather vague as to the modality or modalities to which she assigned her hand-kinesthetic method. She was even more obscure as to how she wanted to categorize its inputs into imagery:

It may be questioned whether the word "image" can be applied to recall in terms of the individual's own movements. Since eye, lip, and throat movements are components of visual and auditory recall, we shall use the term image to designate all three types of recall without going into the theoretical discussion. (Fernald, 1943, p. 82)

Fernald did not appear to place much credence in the possibilities of improving modality-based types of functioning. The VAKT approach, associated with her name, is not directly a process training approach, but rather one in which a generally strong process or processes, i.e., those of the hand-kinesthetic nomenclature, is (are) used to bolster and support the major modalities employed in learning, i.e., the auditory and the visual—more basically the visual—when they are poorly developed, weak, enfeebled or impaired:

In more cases of visual or auditory defects, the hand-kinesthetic method . . . serves to build up an adequate apperceptive background, which makes it possible for the child to use effectively such sensory cues as he has. (Fernald, 1943, p. 32)

The results of our investigation seem to indicate that the various visual and auditory perceptual and association deficiencies . . . would disappear if the visual and auditory experiences were supplemented by tactual and kinesthetic experiences . . . normal perception, retention, and memory could be developed by individuals whose failure seems to be due to inability to learn through visual

---

[13] I am interpreting her position per her writings as of 1943.

and auditory channels, if tactual and kinesthetic methods were involved in the learning process.[14] (Fernald, 1943, pp. 166–167)

Interestingly enough, Fernald did not concern herself with precision diagnostics.[15] Though she recognized individual differences in modality-based functioning, she also appeared to believe that the approach to academic remediation, when either visual or auditory "experiences" were not just going right, was to move in with her hand-kinesthetic approach. And while she didn't suggest programs of training that went beyond the kinestheses created by the VAKT, she was of the belief that kinesthetic activation is otherwise massively involved in learning, particularly when difficulties are encountered in apprehension.

In all our extreme cases the individual describes the method by which he is able to learn successfully as one in which the adjustments are represented to himself in terms of hand, lip, throat, and general bodily adaptations. He learns not only reading and spelling, but other things in this way.

Observations of the behavior of our cases during the learning of reading, spelling, foreign language, and other subjects, shows that the individual is actually making overt movements of the hands, lips, and throat when he is attempting to learn any new thing. In reading he attempts to form the words or the letters with his hand and vocalizes the word or the letters with definite throat, lip, and tongue movements. When this is stopped, the learning process is blocked. In other words, he actually needs to form the word with his hand and vocalize it during the initial learning process. (Fernald, 1943, p. 167)

Fernald had no doubt that the kinesthetic method (her kinesthetic method) was the elixir that cured the process problems that ailed you.

In all our cases of total disability of the type called "word-blindness" in the literature we have found that the individual learns rapidly and easily by the kinesthetic method. This applies not only to reading but also to the initial stages of learning anything. (Fernald, 1943, p. 167)

Harold Benjamin, Fernald's editor, in his introduction to her book hailed it as one of the most important products of the "truly revolutionary, scientific movement" in education. In light of the enthusiasm shown for the hand-kinesthetic technique by him and others such as Lewis M. Terman, let us ask ourselves whether kinesthesis has received the recognition Fernald felt was rightfully due it in the years that followed her exposition of its glories. The answer is both yes and no; a fitting one that befits our times.

---

[14] Writing in a behavioristic age, Fernald managed to generally avoid reifying her terms. Note the term "experiences."
[15] Perhaps because she didn't have a test to sell.

A PASSING LOOK AT THE MOTOR MODALITIES

There surely has been no shortage of work directed toward motor training, with physical education becoming more prominent within remedial and special education, and with occupational therapy and physical therapy insisting upon their places, too. For that matter, isn't kinesthesis a prime sense in speech therapy? Yet, it seems to not quite be allowed its place full front with the modalities of vision and speech, even now. At the height of visual training, Barsch could say (1965), "Vision defines distance, color, relationships, textures—and becomes the *true integrating agent* for touch, kinaesthesia and audition" (Meyers and Hammill, 1969, p. 124).

So even from the father of movigenics, vision receives recognition as the regnant sense. While earlier, Gettman could say, "Vision is intelligence" (1962) (Meyers and Hammill, 1969, p. 113). The old observing faculty cannot be dethroned by the motor one. And with audition now clearly making its bid for commercial, if not theoretical honors, movement will clearly remain in third place among the "senses," a trustworthy servant to the other two, but in a supporting rather than a starring role.

MODALITY TRAINING AND THE HANDICAPPED

One final set of observations about the modalities concerns their major position in the training of the mentally handicapped: "Training of the senses"—the phrase, the concept, and the practice were commonplace in almost every type of training and educational approach to the mentally retarded. Even when the mentally retarded were thought to be entirely incurable or uneducable, sense training would still somehow improve them, make them more responsive and responsible, if not smarter and better trained and educated, according to Sherlock and Donkin (1911), Groszman (1917), Inskeep (1926), Descoeudres (1927), and Gesell (who vaguely recommended hand-eye busy work as somehow of value to the retarded in a book written in the 1930s). All seemed to agree that, at the least, perceptual training and perceptual motor training were effective means of "prodding the dull and inert brain" of the retarded child, so "choked with inertia" (Inskeep, 1926). What the sense–realist and naturalist movements had wrought and Itard specifically applied to the mentally retarded was seldom gainsaid.

The curriculum for the mentally retarded in the ungraded schools of Berlin, as developed by Dermoor, was discussed by Descoeudres. That class's schedule is presented below (verbatim) as per her book (Descoeudres, 1927, p. 63).

(a) Training of the senses .... 2 hrs.
(b) Training of the various kinds of attention,
particularly the visual attention[16] (ten-minute
lessons) .... 1 hr.
(c) Handwork (folding, cutting, and especially
modeling)... 6 hrs.
(d) Speech exercises.. 3 hrs.
(e) Exercises in perceptual arithmetic .... 2½ hrs.
(f) Drawing exercises .... 3 hrs.
(g) Froebelian games: (1) individual games
(building, etc.) (2) collective games .... 2½ hrs.
(h) Eurhythmic exercises.................................... 2¼ hrs.
(i) Singing .... 1½ hrs.
      Excursions .... 3 hrs.
      Recreation .... 2½ hrs.
                                   Total (per week)   29¼ hrs.

Count it up, a curriculum that in the bulk is perceptual-motor. There is a clear identification of training the mentally retarded with sensory-motor training, almost exclusively. All this is based upon the notion that this was the way to proceed to help those who surely could have benefitted from some utilitarian instruction, but were denied it on the basis that the sensory-motor level was, if not the only way to go, the major way to go. Tredgold stated the premises of this training in one of the many editions published of his book on mental retardation. This quotation is from the 1917 edition:

It is necessary to pay particular attention to the cultivation of the sensory motor functions. In the ordinary child these are perfected as a result of his own initiative, but in the ament special stimulation is required, not only because of the presence . . . of defects and irregularities of nerve action (which) must be corrected . . . (if) useful work can be accomplished, but because such training affords a most valuable means of developing and coordinating intellectual activity . . . by suitable impressions through eye, ear, skin, muscle, nose and mouth, the range and delicacy of the sensorium are increased, the brain rendered more receptive, the power of discrimination, as well as motor response, encouraged, and a basis supplied for figures, thoughts and ideas. . . . The mental capacity of even the healthy child would be generally improved by a course of sensory training on physiological lines. . . . In the case of the defective mind, such a course of training is usually absolutely necessary. (Inskeep, 1926, pp. 390–391)

---

[16] Do not forget that attention was frequently trained in association with the various modalities.

SOME CONCLUSIONS

To conclude: I would simply like to call to the reader's attention the fact that even the most modern of today's modality-training approaches is redolent of the theories and practices that came to bloom during the nineteenth century and were in full bloom in the earlier decades of the present one. We still have faculties, in S and R form, with associational ties that bind. Galton might need a lexicon to help him understand the newer terminologies of current "modality-speak," having, himself been more familiar with telegraphese than computorese—but the concepts themselves, or even the practices? Not at all. He would not have any problem in grasping them, without the slightest prior briefing, nor would Itard, Séguin, Binet, or the later of the host of process trainers now departed.

Perhaps the antiquarian qualities that seem to characterize so many of our current modality assessment and remediation approaches can be kindly assessed if we view them in terms of the strands and spirals as per some curriculum, the modality ideas of the past repeating themselves in ever more complex and sophisticated terms. But in 1971, Paivo, a most distinguished researcher into imagery concluded that the latter's implications for learning were still only in the speculative stage. While Pressley in a recent review (1977) had to conclude with that familiar lame refrain, ". . . more information is needed if imagery is to have a significant impact on the education of children. The promise is great, but as yet unfulfilled" (Pressley, 1977, p. 616). So it is, not only for imagery, but for the other aspects of modality as well. It is difficult to avoid the conclusion that most of the modality evaluation and remediation efforts of the recent past have represented a long trip to simply come around again to where we were before.

24

The Vanguard of Twentieth Century Remedial and Special Education—Section 1

INTRODUCTION

The next several chapters are dedicated to the process training efforts of men and women, who exemplify special education and remedial process training—and assessment—as it matured during the first half of the twentieth century. There were others who could have been included, but the ones I have chosen will not be faulted. They represent stages in process training over the decades of the early twentieth century. They also represent major early statements on the subject from specific points of view.

I struggled as to the best procedure of presenting them—this or that grouping, by sex, by the type of measurement approach they favored—but none of those considered were fully satisfactory, not even chronological order, since the work of several of our pioneers spanned decades. But it is the latter that is generally followed, if for no other reason that that it gives the "flavor" of process training as the decades of this century unwound.

What one finds in the contributions of all the process trainers is a firm belief when they wrote that the technology was at hand, or anticipated in the very near future, to allow the precise delineation of cognitive processes and the equally precise fitting of developmental and remedial strategems and tactics to children's individual needs. Only here and there a doubt is raised among them; but an occasional nay among many yeas is what it at best amounts to.

At times, the contributions of our pioneers are extensively discussed, despite my awareness that this may wreak undeserved wear and tear upon a reader's attention. I believe, however, that this is justified in order to demonstrate to our present generation of process enthusiasts the dreams their conceptual ancestors held and, perhaps, to invite a greater self-inspection on their parts.

Our review commences with workers whose contributions were largely made during the first two decades of the twentieth century. Their interest was in what we today would call the slow learner and the learning-disabled child, rather than in mental retardation, though they believed that their techniques were applicable to the latter as well. The first three we will discuss—Witmer, Morgan, and Bronner—were generally confident of their results. The last, Woodrow, was a little less secure that disability could be transformed into ability.

WITMER

The name of Lightner Witmer (1867–1956) has been curiously over-looked by academic and professional communities within clinical psychology, school psychology, and special education, despite the major pioneering contributions he made to the constituencies they serve. Witmer himself complained (in a paper written in 1926) that his work had been accorded that sincerest of tribute, imitation, but with very little acknowledgment of him as its source. Recent articles and books have attempted to rectify this neglect. The reader seeking an introduction to Witmer's work is referred to Levine and Levine's accounts of his work (1970).

Lightner Witmer made major contributions both to the education of exceptional children and to psychodiagnostics. His psychological clinic, which had its beginnings in 1896, was the first of its kind in this country.

The incident that inspired Witmer to develop his psychological clinic (at the University of Pennsylvania) related to problems of a learning-disabled child. An elementary school principal, taking one of Witmer's courses at U. of P. and hearing him enthuse about psychology, challenged him to apply psychological "science" to the diagnosis of and remediation of one of her student's spelling problems. Witmer wrote, concerning this case:

> It appeared to me that if psychology was worth anything . . . . it should be able to assist the efforts of a teacher in a . . . case of this kind. (Levine and Levine, 1970, p. 56)

He began working with this child and a few other academically disabled children several hours a week, and from there went on to formally establish the clinic that makes his name particularly important to remedial and special education posterities.

Witmer came out of an early tradition of psychologists who wanted to prove that scientific psychology could and would have practical implications. The *Psychological Review* of 1897 aired a debate between Hugo Munsterberg, the father of applied psychology, and James McKeen Cattell, Witmer's predecessor as Director of the Psychological Laboratories at the University of Pennsylvania. Munsterberg insisted that experimental laboratory psychology was irrelevant to the purposes of instruction. Cattell was equally vehement about its potential value. Witmer was clearly on Cattell's side on the issue. His development of a psychological clinic and his creation of a new journal, by that name, was, he admitted "propagandistic in spirit." His creations were to demonstrate the value of the "new" psychology to education.

In our own time, when the value of school psychology is being seriously questioned in special education circles, it might be heartening to psychologists to once again read Witmer's convictions regarding the value of psychological study and intervention when and wherever school problems present themselves.

For the methods of clinical psychology are necessarily invoked whenever the status of an individual mind is determined by observation and experiment, and pedagogical treatment applied to involve a change.... (Levine and Levine, 1970, p. 57)

Witmer's diagnostic and remedial work proceeded unabashedly on the basis of traditional faculty psychology. The mind possesses a number of broad powers through which is exercised its functions. These are to be trained, remediated, or otherwise brought to fruitful employ.

In his diagnostic armamentarium, Witmer utilized a variety of tests of sensory acuity, memory, and association. For the assessment of performance factors in cognitive functioning, he included several instruments developed by him and standardized by his students, including the Witmer Formboard and the Witmer Cylinders Tests. Though espousing individual observation, he was a pioneer in the utilization of normative data for purposes of diagnostic decision making. Witmer was, then, very much with our own times of psycho-educational assessment.

The position Witmer took regarding training and remediation[1] puts him squarely in the tradition of our old friends, the formal disciplinarians. He made this clear in an article published in the first decade of the century (1908–1909):

I believe that the home and school, chiefly through the neglect of discipline, permit the mind of many children to remain undeveloped during the formative

---

[1] Equated with school psychology at that time.

period. The discipline that is required is not merely that which makes for obedience. . . . It is the discipline . . . that trains the memory, the will, the attention and forms habits of work. [2] (Levine and Levine, 1970, p. 62)

Witmer's position on remediation was that there are likely to be faulty cognitive processes as well as specifically deficient academic ones at work in school failure and that the former take priority in remediation over the latter.

S. W. Parker, one of Witmer's students, recalled his master's procedures in an article published in the Witmer-founded *Journal of the Psychological Clinic* (1917–1918). Albert, the subject of Witmer's training, was 14½ years of age and "sluggish, indifferent and thoughtless." The boy read at a sixth-grade level, spelled at a fifth-grade level, could only manage arithmetic at the rote level, and generally lacked in syntax and comprehension. In addition, he was a "nervous wriggling boy." Witmer soon settled him down so that "For once in his life . . . he sat at his desk absolutely quiet."

Because of Albert's picture of mental confusion and "conspicuous defect in persistent concentration of attention," Witmer decided that weeks of mental discipline were to precede further attempts to provide academic instruction for purposes of content. Albert, since his mind "skimmed" was to be given tasks requiring exactness and completeness. Some of the prescriptive regimen of his first months follow:

1. The memorizing with absolute accuracy of the definitions in Webster's Abridged Dictionary, of words taken from Rice's Rational Spelling Book—fourth year—a very few words each day.
2. The memorizing, word for word, of the illustrative sentences in Rice's Speller containing the words studied.
3. The composition of original sentences containing the words studied.
4. Drill in penmanship in which precision must be rigidly insisted upon.
5. Simple stories like those in Aesop's Fables and Baldwin's Fifty Famous Stories; read and reread every word until every sentence was read with absolute accuracy.
6. Oral and written reproduction of each story until he could reproduce the content of what he had read in a logical and comprehensive manner.
7. The writing of solutions of simple arithmetic problems, to *exercise his reasoning faculty within the limits* of his *very elementary comprehension.* (Levine and Levine, 1970, p. 65)

[2] Habit training, based upon psychological theories of associationism, connectionism, and Dewyism, was a common theme in many of the educational psychology and pedagogical textbooks of the late nineteenth and early twentieth centuries.

This regimen established, Albert was turned over to the ministrations of a teacher-clinician working under Witmer's direction. The results were mixed. Albert's academic work is reported to have improved considerably and his behavior became considerably more manageable and tolerable. He continued to have problems, however, both academically and behaviorally.

In an article entitled "Diagnostic Education" (1917), Witmer himself undertook to diagnose, train, and educate a two-and-a-half-year-old originally diagnosed by Witmer and another authority as being feebleminded. The child's development had been normal until an attack of whooping cough at six months of age, following which the boy progressed at an uneven and retarded pace. At 26 months, he could only creep if someone moved his knees. He was now able to walk uncertainly but could not climb stairs. Given an object to manipulate he would merely stare at it. He could not feed himself and was still in diapers. His vocabulary was limited to three words and he made no effort to imitate actions.

Witmer first worked with the boy in formboard and pegboard exercises, utilizing these for both diagnostic and remedial purposes. The boy's attention appeared to be faulty but his failings were diagnosed as being due to his boredom with such tasks. Witmer then taught the boy to work the boards. On the formboard, coordination improved to the point that 11 inserts were placed without error in 85 seconds. From this Witmer concluded that the boy was sound in respect to retentive memory, analytic attentiveness, imagery, etc. Since, however, his pupil generally lost interest in performance tasks, Witmer decided to move ahead and teach him first the alphabet, then isolated words (with manipulatives) and finally formal reading. It was all done to the tune of mental discipline, Witmer commenting as follows:

> I do not care whether this boy can read or not. I have had him taught reading because it was the best way to engage his interest and train his attention, imagination and memory. (Levine and Levine, 1970, p. 70)

The results of Witmer's efforts staunchly supported the doctrines of both faculty psychology and formal discipline. Between June and October of the year this neurologically impaired, delayed three-and-a-half-year-old, showed dramatic improvement to the point that he could read a primer. It was done haltingly but Witmer believed ". . . that from this time on the acquisition of spelling and reading was only a matter of drill. He can now spell and sound words and will probably be graduated into the first reader by the first of next June" (Levine and Levine, 1970, p. 70).

Whatever else, Witmer's results can be attributed to a master clinician at work (though he appears to have misdiagnosed the child), demonstrating that formal discipline could have remedial as well as developmental effects upon a child's cognitive apparatus—or so it seemed.

Witmer's influence on process training is hard to adjudicate. As indicated earlier, Witmer the man was generally neglected. Nevertheless, a goodly number of students and professionals were exposed to his teaching and writings. May some later developments in process remediation be traced back to his efforts? It is hard to say. The trail remains cold, but at least for now, acknowledgment of his contributions may be made—and past recognition, long overdue, given.

MORGAN

The term "backward child" is a common one in English literature on school problems and the handicapped. A loose generic term, it means what the user chooses it to mean. Sometimes it was and is intended to describe the slow learner or the higher level, educable mentally retarded, or simply poor school performers, students who performed poorly for any number of reasons, including poor health. *The Backward Child* (1914) described by Barbara Morgan may well have constituted an equivalent for what we now call the learning-disabled child. Morgan describes the problems that he presents, and what might be expected if remediation is not forthcoming:

> . . . often a subtle and baffling personality. In the long list of school problems there is none more difficult than his, none which yields more grudgingly to direct attack. He stands between the normal and feebleminded, and the way in which his shortcomings are treated may determine whether he joins ultimately one class or the other. To put it in another way, the backward child must be brought up to the mark; otherwise he will grow to maturity as an incompetent or as a potential criminal. (Morgan, 1914, p. 1)

While often presenting a picture of general, nay of "complete and apparently impenetrable dullness . . . general measures of remediation," said Morgan, do not create "general effects" of value for the backward child (Morgan, 1914, p. 2). For as a matter of fact, in the makeup of every backward child, a specific problem is usually the root cause of his retardation. This cause can be determined, it can be directly attacked, and its removal means the clearing up of the general "haze."

Morgan appeared to be talking about specific learning disabilities. And the way to determine what such disabilities consisted of is by "mental analysis." It is something different from traditional global intelligence testing or education, or—for that matter—medical assessment.

Mental analysis is not a substitute for any of the agencies in the educational field. It does not duplicate the work of the neurologist or medical specialist because it is concerned with mental diagnosis. . . . Neither does the scheme of mental analysis [hers] touch in any way the purposes of the Binet and Simon tests . . . which throw no light on individual peculiarities and offer no suggestions for cure . . . nor . . . meet at any point the system of Dottoressa Montessori, which is devised for the development of young children largely through sense stimulation. (Morgan, 1914, pp. 3–4)

On the basis of such statements, it appears that Morgan was attempting to establish a tradition of psychoeducational assessment and intervention specifically for the learning disabled. This is even more clearly suggested in her further exposition of the principle of mental analysis:

The principle of mental analysis in striking at the cause and not the effect of backwardness, is applied to the use of simple tests which . . . equip the teacher with the means to find out where a child's mind is at fault. While it uses some of the classic Binet and Simon tests, the point of departure is entirely different. The tests have been selected as bringing into play the mental faculties which must be analyzed and in selecting them, it has been a special point to avoid any device which would illustrate the effect of the school training on the child rather than the native ability of the child itself. (Morgan, 1914, pp. 4–5)

It is also clear from the preceding that Morgan was concerned with process rather than educational deficits. These are to be diagnosed through psychological assessment (the child's mind being too "subtle" to be usefully evaluated by neurologists) and trained on the basis of the foundations of experimental training techniques that she had devised; the results of which had clearly demonstrated:

. . . as a person's physical condition is improved by using a prescription of medicine so a mentally backward child can be brought up to par by daily attention to the actual root of his trouble. (Morgan, 1914, p. 6)

Three points in such training are particularly critical: It has to be individual lest the training effects be "blurred"; it has to be for short periods of time to avoid the negative effects of fatigue, and ". . . all devices used have to be focused on the deficiency revealed by the examination."

To determine the specific process deficits at the root of a child's problem, activities must be provided that actually show the child's mind at work ". . . bringing into play mental activities which are fundamental to the thought processes of everyone . . . regardless of intelligence" (Morgan, 1914, p. 8). Morgan had no doubts about the basic processes that constitute the foundations of the mind and are elaborated into higher cognitive structures.

We will regard the child's mind as having roughly four primary processes with which to work:

Sense impressions

Recollections of sense impressions

Association channels which partly determine and partly are determined by them; and

Abstraction processes by which impressions are translated into ideas.

And as the child grows, these fundamental faculties, by increasing and inter-working, elaborate into imagination, reasoning, expression. (Morgan, 1914, p. 9)

Associationism and faculty psychology were clearly hand in glove in Morgan's scheme of things, as they had been for her predecessors.[3]

Morgan did not like her processes to be gross and ill-defined. We see her proclivities towards precision at play in discussions of attention and memory which we take the liberty of excerpting at length to demonstrate the elaborate nature of her conceptions:

. . . in commenting on a child's memory, it is futile to say, "He never seems to remember anything," for it may be that of his three types of memory, two may be fairly normal and will become quite so when the third type is trained. Faulty memory of some kind underlies a great deal of backwardness, but to correct it the teacher must know whether the child has trouble in remembering a series of impressions that come too fast to allow the formation of associations, which is automatic memory; or whether his difficulty is in the conscious effort to memorize by forming associations, which is voluntary memory; or whether both these processes working properly, he cannot seem to hold what he has in mind, which is retentive memory.

One cannot experiment much in memory without realizing how largely it is interwoven with and determined by associations. The whole training of voluntary memory in fact is primarily to increase and direct associations. But most of our associations are unconsciously formed, so that by the time a child has reached the age of ten, he has a considerable mass of associative material and some well-marked tendencies which are worth studying for the clues they give to his habits of thought.

Habits of thought, in turn, depend for their every existence on the process of abstraction, or the translating of impressions into ideas, which is so fundamental that we usually take no account of it. But the teacher who finds a difficulty with arithmetic or with reading will go to the root of the matter if she examines the way in which the child is turning concrete symbols into the ideas of work and number which are expected from him.

. . . sensation and perception, attention and memory, association and abstraction, are to be regarded as structural faculties. They are the very foundation of mental life and the machinery of our every thought from the recognition of a friend to the binomial theorem. These too are the faculties which chiefly concern

---

[3] She spoke of association both as a faculty, engaging and molding other faculties, and as an activity.

the teacher of elementary schools and among which she is apt to find the child's underlying difficulty. But the bare branches of a tree are not its glory, and the framework of a man's mind is not the measure of his personality. Reasoning, expression, and, at the very top, creative imagination, are the expansion, the outflowering, as it were, of memory, association, abstraction, and the rest. And so the faintest signal of activity in these highly endowed faculties must catch the teacher's interest and find her constant encouragement. . . . (Morgan, 1914, pp. 17–20) [4]

Morgan wished to clearly distinguish between the faculties of attention and memory. For one thing, attention is a faculty for immediate use whereas memory is a "faculty for storing ideas and impressions." "Attention is a more primitive type faculty in which actual brain plasticity is a large factor. . . . Whereas memory is more complex and dependent upon learning ". . . a coordination, involving not only attention but association, perception, judgment and innumerable minor faculties besides" (Morgan, 1914, p. 55).

As we have seen, Morgan had three kinds of memory: automatic, voluntary, and retentive. If you wish to train the first, you can have a child repeat rhymes and utilize rhymes. Voluntary memory, however, requires the development of complex associations. Thus a child should not be set to memorizing poetry, but rather be asked to make a verse and rhymes of his own and then memorize them. Committing prose to memory can also be useful since it forces the mind to form new associations.

> The effect is like the increased strength and more precise activities of a muscle. The search for associated ideas in making up rhymes is as much as exercise, a contracting and relaxing, if you will, of unused faculties as a 15 minute practice with dumbbells is to the biceps. (Morgan, 1914, p. 17)

Retention is a separate faculty. Undernourishment is frequently at fault when it fails. "For the rest, the quality brain substance, which only partly determines automatic memory, is at the root of retentive memory" (Morgan, 1914, p. 72).

Morgan found retentive memory rarely requiring special training or benefiting from it. "What appears to be difficulties in retention is probably due to the fact that a pupil's voluntary memory is poor or untrained and that he is overworking his automatic memory" (Morgan, 1914, p. 74).

A simple matter of forgetfulness is to be helped by making initial impressions stronger, i.e., by awakening and multiplying associations. "So that training in automatic and voluntary memory is the most direct way of remedying the ordinary forgetfulness" (Morgan, 1914, pp. 74–75).

While Morgan was most interested in higher cognitive processes, she did not neglect the senses either, specifically their "mental role." She

---

[4] Froebel receives his due!

distinguished, as we moderns are wont to do, between sensations and perceptions, and it was the perceptual level that concerned her.

Morgan was one of the early attenders to the distinctions that are possible between visiles and audiles, though she regarded it a difficult and "indefinite" problem—discovering the sense favored by a child ". . . which sense plays the more important role, and how important that role is. Or as we commonly say, who is the visual-minded or ear-minded. . . ." (Morgan, p. 85).

Nevertheless, Morgan felt that such a determination was of educational importance, particularly its bearing on the teaching of spelling, telling the teacher ". . . whether to teach him spelling phonetically or by visualizing. . . ." Further, the implications of modality preference extended far beyond the class-room to ". . . the reporting of impressions, the formation of personal tastes and other thousand ramifications" (Morgan, 1914, p. 86).

Modality training, visual and auditory, is to proceed through means of multiplying associations. Multisensory training and the engagement of the various modality-based processes with each other and those at higher cognitive levels are also part of her training procedures.

In talking about perception, Morgan cast the term in higher cognitive coinage. Thus she spoke of analytic and synthetic forms of intellectual perception. She also suggested distinctive ways of testing the two and of guiding education on the basis of preferences for one over the other, since both were "constitutionally bound" and thus not particularly susceptible to training.

Abstraction is an important faculty. It is usually deficient in mental defectives. But it may also be a weakness in people with otherwise good ability. Weakness in mathematical abstraction may exist independent of other weaknesses in abstraction. Should we attempt to train it, our efforts should first focus on the formation of simple abstract ideas—independent of concrete things, though beginning with visual manipulation.

Imagination, a higher order process, results out of the interplay of intellect, and emotion, and morality. Its training proceeds through the training of the other intellectual faculties.

Judgment and reasoning are the least independent of all faculties and the most cooperative. Their training should begin, as with the training of most other processes, at elementary concrete levels. However, a "forcing" procedure is often required to make the subject relinquish dependence upon lower faculties to accelerate their usage. Expression in writing, speaking, drawing, and gesture is another faculty, but one that is exercised in the course of schoolwork.

So attention to process rather than content is emphasized throughout Morgan's work.

. . . no test is made of reading, because reading is complex and throws no light on the structure of the mind. But if the examiner finds a poor homogeneous attention or deficient abstraction process, she can infer trouble with reading and at the same time diagnose it. (Morgan, 1914, p. 173)

The following test procedures from Morgan's book *The Backward Child* show the extensive battery of assessment tests already at work in the early decades of the twentieth century vis-à-vis process.

Sensation Tests
   Vision: Sorting coloured worsteds.
   Sound: Estimating relative heights of notes, the number of notes in a chord.
   Visual or ear-mindedness:
            Answering questions like: "What do you think of first when you think of a band?"
   Touch: Distinguishing between feeling of different substances. Sensitivity to distance between points of a pair of dividers.
   Smell: Identifying smells and discriminating between them.
   Taste: Discriminating between salt, bitter, sour, sweet.

Abstraction Tests
   Mathematical processes:
      Solution of sums in mental arithmetic, like $3 + 2 - 1 \times 2 + 3 + 1 \div 3 = ?$
      Number sense: Solution of sums in mental arithmetic, like: What is the number that gives 12 if you add 3 to it?

Association Tests
   Writing a list of ten to thirty common words.
   Answering the first word thought of on hearing the examiner's key word.

Attention Tests
   Simultaneous: (a) Unconscious: The number of pictures on a card noticed by the child while the teacher talks about only one of them. (b) Conscious: The number of pictures noticed by the child when the card is shown him for a few seconds without comment from the teacher.
   Homogeneous: Crossing out letters on a printed page, either a single letter wherever it occurs or two recurring letters, one with a vertical stroke and the other with a dash.
   Disparate: Reading aloud an easy verse and at the same time writing A's on a sheet of paper. More complicated, writing the alphabet at the same time as the reading.

Perception Tests
   Analysis: Answering questions calling for simple identifications and distinctions, like, "Why are paper, sugar, and snow alike?"
   Solving simple analytical word puzzles, like reducing a word such as furniture into fur, in, true.

Answering part-wholes questions.

Synthesis: Answering questions which demand following out to conclusions, like, ''If you saw a horse and wagon standing, and the horse had no harness on, what would you think?''

Working out easy anagrams.

Memory Test

Automatic: Repeating numbers, words, nonsense syllables, beginning with four, and going as high as possible.

Voluntary: Memorizing the order of laying pictures on the table.

Retentive: Must be determined by teacher's observation over a period of time.

Imagination and Invention Tests

Dramatic imagination: Telling a story, (a) fiction, (b) child's own experience.

Imagery: Making ink-blots and telling what they look like.

Invention: Making sentences containing several given words, i.e., street, find, man. Working out the mechanism of some simple instrument, i.e., an elementary typewriter.

Judgment and Reasoning Tests

Elementary form judgment: Making two equal triangles into a square.

Elementary aesthetic judgment: Judging between normal faces and caricatures.

Working out picture puzzles.

Answering catch questions.

Answering questions on general orientation.

Expression Tests

Copying simple outlines.

Writing and then drawing a simple story.

Telling a story, either the child's own experience or some story he has learned.

Tests of Response

Can rarely be made in the classroom or clinic but the examiner can ascertain from teachers or observe in the course of other tests what response (absolute and comparative) the child makes indicating:

Pleasure—pain
Affection
Fear
Anger
Shame
Curiosity
Praise—blame

(Morgan, 1914, pp. 200–205)

No need to comment here that the affective side of functioning was not neglected by Morgan.

Morgan reported great results from her work. Her experience indicated that "backward children" could be brought up to a normal average in their lessons by a half an hour of daily individual training. Nor did the trainer have to be skilled, as long as the diagnosis had been carried out by a competent examiner and explicit and specific training instructions were provided. She felt that a good teacher should develop her own techniques of training for the various faculties. However, a few suggestions were passed along.

In training sensory faculties, visualizing can be effectively trained by showing words and sentences to a child and having him write them from memory: words and sentences should be increased in complexity to develop greater skill. For sound reproduction, the child is to pick out words with certain similar sounds, e.g., *at*. His task can be made more complex by having him pick out two sounds at a time or by using more words.

For training in analytic and synthetic perception, proper questioning will do. Asking why, for example, helps analysis, while anything encouraging invention can promote the mind's synthetic powers. However, since analytic or synthetic turns of mind are relatively engrained and not easily altered by training, one should help the child approach academics by the perceptive mode most convenient and dependable for him.

For training abstraction, estimating measurements is a good training device. For association, a child can sort words according to use or action, e.g., pick out all the words that have to do with summer. Exercises should be increased in complexity till the child is drawing inferences on the basis of his associations. Such devices not only multiply associations but also develop abstraction.

Simultaneous attention can be trained by games such as hiding the thimble; homogeneous attention, by hammering nails in upper left-hand corners of all squares marked out on a board. For automatic memory training, she recommended having a child make a list of common things, i.e., of the furniture in his home kitchen, all the objects in his desk, the tools he uses in carpentry. Repetition of nonsense syllables, numbers, and words were yet others among her recommendations.

Voluntary memory, a more complex affair, may be improved by having a child write original rhymes and learn them by heart. Memorizing prose is also useful, since the child can not overly depend upon rhyme or rhythm, which accompany poetry and are supports for automatic memory.

Imagination benefits from retelling of stories. Illustrating such stories also stimulates it. Invention, regarded as applied imagination, is to be trained for school purposes through picture puzzles calling for consideration of the shapes of the pieces, and by supplying missing words and letters.

Morgan did not recommend training for the higher processes of judgment and reasoning, as they ". . . do not directly affect the child's school work."

> . . . together with expression and response they are part of the working of the environment and all the subtle influences of life outside the schoolroom . . . the teacher . . . had best concentrate her training on the more primary faculties, and the more glaring faults, trusting the finer points to a harmonious coordination. (Morgan, 1914, pp. 206–207)

Let us now examine Morgan's method of diagnosis in its application:

> George Cascio, 15 years old . . . heavy and overgrown. Complained of because of absence from school and backwardness when there. Reported hopeless by the truant officer. Reported as "unable to learn" by the teacher.
>
> Sensation: Normally discriminating in all five senses. His sensitivity to colour over sound is marked, but he appears to be ear-minded.
>
> Abstraction: Accurate in figuring and seems to grasp the mathematical processes.
>
> Association: In groups, is difficult, and tends to be objective.
>
> Attention: Simultaneous attention is poor and easily confused. He remembered two out of eight pictures when looking at the whole card; none when talking about one of the pictures.
>
> Homogeneous attention is good, and persistent.
>
> Disparate, not tested.
>
> Perception: He appears confused in synthetic processes. In analytical questions he perceives clearly, but has some trouble in working out the answers, i.e., they are right, but come slowly.
>
> Memory: His automatic memory is indifferent; five digits is his average.
>
> His voluntary memory is fair, i.e., two out of three times he can get the series of eight right.
>
> His retentive memory is said to be long, but limited in its variety.
>
> Imagination and Invention: His invention is very poor, and his imagination is more quick than clear, i.e., tends to be fantastic, but he has not the dramatic wealth of detail.
>
> Judgment and Reasoning: His elementary judgments are normal, and he has a good deal of certainty and independence.
>
> Expression: He shows a strong preference for drawing as a means of expression, and added to that a very accurate visualization of detail and a good sense of form. He does not incline to narrative, either in talking, writing, or drawing, but when a very simple version of Roland's death was told him the boy drew a spirited picture of a soldier on horseback blowing a horn, with a good deal of detail like the handle of the bugle, the stirrups, and so on. In language he had nothing to offer but the recital of the main facts, which of course was a matter of memory.
>
> He is not given to gesture.

Response: It does not appear on his teacher's account that he shows any very keen affective feelings. His independence of judgment seems to be borne out in a certain indifference either to praise or blame. His teacher describes him as docile and unresponsive. His docility, that is to say, his non-resistant disposition, probably checks the development of his more violent feelings, such as fear, anger, and shame. And his general lethargy of physique is contrary to a pronounced curiosity.

Summing up, therefore, from these general observations, it appears that George has a poor simultaneous attention and an indifferent automatic memory, the effect of which is to cut him off from a great many of those passing impressions which we take for granted will be registered photographically on a person's brain. In school, much of what the teacher says, and many of her explanations pass him by, because these unconscious, involuntary faculties do not work normally. Set him at a job, however, and his homogeneous attention and voluntary memory, conscious faculties, serve him fairly well. For the sake of improving his classroom work, therefore, the first point is the training indicated for simultaneous attention and automatic memory.

Coming to the more elaborated faculties, it is evident that his invention can be quickened, and his imagination greatly developed by utilizing his disposition to draw. There is no sign that he has an overmastering talent which demands technical instruction, but his fondness for expressing himself in that form can be made the means of unfolding his dormant possibilities. In particular, his associations, which are now difficult and objective, will tend to become more free and elastic if he has training in illustrative and imaginative drawing. The very act of thinking out details to the point of putting them into a drawing will enrich his whole idea of a house, for instance, and ever afterward "house" will stand for more possibilities than it did when it was merely a place to go in and out of.

This imaginative drawing, too, will tend to quicken his perceptions. He already has a predisposition to analysis, which the thinking out of details for an idea will sharpen and clarify. And on the other hand, the very expression of his ideas will tend to strengthen his synthetic perceptions, because in any kind of creative work one gets the habit of foreseeing what this or that will lead to, and whether it leads where one wants it to. . . .

Suggested Training:

For simultaneous attention: Hunting for small objects in plain sight.

Describing pictures looked at for a few seconds.

Let the teacher write words, then sentences, showing them to him for three seconds; then taking them away, ask him what was written.[5]

For stimulating other faculties, using drawing facility: Have him draw scenes and then stories in successive scenes, either out of his own head, or from bare facts suggested by the teacher. He must furnish the details himself. (Morgan, 1914, pp. 188–194)

I have discussed Morgan's work in considerable detail because she exemplified so well the early flowering of the psychoeducational process assessment–remediation movement. Rejecting the notion that global con-

---

[5] Remember that Morgan was writing at a time when rote memory was emphasized.

ceptions of intelligence could guide remediation, she believed in the diagnosis of specific processes, their strengths, and weaknesses, and in training and remediating these processes rather than directly addressing academic problems. She was a clear and simple and confidently assertive teacher. She was sure that she could assess that which she said she was assessing and that her remediation techniques could restore *ad integrum* many students otherwise doomed to failure. She was, then, an apostle of the learning disabled, as Séguin was an apostle of the idiots. There were few efforts as elaborate as hers in the years to follow until the sixties and seventies, when the past of process training was to repeat itself with an intensity that Morgan would have certainly applauded. The efforts of Augusta Bronner's were, however, even more extensive—and considerably more sophisticated.

BRONNER

That human beings have particular abilities and disabilities varying more or less—and frequently varying greatly—from the level of normal capacity, is a fact of much psychological interest as well as of great practical educational and social significance. (Bronner, 1917, p. 1)

So begins Augusta Bronner's book *The Psychology of Special Abilities and Disabilities,* a landmark publication for its time and, as was true of Morgan's, a rare early comprehensive text on learning disabilities, as such disabilities are conceived on the basis of psychological processes. [6]

Bronner decried the injustices suffered by children with specific disabilities. True, there were programs for "the crippled, the deaf, the blind, the feeble minded and the epileptic," but this would not suffice.

. . . variations less obvious, but equally as significant can no longer be entirely disregarded. To classify all persons into groups of the normal or the defective is altogether inadequate for the purposes of education and other social adjustments . . . if there are particular abilities and disabilities in various mental traits. (Bronner, 1917, pp. 2–3)

The substance of Bronner's book is particularly concerned with abilities and disabilities as these are manifested by

. . . the individual who is normal except for special mental defects, and . . . the individual who, though in general, mentally below normal, has some special ability which, if developed, might be highly significant for his future welfare. (Bronner, 1917, p. 8)

Bronner was concerned about the excessively facile ways in which

---

[6] Inspired in considerable part by the conceptualizations of William Healy, a psychiatrist who collaborated with Bronner in studies of juvenile delinquency.

pupils were diagnosed as feebleminded. The individual with special cognitive defects, she said:

> . . . is not generally incapable. . . . The extent of the incapacity may be more or less narrow . . . it is conceivable that a person is defective in all memory processes, or that he is normal, let us say, in his visual memory, but decidedly poor in auditory memory, or even that his disability lies in some very narrow sphere of memory, perhaps for numbers only. Obviously it is unfair and of no practical value to call such a person feeble-minded or a "mental defective." (Bronner, 1917, p. 8)

Thus the study of special abilities should seek strengths, as well as weaknesses, and

> . . . it is necessary to test the different mental functions in order that where special abilities exist they may be brought to light . . . a wide enough range of tests must be used to give each individual the chance to display his capacities. (Bronner, 1917, p. 24)

Bronner tried to substantiate her conceptualizations on the basis of Thorndike's work. She seized eagerly upon Thorndike's statement that:

> measurements reveal a high degree of independence of mental functions even where to the abstract psychological theorist they have seemed nearly identical. (Bronner, 1917, p. 19)

From which she drew the following premise:

> . . . one might expect to find special defect or unusual ability in any one of the mental processes, sensation, perception, apperception, judgment and reasoning, as well as the emotions and will . . . processes concerned with motor reactions. . . . Then, too, . . . complex functions, such as foresight and general powers of self-control. We might, also, consider the problem of the speed of mental processes and reactions rather than the character of the product. (Bronner, 1917, p. 13)

Bronner appears to have misread Thorndike in her interpretation of his conceptions of process. Minute and many were the processes he preferred. They were most certainly not the usual faculties—and it was faculties that Bronner was talking about as processes. Faculty history, indeed, flashes before our eyes as we read off her list of processes: "sensation, perception, apperception." It was Thurstone with whom she would have been congenial, not Thorndike.

Anyone who thinks that I.Q. tests have just recently come under fire simply has not kept down with the literature, so to speak. Binet-baiting was an early pastime. There were many of the righteous in the ranks of psychology and education who castigated intelligence tests as being too general, as ignoring the individual character of the child, as being unfair—almost as soon as Binet had shown his fledgling efforts to the world. Any and all of the criticisms we hear today were heard then, and they were just about as vigorous or indignant then as now; and then as now, not altogether wrong, not altogether right. Bronner demurred from any specific criticisms of general intelligence tests ". . . for their inadequacies have already been so widely discussed" (Bronner, 1917, p. 15). Tests of general ability simply did not suffice, in any case, for her purpose.

> None includes tests for a wide range of different functions; indeed many mental functions are not tested at all, and thus we are given very few clues to particular abilities or disabilities. (Bronner, 1917, p. 14)

Fortunately, there were other tests at hand.

> . . . many other tests . . . for the study of various mental processes, many more than can be . . . discussed; the number is almost legion . . . and new ones are being devised rapidly. (Bronner, 1917, p. 15)

From these, she was to take and, to these, she was to add additional tests of her own, to provide a comprehensive understanding of abilities and disabilities. Small wonder that Guilford would later hail her pioneering assessment efforts as anticipating his own (Guilford, 1967).

We see in Bronner's work some of the earliest use of standardized (though not necessarily well-standardized) tests to assess process disabilities—an advance conceptually and technically, though not necessarily practically, from the improvisations of earlier process assessors. The psychometric age was well on its way when Bronner wrote, the belief in mental measurements was high. Bronner was confident of her instruments.

Bronner was a clinician, and a fine clinical tradition it was from which she came. It is a forgetful school psychologist or clinical psychologist who does not remember her work with Healy on the problems of delinquency. It was to be, then, that when she approached differential diagnosis, she would do it on a comprehensive scale—developmental studies, case histories, team approach, ecological assessment, and all the rest, as well as the study of processes. Her book reflects "clinical care." Bronner was also aware that assessment of special abilities and disabilities has to be tempered by understanding of what we now call dyspedagogia, and by the operations of uncontrolled variables.

> . . . negative results may be due to exceedingly varied causes. Irregularity in test results, which on superficial view, might seem indicative of special defect, may be due instead to *poor physical conditions.* (Bronner, 1917, p. 24)

Product versus process was an issue that confronted Bronner, too.

. . . the practicality of an end, in education as elsewhere, and the value of the means used to attain the end can only be determined by the results achieved. The evaluation of accomplishment is a distinct feature of present activities in educational circles, much more so than in any period in the past . . . proof of the tendency to measure educational product is evidenced by the rapidity with which objective scales for measuring achievement in the various school subjects have been evolved . . . it is the product that is being studied not process. Such methods of evaluation are a very practicable help. . . But they throw no light whatsoever upon the reasons for success or failure, nor is much clue given in explanation of the advantage which one method or system has over another. (Bronner, 1917, pp. 43–33)

It was thus to be *cherchez le process* for Bronner; a quest to find which faculties were causing or contributing to failure, which making for success.

Bronner's lists of processes are disorderly ones. They are a hodgepodge of conceptual faculties and reified behaviors rationalized through a mishmash of common sense observations and justified by appeals to "scientific" psychology. To Bronner, the processes she talked about, her special abilities, and disabilities were observable . . . anyone could see them at play if he would observe correctly or test correctly. She was a clinician above all. Confidence intervals, Fisherian statistics, notions of convergent and divergent analysis—none of these had yet emerged to distract her from her speculations and rationalizations. Whatever seemed to assess a process was used to assess a process. Face validity was justification enough to elect a test to one of her batteries. Tests catalogued as well as diagnosed the processes we review below.

Of course perceptual processes were an area of concern to Bronner. However, her conception of perception erratically wavers from page to page in her book. In some places, it is treated as a broad power (or set of powers) based upon the functioning of individual modalities but encompassing both peripheral (sensory) and central (higher cognitive) processes. In other places, a distinction appears to have been made between "external" perception, as conceived in terms of sensory discriminations, e.g., of form, texture, weight, and "inner" perceptual processes which are strongly engaged with imagery, memory, comprehension, and judgment. She used the same test(s) to tap a multitude of processes.

Among the instruments employed to assess visual perception, Bronner included the Binet Memory-for-Designs subtest, which, of course, also taps memory. The Healy Pictorial Completion test is another candidate for one's armamentarium of perceptual assessment devices. The Cross Line and Code tests sample, she believed, visual and motor imagery. Tests of problem solving efforts with the "concrete" not only provide information about a pupil's problem solving abilities but also furnish evidence about the effectiveness of his use of his modalities. Formboards, construction tests, puzzle boxes, Knox cubes, the Stenquist test for mechanical ability, and a variety of devices and techniques adapted from experimental psychology laboratories were recommended for this dual assessment approach.

There are many means of assessing auditory functioning in Bronner's catalog. They include recall of digits and verbal materials, the repetition of difficult sentences and words, the sounding out of words phonetically, spelling, etc.

Apperception, [7] defined as "perception in the light of something which has gone on before" was a process that Bronner believed should be assessed on a variety of levels. The Healy Pictorial Completion test provided an appreciation for the ". . . apperception of ideas expressed in pictorial form. Apperception of ideas is also approachable through use of the Ebbinghaus Mutilated Test and the Trabue scale for the apperception of ideas expressed in written language" (Bronner, 1917, p. 17).

Perception of relationships was a special ability:

> In general we may distinguish between objective relationships, such as those of space and form, and subjective relationships, such as likeness, equality, cause and effect, and other logical relations. It is quite possible that defects may exist in either one or the other and even in both these subdivisions. (Bronner, 1917, p. 159)

Perception of relationships functions both on concrete and abstract levels. Failures therein account for a variety of school problems. Disorientation of time, place, and a "defective form of sense" are signs of distress in this complex process.

Bronner approached the memory faculty as a multimembered constituency; to do so was commonplace by the time she was writing. She distinguished between rote memory and memory for logical material, between auditory and visual memory, between motor and kinesthetic memory, and between immediate and remote recall.

Her tests for immediate memory include several for visual recall, e.g., of geometric forms; several for auditory recall, e.g., syllables, and memory span for digits forward and backward. Also recommended are the memory test from the Terman version of the Binet test, an "auditory–verbal" memory test, a substitution test, the Knox cube test, and the *Aussage* Picture Test.[8] Learning of school subjects and knowledge of the current date are other means to be used to assess memory of the now. [9]

---

[7] Apperception, ". . . the ability to size up a situation and grasp the general meaning of it is exceedingly important in all activities of life." (Bronner, 1917, p. 17). Apperception was defined by Bronner as involving ". . . the relation of one part to another; perception in the light of what has gone before" (Bronner, 1917, p. 17). There is a bit of gestalt psychology in that definition, as well as Herbart, Wundt, etc.

[8] *Aussage* Test: After seeing a picture, with a variety of objects and actions going on, for a brief time, the subject gives an account of it, after which questions are asked concerning the points not recalled.

[9] To some degree, short- and long-term memory were assessed by the same means.

Bronner's tests for long-term (remote) memory are composed of the following: visual memory, logical verbal memory, general information, number processes and combinations, memory for items of time, such as birthday, months of year, telling time, relating past events, and reading of word pictures or by phonetic values.

Bronner regarded *mental representation* as a key faculty. She defined it as per Healy's definition:

> The ability to represent in terms of various imageries a given situation to oneself, and to revolve it over in the mind, seeing its different parts and mentally commenting on their comparisons and relationships. . . . (Bronner, 1917, pp. 155–156)

To Healy it was one of the "most valuable of human faculties." Bronner sought to evaluate it by an examination of a pupil's general management of problems. It is also assessable by the Cross-Line and Code tests.

To test *association* (by this time a faculty of sorts), Bronner recommended both free association tests and controlled association tests such as the Kent Rosonoff which provide "a clue to the speed as well as to the accuracy of the association processes" (Bronner, 1917, p. 18).

What about ability to follow directions? Is it a specific faculty? It is enough of one to assess through the obeying of commands at the seven-year level of the Binet, the instruction box and Knox cube test. The "ability to formulate generalizations, on the basis of repeated experiences" (another loosely construed process or set of processes) is to be evaluated by the Yerkes Multiple-Choice Test. (Bronner, 1917, p. 20).

Reasoning, like memory, was not considered a unitary process by Bronner but rather ". . . a complex activity in which a number of mental processes are involved . . . the ability to form mental representations, to analyze, to compare, to form judgments, all are elements."[10] Several ways are open for an astute examiner to assess its components. Ability to determine "mental similarities or differences" is a factor in reasoning, and pictorial tests of likenesses and differences may be used to evaluate it, while judgment can be assessed via various "sensory" subtests of Binet's scales since ". . . incidental to many tests one can determine the subject's ability to judge" (Bronner, 1971, p. 19).

The important powers of psychomotor control are to be assessed by having the subject place a stylus in an opening without touching the sides of the opening, or by drawing a line between two given lines without touching their edges, or by his placing dots in half-inch squares as rapidly as possible without touching the lines or missing squares.

---

[10] In such discussion, Bronner approximated a more modern version of process, i.e., as an activity, rather than a static trait or capacity.

Bronner debated whether there was a distinct faculty or set of processes to be identified as learning ability, but on second thought, she found the term "learning ability" too inclusive to allow such a distinction to be made. Extreme deficits in learning ability are to be identified as an indication of a general defect or "feeblemindedness."

Still another major "power" for Bronner was that of mental control. An individual's control of actions is dependent upon his control of the mental states leading to action. The emotions tending to arouse actions are to be retrained by the "realm of ideas." And so

It may be fairly well said that defective powers of control of actions may be due, on the one hand, to inability to repress the feelings, that is to lack of emotional control; and, on the other, to failure to arouse inhibiting ideas. From this it may be seen that defective power of control involves both emotional and ideational or volitional aspects of mental life. (Bronner, 1917, p. 167)

Attention, as we know from our previous acquaintance with it in earlier chapters, had an ambiguous position among facultists. Sometimes it was a major faculty on its own, sometimes a state of mind within which (other) faculties operated. Its status was loosely defined by Bronner as ". . . a function of general applicability and a factor in all performance." Also, defects in attention are frequently "concomitants of physical and nervous disorders" and attention ". . . varies so largely with the interest that is felt in various subjects that it is difficult to interpret a lack of it seen in the laboratory as a real defect" (Bronner, 1917, pp. 163–164). Teachers complaining over a pupil's lack of attention should be cautious in making interpretations. Such a deficiency may be situation specific. Further, the child may be simply inattentive because he is an "out-and-out mental defective."

Bronner gave passing attention to the powers of analysis and synthesis and not much more to imagination or inventive ability. The latter two are "exceedingly complex" and ". . . while defects in these powers no doubt lead to important consequences, little is known of the practical implications other than common-sense conclusions." There was limited experience to go on a few tests with proper norms. Further, such powers ". . . are so interwoven with mental representation, foresight, and other processes, that they are difficult to differentiate" (Bronner, 1917, p. 165). Bronner felt secure that "defects" in lower processes could coexist with normal mental ability. She had her doubts about those in higher processes:

Defects in the higher mental processes lead one to doubt whether the individual possessing them can be regarded as sufficiently normal mentally to fall within the group belonging to our discussion, namely normal individuals with special defects. Powers of apperception, reasoning, judgment, mental representation, and foresight, are naturally criteria of intelligence to such an extent that defects in these aspects of mental life would seem to indicate subnormality if not feeblemindedness. (Bronner, 1917, p. 154)

However, she did acknowledge that some individuals who lack one of such mental powers could do well in a number of tasks not "involving the defect."

Bronner was concerned with the role that special abilities played in the problems and achievements of the mentally retarded. On this score, she decried "The belief . . . quite general that all mental defectives are best fitted for handwork." Even among ". . . defectives capacities are often uneven." In particular, it is important that for high-grade defectives intensive studies of their abilities should be carried out. Too often it is assumed ". . . their main training should be in the sensory and perceptual fields . . ." nor are ". . . all feebleminded adapted to education on the motor side" (Bronner, 1917, p. 197). One must look beyond the a priori conclusions and study the child himself! Knowledge of special abilities and disabilities in the retarded can be used to guide their instructional programs, to determine their future vocational directions, and, or course, to compensate for their defects and deficiencies. This was a bold conceptualization for her day.

Bronner's process conceptions are clearly illustrated by a variety of case histories that, from their introductions, show her general lack of distinction between cognitive processes and academic processes. And, lamentably, there is often obscuration as to whether she intended description or inference as to what caused what:

Case 7 . . . inability in number work [that] probably rests on a basis of an exceeding defect in auditory memory for numbers, uncompensated for by training suited to special characteristics. (Bronner, 1917, p. 56)

Case 8 . . . illustration of defect for number work when there is not merely poor auditory memory, but this is combined with poor powers of forming associations with symbolic material. (Bronner, 1917, p. 61)

Case 9 . . . illustrated the fact that with normal ability to form arbitrary associations and with no defect in memory for numbers, there still may be failure in arithmetic because the concept of number is lacking. (Bronner, 1917, p. 65)

Case 11 . . . in the following case, the difficulty is not easy to explain, for we may find almost all of the psychological processes which underlie number work quite normal . . . memory for numbers and powers of arbitrary association are not defective, nor is there any lack of ability to form mental representations. On the other hand, the step from the concrete to the abstract seems never to have been well established. (Bronner, 1917, p. 69)

Case 13 . . . Arthur L., 17 years old, showed on mental examination his inability to grasp number work. At seventeen, he was only in the sixth grade, no doubt because of his special defect for numbers, for he was able to do other types of school work satisfactorily. Writing and spelling were done well, and he read a fairly difficult passage fluently. That he was normal except in arithmetic was shown by the fact that he passed the 12-year Binet tests readily and showed normal powers of analysis and representation, normal powers in dealing with concrete material, and normal control of verbal associations. (Bronner, 1917, p. 73)

Case 14 . . . This case is presented as illustrating defects in special mental processes leading to disability for reading. Here we find a marked deficiency in auditory powers, shown by poor auditory memory and defective discrimination of sound. (Bronner, 1917, p. 92)

In one case where no clear-cut process disabilities could be discerned, process was, nevertheless, invoked to explain that the disability had eluded her—even without evidence. It was still *cherchez le process*.

Case 16 . . . The next problem presented is of great interest because the inability to master reading is so clear and definite, though psychological tests reveal little in explanation. The various mental processes, each tested separately, seem quite normal. In light of this fact we are led to wonder whether in reading there is not involved some subtle synthetic process, which, at the present time, we have no means of studying, but effects of which nevertheless are of extreme significance. This case is being presented without any pretense of solving the problem definitely. It affords a striking commentary on the limitations of our present knowledge. This does not militate however, against the validity of finding special defect, or against appreciation of its practical importance. (Bronner, 1917, pp. 100–101)

It is simply impossible to keep a good process person down!

We have, at this point, completed a comprehensive, though certainly not complete, discussion of Augusta Bronner's process conceptions—we have learned enough, in any case, to ask what her intentions were as to the uses of process knowledge. Bronner was rather modest on such issues. It was not her purpose, she stated, ". . . to offer any specific devices guaranteed to overcome defects or to develop abilities." Indeed, ". . . no general formulae for treatment can be given. . . ." since each problem case requires individual decision-making (Bronner, 1917, p. 220).

However, knowledge of specific abilities and disabilities was essential, if learning problems were to be understood and a pupil's potentials maximized.

The first principle of progress towards the goal of developing each individual in relation to his potential is the recognition of the actual need for individual adjustment. To realize that such a problem exists is to be able to formulate it clearly in one's own mind, to see its significance and its relation to life, is the first step towards its solution . . . the basis of the wise and rational use of all special training is the need for educational diagnosis. Before understanding treatment the ailment must be known; the cause of the trouble must be determined before the steps can be taken towards effective remedy. This is as true of mental peculiarity as of physical troubles, and it applies in educational and vocational life as truly as in any other field. (Bronner, 1917, pp. 220–221)

Admittedly, the tests of her time were not perfect, there were many gaps in knowledge, both diagnostically and educationally, many misunderstood complexities, and difficulty in distinguishing minute individual differences.

Nevertheless,

. . . this does not lessen a whit the value of findings which indicate peculiarities in individual mental functioning. It is part of wisdom to discover all one can of the characteristic mental traits of individuals and to guide practical procedure in the light of these findings. (Bronner, 1917, p. 222)

Knowledge of mental processes—and the strengths and disabilities therein—should be used to guide children's educational programs, to plan their academic careers and their vocational directions. It should also be used to determine those areas where "teaching to strengths" will make a difference and to determine whatever gifts the child might possess that may contribute to his useful development.

What is the degree to which specific defects can be corrected or truly compensated for in lasting fashion? On this score, Bronner was hesitant. She did not forthrightly offer programs of remediation in her book. Individual remediation was to be an individual affair, and there were no guarantees of success.

What can be done to compensate for or to minimize defects can only be determined on the basis of the special conditions that exist in each individual case. In general the balance should be preserved between reasonable expenditure of time and energy and the value of the results that we may hope to achieve. . . . The possibilities of the limitations can be learned only through experimental endeavors with each individual. (Bronner, 1917, p. 224)

Yet,

. . . analysis of the mental processes which are elements in activities for which defect exists would seem to offer the greatest opportunity of rationally attacking the problems of specialized incapacity. (Bronner, 1917, p. 225)

Even though,

The exact degree to which defective powers can be improved is not definitely known, no matter whether the defect concerns perception, memory, association, speed of reactions, or any other phase of mental life. But, definite training and practice are so generally effective . . . that it seems only fair to conclude that even where powers are exceedingly low they can be vastly increased by intensive training. (Bronner, 1917, p. 225)

And so she recommended training of "visual, auditory and motor" memory functions and reasoning, and that children be taught to "master abstractions" to take "the step from the concrete to the abstract" to such purposes ". . . . Specific devices will suggest themselves to every teacher once she is aware of the problem" (Bronner, 1917, p. 226).

Augusta Bronner stands high on the honors list of early representatives of the diagnostic prescriptive movement. She worked in what she regarded as uncharted waters.[11] It was still a time when armchair philosophizing and the flimsiest of experimental evidence sufficed to support one's inferences. Bronner was willing to make allowances for the limitations of both general and personal knowledge, but beyond that she was buoyed by the conviction of the originality and value of her work. It was a world at war when she wrote, but still a world of hope and expectation for better things. Why should she not join in?

Like Binet, Bronner was a clinician as well as a theorist. Like Binet, she was inconsistent, if not downright sloppy, in some of her formulations. Like Binet, she needs no apology for being either. Most of the processes that we today entertain in our test profiles and remediation kits are really not much more sophisticated than hers; they only seem to be because they are jargonized *à la mode*. Worse solutions than Bronner's have been fomented and foisted upon those seeking answers for the learning disabled. Polish up hers—some still glow; they even occasionally manage to provide light.

WOODROW

Herbert Woodrow, who wrote *Brightness and Dullness in Children* (1919), was one of the more thoughtful of writers on the subject of process training. Historically aware and sensitive to theoretical nuances, Woodrow attempted to rationalize processes and process training within the traditions of scientific psychology of his day[12] and according to the regnant laws of factor analysis. In particular, he tried to reconcile traditional faculty doctrine with Spearman's factor theories and Thorndike's "nonfocal" conception of processes, taking from both what he felt were the incontrovertible truths of each and melding them as best he could. That Woodrow believed there are broad distinct processes at work to be tested

[11] She was not particularly appreciative of previous efforts in mental orthopedics.

> None based on anything more than the main laws of mental life, laws which are applicable to all activities rather than to the peculiarities of special cases. In spite of much experimentation, little has been written concerning the training of the separate mental processes other than by practice. (Bronner, 1917, p. 226)

[12] To which he had contributed, particularly in his studies of attention.

and trained is apparent in the following statement, somewhat ambivalent though it may be, about the specificity of process operations.

> Plainly it is impossible to find one mental process that can be identified with intelligence. It is true that certain mental functions, such as attention and reasoning, are more closely related to intelligence than others. It must be remembered, however, that the mind, like the body, functions to a large extent as a single organism, and that the more important mental processes involve all the others . . . in the case of reasoning . . . one's ability depends upon his knowledge; his knowledge in turn is dependent upon his perceptions and memory, and also upon his power of attention . . . we cannot test visual acuity without testing attention . . . all mental processes influence behavior although they do not have equal weight. (Woodrow, 1919, p. 150)

Woodrow discussed the various "capacities" of importance to academic achievement. And in his discussion, he distinguished between simple, fundamental, and complex types of cognitive processes.

> The simpler mental capacities are; sensory capacity, that is the capacity for receiving sensations and discriminating between them; perception, or the observation of external objects; the capacity for imagery, and the capacity for feelings of pleasantness and unpleasantness.[13] (Woodrow, 1919, p. 151)

Operating at a level above these simple processes are the fundamental processes of association, attention, and memory. While in the highest gallery, hard work, we find the complex mental processes, among which Woodrow included reasoning, emotion, and will. There are means, formal and informal, of assessing all. Speaking of association, Woodrow observed:

> The occurrence of one idea, or of any mental process in sequence upon, and as a result of another, is called an association. Since all things are made up of a multitude of such sequences, clearly the processes of association must pervade the entire intellectual life. (Woodrow, 1919, p. 171)

It was an associationistic era, wherein association was invoked to explain mental functioning in all its corners; the force that had once been used to explain away faculties had become a faculty in its own right. Other faculties relied upon its operations. So "every act of memory is one of controlled association . . . memorizing consists simply in the formation of associations" (Woodrow, 1919, p. 180). In testing it (memory) through paired associates learning, memory span, and the learning method, we are assessing associations formed in the past.

---

[13] I have chosen to play down such affective and conative variables in our narrative of the processes, in light of their general exclusion from current psychoeducational concern.

Attention, like association, was another fundamental process, sharing in every mental operation. "It is the great steadying and directing factor of the mind . . . the process which directs the stream (of associations) to a certain course. . ." (Woodrow, 191, p. 185). Tests of perseverance and distractibility are to be used to assess this faculty.

The major, complex cognitive faculty for Woodrow was reasoning. Woodrow found it hard to define but offered the following definition tentatively:

> . . . it is purposive thinking . . . it consists in arriving at a mental solution of a problem through a more or less orderly process of association and selection of ideas. . . . (Woodrow, 1919, pp. 190–191)

Woodrow, unfortunately, found no "very precise" tests of reasoning ability. It could be assessed, generally speaking, in almost all problem-solving activities (arithmetic being perhaps the best school activity for this purpose). He also recommended, however, tests of "logical-mindedness," (which assess cognitive analysis and synthesis) the recognition of absurdities, the ability to define, the ability to interpret pictures and poetry, the ability to form general principles, the ability to distinguish between good and bad reasons, and the ability to distinguish between sound and false conclusions drawn from stated premises. Woodrow found the Binet-Simon Scale to be a storehouse of "logical-mindedness" tests, which could be used to assess reasoning.

Though influenced by Bronner's process training rhetoric, Woodrow, took a very modest position as to the possibilities of process training.

> It remains to consider what it means to train a capacity. In general, it may be said that training cannot increase the fundamental capacities, but simply teaches the child to make the best use of such capacities as he possesses. This training may consist in the formation of very general habits such as habits of concentration of attention, and the most efficient methods of study, or it may consist in specific information, such as the multiplication table. In teaching the child the more general habits, formal exercises may be used. These formal exercises, like exercises for training the senses, that are so prominent in the physiological method,[14] often seem to be aimed at the development of faculties as such. In reality, however, they consist simply in drill for the formation of habits which are useful in a very wide range of situations. To train a child's capacities, then, does not mean to give him *more* memory, *more* attention, or *more* reasoning power,[15] but rather to lead him to memorize that which is most useful, to attend to those things which

---

[14] He so identified the work of Itard, Séguin, Montessori, and Binet.
[15] As per reasoning, "He may be encouraged to exercise his powers and given the chance to acquire the knowledge upon which the success of their exercise is dependent" (Woodrow, 1919, p. 307).

are most worthwhile, and to reason out problems of ever increasing weight. (Woodrow, 1919, p. 296)

Woodrow appeared to be suggesting what could be construed loosely as a behavioristic conception of process training in the latter sentences of the preceding quoted statement. Such an interpretation is further bolstered by another statement concerning the training of attention (a process that was of particular research interest to him).

. . . all that training of attention really means is that, by a change in the conditions under which attention is given, and by a reduction, through habit and familiarity, of obstacles to its application, there may be brought about, in many directions, a greater ease of mental concentration. (Woodrow, 1919, p. 299)

Woodrow, however, was espousing a different cause than behaviorism. He was in fact, basically committed to a deterministic and fundamentally genetic point of view regarding the nature of man's abilities. This is the Galtonian view, common at the time he wrote. Woodrow's views on heredity become explicit in his further discussion of attention:

Capacity for attention is determined mainly by heredity, environment, before the age of school, and by growth. As a general power of the mind, a general capacity or faculty . . . it is as little subject to increase by education or to improvement by training as is general intelligence. (Woodrow, 1917, p. 297)

The spectacular results that Séguin, Montessori, Binet, and Morgan reported (which Woodrow accepted as whole-cloth verities) were due, then, not to the fact that they had strengthened their subjects' faculties but rather that they had taught them to more effectively utilize those faculties in which they were already most effective.

The crucial explanation of the success . . . [of the methods used by Séguin, Montessori, et al.] . . . is not the fact that it trains the mental and physiological functions, but that it is adapted to the capacities possessed by the child, that it exercises the innately strong capacities. (Woodrow, 1919, p. 285)

The sensory capacities and motor movements of both young children and the feebleminded are relatively well developed compared to other, "higher" capacities. The same is true of memory—thus the success obtained in training these capacities:

A child is not so far behind a man in sensory discrimination, as in the ability to concentrate attention or to reason . . . in devoting attention to the education of the senses of a young child, we are training him in the occupations for which, at the time, he is best equipped. . . . Feebleminded and young children have little capacity for judgment and reasoning. Their most valuable asset is rote memory capacity. Its training should, therefore, form a conspicuous part in their education. (Woodrow, 1919, pp. 285–286)

From such statements, we may also draw the sequitur that Woodrow believed in teaching to the strengths, as far as processes were concerned, rather than laboring upon the amelioration of the weaknesses. Teaching to the strengths is, indeed, what he recommended for both cognitively impaired and gifted pupils. Talking about the learning disabled he noted:

> Sometimes a high order of intelligence is accompanied by defects which make it imperative to use . . . the stronger faculties. (Woodrow, 1917, p. 293)

Woodrow was also concerned lest gifted children with specific, rather than general, superiorities be overlooked by their teachers. In such children, while

> . . . the general level of mental capacities may be above normal, only one or a very few of the capacities may be strikingly superior. Of course, no child is equally developed in all of his capacities. One capacity may be very superior while the others may be only slightly so or even mediocre. The superior capacities of exceptional children of this latter type may be easily overlooked by the teacher. . . . Naturally we should desire to prevent a one-sided development, and to produce a child of well-balanced character and intellect. This cannot be done, however, by ignoring the child's special aptitude and attempting to educate him along lines unrelated to his speciality . . . it is necessary to make use of the special talent, to use it and the interests related to it as a starting point, as a base from which to begin our entire educational campaign. . . . (Woodrow, 1919, pp. 291–292)

Woodrow, however, did not fully renounce the notions of traditional process training either, though he treated them in considerably more sophisticated fashion than most.

> Education must accept the capacities of a child as it finds them, and by affording them every exercise possible, make them fit to render their greatest service. This does not necessarily mean that there is no value in formal exercises designed to develop this or that mental function. Memory lessons, attention lessons and reasoning lessons, have their use. They provide a mental technique, methods of mental procedure, which may prove useful in an endless variety of situations. . . . Very likely, it would be wise to provide formal "reasoning training" for exceptionally bright children at the higher mental ages, just as we provide sensory and motor training for children of the lower mental ages. Such exercises could be patterned after . . . tests of logical-mindedness—tests involving the ability to pick out from a number of reasons the best . . . or to select the best conclusion . . . tests of analysis and synthesis, involving the process of pointing out likenesses and differences, and exercises in the formulation of definitions and recognition of absurdities. The possible value of reasoning lessons, imagination lessons . . . and so on, needs further study. (Woodrow, 1919, p. 309)

Nor did he forget that holy grail of modern process training—individualization.

By adapting our methods to the capacities of the child, by basing education upon an inventory of these capacities, we immediately become aware of numerous consequences of the greatest aid to our educational efforts. (Woodrow, 1919, p. 309)

So said he then; so say we now. The dream was; the dream remains.

25
The Vanguard of Twentieth Century Remedial and Special Education—Section 2

INTRODUCTION

The avant-garde of this chapter are three individuals whose work greatly influenced theory and practice in their day: Cyril Burt, Leta S. Hollingsworth, and Harry J. Baker. Of these, Hollingsworth's contributions are now historical shadows. Cyril Burt has recently become a controversial figure, but has always been a significant force in relation to factor analytic theory and nature–nurture controversies concerning the constituents of human ability. Baker's books have generally faded from public consciousness, but his test keeps riding on.

Can we find communalities, besides some rough chronological ordering of these individuals? The answer is yes: first, in terms of the chronology of their writings—all were prolific over at least two decades; second, in terms of their promotion of psychoeducational profiles, those special chartings that provide us with a differential understanding of cognitive and educational abilities. The three subjects of this chapter enthusiastically promoted the use of these devices, though not with an identity of purposes. The present popularity of test profiles owes them something, to be sure.

BURT

Cyril Burt's work in school psychology and remedial and special education has largely escaped notice in the United States, despite his voluminous efforts in these areas. His neglected corpus of work is recommended to the readers of this book, not only because of its historical importance, but because Burt's insights are still cogent for those who are concerned with educational problems.

Of specific concern to us in this chapter are Burt's writings on specific abilities and disabilities. Burt was inconsistent throughout his career in respect to the reality he was willing to allot to these. We know from our acquaintance with his *Factors of the Mind* (1940) that at certain stages of his career he regarded psychological factors (i.e., faculties, processes) as abstractions. However, Cyril Burt, the school psychologist and educationist, inevitably resorted to reifications when dealing with individual differences in children, which is no surprise to us here. He was no more guilty of inconsistency in this respect than Aristotle, Descartes, or Spearman. On occasion, all disclaimed the existence of specific genotypical cognitive power plants in the soul or mind but found themselves cognitively tongue-tied when they tried to describe behavioral phemonena without them. Nor are current antiprocess theorists able to do much better in their out-of-journal parlance.

Burt's writings under scrutiny in this chapter are three: *The Distribution and Relations of Educational Abilities* (1917), *Mental and Scholastic Tests* (1922), and *The Backward Child* (1937).

In the first of these books, Burt attempted to establish the different causes of "educational backwardness." There are a variety of "nonmental" factors. There are also "Intrinsic or Mental Factors (the backwardness being apparently primary or innate). . . ." (Burt, 1917, p. 37). Here he distinguished between "Weak General Ability" and "Weak Specific Ability (inferiority, apparently inborn), of particular mental functions: 'memory,' 'attention,' 'observation,' 'judgment,' 'reasoning,' 'motor co-ordination.' " (Burt, 1917, p. 38).

Burt also described weak general and specific "educational" abilities that were only related to achievement in academic areas. The first affected "efficiency in several school subjects." It was often hereditary, but was "unassociated with marked weakness of general intelligence." It is ". . . often compensated by non-scholastic ability and interests" (Burt, 1917, p. 38).

The second involved "Specific Educational Defect (i.e., inferiority apparently inborn, affecting one group of allied subjects only, often compensated by interest or aptitude in other special directions): chiefly affecting power to manipulate verbal symbols (as in reading, spelling or dictation)" (Burt, 1917, p. 38).

This distinction between different types of learning disabilities, one affecting general life functions, one narrowly confined to academic acquisitions is an interesting one. It would appear that Burt was being influenced by theories of word blindness at the time that his early book was being written. "Weak specific ability," it should be noted accounted for 22% of school failure in Burt's reckoning, while "specific educational defect" accounted for 8%. Weak general ability accounted, quite interestingly, for only 11% of educational problems.

Burt was writing at a time when factor analysis was developing. The correlational coefficient was seeing heavy duty; and, even to the unpracticed eye, the existence of special "factors," common to certain sets of school subjects but relatively lacking in others, was there for the postulation. Burt's own hierarchical ideas of mental organization are clearly on view as early as this time (1917). He found verbal memory factors and mechanical memory ones; "visuokinesthetics," he observed, were factors in arithmetical operations, etc. Burt summarized his opinions regarding the role that various abilities play in school learning:

> First, the abilities and processes involved are far more complex than those who have written on the subject commonly assume. Secondly, similar results are reached by different children by very different mental processes; consequently a child who fails under one method of instruction will often succeed, if a brief study be made of his natural aptitude and operations and another mode of instruction adopted accordingly. Thirdly, similar subjects require very different abilities at different ages and at different stages of operation. (Burt, 1917, pp. 62–63)

Certainly, the preceding statement is one of modernity that requires no additional comment!

In order to help chart the types of abilities and disabilities presented by school children, Burt proudly offered what he called a psychograph. It was to be used to study and compare "the peculiar endowments and deficiences of individual children" and ". . . yield a clear picture of the educational capacities of such individuals" (Burt, 1917, p. 65).

The psychograph was a rather straightforward affair when first proposed, addressing itself entirely to school subjects such as handwork, reading, science, geography, and history. It was to be used to assist teachers in managing the heterogeneity of pupils and to guide individual educational programming. Burt found no purpose in penalizing pupils for specific defects. ". . . a normal or able child should not be kept back in a low class for all subjects, simply because he is deficient in one special branch . . . of school work" (Burt, 1917, p. 74).

Burt argued strongly as well against considering the mentally retarded as an undifferentiated mass of pupils, responding to one particular system of care, one particular system of education.

> Among defectives . . . the distribution of capacity appears to be somewhat more uneven than among normal children. There is less evidence for the assumption that educational ability may be treated as a single mental quality. Such treatment can at present be justified only upon grounds of simplicity and con-

venience. This conclusion . . . is entirely consistent with what I have elsewhere remarked as to the complexity and ambiguity of the current definition of "mental deficiency." For practical purposes it suggests *the importance of further classifying cases of deficiency according to the kind of deficiency, as well as according to its degree.* Some defectives excel in manual subjects, but are unable to master intelligent reading, writing, or calculation; others may so profit from instruction in the latter subjects as eventually to become fit for re-transference to the ordinary schools; others may be afflicted with special defects, such as those described as "word-blindness" or "number-defect"; others, again, may be unable to acquire manual dexterity or to use tools with safety or skill. These different types should be sorted out in an observation class, and eventually transferred to classes specially suited to their special kind of ability or defect. (Burt, 1917, p. 63)

This issue, i.e., of not treating the mentally retarded as a homogeneous group was expanded in Burt's second book, *Mental and Scholastic Tests* (1922), into a plea to distinguish the learning disabled from the mentally retarded.

A child, who suffers merely from a specialized disability in reading and spelling, such as so-called "word-blindness," is to be carefully distinguished from one who is in every respect mentally defective. (Burt, 1922, p. 265).

This second book provides additional insights into the modernity of Burt's views on learning problems. He was buoyed by the promise of the rapid advances in experimental psychology and psychometric research. The facts obtained from these scientific endeavors would inaugurate an age of education within which the individual capacities of children could finally be addressed. The "new" psychology would not rest upon the clichés of armchair speculations or be content with generalizations about the laws of the mind. It would investigate the individuation of those laws within practical application and result in schools able to flexibly adapt to changing pupil needs, as opposed to those which still sought to bend pupils to their will. Writing of this new psychology in *Mental and Scholastic Tests,* Burt proclaimed its promise:

It is content to define the limited powers of this child and of that, not the ultimate potentialities of children as such. It seeks to formulate aims proportioned to those limited powers, not the ideal aims of an ideal school in an ideal society. (Burt, 1922, p. 265)

As a result, instructors in schools will be able to free themselves from the lockstep conformity that has always frustrated pupils' changing needs. Instruction, Burt said,

. . . should be individualized, not universalized; adaptable as clay, not rigid as a clamp; evolved progressively from week to week, modified for this purpose and reversed for that, not written down once for all cases and occasions in a book. (Burt, 1922, p. 265)

Burt explained his position concerning human abilities as they manifest themselves in school. In the following statement, we find again his insistence that specific deficiencies are not to be confused with and taken as signs of the general disability of retardation.

. . . educational attainments depend largely upon capacities of two kinds: first a common or general capacity, entering into every subject in different degree, but best exhibited in those that need thought-processes of a higher order, such as the comprehension of reading matter among young children, and, among older children, problem arithmetic and literary (or rather logical) composition; secondly, specific capacities—such as arithmetic ability, linguistic ability, and music ability—entering into only a small group of subjects. A child who is deficient in the former will be backwards in all subjects, most backward in those subjects most dependent upon this central capacity [for example, the subjects first named], least backward in those subjects least dependent upon it (such as manual and musical subjects). A child who is deficient in one of the specific capacities alone will be backward in the limited group of implicated subjects, and in none but these. (Burt, 1922, p. 266)

Whereas in his first book (1917), Burt was prone to stay on the surface concerning the educational problems he had studied, he was, in his second major book, *Mental and Scholastic Tests* (1922), ready to address the psychological processes that underlie academic behavior.

. . . the examiner should go further still and test the underlying psychological capacities. His end is only reached when he has probed beneath the scholastic abilities and scholastic defects, and has, wherever possible, observed and measured the deeper and simpler functions, the elementary intellectual processes, that together make up the activities of the school. He should remember always that linguistic ability and arithmetical ability, even the ability to read and to add, are themselves highly complex functions; and that in mental life there are always more ways than one of learning to do one thing. (Burt, 1922, p. 265)

Burt cautioned against excessive precision in attempting to precisely discriminate specific disabilities in young children, a caution that is too often overlooked nowadays.

. . . below the age of about ten, it must be peculiarly difficult to diagnose a special or localized disability, as it is undoubtedly difficult to discover special or localized talents. Specialization is, during early childhood, the exception rather than the rule. Young turtle, said Epicurus, is every kind of meat in one—fish, fowl, pork, venison; but old turtle is just plain turtle. Similarly the young child contains in fresh and dormant essence the germ of every faculty. Age alone betrays our idiosyncrasies. (Burt, 1922, p. 265)

Despite such reservations, Burt recommended that teachers, nevertheless, be alert for learning problems in young children.

. . . the teacher should always take into consideration their possible existence. Many young children committed to special schools for the mentally deficient prove afterwards to have been cases of specialized defect. (Burt, 1922, p. 265)

I cannot resist the opportunity of presenting a lengthy quote from Burt's 1922 book concerning the educator's responsibilities in respect to pupil assessment and diagnosis. Burt's statements appear most appropriate to our own age of would-be precision evaluation.

If the child proves to be backward in such a subject as reading and spelling, the teacher should first hold in mind two truths; the one, that any single mental function (as visual memory or memory for sounds) that enters as a subordinate component into the total process of reading may by its own ineffectiveness render ineffective the larger process in its entirety; the second, that one or another of many different mental functions may assume the office of the ineffective function, if only the means of teaching and the mode of learning be appropriately changed. The duty of the teacher, therefore, is to find what element is out of gear, and then to seek another element to fill its place.

He will enquire, to begin with, whether the cause of the backwardness is extrinsic—due to ill health, irregular attendance, or an illiterate home; or, on the other hand, intrinsic—due to causes residing in the child himself. If it is intrinsic, he will proceed to ask: is the disability predominantly moral or temperamental—due to lack of industry or lack of interest, to want of motive, or to want of care—or is it predominantly intellectual? And if intellectual, is it one of many symptoms of an all-pervasive backwardness, crippling general intelligence in each of its many forms; or is it a specific disability affecting the linguistic subjects alone, or it may be even, simply, reading alone—suggesting, in fact, what is, in extremer cases, sometimes designated "word blindness." In such a case, is the backwardness due perhaps to defective sensation—to partial deafness, or to imperfect vision uncorrected by appropriate spectacles? Is it due to defective perception—to an imperfect analysis of forms seen or of sounds heard, of words uttered by his own lips or of movements traced by his own hand? Is it due to a difficulty in retaining these sense–perceptions, or rather the memories of the forms, sounds, and movement feelings fully sensed and distinctly perceived?

And, if the difficulty be a difficulty of memory, it must be further recollected that memory, too, is of many forms. Some children may be unable to evoke memory-images of a particular kind; many visualizers cannot call up sounds; many audiles cannot visualize; many carry memories best in a motor form—a recollection of movements traced by the hand, or of postures assumed by tongue and lips. Others, again, are defective in recognition memory; they can evoke images, that is, they can imagine; but they cannot identify. Some have poor short-distance memories; some poor long-distance memories. Some have poor rote memories and learn bare facts only after an exceptional amount of drill. Some have poor rational memories and learn empirical data better than logical principles. Each of these different modes of memory should be separately tested. Very frequently the weakness lies in long-distance mechanical memory: the central difficulty is to preserve for long periods the arbitrary associations between the several abstract symbols—between the word as seen, as uttered, as heard, and as written—or between any of these abstract symbols and the concrete meaning symbolized (whether that meaning be apprehended as clearly as a visual picture or implicitly as definable through words) or, finally, between the several elements which comprise one and the same abstract symbol, which are apprehended in one and the same mental form, and which require to be associated in the correct and proper order, for example, the successive letters of a given word.

There is, it will be seen, a bewildering network of interweaving associations. And, as the electrician will disengage and inspect in turn every relay in a faulty circuit, so the teacher should test each type of connection, one by one, between all possible pairs—visual with articulatory, visual with graphic, auditory with articulatory, auditory with graphic, articulatory with visual, articulatory with graphic, ideational with graphic, with visual, with auditory, and with articulatory. He must note which mode of association is feeblest, and so tends to throw the whole series out of action. He must also note which mode is most easily formed, most permanently retained. He will then in his teaching appeal to the stronger and distrust the weak.

But even here the analysis is not yet at an end. The mind is something more than a consecutive string of associations. It is a hierarchy of systems within systems. Each mental process is to be conceived rather as the functioning of a complex mechanism than as the mere percolation of a simple conduit. Every act of learning consists in the organization of a mental schema—of an "neurogram" or a "psycho-physiological disposition," to borrow the technical jargon—not in the mere addition of one link to another in a long chain. The mind of the backward or defective child is preeminently weak in this very capacity for mental organization, in the constructing of such psychical systems. He fails not so much in power to associate as in power to integrate; not so much in the capacity to hook, as it were, "C" mechanically on to "A" and "A" mechanically onto "T," as in the capacity to synthesize in order the letter-sounds, "C-A-T," both with each other and with the letter-forms, and the two groups in turn with word-form and word-sound as a whole, and each and all with meaning—with mental picture, or generic idea—until the whole arrangement can operate as a compound unit of implicitly apprehended parts. (Burt, 1922, pp. 284–285)

Even individualized instruction can be expected to fail, said Burt, if not guided by a careful diagnostic understanding of the pupil.

. . . even for the backward, individual teaching may be no less wasteful—it will, indeed, be more wasteful—than class teaching, unless it follows the appropriate method. And the appropriate method can only be discovered by an intensive study of the special needs of each particular child. Individual teaching, in short, presupposes individual observation. . . . The sound method for a child is that method by which he learns most successfully; and what is sound for most children, may be unsound for the remainder. (Burt, 1922, p. 289)

Burt, if we recall our review of his earlier book, was concerned that special abilities be recognized. He repeated this concern in *Mental and*

Scholastic Tests. The principles of compensatory education are clearly set forth therein, i.e., in respect to utilizing a sound or superior ability to compensate for a deficient one.

> . . . special tests may reveal what in a given child are the mental capacities we may most successfully rely upon, and what we cannot entirely trust. Let me here emphasize that it is not sufficient to discover disabilities. We are too prone to look for backwardness and to emphasize deficiency. In the most backward and in the most defective we should still search also for unusual abilities and special gifts and abilities that may compensate for defects, that may offer help to appropriate training, and hold out hope for successful development. (Burt, 1922, p. 299)

In lieu of completely reliable measurement instruments to accomplish the task of assessment for instruction, Burt advised that: "The teacher . . . rid himself of the assumption that for a given subject there is one sound method; and test each method anew upon each backward individual (Burt, 1922, p. 299). What he recommended was an in situ task analysis to be carried out with each individual pupil:

> . . . the plan . . . may be termed experimental teaching. Essentially it consists of individual instruction carried out by constantly varied devices and by widely diversified methods; but it is to be accompanied always by a close observation of the child's spontaneous method of attack, and by a detailed study of the ways which the child can, does, and will by preference, follow and adopt in learning a given piece of work; and it is to be succeeded always by an intensive training in the most defective operations by means of the least defective channels. (Burt, 1922, p. 268)

Burt's *The Backward Child* was one of a series of books he wrote on exceptional children. It was one of the most successful, too, going through a considerable number of printings, though the concepts remained essentially stable from one to another. The edition upon which we based our account and from which I am quoting is that of 1937.

Backwardness was defined by Burt in this volume in a fashion that takes in almost any type of problem manifesting itself in academic failure. Burt was continuing the tradition we first observed with Barbara Morgan. The condition of backwardness is due, he said, to defects or disabilities that are ". . . either general or limited; general and widespread, when they spring from undeveloped intelligence; limited and narrow when they spring from a lack of some specialized aptitude" (Burt, 1937, p. 11). Thus we observe in *The Backward Child* that Burt's concern about differentiating specific from general defects was still quite intense. There are those, he said, ". . . who are the victims of nothing but some special disability . . . these are primarily backward in one school subject only, or in one type of mental process and no other" (Burt, 1937, p. 12).

Burt was, within this book, continuing his commitment to assessing and prescribing for the various functions of his pupils, both general and specific. Like in his earlier writings, his approach to the latter is in the tradition of late nineteenth century faculty psychology. There is to be assessment of the most elementary processes first—sensation, perception, and motor functions of a simple sort—and then the progression is to proceed into higher processes, ending with thought and reasoning. Perhaps, because he was so intent on precision assessment from the lowest to highest levels of cognition, he was not content with the tools currently available for the comprehensive undertaking he believed was essential to educational planning.

For many functions of the mind have as yet not standardized methods of measurement, and most of the existing methods are too cumbersome for use outside the laboratory. (Burt, 1937, p. 464)

Not only were existing methods too often cumbersome; they were also too often imprecise. Of the tests that presumed to isolate separate functions or processes, he remarked:

. . . it is questionable . . . whether they . . . really isolate the capacities after which they are familiarly named. . . [so as to]. . . enable us to watch more clearly certain aspects of the mind at work in definite and comparable situations. (Burt, 1937, p. 464)

He was too much of a pragmatist, however, to reject what instruments were available. If they were not available for his purposes, he was perfectly willing to improvise some of his own.

In modality assessment, Burt insisted upon clearly distinguishing between what he regarded as sensory and motor functions and those he regarded as "mental." For example, he noted, a child's eyesight may be perfectly normal and yet the child will fail to discriminate the various shapes and forms encountered in schoolwork. Similarly, a child may hear sounds adequately and fail to be able to compare and analyze various sound patterns. None of this was new as he observed it (even in light of his own previous writings); however, it was newer than it is today, when we continue to marvel at such distinctions.

As I observed earlier, Burt's approach to processes in *The Backward Child* has a traditional faculty psychology flavor about it. This is again apparent in his treatment of attention, the separation of which, from other faculties, perplexed him, as it had many faculty psychologists of the past. And as was done in the past, and again in the future, he recommended that ". . . tests of perceptual capacity be in part tests of attention" (Burt, 1937, p. 478).

Burt also made some attempts to directly measure attention, whatever that was, though his direct assessments were still modality based.

(How could they be other?) For evaluating scope of attention, he recommended tachistoscopic presentation of slides with irregularly placed dots, which a testee is to enumerate following their disappearance. For assessing duration of attention, he suggested having the testee tap dots on a tape passing by them at regulated speeds, and via cancellation tests.

Burt discussed the higher cognitive processes, also called powers, abilities, and activities, as ". . . resting upon sensation, perception, and attention."[1] Their development depends upon "the association of ideas," mechanical and logical. He did not regard association as a faculty on its own.

Among the higher faculties with which Burt was most concerned was memory; no matter what one's age was, memory as an act, if not a faculty, could not be ignored. He recommended attention to it, both in terms of the ability to "memorize" and in terms of long-term reproduction. The latter is a matter of "old associations," the former one of "new associations."

Burt wished to assess memory from all standpoints, new and old. Distinctions aplenty were available to him concerning memory, which has always been accommodating to those who like their processes many and finite. Thus, discriminations are to be made between mechanical (rote) and logical memory, between short-distance (immediate) and long-distance (delayed) memory. The instruments for all of this should be commonplaces in our memories by now—substitution tests, digits, sentences, and stories to recall.

The term "habit formation" appears in *The Backward Child* as ". . . an essential to the acquisition of what are termed skills" (Burt, 1937, p. 503). Whether it was to be considered a distinct set of processes (or a faculty of some sort) is unclear; again, it is an "activity" that is hardly new by the standards of previous faculty psychologists. Did Burt intend a figure of speech in talking about *it*? It is simply not clear.

Modality training was important to Burt's point of view in *The Backward Child,* as to those expressed in earlier writings. "Different children . . . learn best by different channels," (Burt, 1937, p. 505). And there are the special needs of visiles and audiles and of techniques properly adapted to modality problems. He with poor visual imagery will be likely to have trouble when taught with pure phonic methods. Nonvisualizers are inclined to have trouble with arithmetic. A bright child can usually compensate for his deficiencies "hit upon some other means or channel" while the ". . . dullard is doubly penalized" (Burt, 1937, p. 517).

---

[1] It is hard to reconcile the Burt who wrote this way and the Burt who wrote *The Factors of the Mind* and other articles on cognitive assessment. Burt wore a number of hats in facile fashion.

As in earlier books, Burt made the distinction in *The Backward Child* (a classic and forever continuing distinction in psychology) between higher and lower cognitive processes, relating them to differences in the type of imagery employed, abstract or concrete. It is difficult to think that he was not leafing through a traditional process text of the past to base his ideas upon. His means of assessing higher cognitive processes—and of improving them—you, the reader, should be able to anticipate by now. And if not, there is almost everywhere at least one edition of *The Backward Child* available in a college or university library. It is, in respect to processes, the least innovative of the three books we have examined. In terms of an overall approach to the child or youth with learning problems, however, it has considerable merit.

HOLLINGSWORTH

Leta S. Hollingsworth is a most interesting entry in the history of processes and process training. This great lady of twentieth century psychology and special education was greatly concerned with these topics. She wrote *The Psychology of Special Disability in Spelling* (1918), had a chapter on special abilities in her book on exceptional children, *The Psychology of Subnormal Children* (1920), and then, in 1923, published her definitive statement on processes in *Special Talents and Defects*.

Cognitive processes, yes? Cognitive processes, no. At least, not too many of them or much about them, despite books and chapter titles suggesting a harvest of such.

It was not that Hollingsworth was insensitive to the possibilities of process formulations. Hardly! She was writing at a time when the conceptual air was thick with them. But Hollingsworth was product oriented and insistent upon operationalizing her concepts via product.

Attempting to define function (which is a behavioral derivation of faculty doctrine) she made her product orientation quite clear.

[A mental function] must be judged by its product, the measurement of performance is the only approach there is, or probably will ever be to the measurement of the mind . . . it is impossible to identify or measure any such function as "the reason," "the memory," "the observation," . . . "the will," and similar supposed entities. (Hollingsworth, 1923, p. 4)

Wherefore, a mental function is to be defined as ". . . *an actually or possibly observable event in behavior"* (Hollingsworth, 1927, p. 4).

Throughout most of her writing, Hollingsworth avoided the familiar traps of reification to an unusual extent—particularly, when one considers the time period within which she wrote. Her functions were clearly operationalized and without excessive inferential baggage. And when she reported tests of functions, she usually did so in terms of rather concrete test behaviors, with seldom an invocation of a hypothetical process to explain them, ". . . memorizing digits, detecting absurdities, and reading English print are examples of mental functions" (Hollingsworth, 1923, p. 4).

Nor did Hollingsworth fall into the niceties of definition that all too often obscure fact and meaning and create illusions of precision in process theory. For she recognized that processes were, at their ultimate delivery point, words and, as such, highly susceptible to distortions.

> Other terms which are used to refer to performances or "events in behavior," are *abilities* and *capacities*. A prolonged discussion might be conducted, in an attempt to assign different technical meanings to these words, and to bring out fine shades of distinction among them. For instance, it might be claimed that "ability" should be reserved to signify capacity *plus* the skill acquired by practice, if any; while "capacity" should mean the innate aptitude, apart from all training. However, since capacity in this sense can never be known, but can only be inferred from the degree of actual performance, under controlled conditions, it hardly seems necessary to maintain such distinctions for our purpose. Refinements of nomenclature will, therefore, be avoided, and the terms *mental function, capacity,* and *ability* will be used interchangeably, to denote performance which depends on the inborn integrity and sensitivity of the individual. (Hollingsworth, 1923, pp. 4–5)

Hollingsworth's formulations of functions relied upon the theoretical formulations of first Thorndike and then Spearman. A strong allegiance to Thorndike is particularly evident in her first book on the topic, *The Psychology of Special Disability in Spelling* (1918), published, incidentally, by Teachers College, Columbia University. In this book, regarding improvement in spelling ability she states:

> English spelling must be acquired by the formation of hundreds of specific bonds and cannot be acquired by the formation of a comparatively few fundamental bonds. If a child has not formed the specific bonds involved in spelling "eight," there is no help . . . for him in the possession of a thousand other words. . . . In order to increase a child's ability to spell . . . words he must be taught specific words; must form those specific bonds. (Hollingsworth, 1918, p. 66)

We see in this early statement her rejection of a traditional view in favor of classic Thorndike associationism. The processes of learning as formulated per Thorndike, are also clearly evident in a chapter (in her book on spelling) entitled "Contribution to the Theory of Special Linguistic Defect."

1. An object, act, quality, etc., is "bound" to a certain sound, which has often been repeated while the object is pointed at, the act performed,

etc. In order that the bond may become definitely established it is necessary (a) that the individual should be able to identify in consciousness the object, act, quality etc., and (b) that he should be able to recollect the particular vocal sounds which have been associated therewith.

2. The sound (word) becomes "bound" with performance of the highly complex muscular act necessary for articulating it.

3. Certain printed or written symbols, arbitrarily chosen, visually representing sound combinations, become "bound" (a) with the recognized objects, acts, etc., and (b) with their vocal representatives (so that when these *symbols* are presented to sight, the word can be uttered by the perceiving individual). This is what we should call the ability "to read" the word.

4. The separate symbols (letters) become associated with each other in the proper sequence, and have the effect of calling each other up to consciousness in the proper order. When this has taken place, we say that the individual can *spell orally*.

5. The child, by a slow, voluntary process, "binds" the visual perceptions of the separate letters with the muscular movements of hand, arm, and fingers necessary to *copy* the word.

6. The child "binds" the representatives in consciousness of the visual symbols with the motor responses necessary to produce the written word spontaneously, at pleasure. (Hollingsworth, 1918, pp. 79–80)

Hollingsworth illustrated the above principles through a reinterpretation of case histories, drawn from the work of Broca and Dejerine and other neurologists, which she interpreted in terms of bond theory. One such case is the following:

. . . a man sixty-eight years of age, of more than ordinary intelligence and culture, with partial right lateral hemianopsia, with complete hemiachromatopsia. There was preservation of ability to read figures and to calculate, and there was no disturbance of articulate speech. There was also perfect preservation of spontaneous writing and of writing from dictation. The patient could thus write whole pages correctly.

But *writing from a copy was very difficult and defective.* There was no impairment of general intelligence, but the ability to read words was lost. (Hollingsworth, 1918, p. 83)

As interpreted paradigmatically a la Thorndike, this patient had

lost . . . bonds noted under (3), (4), and (5). *The bonds between printed or written symbols and objects, acts, etc., were destroyed; the bonds between printed or written symbols and their vocal representatives were destroyed; the bonds between the visual perceptions of the separate letters and the muscular movements of the arm, hand and fingers necessary to copy the word, were destroyed; all other bonds remained intact.* (In this case we note the peculiar fact that though the bonds between visually presented *words* and *concepts* were destroyed, the bonds between visually presented *numerals* and *concepts* were *not* destroyed.) (Hollingsworth, 1918, p. 85)

Thusly, Hollingsworth, in her early writing, skirted faculties to an extraordinary extent for someone writing ca. 1918 about learning disabilities, and this because of her commitment to Thorndike's brand of associationism. Later she was to receive encouragement to the same purpose from Spearman, whose factor theories were dominant ones at the time *Special Talents and Defects* (1923) was written.

While Spearman's "general factor" would seem to be entirely antithetical to Thorndike's specific bond theory, Spearman did allow for specificity in his theorums. He did not like the broad specific factors (so easily identified with faculties), to be sure, but after factoring out g, he had found s's. As he was quoted by Hollingsworth:

All branches of intellectual activity have in common one fundamental function (or group of functions) whereas the remaining or specific elements of the activity seem in every case to be wholly different from that in all others. . . . (Hollingsworth, 1923, p. 15)

True, neither Spearman nor Thorndike in their written to's and fro's had seen any particular grounds for conciliation. Commenting on Spearman's insistence that g expressed most of the variance relative to abilities, Thorndike and his collaborators saw an entirely different picture.

One is almost tempted to replace Spearman's statement by the equally extravagant one that there is nothing whatever common to all mental functions. . . . (Hollingsworth, 1923, p. 16)

However, things had quieted down a bit when *Special Talents and Defects* was being written so that Hollingsworth could state:

During the twenty years which have elapsed since the first interpretations were set forth there have been modifications of each hypothesis, in the direction of mutual reconciliation. (Hollingsworth, 1923, p. 17)

This was not completely true—at least, not unless one wished to stretch some points. But it was true enough for her purpose, which was to interpret school performance both in terms of general ability and in terms of specific functions.

General intelligence is now measured, for practical purposes. . . . Nevertheless, there are, as Thorndike maintained and maintains, mental functions, standing in which is hardly predictable from knowledge of other capacities. In rare cases there may be complete discrepancy in ranks between performance in one task and performance in other tasks, with equal training. These are the cases of special talents and defects. . . . (Hollingsworth, 1923, p. 34)[2]

Yet, early Thorndike was adamantly set against faculties and transfer of training and formal discipline, and early Thorndike would have condemned, except for classificatory purposes, broad types of cognitive factors. Later, Thorndike didn't find much attractive about broad proccesses either, even though he gave "identical elements" more latitude in their interpretation. But extreme specificity—denying group factors altogether wouldn't have allowed Hollingsworth any "special talents and defects." Or would they have? Thorndike's writings, like other bibles, permitted several interpretations.

Hollingsworth recommended that the study of mental pathology become a major approach to the study of special abilities.

For the study of mental decay, when carried out by adequate methods, extremely difficult of attainment, is sure to throw light on the relationships among mental functions. From it we shall learn whether some functions remain intact, with impairment of other functions. (Hollingsworth, 1923, p. 26)

For the study of special abilities in a school context, she recommended various test approaches. The psychometric technology to identify both specific disabilities and special abilities was (with qualification) available:

Although much further research is required before we can identify all the mental functions which are incoherent with general intelligence. We already have some knowledge of the matter useful for the welfare of school children. (Hollingsworth, 1923, p. 37)

She opted for psychographs of the mental functions to be studied.[3] Following her psychograph, left to right, we find the following functions named: grip, tapping, coordinator, profile, Séguin board, Stenquist, cancellation, substitution, community of ideas, word building, completion, vocabulary, cube limitation, digit span, digits reversed, verbal memory, opposites, calculation, directions.

These "functions" are essentially free of any conceptual flesh and stand in stark contrast to those familiar to us from the work of earlier pioneers in process assessment and training. Hollingsworth had been too strongly influenced by Thorndike and Spearman to tread the florid process paths taken by many of her predecessors—Bronner, for example.

The abilities revealed by the psychograph and the I.Q. are to be used to interpret the special disabilities and abilities of schoolwork—once

---

[2] It is worthy of comment that Hollingsworth seemed to interpret Thorndike, in this instance, as supporting some type of specific trait theory (Bronner had done the same).
[3] Made popular by Burt.

again, not hypothetical cognitive processes; once again, observable—abilities in reading, spelling, arithmetic, drawing, and music.

As to the nature of abilities, general and specific, Hollingsworth felt genetics explained the large part of them. And because the entire nervous system is determined by common genetic and constitutional factors, covariation rather than disparity holds, even for specific abilities in most instances. Great variation is an exception.

Although we cannot state with precision the frequency with which marked special gifts occur among the stupid, or marked special deficiencies occur among the highly intelligent, we know that such cases are quite rare. It is necessary to remind ourselves constantly of this fact, because it would gratify the demand for justice and fair play to find that special gifts are freely distributed among the generally inferior, and special defects frequently found among the superior. The truth which satisfies our desires need be stated but once, to be apprehended and remembered. The truth which offends kindliness, self-interest, or cherished beliefs, and is hence unsatisfying, requires emphasis. Threrefore we must take particular care to bear in mind throughout the whole of our discussion of special talents and defects, that we are dealing with comparatively rare phenomena. The distribution of abilities, as determined by biological law, does not correspond to our concept of fair play. Nearly all stupid persons are inferior in all capacities. The great majority of gifted persons are superior in nearly all their abilities. The majority of human beings are neither markedly inferior nor markedly superior, but are "typical" (not far from the median or average) in all respects. (Hollingsworth, 1923, pp. 44–45)

What were the possibilities of cognitive training, at any level? Addressing herself to the question "Can an Intellect Be Trained as a Unit?" (Hollingsworth, 1923, p. 28), she decided against it; after all, Spearman's g was something else than intellect which ". . . is not a unit, but a complex of many capacities coinciding mysteriously in amount to a very marked extent in an individual," and training the mind as a unit seemed to her to smack of formal discipline all over again, which was anathema to Thorndike, with whose concepts she was generally in concordance. Within what appears to be general intelligence, "Each function has elements special to itself, and some functions are very highly specialized as regards the amount of transfer or training from them to others, or from others to them" (Hollingsworth, 1923, p. 28).

On the other hand, she was not too optimistic about training special abilities, either. She was a naturalist, who didn't have much hope for nurture.

The question arises: Can . . . special talents be acquired, or the special deficiencies be overcome, by any course of training? Scientific psychology tends more and more strongly to the conclusion that psychology and education can do nothing to alter the amounts or relationships of innate mental endowment. They can but measure endowment and give it training suited to its requirements. The history of Séguin's formboard seems to illustrate the evolution of the point of view on this question. About sixty years ago this formboard was hopefully used as a supposed *means of altering* original endowment. Feebleminded children were given exercises in placing and replacing the blocks in it, in order that they might become more intelligent. Today this formboard is used as a *means of gauging* original endowment. Psychology cannot create endowment; it can merely measure and describe it. Education cannot bestow mental gifts; it can only utilize such as are innately present within the organism. Talent and genius can be created in children only by the procreation of parents, who are the biological carriers of extraordinary endowment. (Hollingsworth, 1923, p. 60)

It would be journalistically satisfying to conclude that Hollingsworth's spartan description of processes (i.e., functions, etc.) and her unwillingness to allow them to improve with training is responsible for the general neglect of her work. Instead, it is, of course, syndromatic of special education's general neglect of its past.[4] Morgan and Bronner— surely no two had ever committed themselves more diligently to the cause of processes and process training. And yet acknowledgment of their work is rarely given.

It is probably just as well for process proponents that Morgan, Bronner, and Hollingsworth are forgotten. Too much attention to the first two might arouse an embarrassing "Why it's all been done before!" While Hollingsworth's reduction of abilities to the bare bones of assessed behavior and her dismissal of process training might arouse anxieties lest her way be the right one for the study of academically related processes to pursue.

BAKER

Harry J. Baker, a clinical psychologist in the Detroit Public Schools, was author or coauthor of a number of major texts which included such subjects as childhood exceptionality (1944), behavior problems (1935), learning characteristics (1927), and learning problems (1929). He is perhaps best known among the present generation of remedial and special educators as the codeveloper (with Beatrice Leland) of the *The Detroit Tests of Learning Aptitude* (1935).

Baker's interest in cognitive abilities was expressed early in his

---

[4] The frequently hailed antiquarian by Kirk and Frostig, for example, is Binet. While I share their appreciation and fondness for the great man, I also suspect that his ghost is called to testify in favor of current process diagnostics and training more on the basis of his fame as the originator of a most famous intelligence test than on the basis of any success he had demonstrated in specific process assessment and training.

career (1922).[5] His concern with their diagnosis and their training is of interest here, specifically as expressed in his two books on the subject, *Characteristic Differences in Bright and Dull Pupils* (1927) and *Educational Disability and Case Studies in Remedial Teaching* (1929).[6]

Like Woodrow, Baker appears to have been influenced in his thinking by factor analytic concepts. More than Woodrow, he was ambivalent whether to opt for general intelligence or specific faculties.

In the first of his two books on the subject, *Characteristic Differences in Bright and Dull Pupils,* Baker allowed the possible operations of specific cognitive faculties but in general supported the greater importance of the general faculty.

> Those who have had little or no training in psychology try to explain success or failure in terms of special mental faculties. For example; a pupil who is backward may be described as "backward on account of poor memory." But if we examine "memory" very closely, it may have in it certain elements of association and reasoning. So it is difficult to state just what are the limits of pure memory or where it merges into some other faculty. If memory is closely allied to reasoning, to association, or to other mental faculties, the improvement would necessitate the improvement of other faculties. This improvement would probably mean that general intelligence has also been improved. (Baker, 1927, pp. 24–25)

According to the Baker of this book, general ability accounts for most of the variance in learning and school performance. It is probably nearer to the truth to describe brightness or dullness in terms of general intelligence than in terms of the operation of special faculties. Sometimes special faculties may act in powerful ways, but they cannot permanently offset the effect of general intelligence; they may hinder but they rarely assist its operations.

Intelligence, that super process, is the faculty in charge of all others, according to Baker.

> Special mental faculties are quite subservient to the effects of general intelligence. They are in reality secondary factors in successful learning . . . subfactors in general intelligence. . . . (Baker, 1927, p. 25)

General intelligence, however, can be better understood by an understanding of special abilities. Those that Baker was then interested in ranged beyond the faculties associated with the modalities. They are those of the "higher" cognitive sort. He discussed several in detail: The faculty of association, so important to learning, he found to be closely

---

[5] In an article in the *Journal of Applied Psychology* entitled "Mental Tests as an Aid in the Analysis of Mental Constitution."

[6] Curiously, these issues are generally ignored in his other books. Nor can the test manual for the Detroit tests be said to overly concern itself with them.

related to and dependent upon memory and reasoning. Memory, he warned, should not be regarded as a simple unitary faculty, it ". . . may be classified according to the sense organs by which the impressions are received, e.g., auditory memory, visual memory, motor memory, and several others. . . ." it could also be classified on the basis of "rote memory" and "logical memory," "immediate memory" and "delayed memory" (Baker, 1927, p. 25).

As did many of his distinguished predecessors, Baker regarded simple rote memory as the particular type of memory process(es) with which the mentally dull were most comfortable. He did not find any important differences between the bright and dull students in respect to their comparative efficiency in auditory or visual rote memory, and engaged in a little speculation about aptitude-treatment interactions:

> . . . there is no evidence that auditory memory is the best method for bright and visual memory for dull pupils, or *vice versa*. The relative keenness or receptivity of the ear as compared to the eyes is not characteristic of any intelligence level. (Baker, 1927, p. 27)

So much so for visiles and audiles. However, "Bright pupils do surpass dull pupils in delayed recall, especially when they can associate many other factors to assist them" (Baker, 1927, p. 27).

The faculty that most intrigued Baker was reasoning. This is the faculty most clearly related to brightness and dullness. However,

> Reasoning is dependent upon so many other faculties that it can scarcely be considered as a separate faculty. . . . It is very similar in many respects to general intelligence, in that it makes demands upon the more complicated centers of thoughts. (Baker, 1927, p. 27)

As to attention, this favored process of so many, it was demoted by Baker from faculty status:

> It is not a trait or faculty, but is a condition under which mental action functions. Good attention involves steady concentration on the purpose, whereas in poor attention, the object of attention may pass entirely from the mind. The attention of dull students is often described as "very poor," that of bright pupils as "good." It is very doubtful whether these observations correctly indicate the natural tendencies of bright and of dull pupils. (Baker, 1927, pp. 28–29)

The quality of attention, in any case, really is a consequence of action, rather than a power in and of itself. Interest a pupil so he focuses his ability on a subject and you have good attention. Overload poor students and ". . . they pay little attention to what they do not understand or cannot comprehend" (Baker, 1927, p. 29).

Baker observed that special disabilities minimally affected a bright student, e.g., the one

. . . who has a special mental disability . . . which is definitely below the level of his general intelligence. In such a case the pupil usually seems to suffer very little from this special deficiency. In fact, instead of being handicapped, he often uses his other mental faculties to circumvent the weak spot in his mental armor. For example, if a defect occurs in visual rote memory. The pupil translates the visual units into auditory units by repeating aloud what has been presented to him visually, and thus gets an impression upon his mental "field" where it is more easily and clearly received. Adults of average or superior intelligence use this device constantly. They learn by experience in what ways their special defect may be overcome. The bright mind is able to find means of circumvention, by the very fact of its great resourcefulness and versatility. Here the chain is really not as weak as its weakest link. (Baker, 1927, p. 22)

The dull pupil is another case entirely, i.e., when ". . . the special disability is much below the general low level of the dull pupil's mind."

In this case, the disability is a serious handicap, for the dull mind lacks the resourcefulness to circumvent the weakness. If the weak trait in question is called upon, the dull pupil is at a complete loss; he does not know how to substitute some other faculty and thus to proceed successfully. One of the most important requirements for the successful teacher of dull pupils is the ability to discover these particular weaknesses and patiently to show the pupil how to proceed along other avenues. (Baker, 1927, p. 23)

Baker advised about pupils with strong special abilities, those dull or bright. For the dull student, a strong faculty can be both an asset and a liability. It is an asset in that it provides the dull pupil with confidence in his abilities. If his faculty of rote memory is particularly strong, a dull student may make very good progress in learning realms "that are not much above the rote level." However,

The special talent is often a liability to the dull pupil because he used it indiscriminately to the detriment of his general mental and educational progress. It is a frequent observation of teachers that dull pupils seem to excel other pupils in the early elementary grades, but come to a sudden standstill when the schoolwork requires general powers of reasoning and association. On account of lack of judgment, the special talent is exploited in ways which build up the present at the expense of the future. Teachers will often do well to discourage, rather than to encourage, the exploitation of special ability in dull pupils. (Baker, 1927, p. 23)

The bright student with a "special talent" is something else altogether:

Superior minds do not tend to branch out in any direction to excess, and therefore, seldom abuse the advantages which they have. The special talent is used by the bright pupil to explore and to scout far into new fields, but the building up of workable lines of communication to the settled and familiar fields is not neglected. Under such circumstances the special talent is a general tonic for the bright mind and gives it a desirable emotional tone. The real advance of civilization is probably bound up with the proper use of special talent of superior minds. (Baker, 1927, p. 23)

In any case, general intelligence still explains more than special abilities:

> When, nevertheless, special mental faculties are given careful examination and study, they appear to be subsidiary aspects of general intelligence, and as such subsidiaries, cannot operate to offset general intelligence except within quite narrow limits. They serve chiefly to furnish a convenient terminology to illuminate the operations of general intelligence. To the extent to which they have special effects of their own, they should be studied in reference to those activities. (Baker, 1927, p. 29)

It is quite another Harry Baker who greets us from the pages of his second book, *Educational Disability and Case Studies in Remedial Education* (1929), whose copyright is but two years after the first we discussed. It is the Baker we have come to associate with the Detroit Tests of Learning Aptitude—still some time away.

In his second book, Baker came out clearly in favor of special and specific abilities. He even appears to have forgotten the hesitancies he himself expressed about them in his earlier work. As witness his statement:

> The writer believes that special faculty psychology has unjustly been in general disrepute for some time. The higher statistical validity of measures of general intelligence and the lack of adequate norms for special tests have been chiefly responsible for this condition. Special faculty psychology has great possibilities if used to supplement measures of general intelligence. The only means of complete mental diagnosis will be through the maximum utilization of tests of special mental abilities. A further objection to special ability tests is that mental processes cannot be isolated and measured so that one test may be said to measure association distinctly without memory, and another measure judgment without reasoning. While there is undoubtedly overlapping of processes in some of the special tests, the trait in question often stands out quite distinctly and dominates the mental activity in question, (Baker, 1929, p. 32)

In his later book Baker recommended that the Stanford-Binet test be used to assess abilities and disabilities.

> Although Terman emphasizes that the Stanford-Binet test measures general intelligence rather than specialized abilities, psychologists recognize that it has certain diagnostic values for special abilities and disabilities . . . the comprehension questions may be considered independently of the remainder of the test as a miniature scale of comprehension. Memory tests for numbers or for sentences also form special test series in that psychological trait . . . knowledge of numbers, of right and left, and of time may be conveniently assembled as a partial means of orientation. . . . (Baker, 1929, pp. 31–32)

Thus, Baker's testing of specific faculties began with various subtests from the Binet, e.g., its vocabulary and free association tests (from the 1917 version). To his borrowings from the Binet he added an Opposites test, assessing controlled association, and an Orientation test, addressing three types of orientation: [7]

(1) allopsychic, or knowledge of general environment; (2) autopsychic, or knowledge of self; and (3) time orientation. (Baker, 1929, p. 33)

Baker's process testing did not neglect memory. For auditory rote memory, he employed words rather than digits. For visual rote memory, he employed a test in which pictures of objects increasing in number were first shown and then removed, with the pupil expected to name what he had seen. The readers will remember similar ones used by Baker's predecessors, though sometimes to measure different processes.

For evaluating judgment, Baker found the Porteus Maze test useful. The Whipple-Healy Tapping test (in which the testee is asked to place a dot in as many squares as possible within a half-minute span) was recommended for assessing speed of motor reaction time, which he considered a special mental factor.

Baker made a valiant effort "to trace the relationship between mental defects and educational defects." Thus he found achievement in arithmetic was correlated with "unusual ability" or disabilities in the "mental traits" assessed by the free association, visual rote memory, orientation, maze, and motor tapping tests, but not with the "trait" represented by the vocabulary test. More precisely, poor mastery of simple arithmetic combinations was found to be related to poor performance on all of these tests, whereas only poor performance on the free association test was related to incorrect use of arithmetic processes.

Baker made similar analyses for other areas of academic work. Students who constantly erred in spelling by transposing letters also did poorly on the orientation tests, while carelessness in spelling was related to general carelessness, lack of judgment, and foresight on the Porteus Maze test. In reading, word callers were found to be weak in association as assessed by the opposites test, while a low level of efficiency in phonics was related to poor vocabulary and to weak auditory and visual rote memory. Good handwriting was accompanied by good visual memory, and high

---

[7] Does orientation constitute an ability or set of abilities? Should they be considered broad cognitive–affective traits? It is not clear as to what status Baker elevated his trio. However,

Poor powers of orientation affect scholarship as well as non-school activities, and many cases have been found in which poor orientation has been able to nullify higher level of general mental age in trying to master schoolwork. (Baker, 1929, p. 34)

scores on Porteus Mazes and in motor tapping. Poor handwriting was accompanied by poor free association scores, poor auditory rote memory, and orientation, ". . . all of which seem to be perfectly logical and expected relationships once they have been discovered by objective data" (Baker, 1929, p. 43).

After such analyses, Baker presented his conclusions concerning the relationship of special mental disabilities to the educational disabilities. With all due apologies, because of limited data and too few cases, he offered the following observations:

> Disability in Binet Free Association is related to defects in arithmetic, spelling and reading. Association is an important psychological trait in all school subjects. Rote memory plays an important role in several of the learning situations, and defective visual rote memory.
>
> Disability in orientation is significantly correlated with poor general mastery of arithmetic and spelling. In both of these subjects the elements must be combined in logical relationships for successful performance, and orientation deals with relationships. This close affinity between elements in the school subjects and in general situations outside of the school is quite remarkable, constituting a good argument for better child training in the home in the development of responsibility.
>
> Poor judgment on the Porteus Maze Test and poor muscular control on the Motor Tapping Test are also significantly correlated with failure in arithmetic and spelling. These tests measure a certain type of reckless or careless procedure which is especially fateful to the exactness of these two subjects. (Baker, 1929, pp. 44–45)

Baker, working without acknowledgment of predecessors or contemporaries, then rediscovered the diagnostic prescriptive wheel. He completed his chapter on the "Relationship of Educational and Mental Factors" with a statement to the effect that:

> Some of these trait relationships have very logical connections and furnish a fruitful basis for the correction of defects and also in determining the underlying factors in the psychology of the various elementary school subjects. (Baker, 1929, p. 45)

Baker's work was not to end in didactic inquiries. It ultimately was to be applied to improve the remedial efforts of coaching teachers in the Detroit public schools.

Baker provided these teachers with individual pupil profiles based on the results of his specific ability tests (together with age and educational achievement test results).

> The evidence from the coaching teachers shows that this specific information with regard to abilities and disabilities was very helpful in analyzing the exact difficulties of pupils. . . . (Baker, 1929, pp. 37–38)

Baker's interest in cognitive processes vis-à-vis remedial education lay in understanding the relationship of mental defect to educational defect so as to guide the remedial "coaching (tutoring) process." (He did not, however, recommend direct process remediation.) Arming a group of coaching teachers with his test profiles, he found that, in 89 cases they coached, there were "40 restorations out of 89 disabilities. . . ." (Baker, 1929, p. 78)

Let us quote some observations relative to specific mental abilities in the diagnoses of these cases. In Case 37, a boy of nine years and five months of age, I.Q. 75:

> Porteus Maze . . . score of 7-6 reflected his lack of general initiative which in turn may have been based upon poor physical vitality. His highest scores were 10-3 on Visual and Auditory Rote Memory. He had learned to rely on these memory factors to the detriment of other mental faculties. His defect in other mental functions was noticeable in his responses on the Binet examination. (Baker, 1929, p. 151)

For this case, the results of his mental analysis were used to guide the instructional-remedial process and to assist the teacher in understanding those of the boy's problems which were fundamentally irremediable.

In still another case, that of a girl nine years six months old with a Binet score of 86, the following results were found:

> Mental: Her mental profile showed unusual variation in test scores. Her low score of 7-6 on Porteus Maze reflected her impulsiveness and lack of foresight. The scores of 8-3 in Visual, and 8-9 in Auditory Rote Memory disclosed weakness that greatly affected her failure in the early primary grades. Her score of 11-0 on Orientation showed initiative and ability to manipulate her environment, while 11-3 in Motor Tapping gave her a false idea of general superiority based solely on one phase of her ability. Her ready tongue showed its unusual powers on the Binet Free Association with a score of 12-0. We were able to get an unusually clear picture of her personality from this combination of her mental traits. Generally she made a better showing on special tests than on the Binet which involves more power of analytical reasoning.
>
> The girl's process test results were used to understand her educational problems. In reading, her impulsive nature and erratic habits caused her to extemporize in a jerky and bizarre manner. Poor rote memory depleted her stock of sight words and made her case more hopeless in some respects than if she had never had any experience with reading. In spelling the double defect of visual and auditory memory combined to reduce her mastery of this subject nearly to the zero point. (Baker, 1929, pp. 149–150)

Still another case, a boy with a chronological age of nine years, eleven months, and an I.Q., of 92:

> His greatest defect was in Binet Free Association with a score of 6-4. . . . His score of 8-6 on Porteus Maze probably reflected of the poor judgment which

he had shown in many situations. He was weak in Auditory Rote Memory . . . but was exceptionally good in Visual. . . .

In arithmetic he made many careless errors on the types of processes and also in the vocabulary of problems. He was quite poor in combinations and this result was probably related to poor auditory memory. The same mental disability affected his work in spelling, for he was a poor listener and omitted all auditory steps in studying. His knowledge of phonics was very poor. . . .

Some phonic drill was provided which aided him in reading and also in spelling . . . and he was drilled on the use of Auditory steps in studying. He spelled words aloud at home, and listened to oral work from others. The coaching teacher also trained him on a span of Auditory words which made him more observant . . . in arithmetic . . . he exercised more care in the selection of processes. The drill on auditory material assisted in mastery of the simple combinations. . . . (Baker, 1929, pp. 144–145)

In the summary and conclusion of his second book of processes and their disabilities, Baker emphasized the importance of studying educational and mental cognitive disabilities in tandem.

Too frequently . . . the problem of coaching has been approached from the mental side alone, or the educational side alone. There are significant relationships between educational and mental disabilities . . . which should be investigated. . . . In brief, if a method of instruction depends upon a specific trait such as Auditory Rote Memory, and if this trait is lacking in some cases, instruction is almost certain to fail under such conditions. (Baker, 1929, p. 164)

Baker was soon to bring forth (with Leland) The Detroit Tests of Learning Aptitude, which is an instrument that makes common sense and creates a feeling of knowingness in its user. Despite the competition of recent more glittering contenders in the field of special abilities, the Detroit holds a loyal retinue gathered in the past and, without any great fanfare, continues to attract new converts.

26
The Vanguard of Twentieth Century Remedial and Special Education—Section 3

This chapter is dedicated to the work of two educators whose efforts were directed solely to the mentally retarded, Alice Descoeudres, a Belgian, writing in the closing years of the 1920s, and John Duncan whose book appeared during World War II. While there are no clear classifications to be offered for the populations they worked with, it would appear that Descoeudres was concerned with pupils who were in the high trainable–low educable range (if we may use terms that are rapidly becoming extinct), while Duncan worked with high educable, and, perhaps slow learner pupils.

Both Descoeudres and Duncan were heavily committed to sensory–motor education, though, as will be seen, with different philosophies for starting point. Both exemplified traditions of sense and body training, albeit with different objectives and goals. Both clearly anticipated the directions that future work would take with the retarded, though their writings now sound simplistic and antiquarian, in terms of the industrial society within which the retarded, as well as the normal, must now dwell.

DESCOEUDRES

The name of Alice Descoeudres and her book *The Education of Mentally Deficient Children* have been brought, most extensively, to the attention of modern special educators by Kirk and Johnson, who discussed her work in the first edition of *Educating the Retarded Child* (1951). Our interest in her work is limited to her contributions to process training.

Descoeudres's philosophy (and practices) of education proceeded along lines that had been previously delineated within general and special education. She based her pupils' training on their natural activities, in the traditions of Rousseau, Froebel, and John Dewey. The correlation method that she employed had its roots in Herbart as well. The object lesson of which she was fond was Pestalozzian in origin. Descoeudres's emphasis upon physical education and body movement for learning is in direct lineal relationship to Séguin, while the use she made of recreation, games, walks, gardening, and practical tasks to develop mind and body was the result of her tutelage by Decroly. Her heritage from formal discipline has been briefly noted by Kirk and Johnson.[1] Her techniques of perceptual training are multiparented.

In short, Descoeudres was an imaginative eclectic. She freely borrowed from predecessors, and from colleagues Decroly and Rouma in particular. What she borrowed, she freshened and extended in a variety of ways to meet the special needs of the children she instructed. Her work still deserves a reading. Her contributions to process training should be acknowledged.

Having thus introduced Descoeudres, and recommending the more extensive introduction in Kirk and Johnson's book to readers interested in reacquainting themselves with her work, let us now more precisely examine her writings about process training. She placed this work, in fact, all of her work with the retarded clearly in the tradition of the *education nouvelle* which began with Itard and extended into the work of Decroly. Her statement:

> The characteristics of special teaching are precisely those advocated by the exponents of the new pedagogy—more movement, more manual work, less talk, and much more extensive use of the perceptive powers. (Descoeudres, 1928, p. 15)

Descoeudres distinguished, as had Decroly her mentor before her, between didactic instruction "intended to provide the pupil with the knowledge that is indispensable for life" and a program of *psychological gymnastics* "which aims at exercising the various mental functions and their reciprocal reactions" (Descoeudres, 1928, p. 59). It is the gymnastics that will improve cognitive functioning.

Perception played a central role in all of Descoeudres's training efforts. She recommended that the perceptual powers be trained first, for

---

[1] "In Descoeudres's system we find a combination of formal exercises and modern philosophy of teaching through experiences" (Kirk and Johnson, 1951, p. 92).

their own sake, second, to reach and train other cognitive powers, and third, as a means through which pupils may acquire instructional content. Very particular importance, she noted,

> . . . must be attached to *perceptual knowledge*[2] and *sensory training.* Perceptual training must penetrate even into the ultimate elements on which the individual perceptions depend. It should analyze, dissect, and investigate. Its objects should be (a) to add precision to knowledge already acquired, (b) to create new knowledge, (c) to improve, enable, and enrich verbal expression, etc. . . . (Descoudres, 1928, p. 70)

Descoeudres distinguished clearly between end-organ deficiencies in the senses and the "perceptive" power of an organ. Whereas an end organ itself might not be susceptible to correction, the cognitive processes associated with its operation can be trained, ". . . experiments have shown that if the sensory power itself cannot be developed by exercise, the power of perception can, by way of compensation, be educated and improved" (Descoeudres, 1928, p. 71). Higher cognitive powers can also be educated and improved, along with and through training of a perceptual nature. Attention is a particularly important process phenomenon to be remediated in the mentally retarded, since retardates' academic progress is disrupted by distractability and disinhibition. Because attention is associated with visual, auditory, and motor processes, the training of attention can not usually be separated from the training of modalities—they are "essentially the same thing." Modality and motor training offer the major means of improving the higher faculties of observation, comprehension, memory, and will.

Whatever the cognitive training, it is to proceed, where and when possible through activity. "Whenever the lesson admits of it . . . the faculty of movement[3] should be brought into play in its entirety" (Descoeudres, 1928, p. 54). The impression one gains from reading her book is one of constant movement. Her pupils may not have had their cognitive powers improved through the training she gave them, but they most certainly were kept very busy, particularly through participation in games.

The game approach to instruction was a major indebtedness that Descoeudres acknowledged to Decroly. She had high praise for it.

[2] Her emphasis on perceptual knowledge was in the naturalist tradition—nothing new. Children should learn from their experiences and through concrete media as opposed to "book learning."

[3] We should not forget that movement (motor activities) by a variety of names has played important roles within doctrines, including those of classical faculty psychology, and was also construed as a modality.

Dr. Decroly and his fellow-workers have evolved a series of *educational games,* applying the principles established by the great pioneers in the education of the mentally defective, such as Itard, Séguin and Bourneville. The main value of these games arises from the fact that they have been devised with complete scientific exactness, starting from the defects observed in children, and seeking to cure them in accordance with psychologic laws. (Descoeudres, 1928, p. 73)

Games exercise attention, develop sensory skill and power of observation; they lead to a child independently *"working by himself"* and all other good things. They also serve to *"check the knowledge"* acquired by the child, providing corrective self-feedback. To train is to test, just as tests serve to train. [4] Games are:

. . . valuable to the teacher . . . either to determine the mental level of the newcomer on entering the class or institution, or to measure his progress, by noting the time taken, the amount of hesitations, and the number of mistakes. (Descoeudres,1928, p. 74)

Within her programs of modality (and cognitive training), Descoeudres gave exercise of the visual sense priority. Training related to the sense of hearing was second in emphasis, followed by that of the muscular sense and the sense of touch. The development of taste and smell was given least priority.

In keeping with Decroly's precepts, Descoeudres used a variety of games at all levels of such training. For the "visual sense" (and training through it, as well, the powers of visual attention) there were games for (a) shapes and colors, (b) shapes alone, (c) colors alone, (d) size, (e) direction, and position of objects, and (f) the observation of natural phenomena. "Lotto" games were a particular preference of Descoeudres. Sorting, completion of different types of pictures, picture puzzles, and color dominoes were other frequent choices.

A major emphasis in Descoeudres's approach to education was "naturalist" training, in which she drew from Decroly's techniques and Rousseau's theories. Some of the means she devised for this training are artificial in nature: In The Sun and Shadow Game, various landscapes, monuments, and other landmarks are depicted on a picture. The child, observing the shadows thrown by the objects, has to place a small cardboard disk representing the sun on the side opposite to the shadows in the picture. In The Wind Game, there are three similar landscapes. The child places inscriptions upon them to the effect "no wind," "north wind," "and south wind," after orienting the landscapes to north-south. Then, after making various personal outdoor observations, the child puts various items

---

[4] As Montessori had specified.

on the cards, placed vertically or leaning to one side or the other in response to the direction from which the wind was blowing. These items include trees, puffs of smoke flags, wash hanging from a line, and three figures, one walking quietly along with his hat on, the two others chasing their hats in opposite directions.

Other games that she developed in the same genre are directed toward having the pupils attend to where and why snow melted quickest, why it disappeared in one spot while remaining in another, why it remained white in some places while in the other patches it became soiled, etc. She even devised a game dealing with phases of the moon. These games trained visual attention. It was—to her—

> . . . obvious that learning to see and appreciate differences of increasing fineness—in short, to observe—is the primary condition for the acquisition and retention of knowledge. This is the case in all grades and in all branches of teaching . . . exercises . . . suitable for preparing young children and defectives for learning to read and spell . . . involve the differentiation of concrete . . . elements as a preliminary to the study of abstract signs. (Descoeudres, 1928, p. 86)

Again in the naturalistic tradition, pupils were required to observe "natural" phenomena, for example:

> . . . to distinguish shades of colour in sky, clouds, trees, and . . . different kinds of green in the country, to distinguish sunlight and shadow and the movements of the shadow and the sun; to note apparent distortions of objects seen in perspective; given a leaf and asked to find another one like it in the garden or to discover the trees to which the fallen leaves belong; to arrange his companions in order of size, colour of hair; to take observation walks . . . for teaching the children to see, to look at, and to think about what they see. (Descoeudres, 1928, p. 87)

In this genre, she assigned observation tasks to her pupils in which they listed and categorized things seen, heard, etc., in their home, e.g., all things made of iron, wood, or glass, or what about the house was wet by rain when it fell, etc.

One of Descoeudres's exercises for the powers of observation had pupils assume the different positions and attitudes of figure drawings; or copy them in their own drawings. In one variant, details were repeatedly added, the children keeping their eyes shut as this was done. Following each addition, the children opened their eyes and by word or gesture indicated what was added; the figures could also be altered, rather than added to. Observation of differences was specifically trained by showing two figures that were identical—except for one detail, which the children had to either draw or describe. These lessons in visual "attention," Descoeudres observed:

. . . have undoubtedly helped to increase the children's visual acuteness and rapidity of perception, while at the same time they were creating habits of observation and attention, the good results of which are apparent in every lesson as well as in life itself. (Descoeudres, 1928, p. 92)

Descoeudres also believed in exercising visual memory. Things can be shown, hidden, and then identified in their absence or upon reviewing; their numbers and positions can be changed or delays introduced to increase the difficulty levels of such training. Descoeudres's inheritance from naturalism influenced her choice of materials for such training, e.g., Easter eggs, different cereals and flowers, and pictures of birds.

She adopted her exercises for auditory training from Rouma, but they really go back in their ultimate lineage to Itard and Séguin. So, for example, the identification of different objects, e.g., bell, whistle, watch, key ring, glass, money, from the sounds they made when swung, blown, listened to, tapped, dropped, or otherwise rendered acoustic. Discrimination of sounds proceeded from the gross to the fine: e.g., at one end of the continuum, a key and a rubber ball dropped for comparison purposes; and at the other end of the continuum, two coins of similar size dropped. Also included in auditory training was the distinction of the step of an adult from that of a child, the identification of classmates by their voices, establishing the number of children who were counting aloud; singing or reciting (all without the aid of vision of course); the reproduction of different rhythms tapped out by teachers; and phonic exercises.

The sense of touch and the "muscular sense" were given appropriate recognition by Descoeudres, though she appears to have been casually ignorant (or at least not acknowledging) of earlier theorists and contributors in these realms other than those familiar to her from the French-Belgian traditions and training.

Modern pedagogy is inclined to recognize that the importance of the visual sense has too long been overemphasized at the expense of the muscular and tactile senses. If we only see how quite a young child becomes aware of the outside world by touching and feeling and handling everything he meets, or if we think of the important part played by the muscular sense in the development of the intellect, we shall be rightly astonished that schools have so long limited the use of these senses to the art of holding a pencil or a pen. (Descoeudres, 1928, p. 96)

Again Descoeudres was following in the footsteps of her master, Decroly, who had strongly emphasized the importance of "visual-motor" exercises in educating the mentally retarded. Decroly had said:

They [visual-motor exercises] occupy the children in a completely active manner, and fix and retain their attention by the variety of the sensory stimuli to which they give rise. Owing to this very fact, the children enjoy them more than all the other exercises. Moreover, they develop their elementary logical sense by the natural observation of the mistakes they make. Among these exercises we find not only the most elementary occupations but also the most complicated processes of logic and reasoning. (Descoeudres, 1928, p. 96)

Descoeudres distinguished the tactile sense from the visual-motor. It is one of "touch" rather than fine motor execution.

The sense of touch was to be trained through a variety of physical and handiwork activities. It was also to be provided . . . some exercises . . . in its strict sense. (Descoeudres, 1928, p. 95)

The exercises to us, again, are hardly novel. A number of articles in duplicate are collected in a box and the pupil is required to select from them those that match the ones placed in his hand; or he is required to recognize and discriminate different items by touch, e.g., various vegetables and fruits, coins of different sizes, cut-out alphabet letters and numbers; or requested to fit boxes of different sizes, one into the other. Then there is the classification of things on the basis of roughness and smoothness, hardness and softness, and thickness. Lotto games were used for tactile purposes, employing common objects of different sizes and geometric shapes. A peg game for touch training required insertion of pegs into different holes. Ordinary "visual" academic training games were, for tactile training purposes, played with eyes shut.

Taste and smell were rather summarily handled by Descoeudres since they ". . . have less pedagogical value and less practical utility . . . than the other senses" (Descoeudres, 1928, p. 101). Training was carried out, nonetheless, to help pupils discriminate potentially harmful substances and to develop verbal concepts associated with these senses. Pupils were taught to recognize the taste of different foods, to discriminate beverages and breads, ". . . to recognize fruit and vegetables; to recognize the same food cooked and prepared in different ways. To recognize salt, sweet, acid and bitter flavors; to be able to arrange solutions of various degrees of sweetness in their order of intensity" (Descoeudres, 1928, pp. 100, 101). They were trained to recognize (without seeing or touching) the odor of different flowers, fruits, vegetables, spices, beverages and other liquids, meats, pharmaceutical preparations, and plants. In advanced training, they distinguished ". . . entirely by smell between two substances mixed together" (Descoeudres, 1928, p. 101).

Descoeudres firmly believed, as did Decroly, that physical training has a cognitive exercising effect as well as a physical one. Its effects are very broad.

. . . movement is one of the indispensable factors in the growth of intelligence. Its advantages are equally great as a preparation for schoolwork [handwork, drawing, and writing]. These subjects yield such deplorable results with defectives for the very reasons that the requisite systematic creation of manual dexterity is lacking. Now gymnastic movements of the body prepare the way for the more restricted movements involved in speech and manual occupations, and are thus preparatory to mental activity . . . well-devised physical training opens up for them new fields of activity. (Descoeudres, 1928, pp. 104–105)

Distinguished for training purposes were natural and systematic training. Natural activities include: ". . . *recreations, games . . . action songs, shower-baths* (very necessary for the poor), and *exercises* in *mimicry,* with or without music" (Descoeudres, 1928, p. 105). Also, walks and excursions and the practical exercises of every day life ". . . formed by the hundred and one little *tasks* that crop up in the classroom every day . . ." (Descoeudres, 1928, p. 106). "Cleaning blackboards, moving chairs, climbing up a ladder, etc. . . . all would do nicely in this last category" (Descoeudres, 1928, p. 106). And, among the best of all, gardening, for, "Few exercises of this kind are so perfectly suitable for defectives . . . which at the same time provides abundant material for perceptual teaching and handwork" (Descoeudres, 1928, p. 106).

For systematic physical training, Descoeudres recommended the *Swedish Drill* system developed by Ling, one claimed by its enthusiasts to be the only one that met the requirements ". . . of pedagogy and psychology" (Descoeudres, 1928, p. 106). An auxiliary training approach suggested was the rhythmic training provided through the Jaques-Dalcroze system which ". . . encourages the training of the muscular sense by the other senses, and vice versa." The method leans heavily on marches, e.g., rhythmical marches, marching with changes of rhythm, marching with alternate beats, marching backward and forward, etc.

Descoeudres also saw to it that the hands were elaborately exercised. First as organs serving a cognitive purpose in their own right, so hands were opened in different directions, specific fingers were bent and straightened; different shapes had to be described with the fingers. Then the hands were exercised for kinesthetic or "touch" processes (not clearly distinguished from one another); so her pupils beat on drums, played castanets, cut sticks of different thicknesses, hammered nails, drove screws, played ball, etc.

Descoeudres also included activities of daily living in her training of hand skills, e.g., dressing skills, cutting up vegetables, and the ordinary manual demands of the classroom. Modeling was prized for hand training because of its three dimensional nature. Threading beads of various types and sizes and cardboard pricking were recommended, since they exercise ". . . the coordination between the muscular sense and the visual sense" (Descoeudres, 1928, p. 126). Making and folding, pleating, pinking, cutting and pasting, paper plaiting (wool, straw, or raffia), embroidering, sewing, crocheting, basket-making, cardboard work, woodwork, carpentry, metalwork and of course, gardening—all serve to teach hand, touch, and kinesthetic senses.[5]

Descoeudres found that drawing, like handwork and manual exercises, also assists ". . . the training of the hand" and to ". . . educate the eye" (Descoeudres, 1928, p. 139). It is also a valuable assessment tool.

> However imperfect it may be, a drawing from nature is of great value in showing the teacher how far the child has really perceived an object, what he has actually seen, what spatial relations he has grasped, and how things appear to him. (Descoeudres, 1928, p. 136)

Modality training leads the way to formal academic instruction in Descoeudres's scheme. Instruction begins with preparation of the mind through modality training and, at high levels, by emphasizing the modality aspects of the various subject areas.

It is important, however, cautioned Descoeudres, to establish distinctions in modality training for those who were "real defectives, and the backward child . . . often physically delicate, unstable, or apathetic . . ." (Descoeudres, 1928, p. 248) but of greater cognitive promise. It would be a mistake, she said, to remain too long at the modality training level with the latter; one should rather ". . . pass on quickly to more complicated work" (Descoeudres, 1928, p. 248). While with the defectives, the converse is true ". . . if we try to go too far . . . we shall find ourselves up against the incapacity of our pupils" (Descoeudres, 1928, p. 249). Her concern about pupils becoming fixated at a sensory-motor stage of development because of overconcentrated training at that level, and hence hindering maturation of higher cognitive processes, did not, however, deter Descoeudres from a strongly "perceptual" approach to academics.

Writing of the *"Psychological Points Involved in Reading,"* Descoeudres gave first place to the "perception of visual signs" since ". . . visual perceptions come before auditory ones" (Descoeudres, 1928, p. 182). And it is games again that she used to train perception in the service of reading. Discriminating and matching letters of the alphabet (lower- and upper-case alphabet letters, cursive and printed) which she considered purely visual tasks were assigned first, succeeded by the matching of handwritten and printed letters of the alphabet. Alphabet dominoes helped her pupils to learn the shapes and orders of the letters. Then followed syllable Lotto and onward and upward.

---

[5] This is what most of special education used to be about academically for most of its children in the days not so long gone by. Making pot holders and popsicle stick birdhouses was perceptual training.

Perception of sounds can be improved for reading purposes, she wrote, through graded exercises with emphasis upon "improving the auditory attention." When children hear a certain sound pattern spoken, they are to clap, or when the teacher tells a story without uttering any sound, they clap whenever they can lip-read a sound they are studying. Descoeudres found the results of such exercises to be most impressive.

I have more than once been astonished by the extent to which the attention has been developed by these two exercises. (Descoeudres, 1928, p. 186)

Descoeudres also recommended sound-blending games for phonic training, familiar items these days. For the kinesthetic, tactile, and visual-motor aspects of reading, there was training of the "motor images required in graphic language," that is to say, handwriting, drawing, and tracing on Montessori sandpaper letters. Typed words were also used to assist a child in forging associations of "graphic impressions with other auditory and visual impressions."

While Descoeudres was extremely loyal to Decroly's educational conceptions, she took issue with him concerning the priorities of the visual sense in reading—though acknowledging its traditional privileged status. The Decroly "natural" method emphasized whole word and phrase recognition as opposed to phonics. The justification for the system, still in debate in Belgium, rested on the fact that sight developed faster than hearing. Descoeudres agreed with Decroly.

. . . our visual perceptions are more numerous, more varied, and more precise than our auditory ones; it is with our eyes that we perceive size, shape, colour, position and distance. A deaf child has a far more complete idea of a bell or a glass, etc., than a blind child—even if they are both assisted by the sense of touch. (Descoeudres, 1928, p. 206)

Still, Decroly's "natural" method is more adapted to "visual" children than to those who favor other modalities.

The natural method . . . is perfectly suitable to children of the visual type, but other sensory types must also be taken into account. My own experience does not permit me to agree with Dr. Decroly when he says that his observations and researches have shown him the most rational course to pursue in this branch of teaching: he ought perhaps to have added, in the interests of accuracy, "with children of the visual type." I have come across children, both backward and defective, who could read letters and syllables, but who could never get hold of the natural method or recognize a word whose constituent parts they had not learned to decipher. Besides, I have had many pupils thoroughly well equipped in the matter of hearing, and keenly interested in sounds, whose ability to grasp and retain shapes was very slight. If we demand, and with so much reason, that normal children should be taught by methods made to suit them, are not such methods still more necessary for defectives, who display such extreme types? (Descoeudres, 1928, p. 212)

In short, modality preferences have to be recognized in the instruction of reading. Reading, in the broad sense, however, is a multisensory affair.

Reading is concerned on the whole chiefly with the association of auditory, visual, motor, and graphic elements. That is to say, it is essentially a matter of memory achieved with more or less trouble with sufficiently numerous repetitions. (Descoeudres, 1928, p. 230)

Since the mentally defective are defective in their "association of ideas," the "fusion of visual, auditory, and motor elements," essential to reading, may be difficult to accomplish with them (Descoeudres, 1928, p. 188).

To foster "fusion," she used type-word games, e.g., the children would associate alphabet letters with pictures of an animal or objects, on the basis of beginning sounds, rather than initial letters or names.

Cognitive processes are clearly visible in Descoeudres's treatment of written language problems which were classified into those relating to:

1. Writing (first introduction to letters), where in problems in perception and motor functioning manifest themselves
2. Copying a text, wherein difficulties of movement and visual representation play complex roles
3. Writing from dictation, where the difficulties are mainly auditory
4. Grammar where the difficulties are those of reasoning (Descoeudres, 1928, p. 217).

To assist the initial teaching of spelling, Descoeudres believed children should illustrate their words with drawings. This helps in the understanding of what has been written. Illustrations also assist in the classification of words, e.g., flowers and fruits, utensils and toys, and help direct the child's mind from the concrete to the abstract. Auto dictation is another method, in which the child's drawings dictate what words he should write out; and, of course spelling games were recommended.

Descoeudres believed that higher cognitive processes, extending beyond mere memory and modality considerations, are essential in arithmetic, where—". . . besides all these associations, we penetrate into the realm of abstraction, generalization, reasoning, and deduction" (Descoeudres, 1928, p. 217).

There need have been no fear, however, that she would neglect the modalities in arithmetic instruction—not this student of Decroly and spiritual granddaughter of Itard, Séguin, and Rousseau.

Ideas of number, like every other manifestation of psychological activity, depend on *sensations* caused by stimuli from outside, and the *images* to which these sensations give rise. These two factors—*sensation* and *image*—are closely connected, and it is through the sense organs that the stimulus caused by material things reaches the brain. . . . In the case of mental imagery, the images of objects that have disappeared are retained by the brain and become our property: we can arrange them as we please. And these images, with the help of actual objects, form the basis of the processes of judgment and reasoning which follow. (Descoeudres, 1928, pp. 230–231)

The arithmetic tests she used were modality based, for example, the Decroly-Degand Tests of Child's Notions of Quantity.

. . . It should be noticed, also, that each of these tests is at the same time a pedagogical exercise that is admirably adapted for establishing the conception of number in all its aspects—visual, auditory, motor, and rhythmic—which is, as we have seen, the ideal to be aimed at with defectives. (Descoeudres, 1928, p. 249)

To train arithmetic concepts, the avenue is also sensory, and Rousseau the mentor. Beyond the names and symbols of the numbers, even the conception of numbers require a firm founding on a modality basis. How to proceed? Descoeudres questioned and answered herself:

To procure sensations as clear, as strong and as numerous as possible, to which senses shall we appeal? We cannot do better than adopt the words of Rousseau: "Make use of every sense and test the various impressions against each other." (Descoeudres, 1928, p. 231)

There are various ways to assist the modalities to obtain "clear, strong and numerous" sensations that will lead to success in arithmetic. To assist the visual modality allow the child to discriminate individual objects first, and then groupings. Spread out things to give a clear conception of number and group visually to create a concept of group. To aid the sense of hearing, use intervals between sounds and rhythms to create the impression of number. Indeed, ". . . facts seem to show that it is advisable to make use of . . . rhythmic dispositions in auditory subjects as a basis for the earliest notion of number" (Descoeudres, 1928, p. 233). And essential to arithmetic learning is proper perception by the tactile and kinesthetic senses.

The sense of touch is the one that convinces us most forcefully and palpably of the presence of things, making us know them by their three dimensions and their various characteristics—shape, surface, weight, temperature consistency. The superiority of this sense to that of sight alone is proved by the fact that the expression "He has grasped" means more than "He has seen." . . . the sense of touch is the first to make its appearance, and . . . the other senses are developed from it by processes of differentiation and adaptation. This is true also in the matter of arithmetic. It is a well-known fact that the blind learn by the sense of touch to count as well as those with sight . . . arithmetic [is] a different thing to one who has handled the things themselves and to one who has only set down figures. If the sense of touch is appealed to the eye is thereby compelled to intervene, whereas sight does not necessarily involve the intervention of touch. It is only in the first of these cases that we get that combination of impressions supplied at the same time by the different senses which leads to the quickest and most complete images. . . . The example of Helen Keller and similar cases go to show that if the sense of touch is intact all the other senses may be deficient without any hinderance to the mental development, whereas a weakening of the sense of touch results in profound intellectual decay. . . . I have known . . . motor associations to be developed in defectives and in normal children of three before they had learned the names of the numbers, and even before they had completely acquired the conception of number . . . thus seriously defective children immediately put up two fingers when they are shown two things . . . though they cannot always name the number *two* . . . and this habit may be considered an excellent one for defectives for strengthening the ideas supplied by sight and hearing with the aid of the muscular sense. (Descoeudres, 1928, pp. 234–236)

Various "touch" training exercises recommended by Descoeudres include stringing different numbers of beads categorized by color, categorizing objects on cards, and grouping plates while placing them in racks. Modeling, paper cutting and pasting she regarded as valuable means of strengthening numerical knowledge acquired in arithmetic lessons through manual activity. While she believed . . .

. . . *drawing* will be a valuable aid to the teaching of arithmetic at a very early stage, for a series of simple movements, executed with the hand, and eventually accompanied by speech, in a loud voice, is one of the best ways of applying the rhythmical sense to the teaching of elementary arithmetic." (Descoeudres, 1928, pp. 265–266)

Deficiencies in arithmetic can be referred back to auditory and verbal difficulties—particularly to association problems, e.g., of auditory and verbal symbols with visual and graphic ones. Children who have persistent difficulty in counting correctly are likely to have problems if while ". . . visual, motor, and graphic images are associated with the number . . . only the verbo-auditory image is still defective" (Descoeudres, 1928, p. 239). And retention of numbers is a great problem for children who are "without auditory memory" (Descoeudres, 1928, p. 239). On the other hand, if other processes were adequate, she did not find visually defective children, as a rule, to have problems in retaining numbers.

The acting of counting, Descoeudres found, was greatly hampered by auditory difficulties.

There is one department of arithmetic in which those afflicted with defects of hearing are faced by great difficulties, and that is the act of counting. Let us consider first the simple act of enumerating the series of numbers. What a strangely defective sense of hearing is revealed by the single fact that after fifteen months at school one pupil still counts "One, two, four," and another "One, two, three, five" after three years at school! Yet apart from daily exercises in arithmetic how many times must these children have heard "One, two, three," "One, two, three, four" accompanying their numerous physical exercises: Some children of this type require innumerable repetitions before the series of numbers from one to four is known, and then a fresh effort of patience is demanded to get from ten to twenty and from twenty to a hundred. It is always the same mistakes that keep cropping up, when they are caused by false associations. There is hardly anything but manifold repetitions that will overcome these difficulties, though the fact that each new number is associated with motor images (the fingers), visual images (numerical diagrams, abacus, etc.), and graphic images (figures) may also facilitate matters by strengthening the inadequate auditory images by associations of a different kind. Thus in dealing with children of a visual type the series of written figures may help them to call up the series of names. (Descoeudres, 1928, p. 241)

Motor difficulties constitute a major deficiency area in respect to lower level mathematics operations (those with which, as a teacher of the mentally defective, Descoeudres was particularly concerned).

Let us now go on to consider *motor difficulties* arising in the act of counting. There are some children who require prolonged exercises, lasting for months, before their hands can be made to work properly in counting or drawing objects at the same time as they are employing speech, either aloud or to themselves. (Descoeudres, 1928, p. 243)

Methods, then, must be at the opposite extreme from verbal ones. They must appeal to all the senses—visual, motor, tactile, and auditory—since it is sometimes one and sometimes another of these senses that is defective. It is by creating very vivid images and trying to associate them strongly that a solid foundation will be laid upon which later work can be based. (Descoeudres, 1928, p. 248)

In this respect, she was following a common tradition that had been established by Froebel. Why take a chance on having left out a particular sense system in teaching? Use them all, train them all, neglect them none—safer, as well as more scientific and holistic and ultra-sensory-motor, in keeping with the age . . . almost any age after it all once began.

Even the fingers are a potential vehicle of multisensory training.

The use of fingers is to be encouraged despite the fear of some that it will lead to permanent dependence on the concrete . . . in fact it can be useful in providing a transition to the abstract for those who are less backward. Having the teacher use all "associates"; the visual perception of the fingers . . . the auditory image of the name and the motor reactions—the teacher shows, the child imitates and hears the sound. . . . (Descoeudres, 1928, p. 272)

But then almost any activity is multisensory.

> The children can be required . . . to draw two or three strokes loudly on the
> blackboard; to throw two things that make a noise, one after the other (a motor
> and auditory exercise at the same time); to place three things down noisily on the
> table, after the teacher; or to tap on three disks placed against the wall—a visual,
> auditory, and motor exercise combined. (Descoeudres, 1928, p. 233)

Descoeudres's book, *Education of Mentally Deficient Children*
(1928), has not been done justice in this short review. I have only briefly
covered her process training efforts, for she was certainly one of the most
comprehensive "methods" people who wrote in the field of childhood
exceptionality.

Concerning the niche she holds in this history, she represents in many
ways the culmination of the sensory-motor tradition within special education. All other process trainers addressed themselves to sensory-motor
diagnosis and training. But none of her generation focused as directly as
she, at least to my reading, on training of and through the sensory and
motor apparatuses for the purpose of making them carry the burden of
education.

While Descoeudres did write about higher cognitive processes, she
did not give them much direct attention, either in diagnosis or in treatment. In part, she was excused from this by her concentration on the
mentally deficient and backward in whom "lower level processes" could
be adjudicated as more important. But Morgan and Bronner were also
concerned with such children and they dealt with higher faculties. And
it was not that Descoeudres was training the higher faculties through the
lower modality and motor ones as did Itard and Séguin, for example,
though she suggested here and there that this might be the road that she
was taking. Some reasons why she neglected the higher processes undoubtedly are to be found in the practical concrete home and garden and
the practical pursuit emphases of Decroly, whose thinking so dominated
hers. Also, Descoeudres appears to have been convinced that the
sensory-motor level was that on which the retarded was most comfortable
and could be taught best. Finally, when and where retarded children were
able to go beyond the simplest levels of skill acquisition, her practical
mind seems to have told her, it was time to neglect processes and concentrate instead upon academic instruction.

DUNCAN

John Duncan's book *The Education of the Ordinary Child* (1943) is
really one concerned with the instruction of the mentally retarded, growing as it did out of the author's experience as Headmaster of the Lankhills

School for the Feebleminded (Hampshire County, England). The title perhaps stems from an introduction to the English edition of the book, one written by W. P. Alexander, Director of Education at Sheffield, England, who was Duncan's conceptual mentor, and asserted that Duncan's techniques, proven successful with the feebleminded "are the most excellent methods for the ordinary child" (Duncan, 1943, p. v).

English educators of the 1930s, such as Alexander, Duncan, and their American cousins, were responsive to the process formulations of factor analysis. However, it was Spearman's drum rather than Thurstone's that they most likely marched to. A World War II examination of Duncan's programs by two distinguished American authorites in psychology and education, Ernest W. Tiegs and Louis P. Thorpe, resulted in a preface to the American edition of his book, published by Ronald Press:

> The English point of view is based upon the well-established but usually ignored fact that children with identical I.Q.'s (or M.A.'s) may nevertheless differ widely in their mental powers and deficiencies. While they have thus accepted the desirability of analyzing composite I.Q.'s and M.A.'s in an effort to determine their significance, the English do not go the whole way with factor analysis studies of the nature and organization of intelligence as advocated by Thurstone and others in this country. Instead, they base their analyses and related educational programs on Spearman's gv (verbal) and gF (concrete and visual) factors. While they thus appear to ignore the fact of other primary abilities, as reported in various American researches, they do so deliberately and with apparent success. They appear to be happy if they can discover even one primary ability as the avenue through which the child may find usefulness and happiness. (Duncan, 1943, p. iii)

Variations on Spearman's themes as conceptually concertized by W. P. Alexander were to guide Duncan. Alexander, who devoted considerable research to "concrete intelligence" had made an effort to apply Thurstone's factors analytic methods in ways compatible with Spearman's g. He, and Duncan after him, acknowledged ". . . only one intelligence—g" (Duncan, 1943, p. 44), and Spearman was its prophet. But this g had process helpers, Duncan pointed out.

> It may operate in conjunction with v (verbal skills) in dealing with words or abstractions, or in conjunction with another special factor, for example F in dealing with things. (Duncan, 1943, p. 44)

Thus we have gv—verbal (abstract, symbolic, etc.) intelligence—assessed by Binet-type tests, and gF—assessed by performance tests.

Alexander recommended as a gF battery, and Duncan followed along: (a) the Cube Construction Test, (b) Alexander's Passalong Test and (c) Kohs's Block Design Test. Each of these tests ". . . does in fact measure the same two factors, g and F, in different amount," in five precise ways. Total scores from the battery were converted into measures of concrete mental age and used to constitute a *"Practical Quotient"* (P.Q.) (Duncan, 1943, p. 44).

Duncan found Alexander's battery of performance tests to have remarkable predictive validity, since they were able to place children in order "according to their practical ability" in such a way as to concur remarkably well with staff opinions and making it "possible to make a prognosis of a defective child's career" with a minimum of effort (Duncan, 1943, p. 45).

Really! gv-gF was one more surfacing of a chronic polarity, albeit one with many facets: innate ideas/sensory learning; bookish instruction/learning through experience; humanist education/commercial vocational; verbal I.Q./performance I.Q.; academic training/life skills curricula; abstract thinking/concrete thinking; and, more recently, left-brain education/right-brain education.

Humanist traditions were strong in Duncan's England. England's enabling law for popular education, the Education Act of 1870, provided for public education but with an academic emphasis. It was thus into a world of words, abstractions, and symbols, for which they had been poorly prepared by tradition or current home circumstances, that many of the children of England's lower urban and rural classes were thrust—there to become 'backward children" or "feebleminded" in ways familiar to us in the United States.

Not only the retarded but also the "ordinary" child was penalized because of the excessive stress placed upon formal academic achievement, even by the lowest forms of the lowest publicly supported schools in England. It was for such children (as well as the retarded) that Alexander and Duncan were urging a return to the concrete and practical in academic instruction.

> For possibly 90% of the population of a country, life is a practical affair. The business of living, which includes earning a living, is for them dependent upon their practical ability rather than on their verbal ability. (Duncan, 1943, p. 58)

For the mentally retarded, indeed for the majority of all school children, they recommended that education should proceed ". . . chiefly on concrete, visual and everyday lines" (Duncan, 1943, p. 60).

Duncan was writing in a tradition that has held the mentally retarded to be more efficient in sensory-motor activities than in verbal-symbolic ones. Itard, Séguin, Montessori, and Binet all believed this, and it was a common observation in many texts of the time in psychology and education. Duncan was also repeating, though inadvertently, the snobbery of the English upper classes, who felt that the working class "common man" was not intended for higher abstract education. In a positive vein, he was, of course, promoting attention to individual differences and the practical life needs of the retarded.

Duncan was also making a distinction—easily overlooked in a casual reading of his book—between intellectual achievement and academic achievement. The latter required good verbal skills together with g (gv). But work could be carried out at "high intellectual levels" by pupils low in gv, if they were strong in gF and their instruction were couched in gF terms; it was a very important issue for Thurstone as well.

Duncan's pupils at Lankhills (some 400 or so) had been adjudicated as feebleminded under England's Education Act. And Duncan believed they represented the dregs of the educable retarded continuum in the regions the school served, since permission for consent for placement in the school was rarely given by parents ". . . in the case of girls if they are useful in the home, and in the case of boys if they are well-behaved at home" (Duncan, 1943, p. 15).

Duncan had no doubts about their retardation (Binet, I.Q.s ranging from 54 to 76 with a mean I.Q. of 66). However, a great number of other observers had their doubts, about the validity of the diagnosis altogether or about the "garden variety" nature of the group. For the pupils' behavior and achievement was distinctly different from that of M.R. populations at other schools. In fact, Duncan's own assessments found that they scored much better, though still low, on such "g" saturated tests as the Raven Matrices and Alexander's Performance Tests (P.Q. range, 67–119; mean, 96).

It is thus hard to consider the pupils at Duncan's school as being traditionally M.R. Alexander's description of their work raises further doubt.

Some of these children who have been certified mentally defective are able, before they leave Lankhills, to do invisible jointing in wood; they can do a series of folk dances with poise and rhythm and without a trace of mistake; from written instructions they can make cardboard models of, for example, a garage; they can take measurements of an actual piece of furniture, reduce it to scale, make a cardboard model and then a model in wood—and so on. The standard of work produced and, even more important, the whole attitude of the children are not those of mentally defectives; nor, in fact, are they defective in terms of g and F.[6] (Duncan, 1943, p. 16)

It was even suggested that there was a difference between urban and rural M.R. children—this by an "eminent psychologist," unidentified, who found the standards of achievement at Lankhills "incredibly high" for mentally defective children, even though measured I.Q. was the same as for their urban counterparts.

Kirk and Johnson felt, too, that Duncan's M.R. population was unusual, particularly in their characterization as having poor verbal but adequate performance skills (Kirk and Johnson, 1951).

[6] *The Educational Needs of Democracy*, by W. P. Alexander (University of London Press).

A. J. J. Ratcliff, M.A., otherwise unidentified by Duncan, thought that there might be a special explanation for why Duncan's groups were so specialized.

> As a result of the skimming of higher gv abilities that has occurred over generations through migration from the country to the towns, is it not possible that the residual rural population may be a reservoir of high gF ability? (Duncan, 1943, p. 226)

From the present vantage point, many of Duncan's pupils, if not the majority, were quite likely socioculturally "retarded" children in whom verbal development had been stunted through lack of adequate opportunity but whose "nonverbal" abilities were at least reasonably well nurtured in the rural environments where they were raised. Duncan, however, seemed to lean to a genetic explanation.

Duncan believed that the gv-gF distinction had important implications for instruction of the mentally retarded or less able normal student. In the realm of process training, he believed that the higher cognitive processes of such children should be trained through gF means of accession. Instructionally, life and vocational skills and academics could be most successfully accomplished if approached through gF means, i.e., the concrete and visual. The message was clear:

> The results from both Alexander's and Raven's tests appear to us a message of hope for all who have the privilege of teaching dull children. The abilities of these children are far higher than many of us have suspected. That their attainments have been low is due to an educational approach through the medium of words, their weakest factor. If the abilities of duller children are to be matched by their attainments, we must set their feet on the gF pathway. (Duncan, 1943, p. 48)

Despite his pride at identifying the gF "pathway" Duncan appeared, in his writings, to be slightly insecure about his neglect of other special abilities.

> . . . attention has been drawn . . . to two main types of ability, the gv type and the gF type. There are, of course, many special abilities. Thurstone has isolated nine primary factors. All teachers know of children who have but one special ability, and they wisely give opportunities for the development of that ability. We shall . . . however, confine ourselves to the two types that appear to present educational pathways of considerable breadth. The gv pathway at present carries most of the traffic. (Duncan, 1943, p. 55)

Duncan was particularly proud of translating Spearman's learning themes into instructional programs for the mentally retarded.

Charles Spearman's principles of cognitive functioning had certainly been honored, prior to Duncan, by English educators. However,

> The conscious interpretation of Spearman's principles into practical exercises, i.e., into exercises in educing visual and concrete relationships, in order to

build up a whole curriculum planned on these basic principles has . . . never been attempted. (Duncan, 1943, p. 61)[7]

These principles, prominent during the 1930s, were: the principle of experience, the principle of relations, and the principle of correlates. Duncan commented:

> Learning, as we see it, is the pupil's activity (a) in observing (one aspect of Experience); (b) in comparing and contrasting (Relations); (c) in applying the relationships observed in order to obtain new knowledge (Correlates); (d) in observing given new "isolates" and bringing them into relation in right sequence with knowledge and skills that have already been acquired (Application); and (e) in planning and thinking in series and sequences. (Duncan, 1943, p. 57)

A good share of Duncan's book is devoted to what would, on face value, be considered prevocational and vocational training, i.e., emphasizing as it does manual and handcraft work. These activities, however, were prized by him for their disciplinary values rather than for their practical utility. His emphasis on disciplinary goals is repeated throughout the book. He chides work that does not ". . . stimulate any intellectual activity. . . . The need is that, in order to stimulate interest and effort, problems should be at the highest possible intellectual level at which a child can work" (Duncan, 1943, p. 51).

He sought out situations that would result in cognitive training:

> Efforts . . . to enable the children to acquire knowledge and skills through the exercise of their intellect in visual and concrete situations, by providing exercises for them to do that would stimulate their greatest abilities. (Duncan, 1943, p. 61)

> . . . exercises . . . which would stimulate intellectual activity—planning, thinking in sequences, grasping relationships. (Duncan, 1943, p. 67)

Since it was cognitive ability rather than skill acquisition that Duncan sought through his training procedures, he had to exercise care that handwork, generally, and crafts, specifically, be utilized which had educational values as opposed to being repetitive, manual busy work. The primary basis for the selection of a particular manual activity for inclusion within the gF curriculum was, consequently, intellectual. Those children who were poor in gv but strong, or at least adequate, in gF were presented with concrete or visual situations in which they had to "think."

Duncan repeatedly emphasized the cognitive training values of his methods as opposed to the purely educational or vocational vantages of other curricular approaches.

---

[7] If Spearman was not altogether happy by concepts borrowed from Thurstone, adulterating his g, he most certainly would have been pleased to see his principles of learning, i.e., principle of experience, principle of relationships, and principles of correlates being taken seriously in special education; as, indeed, they were by Duncan.

We . . . approached Handwork viewing it as a means of education. The criterion of the choice of activities was educational value, and this was sifted further still to a consideration of intellectual value. . . . The fundamental purpose of educating children who appear to have little intellect must surely be to develop such abilities as they have so that they attain their maximum potential intellectual efficiency. We were not in the first place concerned with crafts as such. It was the means—the stimulation of thought, the intellectual activity in solving visual and concrete problems—that came first. . . . (Duncan, 1943, pp. 66–67)

So Duncan was an almost classical formal disciplinarian—albeit of later lineage—when manualism had become respectable. He sought to train the minds of pupils whose avenues of verbal access were limited, but who, if approached through the concrete and palpable, could still have their mental processes—even their higher cognitive processes—properly trained.

His discussion of the educational value of various handwork could have fit into our chapter on formal discipline:

Needlework trains powers of observation and judgment and the senses of form, proportion and colour. It helps to produce staying power, because not only must thought and effort be concentrated . . . but also be carried on . . . to produce a finished result. (Duncan, 1943, p. 100)

In writing about gardening, always dear to an Englishman's heart, Duncan chided his readers to remember that "We must keep in mind . . . the exercising of the child's 'problem-solving apparatus' is more important than his achieving immediate apparently good results" (Duncan, 1943, p. 163), and that horticultural science ". . . entails work in searching, comparing, contrasting, and grasping relationships . . . problems in concrete situations" (Duncan, 1943, p. 181).

In fact, Duncan was insistent that "intellectual" components are to be found in almost any physical activity, if the activity is properly managed. Physical education has ". . . intellectual values . . . not always appreciated" (Duncan, 1943, p. 155). It is "intellectual exercise" as well as physical exercise when systematically carried out. Housekeeping provides ". . . training in good intellectual habits—with the aim of intellectual efficiency. Exercises [housekeeping ones] must therefore give opportunities for planning in sequences, and for independent thought" (Duncan, 1943, p. 110). Country dancing trains a child's "ability to remember and execute 'movements' in proper sequence" (Duncan, 1943, p. 144).

The aim of the most clearly physical of training activities is "much thinking" to achieve a little doing. Whatever is taught must observe this percept. If cognitive training values are not found in a particular activity, it is to be discarded.

Duncan believed that the most effective way of utilizing handwork and other concrete types of training for the purposes of stimulating and developing cognitive functioning is through the programs of systematic curricular management, or what he called the *subjects method.* [8] He asked:

> Is it possible to plan a series of graded exercises of increasing intellectual difficulty to form a whole scheme? . . . of a type in which the manual activity would stimulate intellectual activity—planning, thinking in sequences, grasping relationships. (Duncan, 1943, p. 67)

The answer is yes, if Spearman's principles of education are applied via a gF route.

A rough and partial description of Duncan's procedures in paper and cardboard work illustrates his concepts and procedures in manual curricular development:

1. Initially, pupils are taught simple measurements such as measuring an inch. They are then provided exercises in making inch squares, then create patterns—using the squares, diagonals created with them, and the triangles cut from them.
2. The pupils make actual objects out of paper and cardboard, boxes, furniture, etc., according to several scales on the basis of plans. They are taught to measure, visualize, and conceptualize.
3. The children draw three views and, then, plans on the basis of actual models they have made. They are required to work out and note the measurements for various scales. They make models from their own sketches.
4. The children are given three-view drawings of unknown objects from which they are required to visualize objects. The objects are not actually seen. "Abstract thought," as well as visual powers, is required.
5. A description of a model is given with instructions as to how to make it. (Kirk and Johnson say oral, though Duncan's book appears to indicate otherwise.) The children have to comprehend the instructions, then draw a sketch of three views, inserting appropriate measurements, and then, finally, make the objects depicted.
6. The pupils are presented with a series of problems in grasping relationships (remember Spearman at work here).

It will be seen that the exercises at this stage present a series of problems in grasping relationships:

(i) between a written description of an object and the visual image of it,
(ii) between the visual image of an object and its development,

---

[8] It might be noted that Kirk and Johnson took umbrage with some of Duncan's observations and conclusions. Duncan's work, they said, was essentially an adaptation of ". . . the curriculum of the regular school with greater emphasis on activities in the manual and occupational field" (Kirk and Johnson, 1951, p. 97).

(iii) between actual measurements and scale measurements, and
(iv) between the several parts of the development so as to judge where flaps should be left for joining. (Duncan, 1943, p. 80)

Thus the progression from the simple to the complex, always training the pupil's mind to think, always demanding an additional measure from cognitive processes at each successive stage of training.

This systematic step-by-step training was, remember, used primarily by Duncan to train his pupils' minds. Duncan expected the latter to then function more effectively in academics as well as in manual and technical realms. It was this training of their cognitive powers that enabled his students to academically excel over mentally retarded pupils at other schools—even the best of these. His 14-year-old students could read at the level of a normal 11½-year-old child, while those at other installations (day and residential) were generally arrested at the level of a 7½-year-old.[9]

Duncan did admit that children low in gv could not advance too high in language arts, which depend largely on gv ability (Duncan, 1943, p. 183). Mathematics is another affair altogether, as Alexander had said.

Is it reasonable to suggest that the boy with a fair amount of g and of F may, in fact, be taught what are normally thought of as academic subjects without the use of words, or at least with only such limited use of words as he is able to manage? I believe that the greatest contribution to education at the moment would be the development of what I call F methods, which would enable those pupils who lack v but who have F to make their g manifest by an F approach. Let us consider this in the sphere of mathematics. To prove that the square on the hypotenuse of a right-angled triangle is equal to the sum of the squares on the other two sides, we may employ two methods, one verbal and the other practical. For verbal pupils the appropriate method will be the extension of the necessary lines and the completion of the necessary diagrams which enable comparison of triangles to be carried out. I am not suggesting that this proof is not completely adequate. I am suggesting that it would be equally adequate for practical pupils to cut out the appropriate areas and match them one to the other, thus coming to the same conclusion without the use of words. I have often wondered whether any really good mathematician ever uses words in solving a mathematical problem. It is obvious that he must use words in telling other people about it, but it is one thing to solve a problem and another thing to tell people how it is done. (Duncan, 1943, pp. 201–202)

And so it was that Duncan found that gF procedures were highly successful in taking his pupils through various aspects and stages of mathematical training.

_____
[9] He used a melange of look-say, Decroly whole-word and sentence method, and phonics to instruct them in reading. He found phonics essential, which somehow doesn't fit his visual-manual orientation.

History and geography? Maps, models, costumes, and field trips, all were found to promote gF training. These were not so effective with children who were very low in general ability, but were quite good with those in the middle and upper ranges of retardation.

Duncan's work, upon review, represents, from several standpoints, a regressive detour on the road to process training. However, although it was mental discipline à la *sloyd*, it also consisted of several things quite prescient of late developments in special education: for one, his use of motor training for general cognitive training; for another, his use of psychometrics and psychometric training as a basis for instruction; and third, his systematic hierarchical procedures for skills development.

The successes Duncan claimed appear to have been authoritatively substantiated. While it is quite likely that Duncan did have a unique population in his school—a notion he himself entertained—his results were still quite good. Was it the gF approach or the vigorous systematic control of behavior and superior management of all instruction that was responsible? In Duncan's work, we have a record of an effort that deserves another look.

27
The Vanguard of Twentieth Century Remedial and Special Education—Section 4

This chapter is the last in this book to discuss the contributions of any particular process theorist or trainer in detail. In it we specifically consider the participation of Louis and Thelma Gwen Thurstone, and Samuel A. Kirk in the "process" movement of the years leading up to and immediately following World War II. Beyond their efforts was the modern age of process training, well documented and hardly needing any wordy re-statements.

The Thurstones and Kirk are really compatible traveling companions. They shared the conviction that processes *as revealed by and through tests* would lead the way to more effective means of managing schools and educating pupils. They represented commitments to the belief that specific processes or abilities, rather than global ones are the bases upon which to establish scientific instruction.

For quite a while it appeared that *primary mental abilities* would be the way taken by specificity in educational assessment. The Thurstones certainly believed it. And, as will later be seen in this chapter, young Samuel Kirk was of similar persuasion. That the post World War II direction of factor analysis eventually diverged (in so far as special and remedial education are concerned, at least) from the PMA model by no means should diminish its important historical and psychometric role within education, and, specifically, special education; nor should it be forgotten that Guilford borrowed considerably from Thurstone.

As to the Samuel Kirk that we find in this chapter, he is still experimenting, still looking for the right mix of ideas, assessment techniques, and remedial practices to make a difference with handicapped children. It is one thing to disagree with Samuel Kirk's position on processes. It is impossible to deny homage to special education's most gifted scholar. And so this chapter provides a pleasant introduction, if nothing more, to Kirk's involvement with processes; and perhaps helps us understand the creator of the ITPA at a time when he was still struggling to formulate his process concepts.

THE THURSTONES

Louis Thurstone (1887–1955) is a psychometric immortal. Thelma Gwen Thurstone, his wife, a most formidable woman, with considerable accomplishments of her own. Both are latter-day pioneers in process assessment and remediation. Neglect of this fact (though certainly not by Sam Kirk) may be attributed to several causes. Firstly, the failure of Thurstone's Primary Mental Abilities Test (PMA) to create much enthusiasm in test consumers. Secondly, to the fact that process training efforts based upon the primary abilities that the Thurstones believed were identified by the test were too avant garde for their day, being a sort of head start training prior to headstart itself. Created by Thelma Gwen Thurstone and carried out under her direction, they were intended to train the abilities revealed by the PMA; an anticipation of later efforts vis-à-vis Guilford's cognitive factors.

The publication of T. L. Kelley's *Crossroads in the Mind of Man* had been instrumental in calling attention to the possibility of particular group "mental" factors determining cognitive activity, rather than the general and specific ones favored by Spearman and his followers.[1] Thurstone was probably the most influential of those who proceeded down the paths suggested by Kelley's initial explorations. His theoretical position, and the direction of his work was clearly evident in a statement that he made in 1938.

One of the oldest psychological problems is to describe and to account for individual differences in human abilities. How are these abilities and the great variations in human abilities to be comprehended? And just what is an ability? For centuries philosophers have been free to set up arbitrary classifications of personality types and lists of abilities, and there have been almost as many classifications as there have been writers. The factorial methods have for their object to isolate the primary abilities by objective experimental procedures so that it may be a question of how many abilities are represented in a set of tasks, and whether a particular objective performance represents an ability that is in some fundamental sense primary. (Thurstone, 1938, p. 1)

---

[1] Burt appears to have had conceptual precedence. Though even Spearman and Thorndike had flirted with group-type factors.

A statement some ten years later indicates that Thurstone was, if anything, even more convinced as to the validity of his earlier position. Writing in 1948 about *The Psychological Implications of Factor Analysis,* he opted for specific "primary" mental abilities or faculties for:

> The breakdown of the cognitive intellective functions into primary factors has revealed that the cognitive field represents a large number of functional unities or factors. (Thurstone, 1948, p. 617)

Thurstone generally regarded psychometric notions of general intelligence as obsolescent. He believed that his factor analytic methods opened up new vistas onto a verity of specificities that would replace the I.Q. in academic and vocational planning and prediction. With enough progress,

> . . . we shall have a profile for each person with a very large number of columns. . . . Even in the present state of knowledge we certainly can do much better in appraising the intellective assets of a person than by . . . methods by which each person was described in terms of a single I.Q. (Thurstone, 1948, p. 618)

Thurstone was distinctly annoyed over the dominance of verbal factors in both popular and academic conceptions of "intelligence." He staunchly championed visual, motor, mechanical and other types of nonverbal skills which he believed were too often dismissed as global nonintellective skills. So his complaint:

> It is rather common to hear mechanical aptitude referred to as if it were a single entity, but it is our hypothesis that mechanical aptitude is a complex of abilities. . . . It is our job . . . to discover . . . what those abilities are . . . . we make the hypothesis that mechanical aptitude is mostly in the head. . . . It is rather common in public schools to send the verbally slow learners to technical schools with the idea that, if a boy is sufficiently stupid, he may become a good machinist. This is one of the educational blunders of our generation . . . when a mechanic inspects a piece of machinery . . . and when he diagnoses what is wrong with it, he is using his head and only incidentally his hands. (Thurstone, 1948, p. 175)

This spirited defense of the nonverbal may appear unnecessary from the standpoint of the 1970s. But written at a time when the "blue collar" appeared to many to be a badge of intellectual inferiority it was a worthwhile cause.

Thurstone repeated his protests in favor of the nonverbal on numerous occasions.

It was to be expressed again by Thurstone in his discussion of "learning disabilities." Speaking about the "mental profiles" of primary abilities he had collected with Chicago school children, he presented several case studies of children who were regarded as intellectually inferior when they were, rather, weak in specific verbal factors (faculties).[2]

A boy who was a poor reader was considered to be a dunce by his teachers. His mental profile showed that he had the highest score on Space and Reasoning, and high scores in all other factors except the verbal factor V. His teachers changed their attitudes when they saw his handicap was quite specific. An amusing case was a girl who talked herself out of a number of situations involving truancy and misbehavior by fantastic but plausible stories. When her lies were eventually discovered, it was also found that her mental profile was very low in all factors except one, namely, verbal fluency. (Thurstone, 1948, p. 178)

Thurstone, was firmly convinced that mental profiles drawn upon the basis of his test and others like it would clarify the causes of educational failure and lead the way to remediation.

One of the important educational problems in the first few grades is that a certain proportion of children have difficulty in learning to read. In many cases this difficulty does not seem to be associated with low intelligence, but it seems to be more specific. There is the possibility that the methods of teaching reading should be adjusted to the mental profiles of the children. If it should be found that children of different mental profiles profit from different methods in teaching reading, then the same type of problem can be raised at all subsequent ages. It may be specially important to adjust the teaching methods at the early ages to the mental profiles of the children. . . . It requires often considerable insight of the examiner to relate the mental profile to the circumstances of each case, but there is no question but that the profile is more helpful than the I.Q. in the interpretation of educational and behavioral problems. (Thurstone 1948, p. 176)

As to the question of whether cognitive processes lent themselves to training, no equivocation was required as far as he was concerned. "It is one of the common questions about primary abilities whether they can be trained, and the answer is in the affirmative" (Thurstone, 1948, 180).

Thelma Gwen Thurstone who worked with her husband on the primary mental abilities scale and helped to create special versions for younger children, like her husband, was convinced of the modifiability of factors through training and was a prime mover in the development of a curriculum in which kindergarten children's primary abilities were trained in a variety of games and exercises. While her husband foresaw the day when there would be the creation of ". . . similar training material for the primary abilities . . . for the later years in the school curriculum"

---

[2] Thurstone's concerns that people be poorly judged because they were deficient in verbal skills was an enduring one. perhaps a personal issue for him; the author personally heard him make this point in ways that suggested an animus against the verbally glib. The cases mentioned in the quote support this inference.

(Thurstone, 1948, p. 181), such was not to be the case. Despite the distaff Doctor Thurstone's commendable and seemingly successful efforts to raise the cognitive skills of children, and the later commercialization of her training techniques, PMA training efforts more or less trailed away into disuse. But in any case, no threnody is required for the Thurstones' efforts. They wielded considerable influence upon the process training movement. Kirk for one, as we shall see, was most certainly influenced by PMA (1940). Baker may also have been. And while it would be Guilford's acolytes who would lead the factor-analytic way into the diagnosis and remediation of processes in the years to come, much that is best in the SOI model is borrowed from L. L. Thurstone; while the cognitive training of children also owes an undeniable debt to T. G. Thurstone. The formidable husband and wife team of Thurstone and Thurstone are front and foremost among those who have pointed the way.

KIRK

Samuel Kirk needs no introduction in a history of process training. It is interesting to observe, however, that well before his interest in the ITPA, one of America's great special educators had already clearly marked out a path of study into specificities of cognitive functioning.

As far back as 1933, Samuel Kirk was already showing a process bent as he wrote *The Influence of Manual Tracing on the Learning of Single Words in the Case of Subnormal Boys*. A deepened interest is reflected in his 1939 study, *Reading Aptitudes of Mentally Retarded Children*, in which Kirk observed both specific strengths and weaknesses in aptitudes bearing upon reading. In the study, he determined the degree to which the training of specific functions could improve the reading of slow-learning nonreaders, selected from an ungraded class. The emphasis was on "teacher planned and prepared" activities to develop all of the nonreaders' deficient functions (except motor) so as to improve their reading— specifically to improve their scores on the Monroe Reading Aptitude test which was administered on a pre–post basis. The emphasis in training was thus on visual memory, auditory memory, articulation and sentence length—which were found to be deficient on the pre-test. Major improvements on the Monroe test and increased interest in school activities were noted as the result of this "experimental intervention."

In his book *Teaching Reading to Slow-Learning Children* (1940), we find Kirk's utilization of process terms already familiar to us; memory for sentences and ideas; visual memory and visual discrimination; auditory memory and discrimination; and motor ability-popular process terms!

Kirk's interest in learning abilities is clearly demonstrated in this early book.

> . . . since intellectual development and learning ability are the main deficiencies of the mentally retarded child . . . it would appear that greater emphasis should be placed on the study of their learning capabilities and techniques for the most efficient methods of instruction. (Kirk, 1940, p. 21)

In part, his interest in processes (at least as of 1940) appears to have been attributable to his association (in conceptual frameworks at least) with Marion Monroe who provided a foreword for his book. Visual, auditory, motor and language processes were prominent in the aptitudes that Monroe had recognized as critical to the acquisition of reading.

Kirk recommended intensive work on the development of language factors for the mentally retarded vis-à-vis reading utilizing the technologies available in the pre-war years. He also offered various suggestions of his own for process training and remediation.

Training the Memory for Sentences and Ideas included practice in dramatization of stories which ". . . . involve memory for certain phrases and sentences." Exercises involving ". . . the repetition of sentences of increasing complexity. . ." were another means of improving a child's memory ". . . in connection with sentences." Kirk also recommended that songs and poems be memorized as good training for ". . . developing the memory for sentences and ideas." Learning directions in classroom and recreational activities was also found to be useful in training ". . . memory for directions in logical sequence." (Kirk, 1940, pp. 51–53).

Visual training, to improve visual discrimination, for Kirk was essentially an affair of detecting likenesses and differences which would also ". . . involve training of the language function, as well as memory for sentences and ideas." Puzzle work, drawing activities and work in arts and crafts, sorting of objects and pictures, matching words and pictures, play with "words and letters," and recognition of other children's names in writing written-in labels also served to this purpose.

Visual memory, always important to process training theorists, received its fair share of attention from Kirk who suggested that many of the exercises used in visual-discrimination training could also be useful for training memory, e.g., when used in exercising delayed recognition and discrimination. Kirk also believed that visual memory functions can be improved, a la Binet, by showing children patterns or pictures, removing them from view and having them draw them from memory; his children were to be allowed, following their initial drawings, to examine the pictures or designs again and then to complete their drawings more perfectly; complexity of pictures or patterns was to be gradually increased as performances improved, etc.

Auditory discrimination and memory were not neglected by Kirk. They were, he stated, particular areas of deficiency in the mentally retarded children. Both are usually trainable, he wrote, in the same or similar exercises.

Kirk recommended for such purposes that children be blindfolded and then asked to tell what direction a sound was coming from, or that they be required to identify which other children in a class made a particular noise or what type of animal another child might be imitating. Further, he had other children call out the child's name subsequent to which he was to identify them appropriately by name.

Distinguishing various noises, distinguishing and discriminating between different sounds, and so forth, furnish interesting games and constructive activities exercises for the development of auditory memory and discrimination. (Kirk, 1940, p. 56)

Tapping exercises, familiar to us from the ITPA, constituted another methodological medium for training auditory memory in Kirk's repetoire. The teacher, tapped ". . . on the desk, on glass, on paper, on the blackboard, and on other objects in the room. . . ." while the children were looking away (Kirk, 1940, p. 56). The objects used in tapping were then to be identified. (The reader will readily recognize the origins of such auditory training.) A more precise type of exercise recommended is one in which the teacher is required to tap on the desk. ". . . and ask the children how many times you have tapped. Start with two or three taps alternated irregularly and increase the taps to four or five and six, or more." Such training improves "attention to auditory stimuli," as well as increasing ". . . the child's ability to remember what he hears" (Kirk, 1940, p. 57).

Still other auditory training recommended by Kirk consisted of rhyming exercises, the learning of jingles and nursery rhymes. Giving the children directions, increasing in number, for the purpose of executing various acts are other ways in which ". . . they will learn to keep in mind a series of directions." Identifying tunes and singing games further develops ". . . the auditory function." So went some of Kirk's auditory training suggestions.

Kirk did not emphasize motor training to any great degree. For one thing, the motor ability of the mentally retarded is only ". . . slightly inferior to that of normal children. Some abnormal children are even superior to some normal children in this respect. It is therefore not important for teachers of mentally retarded children to develop the motor ability of these children" (Kirk, 1940, p. 59).

Further, Kirk believed that motor ability could be developed ". . . without specific exercises. . ." through regular classroom activities such as ". . . handwork, drawing, writing, and tracing. . . ." Where oculomotor coordination, and left-to-right eye movement in reading are concerned, these would be developed in connection ". . . with reading itself and not by special exercises" (Kirk, 1940, p. 58). It was a pre-Kephart, Frostig, Gettman, Barsch tradition.

But Kirk was looking beyond. He was concerned with (1) the nature of intelligence and (2) the educational activities that would train it. Could factor analysis generate such training? Well, it had been Spearman and his concepts of "general" cognitive functioning, who had dominated factor analysis in the twenties, but now the concepts of Louis Thurstone (c. 1938) vied with them for supremacy. And Thurstone, as we know, was having none or as little as g as he could get away with. It was primary factors that he was after and they were interpreted as revealing the basic mental faculties.

An early version of Thurstone's test of primary mental abilities offered possible guidance, Kirk thought, for identifying basic cognitive processes, the training of which would improve intellectual and academic functioning. Kirk observed:

> Probably the curriculum of a special class of young mentally retarded children should include games and activities which will develop the primary mental abilities. . . . For example, young children may be trained in *perceptual speed* through exercises in finding a picture among a series of pictures, or an item in a large picture. Similar mental exercises and games can be formulated for all of the primary mental abilities. (Kirk, 1940, p. 47)

He was not altogether sure, however, that he was on the right track.

> Since no one has attempted to train the primary mental abilities, it is not known whether such training is possible. Furthermore, training of specific functions may not transfer to other mental abilities. . . . However, recent evidence on the educability of intelligence is a hopeful sign. (Kirk, 1940, pp. 47–48)

As we now know, it was Osgood rather than Thurstone who was to eventually guide Kirk's exploration of processes. But the beginnings of his interest, as we have just seen, were apparent well before the appearance of the ITPA, which, in retrospect, appears as the capstone of Kirk's long-term interests in specific processes.

28
Post-World War II Developments in Process Training of the Cognitively Impaired

Some of the post-World War II interest in process assessment and re-mediation has already been reviewed in earlier chapters, in which we called attention to some of the lesser attended concerns and efforts in this area. Those under review in this chapter are by and large familiar ones to most students of remedial and special education. They will, on this basis not receive any great degree of exposition but will, in effect, serve as a bridge to the works of Otto and McMenamy (1966), Meyers and Hammill (1969), Lerner (1976), etc., to which the student of process remediation may turn for the current appreciation of the process scene.

This narrative "breaks" somewhere around 1950, which the author regards as an appropriate, though admittedly arbitrary, point from whence begins contemporary special education.

Initial post-World War II special education was not geared, to any great extent, to subtleties of psychological diagnosis and practice. In Pennsylvania, for example, education laws called for classes for the blind, deaf, and the mentally and physically handicapped. There was no place for the emotionally disturbed, brain injured, or what would later come to be called the learning disabled. Neither was there a place for the trainable, or severely or profoundly retarded. Not much in the way of good program-ming in special education either in most places in America.

There was, however, considerable interest in processes during the late 1940s in medical and psychological quarters. World War II had created a vast pool of neurologically damaged individuals for physicians and behavioral scientists to study. It was on the basis of work with brain-injured war veterans that many of our current insights as to cognitive processes were to emerge. Much of A. R. Luria's work was based upon experience with brain-injured veterans. Chalfont and Schefflin's considerable review of *Central Processes Disfunctioning in Children* (1969), so influential in later formulating process doctrine for special education, was based upon Luria's work. So the field of modern-day learning disabilities can trace its lineage back to tank battles at Minsk and to sniper bullets at Stalingrad. But for that matter, it finds its roots even further back, in World War I, whose head injury cases led to the insights of Kurt Goldstein,[1] Paul Schilder, Lev Semyonovich Vygotsky, and the like—all of which brings us up to the initial work of Strauss and Lehtinen,[2] which acutely focused attention on the cognitive impairments that were sequelae of brain injury in children (1947).

STRAUSS AND LEHTINEN

The work of Alfred A. Strauss and Laura Lehtinen burst upon the world of special education with considerable force. It can even be considered epochal, proposing as it did differential instruction for cognitively impaired children based upon (1) differences in etiology and (2) differences in the nature of specific cognitive impairments. The "true" mental retardate (we were still calling them garden variety in those days) is generally low in ability. The brain-injured pupil shows marked unevenness in cognitive functioning and specific process impairments. So it went. No matter that Seymour Sarason was able to punch holes in some of Strauss and Lehtinen's conclusions (1949). They made their point: Process disorders were to be reckoned with. And process disorders had something to say about the type of instruction the child suffering from them was to receive.

Certainly, one would expect a rather sophisticated appreciation of processes and process disorders fron such a distinguished scholar as Strauss and such a canny educator as Lehtinen. And if we read their *Psychopathology and Education of the Brain Injured Child* (Volume I, 1947, Volume II, 1955), we find a refurbishing of old process ideas in terms of a modern conceptualization strongly influenced by Gestalt psychology and "field" theory. We also find clear anticipations of Cruickshank, Kephart, and Frostig, who, to be sure, have acknowledged their debts to these two masters.

---

[1] Whose processes tended to be broad in nature.
[2] Whose work owes much to that of Heinz Werner, another gestaltist in the tradition of Goldstein.

It was perceptual processes that were first and foremost in Strauss and Lehtinen's considerations, as was to be expected from authors writing in a gestaltist vein. So in their 1947 book we read of visual and auditory perception and of visual and auditory imagery and, of course, of problems and disabilities therein. We also read of a factor (process or processes) school psychologists were to increasingly emphasize in their reports during the post–World War II years—visuomotor perception ". . . a psychological function in which we know the brain-injured child is outstandingly handicapped." (1947, p. 154)

It would not do to say that Strauss and Lehtinen reintroduced perception into special education during the early post-war years. Actually, perception has always hung about in almost any type of training practice offered the handicapped. But most surely, the concept of perception, perception as a construct, had languished somewhat in special education circles in the thirties and forties, as can be attested to by a general lack of attention to it within general introductory texts concerning exceptional children. There is little doubt that attention to "perceptual problems" quickened as a result of Strauss and Lehtinen's work.

BENDER

Let us also recognize the importance of Lauretta Bender to the clinical and educational awareness of perceptual and visual-motor disorder. The increasing popularity of the Bender-Gestalt test within psychiatric and neurological clinics and with school psychologists following World War II resulted in the detection of ever greater numbers of children suffering from academic or behavioral problems who also had "visual motor problems" or "perceptual" problems. The Bender-Gestalt Test played a major role in psychologists' diagnoses of brain injury as well, i.e., based on the assumptive relationships of visual-perceptual and visual-motor difficulties to neurological pathologies.

Neurologists, scrounging around for "soft signs," were also known to peek at the psychologists' reports for such presentments before formulating their own diagnosis of neurological dysfunction. Were one to go back and review the records of those hoards of children who were diagnosed as neurologically impaired in the 1950s and the 1960s by psychologists and neurologists, one would find that Lauretta Bender's test results were often at the bottom line of the diagnosis. The ease and facility of the test's administration and the quick inferences permitted by it were, in large part, responsible. Of course, too, the test results were often indicative of problems and did have predictive validity, as is also true today. The "Bender" remains a most useful instrument. But in the hands of the naive it generated a great deal of nonsense. Brain damage, thy name was lesion, thanks to the "Bender." [3] Blessedly, current interpretations of its results tend to be more judicious.

WECHSLER

This brings us to the Wechsler tests as a major contribution to the process training movement, one that is recognized in practice but without too much thought given to it beyond that.

The Stanford-Binet test had long reigned as the monarch of cognitive measurement when Wechsler appeared on the scene. Binet test scatter offered the possibilities of specific diagnostic implications. Indeed, the Binet, an omnibus test, has manifest face-value specificity in its subtests, so why not interpret it thusly? A variety of people did, prior to World War II, including Harry Baker (1929). But the Binet was not really intended for such purposes. Terman had decried such efforts with the test he had painstakingly created and validated (with the help of Maude Merrill and countless graduate assistants) to assess general ability. Quinn McNemar put the onus on scatter analysis from the standpoint of his statistical analysis (1942). And so the Binet languished as an instrument to be used to assess specific process assessments, though Mary Meeker (1965) and Robert Valett (1965) attempted valiantly to use it for such purposes. Then along came the Wechsler tests, which accomplished what the Binet could not and would not do.

When Form 1 of the Wechsler Intelligence Scale for Adults first appeared on the scene, it was intended to provide a technique more suitable for adults than was the Stanford Binet with its presumed plateau of intelligence ca. age 16 and its notions of mental age, which David Wechsler despised.

The Wechsler scales were clearly intended by Wechsler to investigate first and foremost that illusive process called general intelligence.[4] But they also clearly allowed a breakdown of intelligence on the basis of separate types of functioning, capacity, and ability—though these types were quite broad and still saturated with general intelligence. Differential diagnoses and cognitive descriptions could be generated from discriminated subtest differences obtained from the Wechsler scales. All sorts of elegant and fancy—and fanciful—test analyses and interpretations were to be had. If one ever wants to learn how to squeeze a Wechsler test for

---

[3] With apologies to Joseph Heller.
[4] Wechsler's musings about intelligence approach the mystical levels invoked by Spearman in talking about g (1939).

interpretation, he should read David Rappaport's classic volumes *Psychodiagnostics* (1946a, 1946b), bibles for the clinical psychologists of their day.

As later forms of the Wechsler scales appeared, among them the several forms for children, factor analysts and clinical psychologists alike generated processes to fit its subtests or "factors." One sure reason for the tests' increasing popularity vis-à-vis the Binet was that they allowed specific types of interpretation based upon what appeared to be precise process discriminations (for and against which a considerable literature has been generated). George is strong in comprehension but weak in spatial-synthetic analysis, Susie has poor attention and is deficient as well in psychomotor speed. School psychologists, in some cases, found it easier to simply send along a list to teachers telling them what processes were associated with the various subtests of the Wechsler Intelligence Scale for Children (WISC) to allow them to draw their own conclusions and save some writing time. Quite naturally, instruction books were also generated to teach or to correct the processes revealed by the Wechsler.

None of these remarks are to be construed as criticism of the Wechsler tests, which are fine instruments and whose usefulness in process discrimination (e.g., verbal from performance factors) has been as successful as any of the more recent types of more specific of process tests. What I am trying to simply highlight is that the Wechsler tests played a profound role in conditioning the minds of clinicians and educators to the possibilities of "accurately" assessing processes vis-a-vis tests. The enormous acceptance of such later "process" tests as those of the Frostig type and the ITPA was very much predicated, I believe, on the basis of groundwork done by the Wechsler tests. Also to be noted are the excesses of the psychometrically unwashed in interpreting the Wechsler tests; their flights of interpretive fancy often reached apogees of bizarreness. A few courses of psychometrics had created a battalion of would-be school psychologists and counselors who, with undaunted faith in inter-subtest scatter, blithely diagnosed autism or schizophrenia or brain damage in many a confused but normal little child. The lesson of such excesses has, unfortunately, yet to be learned.

AND UP TO THE PRESENT

Processes were clearly in the catbird seat by the 1960s in special education. Wepman and Osgood,[5] to mention two particularly influential figures in language assessment, appeared amidst a new era of "diagram

---

[5] Osgood's notions of decoding, association and encoding would have been quite congenial to Bain, Hughlings, Jackson and Ferrier—and why not, since Osgood was an associationist.

makers." They explained a great deal, or at least seemed to be doing so, and various tests and training capitalized on their insights.

Visual processes continued to maintain their popularity in this resurgence of process interest with special education. So much was visual perception emphasized in the early days of the latest groundswell of enthusiasm for processes within special education, that when one entered the exhibit halls of the Council for Exceptional Children for annual meetings, sunglasses would have been advisable—such was the dazzle of the visual modality nostrums on display. Cure a visual process and learn to read, they all suggested. Visual process training kits were everywhere; but not a curriculum to teach.

And so we move from Bender to Benton (1955) to Frostig (1964) and consider a great many other people in between. Gross motor and kinesthesic processes again received their due by Roach and Kephart (1966) and in the poetical writings of Raymond Barsch (1965). The auditory was given its due most prominently for school people by the ITPA but, of course, by Myklebust too.[6] The field of learning disabilities emerged as a field based upon process theorems, with a strong perceptual and motor bias. Perceptual training, creeping and crawling, trampoline bouncing, sandpaper letters, parquet blocks, the new scientific pedagogies were now on hand . . . actually not much more in substance or basic form than the old "new" pedagogies that have earlier been hurled at the reader in this book. Amnesia is the mother of invention.

Bateman enthusiastically explained what the new scientific pedagogy would mean to the teacher. She would no longer have to worry about I.Q.s or medical diagnoses of brain injury.

> If each child has posted on the front of his desk a profile view of his present level of development in areas such as understanding what he hears, categorizing ability, visual memory, etc. with the normal developmental sequence of ability in each area clearly spelled out, she (the teacher) would see at a glance (a) where the child is, (b) what step comes next and (c) types of classroom activities suitable to move him a bit higher up the ladder. (Bateman, 1964, p. 25)

This time, however, there was learned research to back it all up, this new scientific pedagogy. What such research all boiled down to is something else. Hammill and his associates began an assiduous collection of the investigations into process training and came to the conclusion that it came up somewhat short. Those who believed in processes, e.g., Frostig, Kirk, and Minsloff, disagreed. But I am now going against my intent to not poke into the present process scene within this chapter any more than necessary to provide a closing chapter to a chronology. Let me stop, then, for now. I will editorialize in the following and concluding chapter.

---

[6] Auditory perception appears to be particularly flourishing these days.

Part IV

Conclusion

29
Some Conclusions about Process Training

My historical review of processes and process training has been left deliberately incomplete so as to avoid the debate that continues as these final pages are being written. Approximately a decade has passed since I wrote the first of several position papers on the subject, which remains one of continued and intense interest to me. I believe that my own statements and those of current process and antiprocess camps are not quite ready for an efficient or fair ordering. There are observations about it all, however, that can be made without heat, passion or, for that matter, conviction that they are altogether correct.

We have seen that process training is, in fact, one of the oldest forms of education and that, despite periodic discontinuities in its practice, it has continued unabated into our own day. Its philosophies and precepts must certainly have had a powerful appeal and conviction to survive so many centuries, fashions, opinions, and attacks—and they continue to do so. For let the behaviorists insist, as they will, that all we should do is devote our attention to the here and now of inputs and responses, all of us (including the behaviorists) cling to the belief that there is something within us that is more than gristle and bone, more than sensation and response. To the process trainer, it is the mind and its powers, i.e., abilities, capacities, faculties—processes. And to the process trainer, these seem important, in fact, fundamental, to train; and usually in a way that takes precedence over direct instruction in some skill, academic or otherwise. It was what Socrates and Plato said and what Itard, Séguin, Montessori, and Binet reiterated. It is what the Frostigs, Kirks, Kepharts, seem to have been saying more recently. Are their processes hypothetical? They can be operationalized to give them conceptual flesh. Does process training fail? There is evidence that it works as well. The debate goes on, it always goes on.

Why has process training been so powerful a force on the special education scene in recent years? An interesting insight has been provided on the matter by Kane and O'Brien in their discussion of the fluctuating fortunes of formal discipline. Their statement permits generalization to all process training views of education. There is a resurgence of interest in it, they note ". . . in periods when some particular dominating curriculum in the schools has fallen into a rut of staleness and dead routine" (Kane and O'Brien, 1954, p. 196).

Let us paraphrase their observations within the context of modern special education. The younger generation in this field finds itself inundated with curricula, technologies, and assessment devices undigestible in their numbers and claims. It was not so, not so many years ago, when the making of potholders and popsicle-stick bird nests constituted much of curriculum within many of our special education classes, classes that were special largely in the experience of segregation they offered. There was very little that special education could show in those antediluvian years to justify its existence as an instructional vehicle for the cognitively handicapped. Special education was maintenance education; much of its achievement lay in the fact that mentally handicapped children were being educated at all.

We were too busy, then, in simply providing services to ask ourselves many questions about the values of those services. Accountability for special education teachers was something that they had to be largely concerned about on April 15 of each year. Supervision was a matter of public relations by the itinerant ignorant as much as anything else. Not that decent, and even exemplary, instruction did not go on here and there, particularly when charismatic leaders such as Cruickshank took an interest. But articles asking what is special about special education rarely received a positive answer, if we were honest with ourselves.

And so the appearance of process and process training (i.e., those efforts by Kephart and Frostig and those constituted within the ITPA mold) was, to special education, rain upon parched land reviving enthusiasm, restoring hope, galvanizing programs of intervention. They deserve much credit on this account. Read Barbara Bateman's landmark article in *Exceptional Children* (1964) if you wish to recapture some of the spirit of that time. The new scientific pedagogy was going to revitalize education, provide individual prescriptive correctives for learning problems, reclaim the cognitively impaired. Down with models of general intellectual incompetency! Down with medical models of noneducational etiology! The promised land was at hand. Alas, neither Moses nor we ever crossed to the other side.

Now we have seen still another revolution, that of behavioral objectives, contingency management, applied behavioral analysis, criterion-referenced measurement, *und so weiter*. These are instructional tools for educating and training the handicapped that have caused a resurgence of "curriculum" (here considered in its broadest terms) from that for the severely handicapped to that for the learning disabled. With "curriculum" resurgent, processes (faculties) no longer seem so important. Where once they were hailed as hypothetical constructs, they are often condemned on the same grounds (Smith and Neisworth, 1975).

That the process training camp might be in some disarray may be suggested by the diminishing number of "process training" articles within special education journals. Is its cause in any danger? The answer is most assuredly to the contrary. There is scarcely a day when some new process training approach is not spewed forth by the commercial enterprises that serve special and remedial education. Nor is early childhood education neglected a whit in all this process attention to those with learning problems. Parents and teachers still respond to the concept. Perception is still a magic word. And if processes are a bit uneasy, at present, concerning their abodes within test profiles, they are welcome visitors to split-brain halves. No one by now can be unaware that the education of old has neglected the right brain, so it's off to train the right brain we now go. And processes are making new territorial gains within cognitive psychology (Resnick, 1976). Even amidst the most "objective" circles of education, we find process training, succubuslike, surviving, attached to other technologies.

A prime example of this is to be found in behavioral objectives. Presumably, they serve to focus attention upon external behaviors and goals, and within special education, they are to be used to control, manage, and direct instruction. But what happened in so many places is that objectives suddenly become endowed with developmental properties and are regarded as stages through which pupils must proceed. When this happens, and it so often does happen, objectives become processes, more modern than the faculties of memory or imagination admittedly, but processes nonetheless, and training by objectives has become, yes, process training.

Process training has always made the phoenix look like a bedraggled sparrow. You cannot kill it. It simply bides its time in exile after being dislodged by one of history's periodic attacks upon it and then returns, wearing disguises or carrying new noms de plume, as it were, but consisting of the same old ideas, doing business much in the same old way.

Writing in 1929, Spearman made one of his many observations regarding the durability of faculty constructs:

> . . . we find the doctrine of "faculties" everywhere mentioned in terms of the keenest reprobation. Such hostility, however, shows itself on closer examination to be still freely accepted under very numerous synonyms. . . . Despite all protests to the contrary, this ancient doctrine has in good truth not even yet been abandoned. Modern authors seem, rather, to be incapable of abandoning it. (Spearman, 1929, p. 25)

Modern authors (ca. 1978) seem also to be incapable of abandoning the idea that they can train the mind and its parts. I must admit, myself, to being prejudiced in this direction. The problem is, as far as I am concerned, that when I am training the mind and its parts, I am not sure of exactly what I am training. And I am always in danger of believing in what I do. There is the rub, there is my concern.

There is nothing wrong with talking about training the mind (or its parts) or remediating them, or building upon them, or whatever, if we recognize the hypothetical nature of our terms. But reification of such terms seems inevitable, and the hypothetical becomes real, and sooner or later we find ourselves training processes instead of teaching people—training perception and memory and reasoning, instead of teaching people to perceive better, to remember better, to reason better.

Is this all a game of words? I think not. For the enormous investment in process training made by special education in developing and remediating children's "processes" some years ago represented a wide and distant detour on the road toward remediation. Excessive interpretation of flimsy research results and unwarranted extrapolations of factor-analytic theory and data led the way, fostering an air of scientism that masked the nature of practices that are ancient in their origins, and have been repeated throughout history only to be found wanting over and over again in their resuscitations—old wine in very leaky new bottles.

True, the imprimaturs of some of the finest minds in psychology, education, and special education have supported, and continue to support, process training practices. But examined closely, I believe their arguments rest on metaphorical or metaphysical grounds, rather than on concrete substantive ones. We will not argue one's rights to figures of speech or to personal beliefs. But the practices they foster are, however, quite another affair. On this count, process has done rather poorly of late.

Regarding efforts to separate and train processes from content in general education, Ebel had the following to say:

> There is an effort to separate the process of thinking from the content of the thoughts and to give priority to the process over the content in specifying the objectives of education. It seems to me that such separation is impossible. As I

consider what goes on in schools and colleges, I find few instances in which processes of thinking are taught separately from the content to be thought about. Reviewing my own education, it seems that I always learned process and content together; in reading, arithmetic and grammar; in Latin, geometry, and physics; in measurement, statistics, and philosophy. That is why in my own teaching I do not try mainly to develop abstract cognitive skills in my students, or to cultivate abstract higher mental processes. Instead I try to help them build solid, comprehensive structures of knowledge. Of course, these structures include knowing how to do, as well as knowing what is so. But the emphasis is squarely on knowing. (Ebel, 1974, p. 487)

Regarding efforts to train cognitive processes within special education, I have written in a similar vein:

Cognitive training represents a commitment to insecurely identified, unverifiable, hypothetical constructs, and too many at that. Cognitive constructs do not represent legitimate processes for training; except in the broadest construction of the term. Cognitive theory and research do have much to say about the ways in which we learn, some of it potentially useful, and much of its useless. However, the value of such theory and research in education will not be determined through in-out experiments or correlational studies, but on the basis of how they assist in positively modifying the instructional process, in helping determine the types of individual dispositions that contribute to readiness or lend themselves to particular types of instruction or the degree to which they provide insight into curriculum and techniques of instruction and suggest means of altering them in positive fashion. Cognitive theory, in so far as it can translate into instructional practices, may be useful, but I do not see the utility of training hypothetical constructs. Cognition is part and parcel of almost everything we do. . . . In so far as we do things better we are functioning better cognitively—whatever functioning cognitively may mean. . . . We don't need to train cognitive processes directly to train cognition. . . . In special education we train cognition best through training toward utilitarian goals. (Mann, 1974, p. 190)

To the question "Does cognitive training work?" I have answered hyperbolically:

Does it work? But, of course, it works, if you mean can we show successes for cognitive training intervention. For, yes, almost every intervention approach has its successes . . . and cognitive training approaches are likely to positively affect some of the behaviors relevant to the training and education of the handicapped—and of the gifted. . . . There is some transfer of training! There are good general habits that can be trained under one condition, e.g., ones defined by cognitive constructs, that will bear fruit in others, and there are specific skills that we can train under one rubric, which will emerge under others. But let us not fool ourselves that we have trained some processes, or strengthened them or remediated them, to accomplish our successes, when in fact we have simply been training an individual to do things in one situation that has similarities to another, that will improve his performance in the other. And I would promulgate here the cliché that we would have been better off training directly for and in the other in the first place, if the improvement in functioning there was the eventual aim of our training. . . . If training "cognitive processes" will improve academics, training in academics (in the broad sense) will improve cognitive processes.[1] And the goals and objectives of academics are far more visible and valid than those of cognitive skills and strategies in education. . . . (Mann, 1974, p. 106)

I claim no originality in such statements. But they apparently have to be repeated periodically, the memory of the old being fallible, the recall capacities of the young being unwilling. It is not just the past that we do not seem to remember, but as Marie Antoinette's maid pointed out, even yesterday. And so we repeat and repeat and again repeat the outworn, the discredited, the valueless.

There is no form without content, as Aristotle said, no process of learning external to the substance of learning. We can most certainly help children to perceive better, to carry out motor functions better, to remember better, and so on. But we will not be doing so through the remediation of any particular type of ability—except in the metaphorical sense. No matter, too, what part of the individual is impaired, that individual still functions as one, as Hughlings Jackson once told us. And we can only train him as one, despite how hard we may seek to isolate a particular aspect of that one.[2]

Let me echo Thorndike's statement regarding the place of processes within education:

I do not require them . . . partly because I do not believe the mind is composed of such and partly because in any case there are more urgent needs. (Ebel, 1974, p. 104)

Those urgent needs should be for us the training or remediation of our pupils in those skills required for productive living in and outside of school—and, when possible, the impartation of knowledge and wisdom to them that will make their lives more than a mere pursuit of reinforcements. In so doing, as we engage our pupils in instruction, we will also engage those processes of theirs that are appropriate to that instruction. For if our pupils come along, surely their processes will not be left behind.

[1] Formal discipline lurks in the hearts of all of us.
[2] Descartes lurks in the hearts of all of us.

References

Adams, J. *The Herbartian psychology applied to education*. Boston: D. C. Heath & Co., 1907.

Albrecht, F. M. A reappraisal of faculty psychology. *Journal of the History of the Behavioral Sciences*. 1970, *6*, 36–40.

Anastasi, A. Review of Thurstone, T. G., & Thurstone, L. L. Test of Mental Alertness. In O. K. Buros (Ed.), *The Third Mental Measurements Yearbook, N. J.*, New Brunswick. New Jersey: Rutger University Press, 1949.

Adler, M. J. In defense of the philosophy of education. In N. B. Henry (Ed.), *Philosophies of education*, Forty First Yearbook of NSSE, Chicago: Univ. of Chicago Press, 1942.

Aristotle. *De Anima*. In G. Murphy & L. B. Murphy (Eds.), *Western psychology*. New York: Basic Books, 1969.

Bain, A. *Education as a science*. New York: D. Appleton and Co., 1879.

Baker, H. J. *Characteristic differences in bright and dull children*. Bloomington, Ill. The Public School Publishing Co., 1927.

Baker, H. J. *Educational disablity and case studies in remedial teaching*. Bloomington, Ill.: The Public School Publishing Co., 1929.

Baker, H. J. & Traphagen, V. *The diagnosis and treatment of behavior problem children*. New York: Macmillan, 1935.

Baker, H. J. *Introduction to exceptional children*. New York: Macmillan, 1944.

Baldwin, J. *Psychology applied to the art of teaching*. New York: Appleton, 1896.

Ball, T. S. *Itard, Séguin, and Kephart*. Columbus, Ohio: Merrill, 1971.

Bateman, B. Learning disabilities—yesterday, today, and tomorrow. *Exceptional Children*, 1964, *31*, 167–168.

Beck. R. H. *A social history of education*. Englewood Cliffs, N.J.: Prentice-Hall, 1965.

Bennett, C. E. & Bristol, G. P. *The teaching of Latin and Greek in the secondary school*. New York: Longmans, Green and Co., 1906.

Bentley, M. The psychological antecedents to phrenology. *Psychological Monographs*, 1916, *21*(72) 102–115.

Berlin, I. *The age of enlightenment—the eighteenth century philosophers*. Boston: Houghton Mifflin, 1956 (quoted Gutch, 148).

543

Black, H. C., & Lottich, K. V., & Seckinger, D. S. *The Great Educators*. Chicago: Nelson-Hall Co., 1972.

Bode, Boyd Henry. *How we learn*. Boston: D. C. Heath & Co., 1940.

Bolzan, E. L. *Almira Hart Lincoln Phelps: her life and work*. Lancaster: Science Press Printing Co., 1936.

Boring, E. G. *A history of experimental psychology*. New York: Appleton-Century-Crofts, 1950.

Boyd, W., & King, E. J. *The history of western education*. New York: Barnes & Noble, 1973.

Brett, G. S. *History of psychology*. R. S. Peters, (Ed.), London: Allen & Unwin. 1951.

Broadbent, D. E. Division of function and integration of behavior. In F. O. Schmitt & F. G. Worden (Eds.), *The neurosciences: Third study program*. New York: MIT Press, 1974, 31–64.

Broca, P. P. Remarks on the seat of the faculty of articulate language, followed by an observation of aphasia (1861). Trans. G. VanBonin in *Some papers on the cerebral cortex*, 49–72, Charles Thomas, Springfield, 1960.

Brooks, G. P. The faculty psychology of Thomas Reid. *Journal of the History of the Behavioral Sciences*. 1976, *12*, 65–77.

Bronner, A. *The psychology of special abilities and disabilities. Boston: Little, Brown & Co., 1917*.

Browning, O. *Aspects of education*. New York: Industrial Education Association, 1888.

Brubacher, J. S. *A history of the problems of education* (2nd ed.). New York: McGraw-Hill, 1966.

Brueckner, L. J. & Melby, E. O. *Diagnostic and remedial teaching*. Boston: Houghton Mifflin, 1931.

Bruner, J. S. *The process of education*. Cambridge, Mass.: Harvard University Press, 1961.

Burnham, W. H. *The normal mind*. New York: Appleton, 1924.

Bruner, J. S. *The process of education*. Cambridge, Mass.: Harvard University Press, 1961.

Burt, C. *The distribution and relations of educational abilities*. St. Albans, England. P. S. King & Son, Ltd., 1917.

Burt, C. *Mental and scholastic tests*. London: P. S. King & Son, Ltd., 1922.

Burt, C. *The backward child*. New York: Appleton-Century, 1937.

Burt, C. *The factors of the mind*. London: University of London Press, 1940.

Burt, C. The meaning and assessment of intelligence. *Eugenics Review, 47*, 1955b, 81–91.

Burt, Cyril. The evidence for the concept of intelligence. *British Journal of Educational Psychology*, 1955a, *25*, 158–177.

Burton, W. *The culture of the observing faculties*. New York: Harper, 1865.

Buss, A. T., & Poley, W. *Individual differences: Traits and factors*. New York: Gardner, 1976.

Butts, R. F. *Cultural history of western education*, New York: McGraw-Hill, 1955.

Calkins, N. A. *Manual of object teaching*. New York: Harper, 1882.

Carroll, H. A. *Generalization of bright and dull children*. New York: Teachers College Contributions to Education, No. 489, 1930.

Cattell, R. B. *Abilities: Their structure, growth, and action*. Boston: Houghton Mifflin, 1971.

Chalfont, J. C., & Schefflin, M. *Central processing dysfunction in children. A review of research*. Bethesda, Md.: National Institute on Neurological Diseases and Stroke, 1969.

Chapman, J. C., & Counts, G. S. *Principles of education*. Boston: Houghton Mifflin, 1924.

Cole, L. *A history of education*. New York: Holt, Rinehart & Winston, 1950.

Cole, P. R. *A history of educational thought*. London: Oxford University Press, 1931.

Colvin, S. S. *The learning process*. New York: Macmillan, 1911.

Conford, F. M. *Plato's cosmology*. London: Routledge and Kegan Paul Ltd. Broadway House.

Cremin, L. A. *The transformation of the school*. New York: Knopf, 1961.

Das, J. P., & Kirby, J., & Harman, R. F. Simultaneous and successive syntheses: An alternative model for cognitive abilities. *Psychological Bulletin,* 1975, *82*(1), 87–103.

Davies, J. D. *Phrenology fad and science*. New Haven: Yale University Press, 1955.

da Vinci, L. *Selections from the notebooks of Leonardo da Vinci*. Irma A. Richter (Ed.). Oxford, England: Oxford University Press, 1952.

DeGuimp, R. *Pestalozzi, his life and work*. New York: D. Appleton & Co., 1901.

Descoeudres, A. *The education of mentally defective children*. Boston: Heath, 1928.

Dewey, J. *Democracy and education*. New York: Macmillan, 1916.

Dewey, J. *How we think*. Boston: D. C. Heath & Co., 1933.

Dexter, T. F. G., & Garlick, A. H. *Psychology in the schoolroom*. New York: Longmans, Green, 1902.

Douglass, A. A. *Secondary education*. Boston: Houghton Mifflin, 1927, p. 352.

Drever, J. *An introduction to the psychology of education*. New York: Longmans, Green, 1922.

Drever, J. Some early associationists, in Wolman, B. J. (Ed.). *Historical Roots in Contemporary Psychology*. New York: Harper & Row, 1968, 11–28.

DuBois, P. H. *A history of psychological testing*. Boston: Allyn & Bacon, 1970.

Duncan, J. *The education of the ordinary child*. New York: Ronald, 1943.

Ebel, R. L. And still the dryads linger. *American Psychologist,* 1974, *29*, 485–492.

Eby, F. *The development of modern education*. Englewood Heights: Prentice-Hall, 1934.

Evans, E. G. S. *Modern educational psychology: An historical introduction*. London: Routledge & Kegan Paul, 1969.

Eysenck, H. J., Cyril Burt. *British Journal of Mathematical and Statistical Psychology,* 1972, *25*, i–iv.

Fernald, G. M., & Keller, H. The effect of kinaesthetic factors in the development of word recognition in the case of non readers. *Journal of Educational Research,* 1921, *4*, 355–377.

Fernald, G. M. *Remedial techniques in basic school subjects*. New York: McGraw-Hill, 1943.

Fernald, M. R. The diagnosis of mental imagery. *Psychological Review,* Monograph Review Supplement, Vol. *14*, No. 58, 1912.

Ferrier, D. *The functions of the brain*. London: Smith, Elder, 1876.

Ferrier, D. *The functions of the brain,* 2nd ed. London: Smith & Elder, 1886.

Ferrier, D. *The localization of cerebral disease*. London: Smith, Elder, 1878.

Ferrier, D. The localization of functions in the brain, (MS)—communicated by J. B. Sanderson, Archives of Royal Society. March 5, 1874, AP56.2, abstract in Proc. R. Soc. 22 (1874a) 229–32.

Fowler, T. *Locke's conduct of the understanding*. Oxford: Clarendon Press, 1901.

Freeman, F. N. *Mental tests*. Boston: Houghton Mifflin, 1939.

Fritsch G. & Hitzig, E. On the electrical excitability of the cerebrum (1870), Trans. G. VonBonin, in *Some Progress in the Cerebral Cortex,* 73–96. Springfield: C. Thorn, 1960.

Froebel, F. *Autobiography of Friederick Froebel,* Trans. E. Michaelis and H. A. Moore. London: Swan Sornenschein, 1886.

Froebel, F. *The education of man,* Trans. W. W. Hailman. New York: D. Appleton & Co., 1909.

Frost, S. E., Jr., & Bailey, K. P. *Historical and philosophical foundations of western civilization* (2nd ed). Columbus, Ohio: Merrill, 1973.

Gage, N. L., & Berliner, D. C. *Educational psychology.* Chicago: Rand McNally, 1975.

Garrison, K. C., & Kingston, A. J., & McDonald, A. S. *Educational psychology.* New York: Appleton-Century-Crofts, 1964.

Gassaniga, M. S., & Bogen, J. E., & Sperry, R. W. Dyspraxia following divisions of the cerebral commissures. Archives of Neurology, 1967 *16,* 606–612.

Goldstein, K. *The organism. A holistic approach to biology.* New York: American, 1939.

Good, H. G., & Teller, J. D. *A history of western education.* New York: Macmillan, 1969.

Goodenough, F. L. *Mental testing.* New York: Rinehart, 1949.

Gorfinkle, J. E. *The eight chapters of Maimonides on ethics—A psychological and ethical treatise.* New York: Columbia University Press, 1912.

Graves, F. P. *Great educators of three centuries.* New York: AMS Press, 1912.

Graves, F. P. *A history of education during the Middle Ages.* New York: Macmillan, 1919.

Graves, F. P. *A student's history of education,* New York: Macmillan Co., 1915.

Greeley, H. Education: Its motives, methods and ends. *Pa. Sch. Journal,* Nov. 1857, *VI,* 158.

Green, V. A. *Life and works of Pestalozzi.* London: University Tutorial Press Ltd., 1913.

Groszmann, M. P. E. *The exceptional child.* New York: Scribners, 1917.

Gutek, G. L. *Pestalozzi and education.* New York: Random House, 1968.

Halleck, R. P. *Psychology and psychic culture.* New York: American, 1895.

Halleck, R. P. *The education of the central nervous system.* New York: Macmillan, 1897.

Hamlyn, D. W. *Sensation and perception.* New York: Routledge & Kegan Paul, 1961.

Harris, W. T. *Psychological foundations of education.* New York: Appleton, 1898.

Head, H. *Aphasia and kindred disorders of speech.* (Vol. I). Cambridge University Press, 1926a.

Head, H. *Aphasia and kindred disorders of speech.* (Vol. II). Cambridge University Press, 1926b.

Herbart, J. F. *ABC of severe perceptions and minor pedagological workers.* Trans. W. J. Eakoff. New York: D. Appleton & Co., 1903.

Hinsdale, R. B. *Horace Mann and the common school revival.* New York: 1898.

Holman. H. *Pestalozzi: An account of his life and works.* New York: Longmans, Green & Co., 1908.

Hollingsworth, L. S. *The psychology of special disability in spelling.* New York: Teachers College, Columbia University, 1918.

Hollingsworth, L. S. *The psychology of subnormal children.* New York: Macmillan, 1920.

Hollingsworth, L. S. *Special talents and defects.* New York: Macmillan, 1923.

Hopkins, L. P. *Educational psychology: A treatise for parents and educators.* Boston: Lee and Shephard, 1886.

Humphrey, G. & Humphrey, M. *The wild boy of Aveyron.* New York: Appleton Century Crofts, 1932.

Hunt, J. On the localization of the functions of the brain with special reference to the faculty of language. Part 1. *The Anthropological Review,* 1868, *6,* 329–345.

Hunt, J. On the localization of the functions of the brain with special reference to the faculty of language. Part II. *The Anthropological Review,* 1869, *7,* 100–116.

Hutchins, R. M. *The higher learning in America.* New Haven: Yale University Press, 1936.

Huxley, T. H. *Science and education.* New York: American Home Library Co., 1902.

Innskeep, A. D. *Teaching dull and retarded children.* New York: Macmillan, 1926.

Jackson, H. J. *Selected writings of John Hughlings Jackson.* J. Taylor (Ed.) London: Hodder and Stoughton, 1931a.

Jackson, H. J. *Selected writings of John Hughlings Jackson.* J. Taylor (Ed.) London: Hodder and Stoughton, 1931b.

Jasper, H. H. Evolution of conceptions of cerebral localization since Hughlings Jackson. *World Neurology,* 1960, 97–109.

John, E. R. & Schwartz, E. L. The neurophysiology of information processing and cognition. In M. R. Rosenzweig & L. W. Porter *Annual Review of Psychology.* (Vol. 29), 1978, Palo Alto: 1–30.

Kagan, J., & Kogan, N. Individual variation in cognitive processes. In P. H. Mussen (Ed.), *Carmichael's Manual of Child Psychology* (3rd ed.). New York: Wiley, 1970, 1273–1353.

Kamin, L. J. *The science and politics of I.Q.* Potomac, Md.: Lawrence Erlbaum Associates, 1974.

Kane, W. T., & O'Brien, J. J. *History of education.* Chicago: Loyola University Press, 1954.

Keatinge, M. W. *Comenius.* New York: McGraw Hill, 1931.

Keatinge, M. W. *The great didactics of John Amos Comenius.* London: Amos & Charles Block, 1896.

Kelley, T. L. *Crossroads in the mind of man: A study of differentiable mental abilities.* Stanford, Cal.: Stanford, 1928.

Kilpatrick. H. *The Montessori system examined.* Boston: Houghton Mifflin, 1914.

Kirk, S. A. *Teaching reading to slow learning children.* Boston: Houghton Mifflin, 1940.

Kirk, S. A., & Johnson, G. O. *Educating the retarded child.* Cambridge, Mass.: Houghton Mifflin, 1951.

Klein, D. B. *A history of scientific psychology.* New York: Basic Books, 1970.

Kleist, K. *Sensory aphasia and amusia.* New York: Pergamon, 1962.

Lane, H. *The wild boy of Aveyron.* Cambridge: Harvard University Press, 1976.

Lashley, K. S. *Brain mechanisms and intelligence.* Chicago: University of Chicago Press, 1929.

Laslett, P. *John Locke: Two treatises of government.* London: Cambridge Press, 1960.

Lerner, J. W. *Children with learning disabilities.* Boston: Houghton Mifflin, 1976.

Lesky, E. Structure and function in Gall. *Bulletin of the History of Medicine, 44,* 297–314, 1970.

Levine, M., & Levine, A. A. *social history of helping services.* New York: Appleton-Century-Crofts, 1970.

Locke, J. *An essay concerning human understanding.* 1st Ed. 1690, 4th Ed. 1700, 5th Ed. 1706. London: J. M. Dent, 1961.

Lowell, E. J. *The eve of the French revolution.* Boston: Houghton Mifflin, 1892.

Lucas, C. J. *Our Western educational heritage.* New York: Macmillan, 1972.

Luria, A. R. *Higher cortical functions in man.* New York: Basic Books, 1966.

Luria, A. R. *The working brain.* New York: Basic Books, 1973.

MacLeod, R. B. *The persistent problems of psychology.* Pittsburgh: Duquesne University Press, 1975.

MacQuorqudale, K., & Meehl, P. E. On a distinction between hypothetical constructs and intervening variables. *Psychological Review,* 1948, *55,* 95–107.

Mandler, J. M., & Mandler, G. *Thinking: from association to Gestalt.* New York: Wiley, 1964.

Manenholz, Bulow. *Reminiscences of Friederick Froebel.* Trans. Horace Mann. Boston: Lothrop, Lee & Shepherd, 1895.

Mann, L. Cognitive training: A look at the past and some concerns about the present. In K. F. Kramer and R. Rosononke (Eds.) *State of the Art, Proceedings,* Lexington, CORRC, 1974.

Mayer, F. *A history of educational thought.* Columbus, Ohio: Merrill,, 1960.

Mayer, F. *Road to modern education.* New Haven: College & University Press, 1966.

McCabe, L. R. *The American girl at college.* New York: Dodd, Mead & Co., 1893.

McCord, C. P. Bumps and dents in the skull. *Archives Environmental Health, 1969, 19,* 224–229.

McHenry, L. C., Jr. *Garrison's history of neurology.* Springfield, Ill.: Thomas, 1969.

McNemar, Q. *The revision of the Stanford-Binet scale.* Boston: Houghton Mifflin, 1942.

Meyer, A. E. *An educational history of the western world.* New York: McGraw-Hill, 1965.

Meeker, M. O. A procedure for relating Stanford Binet behavior samplings to Guilford's structure of intellect. *Journal of School Psychology, 1965,* 3, 26–36.

Monroe, W. S. *Comenius and the beginning of educational reform.* New York: Arno, 1971.

Montessori, M. *The absorbent mind.* New York: Delta, 1967.

Montessori, M. *The Montessori method.* English Trans. A. George. New York: Stokes, 1912.

Morgan, B. P. *The backward child.* New York: Putnam's, 1914.

Mulhearn, J. *A history of education* (2nd ed). New York: Ronald, 1959.

Mulhearn, J. *A history of secondary education in Pennsylvania.* Lancaster, Pa.: Science Press Pringing Co., 1933.

Murphy, G., & Kovach, J. *Historical introduction to modern psychology.* New York: Harcourt Brace Jovanovich, 1972.

Murphy, G. & Murphy, L. B. (Eds.) *Western psychology.* New York: Basic Books, Inc., 1969.

Nakosteen, M. *The history and philosophy of education.* New York: Ronald, 1965.

National Education Association. *Report of the committee of ten on secondary school subjects.* New York: American Book Co., 1894.

Neisser, U. *Cognitive psychology.* New York: Appleton-Century-Crofts, 1967.

Norsworthy, N. *Formal training: New York teaches monograph.* New York: Columbia University Press, 1902.

Norsworthy N., & Whitley, M. T. *The psychology of childhood.* New York: Macmillan, 1920.

Orata, P. T. Transfer of training and educational pseudo-science. *The Mathematics Teacher, XXVIII*(5), 155–161, 1949.

Otto, W., & McMenamy, R. A. *Corrective and remedial teaching.* Boston, Houghton Mifflin, 1966.

Pai, Y. *Teaching, learning, and the mind.* Boston: Houghton Mifflin, 1973.

Parker, F. W. *Talks on pedagogics.* Kellog, 1894.

Parker, S. C. *The history of modern elementary education.* Totowa, New Jersey: Littlefield, Adams, 1970. (Originally published, 1912.)

Pestalozzi, J. H. *How Gertrude teaches the children.* Trans. L. E. Holland & F. C. Turner. Syracuse: C. W. Bardeen, 1894.

Pestalozzi, J. H. *Leonard & Gertrude.* Trans. E. Channing. Boston: D. C. Heath & Co., 1906.

Phelps, A. H. *Lectures to young ladies.* Boston: Carter Herdee & Co., 1833.

Pounds, R. L. *The development of education in western culture.* New York: Appleton-Century-Crofts, 1968.

Power, E. J. *Main currents in the history of education.* New York: McGraw-Hill, 1970.

Pratt, C. Faculty psychology. *Psychological Review,* 1929, *36,* 142–171.

Pressley, M. Imagery and childrens' learning: Putting the picture in developmental perspective. *Review of Educational Research,* 1977, 47(4), 585–622.

Quick, R. H. *Some thoughts concerning education by John Locke.* London: Cambridge University Press, 1895.

Rapaport, D. *Diagnostic psychological testing* (Vol. I). Chicago: Year Book Publishers, 1946a.

Rapaport, D. *Diagnostic psychological testing* (Vol. II). Chicago: Year Book Publishers, 1946b.

Ratner, J. (Ed.) *The philosophy of Spinoza—Selected from his chief works.* New York: The Modern Library, 1927.

Rein, W. *Outline of pedagogics.* Syracuse: C. W. Borden, 1895.

Resnick, L. B. (Ed.), *The nature of intelligence.* New York: Haldstead Press, Division of John Wiley & Sons, 1976.

Riegel, K. F. The dialectics of human development. *American Psychologist,* 1976, *31,* 689–700.

Riese, W. An outline of a history of ideas in neurology. *Bulletin of the History of Medicine,* 1949, *XXIII*(2), 111–136.

Riese, W., & Hoff, E. C. A history of the doctrine of cerebral localization. Part I. *Journal of the History of Medicine & Allied Sciences.* 1950, *5,* 50–71.

Riese, W., & Hoff, E. C. A history of the doctrine of cerebral localization. Part II. Methods and main results. *Journal of the History of Medicine & Allied Sciences.* 1951, *6,* 439–469.

Riese, W. *A history of neurology.* New York: M. D. Publications, 1959.

Riesman, D. & Jencks, C. *The academic revolution.* New York: Doubleday & Co., 1968. 1968.

Robinson, H. M. *Why pupils fail in reading.* Chicago: The University of Chicago Press, 1937.

Rousseau, J. J. *Emile.* Trans. B. Foxley. New York: E. P. Dutton and Co., 1911.

Rousseau, J. J. *Emile.* Trans. W. H. Payne. New York: Appleton-Century-Crofts, 1892.

Rusk, R. *Doctrines of the great educators.* New York: St. Martin's, 1969.

Russell, J. E. *German higher schools.* New York: Longmans, Green, 1907.

Sahakian, W. S. *History and systems of psychology.* New York: Halstead Press, Division of John Wiley & Sons, 1975.

Sandiford, P. *Educational psychology.* Longmans, Green, 1928, 298.

Sarason, S. B. *Psychological problems in mental deficiency.* New York: Harper, 1949.

Saucier, C. A. *Introduction to modern views of education.* Boston: Ginn, 1937.

Sears, W. P. *The roots of vocational education.* New York: Wiley, 1931.

Séguin, E. *Idiocy and its treatment by the physiological method.* New York: William Wood, 1866.

Séguin, E. Origins of the treatment and training of idiots. *American Journal of Education.* 1856, *2,* 145–152.

Sherlock, E. B. *The feeble-minded.* London: Macmillan, 1911.

Shovey, P. A symposium on the value of humanistic, particularly classical, studies. The classics and the new education III. The case for the classics. *School Review.* Nov. 1910, *XVIII,* 598, 607, 608.

Smith, R. M., & Neisworth, J. T. *The exceptional child: A functional approach.* New York: McGraw-Hill, 1975.

Spearman, C. *The nature of "intelligence" and the principle of cognition.* London: Macmillan, 1923.

Spearman, C. *The abilities of man: Their nature and measurement.* London: Macmillan, 1927.

Spearman, C. *Psychology down the ages* (Vol. I). London: Macmillan, 1937a.

Spearman, C. *Psychology down the ages* (Vol. II). London: Macmillan, 1937.

Spencer, H. *Education: Intellectional, moral, and physical.* New York: A. L. Burt, 1860.

Sperry, R. W. Split-brain approach to learning problems. In G. C. Quarton, T. Melnechuk, & F. O. Schmitt (Eds.) *The neurosciences: A study program.* New York: Rockefeller University Press, 1967.

Sperry, R. W. Hemisphere deconnection and unity in conscious awareness. *American Psychologist,* 1968, *23,* 723–733.

Sperry, R. W. Hemispheric specialization of mental faculties in the brain of man. In M. P. Douglas (Ed.) *36th Yearbook of Claremont Reading Conference.* Claremont, California: Claremont Graduate School, 1972.

Sperry, R. W. Lateral specialization in the surgically separated hemispheres. In F. O. Schmitt & F. G. Worden (Eds.) *The neurosciences: Third study program.* New York: MIT Press, 1974.

Spoerl, H. D. Faculties versus traits: The solution of Franz Joseph Gall. *Character and Personality.* 1936, *4,* 216–231.

Sternberg, R. J. *Intelligence, Information processing, and analogical reasoning: The componential analysis of human abilities.* Hillsdale, N.J.: Erlbaum, 1977.

Strauss, A. A., & Lehtinen, L. E. *Psychopathology and education of the brain-injured child.* New York: Grune & Stratton, 1947.

Thorndike, E. L. *Education: A first book.* New York: Macmillan, 1912.

Thorndike, E. L. *Educational psychology.* New York: Columbia University Press, 19131.

Thorndike, E. L. *Educational psychology* (Vol. II). New York: Teachers College, Columbia University, 1913.

Thorndike, E. L. *Notes on child study.* New York: The Macmillan Co., 1903, 50.

Thorndike, E. L. *Principles of teaching.* New York: A. G. Seiler, 1906.

Thurstone, L. L. *The nature of intelligence.* London: Routledge & Kegan Paul, 1924.

Thurstone, L. L. Multiple factor analysis. *Psychological Review,* 1931, *38,* 406–427.

Thurstone, L. L. The vectors of the mind. *Psychological Review,* 1934, *41,* 1–32.

Thurstone, L. L. *Primary mental abilities.* Chicago: University of Chicago Press, 1938.

Thurstone, L. L., & Thurstone, T. G. *The Chicago tests of primary mental abilities: Manual of instructions.* Chicago: Science Research Associates, 1943.

Thurstone, L. L. Psychological implication of factor analysis. *American Psychologist,* 1948, *3,* 402–408.

Tizard, B. Theories of brain localization from Flourens to Lashley. *Medical History,* 1959, *3,* 132–145.

Ulich, R. *Three thousand years of educational wisdom-selections from great documents.* Cambridge: Harvard University Press, 1947.

Valéry, P. *The living thoughts of Descartes.* Philadelphia: David McKay Co., 1947.

Valett, R. E. *A profile for the Stanford-Binet (L-M).* Chicago: Consulting Psychology Press, 1965.

Vernon, P. E. *Intelligence and cultural environment.* London: Methuen & Co., Ltd., 1969.

Wallace, A. R. *The wonderful century.* New York: Dodd, Mead & Co., 1899, 193.

Walker, A. E. *A history of neurological surgery.* New York: Hafner, 1967.

Wallin, J. E. *The education of handicapped children.* Boston: Houghton Mifflin, 1924.

Watson, R. I. *The great psychologists.* Philadelphia: Lippincott, 1963.

Wechsler, D. *The measurement and appraisal of adult intelligence* (4th ed.). Baltimore: Williams & Wilkins, 1958.

Wepman, J. *Recovery from aphasia.* New York: Ronald, 1951.

Wilhelm II. Emperor's address to the commission on school reform. Reichs Anzeiger. *Educational Review.* Feb. 1891, I, 202f.

Wolf, T. H. *Alfred Binet.* Chicago: The University of Chicago Press, 1973.

Wolman, B. B. The historical role of Johann Friederich Herbart. In B. B. Wolman (Ed.) *Historical roots of contemporary psychology.* New York: Harper, 1968, 29–48.

Woodrow, H. *Brightness and dullness in children*. Philadelphia: Lippincott, 1919.

Woodworth, R. S., & Sheehan, M. R. *Contemporary schools of psychology*. New York: Ronald, 1964.

Woody, T. *A history of women's education in the United States*, II. New York: Science Press, 1929.

Woody, T. *Liberal education for free men*. Philadelphia: University of Pennsylvania Press, 1951.

Young, R. M. The functions of the brain: Gall to Ferrier (1808–1886) *Isis*, 1968, *59*, 251–268.

Young, R. M. *Mind, brain and adaptation in the nineteenth century*. Oxford, England: Clarendon Press, 1970.

Index

Gage, N. L., & Berliner, D. C. *Educational psychology*. Chicago: Rand McNally, 1975.

Garrison, K. C., & Kingston, A. J., & McDonald, A. S. *Educational psychology*. New York: Appleton-Century-Crofts, 1964.

Gassaniga, M. S., & Bogen, J. E., & Sperry, R. W. Dyspraxia following divisions of the cerebral commissures. Archives of Neurology, 1967 *16*, 606–612.

Goldstein, K. *The organism. A holistic approach to biology*. New York: American, 1939.

Good, H. G., & Teller, J. D. *A history of western education*. New York: Macmillan, 1969.

Goodenough, F. L. *Mental testing*. New York: Rinehart, 1949.

Gorfinkle, J. E. *The eight chapters of Maimonides on ethics—A psychological and ethical treatise*. New York: Columbia University Press, 1912.

Graves, F. P. *Great educators of three centuries*. New York: AMS Press, 1912.

Graves, F. P. *A history of education during the Middle Ages*. New York: Macmillan, 1919.

Graves, F. P. *A student's history of education,* New York: Macmillan Co., 1915.

Greeley, H. Education: Its motives, methods and ends. *Pa. Sch. Journal,* Nov. 1857, *VI,* 158.

Green, V. A. *Life and works of Pestalozzi*. London: University Tutorial Press Ltd., 1913.

Groszmann, M. P. E. *The exceptional child*. New York: Scribners, 1917.

Gutek, G. L. *Pestalozzi and education*. New York: Random House, 1968.

Halleck, R. P. *Psychology and psychic culture*. New York: American, 1895.

Halleck, R. P. *The education of the central nervous system*. New York: Macmillan, 1897.

Hamlyn, D. W. *Sensation and perception*. New York: Routledge & Kegan Paul, 1961.

Harris, W. T. *Psychological foundations of education*. New York: Appleton, 1898.

Head, H. *Aphasia and kindred disorders of speech*. (Vol. I). Cambridge University Press, 1926a.

Head, H. *Aphasia and kindred disorders of speech*. (Vol. II). Cambridge University Press, 1926b.

Herbart, J. F. *ABC of severe perceptions and minor pedagological workers*. Trans. W. J. Eakoff. New York: D. Appleton & Co., 1903.

Hinsdale, R. B. *Horace Mann and the common school revival*. New York: 1898.

Holman. H. *Pestalozzi: An account of his life and works*. New York: Longmans, Green & Co., 1908.

Hollingsworth, L. S. *The psychology of special disability in spelling*. New York: Teachers College, Columbia University, 1918.

Hollingsworth, L. S. *The psychology of subnormal children*. New York: Macmillan, 1920.

Hollingsworth, L. S. *Special talents and defects*. New York: Macmillan, 1923.

Hopkins, L. P. *Educational psychology: A treatise for parents and educators*. Boston: Lee and Shephard, 1886.

Humphrey, G. & Humphrey, M. *The wild boy of Aveyron*. New York: Appleton Century Crofts, 1932.

Hunt, J. On the localization of the functions of the brain with special reference to the faculty of language. Part 1. *The Anthropological Review,* 1868, *6,* 329–345.

Hunt, J. On the localization of the functions of the brain with special reference to the faculty of language. Part II. *The Anthropological Review,* 1869, *7,* 100–116.

Hutchins, R. M. *The higher learning in America*. New Haven: Yale University Press, 1936.

Huxley, T. H. *Science and education*. New York: American Home Library Co., 1902.

Innskeep, A. D. *Teaching dull and retarded children*. New York: Macmillan, 1926.

Jackson, H. J. *Selected writings of John Hughlings Jackson*. J. Taylor (Ed.) London: Hodder and Stoughton, 1931a.

Jackson, H. J. *Selected writings of John Hughlings Jackson*. J. Taylor (Ed.) London: Hodder and Stoughton, 1931b.